THE NEW PENGUIN GUIDE TO LONDON

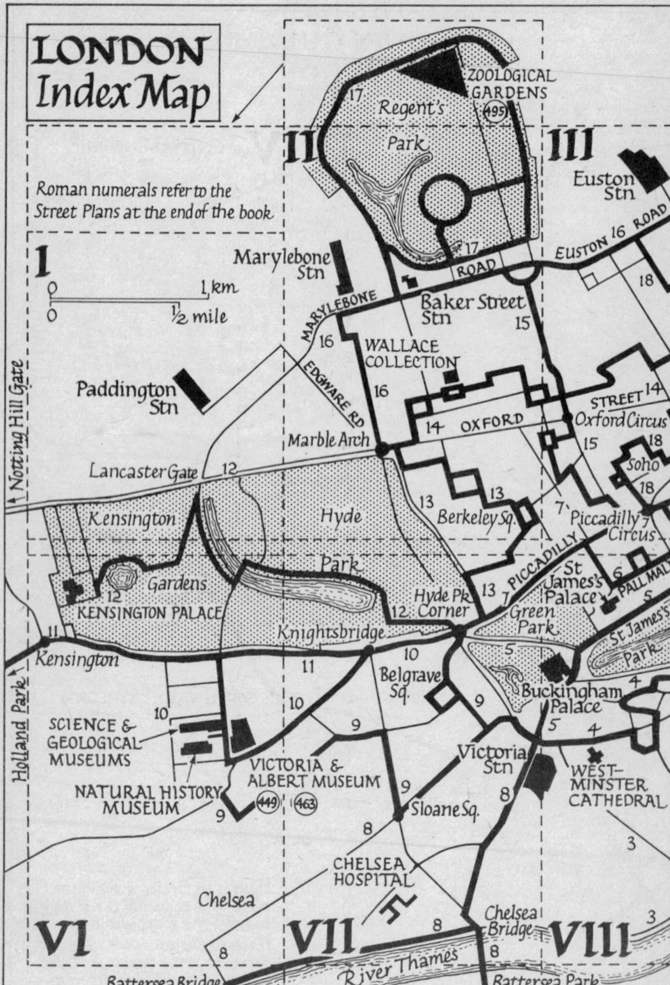
LONDON
Index Map
Roman numerals refer to the Street Plans at the end of the book
0 1 km
0 ½ mile
I
II
III
VI
VII
VIII
ZOOLOGICAL GARDENS
495
Regent's Park
Euston Stn
EUSTON ROAD
Marylebone Stn
MARYLEBONE ROAD
Baker Street Stn
WALLACE COLLECTION
EDGWARE RD
Paddington Stn
Notting Hill Gate
Marble Arch
OXFORD STREET
Oxford Circus
Soho
Lancaster Gate
Kensington Gardens
Hyde Park
Berkeley Sq.
Piccadilly Circus
PICCADILLY
St James's Palace
PALL MALL
KENSINGTON PALACE
Hyde Pk Corner
Green Park
St James's Park
Knightsbridge
Kensington
Holland Park
Belgrave Sq.
Buckingham Palace
SCIENCE & GEOLOGICAL MUSEUMS
NATURAL HISTORY MUSEUM
VICTORIA & ALBERT MUSEUM
449
463
Victoria Stn
WEST-MINSTER CATHEDRAL
Sloane Sq.
CHELSEA HOSPITAL
Chelsea
Chelsea Bridge
River Thames
Battersea Bridge
Battersea Park

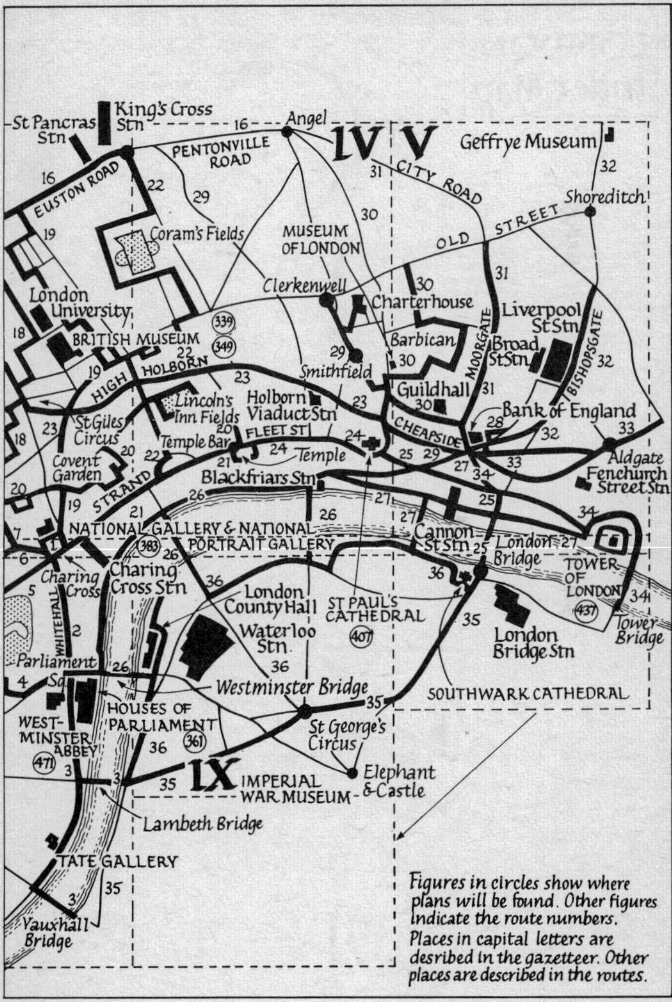

Figures in circles show where plans will be found. Other figures indicate the route numbers. Places in capital letters are desribed in the gazetteer. Other places are described in the routes.

THE NEW PENGUIN GUIDE TO

LONDON

F. R. BANKS

NINTH EDITION

PENGUIN BOOKS

Penguin Books Ltd, Harmondsworth, Middlesex, England
Viking Penguin Inc., 40 West 23rd Street, New York, New York 10010, U.S.A.
Penguin Books Australia Ltd, Ringwood, Victoria, Australia
Penguin Books Canada Limited, 2801 John Street, Markham, Ontario, Canada L3R 1B4
Penguin Books (N.Z.) Ltd, 182–190 Wairau Road, Auckland 10, New Zealand

Published by Penguin Books as *The Penguin Guide to London* 1958
Second edition 1960
Third edition 1963
Fourth edition 1968
Fifth edition 1971
Sixth edition 1973
Seventh edition 1977
Reprinted 1978
Reprinted with revisions 1979
Eighth edition published under the present title 1982
Reprinted with revisions 1984
Ninth edition 1986

Photoset by Rowland Phototypesetting Ltd,
Bury St Edmunds, Suffolk
Printed and bound in Great Britain by
Cox & Wyman Ltd, Reading

CONTENTS

MAPS AND PLANS

FOREWORD

The Penguin Guide to London, now in its ninth edition, is divided into four main parts. The first opens with a brief introduction to the capital, telling something of its places of interest and offering advice on how visitors may employ their time to the best advantage, followed by sections dealing with such practical matters as railway and bus services, car parking, hotels and restaurants, postal services, information offices and other useful addresses, entertainments, sport, and shopping. At the end of this part are suggestions for further reading and study.

The next part consists of a series of short routes which may be followed on foot (or partly by bus) covering the whole of central London in detail and taking in the many fine public and other buildings, parks and squares, interesting churches and small museums, and other places well worth seeing. The routes are arranged to start and finish at noted traffic points, and each may very conveniently be followed from end to end. They also mostly intersect at a number of points, so that, by comparing the index map at the front of the book, parts of several routes may easily be combined to make a longer or shorter round excursion.

The third part of the book is a gazetteer of the most important places of interest, such as Westminster Abbey, St Paul's Cathedral and Southwark Cathedral, the Tower of London and the Houses of Parliament, the great national museums and art galleries, the Royal Hospital, Chelsea, Kensington Palace, and the Zoological Gardens (the London Zoo). The fourth part, expanded in this edition, describes the places most worth visiting in the suburbs of London, and this is followed by a brief section about Greater London. The very full index of places and persons is preceded by a glossary of the architectural terms used in the book, which have been kept as simple as is consistent with accuracy and clarity.

The guide is well supplied with maps and plans. The street plan of central London on nine pages at the back of the book covers practically the whole of this part of the capital described in the text. In addition, there are maps showing the best road routes into and around

London, the railway systems, and the bus routes and theatres and cinemas in the central area. Plans of the National Gallery, the British Museum and the Victoria and Albert Museum, Westminster Abbey and St Paul's Cathedral, the Houses of Parliament, the Tower and the Zoological Gardens will be found adjoining the descriptions of these places in the guide. The Index Map at the front of the book shows the arrangement of the routes and the page numbers of the various maps and plans. All the maps are based on the Ordnance Survey map with the sanction of the Controller of H.M. Stationery Office, but are amended and added to in order to bring them into line with the requirements of the guide.

London, as the capital of England and the heart of the Commonwealth, is by general agreement the most fascinating and interesting city in the world. As the centre of administration, the court, the law, learning, fashion and pleasure, it occupies a unique position in the nation's life. An attempt has been made to deal with as wide a range of topics as is possible in the guide, consideration being given to the great public occasions and the military and civic pageantry indissolubly connected with the capital, and to the seasonal and occasional events and customs that lend colour and atmosphere to the everyday scene, as well as to the wealth of historical and literary associations.

In preparing successive editions of the guide the author has explored the whole of the area described on foot and has visited every building where the stranger may expect to gain admittance at any time. Full consideration has been given to the vast amount of new building, both public and private, that is still going on and to the many other changes that are taking place in the capital. It must be stressed, however, that changes take place frequently and rapidly in London, almost week by week in fact, and the hope that the guide will be free from errors and omissions is beyond the realms of possibility. All indeed that an author can wish for is that by constant and careful research and diligent 'field work' he may reduce the errors to a minimum.

Continuing inflation means that any prices that could be quoted in the guide would quickly be rendered out of date. On the whole, therefore, prices have been omitted from this edition. When included, they will at least give readers an approximate idea of how much they may expect to pay.

The author's grateful thanks are owed once again to many anonymous helpers: to officials of the Greater London Council, the London

Transport Board, and the London Visitor and Convention Bureau, to the directors of museums and galleries and their staffs, librarians and church officials, clerks of the City guilds, secretaries of companies, institutions, and societies, and private individuals, all of whom answered carefully and courteously the many questions put to them. The author and publishers again thank the correspondents who have made helpful comments and will be most grateful for any further suggestions for the correction and improvement of the guide, as well as for any material that will assist in keeping it up to date.

While this new edition was being prepared, a bill was introduced in Parliament with the object of abolishing the Greater London Council and dividing its responsibilities among the various borough councils. The effects of this reorganization, should the bill become law, could not be foreseen.

ABBREVIATIONS. The following abbreviations are used in the guide:

adm. = admission
b. = born
d. = died
ft = feet
G.L.C. = Greater London Council
in. = inches
l. = left
L.C.C. = London County Council
m. = mile
N.T. = National Trust
p. = page
r. = right
R. = rooms
yds = yards

Places shown in bold type in the routes are described in the gazetteer of Places of Interest.

AN INTRODUCTION TO LONDON

London, the capital of England and the mother city of the British Commonwealth of Nations, is situated on the river Thames, about forty miles in a straight line, or fifty miles by water, from its mouth at the Nore. It is divided into two unequal portions by the river, the more important part, with most of the chief buildings, standing on the north bank.

The capital is built mainly on a tract of undulating dark brown or grey clay ('London Clay'), which extends along the river valley from about Windsor to the coasts of Kent and Essex. The clay is broken here and there by beds of sand or gravel, forming shelves on both sides of the Thames on which were established the original settlements that grew together to make the city of London. These beds rise as low hills at certain places around the perimeter of inner London, such as Highgate, Hampstead, and Harrow on the north side, and Wimbledon, Sydenham, and Blackheath on the south.

The term 'London' has no single specific meaning. It was originally restricted to the City of London proper (still referred to distinctively as 'the City'), which has an area of only 677 acres and a residential population of 5,300, but daily absorbs about 350,000 commuters. Other districts were once separate communities: Westminster was in fact named from its position in relation to the City. But with the growth of the capital from the Middle Ages onwards – an expansion that has continued steadily ever since, impeded only by fire and war – the surrounding districts were absorbed one by one into the 'great wen' to make up the vast metropolis we have today.

The County of London, the 'youngest' county in England (until 1974), was formed in 1888 out of parts of the counties of Middlesex, Surrey, and Kent. It was placed under the jurisdiction of the London County Council (the 'L.C.C.'), which superseded the Metropolitan Board of Works, an authority elected by some forty-two 'vestries' or district boards. In 1899 the functions of these vestries were transferred to twenty-eight Metropolitan Boroughs, and in 1900 one of these was created the City of Westminster.

By the mid 20th century, the development of transport facilities, combined with the increasingly rapid expansion of the built-up areas around the County of London, made the neighbouring parts of the 'Home Counties' in effect an extension of the capital. In 1965, in recognition of this, the new administrative district of GREATER LONDON was created, with an area of 620 square miles, the estimated population of which is 6,735,900. Extending for about fifteen to eighteen miles in every direction from Charing Cross, the official centre of the metropolis, it embraces the old county of London, the whole of Middlesex and parts of Hertfordshire, Essex, Surrey, and Kent.

At the same time, the London County Council was superseded by the Greater London Council (the 'G.L.C.') and the metropolitan boroughs and the local administrative units formerly in these counties were amalgamated and redivided into thirty-two new London Boroughs, each with its own mayor and council. In consequence, the names of some of the old boroughs have disappeared (St Marylebone, Holborn, Finsbury, and St Pancras, for instance), others have retained their names but have greatly extended their boundaries (Westminster, for example, now includes St Marylebone and Paddington), while others have been given unfamiliar names, such as Camden and Tower Hamlets. The old names are not likely to go out of use for their districts, any more than have the names of smaller areas, vaguely delimited but of distinct personality, such as Mayfair, Soho, Bayswater, and Bloomsbury. Hampstead will still be called Hampstead, though officially part of the borough of Camden.

A list of the London Boroughs with their officially estimated populations is given on p. 534. Many of the activities of the L.C.C. were transferred to the new G.L.C. (compare p. 329), but those concerning health, welfare, libraries, and children's services were brought under the jurisdiction of the London Boroughs, as was education, except that the twelve Inner London Boroughs were combined for this purpose. The City of London continues to be administered separately by its Corporation (as it always has been), but in addition it enjoys the powers of the London boroughs and shares a seat on the G.L.C. with the City of Westminster.

The CITY OF LONDON, the oldest administrative unit in the larger London, still occupies a site (the 'square mile') approximating to that of Norman London. A corporate county in its own right, it is governed by the Corporation of the City of London, consisting of the 'Mayor and Commonalty and Citizens'. The corporation acts through the Court of Common Council, presided over by the Lord Mayor (see p.

275) and comprising twenty-four other Aldermen, who hold office for life (or until they resign), and the Common Councilmen, who are elected annually by the ratepayers and who now number 134. In addition there are two Sheriffs (compare p. 291), whose forerunners served as the 'port-reeves' or chief magistrates of London and Middlesex. The City is divided into twenty-five wards, each under its alderman, who is also a Justice of the Peace; the names of some of the wards (Vintry, Cordwainer, Candlewick, Portsoken) still have a strong medieval flavour.

A distinctive feature of the City, and one closely associated with its government, are the Guilds, or LIVERY COMPANIES, so named from the dress or livery adopted by the members of the guilds as early as the 14th century. There are now ninety-six such companies in the City, each with its own Master or Prime Warden, its Clerk and other officials, and about 20,000 liverymen are entitled to vote at the municipal elections. Twelve of the companies are designated 'great'; of these the Mercers' Company is the foremost, while the others, in order of civic precedence, are the Grocers, the Drapers, the Fishmongers, the Goldsmiths, the Merchant Taylors and the Skinners (these two alternating in seniority), the Haberdashers, the Salters, the Ironmongers, the Vintners, and the Clothworkers. The Apothecaries have the most liveries (1,150), the Saddlers the fewest (sixty-five). The larger companies pride themselves on their handsome halls; some of the companies are very wealthy and maintain schools and almshouses, as well as devoting considerable sums to other charities and education, and several of them assist the trades with which they are nominally connected.

The City of London was described by the Roman historian Tacitus in the 1st century A.D. as a 'busy emporium for trade and traders', and this description could have been applied to it at almost any time since. The Saxon burgesses, predecessors of the Common Council, declared their independence after the Battle of Hastings, and William the Conqueror was forced to come to terms with them, proffering a charter which is still preserved. The City remains one of the most important commercial areas in the world, the financial and business centre of the metropolis, with the chief offices of the principal banks, insurance companies, stockbrokers, and mercantile houses. Considerably more than a million people enter the City in a single business day.

The City can still show several lengths of its defensive wall, built originally during the 2nd century A.D., as well as some remains of a Roman fort, earlier than the wall, and of the Temple of Mithras, discovered in 1954. The wall was about two miles long between the points where it abutted on the Thames (at the Tower and near Blackfriars Bridge). Fragments of a further defence work alongside the river have recently been discovered and the position of a Roman bridge has been located. The wall enclosed a settlement of about 330 acres which spread over two low hills – Cornhill, where the city centre was on the site of Leadenhall Market, and Ludgate Hill, where St Paul's Cathedral now stands – and between these a small river, the Walbrook, flowed down to join the Thames. The Romans gave the place its name of *Londinium*, probably derived from a personal or tribal name.

The commercial centre of the City is the open space familiarly known as 'the Bank', from which many busy and congested streets radiate and round which are grouped several imposing buildings: the Bank of England, the most important bank in the world; the Mansion House, the official residence of the Lord Mayor; and the Stock Exchange, the market for the purchase and sale of stocks and shares. The Bank lies almost due north of London Bridge, which crosses the Thames to Southwark and is the successor of the only bridge over the river at London until the 18th century. It is still the farthest downstream, apart from the elaborate Tower Bridge, a masterpiece of engineering whose fancifully decorative appearance has become a symbol of Victorian London. Historic buildings within the City boundaries range from the noble church of St Helen's, of Norman origin, to Guildhall (north-west of the Bank), the home of the City Council and partly of the 15th century, and the magnificent bulk of the 17th-century St Paul's Cathedral, the masterpiece of Sir Christopher Wren, its famous dome one of the sights and landmarks of London. Of the incomparable series of churches rebuilt after the Great Fire (1666) by Wren, many suffered severely from air attack during the Second World War, though some fine examples survived and others have been well restored. On the northern side an exciting new 'city within the city' (the Barbican) has been developed; the Barbican Centre here has a fine theatre and a spacious concert hall, and the Museum of London contains a wealth of exhibits from every part of the capital. On the eastern edge of the City (though not actually within its boundaries) is the great fortress of the Tower of London, the oldest part of which is early Norman work.

The City is bounded on the west, at Temple Bar, by the City of Westminster; on the north-west, at Holborn Bars, by the district (formerly the borough) of Holborn; on the north by Finsbury and Shoreditch; and on the east by Stepney, part of the 'East End' of London, once noted for its docks, an area now being redeveloped for other industrial, as well as residential and recreational, purposes. Temple Bar stands at the point where Fleet Street, the centre of newspaper activity, ascending from the direction of Ludgate Hill, meets the Strand, running eastward from Charing Cross. The Temple, between Fleet Street and the river, is a name covering two Inns of Court or corporate legal societies; it is especially notable for its church, with a Romanesque 'round' nave and a Gothic chancel, well restored after war damage. On the north side of the Strand are the Royal Courts of Justice, a Victorian Gothic edifice better known as the Law Courts, and behind these is Lincoln's Inn, another of the interesting Inns of Court, neighbouring Lincoln's Inn Fields, one of the largest of the many squares in London. To the south of the Strand is Somerset House, a palace rebuilt in the 18th century and now partly occupied by public offices, and lying back from the other side of the street, farther west, are the Theatre Royal, Drury Lane, and the Royal Opera House, London's two largest and best-known theatres. In this region also is Covent Garden, once famous for its fruit and vegetable market, but now given over mainly to leisure activities. One of its buildings now contains the London Transport Museum, and a new Theatre Museum is to be opened in another.

The CITY OF WESTMINSTER includes the greater part of the region known as the 'West End', the residential and fashionable quarter of London, with the best shops, the chief theatres, etc., the most exclusive hotels and clubs, and the principal royal palaces and government offices. It extends from Temple Bar to Chelsea and Kensington, and from beyond Oxford Street on the north to the Thames, though the part east of Charing Cross Road has more in common with the City than with the West End. In everyday usage the name of Westminster is confined to a much smaller region, the neighbourhood of Westminster Abbey, one of the finest Gothic churches in England, practically a cathedral in all but name, and the Houses of Parliament, the seat of British government. Both front on to Parliament Square, from which Millbank leads south to the Tate Gallery, the principal gallery of modern painting and sculpture as well as of British painting in general, while Victoria Street runs south-west towards

Westminster Cathedral, the sumptuous early–20th-century Byzantine-style church of the principal Roman Catholic archbishop in Britain. From Westminster Bridge, near the Abbey, the Victoria Embankment, lined by gardens, follows the curve of the Thames to Blackfriars Bridge and the City.

Parliament Square is connected with Charing Cross by the broad Whitehall, lined by many of the chief government offices and traversing the site of the royal palace of the same name. Of this, however, little remains apart from the 17th-century banqueting house, a splendid work of Inigo Jones. Charing Cross, the centre of London for the tourist, opens into Trafalgar Square, with the tall Nelson's Column. To the north of this is the National Gallery, containing an unrivalled collection of paintings of practically every school and period, adjoined by the National Portrait Gallery, containing an interesting assembly of British historical portraits, and facing these is the well-known 18th-century church of St Martin-in-the-Fields.

To the west of Whitehall is the delightful St James's Park, and to the south of this is Queen Anne's Gate, the finest street of the early 18th century in London. The park is bounded on the north by The Mall, a spacious avenue which leads south-west from Charing Cross past St James's Palace, a Tudor royal residence, to Buckingham Palace, the principal mansion of the sovereign. The Queen's Gallery, on its south side, holds a changing exhibition of treasures from the royal collection. To the north, cut through by Pall Mall and limited on the east by the Haymarket and on the west by Green Park, is ST JAMES'S, the home of the aristocracy and men of fashion since the 17th century, and famous for its clubs. Piccadilly, which traverses it on the north, is one of the most fashionable streets in London, with many of the most exclusive shops. Its principal building is Burlington House, the headquarters of the Royal Academy of Arts and several learned societies. Regent Street, running north from Piccadilly Circus, and Oxford Street, farther north, are the most popular shopping streets of London, and Portland Place, the extension of Regent Street, is a fine boulevard of the late 18th century, laid out by the brothers Adam. MAYFAIR, bounded approximately by Regent Street, Oxford Street, and Park Lane, took its name from an ancient fair held annually. This district, declared Sydney Smith, the 18th-century wit, 'enclosed more intelligence and ability, to say nothing of wealth and beauty, than the world had ever collected into such a space before'. It still contains some characteristic residences, though many have given way to large hotels and blocks of flats and offices.

Hyde Park and Kensington Gardens, to the west, together form the largest open space in Central London. Kensington Palace, on the west side of the gardens, was the birthplace of Queen Victoria, and its state rooms have been carefully restored in their former style. To the south of Hyde Park is the aristocratic district of BELGRAVIA, laid out in the early part of the 19th century and still largely unspoiled, and farther west is KENSINGTON, one of the few royal boroughs and a greatly favoured residential quarter. South Kensington is well known for its important museums – the Victoria and Albert Museum, an unrivalled collection of applied art of all kinds, and the adjacent Natural History, Geological, and Science Museums, all well worth visiting – and for the Imperial College of Science and Technology, now extended to cover most of the site formerly occupied by the Commonwealth Institute (transferred to Holland Park). CHELSEA, a fashionable residential district in the 17th–18th centuries and now favoured by artists and young people, lies between Kensington and the river. It has many attractive old streets and houses, and a pleasant riverside promenade, stretching west from Chelsea Bridge and passing the grounds of the Royal Hospital, founded for veteran soldiers by Charles II and occupying a fine building by Sir Christopher Wren.

To the north of Hyde Park is PADDINGTON, a residential district mostly laid out to a uniform plan during the first half of the 19th century, but including BAYSWATER, north of Kensington Gardens, with many hotels and boarding-houses. To the east of Edgware Road and north of Oxford Street is MARYLEBONE (officially St Marylebone, pronounced 'Marry-le-bun'), another mainly residential district, with numerous secluded streets and squares of the 18th century. Its most interesting building is Hertford House, in Manchester Square, containing the Wallace Collection, the finest privately-formed art collection in London, but the property of the nation. The district is adjoined on the north by Regent's Park, another large and attractive open space, with the popular Zoological Gardens (now officially named the London Zoo) on its north side. In its east part, near Tottenham Court Road, is the British Telecom Tower, the most distinctive building in London.

On the south side of Oxford Street and east of Regent Street is the congested district of narrow bustling streets known as SOHO, the principal foreign quarter of central London, where almost every nationality is to be found and many languages are spoken: French and Italian long predominated, though Soho also has a large Chinese population. Well known for its restaurants, it extends south as far as Leicester Square, the centre of a theatrical neighbourhood, and the settlement has spread north across Oxford Street to the vicinity of Charlotte Street. Farther east is HOLBORN (pronounced 'Ho-burn'), a district deriving its name from the valley on its east side through which the Fleet River flowed. The region north of New Oxford Street, known as BLOOMSBURY, once consisted of quiet squares and interconnecting streets, laid out in the 18th and early 19th centuries, and favoured by successful merchants and professional men. It is now best known as the home of two important institutions: the British Museum, the national museum of archaeology and ethnography, unsurpassed for the wealth and interest of its collections, and the University of London, which has been expanding steadily over the last five decades. To the north of Holborn is ST PANCRAS, best known for its large railway termini, though it has a fine church of the Regency period.

To the north-east of Holborn, and traversed by Farringdon Road, which ascends from the valley of the vanished Fleet River, is the district of SMITHFIELD, best known for its meat market. The church of St Bartholomew the Great near by is the oldest ecclesiastical building in London, excepting the chapel in the Tower of London. Adjoining on the north is CLERKENWELL, long known for its watchmakers, opticians, and jewellers. Charterhouse here has been a hostel for poor gentlemen since the 17th century. Farther north is FINSBURY, the home of the City University, and some distance east is SHOREDITCH, well known for its cabinet makers. To the south-east of this is SPITALFIELDS, once famous for its silk weavers, many of whose houses have recently been well restored. To the south-east again, and east of the City, is the 'East End' of London, long notorious as a poverty-stricken quarter, but much of it has experienced great changes in recent years.

London south of the Thames is a busy commercial and industrial quarter of much less interest than the north side. SOUTHWARK (pronounced 'Suth-ark'), extending along the bank of the river from London Bridge to west of Blackfriars Bridge, has a cathedral that is the most notable Gothic building in London, except for Westminster Abbey. In the Middle Ages Southwark became a flourishing borough (in common parlance it is still 'the Borough') and in Elizabethan and

Jacobean times it was famous for its riverside theatres, associated with Shakespeare. LAMBETH, farther upstream opposite Westminster, contains Lambeth Palace, the London residence of the Archbishop of Canterbury, partly medieval, and the Imperial War Museum, with exhibits of all kinds illustrating the two World Wars and other 20th-century conflicts. Facing the river north of Westminster Bridge are County Hall, the seat of the G.L.C., and the Royal Festival Hall, a splendid modern concert hall, overlooked by the vast Shell Centre, one of the more obvious of the many new examples of commercial architecture in London. Downstream from Waterloo Bridge is the distinctive building of the National Theatre (three theatres under one roof), opened in 1976. Upstream from Vauxhall Bridge are the prominent buildings of the New Covent Garden Market, the principal market in London for fruit, vegetables, and flowers.

In the seemingly unrelieved mass of building that spreads out in every direction from inner London are other places of interest that should not be overlooked. Particular mention may be made of CHISWICK, an 18th-century suburb fronting the Thames; HAMPSTEAD, with many old houses, its famous Heath and the charming Kenwood House; HIGHGATE, a 'village' survival on a neighbouring hill; ISLINGTON, growing in favour as a residential quarter, with squares and terraces of the 18th and early 19th centuries; GREENWICH, on the south bank of the Thames downstream, well known for its Royal Naval College, its park, and its National Maritime Museum; and DULWICH, still a rural retreat, with a noted picture gallery.

London is popular with visitors at any period of the year, winter almost as much as summer. Much the best time to explore the capital is the spring, when the trees in the parks and squares are coming into leaf and the atmosphere is still fresh and cool. As the summer progresses, the sights and places of interest tend to become more crowded. By the middle of July the great migration of Londoners to the sea and country has begun, but the city is then invaded by tourists, especially from America and the Commonwealth, though increasingly from the Continent, too, for whom August and September are the favourite months. October, after most of the crowds have departed, is another pleasant time in London.

EXPLORING LONDON

London is so large and intricate and its interests are so extensive that the visitor cannot hope to obtain even a superficial impression of it in much less than a week, and a more detailed exploration will take at least a full month (the enthusiast will say a year, if not a lifetime!). Those with limited time at their disposal may well despair of gaining an adequate acquaintance with the many sights and treasures that London holds. Most of the more important features of interest, however, are confined to central London, the area to which the major part of this guide is devoted.

The stranger freshly arrived in London cannot do better than remember W. E. Gladstone's much-quoted advice to a group of American travellers: 'The way to see London is from the top of a bus – the top of a bus, gentlemen.' A modest outlay on bus fares will enable visitors to see at least the main streets, in rather better fashion than by car or taxi, and to form a mental picture of the layout of the capital, with the positions of the most important public buildings. They will find that two main thoroughfares run from west to east to converge at the Bank, the centre of the City, and a journey by bus along one of these, returning by the other, will be found quite a satisfactory introduction to London. The more northerly thoroughfare, beginning at Marble Arch, at the north-east corner of Hyde Park, follows Oxford Street, Holborn, Newgate Street, and Cheapside in a continuous line, passing a little south of the British Museum and just north of St Paul's Cathedral. The second through route starts at Hyde Park Corner, south-east of the park, and traverses Piccadilly eastward to beyond Piccadilly Circus, then turns southward via the Haymarket to Charing Cross, the hub of the West End, there taking up its eastward direction via the Strand, Fleet Street, and Cannon Street, and passing immediately south of St Paul's. These two long thoroughfares are joined by numerous roads running north and south, of which the most important are Park Lane, Bond Street, and Regent Street in the West End, Charing Cross Road and Kingsway (with Aldwych) in the central area, and Chancery Lane at the City's edge. A grasp of the relationship of all these streets, combined with the knowledge that the

Thames flows from west to east (except for a sharp northward bend between Vauxhall Bridge and Waterloo Bridge), and travellers are equipped to begin the exploration of London in more detail. They could then make Charing Cross and the Bank their chief centres, striking out in every direction from these, a plan followed more or less in the descriptions of the routes in this guide.

The traveller who is merely passing through London and can devote only a single day to the capital can hardly hope to receive an adequate impression. The following route (followed, if feasible, on foot) takes in as many of the most interesting streets and buildings as is possible.

Charing Cross to Whitehall, Houses of Parliament, Westminster Abbey, St James's Park and Palace, Buckingham Palace, Green Park, Piccadilly, Piccadilly Circus, Leicester Square, the National Gallery, and Charing Cross, then to the Strand, the Temple, Fleet Street, Ludgate Hill, St Paul's Cathedral, Cheapside, Bank of England, London Bridge, Lower Thames Street, and the Tower.

Visitors with two days at their disposal can try the following routes:

FIRST DAY. Charing Cross to Whitehall, Houses of Parliament, Westminster Abbey, Queen Anne's Gate, Westminster Cathedral, Buckingham Palace, St James's Park and Palace, Piccadilly, Hyde Park Corner, Hyde Park, Marble Arch, Wallace Collection, Oxford Street, Regent Street, Piccadilly Circus, Haymarket, the National Gallery, and Charing Cross.

SECOND DAY. Charing Cross to the Strand, the Temple, Fleet Street, Ludgate Hill, St Paul's Cathedral, Cannon Street, London Bridge, Southwark Cathedral, Lower Thames Street, the Tower, Fenchurch Street, Lombard Street, the Bank of England, Cheapside, Guildhall, Museum of London, Barbican Centre, St Bartholomew's Church, Holborn, Lincoln's Inn, Kingsway, Soho, Leicester Square, and Charing Cross.

The visitor who spends a week in London can devote considerably more time to the individual sights. Perhaps the best plan, if the weather is suitable, is to see the outdoor places of interest in the mornings, when the air is crisper and the streets rather less crowded, and visit the museums, galleries, and other indoor 'sights' after lunch, particularly if the afternoons are warm. The evenings could then be spent in the parks, or at the theatre or some other place of entertainment. Alternatively, the days could be arranged on the following plan.

FIRST DAY. Charing Cross to Whitehall, Banqueting House, Houses of Parliament, Westminster Bridge, County Hall, Albert Embankment, Lambeth Palace, Lambeth Bridge, Tate Gallery, Millbank, Westminster Abbey, Queen Anne's Gate,

St James's Park, and Charing Cross. — SECOND DAY. Charing Cross to The Mall, St James's Palace, Buckingham Palace, Queen's Gallery, Westminster Cathedral, Victoria, Belgravia, Hyde Park Corner, Piccadilly, St James's Square, and Charing Cross. — THIRD DAY. Hyde Park Corner to Knightsbridge, Brompton Oratory, Victoria and Albert Museum, Natural History Museum or Science Museum, Kensington Gardens, Kensington Palace, the Serpentine, and Hyde Park Corner. — FOURTH DAY. Hyde Park Corner to Mayfair, Oxford Street, Wallace Collection, St Marylebone Church, Regent's Park, and the Zoological Gardens, then via Portland Place and Regent Street to Piccadilly Circus. — FIFTH DAY. Charing Cross to the National Gallery, Leicester Square, Soho, British Museum, London University, Russell Square, Southampton Row, Lincoln's Inn, Kingsway, Aldwych, Victoria Embankment, and Charing Cross. — SIXTH DAY. Charing Cross to the Strand, Covent Garden, the Temple, Fleet Street, Ludgate Hill, Old Bailey, St Bartholomew's Church, the Barbican Centre, Museum of London, St Paul's Cathedral, Cheapside, Guildhall, and the Bank of England. — SEVENTH DAY. The Bank to London Bridge, Southwark Cathedral, Guy's Hospital, London Bridge, Lower Thames Street, the Tower, All Hallows Church, Fenchurch Street, Lombard Street, and the Bank.

Visitors with more than a week at their disposal may prefer to follow the detailed routes given in this guide. Those wishing to draw up their own itineraries should take into account the following points.

Museums, galleries, and public institutions are almost invariably closed on New Year's Day, Good Friday, May Day Monday, Christmas Eve and Day, and Boxing Day, and on *Sunday mornings*, but the London Transport Museum, Madame Tussaud's Waxworks and the London Planetarium, the Ship Collection at St Katharine's Docks, the Tower Bridge Walkway, and the Zoological Gardens are open then. The Faraday Museum in the Royal Institution is open on *Tuesdays and Thursdays* only, the Ambulance Museum in St John's Gate on *Tuesdays*, *Fridays and Saturdays* only, the House of St Barnabas and the Royal Mews on *Wednesdays and Thursdays* only, Chelsea Physic Garden (April–October) and Linley Sambourne House on *Wednesdays and Sundays* only, the Great Hall of Eltham Palace on *Thursdays and Sundays* only, and the Bear Gardens Museum and Lancaster House on *Saturdays and Sundays* only.

Charlton House, the London Diamond Centre, the National Sound Archive, the Stock Exchange, the Telecom Technology Showcase, the Thomas Coram Foundation, and Well Hall are closed on *Saturdays* and some of the smaller places of interest are closed on *Sundays*. The Blewcoat School and the National Postal Museum are closed on *Saturdays and Sundays*, the Soane Museum on *Sundays and Mondays*, the Banqueting House, the Crafts Council Gallery, the Dulwich College Gallery, the Geffrye Museum, the Institute of Contemporary Arts, the London Toy and Model Museum, the Museum of London, the National Museum of Labour History, and the Queen's Gallery on *Mondays*, Carlyle's House on *Mondays and Tuesdays*, the Wellington Museum on *Mondays and Fridays*, the Jewish Museum on *Mondays and Saturdays*, Greenwich Church on *Wednesdays*, the Royal Naval College on *Thursdays*, Fenton House on *Thursdays and Fridays*, and the Museum of Childhood, Bethnal Green, and the Victoria and Albert Museum on *Fridays*.

The Houses of Parliament (see p. 358) *were closed to the public at the time of this revision and no date had been announced for their re-opening.*

Advance arrangements must be made in writing to see the Bank of England, the Broadcasting Gallery of the I.B.A., Canonbury Tower, Charterhouse, the College of Arms, Gray's Inn, the Hunterian Museum, Lambeth Palace, Lincoln's Inn, Lloyd's, the Mansion House, Marlborough House, the Royal College of Music (Donaldson Museum), and Trinity House. Where places are normally open to parties only it is sometimes possible for an individual visitor to make arrangements to be attached to a party.

Most (though not all) of the national museums and galleries provide facilities (lifts, wheelchairs, etc.) for the disabled, but in some the facilities are quite inadequate and it is advisable to make inquiry in advance (to the director or information officer).

ART COLLECTIONS. Visitors (especially foreign visitors) who naturally expect to find the national collection of British paintings in the NATIONAL GALLERY will be disappointed. Though a selection of British works (mainly of the 18th and 19th centuries) is shown here, the gallery is chiefly concerned with foreign paintings (down to the late 19th century), and the main collection of British paintings (of all periods) is at the TATE GALLERY. Here also are the national collections of modern foreign paintings and modern sculpture. Many fine 'Old Masters' can be seen at the WALLACE COLLECTION, the COURTAULD INSTITUTE GALLERIES (which also shows some well-known French Impressionists and Post-Impressionists), the VICTORIA AND ALBERT MUSEUM (where, too, the Raphael Cartoons are on permanent loan), KENWOOD HOUSE, adjoining Hampstead Heath, and the DULWICH COLLEGE GALLERY in south London, and the SOANE MUSEUM has some famous Hogarths. Historical portraits are shown at the NATIONAL PORTRAIT GALLERY, and also, with other relevant paintings, at the IMPERIAL WAR MUSEUM, the NATIONAL ARMY MUSEUM, and the NATIONAL MARITIME MUSEUM at Greenwich. A selection of the royal paintings, etc. (changed periodically), is shown in the QUEEN'S GALLERY, Buckingham Palace Road.

The CITY CHURCHES are mostly open on Monday–Friday and closed on Saturdays, but some are open for a few hours only during the middle of the day. In 1954 the number of parishes in the City was reduced from 108 to twenty-four, and fifteen churches were nominated as GUILD CHURCHES. These have been assigned to specific purposes (St Lawrence Jewry, for instance, is the official church of the Corporation of London) and they may not be open on Sundays for visitors or service. The halls of the CITY LIVERY COMPANIES can often be seen by previous arrangement with the Clerks and some of them are thrown open to the public on a few days in the year. For these occasions particulars and tickets are obtainable in advance from the City of London Information Centre (see p. 73). The most interesting halls are those of the Apothecaries, the Fishmongers, the Goldsmiths, the Skinners, the Stationers, and the Vintners.

Admission To Places Of Interest. The following list gives the times and conditions of admission to the principal sights of central and suburban London. The most important museums, galleries, etc., are indicated by an asterisk (*). Children, students, and pensioners are usually admitted at half-price where a charge is made.

All Hallows by the Tower, Mondays–Fridays 9 to 6, Saturdays 11 to 6, Sundays 12.30 to 6; Apsley House, see Wellington Museum; Artillery Museum, see Rotunda Museum.

Bank of England, see p. 274; Bankside Gallery, Tuesdays–Saturdays 10 to 5, Sundays 2 to 6 (closed between exhibitions); *Banqueting House, Tuesdays–Saturdays 10 to 5, Sundays 2 to 5; Barbican Art Gallery, Tuesdays–Saturdays 10 to 6.45, Sundays and Bank Holidays 12 to 5.45 (closed between exhibitions); Bear Gardens Museum, Saturdays and Sundays 10.30 to 5.30 (Mondays–Fridays by appointment only); H.M.S. Belfast, daily 11 to 5.50 (in winter to 4.30); Bethnal Green Museum, see Museum of Childhood; Blewcoat School, Mondays–Fridays 10 to 5.30 (Thursdays to 7); British and Foreign Bible Society, Mondays–Fridays 10 to 4 (free); British Crafts Centre, Mondays–Fridays 10 to 5.30, Saturdays to 4 (free; closed between exhibitions); *British Library, see p. 336; *British Museum, see p. 336; Brixton Windmill, daily 9 to dusk; Broadcasting Gallery, Mondays–Fridays at 10, 11.30, 2.30, and 3.30 (guided tours; free); Building Centre, Mondays–Fridays 9.30 to 5.30, Saturdays 10 to 1 (free); Burgh House, Wednesdays–Sundays 12 to 5, Bank Holidays 2 to 5 (free; closed between exhibitions); Burlington House, see p. 85.

Cabinet War Rooms, Tuesdays–Saturdays and Bank Holiday Mondays 10 to 5.50 (last adm. at 5.15); Camden Arts Centre, weekdays 11 to 6 (to 8 on Fridays), Sundays 2 to 6 (free; closed between exhibitions); Canonbury Tower, usually on application to the Warden; Carlyle's House, April–October, Wednesdays–Sundays and Bank Holiday Mondays 11 to 5; Cecil Sharp House, weekdays 9.30 to 5.30 (free); Central Criminal Court, on Saturdays at 11, on other weekdays (when the court is not sitting) at 11 and 3 (free; to the public galleries, see p. 246); Central Hall (Imperial Collection), weekdays 10 to 6; Ceylon Tea Centre, weekdays 10 to 6 (free; closed between exhibitions); Charlton House, Mondays–Fridays 9 to 5, Saturdays by appointment (telephone 856–3951; gardens open daily, free); Chartered Insurance Institute Museum, Mondays–Fridays 9.15 to 5.15 (free); *Charterhouse, usually April–July, Wednesdays at 2.45, by arrangement with the Registrar; Chelsea Physic Garden, April–October, Wednesdays and Sundays 2 to 5; *Chelsea Royal Hospital, see p. 354; *Chiswick House, daily 9.30 to 6.30 (mid-October –mid-March, Wednesdays–Sundays 9.30 to 4); College of Arms, see p. 354; *Commonwealth Institute, weekdays 10 to 5.30; Sundays 2 to 5 (free); Coram Foundation, see Thomas Coram Foundation; *Courtauld Institute Galleries, weekdays 10 to 5, Sundays 2 to 5; Courtauld

INSTITUTE OF ART, see Home House; CRAFTS COUNCIL GALLERY, Tuesdays –Saturdays 10 to 5, Sundays 2 to 5 (free); CROSBY HALL, weekdays 10 to 12 and 2 to 5, Sundays 2 to 5 (free); CUMING MUSEUM (Southwark), weekdays 10 to 5.30 (Thursdays to 7, Saturdays to 5; free); *CUTTY SARK (Greenwich), weekdays 11 to 6 (in winter to 5), Sundays from 2.30.

DESIGN CENTRE, Mondays and Tuesdays 10 to 6, Wednesdays–Saturdays 10 to 8, Sundays 1 to 6 (free); DICKENS HOUSE, weekdays 10 to 5; DR JOHNSON'S HOUSE, weekdays 11 to 5.30 (October–April to 5); DR WILLIAMS'S LIBRARY, usually Mondays–Fridays 10 to 5 (Tuesdays and Thursdays to 6.30), on application; DONALDSON MUSEUM, see Royal College of Music; *DULWICH COLLEGE GALLERY, Tuesdays–Saturdays 10 to 1 and 2 to 5, Sundays 2 to 5.

ELTHAM PALACE, Great Hall, Thursdays and Sundays 11 to 7 (November–March to 4; free).

FENTON HOUSE (Hampstead), April–October, Saturdays–Wednesdays 11 to 6 (Saturdays and Sundays 2 to 6 in March); FRIENDS' HOUSE, Mondays–Fridays 9.30 to 5.30, Saturdays 9 to 4.30 (by appointment).

GEFFRYE MUSEUM, Tuesdays–Saturdays and Bank Holidays 10 to 5, Sundays 2 to 5 (free); *GEOLOGICAL MUSEUM, see p. 414; GIPSY MOTH IV (Greenwich), weekdays 10.30 to 6 (in winter to 5), Sundays from 2.30; GRAY'S INN, Hall, Chapel and Library, usually on application to the Under-Treasurer (to the gardens, May–September, daily 12 to 2.30; free); GREENWICH CHURCH, daily (except Wednesdays) 10 to 12.30 and 2 to 4; GUARDS' CHAPEL, see Royal Military Chapel; *GUILDHALL, Great Hall, weekdays 10 to 5 (Sundays also in May–September), Art Gallery, weekdays 10 to 5 (closed between exhibitions), Clock Museum, Mondays–Fridays 9.30 to 4.45 (all are free); GUINNESS WORLD OF RECORDS, Mondays–Thursdays 10 to 10, Fridays–Sundays 10 to 11 (last admission one hour before).

HAYWARD GALLERY, Mondays–Wednesdays 10 to 8, Thursdays–Saturdays 10 to 6, Sundays 12 to 6; HOGARTH'S HOUSE (Chiswick), weekdays 11 to 6, Sundays 2 to 6 (in winter to 4; free; closed first two weeks in September and last three in December); HOME HOUSE, Mondays–Fridays 10 to 5, in vacation (free; closed for ten days at Easter and Christmas); HORNIMAN MUSEUM (Forest Hill), weekdays 10.30 to 6, Sundays 2 to 6 (free); HOUSE OF ST BARNABAS, Wednesdays 2.30 to 4.15, Thursdays 11 to 12.30 (or by appointment for parties only; gratuity); *HOUSES OF PARLIAMENT, see p. 358; HUNTERIAN MUSEUM, Mondays–Fridays 10 to 5 (on written application; free; closed during August).

IMPERIAL COLLECTION, see Central Hall; *IMPERIAL WAR MUSEUM, see p. 368; INNER TEMPLE HALL, usually Mondays–Fridays 10.30 to 11.30 and 3 to 4 (except during vacations); INSTITUTE OF CONTEMPORARY ARTS, Tuesdays –Sundays 12 to 11 (art gallery to 9).

JEWEL TOWER, weekdays 9.30 to 6.30 (mid-October–mid-March to 4); JEWISH MUSEUM, Tuesdays–Thursdays 10 to 4, Fridays and Sundays 10 to 12.45 (free; closed on Jewish holy days).

KEATS HOUSE (Hampstead), weekdays 10 to 1 and 2 to 6, Sundays and Bank

Holidays 2 to 5 (free); KENSINGTON EXHIBITION CENTRE, daily 11 to 6 or 7 (closed between exhibitions); *KENSINGTON PALACE, see p. 371; *KENWOOD HOUSE (Hampstead), daily 10 to 7 (February, March, and October to 5, November–January to 4; free), to park and gardens, 8 to dusk; KODAK GALLERY, Mondays–Fridays 9 to 4.45 (free; closed between exhibitions).

*LAMBETH PALACE, open occasionally for conducted parties or by arrangement with the Chaplain; LANCASTER HOUSE, Easter–mid-December, Saturdays, Sundays, and Bank Holidays, 2 to 6 (except when used for government functions); LAW COURTS, see p. 231; LEIGHTON HOUSE, weekdays 11 to 5 (to 6 for special exhibitions; free); *LINCOLN'S INN, Halls and Library, on previous written application only, Chapel and Gardens, Mondays–Fridays 12 to 2.30 (free); LINLEY SAMBOURNE HOUSE, March–October, Wednesdays 10 to 4, Sundays 2 to 5 (at other times on application to the Victorian Society, 1 Priory Gardens, W4); LIVESEY MUSEUM (Southwark), weekdays 10 to 5 (free; closed between exhibitions); LLOYD'S, by appointment or by introduction from a member; LONDON DIAMOND CENTRE, Mondays–Fridays 9.30 to 5.30 (Saturdays 9.30 to 1.30 by arrangement); LONDON DUNGEON MUSEUM, daily 10 to 5.45 (October–March to 4.30); LONDON PLANETARIUM, daily 11 to 4.30 (performances every hour; see also Madame Tussaud's); LONDON TAXI MUSEUM (Brixton), Mondays–Fridays 9 to 5, Saturdays 9 to 12 (free); LONDON TOY AND MODEL MUSEUM, Tuesdays–Saturdays and Bank Holidays 10 to 5.30, Sundays 11 to 5; LONDON TRANSPORT MUSEUM, daily 10 to 6; LONDON ZOO, see Zoological Gardens; LORD'S CRICKET MUSEUM, 10.30 to 5 on match days only (out of season tours by arrangement).

MADAME TUSSAUD'S WAXWORKS, daily 10 to 5.30 (July and August to 6; closed Christmas Day only; combined ticket with London Planetarium obtainable); MALL ART GALLERIES, weekdays 10 to 5 (occasionally on Sundays; closed between exhibitions); MANSION HOUSE, for organized parties only, on written application to the Lord Mayor's secretary; MARLBOROUGH HOUSE, conducted tours only, including the Queen's Chapel, by previous arrangement with the Administration Officer; MIDDLE TEMPLE HALL, usually Mondays–Fridays 10 to 12 and 3 to 4.30 (Saturdays by appointment only); MONUMENT, weekdays 9 to 5.40 (October–March to 3.40), Sundays 2 to 5.40 in May–September only; MUSEUM OF CHILDHOOD, Mondays–Thursdays and Saturdays 10 to 6, Sundays 2.30 to 6 (free); MUSEUM OF GARDEN HISTORY, Mondays–Fridays 11 to 3, Sundays 10.30 to 5 (free); *MUSEUM OF LONDON, see p. 374; MUSEUM OF MANKIND, weekdays 10 to 5, Sundays 2.30 to 6 (free).

NATIONAL ARMY MUSEUM, see p. 354; *NATIONAL GALLERY, see p. 380; *NATIONAL MARITIME MUSEUM (Greenwich), Mondays–Fridays 10 to 6 (in winter to 5), Saturdays 10 to 6, Sundays 2 to 5.30 (in winter to 5); NATIONAL MUSEUM OF LABOUR HISTORY (Limehouse), Tuesdays–Saturdays 9.30 to 5, Sundays 2.30 to 5 (free); *NATIONAL PORTRAIT GALLERY, see p. 391; NATIONAL POSTAL MUSEUM, Mondays–Thursdays 10 to 4.30, Fridays 10 to 4 (free); NATIONAL SOUND ARCHIVE, Mondays–Fridays 10 to 4.30 (to 9 on

Thursdays; by appointment); *National Theatre, conducted tours on weekdays at 10.15 and 12.45, and (except on Wednesdays and Saturdays) at 12.30 and 5.30; *Natural History Museum, see p. 399.

Old Bailey, see Central Criminal Court; Old Royal Observatory (Greenwich), as for the National Maritime Museum; to Planetarium, Mondays, Tuesdays, Thursdays, and Fridays at 2.30 and 3.30 (additional programmes on Saturdays in summer); Old St Thomas's Hospital, Operating Theatre, Mondays, Wednesdays, and Fridays, 12.30 to 4; Orangery (Kensington Gardens), as for Kensington Palace.

*Percival David Foundation of Chinese Art, Mondays 2 to 5, Tuesdays–Fridays 10.30 to 5, Saturdays 10.30 to 1 (free); Photographers' Gallery, weekdays 11 to 7, Sundays 2 to 6 (free); Planetarium, see London Planetarium and Old Royal Observatory; Pollock's Toy Museum, weekdays 10 to 5; Post Office Tower, see Telecom Tower; Prince Henry's Room, Mondays–Fridays 1.45 to 5, Saturdays to 4.30 (free); *Public Record Office Museum, closed for restoration in 1985.

Queen's Chapel, see Marlborough House; Queen's Chapel of the Savoy, Tuesdays–Fridays 11.30 to 3.30 (closed August and September); *Queen's Gallery, Tuesdays–Saturdays and Bank Holidays 11 to 5, Sundays 2 to 5.

Ranger's House (Blackheath), daily 10 to 5 (November–January to 4; free); Roman Fort, West Gate, first Tuesday in each month, 10.30 to 12, third Friday 2.30 to 4.30; Rotunda Museum (Woolwich), Mondays–Fridays 12 to 4 or 5, Saturdays and Sundays from 1 (free); Royal Academy, see p. 85; Royal College of Music, Donaldson Museum, Wednesdays 11 to 4 during term, on application to the Curator; Royal Courts of Justice, see p. 231; *Royal Hospital, Chelsea, see p. 354, Royal Institute of British Architects, Heinz Gallery, Mondays–Fridays 11 to 5, Saturdays 10 to 1 (free; closed between exhibitions); Royal Institution, Faraday Museum, Tuesdays and Thursdays 1 to 4 (at other times by arrangement); Royal Mews, Wednesdays and Thursdays 2 to 4 (except during Ascot Week); Royal Military Chapel, weekdays 10 to 3.30; *Royal Naval College (Greenwich), Chapel and Painted Hall, daily (except Thursdays) 2.30 to 5 (free); Royal School of Needlework, Mondays–Fridays 9.30 to 5.30 (free); Royal Society of Arts, Hall, weekdays on application, after 9.30 (when not in use).

St Andrew-by-the-Wardrobe, Mondays–Fridays 7 to 6, Sundays 10 to 6; St Andrew's, Holborn, Mondays–Fridays 8.15 to 5.30; St Bartholomew the Great, daily 8.30 to dusk; St Bride's, Fleet Street, daily 9 to 5; St Catherine's House, see p. 235; St Clement Danes, daily 8 to 5; St Clement's Eastcheap, Mondays–Fridays 9 to 4.30; St Edmund the King, Mondays–Fridays 8.30 to 4.15; St Giles Cripplegate, Mondays–Fridays 9.30 to 2, Sundays 7.45 to 12 and 2.30 to 5; St Helen's, Bishopsgate, Mondays–Fridays 9 to 5, Saturdays and Sundays 1 to 4; St James Garlickhithe, Mondays–Fridays 10 to 5, Sundays 2.30 to 6; St James's, Piccadilly (Church Hall), weekdays 10 to 6,

Sundays 12 to 6; ST JOHN'S GATE (Ambulance Museum), Tuesdays, Fridays, and Saturdays 10 to 6 (free; tours, including St John's Church, at 11 and 2.30); ST KATHARINE ROYAL FOUNDATION (Stepney), usually on application to the Master (free); ST KATHARINE'S DOCKS, Ship Museum, daily 10 to 5; ST LAWRENCE JEWRY, Mondays–Fridays 7.45 to 5, Saturdays and Sundays 2 to 5; ST MAGNUS THE MARTYR, Tuesdays–Fridays 10.30 to 4; ST MARGARET LOTHBURY, Mondays–Fridays 8.30 to 4.30; ST MARGARET PATTENS, Mondays–Fridays 9.30 to 4.30; ST MARGARET'S, Westminster, daily 9.30 to 4.30; ST MARTIN-WITHIN-LUDGATE, Mondays–Fridays 10 to 3; ST MARY ABCHURCH, most weekdays 10 to 4, Sundays 2 to 4; ST MARY ALDERMARY, Tuesdays–Fridays 10.30 to 3.30; ST MARY-AT-HILL, Tuesdays–Thursdays 1 to 2.30 (except during August); ST MARY-LE-BOW, Mondays–Fridays 9 to 4; ST MICHAEL, PATERNOSTER ROYAL, Mondays–Fridays 8.30 to 6; ST MICHAEL'S CORNHILL, Mondays–Fridays 8 to 5, Sundays 10 to 1.30; ST PAUL'S CATHEDRAL, see p. 404; ST PETER'S CORNHILL, Mondays–Fridays 10 to 4 (except during August); ST STEPHEN, WALBROOK, under restoration in 1985; ST VEDAST'S, Foster Lane, Mondays–Fridays 6 to 6, Saturdays 6.30 to 9, Sundays 7 to 1.30; SAVOY CHAPEL, see Queen's Chapel of the Savoy; *SCIENCE MUSEUM, see p. 414; SERPENTINE GALLERY, Mondays–Fridays 10 to 6, Saturdays and Sundays 10 to 7 (November–March to dusk; free; closed between exhibitions); SHELL CENTRE, Viewing Gallery, closed until further notice; SILVER VAULTS, Mondays–Fridays 9 to 5.30, Saturdays (except before Bank Holidays) 9 to 12.30 (free); *SIR JOHN SOANE'S MUSEUM, Tuesdays–Saturdays 10 to 5 (free); SOMERSET HOUSE, see p. 229; SOUTH LONDON ART GALLERY (Camberwell), Tuesdays–Saturdays 10 to 6, Sundays 3 to 6 (free; closed between exhibitions); *SOUTHWARK CATHEDRAL, see p. 422; STOCK EXCHANGE, Public Gallery and Cinema, Mondays–Fridays 9.45 to 3.15 (free).

*TATE GALLERY, see p. 426; TELECOM TECHNOLOGY SHOWCASE, Mondays–Fridays 10 to 5 (free); TELECOM TOWER, Viewing Gallery, closed until further notice; *TEMPLE, see Inner Temple Hall and Middle Temple Hall; *TEMPLE CHURCH, weekdays 10 to 5, Sundays 2 to 4; THAMES FLOOD BARRIER CENTRE, daily 10.30 to 6 (October–March to 5); THEATRE MUSEUM, Covent Garden, to be opened in 1986; THOMAS CORAM FOUNDATION (formerly the Foundling Hospital Offices), Mondays–Fridays 10 to 4 (except when used for conferences); TOWER BRIDGE WALKWAY and Museum, daily 10 to 6.30 (November–March to 4.45); *TOWER OF LONDON, see p. 434; TRINITY HOUSE, occasionally on written application to the Secretary (parties only).

UNIVERSITY COLLEGE, Flaxman Gallery and Flinders Petrie Egyptology Collection, usually Mondays–Fridays 9 to 5.

VICTORIA AND ALBERT MUSEUM, see p. 447.

*WALLACE COLLECTION, see p. 465; WELL HALL (Eltham), daily (except Saturdays) 11 to 4.30; *WELLINGTON MUSEUM, Tuesdays–Thursdays and Saturdays 10 to 6, Sundays 2.30 to 6; WESLEY'S CHAPEL, daily 9 to dusk; WESLEY'S HOUSE, weekdays 10 to 4, Sundays after service at 11; *WESTMINSTER ABBEY, see p. 469; *WESTMINSTER CATHEDRAL, see p. 488; *WESTMINSTER HALL, see p. 358; WESTMINSTER SCHOOL, usually on application to Bursar, during school holidays; WHITECHAPEL ART GALLERY, daily (except Mondays) 10 or 11 to 5 (Wednesdays to 8; free; closed between exhibitions); WHITEHALL PALACE, see Banqueting House; WOODLANDS ART GALLERY (Greenwich), Mondays, Tuesdays, Thursdays, and Fridays 10 to 7.30, Saturdays 10 to 6, Sundays 2 to 6 (closed between exhibitions).

*ZOOLOGICAL GARDENS see p. 492.

Times and conditions of admission are liable to change. The latest information should be sought from the London Visitor and Convention Bureau (see p. 72).

PLACES OF INTEREST TO CHILDREN: H.M.S. *Belfast* (adm., see above); Museum of Childhood, Bethnal Green; Buckingham Palace and the Horse Guards (Changing of the Guard); *Cutty Sark*; Geffrye Museum; Kensington Palace (Princess Victoria's dolls and toys); London Toy and Model Museum; London Transport Museum; Madame Tussaud's and the London Planetarium; National Maritime Museum and Planetarium (Greenwich); Natural History Museum; Peter Pan statue and the Round Pond (Kensington Gardens); Pollock's Toy Museum; Royal Mews; Science Museum (children's gallery, etc.); Tower Bridge Walkway; Tower of London; Trafalgar Square; Zoological Gardens.

MAPS AND ATLASES. The street plan of central London at the end of this guide will be found adequate for general use by the tourist and holiday-maker. The best map of London is that contained in the *Reference Atlas of Greater London*, published by Messrs John Bartholomew & Son Ltd (13th edition, 1968). The whole of Greater London is drawn on a scale of 4 in. to 1 m., and the central area (extending from the Houses of Parliament to the Tower) on a scale of 10 in. to 1 m., while the environs, reaching as far north as St Albans, south to Reigate, east to Tilbury, and west to Windsor, are included on a scale of 2 in. to 1 m. In addition there are general and administrative maps, and an index of over 62,000 names. This atlas is at present out of print, but it may be consulted at public libraries.

Smaller maps, easy to carry about, include Bartholomew's *Everyone's London Street Plan*, on a scale of 1 to 15,000 (about 4¼ in. to 1 m.), covering inner London from Hampstead to Clapham Common and from Kew Bridge to Tower Bridge. Bartholomew's *Central London Pocket Map* covers London from Primrose Hill to Battersea Park and from Olympia to Tower Bridge, on a scale of 1 to 10,000 (about 6½ in. to 1 m.), and the same company's *London Plan*, on a scale of 3¾ in. to 1 m., extends from Hammersmith to Greenwich and from Hampstead to Denmark Hill. All these maps have indexes.

Other maps are published by the Geographers' A–Z Map Company (whose showrooms are at 28 Gray's Inn Road, Holborn, WC1), including a *Super Scale Map of London* (9 in. to 1 m.), a *London Map* on a scale of 6 in. to 1 m., and the *Premier Map of London* (3 in. to 1 m.), and by Geographia/Nicholson (17 Conway Street, W1), including the *London A1 Master Street Plan* (1 to 20,000 or 3⅙ in. to 1 m.). Pocket Atlases, with indexes, are published by these companies and by the Ordnance Survey, whose *A B C London Street Atlas* (6 in. and 3½ in. to 1 m.) covers the whole of Greater London. Other maps on various scales are published by Messrs George Philip of 12 Long Acre, WC2, among them the *Touring Map of London* (5 in. and ¾ in. to 1 m., with index).

Useful maps for motorists are Bartholomew's *London To and Through* (1 in. and ¼ in. to 1 m.) and *50 Miles round London* (1 to 250,000 or about ¼ in. to 1 m.), Geographia's *One Way London* (1 to 10,560), the *AA Map of London* (1 in. and ⅐ in. to 1 m.), the Geographers' A–Z *Main Road Map of London* (1 in. to 1 m.), and the *RAC's London Region* map (1 to 100,000 or about ⅝ in. to 1 m.). Sheet 9 of the Ordnance Survey *Routemaster Map* (¼ in to 1 m.) covers the approaches to London from Harwich, Dover, and other south-east ports. Bartholomew's *National Map* series (1 to 100,000) is useful for motorists and cyclists, but the best maps for the country around London (especially for walkers) are those in the Ordnance Survey *Landranger* series (1 to 50,000), which have replaced the popular 1 in. to 1 m. maps. An interesting map and guide to *Roman London* has been published by the Ordnance Survey (2nd edition, 1983).

These maps and atlases are stocked by most booksellers and many stationers. They may also be obtained from Messrs Edward Stanford, 12 Long Acre, WC2 (near Covent Garden). The selling agents for the Ordnance Survey are Messrs Stanford and (for England and Wales) Messrs Cook, Hammond, and Kell, 22 Caxton Street, SW1. Ordnance Survey maps may also be ordered by post from many post offices.

APPROACHES TO LONDON

By Rail. Fast through trains run to London from every important city in Britain and from the principal ports. The 1st class fare is up to fifty per cent more than the 2nd class fare. Children up to five years travel free, those up to sixteen years pay half fares. Single tickets are generally valid for three days (including the day of issue) and return tickets (available for three months) are issued for both classes, generally at twice the single fare, but day, weekend, and monthly return tickets at cheaper fares and other concessions are obtainable. Credit cards may be used to buy tickets.

Seats may be reserved in advance on many trains on application in the inquiry office at the starting-point of the journey and from rail travel agents. Restaurant or buffet cars are attached to most of the long-distance trains. Breakfast, lunch, tea (or high tea), and dinner are obtainable in the restaurant cars (reduced prices for children). Light meals packed for the journey may be obtained at the station or by telephoning Travellers Fare, St Pancras Chambers, NW1 (387–2878, extension 3712). Sleeping accommodation is provided on the principal night trains, but berths should be booked well in advance.

A Passenger Timetable, including all the railway services in Britain (as well as the sea connections to Ireland, the Isle of Wight, and the Channel Islands), is published annually, in May, by the *British Railways Board*, Euston Square, NW1 (PO Box 100; telephone 262–3232), and supplements may be issued from time to time. These are obtainable from the Travel Offices of British Rail and from railway stations and offices. The *A B C Rail Guide* (monthly), on sale at bookstalls and booksellers, gives all the journeys to and from London, as well as the fares. British Telecom's pre-recorded Traveline service provides up-to-date information on rail travel; the telephone number is 246–8021.

The concessions include Family, Senior Citizen, Student, and Young Persons Railcards, available for twelve months. Special facilities are provided by British Rail for disabled and elderly people. Car parks are provided at most stations (at a charge for twenty-four hours), but some are reserved for season-ticket holders on Monday–Friday. Passengers can insure themselves and their luggage at any station for a reasonable fee.

Luggage will be carried free on the railways up to a maximum of 70 kg (154 lb.) for 1st class passengers and 50 kg (110 lb.) for 2nd class (up to half these allowances for children). For excess luggage a charge is made varying according to the weight and the distance travelled. Passengers' luggage will also be collected, conveyed, and delivered in advance by British Rail. Left luggage facilities are provided at the principal stations. The porter expects a 'tip' of about 10–15p for carrying the luggage from the train to the taxi, etc.

BY ROAD. The best road routes into and round London are indicated on the map on the following pages, which also shows places in suburban London described in the guide.

Long-distance coaches ply on all the main roads of Britain, connecting the principal towns and resorts with the capital. The chief terminus in London is the VICTORIA COACH STATION, Buckingham Palace Road, SW1 (Plan VII, D3). Tickets may be bought and particulars of all coach services may be obtained here and at the London Visitor and Convention Bureau (see p. 72). Fares (especially return fares) compare very favourably with those of the railways, but the journey takes longer. Particulars of services are given in the *National Express Coach Guide*, issued twice yearly and obtainable from National Travel (National Bus Company) Ltd, Victoria Coach Station, or from bookstalls, etc. Information about coach travel may be obtained by telephoning 730–0202.

Up-to-date information about coach services is given by British Telecom's Traveline service (246–8021). Cheap day returns may be obtained on certain days by students and pensioners. One suitcase is usually carried free on the coach, but excess luggage is charged extra. For the 'Green Line' Coaches and Country Buses in the neighbourhood of London, see p. 55.

The M25, a new motorway encircling London, is nearing completion in 1985. It will link all the motorways and main roads into the capital, have an extension to Heathrow Airport, and pass under the Thames by the Dartford Tunnels, where some delay may be expected.

BY AIR. HEATHROW AIRPORT (often called London Airport), the landing-ground for the majority of the services to the capital, is fourteen miles west of Hyde Park Corner and adjacent to the M4 motorway. The terminals for *British Airways* services to and from Heathrow have now been established at the airport, and Speedbird House here is the head-office of the company. The addresses of British Airways booking offices in London are given on page 43.

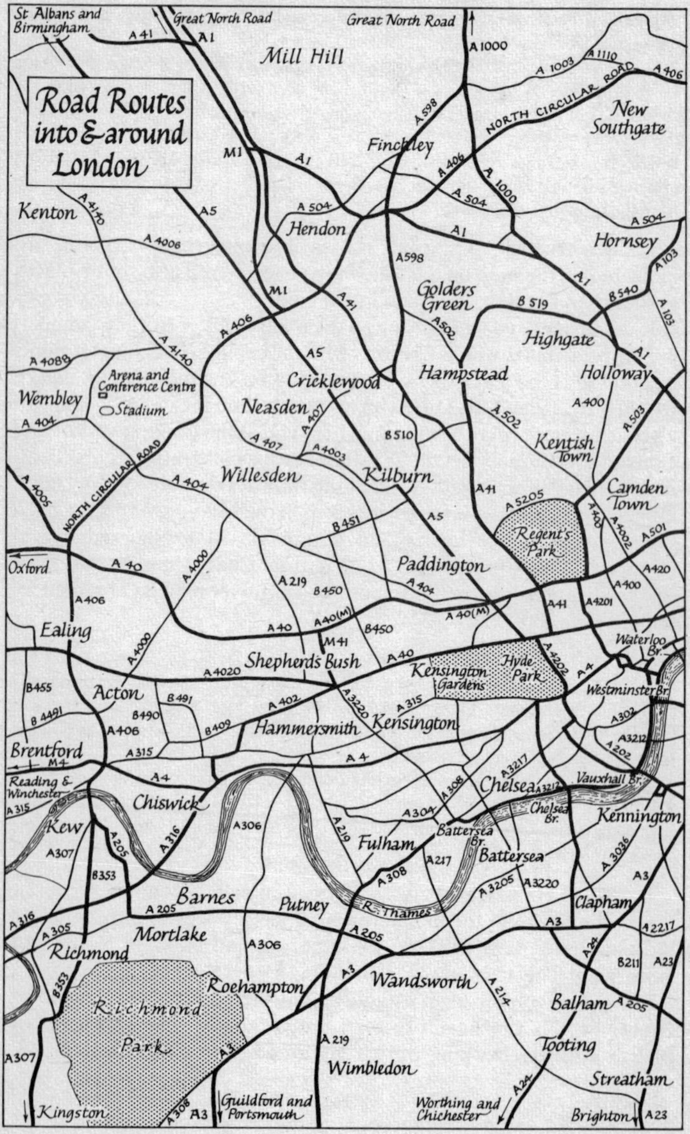
Road Routes into & around London
St Albans and Birmingham
Great North Road
Great North Road
Mill Hill
Finchley
New Southgate
NORTH CIRCULAR ROAD
Kenton
Hendon
Hornsey
Golders Green
Highgate
Hampstead
Holloway
Wembley
Arena and Conference Centre
Stadium
Cricklewood
Neasden
Kentish Town
Willesden
Kilburn
Camden Town
Regent's Park
Oxford
Paddington
Ealing
Shepherd's Bush
Kensington Gardens
Hyde Park
Waterloo Br.
Westminster Br.
Acton
Hammersmith
Kensington
Brentford
Reading & Winchester
Chelsea
Vauxhall Br.
Chelsea Br.
Chiswick
Kew
Battersea Br.
Kennington
Fulham
Battersea
Barnes
Putney
R. Thames
Clapham
Mortlake
Richmond
Wandsworth
Roehampton
Balham
Richmond Park
Tooting
Wimbledon
Streatham
Kingston
Guildford and Portsmouth
Worthing and Chichester
Brighton

APPROACHES TO LONDON

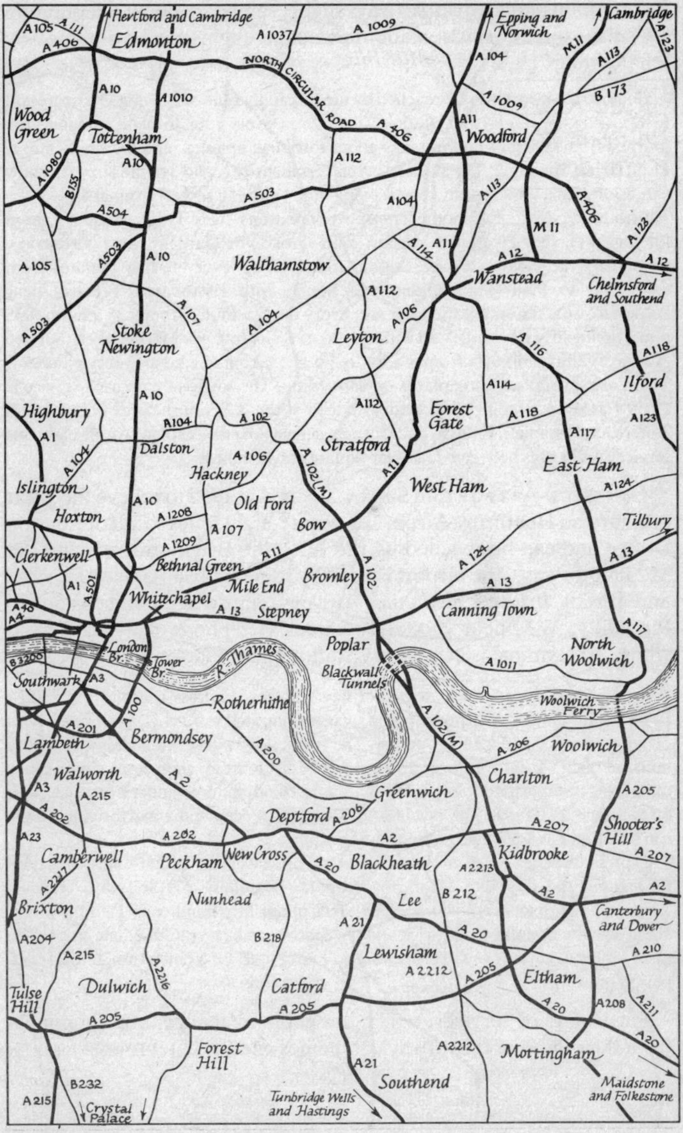

Reservations for British Airways flights can be made by telephoning 897–4000 and information about passenger flights can be obtained by telephoning 759–2525.

Heathrow Airport may be reached by the Piccadilly Line of London Underground to HEATHROW CENTRAL station. Trains run every four to eight minutes, the journey from central London takes about forty-five minutes, and the single fare is £1.50 (£1 on Sundays). The station serves Terminals 1, 2, and 3 of the airport; a new extension of the underground line is being built (1985) to serve Terminal 4.

Airbus Services of London Transport, operating daily (with adequate room for luggage), link Heathrow Airport with Grosvenor Gardens, near VICTORIA STATION, via Victoria Coach Station (Service A1; every twenty minutes from 6.40 a.m. to 9.40 p.m., taking one hour); with Eastbourne Terrace, near PADDINGTON STATION (Service A2; every thirty minutes from 6.35 a.m. to 9.35 p.m., taking fifty minutes); and with EUSTON STATION, via Marble Arch (Service A3; every thirty minutes from 8 a.m. to 5 p.m., taking one hour twenty minutes). There are several stopping places on each route. The single fare on each service is £2.50 (children over five but under sixteen years, £1; return fares double) and American, Canadian, French, and German currencies are accepted. An all-night bus service (N97) runs between Trafalgar Square and Heathrow.

GATWICK AIRPORT, in Surrey, opened in 1958 to relieve the great pressure on Heathrow Airport, is twenty-eight miles south of London Bridge and can be reached by the A23, the Brighton road, and the M23 motorway. The airport is used by some British Airways services and also by *British Caledonian Airways*, whose head office is at 215 Piccadilly, W1, near Piccadilly Circus (telephone 668–4222), and whose air terminal is at Victoria Station (near Platform 12).

A new high-speed train service (the 'Gatwick Express'), from VICTORIA STATION to Gatwick Airport Station, was inaugurated in 1984. The service has its own ticket-office and waiting lounge. The trains leave every fifteen minutes (every hour at night) from Platform 13 or 14 and the journey (non-stop) takes thirty minutes. The fares (2nd class) are £3.30, return £6.60; children under five years, free; up to fifteen, half fares. The 1st class fares are fifty per cent more and through tickets can be bought at any underground station.

Express Coaches connect VICTORIA COACH STATION at half-hourly intervals throughout the day with Heathrow Airport (Flightline 767) and with Gatwick Airport (Flightline 777). The journey takes about fifty minutes to Heathrow and about seventy minutes to Gatwick and the coaches make no intermediate stops. The fares for each service are £2.25 for a single journey, £3 for a day return, and £4 for a period return.

Particulars of services, which are liable to change, are obtainable from the offices of the airway companies and the chief tourist agents.

They are also given in the *ABC World Airways Guide*, published monthly by ABC Travel Guides, Dunstable, Bedfordshire, and obtainable from the publishers, at bookstalls, etc. Up-to-date information on air services is given by the Traveline Service (246–8021). Return tickets are obtainable on most air lines and show a considerable saving in fares. Travellers should make sure what allowance of luggage is permitted free, as the charge for excess luggage may be heavy. Regular services are operated to London from the most important places in the British Isles, as well as from the chief continental centres.

Reservations on *British Airways* flights may be made at 75 Regent Street, W1; 421 Oxford Street, W1; 127 Kensington High Street, W8; 110 Strand, WC2; 101 Cheapside, EC2; 52 Grosvenor Gardens, SW1; Victoria Station (adjoining Platform 13); the Hilton Hotel, Park Lane, W1; the Portman Hotel, Portman Square, W1; and the West London Air Terminal, Cromwell Road, SW7.

The London office of *Aer Lingus* is at 223 Regent Street, W1; of *Pan American Airways* at 193 Piccadilly, W1; and of *Trans World Airlines* at 200 Piccadilly.

TRAVEL AGENTS. The following are the chief London offices of travel agents who for a fee will arrange transport, hotel accommodation, and other matters for the convenience of visitors.

American Express, 6 Haymarket, SW1; *Thomas Cook Ltd*, 45 Berkeley Street, W1; *Frames' Tours*, 80 Southampton Row, WC1; *Lunn-Poly*, 4 Chiswell Street, EC1. These and other companies offer 'package tours' and 'bargain breaks', at cheaper rates.

VISITORS FROM ABROAD are advised to communicate before making arrangements with the representatives of the *British Tourist Authority*, which has offices in Amsterdam, Auckland, Brussels, Chicago, Copenhagen, Dallas, Dublin, Frankfurt-am-Main, Los Angeles, Madrid, New York, Oslo, Paris, Rome, Stockholm, Sydney, Toronto, Vancouver, Vienna, Zurich, and elsewhere.

Aliens staying in London must register three months after their arrival in Britain (within seven days if specifically instructed to do so) at the *Aliens Registrations Office* (open Mondays–Fridays 9 to 5), 10 Lamb's Conduit Street, off Theobalds Road, Holborn, WC1.

TRANSPORT IN LONDON

RAILWAYS. The following are the chief railway termini in London. Almost all are connected by the underground railway system (see map, following) and by bus.

BAKER STREET (Plan II, C2) is the terminus of the Metropolitan line (London Transport) to Amersham, Chesham, Watford, and Uxbridge, and is also on the Bakerloo, Jubilee and Circle lines of the underground.

BLACKFRIARS (IV, E3) is on the Southern Region line (closed on Saturdays and Sundays) that starts from Holborn Viaduct (but a terminus for some trains) and has a station also on the Circle and District lines.

BROAD STREET (V, D2), adjoining Liverpool Street Station (see below), is the terminus of the London Midland Region's 'North London' line to Richmond via Willesden Junction.

CANNON STREET (V, F1) is a terminus of the Southern Region in the City (closed on Saturdays and Sundays) and is connected to a station on the Circle and District lines.

CHARING CROSS (III, F3) is a terminus of the Southern Region in the West End. It is close to Charing Cross station on the Bakerloo, Jubilee, and Northern lines; Embankment station, which is on the Bakerloo, Circle, District and Northern lines, lies to the south on the Victoria Embankment and is reached via Villiers Street, on the east side of the main station.

EUSTON (III, A2) is one of the two principal termini of the London Midland Region, and is connected to a station of the same name on the Northern and Victoria lines.

FENCHURCH STREET (V, F3) is a terminus of the Eastern Region for the Docks and places on Thames-side. It is situated about 300 yds north of Tower Hill station on the Circle and District lines and a quarter of a mile south-west of Aldgate station on the Circle and Metropolitan lines.

HOLBORN VIADUCT (IV, D3) is a City terminus of the Southern Region (closed on Saturdays and Sundays). Its nearest underground stations are St Paul's on the Central line, just over a quarter of a mile east, and Farringdon on the Circle and Metropolitan lines, about a third of a mile north.

KING'S CROSS (III, A3) is the principal terminus of the Eastern Region for long-distance trains to the north. It is linked by subway with St Pancras Station (see below) and is connected to the Circle, Metropolitan, Northern, Piccadilly, and Victoria lines. The new KING'S CROSS MIDLAND City Line Station is in Pentonville Road, about 250 yds east, and may be reached by subway.

LIVERPOOL STREET (V, D2) is the principal terminus of the Eastern Region for East Anglia and is connected to the Central, Circle, and Metropolitan lines.

LONDON BRIDGE (IX, E2) is a terminus of the Southern Region south of the river and has a station on the Northern line.

MARYLEBONE (II, C1), a terminus of the Western Region, mostly for the shorter distance services, is a quarter of a mile west of Baker Street station and is connected to the Bakerloo line.

MOORGATE (V, D1), on the Circle, Metropolitan, and Northern lines, is the terminus of the new British Rail line via King's Cross Midland (see above) to St Albans and Bedford, and of a line to Finsbury Park.

PADDINGTON (I, D2) is the chief terminus of the Western Region, and is connected to the Bakerloo, Circle, District, and Metropolitan lines.

ST PANCRAS (III, A3) is the other principal terminus of the London Midland Region. It is close to King's Cross Station, with which it shares an underground station (see above).

VICTORIA (VII, D3) is the principal West End terminus of the Southern Region, used by boat-trains from Dover, Folkestone, and Newhaven. It is connected to the Circle, District, and Victoria lines.

WATERLOO (IX, B1) is the chief terminus of the Southern Region for trains from the West of England. It is connected to the Bakerloo and Northern lines, and is the terminus of the Waterloo & City line to the Bank, operated (weekdays only) by the Southern Region.

A new bus service of *London Transport* ('Bus Link') connects Waterloo station with Euston, St Pancras, and King's Cross Stations (every fifteen minutes; fare 40p between any two stations, but no change is given). A special bus service links King's Cross, St Pancras, Euston, Paddington, Victoria, and Waterloo Stations on Saturday and Sunday nights. The 'Red Arrow' buses (see below) link some of the main line termini during the day.

INFORMATION OFFICES and refreshment rooms will be found at most of the termini. Information about trains to and from main line stations may be obtained by telephoning 262–6767 (for Paddington Station), 278–2477 (for King's Cross and Moorgate), 283–7171 (for Fenchurch Street and Liverpool Street), 387–7070 (for Broad Street, Euston, Marylebone, and St Pancras), and 928–5100 (for Southern Region stations). Inquiries regarding rail transport may be made also at the *British Rail Travel Centre* (open weekdays 9 to 5), 4–12 Regent Street, south of Piccadilly Circus (Plan III, F2). Tickets may be purchased here and reservations made; tickets may also be bought at any of the main London termini for travel from any other London terminus.

The UNDERGROUND RAILWAYS of *London Transport* provide the quickest and easiest method of getting from one part of the metropolis to another. The nine lines are connected with each other at many points, and with their numerous branches extend to almost every quarter of London (except south of the Thames, better served

RAILWAYS OF LONDON

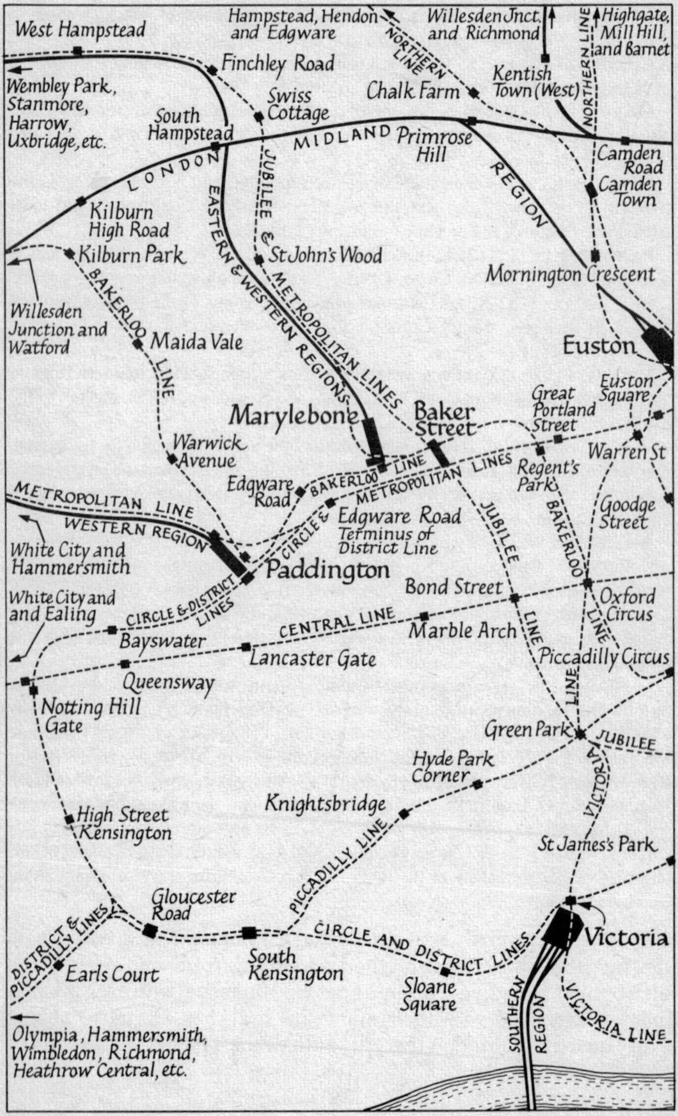

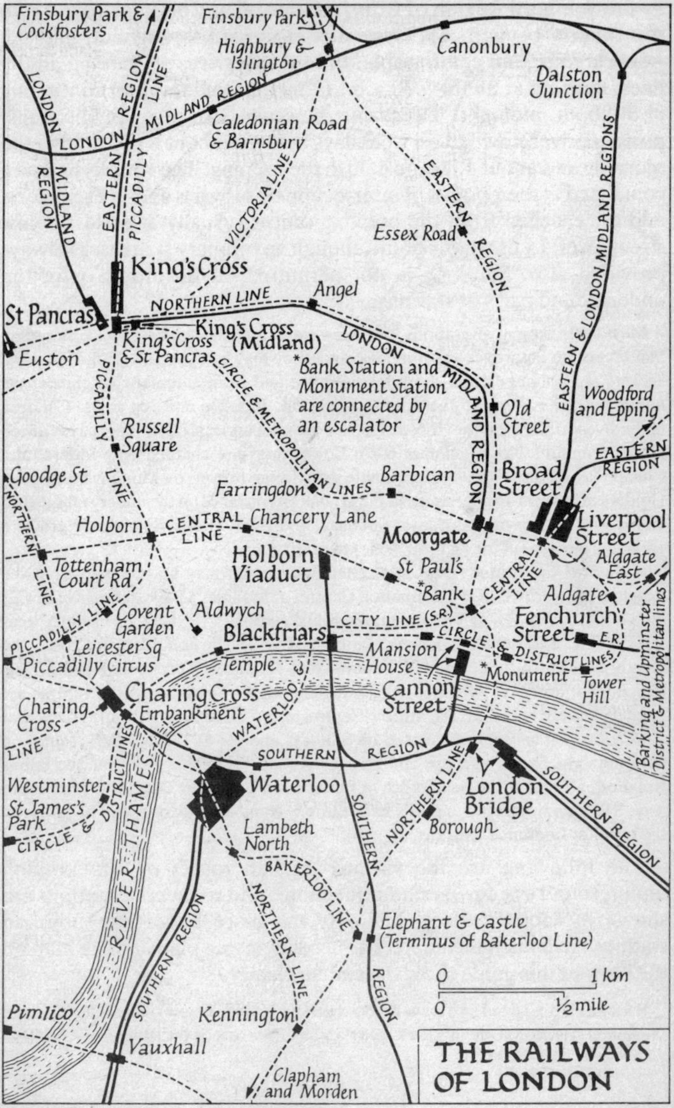

Finsbury Park & Cockfosters
Finsbury Park
Highbury & Islington
Canonbury
Dalston Junction
LONDON MIDLAND REGION
EASTERN REGION
PICCADILLY LINE
LONDON MIDLAND REGION
Caledonian Road & Barnsbury
VICTORIA LINE
EASTERN REGION
EASTERN & LONDON MIDLAND REGIONS
Essex Road
King's Cross
NORTHERN LINE
Angel
St Pancras
King's Cross (Midland)
King's Cross & St Pancras
Euston
LONDON MIDLAND REGION
*Bank Station and Monument Station are connected by an escalator
CIRCLE & METROPOLITAN LINES
PICCADILLY LINE
Russell Square
Old Street
Woodford and Epping
EASTERN REGION
Broad Street
Goodge St
NORTHERN LINE
Barbican
Farringdon
Holborn
CENTRAL LINE
Chancery Lane
Moorgate
Liverpool Street
Holborn Viaduct
Tottenham Court Rd
St Paul's
Aldgate East
*Bank
CENTRAL LINE
Aldgate
Covent Garden
Aldwych
Fenchurch Street
E.R.
PICCADILLY LINE
Leicester Sq
Blackfriars
CITY LINE (S.R.)
CIRCLE & DISTRICT LINES
Mansion House
Piccadilly Circus
Temple
*Monument
Tower Hill
Charing Cross
Cannon Street
Charing Cross LINE
Embankment
WATERLOO & CITY
Barking and Upminster District & Metropolitan lines
SOUTHERN REGION
Westminster
St James's Park
CIRCLE & DISTRICT LINES
RIVER THAMES
Waterloo
NORTHERN LINE
London Bridge
Borough
SOUTHERN REGION
Lambeth North
SOUTHERN REGION
BAKERLOO LINE
NORTHERN LINE
SOUTHERN REGION
Elephant & Castle (Terminus of Bakerloo Line)
0 1 km
0 ½ mile
Pimlico
Kennington
Vauxhall
Clapham and Morden
THE RAILWAYS OF LONDON

by the Southern Region of British Railways) and on some routes into the country beyond. The system is electrified throughout, and the trains are fast and comfortable. Frequent services operate on all the lines, starting at about 5.30 a.m. (7.30 on Sundays) and continuing until about midnight. The trains, however, like other public transport, are overcrowded on weekdays between about 8 and 9.30 in the morning and about 4.30 and 6.30 in the evening. The various lines are connected at their points of intersection by subways and/or escalators, and are reached from the booking-offices (usually at or just below street level) by escalator or lift, though an ordinary staircase is always provided also. Smoking is not permitted on the trains or in the underground parts of stations.

Most trains stop at all stations, but a few stations (indicated below) are closed on Sundays or on Saturdays and Sundays, and some may be closed on public holidays. Tickets are obtained from the booking office and from automatic machines; the minimum fare is 40p and the machines take 5p, 10p, 20p and 50p coins. Children under five years travel free, those of five or over but under sixteen years pay reduced fares (minimum 20p, maximum 60p). Lower fares are charged on Sundays, and Cheap Day Return tickets are available daily (after 10 a.m. on Mondays–Fridays). Holders of *Senior Citizen Railcards* may travel any distance on the underground after 9.30 a.m. (all day on Saturdays, Sundays, and Bank Holidays) for a return fare varying from 40p (in the Central Zone) to £1.50.

A map of the routes (free) and other information may be obtained from the London Transport Travel Information Centres at St James's Park station (VIII, C2; telephone 222–1234), at Victoria underground station (VIII, C1), Piccadilly Circus station (III, F2), Oxford Circus station (III, E1), Euston, King's Cross, and Heathrow Central underground stations, and Heathrow Terminals 1 and 2. The telephone inquiry service operates all day and night. The information centres are open daily from 8.30 a.m. (Heathrow Central from 7.30) until 9.30 p.m., except that the Oxford Circus centre is closed on Sundays and the St James's Park centre on Saturdays and Sundays. Maps and information are obtainable also from the Public Relations Officer at the head office of the London Transport Executive (55 Broadway, SW1), adjoining St James's Park station. Hand luggage only can be taken on the trains of London Transport.

The following are the various through routes on the London underground system. Termini, junctions, and connecting stations are shown in capital letters, but only the more important suburban stations have been included. The accompanying plan and the map on the back of this guide show the system clearly.

BAKERLOO LINE. HARROW & WEALDSTONE (see below), Wembley Central, Willesden Junction, Queen's Park, Maida Vale, PADDINGTON, Edgware Road (see below), Marylebone, BAKER STREET, Regent's Park, OXFORD CIRCUS, PICCADILLY CIRCUS, CHARING CROSS, EMBANKMENT, WATERLOO, Lambeth North, and ELEPHANT & CASTLE. The Edgware Road station is not connected with the station of the same name on the Circle, District and Metropolitan lines. (Service between Queen's Park and Harrow & Wealdstone during rush hours, Mondays–Fridays only.) The service from Harrow & Wealdstone to Watford High Street and Watford Junction is now operated by British Rail.

CENTRAL LINE. EALING BROADWAY, NORTH ACTON (junction for Northolt and WEST RUISLIP), White City, Shepherd's Bush (see below), Holland Park, NOTTING HILL GATE, Queensway, Lancaster Gate, Marble Arch, BOND STREET, OXFORD CIRCUS, TOTTENHAM COURT ROAD, HOLBORN, Chancery Lane (closed on Sundays), St Paul's, BANK (escalator connection to the Monument), LIVERPOOL STREET, Bethnal Green, MILE END, Stratford, LEYTONSTONE (junction for HAINAULT via Wanstead), WOODFORD (junction for Hainault via Chigwell), Loughton, and EPPING (for trains to ONGAR). The Shepherd's Bush station is not connected with the station of the same name on the Metropolitan Line.

CIRCLE LINE (trains run continuously in both directions). PADDINGTON, Bayswater, NOTTING HILL GATE, High Street Kensington, GLOUCESTER ROAD, SOUTH KENSINGTON, Sloane Square, VICTORIA, St James's Park, Westminster, EMBANKMENT, Temple (closed on Sundays), Blackfriars, Mansion House, Cannon Street (closed on Saturdays and Sundays), MONUMENT (escalator connection to Bank), TOWER HILL, ALDGATE, LIVERPOOL STREET, MOORGATE, Barbican (closed on Sundays), Farringdon, KING'S CROSS & ST PANCRAS, Euston Square, Great Portland Street, BAKER STREET, EDGWARE ROAD (see Bakerloo line) and PADDINGTON.

DISTRICT LINE (some trains terminate at the Mansion House or Tower Hill). EALING BROADWAY, EALING COMMON, ACTON TOWN, TURNHAM GREEN (junction for Kew Gardens and RICHMOND), HAMMERSMITH, Barons Court, West Kensington, EARLS COURT – junction for KENSINGTON (Olympia), for Paddington and EDGWARE ROAD (see below) and for WIMBLEDON via West Brompton, Fulham Broadway, and Putney Bridge – GLOUCESTER ROAD and thence as the Circle Line (see above) to TOWER HILL, then ALDGATE EAST, WHITECHAPEL, MILE END, Bow Road, BARKING, and UPMINSTER. This line coincides with the Piccadilly Line from Ealing Common to South Kensington, with the Circle Line from High Street Kensington to Edgware Road, and with the Metropolitan Line from Aldgate East to Barking. The service between Earls Court and Kensington (Olympia) operates only when Olympia is open. Wimbledon station is also on the main line to the south-west from Waterloo.

JUBILEE LINE. STANMORE, WEMBLEY PARK, West Hampstead, FINCHLEY ROAD, Swiss Cottage, St John's Wood, BAKER STREET, BOND STREET, GREEN PARK, and CHARING CROSS.

METROPOLITAN LINE. HAMMERSMITH, Shepherd's Bush (see Central Line), PADDINGTON, EDGWARE ROAD (see Bakerloo Line), BAKER STREET (junction for FINCHLEY ROAD, and HARROW-ON-THE-HILL, from which lines run to UXBRIDGE via Rayners Lane and to Watford, Amersham and Chesham), thence as the Circle Line (see above) to LIVERPOOL STREET (junction for ALDGATE), then ALDGATE EAST and WHITECHAPEL (junction for SHOREDITCH, and for NEW CROSS and NEW CROSS GATE) and as the District Line to BARKING. (Services from Whitechapel to Shoreditch and Barking during rush hours only.)

NORTHERN LINE. (a) *Charing Cross Section:* EDGWARE, Hendon Central, Golders Green, Hampstead, CAMDEN TOWN (junction for Highgate, Finchley Central, and HIGH BARNET or MILL HILL EAST), EUSTON (see below), WARREN STREET, Goodge Street, TOTTENHAM COURT ROAD, LEICESTER SQUARE, CHARING CROSS, EMBANKMENT, WATERLOO, KENNINGTON (see below), Oval, STOCKWELL, Clapham Common, Tooting Broadway, and MORDEN. (b) *Bank Section:* as above from Edgware, etc., to EUSTON, then KING'S CROSS & ST PANCRAS, Angel, Old Street, MOORGATE, BANK (escalator connection to the Monument), London Bridge, Borough, ELEPHANT & CASTLE, and KENNINGTON, and as above to Morden. Through trains run from Edgware, High Barnet, and Mill Hill East to Morden on both sections.

PICCADILLY LINE. HEATHROW CENTRAL, (see p. 42), Hounslow Central, Osterley, ACTON TOWN (junction for EALING COMMON, RAYNERS LANE, and UXBRIDGE), HAMMERSMITH, EARLS COURT, GLOUCESTER ROAD, SOUTH KENSINGTON, Knightsbridge, Hyde Park Corner, GREEN PARK, PICCADILLY CIRCUS, LEICESTER SQUARE, Covent Garden, HOLBORN (junction for ALDWYCH, during rush hours only), Russell Square, KING'S CROSS & ST PANCRAS, Arsenal, FINSBURY PARK, Wood Green, Southgate, and COCKFOSTERS. This line coincides with the Metropolitan Line between Rayners Lane and Uxbridge, and with the District Line from Ealing Common to South Kensington, but trains on the Piccadilly Line do not stop between Acton Town and Hammersmith. (Services from Rayners Lane to Uxbridge during rush hours only.)

VICTORIA LINE. BRIXTON, STOCKWELL, Vauxhall, Pimlico, VICTORIA, GREEN PARK, OXFORD CIRCUS, WARREN STREET, EUSTON, KING'S CROSS & ST PANCRAS, Highbury & Islington, FINSBURY PARK, Tottenham Hale, and WALTHAMSTOW CENTRAL.

Special tickets ('London Explorer Passes'), obtainable from underground stations and London Transport information centres, allow unlimited travel between most underground stations, as well as on all the London Transport red buses (see p. 51). The tickets are available for one, three, four or seven days, and include the transfer by underground or Airbus to Heathrow Airport. The cost varies from £3 (children £1.30), for one day, to £13 (children £5). Other concessions are introduced from time to time on the London Transport underground and bus services.

London south of the Thames is served by the SOUTHERN REGION of British Railways. Frequent services of fast electric trains are operated, connecting at many points, but most of the local trains have 2nd-class compartments only. Cheap Day Return tickets are issued daily between the London termini and the suburban stations, and other concessions include 'off-peak' return tickets, combined tickets for party travel, and special ramblers' tickets. Particulars of all these may be obtained from any railway station and from the *British Rail Travel Centre* or other travel offices.

The CHARING CROSS Station of Southern Region is connected directly with LONDON BRIDGE by way of Waterloo. Another service runs from VICTORIA to LONDON BRIDGE via Battersea Park, Clapham, East Brixton, Denmark Hill, Peckham Rye, and South Bermondsey.

The most important connecting points of the Region in the neighbourhood of London are CLAPHAM JUNCTION (perhaps the busiest junction in the world), where lines from Victoria and Waterloo converge, and EAST CROYDON, where lines from Victoria and London Bridge meet.

The WATERLOO & CITY RAILWAY, operated by the Southern Region, on weekdays only, connects Waterloo with Bank station on the underground system. There is a frequent service of electric trains (from about 7 a.m. to 10 p.m., to 2 p.m. on Saturdays) and the journey takes five minutes. Through bookings can be made to Tower Hill, Liverpool Street, and Moorgate, but no dogs or heavy luggage may be taken.

The LONDON MIDLAND REGION has a useful electric line (the 'North London' line) from Broad Street to Richmond (where it connects with the Southern Region) via Dalston Junction, Highbury & Islington, Camden Road, Hampstead Heath, Finchley Road, Willesden Junction, Acton Central, and Kew Gardens. Another railway, diverging from this at Camden Road, runs via Primrose Hill, South Hampstead, Kilburn High Road, Queen's Park (see the Bakerloo Line above), and Harrow & Wealdstone to Watford Junction. Some trains start at Euston and join this line at South Hampstead. Another railway runs from Moorgate via Old Street (on the Northern line), Essex Road, and Highbury & Islington to Finsbury Park.

BUS SERVICES. The bus routes of *London Transport* make a criss-cross pattern extending over the whole of central London and into the suburbs, where they connect with the London Country bus services reaching far out into the surrounding country. The services of the central area buses, which are coloured red and bear numbers below 300, are frequent, but the vehicles are uncomfortably crowded during the 'rush hours'. Some services are extended on Saturday afternoons or Sundays, or during the peak hours, while others are curtailed on Sundays. A number of all-night services are operated. The buses ply on most routes from about 6.30 or 7 a.m. until between 11 p.m. and midnight.

In inner London (most of the area covered by this guide) and from here to destinations in outer London, the fare varies with the distance travelled. The

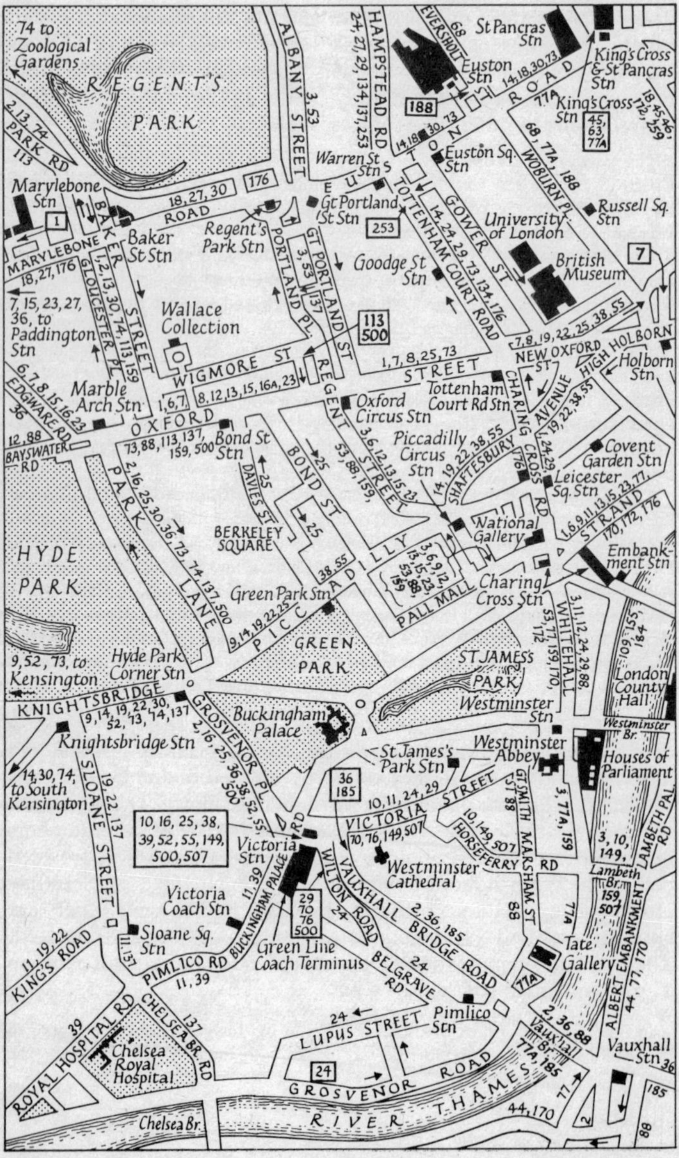
74 to Zoological Gardens
REGENT'S PARK
ALBANY STREET
HAMPSTEAD RD
EVERSHOLT
St Pancras Stn
Euston Stn
King's Cross & St Pancras Stn
King's Cross Stn
EUSTON ROAD
Warren St Stn
Euston Sq. Stn
WOBURN PL.
Russell Sq. Stn
GOWER ST
TOTTENHAM COURT ROAD
University of London
British Museum
Marylebone Stn
BAKER
MARYLEBONE ROAD
Gt Portland St Stn
Regent's Park Stn
PORTLAND PL.
GT PORTLAND ST
Goodge St Stn
Baker St Stn
GLOUCESTER PL
STREET
Wallace Collection
7, 15, 23, 27, 36, to Paddington Stn
WIGMORE ST
REGENT
NEW OXFORD ST
HIGH HOLBORN
Holborn Stn
Marble Arch Stn
EDGWARE RD
OXFORD STREET
Oxford Circus Stn
Tottenham Court Rd Stn
CHARING CROSS RD
AVENUE
BAYSWATER RD
Bond St Stn
BOND ST
DAVIES ST
Piccadilly Circus Stn
SHAFTESBURY
Covent Garden Stn
Leicester Sq. Stn
STRAND
PARK LANE
BERKELEY SQUARE
National Gallery
Embankment Stn
HYDE PARK
PICCADILLY
Green Park Stn
Charing Cross Stn
PALL MALL
WHITEHALL
GREEN PARK
ST JAMES'S PARK
London County Hall
9, 52, 73, to Kensington
Hyde Park Corner Stn
KNIGHTSBRIDGE
GROSVENOR PL.
Westminster Stn
Buckingham Palace
Westminster Br.
Knightsbridge Stn
St James's Park Stn
Westminster Abbey
Houses of Parliament
14, 30, 74, to South Kensington
SLOANE STREET
VICTORIA STREET
GT SMITH ST
MARSHAM ST
LAMBETH PAL RD
HORSEFERRY RD
Victoria Stn
Westminster Cathedral
Lambeth Br.
Victoria Coach Stn
BUCKINGHAM PALACE RD
WILTON ROAD
VAUXHALL BRIDGE ROAD
Sloane Sq. Stn
Green Line Coach Terminus
Tate Gallery
ALBERT EMBANKMENT
KINGS ROAD
PIMLICO RD
BELGRAVE RD
Pimlico Stn
LUPUS STREET
Vauxhall Stn
ROYAL HOSPITAL RD
CHELSEA BR. RD
Chelsea Royal Hospital
Vaux'hall Br.
GROSVENOR ROAD
RIVER THAMES
Chelsea Br.

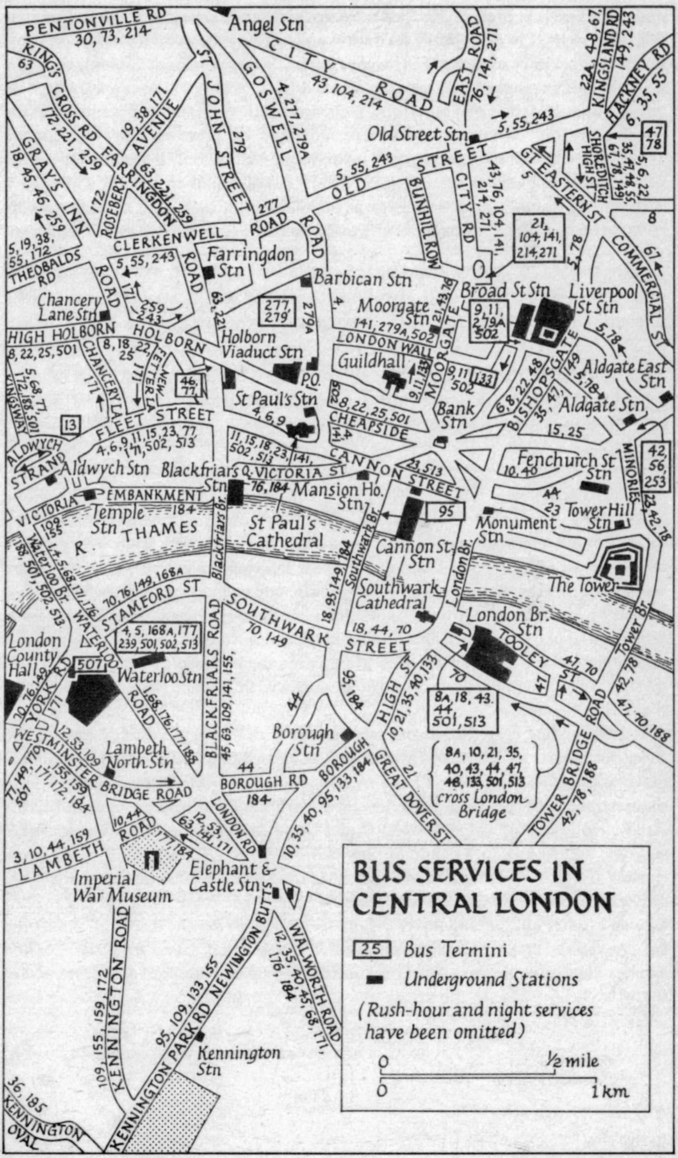
BUS SERVICES IN CENTRAL LONDON
25 Bus Termini
Underground Stations
(Rush-hour and night services have been omitted)
0 ½ mile
0 1 km
PENTONVILLE RD
30, 73, 214
Angel Stn
CITY ROAD
43, 104, 214
KING'S CROSS RD
172, 221, 259
ROSEBERY AVENUE
19, 38, 171
FARRINGDON ROAD
63, 221, 259
GRAY'S INN
18, 45, 46, 259
5, 19, 38, 55, 172
THEOBALDS RD
ST JOHN STREET
279
GOSWELL ROAD
4, 277, 279A
CLERKENWELL ROAD
5, 55, 243
Farringdon Stn
Chancery Lane Stn
HIGH HOLBORN
8, 22, 25, 501
HOLBORN
8, 18, 22, 25
CHANCERY LA
FETTER LA
NEW
KINGSWAY
Holborn Viaduct Stn
Barbican Stn
OLD STREET
5, 55, 243
277
Old Street Stn
EAST ROAD
76, 141, 271
BUNHILL ROW
CITY RD
43, 76, 104, 141, 214, 271
21, 104, 141, 214, 271
GT EASTERN ST
KINGSLAND RD
22A, 48, 67, 149, 243
HACKNEY RD
6, 35, 55
SHOREDITCH HIGH ST
47 78
COMMERCIAL ST
Broad St Stn
Liverpool St Stn
9, 11, 279A 502
Moorgate Stn
141, 279A, 502
MOORGATE
LONDON WALL
Guildhall
277, 279
P.O.
St Paul's Stn
4, 6, 9
46, 77
13
FLEET STREET
4, 6, 9, 11, 15, 23, 77, 171, 502, 513
11, 15, 18, 23, 141, 502, 513
CHEAPSIDE
8, 22, 25, 501
Bank Stn
9, 11, 502
133
BISHOPSGATE
6, 8, 22, 48
35, 47
Aldgate East Stn
Aldgate Stn
15, 25
MINORIES
42, 56, 253
Fenchurch St Stn
10, 40
23 Tower Hill Stn
ALDWYCH
STRAND
Aldwych Stn
Blackfriars Stn
Q. VICTORIA ST
76, 184
Mansion Ho. Stn
CANNON STREET
23, 513
95
Monument Stn
EMBANKMENT
VICTORIA
Temple Stn
R. THAMES
St Paul's Cathedral
Cannon St Stn
The Tower
Blackfriars Br.
Southwark Br.
London Br.
Tower Br.
Waterloo Br.
Southwark Cathedral
London Br. Stn
TOOLEY ST
47, 70
STAMFORD ST
10, 76, 149, 168A
4, 5, 168A, 177, 239, 501, 502, 513
SOUTHWARK STREET
70, 149
18, 44, 70
WATERLOO
London County Hall
507
Waterloo Stn
YORK RD
BLACKFRIARS ROAD
45, 63, 109, 141, 155
HIGH ST
10, 21, 35, 40, 133
8A, 18, 43, 44, 501, 513
TOWER BRIDGE ROAD
42, 78, 188
47, 70, 188
Borough Stn
BOROUGH RD
184
BOROUGH
10, 35, 40, 95, 133, 184
GREAT DOVER ST
8A, 10, 21, 35, 40, 43, 44, 47, 48, 133, 501, 513 cross London Bridge
Lambeth North Stn
WESTMINSTER BRIDGE ROAD
12, 53, 109
LONDON RD
12, 53, 63, 141, 171
LAMBETH ROAD
3, 10, 44, 159
Imperial War Museum
Elephant & Castle Stn
KENNINGTON ROAD
109, 155, 159, 172
NEWINGTON BUTTS
KENNINGTON PARK RD
95, 109, 133, 155
WALWORTH ROAD
12, 35, 40, 45, 68, 171, 176, 184
Kennington Stn
KENNINGTON OVAL
36, 185

minimum fare is at present 25p, but reduced fares are charged for children from five to fifteen years. On most buses the fare is collected by the conductor, but on some (mostly in the outer suburbs) the traveller enters through the front doors and pays the driver. Five passengers are generally allowed to stand on the lower deck (three on buses without conductors), if all the seats are taken. Smoking is permitted on the upper deck only. Stopping-places are indicated by posts bearing the London Transport symbol, but buses will pull up at 'request stops' only if signalled to do so.

A series of single-deck motor-buses ('Red Arrows'; numbered 500 and upwards), with limited seating and few stops, was inaugurated in 1966. The 'flat fare' is 30p, payable on boarding; no change is given and there are no reduced fares for children.

The most important bus routes in central London are shown on the accompanying plan, and the routes in the main streets and to the various places of interest, etc., are given in the text of the guide. Maps of the routes are issued (free) by London Transport and may be obtained from the inquiry offices, etc. Most stopping-places in central London display notices giving the service frequencies and the times of the first and last buses, and full timetables are shown for the less frequent routes.

Special daily tickets, 'Red Bus Rovers', which allow unlimited travel on all London buses, and 'London Explorer' passes, which allow unlimited travel on buses and underground trains in the G.L.C. area, can be purchased from bus garages, underground stations, and London transport information centres. Bus passes are obtainable for periods of one week, one month, and one year, and 'Travelcards' (for use on buses and underground trains) for periods of one week, one month, three months, and one year. Both allow unlimited travel within certain zones. The price is dependent on the number of zones to be entered and passport-sized photographs must accompany applications. None of these special tickets and passes can be used on the Airbus Services.

A circular bus tour (about one and a half hours), operated daily by London Transport, starts at least every hour from 9 a.m. to 8 p.m. (to 4 in winter) from the Haymarket (east side, near Piccadilly Circus) and Victoria Street (near Victoria Station); from 10 to 5 (summer only) from Park Lane (west side, south of Marble Arch), Holles Street (near Oxford Circus), and Marylebone Road (Baker Street station); and from 2 to 9 (summer only) from Leicester Square. Most of the tours starting from the Haymarket and Victoria Street are accompanied by guides, but only a few of those from the other departure points. The payment of £3.25 (£4.25 for a guided tour; children under sixteen, £1.50 and £2.50) may be made on joining the bus, or tickets may be obtained in advance (at cheaper rates) from the London Transport information centres. *London Crusader* buses (coloured green and white) follow a similar route to the above tour and charge the same rates, but leave from outside the National Gallery in Trafalgar Square.

A circular tour of London is operated daily throughout the year by *Culture Bus*

Ltd, every thirty minutes from about 9 a.m. to about 6 p.m., stopping at Trafalgar Square, Hyde Park Corner, the South Kensington museums, Marble Arch, Marylebone Road, the British Museum, St Paul's, the Museum of London, the Bank, the Tower, the National Theatre, and the Tate Gallery. The service is continuous and the round trip takes nearly two hours; the fare is £3 (children from five to fourteen years £2; family tickets £8.50). The bus may be boarded and left at any of a number of recognized stopping places, and the journey may be broken and the service rejoined later without extra charge. Tickets may be obtained on the buses (no change given) or from the office of the company at 21 Elizabeth Street, SW1 (telephone 730–9273), near Victoria Coach Station. Tours are arranged also by *London Cityrama*, Silverthorne Road, Battersea, SW8 (720–6663), and other companies.

The GREEN LINE COACHES mostly run right across the capital from one side to the other, reaching many places well out in the country (Aylesbury, Guildford, Tunbridge Wells, etc.). These coaches are much faster than the ordinary buses, but they will stop in London only at the points so indicated (fewer than the bus stops) and the fares are proportionately higher. Timetables of the services and a map of the routes (free) are obtainable from the London Transport Travel Information Centres and the Green Line inquiry office at Eccleston Bridge (near Buckingham Palace Road, Victoria). The principal stopping-points in central London are Buckingham Palace Road, Eccleston Bridge, Hyde Park Corner, Marble Arch, Baker Street station, Oxford Circus, and Aldgate.

The COUNTRY BUSES, coloured green and bearing numbers from 300 to 499 and 800 upwards, extend from the outer suburbs as far afield as Bishop's Stortford, Letchworth, Dunstable, Aylesbury, West Wycombe, Windsor, Guildford, Horsham, East Grinstead, Tonbridge, and Gravesend. Information regarding services, etc., on the Country Buses and the Green Line Coaches can be obtained from *London Country Bus Services*, Lesbourne Road, Reigate, Surrey (telephone 07372–42411).

'Golden Rover' tickets are obtainable daily (Mondays–Fridays after 9 a.m.) from the conductors for unlimited travel on Green Line coaches and Country Buses. They cost £3.20 each (children under sixteen, £1.60). Cheap day and weekend return tickets are also available, during the same times.

COACHES. Conducted Coach Tours are operated by *London Transport* on weekdays throughout the year round London (about seven hours), taking in Westminster Abbey, St Paul's Cathedral, and the Tower of London (£21.50, children under fourteen £13.50, including lunch); in the morning through the West End (about three hours), taking in Westminster Abbey (£8, children £5); and in the afternoon through the City (about three hours), including St Paul's and the Tower (£10, children £6). The coaches start from the Wilton Road Coach Station, south-east of Victoria Station; tickets may be obtained from the London Transport information centres, from the London Visitor Bureau, from Victoria Coach Station, and from National Bus Offices; and the fares include the admission charges where applicable. Special coaches connecting with these and other tours arranged by

London Transport pick up at King's Cross Station, Marble Arch, and other places.

Coaches also ply in summer from London on day and half-day excursions to places of interest over a wide area. Particulars are obtainable from travel agents and information bureaux. London Transport operate tours to Hampton Court, Windsor Castle, Brighton, Canterbury, Cambridge, Oxford, Stratford-upon-Avon, and other places within a day's reach of London. Conducted tours are arranged also by *American Express*, *Thomas Cook Ltd*, and *Frames' Tours* (see p. 43), and by *National Travel* (Victoria Coach Station), *Evan Evans' Tours* (27 Cockspur Street, SW1), and other companies.

MOTOR-LAUNCHES ply daily on the Thames from about April to October and provide a pleasant method of exploring the river and its neighbourhood. Services are operated from WESTMINSTER PIER (Plan VIII, B3) from 10 a.m. every twenty minutes downstream to the Tower of London (Tower Pier) and to Greenwich, and about every thirty minutes upstream to Kew (for Kew Gardens), less frequently to Richmond and Hampton Court. Similar services are operated from CHARING CROSS PIER (VIII, A3) and the FESTIVAL PIER, in front of the Royal Festival Hall (IX, A1), to Tower Pier and Greenwich, and from TOWER PIER (IX, D3) to Westminster and Greenwich. All of these services (except those to Kew and Hampton Court) also operate in winter. Return tickets are available, at a reduced cost, and children under sixteen are carried at about half fare. Round trips (of about an hour) and evening cruises are arranged in summer. Further information regarding the services may be obtained from the *Westminster Passenger Service Association*, Westminster Pier, Victoria Embankment, SW1 (telephone 930–2062 and 4097), and *Charing Cross River Services*, Charing Cross Pier, Victoria Embankment, WC2 (telephone 930–0971).

Other cruises on the river are operated by *London Launches Ltd*, from Westminster Pier to the Thames Flood Barrier (telephone 740–8263). Cruises including dinner or supper are arranged by *Catamaran Cruisers* (839–2349), *Tidal Cruisers* (722–9132), and other companies. Combined coach and river tours, starting from Victoria Coach Station, are arranged by *London Transport*.

Water-buses are operated on the REGENT'S CANAL by the *London Waterbus Company* (Camden Lock, off Chalk Farm Road, NW1; telephone 482–2550), daily, between April and early October, from 'Little Venice', Paddington (Plan I, C2), through Regent's Park to the Zoological Gardens and Camden Lock (beyond I, A3), leaving and returning hourly from 10 a.m. to 5 p.m. A limited service is operated on Saturdays and Sundays and during school holidays in winter. The single journey takes forty-five minutes (thirty minutes from Little Venice to the Zoo); reduced fares are charged for children under sixteen and return tickets are obtainable, as well as single tickets including the admission charge to the Zoo.

Cruises by narrow boat are operated on the canal, daily, from Easter to October, starting from Blomfield Road, near Little Venice, and plying through Regent's Park to Camden Lock (about one and a half hours, including return cruise). Particulars can be obtained from *Jason's Trip* (60 Blomfield Road, W9; telephone 286–3428). Other trips by narrow boat are operated every afternoon from Easter to October, from Camden Lock through the Zoo to Little Venice and return (information from *Jenny Wren Cruises*, 250 Camden High Street; telephone 485–4433), and from Camden Lock along the eastern part of the Regent's Canal to Limehouse Basin, by *Eastern City Canal Ferries* (152 Sewardstone Road, EC2; telephone 981–4678). Advance booking is advisable on all these cruises.

TAXICABS ply on the main streets of London or can be hired from taxi-ranks or by telephone. Fares are indicated by meters, and if the meter-flag is up or the indicator 'Taxi' or 'For Hire' is lit the driver may be hailed, but he is under no obligation to accept a passenger unless the taxi is stationary. The charge for hire varies according to the distance covered, but the minimum is 80p. A small extra charge (for the whole hiring) is made for each additional person, but two children under ten years count as one person. Each article of luggage carried outside is charged extra (more for heavy or awkward articles). The driver expects a tip of about fifteen per cent of the fare (15p for a short journey), proportionately more if he helps with the luggage. If the journey begins or ends between midnight and 6 a.m., an extra charge on the fare is payable. For journeys over six miles the fares are normally arranged by agreement.

The taxi fare from central London to Heathrow Airport works out at between £10 and £18. The telephone numbers of local taxi-ranks are given in the London telephone directory 'Yellow Pages' under the heading 'Taxis'. Taxis may also be hired from radio-taxi companies by telephoning 286–0286, 286–4848, or 272–3030. Mini-cabs are not allowed to pick up passengers in the streets, but may be hired by telephone (828–4422).

PRIVATE CARS, with qualified chauffeurs, may be hired in London by the hour, day, or week, and for special occasions. Most hiring companies will meet trains, boats, or aircraft by prior arrangement. The charge varies considerably according to the size and make of car, and the period of hiring. Intending hirers should make sure that fully comprehensive insurance is included.

Cars may be hired for collection at airports and railway termini by telephoning *Godfrey Davis Europcar* on 950–4080 (on 897–0811 for Heathrow Airport, 0293–

31062 for Gatwick Airport). The company has offices in Birmingham, Bristol, Manchester, Southampton, Glasgow, and Dublin, and will also provide cars with chauffeurs (telephone 834–6701). Cars may also be hired from *Car Hire Centre*, 23 Swallow Street, near Piccadilly Circus, W1 (734–7661), *Chelsea Car Rental*, Sloane Avenue, SW3 (581–2255), *Huntsworth Hire*, 3 Huntsworth Mews, off Gloucester Place, NW1 (402–4650 and 258–1996), and other companies.

CAR PARKING. The regulation of the motor traffic is still a serious problem in the increasingly congested streets of London, but has been tackled in three ways: by the introduction of a system of one-way traffic, by the provision of parking meters in the streets, and by the building of 'multi-storey' or underground car parks. Street parking is restricted all over central London and some streets are closed to traffic. Oxford Street, for instance, is closed to car users on weekdays between 7 a.m. and 7 p.m.

PARKING METERS have been installed in every part of central and suburban London. The meters mostly take 10p and 50p coins, and the charge is usually for a maximum allowable period of two hours, but four-hour and five-hour meters will be found on the Victoria Embankment and in the Victoria, Bayswater, Marylebone, and Bloomsbury areas, and ten-hour meters in Holborn and elsewhere. The system operates from 8.30 a.m. to 6.30 p.m. on Mondays–Fridays and 8.30 to 1.30 p.m. or 6.30 p.m. on Saturdays; no charge is made on Saturday afternoons in some areas and on Sundays and Bank Holidays. Parking in some areas is reserved for residents only. Free parking is permitted in certain places in Hyde Park and Regent's Park (not between 10 and 11 a.m. on Mondays–Fridays).

CAR PARKS. Many large public car parks, in multi-storey blocks or underground, have been constructed in central London in recent years, alleviating to some extent the appalling congestion of parked cars. That in HYDE PARK (Plan II, E2), with room for 1,100 cars and a subway to Marble Arch station, may be specially mentioned. The charges at these car parks vary considerably (with a minimum period of two hours or more in some parks), but may be reckoned to work out at approximately £7 for a day. Weekly terms can be arranged at some car parks. Many of the larger hotels also have underground car parks.

The *Automobile Association* publishes a booklet, *Parking in London*, giving particulars of the public car parks in central London (with a map) and of parking near the main approaches to the capital by railway, as well as other useful information. Particulars may be obtained also from *National Car Parks Ltd*, 21 Bryanston Street, Marble Arch, London W1 (telephone 499–7050).

HOTELS AND RESTAURANTS

Hotels of almost every grade will be found in most parts of London, but especially in the west and south-west quarters. Though several new hotels have been built in recent years, there is still a great shortage of accommodation and visitors are advised that it is essential to secure rooms as early as possible in advance. The lists below make no claim to be complete and the omission of a name certainly implies no condemnation. It is inevitable, owing to lack of space, that mostly the larger and better-known hotels are included, but there are many smaller hotels, offering adequate accommodation for rather lower charges, particularly in the relatively quieter areas of Kensington, Bayswater, and Bloomsbury, while even more reasonable accommodation is obtainable in the outer suburbs, at the expense of time spent in getting to the centre of London.

The charges for hotel accommodation fluctuate very considerably. The handbooks of hotels mentioned below may be consulted, and a small outlay in postage or on telephone calls will result in first-hand information regarding the type of accommodation that can be offered and the charges made. In any case it is advisable always to verify charges before booking rooms. The 'room-and-breakfast' charge quoted by hotels is for a single room and normally includes a bath and an 'English' breakfast; a reduction can sometimes be obtained if a light ('Continental') breakfast is taken. The 'en pension' charges quoted for board and lodging are for a stay of one week, unless indicated otherwise; most hotels, however, will arrange a charge for a shorter period, though not usually of less than three days. The pension charges include both lunch and dinner (though not invariably tea), but this arrangement is generally inconvenient for holiday visitors, who will probably wish to take some at least of their meals elsewhere. Bills are presented weekly, and visitors are expected to vacate their rooms before noon on the day of departure, otherwise an extra day may be charged for.

Handbooks of Hotels are published annually by the *English Tourist Board* (4 Grosvenor Gardens, SW1) and the *British Hotels and Restaurants Association*, and by *Ashley Courtenay Ltd* and other companies, and are obtainable from bookstalls, etc. The *Automobile Association*'s members' handbook also lists hotels. The *Good Hotel Guide*, published annually, gives particulars of recommended hotels.

Reservations may be made through a growing number of booking agencies. These include *Concordia Hotel Reservations*, 52 Grosvenor Gardens, SW1 (telephone 730–3467), *Hotel Bookings International*, 65 Pound Lane, NW10 (459–1212), *Hotel Booking Service*, 13 Golden Square, W1 (437–5052), *Hotelguide*, 8 Charing Cross Road, WC2 (836–5561), and *Hotel Reservation Centre*, 10 Buckingham Palace Road, SW1 (829–1849). Hotel reservation offices will be found at Victoria, Waterloo, and Liverpool Street Stations, and at Heathrow Airport. The *London Visitor and Convention Bureau* (see p. 72) also maintains a hotel information and booking service.

In the lists that follow, the hotels are arranged under their postal districts, then in alphabetical order. All (or almost all) the bedrooms in these hotels have private bathrooms attached.

Hotels in the district W1 (Piccadilly, Park Lane, Mayfair, and Oxford Street): ATHENAEUM (110 R.), 116 Piccadilly; BRISTOL (190 R.), Berkeley Street; BRITANNIA (440 R.), Grosvenor Square; BROWN'S (130 R.), Albemarle Street; CHESTERFIELD (120 R.), Charles Street; CHURCHILL (490 R.), Portman Square; CLARIDGE'S (250 R.; all suites), Brook Street (Route 13); CLIFTON-FORD (230 R.), Welbeck Street; CONNAUGHT (100 R.), Carlos Place (off Grosvenor Square); CUMBERLAND (890 R.), Marble Arch, Oxford Street; CURZON (70 R.), Stanhope Row, Park Lane; DORCHESTER (280 R.), Park Lane (Route 13); DURRANT'S (100 R.), George Street; FLEMING'S (125 R.), Half Moon Street; GROSVENOR HOUSE (480 R.), Park Lane; HOLIDAY INN (240 R.), George Street; INN ON THE PARK (230 R.), Hamilton Place, Park Lane; INTER-CONTINENTAL (500 R.), Hamilton Place, Piccadilly; LONDONDERRY (140 R.), Park Lane; LONDONER (250 R.), Welbeck Street; LONDON HILTON (500 R.), Park Lane (Route 13); LONDON MARRIOTT (275 R.), Grosvenor Square; MANDEVILLE (165 R.), Mandeville Place; MAY FAIR (390 R.), Berkeley Street (Route 7); MONTCALM (115 R.), Great Cumberland Place; MOUNT ROYAL (700 R.), Bryanston Street, near Marble Arch; NEW PICCADILLY (290 R.), Piccadilly and Regent Street; PARK LANE (280 R.), Piccadilly; PORTMAN INTER-CONTINENTAL (275 R.), Portman Square; RATHBONE (60 R.), Rathbone Street, north of Oxford Street; REGENT CREST (350 R.), Carburton Street, Marylebone; REGENT PALACE (1030 R.), Piccadilly Circus; RITZ (130 R.), Piccadilly (Route 7); ROYAL ANGUS (90 R.), Coventry Street; ST GEORGE'S (85 R.), Langham Place; SAVOY COURT (100 R.), Granville Place, near Oxford Street; SELFRIDGE (300 R.), Orchard Street (above Selfridges department store); SHERLOCK HOLMES (150 R.), Baker Street; WASHINGTON (160 R.), Curzon Street; WESTBURY (270 R.), New Bond Street.

W2 (Bayswater and north of Hyde Park): BAYSWATER FAIRWAY (115 R.), Princes Square; CHARLES DICKENS (190 R.), Lancaster Gate; EDEN PARK (135 R.), Inverness Terrace; GREAT WESTERN ROYAL (160 R.), Paddington Station; HENRY VIII (110 R.), Leinster Gardens; HYDE PARK TOWERS (110 R.),

Inverness Terrace; LEINSTER TOWERS (170 R.), Leinster Terrace; LONDON EMBASSY (190 R.), Bayswater Road; LONDON METROPOLE (550 R.), Edgware Road; PARK COURT (440 R.), Lancaster Gate; PARK PLAZA (280 R.), Lancaster Gate; PEMBRIDGE COURT (35 R.), 34 Pembridge Gardens; PHOENIX (130 R.), Kensington Gardens Square; POST HOUSE (175 R.; motel), Bayswater Road; ROYAL LANCASTER (440 R.), Lancaster Terrace; VICEROY (50 R.), Lancaster Gate; WHITE'S (60 R.), Lancaster Gate.

W8 (Kensington): KENSINGTON CLOSE (530 R.), Wright's Lane, off Kensington High Street; KENSINGTON PALACE (310 R.), De Vere Gardens; LONDON TARA (840 R.), Scarsdale Place, Wright's Lane; ROYAL GARDEN (430 R.), Kensington High Street.

W11 (North Kensington): HILTON INTERNATIONAL (610 R.), Holland Park Avenue; PORTOBELLO (25 R.), 22 Stanley Gardens.

W14 (West Kensington): ROYAL KENSINGTON (410 R.), 380 Kensington High Street.

SW1 (Westminster, St James's, Victoria, and Belgravia): BELGRAVIA-SHERATON (90 R.), Chesham Place; BERKELEY (180 R.), Wilton Place, Knightsbridge; CADOGAN (75 R.), 75 Sloane Street; CAVENDISH (255 R.), Jermyn Street, Piccadilly; DUKE'S (50 R.), 35 St James's Place; EBURY COURT (40 R.), 26 Ebury Street; ELIZABETH (25 R.), 37 Eccleston Square; GORING (100 R.), Beeston Place, Grosvenor Gardens; GROSVENOR (360 R.), Victoria Station; HOLIDAY INN (215 R.), 17 Sloane Street; HYATT CARLTON TOWER (240 R.), Cadogan Place; HYDE PARK (200 R.), Knightsbridge; KNIGHTSBRIDGE GREEN (20 R.), 159 Knightsbridge; LOWNDES (80 R.), 20 Lowndes Street, near Cadogan Place; ROYAL COURT (100 R.), Sloane Square; ROYAL HORSEGUARDS (280 R.), Whitehall Court; ROYAL WESTMINSTER (135 R.), Buckingham Palace Road; ST ERMIN'S (240 R.), Caxton Street; ST JAMES'S (520 R.), Buckingham Gate; SHERATON PARK TOWER (295 R.), 101 Knightsbridge; WILBRAHAM (50 R.), 1 Wilbraham Place.

SW3 (Knightsbridge): BASIL STREET (100 R.), 8 Basil Street; CAPITAL (60 R.), 22 Basil Street.

SW5 (Earls Court): BARKSTON (70 R.), 36 Barkston Gardens; GEORGE (145 R.), Templeton Place; HOGARTH (90 R.), Hogarth Road; LONDON INTERNATIONAL (420 R.), Cromwell Road.

SW7 (South Kensington): BAILEY'S (155 R.), 140 Gloucester Road; BLAKE'S (70 R.), 33 Roland Gardens; CRANLEY GARDENS (90 R.), Cranley Gardens; EMBASSY HOUSE (70 R.), 31 Queen's Gate; FORUM (915 R.), 97 Cromwell Road; GLOUCESTER (550 R.), Harrington Gardens; JOHN HOWARD (30 R.), 4 Queen's Gate; KENSINGTON FAIRWAY (90 R.), 117 Cromwell Road; LONDON PENTA (910 R.), Cromwell Road; NORFOLK (100 R.), Harrington Road; NUMBER SIXTEEN (25 R.), 16 Sumner Place; ONSLOW COURT (145 R.), 109 Queen's Gate; REGENCY (195 R.), 100 Queen's Gate; VANDERBILT (100 R.), 76 Cromwell Road; and others in this district.

WC1 (Bloomsbury and neighbourhood): BLOOMSBURY CREST (250 R.), Coram

Street; IMPERIAL (460 R.), Russell Square; KINGSLEY (170 R.), Bloomsbury Way; LONDON RYAN (210 R.), Gwynne Place, King's Cross; MARLBOROUGH CREST (175 R.), Bloomsbury Street; ROYAL NATIONAL (780 R.), Bedford Way; ROYAL SCOT (350 R.), 100 King's Cross Road; RUSSELL (320 R.), Russell Square (Route 19); Y HOTEL (170 R.), 112 Great Russell Street; and many others.

WC2 (Charing Cross, Strand, and neighbourhood): CHARING CROSS (220 R.), Charing Cross Station; DRURY LANE (130 R.), Drury Lane; HOWARD (130 R.), Temple Place; PASTORIA (50 R.), St Martin's Lane; ROYAL TRAFALGAR (110R.), Whitcomb Street; SAVOY (200 R; all suites), Strand (Route 21); STRAND PALACE (790 R.), Strand; WALDORF (310 R.), Aldwych.

NW1 (Marylebone, etc.): HAREWOOD (90 R.), Harewood Row, near Marylebone Station; KENNEDY (320 R.), Cardington Street, near Euston Station; WHITE HOUSE (590 R.), Albany Street, near Regent's Park.

N1: GREAT NORTHERN (60 R.), King's Cross Station.

EC2: GREAT EASTERN (145 R.), Liverpool Street Station.

E1: THE TOWER (840 R.), St Katharine's Way (in the World Trade Centre, Route 34).

SUBURBAN HOTELS: *Carnarvon* (150 R.), Ealing Common, W5; *Clarendon* (160 R.), 8 Montpelier Row, Blackheath, SE3; *Cunard International* (640 R.), Shortlands, Hammersmith, W6; *Garth* (30 R.), 70 Hendon Way, Cricklewood, NW2; *Hendon Hall* (50 R.), Ashley Lane, Hendon, NW4; *Holiday Inn* (300 R.), King Henry's Road, Swiss Cottage, NW3; *Kenton House* (50 R.), 5 Hillcrest Road, Ealing, W5; *Ladbroke Clive* (80 R.), Primrose Hill Road, Hampstead, NW3; *Ladbroke Westmoreland* (350 R.), 18 Lodge Road, St John's Wood, NW8 (near Lord's Cricket Ground); *Lily* (100 R.), 23 Lillie Road, West Brompton, SW6; *London Park* (380 R.), Longville Road, Elephant & Castle, SE11; *Post House* (140 R.; motel), Haverstock Hill, Hampstead, NW3; *Sandringham* (15 R.), 3 Holford Road, Hampstead Heath NW3; *Swiss Cottage* (60 R.), 4 Adamson Road, NW3; *West Centre* (495 R.), Lillie Road, Fulham, SW6.

BOARDING-HOUSES, some describing themselves as private hotels, are to be found in all the residential parts of London, as well as in the suburbs. They vary considerably in their charges and in the quality of the accommodation offered, and a recommendation from someone known to the visitor is advisable. The letting rooms are generally limited in number and in many cases are booked early in the season, if not all the year round. There are satisfactory boarding-houses in Bayswater, to the north of Hyde Park, and in Kensington, especially in the neighbourhood of Cromwell Road and Earls Court. Numerous cheaper and rather plainer boarding-houses exist in Bloomsbury, with proportionately lesser charges. The visitor should come to an arrangement at the outset regarding the provision of lunch and tea.

Residential Hotels or blocks of flats, with suites of furnished apartments, and in some cases with restaurants and room attendance ('service flats'), have been built in many quarters of London. The most palatial (and most expensive) are in Kensington and Bayswater; in less exclusive quarters charges are proportionately less. Meals may usually either be taken in the restaurant or be ordered from it. Some of the larger blocks of flats are equipped with private bathrooms, bars and lounges, games rooms and swimming pools, and garages. Furnished Apartments are obtainable also in private houses, and are advertised by house-agents and accommodation bureaux and in the newspapers. The most expensive apartments are in St James's and Mayfair (the neighbourhood of Piccadilly and Oxford Street), where meals can often be supplied if arranged. Cheaper rooms are numerous in Bloomsbury and elsewhere, but breakfast is generally the only meal that can be provided.

Furnished Houses, obtainable in parts of the suburbs, are usually fairly expensive, and are best sought through a reliable house-agent. Plate, cutlery, and linen are generally provided, but are charged as 'extras'. *Universal Aunts*, 250 King's Road, SW3 (telephone 351–5767), have lists of furnished flats, and will also make suitable arrangements for those who wish to stay as paying guests with a private family in London. The *London Visitor Bureau* (see p. 72) also keeps a register of householders in and around the capital who can offer accommodation to overseas visitors (an early inquiry is advisable), and maintains a 'low budget' accommodation service at its Victoria Station information office. Members of the *Youth Hostels Association* (London office, 14 Southampton Street, Strand, WC2) will find hostels in Holland Park, Kensington (Route 11), and the St Paul's Choir House (Route 24), and at Highgate (84 Highgate West Hill, N6) and Earls Court (38 Bolton Gardens, SW5).

Restaurants, cafés, and tea-rooms of every size, grade and range of price abound in London, the most favoured regions being the Piccadilly area, Soho, and Kensington. All the principal hotels have restaurants and grill-rooms to which non-residents are admitted, and some hotels will provide theatre suppers. Alcoholic liquor may be obtained only during the licensing hours, except by residents in their hotels. Most restaurants which have no licence will send out for drinks (small tip expected). Smoking is permitted almost everywhere, and evening dress is required only at a few of the more exclusive restaurants. At these and other first-class restaurants tables can usually be booked in advance.

The most expensive restaurants will be found in the neighbourhood of Piccadilly and Regent Street. Here the cuisine is mainly French or Italian, and meals are generally served à la carte; elsewhere table d'hôte meals can usually be obtained or arranged. Foreign restaurants, especially in Soho, are often unpretentious, but are greatly favoured for their cooking and unusual dishes, though the charges here, as elsewhere, vary considerably from place to place, and a previous inquiry should preferably be made. The grill-rooms attached to hotels and restaurants, particularly in the West End, are popular for lunch. Restaurants in the City, including some well-known and old-fashioned taverns, are usually open only on weekdays for lunch. The fare here is generally plainer, though well-cooked, and the special 'plat du jour' offered can be recommended. Good plain luncheons may be obtained at reasonable charges at many public houses.

The restaurants recommended below are arranged alphabetically under their postal districts. Only a selection can be given, and here again the omission of a name implies no condemnation. Some restaurants are closed on Saturdays or Sundays, while some are open for lunch or dinner only on those days, and it is as well to telephone in advance, booking a table at the same time, if possible. Specialities are mentioned in brackets. Particulars of recommended restaurants are given in *The Good Food Guide*, published annually.

W1 (Mayfair and north of Piccadilly): BENTLEY'S, 11 Swallow Street (English fare); CAFÉ ROYAL, 68 Regent Street (French); GAYLORD, 16 Albemarle Street (Indian); GEETANG'S, 23 Brook Street (Indian); GREENHOUSE, 27a Hay's Mews (English, French); GOLDEN CARP, 8a Mount Street (French, vegetarian); ICI PARIS, 2a Duke Street (French); JUSTIN DE BLANK, 54 Duke Street; LA NAPOULE, 8 North Audley Street (French); LANGAN'S BRASSERIE, Stratton Street; LE GAVROCHE, 43 Upper Brook Street (French); MARQUIS, 121a Mount Street (Continental); MIRABELLE, 56 Curzon Street (French); SAGA JAPANESE, 43 South Molton Street (Japanese); SCOTT'S, 20 Mount Street (English, French; noted for shellfish); SOVEREIGN, 17 Hertford Street (French); SWISS CENTRE, 2 New Coventry Street (International); TANDOORI, 37a Curzon Street (Indian); TIBERIO, 22 Queen Street (Italian; dancing); TOKYO, Swallow Street (Japanese); VEERASWAMY'S, 99 Regent Street (Indian); VENDÔME, 20 Dover Street (French; shellfish); WOLFE'S, 34 Park Lane (American).

W1 (Soho and neighbourhood): AU JARDIN DES GOURMETS, 5 Greek Street (French); BRAGANZA, 56 Frith Street (French; fish); CHEZ VICTOR, 45 Wardour Street (French); CHOY'S, 45 Frith Street (Chinese); CRANK'S, 8 Marshall Street (vegetarian); GAY HUSSAR, 2 Greek Street (Hungarian); GENNARO'S, 44 Dean Street (Italian); HOSTARIA ROMANA, 70 Dean Street (Italian); KETTNERS, 29 Romilly Street (old-established); LA CUCARACHA, 12 Greek Street (Mexican); LA TERRAZZA, 19 Romilly Street (Italian); LA VALBONNE, 62 Kingly Street (French,

Italian); LEONI'S QUO VADIS, 26 Dean Street (Italian); L'ÉPICURE, 28 Frith Street (French); MARTINEZ, 25 Swallow Street (Spanish); OSTERIA LARIANA, 49 Frith Street (Italian); PETER MARIO, 47 Gerrard Street (English, Italian); ROMANO SANTI, 50 Greek Street (Italian); RUGANTINO, 26 Romilly Street (Italian); VENEZIA, 21 Great Chapel Street (Italian); WHEELER'S, 19 Old Compton Street (French; shellfish).

W1 (Marylebone and north of Oxford Street): ANEMOS, 34 Charlotte Street (Greek); ANTOINE'S, 40 Charlotte Street (French; fish, oysters); CAMPAGNA, 31 Marylebone High Street (Italian); CRAWFORDS, 10 Crawford Street (English, Continental); FISHERMAN'S WHARF, 73 Baker Street (French; fish); GENEVIEVE, 13 Thayer Street (English, French); HELLENIC, 30 Thayer Street (Greek); IL BARBINO, 64 Seymour Street (Italian); KERZENSTÜBERL, 9 St Christopher's Place, Wigmore Street (Austrian); LACY'S, 26 Whitfield Street (English, French); LE PETIT MONTMARTRE, 15 Marylebone Lane (French); L'ÉTOILE, 30 Charlotte Street (French); MASAKO, 6 St Christopher's Place; MIKADO, 110 George Street (Japanese); RUE ST JACQUES, 5 Charlotte Street (French); TRATTORIA DEI PESCATORI, 57 Charlotte Street (Italian); VECCHIO PARIOLI, 129 Crawford Street (Italian, Continental); WHITE TOWER, Percy Street (Greek).

NW1: CHALCOT'S, 49 Chalcot Road; TONINO, 12 Glentworth Street (Italian).

W2 (Bayswater and north of Hyde Park): CHEZ FRANCO, 3 Hereford Road (French, Italian); CONCORDIA, 29 Craven Road (Continental); FOURNAKI, 10 Moscow Road (Greek); KALAMARAS, 66 and 76 Inverness Mews (Greek); LOTUS HOUSE, 61 Edgware Road (Chinese); MANDARIN KITCHEN, 14 Queensway (Chinese); MIGNON HUNGARIAN, 2 Queensway Corner (Hungarian); MOURINO'S, 58 Porchester Road (Spanish); PEKING, 3 Westbourne Grove (Chinese); ROMANTICA TAVERNA, 12 Moscow Road (Greek); TRAT WEST, 143 Edgware Road (Italian).

W8 (Kensington): ALCOVE, 17 High Street (French); AL GALLO D'ORO, 353 High Street (Italian); ARK, 35 High Street (French); BAHN THAI, 35 Marloes Road (Thai); BISTINGO, 45 High Street (Italian); CASA PORELLI, 1a Launceston Place (Italian); FU TONG, 29 High Street (Chinese); GATAMELATA, 343 High Street (Italian); HOLY COW, 38 Church Street (Indian); IL BARBINO, 32 Church Street (Italian); JIMMIES, Palace Barracks, Church Street (English); LA PAESANA, 30 Uxbridge Street (Italian); LA TOQUE BLANCHE, 21 Abingdon Road (French); LE BISTINGO, 7 High Street (French); LE BRESSAN, 14 Wright's Lane (French); MEDUSA, 38c Church Street (International); SAILING JUNK, 59 Marloes Road (Chinese).

SW1 (St James's and south of Piccadilly): A L'ÉCU DE FRANCE, 111 Jermyn Street (French); ARLINGTON, Arlington Street (International); FRANK'S, 65 Jermyn Street (mainly Italian); LAFAYETTE, 32 King Street; OVERTON'S, 5 St James's Street (English, French; oysters, fish); WHEELER'S, 12a Duke of York Street (French); WILTON'S, Jermyn Street (fish, game).

SW1 (Belgravia and neighbourhood): CARAFE, 15 Lowndes Street (French; fish); GAVVERS, 61 Lower Sloane Street (French); LES TROIS CANARDS, 14

Knightsbridge Green (French); MARCEL, 14 Sloane Street (French); MR CHOW, 151 Knightsbridge (Chinese); PIG AND WHISTLE, 14 Little Chester Street (English); SALLOOS, 62 Kinnerton Street (Indian).

SW1 (Victoria and Pimlico): EATONS, 49 Elizabeth Street (Continental); KUNDAN, 3 Horseferry Road (Indian, Pakistani); LA FONTANA, 101 Pimlico Road (French, Italian); L'AMICO, 44 Horseferry Road (Italian); LA POULE AU POT, 231 Ebury Street (French); LOCKETS, Marsham Court, Marsham Street (English); MASSIMO'S, 42 Buckingham Palace Road (Italian); MIJANOU, 143 Ebury Street; MIMMO D'ISCHIA, 61 Elizabeth Street (Italian); OVERTON'S, 4 Victoria Buildings, Terminus Place (English, French); POMEGRANATES, 94 Grosvenor Road (International); RISTORANTE ITALIANO, 89 Pimlico Road (Italian); TATE GALLERY, Millbank (English).

SW3 (Chelsea): CHOY'S, 172 King's Road (Chinese); DON LUIGI, 316 King's Road (Italian); IL GIRASOLE, 126 Fulham Road; LA TANTE CLAIRE, 68 Royal Hospital Road (French); LE FRANÇAIS, 259 Fulham Road (French); LE GOURMET, 312 King's Road (International); SAN QUINTINO, Radnor Walk (Italian).

SW3 (Brompton, etc.): AL BEN ACCOLTO, 58 Fulham Road (Italian); AU BON ACCUEIL, 25 Elystan Street (French); BEWICK'S, 87 Walton Street (French); BROMPTON GRILL, 243 Brompton Road (French); CLAUDIN'S, 85 Sloane Avenue (Italian); DAPHNE'S, 112 Draycott Avenue (French); DRAKE'S, 2a Pond Place, Fulham Road (English); ENGLISH HOUSE, 3 Milner Street (English); GEORGE AND DRAGON, 256 Brompton Road (fish, grills); KEN LO'S, 67 Elystan Street (Chinese); LE SUQUET, 104 Draycott Avenue (French); MA CUISINE, 113 Walton Street (French); PARKES, 5 Beauchamp Place; SAN FREDIANO, 62 Fulham Road (Italian); SHANGRI-LA, 233 Brompton Road (Chinese); TANDOORI, 153 Fulham Road (Indian); WALTON'S, 121 Walton Street (International).

SW5 (Earls Court, etc.): ARTISTE AFFAMÉ, 243 Old Brompton Road (French); IL PALIO DE SIENA, 133 Earls Court Road (Italian); READ'S, 152 Old Brompton Road; TIGER LEE, 251 Old Brompton Road (Chinese).

SW7 (South Kensington): GONDOLIERE, 3 Gloucester Road (Italian); HILAIRE, 68 Old Brompton Road; JAMSHID, 6 Glendower Place (Indian); MONTPELIANO, 13 Montpelier Street (Italian); SHEZAN, 16 Cheval Place, off Montpelier Street (Indian); STABLE, 123 Cromwell Road (French, Italian).

WC1 (Bloomsbury): IL FORNELLO, 150 Southampton Row (Italian); SPAGHETTI HOUSE, 20 Sicilian Avenue (Italian).

WC2 (North of Charing Cross): BEOTY'S, 79 St Martin's Lane (Greek, French); CELLIER DE MEDICI, 8 Mays Court, St Martin's Lane (International); CHEZ SOLANGE, 35 Cranbourn Street (French; music); DICKENS ROOM, Mercer Street; GIOVANNI'S, 10 Goodwin's Court, St Martin's Lane (Italian); IVY, 1 West Street (French); LA BUSSOLA, 42 St Martin's Lane (Italian; music); LAGUNA, 50 St Martin's Lane (Italian); MANZI'S, 1 Leicester Street; MON PLAISIR, 21 Monmouth Street (French); SHEEKEY'S, 28 St Martin's Court, Charing Cross Road (English); SHUTTLEWORTH'S, 1 Aldwych (International); TOURMENT

D'AMOUR, 19 New Row, off St Martin's Lane; TROTA BLU, 48 Cranbourn Street (Italian).

WC2 (North of the Strand): BOULESTIN, 25 Southampton Street (French); INIGO JONES, 14 Garrick Street (French); INTERLUDE DE TABAILLAU, 7 Bow Street (French); LA SCALA, 35 Southampton Street (Italian); L'OPÉRA, 32 Great Queen Street (French); NAG'S HEAD, 10 St James's Street, Covent Garden (theatrical clientele); RULE'S, 35 Maiden Lane (theatrical clientele); SIMPSON'S, 100 Strand (English); TERRAZZA-EST, 125 Chancery Lane (Italian); THE GRANGE, 39 King Street (French); THOMAS DE QUINCEY'S, 36 Tavistock Street (French); TUTTONS, 11 Russell Street.

EC1 (Smithfield): BARLEYMOW, 50 Long Lane (English); BUBBS, 329 Central Markets (French).

EC2 (City): BARON OF BEEF, Gutter Lane, Gresham Street; BIRCH'S, 3 Angel Court, Throgmorton Street; LE POULBOT, 45 Cheapside (French); OLD DR BUTLER'S HEAD, Mason's Avenue, Coleman Street; PALMERSTON, 49 Bishopsgate (noted grill-room); WILLIAMSON'S TAVERN, 1 Grovelands Court, Cheapside.

EC3 (City, east of Bank): CITY TIBERIO, 8 Lime Street (Italian); GEORGE AND VULTURE, 3 Castle Court, Lombard Street (well-known chop-house); SIMPSON'S, 38½ Cornhill; WHEELER'S, 9 Fenchurch Buildings, Fenchurch Street (French); WHEELER'S CITY, 19 Great Tower Street (French).

EC4 (City, west of Bank): COCK TAVERN, 22 Fleet Street; LE GAMIN, 32 Old Bailey (French); MERMAID THEATRE, Puddle Dock; OLD CHESHIRE CHEESE, Wine Office Court, 145 Fleet Street; PRINCESS ELIZABETH, off Swan Pier, near London Bridge; SAMUEL PEPYS, 48 Upper Thames Street; SWEETING'S, 39 Queen Victoria Street (excellent fish).

SE1 (South Bank): GEORGE, 77 Borough High Street; NATIONAL THEATRE, South Bank; SOUTH OF THE BORDER, 8 Joan Street, Waterloo (English, French, with roof garden).

SUBURBAN RESTAURANTS: *Alonso's*, 32 Queenstown Road, Battersea, SW8 (French, Spanish); *Anna's Place*, 30 Mildmay Park, N1; *Ararat*, 249 Camden High Street, NW1 (Greek); *Au Bois St Jean*, 122 St John's Wood High Street, NW8 (French); *Bagatelle*, 5 Langton Street, Chelsea, SW10 (French); *Barbarella*, 428 Fulham Road, SW6 (Italian); *Canaletto*, 451 Edgware Road, W2 (Italian); *Carlos Place*, 855 Fulham Road, SW6 (French); *Chalk and Cheese*, 14 Chalk Farm Road, NW1 (English, French); *Chez Moi*, Addison Avenue, Holland Park, W11 (French); *Chez Nico*, 129 Queenstown Road, SW8 (French); *Frederick's*, Camden Passage, Islington, N1 (International); *Gastronome One*, 311 New King's Road, SW6; *Hungry Horse*, 191 Fulham Road, SW10 (English); *La Croisette*, 168 Ifield Road, SW10 (French); *La Famiglia*, 7 Langton Street, SW10 (Italian); *La Gaffe*, 107 Heath Street, Hampstead, NW3 (French); *La Jardinière*, 148 Holland Park Avenue, W11 (French); *La Pomme d'Amour*, 128 Holland Park Avenue, W11 (French); *L'Arlequin*, 123 Queenstown Road, SW8 (French); *L'Artiste Assoiffé*, 122 Kensington Park Road, W11 (French); *Leith's*, 92 Kensington Park Road (International);

L'Olivier, 116 Finborough Road, SW10 (French); *Martin's*, 88 Ifield Road, SW10; *Monsieur Thompson's*, 29 Kensington Park Road, W11; *Oslo Court*, Prince Albert Road, St John's Wood, NW8 (Balkan); *Peters*, 65 Fairfax Road, Swiss Cottage, NW6 (French); *Quincy's*, 675 Finchley Road, NW2; *Sabras*, 263 Willesden High Road, NW10 (vegetarian); *Salamis*, 204 Fulham Road, SW10 (Greek); *San Carlo*, 2 High Street, Highgate, N6 (Italian); *Turpins*, 118 Heath Street, Hampstead, NW3 (English); *Van B's*, 306b Fulham Road, SW10.

Inexpensive meals may be obtained at the chains of restaurants established by Messrs J. Lyons & Co. (excellent tea), The Aerated Bread Co. ('ABC'), the Express Dairy Co., Kardomah, Kenco Coffee Houses, and other companies. Restaurants will also be found in all the large department stores. Reasonably priced meals may be obtained at the chains of restaurants owned by Angus Steak Houses, the Pizza Express Group, and Quality Inns.

TEA-ROOMS. Tea can be obtained at most of the hotels, many of the restaurants (practically all the lower-priced restaurants), in the principal stores, and at numerous cafés. It is served out-of-doors in summer in Hyde Park, Kensington Gardens, Regent's Park, and the Zoological Gardens. Light refreshments and 'snacks' may be purchased here, in St James's Park and several other public parks, and in the Victoria Embankment Gardens. Tea-rooms are mostly closed on Saturday afternoons and Sundays in the City.

PUBLIC HOUSES. A feature of London life in recent years has been the growth in popularity of the public house as a place to eat as well as to drink in sociable surroundings. The following is a selection only of the many London pubs of character where meals or light refreshments of good quality may be obtained, generally at reasonable prices. Some pubs do not serve full meals, and they rarely serve meals on Sundays, when, however, snacks can usually be obtained at the bar.

ALBERT, 52 Victoria Street, SW1; ANCHOR, Bankside, Southwark, SE1; BARLEY MOW, 82 Duke Street, off Oxford Street, W1; BLUE POSTS, 6 Bennet Street, off St James's Street, SW1; BRICKLAYERS' ARMS, 6 New Quebec Street, off Gloucester Place, W1; BUNCH OF GRAPES, 207 Brompton Road, SW3; CADOGAN ARMS, 298 King's Road, SW3; CAPTAIN'S CABIN, Norris Street, off Haymarket, SW1; CASK AND GLASS, 39 Palace Street, SW1; CHELSEA POTTER, 119 King's Road, SW3; CLARENCE, 53 Whitehall, SW1; COCK AND LION, 62 Wigmore Street, W1; CROSS KEYS, Lawrence Street, SW3; DICKENS INN, St Katharine's Docks, E1; DOVER CASTLE, 43 Weymouth Mews, near Portland Place, W1; FOUNDER'S ARMS, Bankside, SE1; GRENADIER, 18 Wilton Row, off

Wilton Crescent, SW1; Horse and Groom, 128 Great Portland Street, W1; King's Arms, 77 Buckingham Palace Road, SW1; King's Arms, Shepherd Market, W1; Marlborough Head, 24 North Audley Street, W1; Masons' Arms, 58 Devonshire Street, W1; Moore Arms, 61 Cadogan Street, SW3; Museum Tavern, 49 Great Russell Street, WC1; Old Rising Sun, 79 Marylebone High Street, W1; Prince Albert, Princess Road, NW1; Red Lion, 1 Waverton Street, Charles Street, W1; Rose and Crown, 2 Old Park Lane, W1; Running Footman, 5 Charles Street, W1; Scarsdale Arms, Edwardes Square, W8; Shepherds Tavern, 50 Hertford Street, W1; Sherlock Holmes, 10 Northumberland Street, WC2; Six Bells, 197 King's Road, SW3; Swan, 66 Bayswater Road, W2 (north of Hyde Park); Swan, Cosmo Passage, Southampton Row, W1; Talbot, 1 Little Chester Street, near Grosvenor Place, SW1; Two Chairmen, 39 Dartmouth Street, SW1; White Horse, Fetter Lane, EC4; White Horse, 45 Rupert Street, W1.

Suburban Pubs include the *Angel*, 21 Rotherhithe Street, Bermondsey; *Bull & Bush*, North End Road, Hampstead; *Canonbury Tavern*, 21 Canonbury Place, Islington; *Dove*, 19 Upper Mall, Hammersmith; *Flask*, Flask Walk, Hampstead; *Flask*, 77 West Hill, Highgate; *Freemason's Arms*, Downshire Hill, Hampstead; *Jack Straw's Castle*, North End Way, Hampstead; *Mayflower*, 117 Rotherhithe Street; *Old Ship*, 25 Upper Mall, Hammersmith; *Old Swan*, 116 Battersea Church Road, Battersea; *Pied Bull*, 1 Liverpool Road, Islington; *Prospect of Whitby*, 57 Wapping Wall (facing the Thames); *Spaniards*, Spaniards Road, Hampstead; *Star & Garter*, 44 Upper Street, Islington; *Swiss Cottage*, 98 Finchley Road, Hampstead; *Town of Ramsgate*, 62 Wapping High Street (facing river); *Trafalgar*, Park Row, Greenwich.

Licensing Hours. Alcoholic liquor may not be sold in London before 11 a.m. or after 11 p.m.; there must be a break of two and a half hours from 3 p.m.; and there is a limit of nine hours per day. The usual 'permitted' hours are from 11 a.m. to 3, and from 5.30 to 11 (for pubs in the City of London, from 11.30 a.m. to 3, and from 5 p.m. to 11). Sunday hours are from 12 noon to 2 or 2.30 and from 7 to 10 or 10.30.

Gratuities in restaurants may be reckoned at about ten–twelve per cent of the bill, rather more at the higher-class establishments. Many of these automatically add a surcharge or 'service charge' to the bill, while some of the lower-priced tea shops do not encourage tipping, but maintain a 'staff-box' near the cash desk. In hotels, tips should amount to about ten–fifteen per cent of the total charge, which may still be distributed personally in some hotels, though it is a growing practice to add a stipulated service charge to the visitor's bill. In this case, tips are still expected for special services, such as carrying the luggage to the taxi or carpark.

POST OFFICES, INFORMATION BUREAUX, AND USEFUL ADDRESSES

POST OFFICES. London is divided into eight postal districts, distinguished by their initials: EC (East Central), WC (West Central), W, NW, N, E, SE, and SW. These districts are further divided into delivery office areas, each distinguished by a number, the head-office of the district being in the area numbered '1'. These areas have been divided again into smaller delivery areas which have postal code letters and numbers. Letters, etc., addressed to London should bear at least the postal district initials and the area number (e.g., NW1, EC4, W12) and preferably also the postal code, where this is known. For example, the address of the London Transport head-office should be given as 55 Broadway, London SW1H OBD.

The LONDON CHIEF OFFICE (formerly the 'General Post Office') is in King Edward Street, EC1 (Plan IV, D3), and its telephone number is 432–1234. It is open for all kinds of postal and telegraph business on Monday–Friday from 8 a.m. to 7 p.m. (Saturdays from 9 to 12.30), except on public holidays. The TRAFALGAR SQUARE branch office, 22–28 William IV Street, WC2 (near St Martin's; III, F3), is open daily from 8 a.m. to 8 p.m. for all kinds of business, and also keeps open from 10 a.m. to 5 p.m. on Sundays and public holidays (except Christmas Day). Other post offices in London are normally open on Monday–Friday 9 a.m. to 5.30 p.m., and on Saturdays to 12.30 or 1, but many offices in the suburban area close also at 12.30 or 1 on the local early closing day, and others in the central business area are closed all day on Saturday. Only the Trafalgar Square office is open on Sunday.

The principal delivery of letters, etc., is made between about 7 and 9 a.m., but there is usually a second delivery later in the morning, and further business deliveries are made in the central areas. There is no Sunday delivery of letters or parcels, and no collection is made after Saturday morning until Monday morning. The inland telegram service was replaced in 1982 by a new telemessage service (see below).

The postal charges at present (1985) are 17p for first-class mail, 12p for second-class mail. A certificate of posting will be issued free on request at the post office, and a record of delivery is provided for inland letters for a fee of 20p (payable at the time of posting). Express letters and parcels (carried by special messenger) may be sent from the more important post offices in London for an additional fee of £1.50. Packets may be registered at any post office against loss; the compensation depends on the fee paid, but compensation for money lost in the post is paid only if it has been sent in a special Registered Letter envelope, obtainable at the post office.

The *Datapost* service of the Post Office provides a guaranteed delivery for important documents and packages on the same day in many areas ('Sameday' service) or on the next day in any part of Britain ('Overnight' service). The *Royal Mail Special Delivery* service ensures the delivery next day of first-class letters and packets, for a fee of £1.50. The *Swiftair* service offers an express delivery of air-mail letters and packets to most parts of the world, for an additional fee of £1.50 above the normal postal rates.

Full particulars of all post office services are given in the *Post Office Guide* published annually in November (supplements are issued free, from time to time), and obtainable from H.M. Stationery Office (49 High Holborn, WC1) and from the chief post offices. Complete lists of post offices (with their addresses and telephone numbers) are given under 'Postal Services' in the 'Yellow Pages' of the telephone directory.

POSTE RESTANTE. Correspondence marked 'poste restante' or 'to be called for' may be addressed to the London Chief Office or to any branch office, of which there are generally several in each district. Proof of identity is required before letters are given up to the addressee. Letters are kept for a fortnight (for one month, if from abroad), for up to three months by special arrangement, but the poste restante system must not be used for more than three consecutive months. Letters bearing no district initials will be delivered to the London Chief Office, while those without an area numeral go to the district head-office.

PARCELS handed in at any post office will be delivered to any address in Great Britain and Northern Ireland for a charge varying according to the weight, from 1 kg (just over 2 lb.) up to 25 kg (about 55 lb.), the maximum weight. Parcels above this limit will be collected from any address and delivered by *British Rail*, who have two services: *Red Star Parcels* (Room 4a, Melbury House, Melbury Terrace, NW1) and *City Link Parcels* (King's Cross Freight Terminal, York Way, N1; telephone 837–8822). Parcels will also be conveyed in the London area by *Roadline*, whose parcels office is at Willow Walk, Bermondsey, SE1 (telephone 237–3555); for the City at Macclesfield Road, EC1 (telephone 253–7677). The charge varies according to weight and size (7 kg is the minimum weight), though bulky parcels may be charged fifty per cent more.

TELEPHONE facilities will be found at many post offices, shops, and railway stations (including the chief underground stations), and there are numerous kiosks in the street. The standard charge for a local call is 6p for two minutes, increasing to 12p for the next two minutes, and so on. Reduced rates are charged before 8 a.m. and after 6 p.m. (all day on Saturdays and Sundays) and higher rates are charged between 9 a.m. and 1 p.m. (Monday–Friday). Public call boxes, including those of the new 'payphones', mostly take 10p and 50p coins (some take 2p coins also). New telephones with machines for use with credit cards have been installed at the airports and the chief railway stations. A system of all-figure dialling is in force throughout the London area; the head office of the Metropolitan Police in Victoria Street, for instance, is dialled 230–1212. Callers outside London must first dial 01.

Telemessages can be sent by telephone to any part of Britain by dialling 190 (100 if outside London) and asking the operator for the Telemessage service. To ensure delivery the next working day (including Saturday), the message must be telephoned before 10 p.m. (7 p.m. on Sundays and Bank Holidays). A telemessage costs £3 for the first fifty words and £1.50 for each subsequent group of fifty words; the name and address are sent free, but Value Added Tax (V.A.T.) is charged on the message. Telemessages may also be sent by the Telex service, and the telemessage service has been extended to many places abroad.

Further information on the telephone services may be obtained from the *Telephone Directory: London Postal Area*, or by telephoning 437–8060 (Central Area) or 921–8888 (City Area).

Information about events of interest to take place in London on the same day may be obtained by dialling 246–8041, events of interest to children by dialling 246–8007, the correct time by dialling 123, a weather report by dialling 246–8091, and travel information by dialling 246–8021.

INFORMATION BUREAUX. The head-office of the LONDON VISITOR AND CONVENTION BUREAU (which in 1985 replaced the London Tourist Board) is at 26 Grosvenor Gardens, Victoria, SW1 (telephone 730–3488). The bureau maintains information offices, with assistants speaking several languages, at *Victoria Station* (on the north-west side), open daily, 9 a.m. to 8.30 p.m. (July and August, 8.30 a.m. to 10 p.m.), at *Selfridges*, Oxford Street, W1, and *Harrods*, Brompton Road, SW3 (these two open during shop hours), and at *Heathrow Central Station*, open daily, 9 a.m. to 6 p.m. Here the visitor can obtain information on London, concessionary tickets for underground and bus journeys, and tickets for theatres and concerts. The assistants will also arrange hotel and boarding-house accommodation.

The BRITISH TOURIST AUTHORITY concerns itself particularly with visitors from abroad, but it no longer has an information office in London. Its administrative office is at Thames Tower, Black's Road, Hammersmith, W6 (telephone 846–9000), and it maintains numerous offices in every part of the world (see p. 43). The authority publishes a monthly magazine, *In Britain*, giving particulars of forthcoming events and other information.

The GREATER LONDON COUNCIL maintains a Tourist and Leisure Information Centre at 25 Shaftesbury Avenue, W1 (near Piccadilly Circus; Plan III, F2), open daily from 10 a.m. to 8 p.m. (telephone 437–1384; for the bookshop 437–1304). Information about any aspect of the capital may be sought here and tickets may be bought for the South Bank concert halls and for events under the jurisdiction of the G.L.C.

The CITY OF LONDON INFORMATION CENTRE, on the south side of St Paul's Cathedral, at the corner of Godliman Street (Plan IV, E3), is open Monday–Friday 9.30 to 5, Saturday 9.30 to 5.30 (telephone 606–3030). Here publications and information relevant to the City may be readily obtained, including a monthly diary of events (free).

Official guide-maps have been set up here and there in the main streets of central London. Inquiries regarding public transport in London should be made to the *London Transport Executive*; for railways elsewhere in Britain they should be made to the British Rail travel office or to the inquiry offices at the principal termini.

AUTHORIZED GUIDES to the sights of London may be obtained through the London Visitor Bureau (see above), and from the *London Appreciation Society* (see p. 75), *Universal Aunts* (see p. 63), and *Take-a-Guide*, 85 Lower Sloane Street, SW1 (730–9144). Bona fide guides are distinguishable by their oval blue and silver badges.

Tours for Children (between five and fifteen years) are organized by *Junior Jaunts*, 4a William Street, Knightsbridge, SW1, to a variety of places of interest (telephone 235–4700). Walking Tours are arranged by *London Walks* (telephone 882–2763), *Discovering London* (0277–213704), *Guided London Outings* (405–6191), the *Streets of London* (882–3414), *Citisights* (archaeological; 241–0323), and *London Suburban Tours* (554–2904). Useful guides are 'London for the Disabled', published for the *Central Council for the Disabled* (25 Mortimer Street, W1; 637–5400), and 'London Made Easy' (for people over sixty), and 'Children's London', these two published by the London Visitor Bureau.

USEFUL ADDRESSES. The following lists give some addresses which may be useful to the visitor to London. Addresses, both business and private, may be found in the *London Telephone Directory* (see above) and in *Kelly's Post Office London Directory*, published annually and available at public libraries, etc.

The addresses and other particulars of people of rank and eminence are given in *Who's Who*, published annually and similarly available. The addresses of American residents in London are contained, together with other information of relevance to visitors from the United States, in the *Anglo-American Year Book*, published by the American Chamber of Commerce at 75 Brook Street, W1.

COMMONWEALTH HIGH COMMISSIONERS: *Australia*, Australia House,

Strand, WC2; *Bangladesh*, 28 Queen's Gate, SW7; *Canada*, 1 Grosvenor Square, W1; *India*, India House, Aldwych, WC2; *New Zealand*, New Zealand House, Haymarket, SW1; *Sri Lanka*, 13 Hyde Park Gardens, WC2; etc.

EMBASSIES AND CONSULATES: *United States*, 1 Grosvenor Square, W1; *Ireland* (Republic), Embassy, 17 Grosvenor Place, SW1; *Austria*, 18 Belgrave Mews West, SW1; *Belgium*, 103 Eaton Square, SW1; *Bulgaria*, 186 Queen's Gate Gardens, SW7; *Czechoslovakia*, 25 Kensington Palace Gardens, W8; *Denmark*, 55 Sloane Street, SW1; *Finland*, 38 Chesham Place, SW1; *France*, 58 Knightsbridge, SW1; *Germany* (Democratic Republic), 34 Belgrave Square, SW1, (Federal Republic), 23 Belgrave Square, SW1; *Greece*, 1a Holland Park, W11; *Hungary*, 35 Eaton Place, SW1; *Iceland*, 1 Eaton Terrace, SW1; *Italy*, 14 Three Kings Yard, Davies Street, W1; *Luxemburg*, 27 Wilton Crescent, SW1; *Netherlands*, 38 Hyde Park Gate, SW7; *Norway*, 25 Belgrave Square, SW1; *Poland*, 47 Portland Place, W1; *Portugal*, 11 Belgrave Square, SW1; *Romania*, 4 Palace Green, W8; *South Africa*, South Africa House, Trafalgar Square, WC2; *Spain*, 24 Belgrave Square, SW1; *Sweden*, 11 Montagu Place, W1; *Switzerland*, 16 Montagu Place, W1; *U.S.S.R.*, 13 Kensington Palace Gardens, W8; *Yugoslavia*, 5 Lexham Gardens, W8; etc.

BANKS are open in London on Monday–Friday from 9.30 a.m. to 3.30 p.m. (3 p.m. in the City) and are closed on Saturdays, Sundays, and Public Holidays. Some branches in the West End open on Saturdays from 9 or 9.30 to 12 or 12.30 and keep open later for at least one evening a week (usually Thursday), until 6 or 8 p.m. The following are the head offices in London of the principal English banks, most of which have numerous branches throughout the city and suburbs. The chief Scottish, Irish, and American banks also have London offices or are represented in London by English banks.

BARCLAYS BANK, 54 Lombard Street, EC3; COUTTS & CO., 440 Strand, WC2; LLOYDS BANK, 71 Lombard Street, EC3; MIDLAND BANK, Poultry, EC2; NATIONAL WESTMINSTER BANK, 41 Lothbury, EC2; WILLIAMS & GLYN'S (now part of the Royal Bank of Scotland), 20 Birchin Lane, Cornhill, EC3.

TRAVELLERS' CHEQUES may be changed at any bank, at the Trafalgar Square and certain other post offices, at some of the larger hotels and department stores, at King's Cross, Paddington, and Victoria Stations and certain underground stations, and at independent bureaux de change, such as *Thomas Cook's Chequepoint Services*, 37 Coventry Street, W1 (always open).

CLUBS. The social and political clubs, many of which have flourished for well over 100 years, are a feature of London life. Below are the addresses of the best known (in the SW1 postal area unless another area is given). Largely frequented for their social advantages, all have comfortable premises with excellent licensed restaurants.

Entrance fees and subscriptions vary greatly and most of the clubs are exclusive, but members may generally entertain their friends (including ladies, in the majority of clubs). Clubs connected with sporting activities are included in the section on 'Sport in and around London'.

ALPINE, 74 South Audley Street, W1 (mountaineering); ARMY & NAVY, 36 Pall Mall; ARTS, 40 Dover Street, W1 (art, literature, and science); ATHENAEUM, 107 Pall Mall (the premier literary club); AUTHORS', 40 Dover Street, W1; BOODLE'S, 28 St James's Street; BROOKS'S, 60 St James's Street (Liberal); CALEDONIAN, 9 Halkin Street (Scottish); CARLTON, 69 St James's Street (the leading Conservative club); CAVALRY AND GUARDS, 127 Piccadilly, W1; CITY OF LONDON, 19 Old Broad Street, EC2 (exclusive); CITY UNIVERSITY, 50 Cornhill, EC3; EAST INDIA, DEVONSHIRE, SPORTS AND PUBLIC SCHOOLS, 16 St James's Square; FARMERS', 3 Whitehall Court; GARRICK, 15 Garrick Street, WC2 (dramatic and legal); GRESHAM, 15 Abchurch Lane, EC4 (merchants, etc.); LANSDOWNE, 9 Fitzmaurice Place, W1; NATIONAL LIBERAL, 1 Whitehall Place; NAVAL & MILITARY, 94 Piccadilly, W1; ORIENTAL, Stratford House, Stratford Place, W1; PORTLAND, 42 Half Moon Street, W1; PRATT'S, 14 Park Place; REFORM, 104 Pall Mall (the leading Liberal club); ROYAL AIR FORCE, 128 Piccadilly, W1; ROYAL AUTOMOBILE, 89 Pall Mall; ST STEPHEN'S CONSTITUTIONAL, 34 Queen Anne's Gate (Conservative); SAVAGE, 9 Fitzmaurice Place, W1 (arts, science, and law); SAVILE, 69 Brook Street, W1; TRAVELLERS', 106 Pall Mall; TURF, 5 Carlton House Terrace; UNITED OXFORD & CAMBRIDGE UNIVERSITY, 71 Pall Mall; UNIVERSITY WOMEN'S, 2 Audley Square, South Audley Street, W1; WHITE'S, 37 St James's Street.

The AMERICAN CLUB and the AMERICAN WOMEN'S CLUB, both at 95 Piccadilly, W1, cater for Americans in London.

SOCIETIES. The following are among the societies that may be of particular interest to the Londoner. Visitors are usually made welcome at meetings, etc., on introduction by a member.

The LONDON SOCIETY (secretary, Room G210, The City University, Northampton Square, EC1) was founded in 1912 'to stimulate wider concern for the beauty of the capital city, for the preservation of its charms and careful consideration of its developments'; it arranges meetings, lectures, and visits, and publishes a journal. THE LONDON APPRECIATION SOCIETY (17 Manson Mews, SW7), founded in 1932, also arranges visits to places of interest of all kinds in and around the capital and issues a journal (reduced subscription for country members). The LONDON AND MIDDLESEX ARCHAEOLOGICAL SOCIETY (Museum of London, London Wall, EC2), established in 1855, likewise arranges visits, lectures, etc., publishes transactions, and maintains a useful library at the Bishopsgate Institute. The LONDON TOPOGRAPHICAL SOCIETY (Bishopsgate Institute; see below), founded in 1898, publishes facsimiles of maps and records of the history and topography of London. The CITY HERITAGE SOCIETY (404 Gilbert House, Barbican, EC2), founded in 1973, aims to promote high standards of planning and architecture and to preserve features of historical interest. It arranges lectures, visits, and social occasions. The CITY OF LONDON SOCIETY (117 Old Broad Street, EC2) was founded in 1952 with the primary object of 'demonstrating that the business activities of the City are vital to the flow of trade throughout the world'; it organizes lectures, films, etc., and interesting walks through the City, etc. The CITY OF LONDON ARCHAEOLOGICAL SOCIETY (28 Rothesay Avenue, SW20) was founded in 1964 (as the City of London Excavation Group) to organize the excavation of Roman and other sites by groups of volunteers. In addition, there are many local societies, most of which arrange visits, lectures, etc. Among the literary societies in London are the DICKENS FELLOWSHIP (48 Doughty Street, WC1) and the WILLIAM MORRIS SOCIETY (Kelmscott House, 26 Upper Mall, Hammersmith, W6).

The NATIONAL TRUST (36 Queen Anne's Gate, SW1) owns an increasing number of fine houses, attractive open spaces, etc., in London and its neighbourhood and deserves the support of every lover of the English scene. It issues a list of its properties (free to members) and the annual subscription entitles members to free access to National Trust properties where a charge is normally made. Subscribers to the NATIONAL ART-COLLECTIONS FUND (20 John Islip Street, SW1; established in 1903) enjoy particular advantages, including admission without formality to the Reading Room and Students' Rooms of the British Museum, the Library and Students' Rooms of the Victoria and Albert Museum, and the Library of Westminster Abbey. Both these bodies arrange visits, etc., for their members, on some occasions to places not otherwise accessible. Members of ENGLISH HERITAGE (PO Box 43, Ruislip, Middlesex) are allowed free admission to many interesting properties now or formerly administered by the Department of the Environment. In London these include the Tower; the Chapter House and Pyx Chamber of Westminster Abbey; the Banqueting House (Whitehall); the Jewel Tower; Lancaster House; Kensington Palace and Orangery; Chiswick House; and the Great Hall of Eltham Palace.

Societies worth the attention of overseas visitors to London are the ENGLISH-SPEAKING UNION, 37 Charles Street, W1; the ROYAL OVER-SEAS LEAGUE, Over-Seas House, Park Place, SW1; the ROYAL COMMONWEALTH SOCIETY, Northumberland Avenue, WC2; and the VICTORIA LEAGUE, 18 Northumberland Avenue, WC2.

INSTITUTES. The following institutes in or near central London offer social and recreational facilities, etc.: BISHOPSGATE INSTITUTE, 230 Bishopsgate, EC2; CITY LITERARY INSTITUTE, Stukeley Street, Drury Lane, WC2; MARY WARD CENTRE, Tavistock Place, WC1; MORLEY COLLEGE, 61 Westminster Bridge Road, SE1; POLYTECHNIC OF CENTRAL LONDON, 309 Regent Street, W1; ST BRIDE FOUNDATION INSTITUTE, Bride Lane, Fleet Street, EC4; ST MARYLEBONE LITERARY INSTITUTE, 248 Marylebone Road, NW1; WORKING MEN'S COLLEGE, Crowndale Road, NW1. Particulars of these and other institutes (many of which also offer courses of study in art, literature, languages, etc.) may be obtained from the Education Officer, County Hall, SE1, except in the City (EC districts), where application should be made direct.

LIBRARIES. Public libraries, where books of reference, magazines, and newspapers may be consulted without charge, are maintained by all the London boroughs and several of the institutes. At some libraries books may be borrowed by arrangement through one's own library. The libraries in central London include the new BARBICAN LIBRARY (open weekdays 9.30 to 5.30, Tuesdays to 7.30, Saturdays to 12.30); BISHOPSGATE INSTITUTE (see above; good London collection); GUILDHALL LIBRARY, Guildhall, EC2 (reference only; fine London Collection), with the City Business Library (open Mondays–Fridays 9.30 to 5); HOLBORN LIBRARY, Theobalds Road, WC1; MARYLEBONE LIBRARY, Marylebone Road, NW1; ST BRIDE PRINTING LIBRARY, at the St Bride Institute (see above); VICTORIA LIBRARY, 160 Buckingham Palace Road, SW1; and WESTMINSTER REFERENCE LIBRARY, St Martin's Street, Leicester Square, WC2.

The best of the subscription libraries is the LONDON LIBRARY, 14 St James's Square, SW1. Members living within twenty miles of the library are allowed to borrow ten volumes at a time (other members, fifteen volumes). The PATENT OFFICE contains a valuable library of technical books and journals accessible without formality, now part of the BRITISH LIBRARY (compare p. 338). The NATIONAL MONUMENTS RECORD (23 Savile Row, W1) have amassed a collection of drawings, photographs, etc., freely accessible to visitors. Collections available to students and research workers (usually on written application to the director) include those of the British Library, the Catholic Central Library (47 Francis Street, SW1), the Commonwealth Institute, County Hall, Dr Williams's Library, the Geological Museum, the Imperial War Museum, Lambeth Palace, the Marx Memorial Library, the National Maritime Museum, the Natural History Museum, the Science Museum, Sion College, the Victoria and Albert Museum, Wesley's Chapel, and Westminster Abbey.

The NATIONAL BOOK LEAGUE, 45 East Hill, Wandsworth, SW18, has a library, information bureau, and licensed refreshment room, publishes book lists, and arranges interesting exhibitions. The rooms are open to visitors on Mondays–Fridays 9.30 to 5. The ARTS COUNCIL POETRY LIBRARY, at the council's headquarters at 105 Piccadilly, W1, is open to visitors on Mondays–Fridays 11 to 5 (Wednesdays and Fridays to 7). The services of ASLIB (formerly the Association of Special Libraries and Information Bureaux; 26–27 Boswell Street, WC1) include an information bureau with a special section for industrial inquiries, a lending library, a panel of translators, and the publication of book lists and a 'Journal of Documentation', mostly for companies and institutions who are members.

ENTERTAINMENTS

THEATRES. Evening performances generally begin at 7.30 or 8, and end between 10 and 10.30. Matinées, beginning usually at 2.30 or 3, are given at most theatres on one or two afternoons of the week, and many have an early evening performance on Saturdays, starting between 5 and 6 p.m., in which case the later evening performance is put back to 8.15 or 8.45.

Particulars of times, etc., are displayed on posters and given in the newspapers and in the *London Theatre Guide*, which is published fortnightly by the *Society of West End Theatre* (Bedford Chambers, Covent Garden, WC2) and displayed at air terminals, railway stations, and theatre booking-offices. The telephone numbers of Theatre Booking-Agents are given in the 'Yellow Pages' of the London directory. Tickets can also be obtained from the *London Visitor Bureau* and by telephoning *Ticketmaster* (379–6433), who also reserve car parking spaces. In Leicester Square there is a theatre booth selling available tickets at half-price plus a 75p service charge (open 12 to 2 for matinées, 2.30 to 6.30 for evening performances).

The most expensive seats are in the Stalls and Dress Circle; the Upper Circle is less expensive and the Gallery has the cheapest seats. Most theatres have boxes, holding from three to six persons. Seats (except for the gallery) may be secured in advance, either direct or by telephone from the theatre box-office (open from 10 a.m.), or from one of the numerous booking-agents. These charge a commission of about twenty per cent for each ticket, but often have at their disposal better seats than can be obtained at the box-offices. For the gallery it is usually necessary to queue before the performance, and this sometimes entails a long wait. For the more popular plays, etc., the booking of seats at the earliest possible moment is essential. Credit cards may be used for booking seats at most theatres.

The following are the theatres in or within easy reach of central London (see plan on p. 81).

ADELPHI, Strand, WC2; ALBERY, St Martin's Lane, WC2; ALDWYCH, WC2; AMBASSADORS, West Street, off Cambridge Circus, WC2; APOLLO, Shaftesbury Avenue, W1; APOLLO VICTORIA, Wilton Road, SW1 (near Victoria Station); ASTORIA, Charing Cross Road, WC2; BARBICAN, Barbican Centre, EC2 (see below); COMEDY, Panton Street, Haymarket, SW1; CRITERION, Piccadilly

Circus, W1; DONMAR WAREHOUSE, Earlham Street, WC2; DRURY LANE (Theatre Royal), Catherine Street, Aldwych, WC2; DUCHESS, Catherine Street, WC2; DUKE OF YORK'S, St Martin's Lane, WC2; FORTUNE, Russell Street, Covent Garden, WC2; GARRICK, Charing Cross Road, WC2; GLOBE, Shaftesbury Avenue, W1; HAYMARKET (Theatre Royal), Haymarket, SW1; HER MAJESTY'S, Haymarket, SW1; JEANNETTA COCHRANE, Southampton Row, WC1; LYRIC, Shaftesbury Avenue, W1; MAGIC CASTLE, Earlham Street, WC2; MAYFAIR, in the May Fair Hotel, Berkeley Street, W1; MERMAID, Puddle Dock, EC4 (IV, E 3; with restaurant); NATIONAL, South Bank, SE1 (IX, A 1); NEW LONDON, Parker Street, Drury Lane, WC2; OLD VIC (IX, B 2), Waterloo Road, SE1; OPEN AIR THEATRE (II, A 2), Regent's Park, NW1; PALACE, Cambridge Circus, Shaftesbury Avenue, W1; PALLADIUM, Argyll Street, Oxford Circus, W1; PHOENIX, Charing Cross Road, WC2; PICCADILLY, Denman Street, Piccadilly Circus, W1; PRINCE EDWARD, Old Compton Street, Soho, W1; PRINCE OF WALES, Coventry Street, Piccadilly Circus, W1; QUEEN'S, Shaftesbury Avenue, W1; ROYAL COURT (VII, D 2), Sloane Square, SW1; ROYALTY, near Kingsway, WC2; ST MARTIN'S, West Street, off Cambridge Circus, WC2; SAVOY, Savoy Court, Strand, WC2; SHAFTESBURY, Shaftesbury Avenue, WC2; STRAND, Aldwych, WC2; VAUDEVILLE, Strand, WC2; VICTORIA PALACE (VIII, C1) Victoria Street, SW1; WESTMINSTER (VIII, C 1). Palace Street, Buckingham Palace Road, SW1; WHITEHALL, Whitehall, near Charing Cross, SW1; WYNDHAM'S, Charing Cross Road, WC2.

The Barbican Theatre (p. 295) is now the London home of the Royal Shakespeare Company. Shakespeare is given also at the *National Theatre*, at the *Open Air Theatre* (about June–September), and occasionally at other theatres. The *Royal Court* is noted for contemporary plays. The *Drury Lane* (especially), *Adelphi*, *Astoria*, and *Palace* theatres are well known for musical shows. The *Palladium*, the *Prince of Wales*, and the *Victoria Palace* are often given over to variety. The *Mermaid* (see Route 27) and the *Barbican* are the only theatres in the City.

SMALLER THEATRES and Theatre Clubs exist mainly for the purpose of staging new or unusual plays. They include the ARTS THEATRE CLUB, Great Newport Street, off Charing Cross Road, WC2 (the home also of the UNICORN THEATRE CLUB for children); BLOOMSBURY, University College, WC1 (entrance from Gordon Street); DRILL HALL, Chenies Street, off Tottenham Court Road, WC1; PLAYERS (theatre club), Villiers Street, Charing Cross, WC2 (old-time variety); SHAW, St Pancras Library, Euston Road, NW1; SOHO POLY, 16 Riding House Street, W1 (near Great Portland Street); THEATRE UPSTAIRS, at the Royal Court Theatre (see above); and the YOUNG VIC, the Cut, Waterloo Road, SE1. Patrons of the theatre clubs must be members, but visitors may usually become temporary members for a nominal fee.

Plays, etc., are also given from time to time at the COCKPIT THEATRE and Arts Workshop, Gateforth Street, NW8 (near Lisson Grove); THE PLACE, Duke's Road, Euston, WC1; the INSTITUTE OF CONTEMPORARY ARTS (see p. 32); and elsewhere.

SUBURBAN THEATRES: ALBANY, Douglas Way, Deptford, SE8; ALMEIDA,

Almeida Street, Islington, N1; BUSH, 2 Goldhawk Road, Shepherd's Bush, W12; GREENWICH, Crooms Hill, Greenwich, SE10; GREENWOOD, 55 Weston Street, near London Bridge, SE1; HALF MOON, Mile End Road, Whitechapel, E1; HAMPSTEAD, Avenue Road, next to Swiss Cottage Station, NW3; KING'S HEAD, 115 Upper Street, Islington, N1; LYRIC, near Hammersmith Broadway, W6; NEW END, 27 New End, Hampstead, NW3; OVAL HOUSE, 52 Kennington Oval, SE11; RIVERSIDE STUDIOS (see p. 85); ST GEORGE'S, 49 Tufnell Park Road, Islington, N7; THEATRE ROYAL, Angel Lane, Stratford, E15; TOWER, Canonbury Place, Islington, N1 (repertory club); TRICYCLE, 269 Kilburn High Road, NW6. The prices of admission to these are considerably lower than for West End theatres. The *Little Angel*, in Dagmar Passage, Cross Street, Islington, N1, is a marionette theatre, with performances on Saturdays and Sundays (and Mondays–Fridays during school holidays) at 3 (advance booking necessary).

Theatres farther afield that may be recommended include the *Ashcroft*, Fairfield Hall, Park Lane, Croydon, Surrey; *Churchill* and *New*, both in High Street, Bromley, Kent; *Orange Tree*, near Richmond underground station; the *Polka Children's Theatre*, 240 The Broadway, Wimbledon; *Questors*, Mattock Lane, Ealing, W5; *Richmond*, The Green, Richmond, Surrey; *Wimbledon*, The Broadway, SW19; and the *Yvonne Arnaud*, Millbrook, Guildford, Surrey.

Pantomimes on ice are presented, during the Christmas season, at WEMBLEY STADIUM, Middlesex (Wembley Park and Wembley Complex stations).

POETRY READINGS (frequently with music) are given at the NATIONAL POETRY CENTRE, 21 Earls Court Square, SW5 (Route 9), at the *National Theatre* and in the *Purcell Room* on the South Bank, and in summer in the Orangery in *Holland Park*, at *Kenwood House*, and the *Ranger's House*, Blackheath (see below). Information may be obtained from the Arts Council Poetry Library (telephone 629–9495).

OPERA AND BALLET. The ROYAL OPERA HOUSE, more familiarly known as the Covent Garden Theatre (Plan III, E3), in Bow Street, WC2, is the home of the Royal Opera Company. Performances, in the original languages, with international artists, alternate with ballet by the Royal Ballet (formerly the Sadler's Wells Ballet), which has acquired world fame. Evening performances generally begin at 7 or 7.30 and matinées (usually on Saturdays) at 2. The prices for seats vary considerably: the cheapest are in the gallery, the most expensive in the grand tier and the boxes. Booking arrangements, etc., are the same as for the West End theatres, but very early application is advisable, especially for the ballet.

The COLISEUM THEATRE (Plan III, F3), in St Martin's Lane, WC2, near Trafalgar Square, is the home of the English National Opera Company (formerly the Sadler's Wells Opera Company), which specializes in opera in English. Performances usually begin at 7

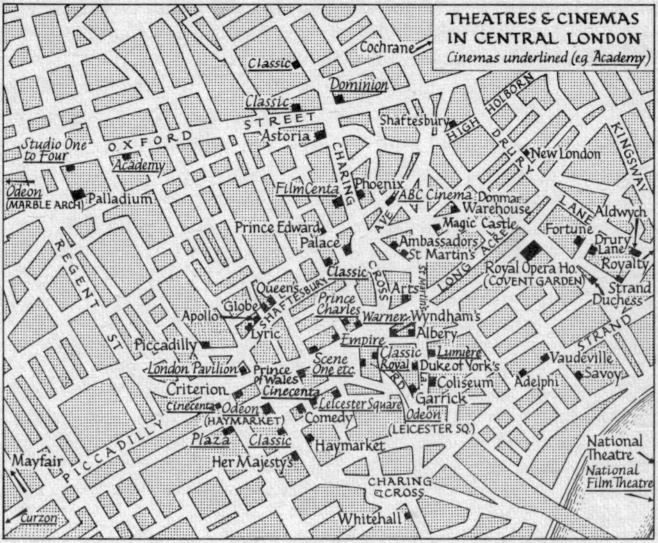

or 7.30 p.m., and there are no matinées (except during the Christmas season). Prices of admission are lower than for Covent Garden, and season tickets are obtainable. The Royal Ballet or the London Festival Ballet usually performs here for a season in the summer. Opera (in English) and ballet are also given (at cheaper prices) at the SADLER'S WELLS THEATRE (Plan IV, A2), in Rosebery Avenue, Islington, EC1 (evenings at 7.30, Saturdays also at 2.30).

Short seasons of opera and ballet are given from time to time at the Drury Lane and other theatres; at the Royal Festival Hall (see below); at the Dominion Cinema; at the LONDON OPERA CENTRE, Commercial Road, Stepney, E1; and in summer at the Open Air Theatre in the forecourt of HOLLAND PARK, and in Battersea Park. Excursions are arranged by travel agents, etc., to the fashionable summer season of opera at Glyndebourne, near Lewes, in Sussex.

CINEMAS. Performances in central London usually begin at about 2.30 (Sundays at about 4.30) and run continuously until about 11 p.m., though some cinemas have late-night showings (at about 11) on Fridays and Saturdays. The prices of admission vary, and certain seats may be reserved in advance at a few cinemas. After a season in the West End, many British and American films have a round of two or more weeks in the suburbs: first in North London, then south of the Thames. The performances here run at about the same times as the West End, but prices are considerably lower. The following are the principal cinemas in central London (see plan, p. 81).

ABC, Shaftesbury Avenue, W1; ACADEMY, 165 Oxford Street, W1; BARBICAN, Barbican Centre, EC2 (V, C1); CINECENTA, Panton Street, SW1; CINECENTA, Regent Street, SW1; CLASSIC, Haymarket, SW1; CLASSIC, Oxford Street, W1; CLASSIC, Shaftesbury Avenue, W1; CLASSIC, Tottenham Court Road, W1; CLASSIC ROYAL, Charing Cross Road, W1; CURZON, Curzon Street, Mayfair, W1; DOMINION, Tottenham Court Road, W1; EMPIRE, Leicester Square, W1; FILMCENTA, Charing Cross Road, WC2; GATE BLOOMSBURY, Brunswick Square, WC1 (III, B3); LEICESTER SQUARE, Leicester Square, W1; LONDON PAVILION, Piccadilly Circus, W1; LUMIÈRE, St Martin's Lane, WC2; MINEMA, 45 Knightsbridge, SW1 (VII, B2); ODEON, Haymarket, SW1; ODEON, Leicester Square, WC2; ODEON, Marble Arch, W1; PLAZA, Regent Street, SW1; PRINCE CHARLES, Leicester Place, WC2; SCENE ONE TO FOUR, Swiss Centre, Leicester Square, W1; STUDIO ONE TO FOUR, 225 Oxford Street, W1 (near Oxford Circus); TIMES CENTA, Baker Street Station, NW1 (II, C2); WARNER, Leicester Square, WC2.

Of suburban cinemas, the best known is the EVERYMAN, at Hampstead, which specializes in old and foreign films. Others include the GATE Cinema at Notting Hill Gate, the CLASSIC Cinema and the CHELSEA Cinema, both in King's Road, Chelsea, the ODEON in Kensington High Street, THE SCREEN on Islington Green, the CAMDEN PLAZA, near Camden Town station, and the SCREEN ON THE HILL, Haverstock Hill, opposite Belsize Park station.

The NATIONAL FILM THEATRE, on the South Bank, Waterloo, SE1 (Plan IX, A1), is open daily to members of the British Film Institute (81 Dean Street, W1), who may reserve seats in advance. The facilities for full members include a licensed club and a library of books and film stills. Performances are normally at 6.15 and 8.30 p.m. (Saturdays and Sundays also at 4). The London Film Festival is held here annually in November–December. Films on various aspects of art are shown at the INSTITUTE OF CONTEMPORARY ARTS (see below) and relevant films are shown also at the COMMONWEALTH INSTITUTE (see p. 31) and at many of the national museums and galleries.

CONCERTS AND OTHER MUSIC. Orchestral concerts are given at the ROYAL FESTIVAL HALL (Plan IX, A1), South Bank, Waterloo, SE1, one of the finest concert halls in Europe, both artistically and acoustically, and the concert hall in the BARBICAN CENTRE (V, C1), Silk Street, EC2. Concerts take place at one or other of these halls, if not both, almost every evening throughout the year, starting usually at between 7.30 and 8 p.m. Tickets are obtainable at the respective box-offices and at theatre booking-agents, etc. Concerts are also given in the Festival Hall on Sundays, starting at 3 or 3.15, and lunch-time concerts and recitals are given on most weekdays in the Barbican Hall, starting at 1 p.m. and lasting about an hour. The Sir Robert Mayer Concerts (founded in 1923) and the Ernest Read Concerts (founded in 1944), both for children, given on Saturday mornings in the Festival Hall, are a valuable feature.

Concerts are also given regularly at the ROYAL ALBERT HALL (VI, B2), Kensington Gore, SW7, starting usually at 7.30, and (more intimately) at ST JOHN'S, SMITH SQUARE (VIII, D3), in the evenings at 7.30 and at lunch-time (especially on Mondays) at 1 p.m. The Promenade Concerts given nightly (except Sundays) at the Albert Hall for eight weeks in the summer (mid-July to mid-September) are very popular. Details of all concerts, recitals, etc., are published in the Saturday editions of *The Times* and the *Daily Telegraph*, and on Sunday in the *Observer* and the *Sunday Times*.

Concerts are given from time to time at the BANQUETING HOUSE, Whitehall (Route 2); the BLOOMSBURY THEATRE (see above); the CAMDEN TOWN HALL (Route 16) and other municipal halls; the CENTRAL HALL, Storey's Gate (Route 4); the FAIRFIELD HALLS, Park Lane, Croydon (Surrey); the GUILDHALL SCHOOL OF MUSIC, in the Barbican (Route 30); MORLEY COLLEGE, Westminster Bridge Road (Route 35); the ROYAL ACADEMY, Burlington House (see below); the ROYAL COLLEGE OF MUSIC, Prince Consort Road (Route 10); the ROYAL NAVAL COLLEGE, Greenwich; the ROYAL OPERA HOUSE (see above); ST MARTIN-IN-THE-FIELDS church (Route 1); and the WEMBLEY CONFERENCE CENTRE (Middlesex).

Open-air concerts are given in summer, on Saturday evenings (at 8) by the lake at KENWOOD, Hampstead Heath (good acoustics); at the CRYSTAL PALACE (Sundays at 8); in Battersea Park, Burgess Park, and Waterlow Park (see Suburban London), and occasionally in Holland Park, Kensington (Route 11).

Recitals of instrumental music and song are given regularly at the QUEEN ELIZABETH HALL (usually at 7.45, Sundays at 3) and the PURCELL ROOM (at 7.30, Sundays at 7), both on the South Bank (see Route 36), and at the WIGMORE HALL (II, D3), Wigmore Street, W1 (evenings at 7.30, Sundays also at 3.30; coffee concerts on some Sunday mornings at 11.30).

Recitals are also given from time to time in GUILDHALL (Route 30); at CONWAY HALL, Red Lion Square, WC1 (on Sundays); on Sunday evenings (at 7.30) in summer at KENWOOD HOUSE (Hampstead Heath) and the RANGER'S HOUSE

(Blackheath); and occasionally at the COMMONWEALTH INSTITUTE and elsewhere.

Lunch-time recitals are given weekly at the BISHOPSGATE INSTITUTE (V, D3), 230 Bishopsgate, EC2 (Tuesdays 1.5 to 1.50 p.m.), and less frequently in GUILDHALL and at the GUILDHALL SCHOOL OF MUSIC. They are also given (at least monthly) in the following churches, starting at 1 to 1.15 and lasting for an hour or less: HOLY SEPULCHRE (Fridays), ST ANNE AND ST AGNES (Mondays or Fridays), ST BOTOLPH ALDGATE (Tuesdays), ST GEORGE'S, HANOVER SQUARE (Thursdays), ST GILES CRIPPLEGATE (Tuesdays), ST JAMES GARLICKHITHE (Thursdays), ST JAMES'S, PICCADILLY (Thursdays), ST LAWRENCE JEWRY (Wednesdays), ST MARGARET PATTENS (Wednesdays), ST MARTIN-IN-THE-FIELDS (Mondays and Tuesdays), ST MARTIN LUDGATE (Wednesdays), ST MARY-AT-HILL (Thursdays), ST MARY-LE-BOW (Wednesdays or Thursdays), ST MARY WOOLNOTH (Mondays), ST MICHAEL'S CORNHILL (Tuesdays), ST OLAVE'S, HART STREET (Wednesdays and Thursdays), and occasionally at other churches.

Organ recitals are given at lunch-time in ST PAUL'S CATHEDRAL (Fridays, usually at 12.30) and SOUTHWARK CATHEDRAL (Mondays and Tuesdays, at 1.10), and at ALL HALLOWS BY THE TOWER (usually Thursdays, 12.15 and 1.15), HYDE PARK CHAPEL, Exhibition Road, South Kensington (daily at 1.15), ST BOTOLPH ALDERSGATE (Wednesdays), ST BRIDE'S, Fleet Street (Wednesdays), ST GILES CRIPPLEGATE (Thursdays), ST JAMES GARLICKHITHE (Thursdays), ST MARY-AT-HILL (Thursdays), and ST MICHAEL'S, Cornhill (Mondays, 1). Organ recitals are given in the evening at the ROYAL FESTIVAL HALL (on Wednesdays at 5.55) and the ROYAL ALBERT HALL (Thursdays, 7.30), and in ST PAUL'S CATHEDRAL (Thursdays, 6), and occasionally at other churches. Further particulars of recitals in the City may be obtained from the City of London Information Centre.

CHURCHES noted for music at their services include *All Saints'*, Margaret Street (near Oxford Circus); *St James's*, Piccadilly; *St Paul's Cathedral*; *St Paul's*, Knightsbridge; *St Peter's*, Eaton Square; *Southwark Cathedral*; the *Temple Church*; *Westminster Abbey*; *Westminister Roman Catholic Cathedral* and *Brompton Oratory*; and the *Church of the Immaculate Conception*, Farm Street, Mayfair.

CONCERTS by BRASS BANDS, etc., are given in summer in the Victoria Embankment Gardens, near Charing Cross (twice daily, at 12.30 or 3 and 6 or 6.30); on the steps of St Paul's Cathedral (Thursdays at 12); in Lincoln's Inn Fields (Tuesdays and Thursdays, 12.30 to 2); at Tower Place, west of Tower Hill (Fridays, 12 to 2); in St James's Park (see Route 5), Hyde Park and Kensington Gardens (Route 12), Regent's Park (Route 17), Greenwich Park (June to August; Sundays, 3 to 4.30 and 6.30 to 8); and other parks. Concerts of light music, etc., are given in the Jubilee Gardens (Route 36) and several of the suburban parks, and concert parties perform on Clapham Common and in various parks on summer evenings. Particulars of all the activities that take place in the parks, etc., under the control of the Greater London Council are contained in a booklet (*What's On*) published by the Department for Recreation and the Arts and obtainable from County Hall, SE1. Information may also be obtained by telephoning the G.L.C. on 633–1707.

ART EXHIBITIONS. Apart from the permanent exhibitions of paintings, etc., at the National Gallery and elsewhere (compare p. 30), loan exhibitions are held at certain galleries and by various societies. The best known of these is the 'Summer Exhibition' of the ROYAL ACADEMY OF ARTS, held at Burlington House, Piccadilly, W1 (Plan III, F1), from the first Monday in May usually until August, and open daily from 10 a.m. to 6 p.m. Loan exhibitions of the greatest interest are also arranged by the Royal Academy, especially in winter, and are open at the same times. Other important loan exhibitions are arranged frequently at the TATE GALLERY (times, see p. 426), the BRITISH MUSEUM (of applied art), the NATIONAL GALLERY, the VICTORIA AND ALBERT MUSEUM, and the HAYWARD GALLERY (adm., p. 32) on the South Bank.

Other temporary exhibitions (generally free) are arranged at the BARBICAN ART GALLERY (in the Barbican Centre); the BRITISH MUSEUM (Prints and Drawings); the COMMONWEALTH INSTITUTE (Route 11); and the GUILDHALL ART GALLERY; in the Ice House and the Orangery in HOLLAND PARK; at the IMPERIAL WAR MUSEUM; the INSTITUTE OF CONTEMPORARY ARTS (Route 6); LEIGHTON HOUSE, Kensington (Route 11); the NATIONAL PORTRAIT GALLERY; the QUEEN'S GALLERY, Buckingham Palace; the SERPENTINE GALLERY in Kensington Gardens; and the WHITECHAPEL ART GALLERY (Route 33); and by the WARWICK ARTS TRUST, 33 Warwick Square (Route 3). All these are in central London. Outside central London similar exhibitions are held at the BATTERSEA ARTS CENTRE, Lavender Hill, SW11; the CAMDEN ARTS CENTRE, Arkwright Road, Hampstead, NW3; the Dutch Barn in HORNIMAN GARDENS (adjoining the Horniman Museum); KENWOOD HOUSE on Hampstead Heath; RIVERSIDE STUDIOS, Crisp Road, Hammersmith, W6; and the SOUTH LONDON ART GALLERY, Peckham Road, Camberwell, SE5.

In addition, annual exhibitions are held (usually for about a month each) at the galleries (at 17 Carlton House Terrace, SW1) of the FEDERATION OF BRITISH ARTISTS, which includes the *Royal Institute of Oil Painters*, the *Royal Institute of Painters in Water-Colours*, the *Royal Society of British Artists*, the *Royal Society of Portrait Painters*, and the *New English Art Club*; and by the *Royal Society of Painter-Etchers and Engravers* and the *Royal Society of Painters in Water Colours*, both at the Bankside Gallery, Southwark (see Route 36).

Smaller art exhibitions, not to be overlooked, are held almost continuously at the many galleries and picture-dealers' shops, mainly in the neighbourhood of Piccadilly and Bond Street (adm. usually free). Particulars of the current exhibitions at most of the galleries, public and private, are given in the daily newspapers and in a guide published by *New Exhibitions of Contemporary Art* (152 Narrow Street, Limehouse, E14).

Other art exhibitions are arranged in the Victoria Embankment Gardens (usually in May) and in summer at Kenwood House, Hampstead Heath. Exhibitions of sculpture in the open air are held (usually every three years) either in Battersea Park or Holland Park.

BRASS RUBBING centres have been established at *St James's Church*, Piccadilly (see p. 142; weekdays 10 to 6, Sundays 12 to 6), *Westminster Abbey* (in the cloisters; weekdays only, 9 to 5.30), and *All Hallows by the Tower* (Route 34; weekdays 11 to 5.45, Sundays 12.30 to 5.45).

OTHER EXHIBITIONS AND SHOWS. Exhibitions of widely differing kinds are held frequently at OLYMPIA, Hammersmith Road, Kensington, W14 (adjoining Olympia station), and the EARLS COURT EXHIBITION CENTRE, Warwick Road, SW5 (reached from Earls Court station by a covered passage). For the annual exhibitions, etc., held here and elsewhere, see p. 99; for the flower-shows at the Royal Horticultural Society's Halls, see p. 124.

Permanent exhibitions include that at the DESIGN CENTRE (adm., p. 32), where the display is changed from time to time, and MADAME TUSSAUD'S WAXWORKS; and other exhibitions are held frequently by the NATIONAL BOOK LEAGUE, and at the BRITISH CRAFTS CENTRE, the BUILDING CENTRE, the CEYLON TEA CENTRE, the CRAFTS COUNCIL GALLERY, and THE GLASSHOUSE, 65 Long Acre, WC2.

Dancing, children's shows, and other entertainments in the open air are provided for in many suburban parks managed by the G.L.C.

DANCING AND CABARET are offered by a number of hotels, restaurants, and night clubs, mostly in the neighbourhood of Piccadilly and Regent Street. The night clubs are open to members only; the subscriptions (usually payable forty-eight hours in advance) vary considerably, and inquiry should preferably be made beforehand. Information may be obtained from the London Visitor Bureau. Most of the restaurants and night clubs keep open until the small hours, but no drinks may be served after 2 a.m. (12 on Saturdays). Evening dress is not usually insisted on.

Cabaret is the speciality of the following establishments, all of which provide evening meals and liquid refreshment (dancing may be enjoyed at those designated 'D'): ABA DABA THEATRE (music hall), 328 Gray's Inn Road, King's Cross; BEEFEATER CLUB by the Tower (D), Ivory House, St Katharine's Docks; CALEDONIAN (D), Hanover Street, off Regent Street; COCKNEY CLUB (D), 18 Charing Cross Road; CURZONS (D), 45 Park Lane; FLANAGAN'S RESTAURANTS, 100 Baker Street and 11 Kensington High Street; HIPPODROME (D), Charing Cross Road and Cranbourn Street; SHAKESPEARE'S TAVERN, Black Friars Lane, near Blackfriars Station; STORK CLUB, 99 Regent Street; TALK OF LONDON (D), Parker Street, off Drury Lane; and TIDDY DOLS (D), 2 Hertford Street, off Park Lane. The DONMAR WAREHOUSE THEATRE (see above) stages a late-night cabaret (until 1 a.m.).

SPORT IN AND AROUND LONDON

The Londoner has an unrivalled opportunity of seeing a great many of the principal national sporting events. Particulars of these and of the facilities for individual sports and games are given below, and details of dates and times of the chief events may be obtained from the daily and Sunday newspapers.

ATHLETICS. The championships of the *Amateur Athletic Association* (A.A.A.), open to amateurs of all nations, are held at CRYSTAL PALACE (Crystal Palace and Penge West stations) usually in June or July. The *Women's Amateur Athletic* (W.A.A.A.) championships are also held in June or July, in some years at Crystal Palace. The *Universities* (U.A.U.) championships take place at Crystal Palace in May, and other meetings, including international events, are held here and at the NEW RIVER STADIUM, Haringey (Harringay Stadium station). The *London Amateur Athletic Championships* are usually held in August, alternately at the EAST LONDON STADIUM, in Mile End Park (Mile End station), and the WEST LONDON STADIUM, at Wormwood Scrubs (East Acton station). The *Stock Exchange Walk* from London (Westminister Bridge) to Brighton takes place every May. The *London Walking Championships* are held in Battersea Park (Battersea Park and Queenstown Road stations) in February, and the *London Cross Country Championships* take place at PARLIAMENT HILL (see Bowls, below) in November. The *City of London* New Year's Day road races start from London Wall (Route 30). The enormously popular *London Marathon* of 26 m. 385 yds, instituted in 1981, is run annually in April, starting from Greenwich Park (at 9.30 a.m.) and finishing on Westminster Bridge. The route is via Tower Bridge, the Isle of Dogs, the Victoria Embankment, and The Mall, and the leading runners take a little over two hours.

Particulars of athletic events may be obtained from the *British Amateur Athletic Board*, Francis House, Francis Street, SW1. Those arranged by the *Greater London Council* are given in the G.L.C.'s booklet, *What's On* (see p. 84). Information about these events may also be obtained by telephoning the G.L.C.'s Sportsline (222–8000).

BADMINTON. The All-England championships are held at the WEMBLEY

Conference Centre (Wembley Park and Wembley Complex stations), in March. Badminton may be played at the Seymour Leisure Centre (see Swimming), The Oasis, and the Swiss Cottage Baths, among other places.

Basketball. The international club championships take place at Crystal Palace in December or January, the British championships at Wembley (see above) in March.

Boating (see also Rowing). Boats may be hired on the Serpentine (see Route 12) and on the lakes in Regent's Park (Route 16), Battersea Park, etc., as well as on the Thames from Putney upstream. Sailing may be enjoyed on the Thames and on the Brent Reservoir, between Hendon and Neasden, in Middlesex (near the A5).

Bowls may be played in Hyde Park (see Route 12) and in Battersea Park and many other suburban parks. The *Greater London Championship* finals take place in September, at Parliament Hill (Hampstead Heath and Gospel Oak stations), in Victoria Park (Bethnal Green or Mile End station, then by bus), or at another venue.

Boxing. Professional bouts, under the control of the *British Boxing Board of Control* (70 Vauxhall Bridge Road, SW1), are arranged at the Royal Albert Hall, the arena at Earls Court (Route 9), Wembley (see above), and the Seymour Leisure Centre (see Swimming). The championships of the *Amateur Boxing Association* take place in April or May at Wembley, the junior championships here in March, and the London championships here in April.

Cricket may be watched regularly during the season at Lord's, the headquarters of the *Marylebone Cricket Club* (M.C.C.) and the ground of the *Middlesex Cricket Club*, at St John's Wood, and at the Oval, Kennington, the home of the *Surrey Cricket Club*. Kent play occasionally at Blackheath, and Essex at Leyton, Ilford, and Romford. Other games, such as Oxford v. Cambridge and Eton v. Harrow (both in July), are played at Lord's, and international matches ('test matches') take place here and at the Oval. Club matches may also be watched on Saturdays and Sundays on grounds all around London, especially in the public parks, and cricket weeks are organized by the more important clubs.

Cycling may be enjoyed in delightful country on almost every side of London. The main disadvantages are the appalling congestion on the main roads at weekends during the summer and the long distances that have to be covered from central London to reach open country. Information about pleasure cycling can be obtained from the *Cyclists' Touring Club* (69 Meadrow, Godalming, Surrey). The organizing body for racing is the *British Cycling Federation* (16 Upper Woburn Place, WC1), and national championships and other events take place at the HERNE HILL stadium, Burbage Road (North Dulwich and Herne Hill stations), and at CRYSTAL PALACE (see Athletics, above). The *London to Brighton Bicycle Ride*, in aid of the British Heart Foundation, takes place annually in June.

FENCING. The championships of the *Amateur Fencing Association* are held in April at its headquarters at the DE BEAUMONT CENTRE, 83 Perham Road, West Kensington, W14 (Barons Court station). Other competitions take place at the centre, which is used also by the London Thames Fencing Club.

FOOTBALL (Association) may be watched at the grounds of the following professional league clubs: ARSENAL, Avenell Road, Highbury, N5 (Arsenal station); BRENTFORD, Griffin Park, Brentford (Brentford Central station); CHARLTON ATHLETIC, Selhurst Park, Croydon, SE25 (Norwood Junction and Selhurst stations); CHELSEA, Stamford Bridge, Fulham Road, SW6 (Fulham Broadway station); CRYSTAL PALACE, also at Selhurst Park; FULHAM, Craven Cottage, Stevenage Road, SW6 (Putney Bridge station); MILLWALL, The Den, Cold Blow Lane, New Cross, SE14 (New Cross Gate station); ORIENT, Brisbane Road, Leyton High Road, E10 (Leyton station); QUEEN'S PARK RANGERS, Loftus Road, off Uxbridge Road, W12 (Shepherd's Bush and White City stations); TOTTENHAM HOTSPUR, White Hart Lane, Tottenham, N17 (White Hart Lane and Manor House stations); WATFORD, Vicarage Road, Watford, Hertfordshire (Watford High Street station); WEST HAM UNITED, Boleyn Ground, Green Street, E13 (Upton Park station); WIMBLEDON, Plough Lane, SW19 (Wimbledon and Wimbledon Park stations). International matches are played at WEMBLEY STADIUM (Wembley Park and Wembley Complex stations); the final tie of the *F.A. Cup* takes place here in mid-May and the final of the *Milk Cup* (to be renamed the Littlewoods Challenge Cup) in March. Amateur matches of a high standard may be seen on the grounds (mostly suburban) of clubs in the Gola (formerly the Athenian), the Vauxhall-Opel (formerly the Isthmian), and other leagues; the final of the F.A. Trophy (for non-professional league clubs) takes place at Wembley in March.

GOLF may be played on numerous courses of a high standard in the country around London. Among the best known, where national championships are held, are Moor Park (Hertfordshire), Beaconsfield (Buckinghamshire), Sunningdale (Berkshire), and Camberley Heath, Royal Mid-Surrey (Richmond), Walton Heath, and Wentworth (near Egham), all in Surrey. An introduction by a member is necessary at these and most other private courses, but there are public courses on MITCHAM COMMON (Mitcham Junction station), in RICHMOND PARK (near Roehampton), and in BECKENHAM PLACE PARK (Beckenham Hill station), TRENT PARK (Cockfosters station), and HAINAULT FOREST (Hainault station), in Essex. Putting greens are maintained in many of the public parks.

GREYHOUND RACING. There are tracks in Catford, Hackney Wick, Haringey, Walthamstow, Wembley, Wimbledon, and other places. The Greyhound 'Derby' is run at Wembley in June, and the 'St Leger' in September.

GYMNASTICS. International championships and other events are held at WEMBLEY (see Badminton) and at the ROYAL ALBERT HALL.

HOCKEY of a good standard may be watched at many grounds in and near London, and international matches are played at WEMBLEY STADIUM (see Football, above), at CRYSTAL PALACE (see Athletics), where the London League play-off final takes place, in May, and at WILLESDEN STADIUM, Donnington Road, NW10 (Willesden Green Station).

HORSE RACING. The racecourses nearest London are at EPSOM (Epsom, Epsom Downs and Tattenham Corner stations), KEMPTON PARK (Kempton Park and Sunbury stations), and SANDOWN PARK (Esher station). The chief events are the *Derby Stakes*, for three-year-old colts and fillies, run at Epsom on the last Wednesday in May or the first in June, and the *Oaks Stakes* (for three-year-old fillies) run here on the following Saturday. The fashionable *Ascot Week*, patronized by royalty, is held two weeks later at ASCOT HEATH (Berkshire), when the chief day is Thursday (Gold Cup Day).

MOTOR RACING. The nearest circuit to London is at BRANDS HATCH (on the London–Sevenoaks road, A20). MOTOR-CYCLE RACING also takes place at Brands Hatch; speedway racing on tracks at Hackney Wick, West Ham, and Wimbledon. The world speedway riders championship is held occasionally at Wembley.

RACKETS. The chief competitions take place at QUEEN'S CLUB, West Kensington (see Tennis, below), the Amateur Singles in January, the Amateur Doubles in February, the Public Schools Championships in March, and the Open Singles and Doubles championships in March and April respectively.

REAL TENNIS. The Amateur Singles championships are held, usually at QUEEN'S CLUB, in March, the World Championship in April, and the Professional Singles championship in May.

RIDING may be enjoyed in Hyde Park (Route 12), on Hampstead Heath, on Streatham, Tooting, and Wimbledon Commons, in Dulwich Park, in Hainault Forest, and in Richmond Park. Horses for Hyde Park may be hired at Bathurst Riding Stables (63 Bathurst Mews) and Ross Nye's Riding Establishment (8 Bathurst Mews), north of Lancaster Gate.

ROWING. The principal event of the year is the *Oxford and Cambridge Boat-Race*, rowed in late March or early April (usually just before Easter) on the Thames from Putney to Mortlake (nearly 4¼ m.). The nearest stations are Putney Bridge (for the start), Hammersmith, Barnes Bridge, and Mortlake. The race attracts a great concourse of spectators, who line the river bank or pay for a position in Duke's Meadows, Chiswick, or on an anchored barge or a pier. The *Head of the River Race*, open to all rowing eights and attracting over 200 crews, is rowed either on the same day or one week earlier over the same course, but generally in the opposite direction. The *Schools' Head of the River Race* is rowed from Hammersmith to Putney in March. The *Wingfield Sculls*, the chief event for solo oarsmen, is rowed between Putney and Mortlake, usually in May. *Doggett's Coat and Badge*, presented in 1715 by Thomas Doggett, an actor, is rowed for by Thames watermen each July over a course from London Bridge to Chelsea (4½ m.) Regattas are held on the SERPENTINE, Hyde Park (in August), and on the Thames at Putney and Hammersmith, as well as at Richmond, Twickenham, Kingston, and elsewhere. *Henley Regatta*, the most famous of the Thames regattas, takes place during the first week in July. A Canoe Race is held annually at Easter from Devizes (Wiltshire) to Westminster Bridge (County Hall steps).

RUGBY LEAGUE FOOTBALL is played by the FULHAM club at the Central London Polytechnic ground at Chiswick. The final of the Rugby League Challenge Cup takes place at WEMBLEY STADIUM, in May.

RUGBY UNION FOOTBALL may be watched at many grounds in the neighbourhood of London. Among the best known clubs (all amateur) are the HARLEQUINS, who play at Twickenham (see below), RICHMOND and LONDON SCOTTISH (both at the Richmond Athletic Ground), ROSSLYN PARK (Priory Lane, Upper Richmond Road, SW15), LONDON WELSH (Old Deer Park, Richmond), BLACKHEATH (Rectory Field, SE3), SARACENS (Green Road, Southgate, N14), WASPS (Sudbury, near Wembley), and LONDON

IRISH (Sunbury-on-Thames). Other good clubs are formed from the London hospitals and public-school old boys. International matches, the *English Counties Championship* final (in March), and the *Oxford v. Cambridge University* match (in December) are all played at TWICKENHAM (Twickenham station).

SHOOTING. The principal competitions are held at BISLEY CAMP, near Brookwood (in Surrey), including the National Rifle Championships, in July.

SKATING. There are rinks at the QUEEN'S ICE SKATING CLUB, Queensway, W2 (Bayswater and Queensway stations), and at the SOBELL SPORTS CENTRE (see below), STREATHAM (adjoining Streatham station), WEMBLEY (Empire Pool, where ice hockey may also be watched), and RICHMOND (near Richmond Bridge). Skating may also be possible for short periods in winter on the Serpentine (Hyde Park), the lake in Regent's Park, Hampstead and Highgate Ponds, and elsewhere.

SNOOKER. The Masters Championship takes place in January at the WEMBLEY CONFERENCE CENTRE (see Badminton), and other competitions are held here and at the NEW LONDON THEATRE (Holborn and Covent Garden stations).

SQUASH RACKETS. Competitions are held at the LANSDOWNE CLUB, 9 Fitzmaurice Place, Berkeley Square, W1 (Green Park station), or the ROYAL AUTOMOBILE CLUB in Pall Mall. Squash rackets may also be played at Queen's Club (see Tennis, below), at Lord's Cricket Ground, at The Oasis (see below), at the Swiss Cottage Baths, at Wembley Stadium (see Football), and on courts attached to several of the West End clubs.

SWIMMING. Among the many swimming pools are those at the SEYMOUR LEISURE CENTRE (closed on Sundays), Seymour Place, Marylebone, W1 (Edgware Road and Marble Arch stations); the CHELSEA SPORTS CENTRE, Manor Street, SW3 (Sloane Square station, then by bus); KENSINGTON BATHS, Lancaster Road, W11 (Ladbroke Grove station); THE OASIS, Endell Street, Holborn, WC2 (Holborn station); SWISS COTTAGE BATHS, Winchester Road, NW3 (near Swiss Cottage station); and the ELEPHANT AND CASTLE RECREATION CENTRE, 22 Elephant and Castle, SE1. Privately owned baths include those at several of the larger hotels. Open-air bathing may be enjoyed at The Oasis (weekdays in April–September), in the Serpentine (see Route 12), and at PARLIAMENT HILL (Hampstead), HIGHGATE PONDS (men only), KENWOOD POND (ladies only), and BROCKWELL PARK (Herne Hill) and other public parks. The *London Swimming Championships* take place at CRYSTAL PALACE (see Athletics) in June and July, and other events are held from time to time.

TABLE TENNIS. The *English Open Championships* are held in March or April, sometimes at WEMBLEY (see Badminton), and other national events take place here, at Crystal Palace, and at the Royal Albert Hall. The *London Table Tennis Championships*, in May, were moved to the new BRIXTON RECREATION CENTRE (Brixton station) in 1985.

TENNIS may be played on numerous public courts (hard and grass) in and around London (Hyde Park, Lincoln's Inn Fields, Battersea Park, Swiss Cottage Baths, etc.), and open competitions are held at many places in summer. The *All-England Championships*, with the most coveted prizes of the world on grass courts, take place at WIMBLEDON, Surrey (Wimbledon, Wimbledon Park, and Southfields stations), for a fortnight at the end of June and the beginning of July, and the *Junior Championships of Great Britain* in September. The *London Grass Court Championships* (the traditional overture to Wimbledon) are held at QUEEN'S CLUB, West Kensington (Barons Court station), in June. The *London Hard Courts* championships take place at HURLINGHAM PARK, Fulham (Putney Bridge and Parsons Green stations) in April, and other tournaments are held at Hampstead and elsewhere. Indoor championships are held at WEMBLEY (see Badminton), in November, and at the ROYAL ALBERT HALL, in January.

The NATIONAL SPORTS CENTRE at Crystal Palace (see Athletics) and the MICHAEL SOBELL SPORTS CENTRE in Hornsey Road, N7, offer excellent facilities for those wishing to train or participate in a variety of sports. Organizations that are concerned with the interests of sportsmen include the SPORTS COUNCIL (16 Upper Woburn Place, WC1) and the CENTRAL COUNCIL OF PHYSICAL RECREATION (Francis House, Francis Street, SW1).

GENERAL INFORMATION

SHOPPING. The most fashionable shops (and hence the most expensive) are in Bond Street, Piccadilly, and the neighbouring part of Regent Street. The most popular shopping centre is Oxford Street, but other good shops will be found in Knightsbridge and Sloane Street, in Brompton Road, in Kensington High Street, and in the Strand. Shops in the City (for example, in Cheapside) are hardly inferior and generally less expensive. Among the more secluded shopping areas are the Burlington Arcade (Piccadilly), Jermyn Street (south of Piccadilly), South Molton Street (a pedestrian precinct off Oxford Street), Beauchamp Place (off Knightsbridge), Kensington Church Street, and Covent Garden.

Certain streets have become associated with particular classes of shops: for instance, Bond Street with jewellers and exclusive dress shops, Savile Row with high-class tailors, Oxford Street with department stores, Tottenham Court Road with furniture dealers and electrical suppliers, and Charing Cross Road with second-hand booksellers. Most of the City and West End shops open at 9 a.m. and close at 5.30 or 6 p.m., but some of the large stores keep open on either Wednesday or Thursday until about 7 or 7.30 p.m. In Bond Street and in the City, many of the shops close all day on Saturday; in the suburbs, shops generally close on Wednesday or Thursday afternoon, and keep open all day on Saturday. Most large shops, hotels, and restaurants will accept international credit cards, such as American Express, Access, Eurocard, and Diners' Club.

The following are among the best-known DEPARTMENT STORES, where a great range of articles may be bought:

Army & Navy Stores, Victoria Street, SW1; *Barkers*, Kensington High Street, W8; *Dickins & Jones*, Regent Street, W1; *D. H. Evans*, Oxford Street, W1; *Fortnum & Mason*, Piccadilly, W1 (high-class); *Habitat*, King's Road, Chelsea, SW3; *Harrods*, Brompton Road, Knightsbridge, SW1; *Heal & Son*, Tottenham Court Road, W1; *Peter Jones*, Sloane Square, SW1; *John Lewis*, Oxford Street, W1; *Liberty's*, Regent Street, W1; *Marks & Spencer*, Oxford Street, W1, and many other branches; *Harvey Nichols*, Knightsbridge, SW1; and *Selfridges*, Oxford Street, W1.

MEN'S OUTFITTERS (some of which also have women's departments) include:

Aquascutum, 100 Regent Street, W1; *Austin Reed*, 103 Regent Street, W1, 163 Old Brompton Road, SW3, and 78 Cheapside, EC2; *Beale & Inman*, 131 New Bond Street, W1; *Brown's*, 23 South Molton Street, W1; *Burberrys*, 18 Haymarket, SW1, and 157 Regent Street, W1; *Gieves & Hawkes*, 1 Savile Row, W1, and 18 Lime Street, EC3; *Lillywhite's* (sports outfitters), 24 Regent Street (Piccadilly Circus), SW1; *Moss Brothers*, Bedford Street, Covent Garden, WC2, and 21 Lime Street, EC3; *Savoy Taylors' Guild*, 164 New Bond Street, W1, 32 Hans Crescent, Knightsbridge, SW1, 93 Strand, WC2, and 83 Cheapside, EC2; *Simpson's*, 202 Piccadilly, W1; *Thresher & Glenny*, 14 Lancaster Place, WC2, and 50 Gresham Street, EC2; *Young's*, 185 Wardour Street, W1, 1 Berners Street, off Oxford Street, W1, and 16 Ludgate Hill, EC4; and many others.

Men's clothes may be hired for almost any occasion from *Alkit* of Cambridge Circus, *Moss Brothers* of Covent Garden, and *Young's* of Wardour Street. Women's clothes may also be hired from Moss Brothers and Young's.

'Boutiques' specializing in garments, etc., for young people will be found in Carnaby Street (near Regent Street), Knightsbridge, Kensington High Street, and King's Road, Chelsea. *Hamley's*, of Regent Street, are noted for toys, and the *General Trading Company*, in Sloane Street (near Sloane Square), for fancy goods. Antique shops abound in the neighbourhood of Bond Street, Kensington High Street and Kensington Church Street, and King's Road, Chelsea. The *Arts Council* has a shop selling products related to its interests at 8 Long Acre, Covent Garden, WC2.

Visitors from overseas may buy goods free of Value Added Tax (V.A.T.) at some shops, on the presentation of their passports (though they may have to pay tax on return to their own countries). Particulars of this Retail Export Scheme may be obtained from the principal stores or the British Tourist Authority. The Penguin Handbook, *London Shopping Guide*, by Elsie Burch Donald, is a useful publication.

AUCTIONS of fine and applied art are held regularly by *Bonhams*, Montpelier Street, SW7; *Christie's*, 8 King Street, St James's, SW1, and 85 Old Brompton Road, SW7; *Phillips*, 7 Blenheim Street, New Bond Street, W1; and *Sotheby's*, 34 New Bond Street, W1. Most auction houses will offer a free valuation service, during office hours.

SPECIAL SERVICES. The dispensary of *Boots the Chemists* in Piccadilly Circus (north side; telephone 734–6126) keeps open on weekdays until 8 p.m. An emergency medical service can be obtained at the *Middlesex Hospital*, Mortimer Street (near Oxford Street and Tottenham Court Road; 636–8833), and also (for a fee) at the *Medent Emergency Clinic*, Chapel Place, off Oxford Street north of New Bond Street (499–1991; open Mondays–Fridays 8 a.m. to 8 p.m., Saturdays 8 to 6). *The Spotted Dog*, of 9 Cambridge Street, Pimlico, SW1 (828–7921), is an organization offering expert shopping assistance for foreign visitors to London. *Childminders*, of 67 Marylebone High Street, W1 (935–9763), operate a service of babysitters, as do Universal Aunts (p. 63).

COINAGE. The change over to decimal currency in Britain took place in 1971. The pound remains the basic unit of currency, and it is divided into 100 minor units. The minor unit is the penny, and there are now seven denominations of coins: 1p, 2p, 5p, 10p, 20p, 50p and £1 (a new coin introduced in 1983). The 5p and 10p coins are equivalent to the 1/- and 2/- pieces, but these remain legal tender, as yet. The £5 and £10 notes remain in use, and new £20 and £50 notes have been introduced. The £1 note is still legal tender at the time of writing (1985), but no more notes are being made. Most foreign currencies can be exchanged at the Trafalgar Square and certain other post offices.

MARKETS are an integral part of the London scene and should certainly not be overlooked or avoided by the visitor. The greater part of the wholesale business is conducted early in the day, from about 4 or 5 a.m., when they are best seen, but a retail trade is carried on at least through the rest of the morning. The following are the principal markets: NEW COVENT GARDEN (Plan VIII, F3), vegetables, fruit, and flowers (closed on Saturdays, except in summer); SMITHFIELD (IV, D3), meat, poultry, and provisions (closed on Saturdays); SPITALFIELDS (V, C, D3), vegetables, fruit, and flowers; the BOROUGH MARKET, Southwark (IX, E1), for general produce; and BILLINGSGATE, on the Isle of Dogs, the chief market for fish (closed on Mondays).

STREET MARKETS, offering almost every sort of portable goods for sale, are to be found on weekdays in BERWICK STREET, Soho; CAMDEN PASSAGE, near Islington Green (antiques; Wednesdays and Saturdays only); CHAPEL STREET, Islington (closed on Mondays, but open on Sundays); EAST STREET, Walworth (closed on Mondays and Wednesdays, but open on Sundays); JUBILEE MARKET, Covent Garden (open also on Sundays); KENSINGTON MARKET, Kensington High Street; LAMBETH WALK, off Lambeth Road; LEADENHALL MARKET, off Leadenhall Street (closed on Saturdays); LEATHER LANE, Holborn (closed on Saturdays); LOWER MARSH and THE CUT, Waterloo Road; NEW CALEDONIAN MARKET, Tower Bridge Road (Fridays only); PORTOBELLO ROAD, Notting Hill (noted antique market on Saturdays); ROMAN ROAD, Bethnal Green (open also on Sundays); SHEPHERD'S BUSH (best on Saturdays), and TACHBROOK STREET, Pimlico.

The following are mainly Sunday markets: MIDDLESEX STREET ('Petticoat Lane'), Whitechapel, patronized by a cosmopolitan throng; CAMDEN LOCK, near Camden Town station (open also on Saturdays); COLUMBIA ROAD, Shoreditch; and EARLS COURT, behind the Exhibition Centre.

PUBLIC HOLIDAYS. Banks and business houses in London are closed on Good Friday, as are many shops. All are closed on Christmas Day and on Bank Holidays: New Year's Day, Easter Monday, the first Monday in May, Spring Bank Holiday Monday (usually in late May), the Late Summer Bank Holiday (usually the last Monday in August), and Boxing Day. Theatres and other entertainments remain open on Bank Holiday Mondays, as do the museums and galleries (except the May Day Monday), when, however, they are generally overcrowded. The public transport is also congested on these days.

POLICE. The headquarters of the METROPOLITAN POLICE, who cover the whole of Greater London except the City, are at the corner of Broadway and Victoria Street, SW1 (Plan VIII, C2; telephone 230–1212). The head-office of the CITY OF LONDON POLICE is at 37 Wood Street, near London Wall, EC2 (V, D1; telephone 601–2222). City policemen are to be distinguished by their crested helmets and red-and-white arm-bands: the Metropolitan police wear blue-and-white armbands. Strangers who require directing or information are well advised to 'ask a policeman', whose courtesy has won a worldwide reputation.

LOST PROPERTY should be sought at the nearest Police Station or at the Metropolitan Police Lost Property Office, 15 Penton Street, Islington, N1 (north of Claremont Square, Plan IV, A2), open on Monday–Friday, 9 to 4.30. Inquiries cannot be answered by telephone, and a charge of fifteen per cent of the value of the article is usually levied. Articles left in the trains or buses of *London Transport* should be inquired for at 200 Baker Street, Marylebone, NW1 (open Monday –Friday, 10 to 6). A small charge is made for articles under £1 in value, and a surcharge of ten per cent in the pound on articles of greater value. For articles left on the trains or at the stations of *British Railways*, inquiry should be made of the stationmaster or at the Lost Property office at the relevant terminus.

RELIGIOUS SERVICES. Churches of almost every denomination can be found in London, and only a few of those most likely to appeal to visitors are mentioned below. Several churches in the City hold mid-day services during the week, but on the other hand most of these are closed on Sundays. The times of the Sunday services, preachers, etc., at many churches are given on the preceding Saturday in *The Times*.

CHURCH OF ENGLAND. *St Paul's Cathedral*, see p. 404; *Westminster Abbey*, see p. 469; *Southwark Cathedral*, see p. 422; *Chapel Royal*, St James's Palace, see p. 136 (or alternatively, the *Queen's Chapel*, p. 135); *Queen's Chapel of the Savoy*, 11.15 and 12.30 (except in August and September); *St Clement Danes*, Strand, 8.30, 11, and 12.15; *Guards' Chapel*, 11 and 12; *Gray's Inn Chapel*, 11.15; *Lincoln's Inn Chapel*, 11.30; *Temple Church*, 8.30 and 11.15; *Tower of London* (Chapel Royal), see p. 434; *Royal Hospital*, Chelsea, see p. 354; *Royal Naval College* (Greenwich), 11.

All Hallows-by-the-Tower, 11; *All Saints'*, Margaret Street, 8, 11 (High Mass), and 5.15; *All Souls'*, Langham Place, 9.30, 11, and 6.30; *Chelsea Old Church*, 8, 12, and 6; *Grosvenor Chapel*, 8.15 and 11; *Holy Trinity*, Brompton, 8, 9, 11, and 6.30; *Holy*

Trinity, Prince Consort Road, 8.30, 11, and 12.05; *Holy Trinity*, Sloane Street, 8.30, 10.30, and 12.10; *St Bartholomew the Great*, 9, 11, and 6.30; *St Bride's*, Fleet Street, 8.30, 11, and 6.30; *St George's*, Hanover Square, 8.15 and 11; *St James's*, Piccadilly, 8.30, 11, and 6; *St Margaret's*, Westminster, 8.15, 11, and 12.15; *St Martin-in-the-Fields*, 9.45, 11.15, 4.15, and 6.30; *St Mary Abbots*, Kensington, 8, 9.30, 11.15, 12.30, and 6.30; *St Marylebone*, Marylebone Road, 8, 11, and 6.30; *St Paul's*, Knightsbridge, 8, 9, and 11; *St Peter's*, Eaton Square, 8.15, 10, and 11; *St Vedast*, Foster Lane, 11.

CHURCH OF SCOTLAND. *St Columba's*, Pont Street, 11 and 6.30; *Crown Court Church*, Russell Street, Covent Garden, 11.15 and 6.30.

WELSH CHURCH. *St David's*, St Mary's Terrace, Paddington, 10.30 and 6.30; *St Benet's*, Queen Victoria Street, 11 and 6.

ROMAN CATHOLIC. *Westminster Cathedral*, see p. 488; *Brompton Oratory*, see p. 160; *St George's Cathedral*, Lambeth, 11, 12.15, and 6; *Church of the Immaculate Conception*, Farm Street, Mayfair, 7.30, 8.30, 10, 11, 12.15 (High Mass), 4.15, and 6.15; *SS. Anselm and Cecilia*, Kingsway, 11; *St Etheldreda's*, Ely Place, 11.

NONCONFORMIST (all at 11 and 6.30). BAPTIST: *Bloomsbury Central*, Shaftesbury Avenue (New Oxford Street). METHODIST: *Central Hall*, Westminster; *West London Mission*, Hinde Street; *Wesley's Chapel*, City Road (at 11 only); PRESBYTERIAN: *St John's*, Allen Street, Kensington. UNITARIAN: *Essex Church*, Palace Gardens Terrace, Notting Hill; *Essex Hall*, Strand. UNITED REFORMED: *Regent Square*, off Gray's Inn Road; *St John's Wood Church* (at 9.30 only); *City Temple*, Holborn Viaduct. INDEPENDENT EVANGELICAL: *Westminster Chapel*, Buckingham Gate. SOCIETY OF FRIENDS: *Friends' House*, Euston Road (not at 6.30). — WELSH PRESBYTERIAN: Charing Cross Road, 10.45 and 6. — CHRISTIAN SCIENCE: *Third Church of Christ Scientist*, Curzon Street, Mayfair, and others, 11 or 11.30 and 7.

JEWISH. *Central Synagogue*, Great Portland Street, daily at 8 a.m. (also Friday at 7, Saturday at 9.30); *Marble Arch Synagogue*, Great Cumberland Place, daily at 8 a.m. and 7 p.m. (also Friday at dusk, Saturday at 9.15); *West London Synagogue*, Upper Berkeley Street, Friday at 6 p.m., Saturday at 11; *Liberal Jewish Synagogue*, St John's Wood Road, Friday at 8, Saturday at 11.

PARKS AND GARDENS. London is particularly well served with parks and open spaces accessible to the public. The best known are the Royal Parks, under the control of the Crown: ST JAMES'S PARK and the adjoining GREEN PARK (Route 5), HYDE PARK and the contiguous KENSINGTON GARDENS (Route 12), and REGENT'S PARK (Route 17), which has PRIMROSE HILL on the north. Farther out are GREENWICH PARK in the south-east suburbs (see Suburban London) and RICHMOND PARK, in the south-west.

Other parks and commons and numerous gardens are under the jurisdiction of the G.L.C. or the borough councils. A few of the more interesting and attractive are listed below (with their nearest stations). Open-air entertainments are given in summer in several of the parks and a varied programme of sport is arranged. Facilities are provided in many parks for boating, bathing, tennis, bowls, etc., and light refreshments may generally be obtained.

BATTERSEA PARK (Battersea Park and Queenstown Road stations); BROCKWELL PARK (Herne Hill station); BURGESS PARK, Walworth (Elephant and Castle station); CLAPHAM COMMON (Clapham Common and Clapham South stations); CLISSOLD PARK, Stoke Newington (Manor House station); CRYSTAL PALACE PARK (Crystal Palace and Penge West stations); DULWICH PARK (North Dulwich and West Dulwich stations); FINSBURY PARK (Finsbury Park and Manor House stations); HAMPSTEAD HEATH, with the adjoining Kenwood, Parliament Hill, and Golders Hill (Hampstead, Golders Green, Gospel Oak, and Hampstead Heath stations); HOLLAND PARK (High Street Kensington and Holland Park stations); HURLINGHAM PARK, Fulham (Putney Bridge station); KENNINGTON PARK (Oval station); PECKHAM RYE PARK (Nunhead and East Dulwich stations); RAVENSCOURT PARK, Hammersmith (Ravenscourt Park station); SOUTHWARK PARK, Rotherhithe (Surrey Docks station); STREATHAM COMMON, with the Rookery (Streatham station); TOOTING COMMON (Balham and Tooting Bec stations); VICTORIA PARK (Bethnal Green and Mile End stations); WATERLOW PARK, Highgate Hill (Archway station).

The private GARDENS of a number of houses in and around London are open to the public on certain days in summer, usually from 2 to 6 or 7. The proceeds, administered by the Queen's Institute of District Nursing, are apportioned to the Retired District Nurses' Benefit Fund and the joint gardens committee of the National Trust and the Royal Horticultural Society. Particulars are given in a booklet issued yearly and obtainable from the *National Gardens Scheme* (57 Lower Belgrave Street, SW1).

ANNUAL EVENTS. Below are listed the more important events that take place in or near London at the same (or nearly the same) period each year. For sporting events, see under 'Sport in and around London'. A diary of *London Events & Entertainment* is published from 148 Fleet Street, EC4, and obtainable (free) from Information Centres. Particulars of dates, times, etc., may be also obtained from the London Visitor Bureau or by telephone.

JANUARY: *Earls Court*, International Boat Show; *Olympia*, International Contemporary Art Fair; *Kensington Town Hall*, Antiques Fair; *Wembley Conference Centre*, Model Engineer Exhibition; *Chapel Royal* (6th), Royal Epiphany Offering; *Drury Lane Theatre* (6th), Cutting of the Baddeley Cake; *Trafalgar Square* (30th), Wreath-laying at Charles I's statue, and Ceremony outside *Whitehall Palace.*

FEBRUARY: *Olympia*, Cruft's Dog Show; *Soho*, Chinese New Year Celebrations; *Crystal Palace*, International Canoe Exhibition; *St Etheldreda's Church* (3rd),

Blessing the Throat ceremony; *Westminster Abbey* (22nd), Scouts' and Guides' Founder's Day Service. — SHROVE TUESDAY: *Westminster School*, 'Tossing the pancake'. — ASH WEDNESDAY: *St Paul's Cathedral* (crypt), Stationers' Company attend service.

MARCH: *Camden Town Hall*, etc., Camden Arts Festival; *Earls Court*, Ideal Home Exhibition; *Chelsea Old Town Hall*, Spring Antiques Fair; *St Clement Danes*, Oranges and Lemons Service; *St Bride's*, Bridewell Royal Hospital Service; *Westminster Abbey* (second Monday), Commonwealth Day Service. — EASTER: Tuesday in Holy Week, *St Paul's*, Bach's 'St Matthew Passion'; MAUNDY THURSDAY, *Westminster Abbey* (in occasional years), Distribution of the Royal Maundy; GOOD FRIDAY, *St Bartholomew the Great*, Poor Widows' Dole; EASTER SUNDAY (or thereabouts), *St Bartholomew's* or other church, Bach's 'St John Passion'; *Battersea Park*, Easter Parade; EASTER MONDAY, *Regent's Park*, Harness Horse Parade; *Hampstead Heath*, *Blackheath*, and *Wormwood Scrubs*, Bank Holiday Fairs; Wednesday after Easter Week, *St Lawrence Jewry*, 'Spital Sermon'.

APRIL: *Wembley Conference Centre*, International Model Railway Exhibition; *Barbican Centre*, London Book Fair; *St George's, Hanover Square*, Handel Festival; *St Andrew Undershaft*, John Stow Commemoration Service; *Parliament Square* (19th, Primrose Day), Decoration of Disraeli's statue; *Southwark Cathedral* (23rd, St George's Day), Shakespeare's Birthday Service.

MAY: *Burlington House*, Royal Academy Summer Exhibition (until August); *Grosvenor House*, Royal Caledonian Ball; *Royal Hospital Grounds*, Chelsea Flower Show; *Cutty Sark Gardens*, etc., Greenwich Festival (until June); *St Olave's, Hart Street*, Pepys Commemoration Service; *St James's, Piccadilly*, etc., Piccadilly Festival; *Royal Opera House*, Covent Garden Proms; *Tower of London* (21st), Commemoration of the death of Henry VI; *Royal Hospital, Chelsea* (29th), Founder's Day; AMERICAN MEMORIAL DAY (30th), Wreaths laid at the *Cenotaph*, Lincoln's Statue in *Parliament Square*, and the grave of the Unknown Warrior in *Westminster Abbey*, and service in *Westminster Abbey*. — SPRING BANK HOLIDAY: *Hampstead Heath* and *Blackheath*, Bank Holiday Fairs. — TRINITY MONDAY: *St Olave's, Hart Street*, Trinity House Service.

JUNE: *Horse Guards Parade*, 'Trooping the Colour'; *Olympia*, Fine Arts and Antiques Fair; *Grosvenor House*, Antiques Fair; *Banqueting House* (Whitehall), English Bach Festival; *Spitalfields Church*, Music Festival; *Wembley Stadium*, Military Musical Pageant (biennial; next in 1987); *Clapham Common*, Clapham Village Fête; *Mansion House* (near 24th), Knollys Rose ceremony; MIDSUMMER (24th), *Guildhall*, Election of Sheriffs.

JULY: City of London Festival; *Earls Court*, Royal Tournament; *South Bank*, National Festival of Music for Youth; *Barbican*, Summer in the City Festival; *Brockwell Park*, Lambeth Fair; Swan Upping on the *River Thames*, from Temple Stairs; *Tower Bridge*, Power boats race (to Calais and back); *Royal Albert Hall*, Promenade Concerts (to September).

AUGUST: *Royal Festival Hall*, etc., South Bank Summer Music Festival; *Barbican Centre*, Mostly Mozart Festival; *Hyde Park*, Riding Horse Parade; *Earls Court*, Motor-Cycle Show; *Notting Hill*, Carnival; *Clapham Common* (Bank Holiday and previous Saturday), Greater London Horse Show; *Hampstead Heath*, *Blackheath*, and *Finsbury Park*, Bank Holiday Fairs.

SEPTEMBER: *Guildhall*, City of London Flower Show; *Chelsea Old Town Hall*, Autumn Antiques Fair; *Park Lane Hotel*, Antiquarian Book Fair; *Westminster Bridge*, etc., Thamesday displays on river; *St Margaret's*, Westminster (3rd), Cromwell's Day Service; BATTLE OF BRITAIN DAY (15th), Fly-past of aircraft over London (11 a.m. to noon), and service at *Westminster Abbey* on the following Sunday (11 a.m.); *Guildhall* (28th), Admission of Sheriffs Elect; MICHAELMAS (29th), *St Lawrence Jewry*, Retiring Lord Mayor attends service before the election of the new Lord Mayor in *Guildhall*.

OCTOBER: *Wembley Arena*, Horse of the Year Show, and National Brass Band Festival; *Royal Academy*, Burlington House Fair; *Earls Court*, Motorfair (biennial; next in 1987); *Law Courts* open (about 1st), services at *Westminster Abbey* and *Westminster Cathedral*, followed by a procession through the House of Lords; *St Martin-in-the-Fields* (first Sunday), Costermongers' Harvest Festival; *Holy Sepulchre*, Holborn (about 1st), Scholars of Christ's Hospital attend service and later visit the Mansion House; *Westminster Abbey* (13th), St Edward's Day Pilgrimage; *St Katharine Creechurch* (16th), 'Lion Sermon'; *Trafalgar Square* (21st), Decoration of Nelson's Monument; *St Paul's* (about 24th), National Service for Seafarers.

NOVEMBER: *Hyde Park*, Veteran Car Run (8 a.m.; to Brighton); *Earls Court*, Caravan Camping Holiday Show; *Olympia*, World Travel Market; *Kensington Town Hall*, Kensington Antiques Fair; *Royal Albert Hall*, Schools Promenade Concerts; *National Film Theatre*, London Film Festival (to December); *Houses of Parliament* (about 6th), State Opening by the Sovereign; *Guildhall* (Friday before second Saturday), Admission of Lord Mayor Elect; Second Saturday, Lord Mayor's Show and *Royal Albert Hall*, Royal British Legion Festival of Remembrance; *Whitehall* (second Sunday), Remembrance Day Service at the Cenotaph (10.45 a.m.); *Holy Sepulchre*, Holborn (22nd), St Cecilia's Day Service and Festival; *St Paul's* (Tuesday after Advent Sunday), Handel's 'Messiah'.

DECEMBER: *Earls Court*, Royal Smithfield Show and Exhibition; *Olympia*, International Show Jumping Championships, and National Cat Show; *Royal Hospital, Chelsea*, Ceremony of the Christmas Cheeses; *St Peter's Cornhill* (before Christmas), Nativity Play; Christmas Lights in *Oxford Street* and *Regent Street*; Royal Choral Society carol concerts in the *Royal Albert Hall* and *Guildhall*; Carol Services at *Westminster Abbey*, *St Paul's Cathedral*, *Southwark Cathedral*, in *Trafalgar Square*, etc.; NEW YEAR'S EVE: *Westminster Abbey* and *St Paul's Cathedral*, Watch Night Services (11.30 p.m.), and gathering of exiled Scots outside St Paul's (midnight).

Particulars of the *Camden Arts Festival* may be obtained from the Festival Office, St Pancras Library, 100 Euston Road, NW1 (telephone 388–1394); of the *Spitalfields Festival* from 29 Marmion Road, SW11 (223–9594); of the *Covent Garden Proms* from the Royal Opera House, Bow Street, WC2 (240–1066); of the *English Bach Festival* from 15 South Eaton Place, SW1 (730–1456); of the *City of London Festival* from the Administrator, City Arts Trust Ltd, 64 West Smithfield, EC1 (606–1973);

of *Barbican Festivals* from the Barbican Centre, Silk Street, EC2 (638–4141); and of the *Promenade Concerts* from the Royal Albert Hall, Kensington Gore, SW7.

BOOKS ON LONDON. The following is a selection from the forbidding number of books that have been published dealing with every aspect of the capital. The dates are those of the latest editions.

The *Survey of London* published for the G.L.C. and still in progress (41 vols.; 1900–81) is the standard work, though most volumes stop short at the 19th century. Other large-scale works of historical value are the *Survey of London* in 10 large vols. (1902–12) by Sir Walter Besant, an impressive social and topographical study; *London, Past and Present*, by Henry B. Wheatley (3 vols.; 1891), a historical dictionary arranged street by street; and the *New Survey of London Life and Labour*, edited by Sir H. Llewellyn Smith (9 vols; 1930–35), a valuable social and industrial study.

GENERAL DESCRIPTION. David Piper: *London* (1980). — V. S. Pritchett: *London Perceived* (1962). — Richard Church: *London, Flower of Cities All* (1966). — Colin MacInnes: *London, City of any Dream* (1962). — James Bone: *The London Perambulator* (1925) and *London Echoing* (1948), both illustrated by Muirhead Bone. — Geoffrey S. Fletcher: *The London Nobody Knows* (1962), *Changing London* (1969), etc. — Sir Evelyn Wrench: *Transatlantic London* (1949). — Tony Aldous: *London's Villages* (1980). — Ivor Brown (ed.): *A Book of London* (1961). — D. M. Low (ed.): *London is London* (1949: an anthology). — H. and P. Massingham (eds.): *The London Anthology* (1950).

Gillian Bebbington: *London Street Names* (1972). — Al Smith: *City of London Street Names* (1970). — Margaret Brentnall: *Old Customs and Ceremonies of London* (1975). — Maurice Rickards: *Where They Lived in London* (1972). — Martin Hall: *The Blue Plaque Guide to London Homes* (1976). — Alec Forshaw and Thea Bergström: *Markets of London* (1983). — Sir Oscar Hobson: *How the City Works* (1966). — Robert Gibson-Jarvie: *The City of London* (a financial and commercial history; 1979). — Sir Ernest Pooley: *The Guilds of the City of London* (1945). — Louis T. Stanley: *The Old Inns of London* (1957). — Martin Green and Tony White: *Guide to London Pubs* (1965). — Edwin Course: *London's Railways* (1962). — John R. Day: *The Story of London's Underground* (1969). — R. S. R. Fitter: *London's Natural History* (1945). — John Burton: *The Naturalist in London* (1974).

Books mainly of interest for their photographs: Helmut Gernsheim: *Beautiful London* (1953). — Martin Hürliman: *London* (1956). — J. Allan Cash: *The Pageant of London in Colour* (1958). — Robert Cameron and Alistair Cooke: *Above London* (aerial photographs; 1980). — Paul Johnson: *London from the Air* (1984). — A. F. Kersting and L. C. Spaull: *Portrait of Westminister* (1964). — William Gaunt and Eric de Maré: *The City of Westminster* (1968). — Edwin Smith: *The Living City* (1957). — David Whitehead: *London Then, London Now* (1969). — Gavin Stamp: *The Changing Metropolis, 1839–1879* (1984). — O. J. Morris: *Grandfather's London* (1979). — John Betjeman (ed.): *Victorian and Edwardian London* (1969). — Benny

Green: *The Streets of London* (1983). — Bill Brandt: *London in the Thirties* (1983). — Christina M. Gee: *Hampstead and Highgate in Old Photographs* (1974).

Books on Various Districts and Places. Ian Norrie (ed.): *The Book of Westminster* (1963). — G. S. Dugdale: *Whitehall through the Centuries* (1950). — Hermione Hobhouse: *A History of Regent Street* (1975). — B. H. Johnson: *Berkeley Square to Bond Street* (1952). — Reginall Colby: *Mayfair, a Town within London* (1966). — Neville Braybrooke: *London Green* (the Royal Parks; 1959). — William Gaunt: *Kensington and Chelsea* (1975). — Thea Holme: *Chelsea* (1972). — Geoffrey Evans: *Kensington* (1975). — Gordon Mackenzie: *Marylebone* (1972). — Ann Saunders: *Regent's Park* (1969). — John Lehmann: *Holborn, an Historical Portrait* (1971). — Mary C. Borer: *The Story of Covent Garden* (1984). — Alec Forshaw: *Smithfield, Past and Present* (1980). — Eric de Maré: *London's Riverside* (1958). — Suzanne Ebel and Doreen Impney: *London's Riverside* (1975). — Philip Howard: *London's River* (1975). — Grace Golden: *Old Bankside* (1951). — Harry Williams: *South London* (1949). — David J. Johnson: *Southwark and the City* (1970).

Patrick Cormack: *Westminster: Palace and Parliament* (1981). — Christopher Jones: *The Great Palace* (of Westminster; 1983). — Eric Taylor: *The House of Commons at Work* (1961). — W. R. Matthews and W. M. Atkins (eds.): *A History of St Paul's Cathedral* (1957). — G. H. Cook: *Old St Paul's Cathedral* (1955). — Jane Lang: *Rebuilding St Paul's after the Great Fire of London* (1957). — G. L. Prestige: *St Paul's in its Glory, 1831–1911* (1955). — Lawrence E. Tanner: *The History and Treasures of Westminster Abbey* (1953). — Edward Carpenter (ed.): *A House of Kings* (Westminster Abbey; 1966). — Eric Abbott and others: *Westminster Abbey* (1973). — Bryan Bevan: *Royal Westminster Abbey* (1976). — Derek Hudson: *Kensington Palace* (1968). — Derek Wilson: *The Tower, 1078–1978* (1978). — Sir Frank Francis: *Treasures of the British Museum* (1972). — Philip Street: *The London Zoo* (1956).

F. M. L. Thompson: *Hampstead, Building a Borough* (1974). — Ian Norrie (ed.): *The Heathside Book of Hampstead and Highgate* (1962). — Sonia Roberts: *The Story of Islington* (1975). — Millicent Rose: *The East End of London* (1973). — William J. Fishman: *The Streets of East London* (1979). — R. Douglas Brown: *The Port of London* (1978). — John Pudney: *London's Docks* (1975). — Olive and Nigel Hamilton: *Royal Greenwich* (1969).

History and Antiquities. Geoffrey Trease: *London, a Concise History* (1975). — R. J. Mitchell and M. D. R. Leys: *A History of London Life* (1958). — Robert Gray: *History of London* (1978). — W. R. Dalzell: *Shell Guide to the History of London* (1981). — Michael Hanson: *2000 Years of London* (1967). — Derek Mayne: *The Growth of London* (1952; good short history). — Christopher Hibbert: *London: The Biography of a City* (1969). — John Hayes: *London: a Pictorial History* (1969). — Felix Barker and Peter Jackson: *London, 2000 Years of a City* (1974). — Geo. E. Eades: *Historic London* (i.e., the City; 1966). — Mary C. Borer: *The City of London* (1977).

Ralph Merrifield: *The Roman City of London* (1965) and *London: City of the Romans* (1983). — Peter Marsden: *Roman London* (1980). — John Morris: *Londinivm: London in the Roman Empire* (1982). — Christopher N. L. Brooke: *London,*

800–1216 (1975). — Timothy Baker: *Medieval London* (1970). — D. W. Robertson: *Chaucer's London* (1968). — Harold Priestley: *London, The Years of Change* (1966). — Martin Holmes: *Elizabethan London* (1969). — John Stow: *The Survey of London* (1598), a classic on Elizabethan London (excellent edition in 2 vols. by C. L. Kingsford; one vol. in Everyman's Library). — Norman G. Brett-James: *The Growth of Stuart London* (1935). — Valerie Pearl: *London and the Outbreak of the Puritan Revolution* (1962). — Walter George Bell: *The Great Plague of London, 1665* (1951), and *The Great Fire of London, 1666* (1951). — John Bedford: *London's Burning* (1966). — T. F. Reddaway: *The Rebuilding of London after the Great Fire* (1951). — Bernard Ash: *The Golden City* (London between the Fires, 1666–1941; 1964). — Graham Parry: *Wenceslaus Hollar in England* (1667; 1977).

M. D. George: *London Life in the Eighteenth Century* (1925). — George Rudé: *Hanoverian London, 1714–1808* (1971). — Simon Jenkins: *Landlords to London* (1975). — Douglas Hill: *A Hundred Years of Georgian London* (1970). — Hugh Phillips: *Mid-Georgian London* (1964). — Bryant Lillywhite: *London Coffee Houses* (1963). — Stella Margetson: *Regency London* (1971). — Francis Sheppard: *London, 1808–1870* (1971). — Donald J. Olsen: *The Growth of Victorian London* (1976). — Priscilla Metcalf: *Victorian London* (1972). — L. C. B. Seaman: *Life in Victorian London* (1973). — Gavin Weightman and Steve Humphries: *The Making of Modern London* (2 vols, 1983–4). — Peter Quennell (ed.): *Mayhew's London* (1949; selection from 'London Labour and the London Poor', by Henry Mayhew, 1851). — Albert Fried and Richard M. Elman: *Charles Booth's London* (1969; a social survey, condensed from the original published from 1889 on). — Gustave Doré (ed. by Blanchard Jerrold from original of 1872): *Doré's London* (1971). — Hermione Hobhouse: *Lost London* (1976). — Felix Barker and Ralph Hyde: *London as it Might Have Been* (1982). — P. G. Hall: *The Industries of London since 1861* (1962). — Aubrey Wilson: *London's Industrial Heritage* (1967). — Alastair Service: *London, 1900* (1979). — David Johnson: *The City Ablaze* ('The Blitz'; 1980).

ARCHITECTURE AND TOWN PLANNING. Steen Eiler Rasmussen: *London, the Unique City* (1960). — Alastair Service: *The Architects of London* (1979). — Edward Jones and Christopher Woodward: *A Guide to the Architecture of London* (1983). — Ann Saunders: *Art and Architecture of London* (1984). — Nikolaus Pevsner: *The Cities of London and Westminster* (1973) and *London 2: South* (with Bridget Cherry; 1983), in the Penguin Buildings of England series (*London 3: North-West* and *London 4: North and North-East* in preparation). — Elizabeth and Wayland Young: *Old London Churches* (1956). — Basil F. L. Clarke: *Parish Churches of London* (1966). — Gerald Cobb: *London City Churches* (1977). — Margaret Whinney: *Wren* (1971). — Geoffrey Beard: *The Work of Christopher Wren* (1982). — Kerry Downes: *The Architecture of Wren* (1982) and *Hawksmoor* (1970). — John Summerson: *Georgian London* (1962; delightful architectural survey). — Geoffrey Beard: *The Work of Robert Adam* (1978). — Dorothy Stroud: *Sir John Soane, Architect* (1984). — Terence Davis: *John Nash* (1973). — John Summerson: *The Life and Work of John Nash* (1980). — Hermione Hobhouse: *Thomas Cubitt, Master Builder* (1971). — Donald Olsen: *Town Planning in London in the 18th and 19th Centuries* (1982). —

Simon Jenkins: *A City at Risk* (London's streets; 1970). — Maurice Ash: *A Guide to the Structure of London* (1972).

ART AND THEATRE. Michael Jacobs and Malcolm Warner: *Art and Artists in the British Isles* (1980; section on London). — David Piper: *Artists' London* (1982). — Michael Wilson: *The National Gallery, London* (1977). — John Rothenstein: *The Tate Gallery* (1958). — David Bindman: *Hogarth* (1981). — Raymond Mander and Joe Mitchenson: *The Theatres of London* (1961) and *The Lost Theatres of London* (1968). — Harold Rosenthal: *Two Centuries of Opera at Covent Garden* (1958). — Clive Boursnell and Colin Thubron: *The Royal Opera House, Covent Garden* (1982). — Alexander Bland: *The Royal Ballet* (1981). — Peter Roberts: *The Old Vic Story* (1976). — Dennis Arundell: *The Story of Sadler's Wells, 1683–1964* (1965). — Gerald Norris: *Musical Gazetteer of Great Britain and Ireland* (1981; comprehensive London section). — H. C. Robbins Landon: *Handel and his World* (1984).

LITERARY ASSOCIATIONS. Dorothy Eagle and Hilary Carnell (eds.): *The Oxford Literary Guide to the British Isles* (1977; good London section). — George G. Williams: *Guide to Literary London* (1973). — Samuel Pepys: *Diary*, covering the years 1660–69 (excellent edition in 11 vols. by R. C. Latham and W. Matthews, 1970–83). — Robert Latham: *The Illustrated Pepys* (selections; 1978). — Richard Ollard: *Pepys, a Biography* (1984). — Geoffrey Trease: *Samuel Pepys and his World* (1972). — John Evelyn: *Diary* (1641–1706). — Daniel Defoe: *Journal of the Plague Year* (1722). — James Boswell: *The Life of Samuel Johnson* (1791). — Margaret Lane: *Samuel Johnson and his World* (1975). — Frederick A. Pottle (ed.): *Boswell's London Journal, 1762–3* (1966). — Una Pope-Hennessy: *Charles Dickens* (1970). — Angus Wilson: *The World of Charles Dickens* (1972). — Michael and Mollie Hardwick: *The Charles Dickens Encyclopedia* (1973). — John Greaves and Gwen Major: *The London of Charles Dickens* (1970). — Norman Page: *A Dickens Companion* (1984). — Charles Dickens: *Pickwick Papers* (1837), *Oliver Twist* (1838), *Nicholas Nickleby* (1839), *Barnaby Rudge* (1841), *Dombey and Son* (1848), *David Copperfield* (1850), *Bleak House* (1853), *Little Dorrit* (1857), *Great Expectations* (1861), and *Our Mutual Friend* (1865). — Margaret Forster: *William Makepeace Thackeray* (1978). — W. M. Thackeray: *Vanity Fair* (1848), *Henry Esmond* (1852), and *The Newcomes* (1855).

Periodical publications containing valuable material on the history and topography of London include the *Transactions of the London and Middlesex Archaeological Society*, one part of which is usually issued each year (three Parts make a Volume); the *London Topographical Record*, issued as and when funds allow by the London Topographical Society; and the *Guildhall Miscellany*, published by the Corporation of London. Papers of value on the history and antiquities of London appear also in *Archaeologia*, issued generally every two years by the Society of Antiquaries; the *Archaeological Journal* of the Royal Archaeological Institute; the *Transactions of the Royal Historical Society*; and journals of other societies. These are usually available to members only, but can be consulted at many libraries.

ROUTES IN LONDON

1 Charing Cross and Trafalgar Square

Plans III, F2, 3 and VIII, A2, 3

STATIONS: CHARING CROSS (Plan III, F3), on the Bakerloo, Jubilee, and Northern lines; EMBANKMENT (VIII, A3), on the Bakerloo, Circle, District, and Northern lines; LEICESTER SQUARE (III, E3), on the Piccadilly and Northern lines. — BUSES from every part of London (compare plan, p. 52, and Routes 2, 6, 19, 21). Eastbound buses stop in Duncannon Street, south of St Martin-in-the-Fields; westbound buses in Cockspur Street, south-west of Trafalgar Square, or in the Strand; northbound buses in front of the National Gallery; and southbound buses at the upper end of Whitehall.

CHARING CROSS (Plan VIII, A3), the triangular open space at the head of Whitehall and on the south side of Trafalgar Square, is generally regarded as the hub of London. 'Why, sir,' said Dr Johnson, 'Fleet Street has a very animated appearance, but I think the full tide of human existence is at Charing Cross.' At this point in 1291 Edward I set up the last of the thirteen crosses that marked the stages in the funeral procession of his queen, Eleanor of Castile, from Harby in Nottinghamshire to Westminster Abbey. The cross was taken down in 1647 and its site is now occupied by a fine equestrian STATUE OF CHARLES I, by Hubert Le Sueur, cast in 1633. Before this could be erected the Civil War broke out and it was disposed of as scrap to a brazier who sold 'relics' alleged to have been made from it to Royalist supporters. At the Restoration, however, the statue was produced intact, and it was set up in 1675, on the spot where several of the regicides had been beheaded in 1660 and facing down Whitehall to the scene of Charles I's execution. On 30 January, the anniversary of the king's death, the statue is hung with wreaths by his admirers. The sculptured stone pedestal, by Joshua Marshall, is said to follow a design by Sir Christopher Wren. A bronze plaque set into the pavement in 1955 behind the statue marks the official centre of London, from which mileages are measured.

TRAFALGAR SQUARE (III, F2,3), named in commemoration of Nelson's great naval victory of 1805, was laid out in 1829–41 by Sir Charles Barry, partly on the site of the Royal Mews, claimed by Sir

Robert Peel as the 'finest site in Europe'. The pigeons that inhabit the square are an integral part of the scene, and the square is a popular terminal point for political demonstrations. On the south side rises the NELSON MONUMENT, or Nelson's Column, designed by William Railton (1843), a fluted Corinthian column 167 ft 6½ in. high, surmounted by a colossal statue of Admiral Lord Nelson, 17ft 4½ in. high, by E. H. Baily. On the pedestal at the base are four bronze reliefs, cast from captured French cannon, showing scenes from the battles of St Vincent, the Nile, Copenhagen, and Trafalgar. The four bronze couchant lions by Sir Edwin Landseer (1868) that guard the base were cast from cannon recovered from the wreck of the *Royal George*, which sank at Spithead in 1782 with 'twice 400 men' on board. The monument is decorated every year on the anniversary of the Battle of Trafalgar (21 October).

From the column there is a noble vista down Whitehall to the clock-tower of the Houses of Parliament. To the right (south-west) is a glimpse of Admiralty Arch, the approach to the Mall and St James's Park (Route 5), and farther right is the beginning of Cockspur Street (Route 6), leading to Pall Mall and the Haymarket. To the left (east) opens the entrance to the Strand (Route 21), with Northumberland Avenue (leading to the Victoria Embankment, Route 26) to the right of it.

At the lower corners of Trafalgar Square are statues of Generals Sir Charles James Napier (d. 1853) and Sir Henry Havelock (d. 1857), and near the latter is a curious round stone police box with a lamp often erroneously said to have come from Nelson's flagship, the *Victory*. Behind the Nelson monument are two ornamental fountains (1948) designed by Sir Edwin Lutyens, with bronze groups by Sir Charles Wheeler and William McMillan. Below the parapet on the north are the Imperial Standards of Length of the Board of Trade (inch, foot, two feet, yard, chain, and 100 ft), and bronze busts of Admirals Lord Jellicoe (d. 1935), Lord Beatty (d. 1936), and Lord Cunningham (d. 1962), the last by Franta Belsky (1967). Above the north-east corner of the square is an equestrian statue (without stirrups) of George IV (d. 1830), by Chantrey.

A fir tree, the annual gift of the people of Norway in memory of the hospitality shown their royal family during the Second World War, is set up in Trafalgar Square and illuminated every Christmastide.

Vehicles must proceed round the square in a clockwise direction. Entrances to Charing Cross underground station, at the south-east corner (near the Havelock statue), at the beginning of the Strand, and near the foot of Cockspur Street (west of

Charing Cross), are connected by a subway by which pedestrians may avoid the invariably congested roadways.

Above the north side of Trafalgar Square rises the **National Gallery** (adm., p. 380), in front of which are a bronze statue of James II, with a Latin inscription claiming him as 'King of England, Scotland, France and Ireland', and an ineffectual bronze copy of the marble statue of George Washington by J. A. Houdon at Richmond (Virginia), presented in 1921. On the west side of the square is CANADA HOUSE, the headquarters of the High Commissioner for Canada, built in 1824–7 by Sir Robert Smirke as the Union Club, but reconstructed by Septimus Warwick in 1925. On the ground floor are a library and reading room and an information bureau; a new Cultural Centre was opened in 1982. Canada House now incorporates the adjoining building on the north, also by Smirke (1827), formerly occupied by the Royal College of Physicians. SOUTH AFRICA HOUSE, on the east side of the square, was designed by Sir Herbert Baker (1931–3) and is the headquarters in London of the Republic of South Africa.

Outside are a winged springbok in gilt-bronze by Sir Charles Wheeler, a statue of Bartholomeu Diaz, the explorer who discovered South Africa (by C. L. Steynberg), and sculptures illustrating the flora and fauna and the history of the republic. In the main hall is a tapestry map designed by Macdonald Gill and woven at Merton in Surrey, and the building contains a reference library, a reading room, and an exhibition hall.

At the foot of Charing Cross Road (Route 19), facing the east side of the National Gallery, is ST MARTIN-IN-THE-FIELDS (III, F3), a classical church of 1721–6, the masterpiece of James Gibbs, a follower of Sir Christopher Wren. A church has stood on this site at least since 1222, though the previous building was erected in 1544 for Henry VIII. St Martin's is the parish church of the Admiralty (whose white ensign is flown on state occasions) and also of the Sovereign, most of Buckingham Palace being included in the parish. George I was the first churchwarden of the new church, the only instance of a reigning monarch holding such an office. Notable features of the exterior are the Corinthian portico and the graceful spire, 185 ft high, its weather-vane topped by a crown. The finely decorated interior has piers with Corinthian capitals, and an elliptical ceiling in the nave, the work of Italian craftsmen. The font, dated 1689, in the north aisle, is from the previous church; at the east end is a portrait of Gibbs by Andrea Soldi (about 1740). The pulpit, introduced in 1858, has older stairs attributed to Grinling Gibbons, the famous woodcarver. On the north of the chancel is the Royal Box and on the south that of the Admiralty. Above the chancel arch are the arms of George I, which appear also in the pediment above the portico.

The crypt, entered from the south-west corner of the church, has massive square piers and a plain vault, and contains old memorials, a chest of 1597, the old whipping-post from Charing Cross (1752), and Gibbs' model of the church. A doorway on the south, fashioned as a memorial arch to the 'Old Contemptibles' of 1914–18, admits to a chapel furnished in 1954 as a memorial to H. R. L. Sheppard, vicar of St Martin's in 1914–27 and well known for his welfare work, a tradition ably carried on by subsequent vicars. The sanctuary lamp here was given in memory of George Heriot (d. 1624), founder of the famous school in Edinburgh, who was buried in the churchyard.

Nell Gwyn or Gwynne (d. 1687), the mistress of Charles II, was among the numerous others buried in the churchyard, but this was cleared in 1829 to make way for Duncannon Street. The catacombs, themselves cleared in 1938, were used during the war as an air-raid shelter. The church registers record the baptisms of Francis Bacon (1561), John Hampden (1594), and Charles II (1630), and the marriages of Benjamin West, the American painter (1765), Thomas Moore, the poet (1811), and John Constable (1816).

2 From Charing Cross to Parliament Square (Whitehall)

Plan VIII, A3–VIII, B3

STATIONS: For Charing Cross, see Route 1; WESTMINSTER (Plan VIII, B3), on the Circle and District lines, for Parliament Square. —BUSES Nos. 3, 11, 12, 24, 29, 53, 77, 88, 159, 170, and 172 all ply down Whitehall.

WHITEHALL (VIII, A, B3), the broad thoroughfare which runs south from Charing Cross to Parliament Square (for Westminster Abbey and the Houses of Parliament), is one of the famous streets of the world, named after a royal palace of which little but the banqueting house has survived. Containing many of the principal government offices, it has long been regarded as the administrative centre of the British Commonwealth. On the right as the road descends is the WHITEHALL THEATRE, designed by E. A. Stone (1930), and on the left, farther on, is GREAT SCOTLAND YARD, a street on the site of that part of Whitehall Palace occupied by visiting kings of Scotland and their ambassadors. Later it became famous as the headquarters of the Metropolitan Police, whose offices are now in Victoria Street (Route 4). The former CROWN ESTATE OFFICE (now the legal department of the Ministry of Agriculture), on the south of Great Scotland Yard, is a fine building by John Murray (1910).

On the other side of Whitehall is the rambling building formerly known as the ADMIRALTY (VIII, A2,3), the chief office of the governing body of the Royal Navy. It consists of two adjoining parts, the older (with a classical portico in a small courtyard), by Thomas Ripley (1722–6). This was the Admiralty of Nelson's day, and here the great admiral lay in state after his death at Trafalgar (1805). It is secluded from Whitehall by a charming stone screen designed by Robert Adam in 1760. Behind, a massive pile dominated by its cupolas, is the newer building, put up in 1895–1907 facing the Mall and the Horse Guards Parade. The Admiralty is now occupied by the naval branch of the Ministry of Defence (see Route 26) and other government departments.

On the south of the old building, facing Whitehall, is ADMIRALTY HOUSE (by S. P. Cockerell, 1786), used for government receptions and conferences. Beyond is a building reconstructed in 1967 behind its façades of 1733 and now occupied by the PARLIAMENTARY COUNSEL. Next comes the HORSE GUARDS (VIII, A3), with its picturesque clock-tower, built by William Kent and John Vardy in 1742–53 on the site of a guardhouse for the palace of Whitehall. Two mounted troopers of the Household Cavalry, in their resplendent uniforms, are posted here daily from 10 a.m. to 4 p.m., but are relieved every hour. At 11 a.m. (10 a.m. on Sundays) the ceremony of Changing the Guard is performed, a popular and colourful spectacle lasting about half an hour, and at 4 p.m. daily a dismounted inspection takes place.

The low arch beneath the clock-tower, closed to cars (except those of royalty and a few privileged persons), admits to the HORSE GUARDS PARADE, a broad open space facing the east side of St James's Park. On the north rises the Admiralty building, and on the south are seen the backs of Nos. 10–12 Downing Street, with the Renaissance-style Foreign Office beyond to the right and the Cabinet and Scottish Offices to the left. Two dismounted sentries of the Household Cavalry patrol the archway. On the parade ground near the Horse Guards are equestrian statues of Viscount Wolseley (d. 1913), by Sir W. Goscombe John, and Earl Roberts (d. 1914), a smaller copy of one at Calcutta. On the south side is a statue by John Tweed of Earl Kitchener (d. 1916), and on the west, at the edge of the park, is the GUARDS' MEMORIAL for 1914–18, by G. Ledward and H. C. Bradshaw. The Horse Guards Parade is the scene of the impressive ceremony of 'Trooping the Colour', performed by the Guards' Division and the Household Cavalry before the Queen on her official birthday (usually early in June).

To the south of the Horse Guards Parade is a huge statue of the Earl Mountbatten (assassinated in 1979), by Franta Belsky, unveiled in 1982, showing him in the uniform of Admiral of the Fleet.

On the east side of Whitehall, opposite the Horse Guards, is the imposing pile of the WAR OFFICE (VIII, A3), built by William Young in 1906 as the headquarters of the Army, and now part of the Ministry of Defence. The corner turrets disguise the fact that none of the angles is a right angle. In front is an equestrian statue by Adrian Jones of the Duke of Cambridge (d. 1904), Commander-in-Chief of the British Armies for nearly forty years (1856–95), and on the south is a statue of the eighth Duke of Devonshire (d. 1908), the statesman.

Beyond is the BANQUETING HOUSE (adm., p. 31), the chief surviving part of the royal palace of Whitehall, an early and splendid example of classical architecture, the masterpiece of Inigo Jones. Built in 1619–22, this was the first example completed in England of the style evolved by Andrea Palladio, the Italian architect. Over the entrance in the staircase annexe (added by Wyatt in 1798) is a bust of Charles I, marking the approximate site of the window through which he stepped on to the scaffold in 1649.

The door at the head of the staircase (surmounted by a bust of James I by Le Sueur) admits to the spacious and well-proportioned Banqueting Hall, 110 ft long by 55 ft high and broad, remarkable especially for its nine allegorical ceiling paintings designed for Charles I by Peter Paul Rubens, who received £3,000 and a knighthood for the work. The paintings were done on canvas at Antwerp with the assistance of Jordaens and other pupils, and were completed in 1635. The subject of the large central oval is the Apotheosis of James I, while other paintings symbolize the Benefits of his Government and the Union of England and Scotland. The Hall was carefully restored in 1973 to the original designs of Inigo Jones, as far as possible, and a canopied throne was placed at the south end.

A mansion on this site was purchased in the 13th century as the London residence of the Archbishops of York. Frequently altered and improved, it was known as York House until the downfall of Cardinal Wolsey in 1529, when it was seized by Henry VIII, who enlarged it and changed its name to WHITEHALL PALACE. The Tudor palace, which covered a large area now bisected by Whitehall and extending east to the river, became for a century and a half the chief residence of the court in London. Henry VIII was married here to Anne Boleyn in 1533 and here he died in 1547.

Elizabeth I was taken from the palace to be a prisoner in the Tower, but returned in triumph on her accession as queen. In a new banqueting house, built in 1581, the first performance of Shakespeare's *Othello* is believed to have been given in 1604. The house was rebuilt in 1605 and here in 1612 Elizabeth, daughter of James I, was betrothed to Frederick V, Count Palatine of the Rhine, the great-grandfather of George I and ancestor of the present royal line. After this building had been destroyed by fire in 1619, plans for a new palace were drawn up for James I by Inigo Jones, but only the Banqueting House was completed. From a window in an annexe on the north of this (since demolished) Charles I stepped to his execution in 1649. Oliver Cromwell took up his residence as Lord Protector in the palace, with John Milton as his secretary; here he refused the crown of England and here he died in 1658. After the Restoration the court returned to the palace, which became a centre of revelry and intrigue, as related by Pepys and others, until Charles II died here in 1685. The weathercock was placed at the north end of the roof by James II to show, it is said, whether the wind was favourable to the voyage of William of Orange. In 1688 he 'stole away from Whitehall by the Privy Stairs' and in the following year the crown was offered here by the Lords and Commons to William and Mary. The new king transferred his residence to Kensington Palace and in 1698 the old palace was burned to the ground, apart from the Banqueting House. In 1724 this was converted by George I into a Chapel Royal, but it was never consecrated and in 1890 it was granted by Queen Victoria to the ROYAL UNITED SERVICE INSTITUTION (founded in 1832), whose museum was housed here from 1895 to 1962. The offices and library of the Royal United Services Institute for Defence Studies, its successor, are in an annexe on the south added after 1890 by Sir Aston Webb.

Gwydyr House, next to the Banqueting House, was built by John Marquand in 1772 and is now the WELSH OFFICE. Dover House, now the SCOTTISH OFFICE (VIII, B3), opposite, was built by James Paine in 1755 and has a portico over the pavement added by Henry Holland (1787). In front is a much-criticized equestrian statue of Earl Haig (d. 1928), by A. F. Hardiman, and farther on is the CABINET OFFICE, formerly the Treasury, built by Kent in 1737, but extended by Sir John Soane in 1827 and given a new façade by Sir Charles Barry in 1847.

The Cabinet Office contains also the offices of the First Lord of the Treasury (a position usually combined with that of Prime Minister) and of the Chancellor of the Exchequer. At the north end is the office of the PRIVY COUNCIL, the private council of the sovereign, comprising princes of the blood, high officers of State, and certain Members of Parliament appointed by the Crown. At the south end, with its entrance in Downing Street, is the office of the Judicial Committee of the Privy Council. This is the highest Court of Appeal for disputes in those countries of the Commonwealth that have no supreme courts of their own. In the building also is the PAYMASTER GENERAL'S OFFICE, formed in 1835.

DOWNING STREET (VIII, B3), famous out of all proportion to its unimposing appearance, is named after its builder, Sir George Downing (d. 1684), who graduated at Harvard in 1642 and became secretary to the Treasury. No. 10, with an unpretentious exterior, is the official residence of the Prime Minister and its Cabinet Room (on the ground floor) has been the scene of many momentous meetings. The house was offered by George II in 1732 to Sir Robert Walpole, the first prime minister in the modern sense, who insisted that it be annexed to his office instead. Walpole lived here in 1735–42, but the front part of the house was rebuilt, probably by Kenton Couse, in 1766–74. The dining rooms of No. 10 and No. 11, next door (the official residence of the Chancellor of the Exchequer), were redesigned in characteristic style in 1825 by Soane.

The Cabinet Office and Nos. 10–11 Downing Street were rebuilt behind their façades in 1960–64 to the designs of Raymond Erith, but with most of the historic features incorporated. No. 12, adjoining, the office of the Chief Government Whip, was completely rebuilt. During the demolition of the old buildings, remains of the Tudor palace of Whitehall (about 1530) were brought to light, including part of the great hall converted by Henry VIII into a tennis court, which can be seen from Treasury Green, opening off Downing Street. Much Roman and Tudor pottery was found, as well as remains of the wooden structure of a Saxon hall, the first work of this kind to be discovered in London.

Samuel Pepys, the diarist, lived in 1658–60 in Axe Yard, which was approximately on the site of Downing Street, and James Boswell lodged in the street (house long since demolished) in 1762–3.

On the greensward facing the Cabinet Office, and over-shadowed by the main offices of the MINISTRY OF DEFENCE (Route 26), are statues of Sir Walter Raleigh (d. 1618), by William McMillan (1959), and Field-Marshal Viscount Montgomery (d. 1976), by Oscar Nemon (1980). RICHMOND TERRACE, to the south, is a late-Georgian survival of 1825 by Thomas Chawner (under restoration in 1985). Sir Henry Morton Stanley, the explorer, died in 1904 at No. 2.

Rising in the centre of Whitehall is the CENOTAPH (VIII, B3), simply inscribed 'To the Glorious Dead', commemorating all servicemen of the British Empire and Commonwealth who gave their lives in the two World Wars. Designed by Sir Edwin Lutyens, it was first erected temporarily in plaster as a saluting point for the Allied 'Victory March' of 19 July 1919, but in deference to public feeling it was rebuilt in Portland stone for the anniversary of Armistice Day on 11 November 1920. The inscription referring to the Second World

War was added in 1946. A service, attended by the sovereign, leading statesmen, and representatives of the Commonwealth and the armed forces, is held at the Cenotaph on Remembrance Sunday (second Sunday in November), when the two-minute silence in memory of the fallen is observed at 11 a.m.

That part of Whitehall beyond the Cenotaph is known as Parliament Street. On the west side are two large blocks of government offices, divided by King Charles Street, at the farther end of which is a statue of Lord Clive (d. 1774), by John Tweed (1916). The northern block of buildings, designed by Sir George Gilbert Scott (1873), contains the FOREIGN AND COMMONWEALTH OFFICE, formed from two departments combined in 1968.

From the west end of King Charles Street, steps descend towards the entrance to the CABINET WAR ROOMS (adm., p. 31) provided in the basement of the second block of buildings in 1939 for Sir Winston Churchill, the War Cabinet, and the Chiefs of Staff. These rooms were in use from the outbreak of the War until the Japanese surrender in 1945. They include the Cabinet Room, as arranged for a typical meeting of the War Cabinet; the Prime Minister's combined office and bedroom, with the desk at which he made some of his famous broadcasts; the Map Room, where information about war operations was collected; and the Telephone Room, from which Churchill could talk directly to President Roosevelt in the White House.

In the second block of buildings, by J. M. Brydon and Sir Henry Tanner (1900), are the TREASURY, the office of the Lord High Treasurer (in commission since the 18th century), the CENTRAL STATISTICAL OFFICE, part of the Cabinet Office, and other government departments. Parliament Street ends on the south at PARLIAMENT SQUARE (Route 3).

3 From Parliament Square to Lambeth Bridge, the Tate Gallery, and Vauxhall Bridge

Plan VIII, B3–VIII, E2
STATIONS: WESTMINSTER (Plan VIII, B3), on the Circle and District lines; PIMLICO (VIII, E2), and VAUXHALL (VIII, F3), ¼ m. E of Vauxhall Bridge, on the Victoria line. — BUSES Nos. 3, 11, 12, 24, 29, 53, 70, 76, 77, 88, 109, 155, 159, 170, 172, and 184 to Parliament Square; Nos. 3, 10, 149, 159, and 507 cross Lambeth Bridge; Nos. 2, 36, 77A, 88, and 185 cross Vauxhall Bridge. No. 88 runs from Parliament Square to Vauxhall Bridge via Great Smith Street and the Tate Gallery.

PARLIAMENT SQUARE (VIII, B3), the attractive open space at the foot of Whitehall, was laid out by Sir Charles Barry as a kind of garden approach to his new Houses of Parliament. From the north side there is a splendid view of St Margaret's Church with Westminster Abbey towering behind, and of the massive pile of the Houses of Parliament with Westminster Hall in front. In the angle between this and the tall clock-tower is New Palace Yard, with an entrance to Westminster Hall and the members' approach to the House of Commons. Bridge Street, skirting the clock-tower on the left, leads to Westminster underground station and Westminster Bridge (Route 26), while Great George Street runs from the north-west corner of the square to St James's Park (Route 5).

Around the grassy centre of the square are statues of Field-Marshal Smuts (d. 1950), by Sir Jacob Epstein, unveiled in 1956, and of former Prime Ministers: Lord Palmerston (d. 1865); the Earl of Derby (d. 1869); Benjamin Disraeli, Lord Beaconsfield (d. 1881); and Sir Robert Peel (d. 1850). Lord Beaconsfield's statue is decorated with primroses, his favourite flower, on Primrose Day (19 April). Facing the House of Commons is a vigorous statue of Sir Winston Churchill (d. 1965), by Ivor Roberts-Jones (1973). On the west side of the square, from which there is a glimpse of County Hall beyond the river, are statues of George Canning (d. 1827), the Prime Minister, and Abraham Lincoln (d. 1865), the latter a fine replica of the one by Saint-Gaudens at Chicago, presented by the American people in 1920.

Behind the Lincoln statue is the elaborate Renaissance-style façade of the MIDDLESEX GUILDHALL (VIII, B3), the former county hall, built by J. S. Gibson (1905–13), and still the sessions hall for that part of Greater London previously in Middlesex.

The relief over the door is of Henry III granting a charter to Westminster Abbey, that on the left shows the signing of Magna Carta by King John, and that on the right Lady Jane Grey accepting the crown from John Dudley, Duke of Northumberland. Illuminated panels in the entrance hall, signed by King George of the Hellenes, Queen Wilhelmina of the Netherlands, and King Haakon of Norway, commemorate the use of the court rooms by the maritime courts of foreign allies during the Second World War. To the north of the guildhall is the ROYAL INSTITUTION OF CHARTERED SURVEYORS (founded in 1868), who also occupy the fine 18th-century building adjoining in GREAT GEORGE STREET. In this street is the INSTITUTION OF CIVIL ENGINEERS, established in 1818 (with Thomas Telford as its first president) and occupying a building of 1911, and at the beginning of BIRDCAGE WALK, just beyond (compare Route 5), are the INSTITUTION OF MECHANICAL ENGINEERS, founded at Birmingham in 1847 and moved to London in 1877, and the ROYAL INSTITUTE OF PUBLIC ADMINISTRATION, founded in 1922.

To the south of Parliament Square, in the shadow of the great abbey, is ST MARGARET'S CHURCH (VIII, C3; adm., p. 35), the mother-church of the city of Westminster and the parish church of the House of Commons since 1614. Members attend service on certain occasions, when the Speaker occupies the pew in front of the lectern. The church, the most fashionable in London for weddings, was founded in the 11th or 12th century, but was rebuilt in the Perpendicular style in 1504–23 by Robert Stowell, master-mason of Westminster Abbey. The Solemn League and Covenant, whereby the Scottish covenanters promised military aid to the English parliament in return for the establishment of Presbyterianism in England, was signed here in 1643. The church was refaced in Portland stone in 1735 and well restored by Sir George Gilbert Scott in 1878. The west porch was added to commemorate the ministry of Canon Farrar (1876–95), afterwards Dean of Canterbury. Samuel Pepys was married in the church in 1655, John Milton in 1656, and Winston Churchill in 1908. It has been the custom since the 16th century to ring the bells when the sovereign drives past in state.

The magnificent Flemish glass in the east window is thought to have been made at the order of Ferdinand and Isabella of Spain to celebrate the betrothal in 1501 of their daughter, Catherine of Aragon, to Prince Arthur, elder brother of Henry VIII. It was intended for Westminster Abbey, but before it arrived Henry had become king and had married his brother's widow. The glass, dispatched to Waltham Abbey, was bought for St Margaret's in 1758. A range of stained glass windows by John Piper, in the south aisle, was inserted in 1967.

The centre panel of the altarpiece is a copy of Titian's 'Supper at Emmaus', carved in limewood (1753). On the north side of the east door is a brass to Sir Walter Raleigh, who was beheaded in 1618 in front of the Palace of Westminster and is claimed to be interred in the chancel, though it is possible that he may be buried at Beddington, in Surrey. A tablet of 1820 on the right of the door commemorates William Caxton (d. 1491), the father of printing, who was buried in the church or churchyard. The alabaster tomb of Lady Dudley (d. 1600), in the south aisle, is one of several good 16th–17th-century monuments in the church. Farther west is a memorial of 1955 to James Rumsey (d. 1792), an American pioneer of steam navigation, who is buried in the churchyard; it incorporates an epitaph written by Robert Herrick for his niece Elizabeth (d. 1630). At the west end are windows given by Americans in memory of Raleigh (with an inscription by J. R. Lowell) and Milton (inscription by Whittier). In the north wall is a window to Admiral Robert Blake (d. 1657), and on the west wall, outside, is a memorial stone (1966) to Blake, John Pym, and other Parliamentarians whose bodies were thrown into a pit in the churchyard by the orders of Charles II.

The road leaving Parliament Square to the south-east passes between St Margaret's Church, on the right, and Westminster Hall, in front of which stands a fine bronze statue of Oliver Cromwell, by Sir Hamo Thornycroft (1899). To the south of the hall opens OLD PALACE YARD, with a striking equestrian statue of Richard I, by Marochetti (1860). The yard was the scene of the execution of Guy Fawkes and others among the Gunpowder Plot conspirators. To the left are various entrances to the **Houses of Parliament** (adm., p. 358), while to the right is the Henry VII Chapel of Westminster Abbey. With its back to the Chapter House is the NATIONAL MEMORIAL TO GEORGE V (1865–1936), by Sir W. Reid Dick and Sir Giles Gilbert Scott (1947). Nos. 6–7 Old Palace Yard, built in 1754 and until 1864 the Clerk of the Parliaments' House, are now occupied by the Commonwealth Parliamentary Association.

Opposite the huge Victoria Tower of the Houses of Parliament is the entrance to the moated JEWEL TOWER (VIII, C3; adm., p. 32), the last surviving domestic part of the royal Palace of Westminster. Built in 1366, probably under Henry Yevele, who rebuilt the nave of Westminster Abbey, it stood at the extreme south-west corner of the palace (hence its L-shaped plan).

The tower was designed as the treasury for the private jewels, plate, and other valuables of Edward III and as the office of the 'clerk and surveyor of the king's works within the Palace of Westminster', who had charge of them. Here he received accessions to the king's treasure and made disbursement when called on to do so, but after 1547 the royal treasures were dispersed by Edward VI and in 1621 the tower became a repository for the records of the House of Lords. Alterations to suit its new purpose were made in this year and in 1719–26, but in 1864 the records were transferred to the Houses of Parliament and from 1869 until 1938 the tower was occupied by the Weights and Measures Department of the Board of Trade. The building, damaged in an air raid in 1941, was carefully restored in 1948–56. The ground floor rooms have vaults with carved bosses; the upper chambers contain relics and illustrations of the Palaces of Westminster and Whitehall. In a case on the first floor is a Saxon sword of about A.D. 800, discovered during excavations near the Houses of Parliament in 1948, and on the second floor are cases of standard weights and measures.

Abingdon Street, leading south from Old Palace Yard past a garden (with a sculpture by Henry Moore, 1967) over an underground car-park, is continued by MILLBANK to Vauxhall Bridge. On the left are the VICTORIA TOWER GARDENS (VIII, C, D3), from which there are views across the river of St Thomas's Hospital and Lambeth

Palace and Church, as well as of Somerset House and other buildings lining the embankment beyond Westminster Bridge. In the gardens are a bronze statue by A. G. Walker of Mrs Emmeline Pankhurst (d. 1928), leader of the women's suffrage movement, and a fine bronze replica (1915) of the group by Rodin erected at Calais in 1895 and representing the heroic BURGHERS OF CALAIS, who surrendered themselves to Edward III in 1347 rather than witness the destruction of their town.

On the right are the offices of the CHURCH COMMISSIONERS, incorporated in 1836 (as the Ecclesiastical Commissioners) to manage the estates of the Church of England. Dean Stanley Street, farther on, opens to SMITH SQUARE, in the centre of which is the church of ST JOHN THE EVANGELIST, with four unusual baroque towers, built by Thomas Archer in 1721–8 and gutted by bombing in 1941. Carefully restored in 1963–9 (by Marshall Sisson), it is now an arts centre for concerts, lectures, and intimate opera.

On the north side of the square and in the adjoining LORD NORTH STREET are delightful early-Georgian terraces, and other houses of the period will be found farther north, in COWLEY STREET, where No. 4 is the head-office of the SOCIAL DEMOCRATIC PARTY, founded in 1981, and in BARTON STREET, where Vaughan Williams lived at No. 10 (in 1899–1905) and T. E. Lawrence of Arabia lived at No. 14.

LAMBETH BRIDGE (VIII, D3), crossing the Thames to Lambeth (Route 35), was rebuilt in 1929–32 by Sir Reginald Blomfield and G. Topham Forrest, on the site of an ancient horse-ferry.

This is recalled by the name of HORSEFERRY ROAD, which runs west and north from the bridge towards Victoria Street (see Route 4), passing the WESTMINSTER HOSPITAL (VIII, D3), founded in 1716 in Broad Sanctuary. The first London hospital to be supported by voluntary contributions, it was transferred to new buildings here in 1937 (extended in 1966). The medical school, also here, was founded in 1834 and combined with that of Charing Cross Hospital in 1984. Earl Attlee, the Labour Prime Minister, died in the hospital in 1967.

In MARSHAM STREET, leading north from Horseferry Road, is a large building containing the head-offices of the DEPARTMENT OF THE ENVIRONMENT, which is responsible for matters affecting the physical environment, including planning and local government, housing and public building, and the royal parks and palaces, and of the DEPARTMENT OF TRANSPORT, which has responsibility for inland transport services. On the other side of Marsham Street, which is extended by Great Smith Street to Broad Sanctuary (Route 4), is the NINTH CHURCH OF CHRIST SCIENTIST, in a deep red brick, by Sir Herbert Baker (1929).

Facing Lambeth Bridge is IMPERIAL CHEMICAL HOUSE, built by Sir Frank Baines in 1927–9 as the headquarters of Imperial Chemical Industries, the largest British manufacturing company, formed in 1926. THAMES HOUSE, a similar block of offices on the opposite corner, is partly occupied by the DEPARTMENT OF ENERGY, set up in 1974 and controlling the nationalized industries of coal, gas, oil, electricity and atomic energy. Beyond rises the impressive MILLBANK TOWER, one of the tallest buildings in London (thirty-four storeys and 387 ft high), designed by Ronald Ward and Partners (1963) for Messrs Vickers and containing the offices of the National Economic Development Council and the Electricity Council. Millbank follows the bend of the river past the **Tate Gallery** (adm., p. 426), to the south of which is the ROYAL ARMY MEDICAL COLLEGE (1907). It passes PONSONBY PLACE and PONSONBY TERRACE, which have good terraces of about 1850 by Thomas Cubitt, and ends at the approach to VAUXHALL BRIDGE (VIII, E, F3; pronounced 'Vox-'), built in 1906 to the designs of Sir Maurice Fitzmaurice and W. E. Riley, with sculptures representing the Arts and Sciences by F. W. Pomeroy and Alfred Drury. The bridge crosses the river to Vauxhall Station (Route 35).

Near the bridge approach is RIVERWALK HOUSE, by Farmer and Dark (1966), now a Government conference centre. In BESSBOROUGH GARDENS, opposite the bridge, is a fountain (by Sir Peter Shepheard) celebrating the eightieth birthday (1980) of Queen Elizabeth, the Queen Mother. On the north-east side of the square is another terrace of about 1850, and on the north-west side are two prominent blocks of building, that facing DRUMMOND GATE designed by Chapman Taylor Partners (1981–4) and that farther west by William Whitfield and Partners (1976–80). Both blocks are leased to the Metropolitan Police.

VAUXHALL BRIDGE ROAD, a long dismal thoroughfare, runs north-west to Victoria Station (Route 4). On the left is LILLINGTON GARDENS, an unusual but successful estate of the Westminster Council, designed by Darbourne and Darke, and completed in 1973. ST JAMES THE LESS, reached from Moreton Street, is a brick Gothic church by G. E. Street (1861), with a fresco above the chancel arch by G. F. Watts.

A more interesting route to Victoria Station, starting from the west corner of Bessborough Gardens, runs through a district laid out by Thomas Cubitt from 1835 onwards. It follows Bessborough Street to PIMLICO STATION (1968), then Lupus Street, on the left. From the north end of St George's Square (see below), BELGRAVE ROAD runs north-west, with long rows of well-preserved houses of about 1850, now mainly occupied as small hotels. Beyond WARWICK SQUARE, an unspoiled layout of 1843 by Cubitt, Belgrave Road is extended to Eccleston Square (Route 8).

GROSVENOR ROAD goes on from the bridge beside the Thames to Chelsea Bridge (Route 8), skirting the district of Pimlico. It passes ST GEORGE'S SQUARE (by Cubitt, 1844) and DOLPHIN SQUARE, a layout of flats round a central garden (by Gordon Jeeves, 1937), opposite which is the WESTMINSTER BOATING BASE, opened, mainly for young people, in 1975. Farther on are CHURCHILL GARDENS, a large housing estate, one of the first examples of the modern style, designed by Powell and Moya and built in 1946–62, with blocks of flats varying from four to eleven storeys in height, formerly heated by hot water carried directly under the river from the BATTERSEA POWER STATION opposite (by Sir Giles G. Scott, 1929–35), disused since 1983 and possibly to be demolished.

4 From Parliament Square to Victoria

Plan VIII, B3–VIII, C, D1
STATIONS: WESTMINSTER (Plan VIII, B3), ST JAMES'S PARK (VIII, C2), and VICTORIA (VIII, C1), all on the Circle and District lines; Victoria is also on the Victoria line. — BUSES Nos. 11, 24, 29, 70, and 76 ply along Victoria Street; for other buses to Parliament Square, see Route 3; to Victoria, see Route 8. Nos. 10, 149, and 507 run from Lambeth Bridge to Victoria via Horseferry Road.

For PARLIAMENT SQUARE, see Route 3. The wide but short street running south-west from the square, and passing between the Middlesex Guildhall and **Westminster Abbey** (adm., p. 469), is known as BROAD SANCTUARY, a name recalling that it occupies part of the site of the sanctuary or precincts of the abbey, a place of refuge from any monarch who abused his power. Elizabeth Woodville, the queen of Edward IV, sought refuge in the sanctuary on several occasions (compare Shakespeare's *Richard III*) and her son, Edward V, was born here (perhaps in the abbot's lodging) in 1470, but the privilege was abolished by James I. In the open space opposite the west door of the abbey rises a column, 60 ft high, by Sir George Gilbert Scott (1859), commemorating scholars of Westminster School who fell in the Crimean War and the Indian Mutiny. An INTERNATIONAL CONFERENCE CENTRE, to the designs of Powell and Moya, is being built (1985) on the north side of Broad Sanctuary.

The Victorian Gothic archway on the south of Broad Sanctuary admits to DEAN'S YARD (VIII, C2), enclosing the site of the abbey gardens. On the east side are entrances to the Abbey Cloisters and to WESTMINSTER SCHOOL (adm., p. 36), one of the foremost public schools, founded by Elizabeth I in 1560 as a successor to the

Benedictine monastic school mentioned as early as the 14th century. It comprises forty Foundation or Queen's Scholars and about 810 other pupils, including ninety girls (first admitted in 1972). The school occupies much-restored monastic buildings on the east side of Dean's Yard and 17th–19th-century buildings round Little Dean's Yard.

The 14th-century College Hall, adjoining the Dean's Court and still a dining hall, contains a minstrels' gallery and oak tables said to be made from timber salvaged from the Spanish Armada. The Great School Room, or 'School', formerly the monks' dormitory, was damaged from the air in 1941 and rebuilt in 1960. On Shrove Tuesday the old ceremony of 'Tossing the Pancake' takes place here, one boy from each form competing and the boy securing the largest piece being rewarded with a guinea by the Dean of Westminster. Ashburnham House (formerly the home of the Earls of Ashburnham), on the north of Little Dean's Yard, is a 17th-century building with a delightful interior attributed to Inigo Jones. The Dormitory of the Queen's Scholars, designed by Wren but completed by Lord Burlington (1734), was gutted during the war and has been reconstructed internally (1950).

Among the numerous famous pupils of the school may be mentioned Richard Hakluyt, the Elizabethan geographer; the poets Ben Jonson, George Herbert, Abraham Cowley, John Dryden, Matthew Prior, and William Cowper; Sir Christopher Wren, the builder of St Paul's; John Locke, the philosopher; the notorious Judge Jeffreys; the Earl of Mansfield, Lord Chief Justice; Charles Wesley, the Methodist hymn-writer; Warren Hastings, governor-general of India; Edward Gibbon, the historian; Jeremy Bentham, the political economist; the statesman Lord John Russell; and Sir Adrian Boult, first conductor of the B.B.C. Symphony Orchestra (1930). Robert Southey, the poet, was expelled from the school for protesting against flogging. William Camden, the antiquary, was headmaster in 1593–9; Richard Busby, headmaster for fifty-seven years (1638–95), bequeathed his valuable library to the school. The pupils attend a daily service in the abbey, and are entitled to seats at all great ceremonies, including coronations, when they enjoy the privilege of crying 'Vivat' immediately after the crowning of the sovereign.

On the south side of Dean's Yard is CHURCH HOUSE (VIII, C2), rebuilt by Sir Herbert Baker in 1937–40, the headquarters of the General Synod (formerly the National Assembly) of the Church of England, as well as of the House of Laity and the Canterbury Houses of Convocation. It was used for a time as the meeting-place of both the Lords and Commons after the Houses of Parliament were bombed in 1941, and in 1945 it became the headquarters of the Preparatory Commission of the United Nations, the first sessions of the Security Council being held here. Of interest are the fine circular Assembly Hall (restored in 1951 after war damage) and the Hoare Memorial

Hall (no general admission). On the front of the building are the arms of the provinces and sees of England.

VICTORIA STREET, opened in 1851 and running south-west from Broad Sanctuary towards Westminster Cathedral and Victoria Station, has been considerably rebuilt. No. 1, on the left (by Ronald Fielding, 1963), contains the head-office of the DEPARTMENT OF TRADE AND INDUSTRY, which is responsible for carrying out the government's policy concerning commerce and overseas trade, technology and industry, and company legislation. ABBEY HOUSE, opposite (rebuilt in 1979), occupies the site of the Westminster Palace Hotel, where the Act of Union by which the Dominion of Canada was constituted was framed in 1867. Near the west gate of the abbey precincts, which stood hereabouts, was the Almonry, from which monastic alms were distributed, and to this building William Caxton moved his printing press in 1483 from the neighbourhood of the abbey.

At the corner of Tothill Street, to the west of Broad Sanctuary, is the large CENTRAL HALL (VIII, C2), the headquarters of the Methodist Church, built by E. A. Rickards and H. V. Lanchester in 1912. The dome, with a diameter of 90 ft, is the largest in London after St Paul's and the Reading Room of the British Museum. The assembly hall, which has a fine organ and seats for an audience of 2,700, is used for concerts, recitals, and meetings; in 1946 it became the first meeting-place of the General Assembly of the United Nations.

In Central Hall (and entered from Matthew Parker Street, at the back) is the IMPERIAL COLLECTION (adm., p. 32), a glittering display of copies of the crown jewels and regalia, past and present, of Britain, France, and many other countries, in an appropriate setting, as well as copies of famous diamonds.

On the right in TOTHILL STREET is Caxton House, built in 1979 by Chapman Taylor Partners for the DEPARTMENT OF EMPLOYMENT, a government office created in 1968 and superseding the Ministry of Labour, set up in 1916. In DARTMOUTH STREET, on the right farther on, No. 11 is the office of the FABIAN SOCIETY, a Socialist organization founded on the initiative of Edward R. Pease in 1884. Bernard Shaw and Sidney Webb were early members. This street leads to QUEEN ANNE'S GATE (VIII, B2), a quiet close built in 1704 for William Paterson, the original founder of the Bank of England, and the most charming survival in London of the domestic architecture of the period.

No. 3 was the home of Viscount Grey of Fallodon (d. 1933), naturalist and Foreign Secretary. Outside No. 13 is a contemporary statue of Queen Anne (probably by Francis Bird), intended for the portico of St Mary-le-Strand. Admiral Lord Fisher lived at No. 16 as First Sea Lord in 1905–10. No. 18 is the office of the NATIONAL CONSUMER COUNCIL. Lord Palmerston, the Prime Minister, was born in 1784 at No. 20 and Lord Haldane (d. 1928), the statesman and philosopher, lived at No. 28. The home of the ST STEPHEN'S CONSTITUTIONAL CLUB, a Conservative club founded in 1870, is at No. 34.

Nos. 36–8, facing the north-west angle of Queen Anne's Gate, are the headquarters of the NATIONAL TRUST, founded in 1895 by Octavia Hill, Sir Robert Hunter, and Canon H. D. Rawnsley; it now has over one million members. The street turns south, passing the entrance (at No. 50) to the HOME OFFICE, which is concerned in general with internal affairs in England and Wales and occupies a gaunt building of 1977 by Sir Basil Spence. Queen Anne's Gate ends at BROADWAY, the continuation west of Tothill Street. Above St James's Park station here rise the LONDON TRANSPORT EXECUTIVE Offices (VIII, C2), built by Adams, Holden, and Pearson (1929) and decorated with controversial sculptures by Sir Jacob Epstein and (higher up) by Eric Gill and others. Another branch of Broadway runs south from the station to Victoria Street.

Broadway is extended westward by PETTY FRANCE, where John Milton occupied a 'pretty garden-house' in 1651–60 and began *Paradise Lost*. Later tenants were Jeremy Bentham, James Mill, and William Hazlitt, but the house was pulled down in 1877. CLIVE HOUSE, on the left, contains the Passport Office, a branch of the Home Office. Petty France ends at BUCKINGHAM GATE, which leads right to Buckingham Palace and the west end of St James's Park (Route 5) and left to Victoria Street. On the west side is the WESTMINSTER CHAPEL (Independent Evangelical), by W. F. Poulton (1864), with a remarkable interior (entrance from the passage on the south). In Caxton Street, on the east, is the BLEWCOAT SCHOOL (VIII, C2), a delightful little brick building of 1709 for a school founded in 1688. It was bought in 1954 by the National Trust and the single lofty panelled room now contains an information office and shop. The street goes on to the southern branch of Broadway.

On the left, at the junction of Broadway with Victoria Street, are the huge offices (twenty storeys and 225 ft high; by Chapman Taylor Partners, 1967) of the METROPOLITAN POLICE, who brought with them the name of their previous home, NEW SCOTLAND YARD, from the Victoria Embankment (Route 26).

Broadway is prolonged beyond Victoria Street by STRUTTON GROUND, which emerges into Greycoat Place near the north end of Horseferry Road (compare Route 3) and the GREYCOAT HOSPITAL (VIII, C, D2), founded in 1698 as a school for boys and girls, but subsequently enlarged and reconstituted in 1873 as a day-school for girls. The buildings, much damaged by bombing, were restored and again enlarged by Laurence King in 1955. In MAUNSEL STREET, on the right of Horseferry Road, Nos. 26–9 are the headquarters of the CHESHIRE FOUNDATION for the incurably sick, established by Leonard Cheshire in 1955.

In GREYCOAT STREET, south of Greycoat Place, is the large hall (by Easton and Robertson, 1926) of the ROYAL HORTICULTURAL SOCIETY, founded in 1804 by John Wedgwood, Sir Joseph Banks, and others. The society's headquarters, with another hall, are at No. 80 in VINCENT SQUARE, to the south, laid out about 1780. The halls are used for exhibitions, etc., and for numerous flower-shows (open to the public, usually from 10 to 5) held in most months from April to November, and including the society's Great Autumn Show (in September). The centre of Vincent Square is the playing-field of Westminster School. In REGENCY STREET, to the east, at No. 112, are the offices of the SHAFTESBURY SOCIETY, founded in 1844 and now concerned in helping the physically handicapped and the poor.

Both sides of VICTORIA STREET, west of Broadway, have been entirely rebuilt in recent years. On the north, in a range of buildings by Sir John Burnet, Tait & Partners, are the WESTMINSTER CITY HALL, completed in 1966, and KINGSGATE HOUSE, which, like ASHDOWN HOUSE, on the left, contains various divisions of the Department of Trade and Industry. The long façade of a range of shops and offices beyond, designed by C. H. Elsom, Pack & Roberts (1971–5), has been interrupted to allow a vista of **Westminster Cathedral** (adm., p. 488).

Bressenden Place, farther west, opens to STAG PLACE, a pedestrian precinct (1962–4) with a bronze sculpture of a stag (by E. B. Copnall) recalling the name of a brewery previously on this site. The precinct is enclosed by huge office and residential blocks of which the most prominent is PORTLAND HOUSE (twenty-nine storeys and 339 ft high), designed by Howard Fairbairn and Partners (1962) and overshadowing Buckingham Palace in the view from the Green Park side. In Eland House, on the west, are the offices of the OVERSEAS DEVELOPMENT ADMINISTRATION, which deals with the financial and technical assistance given by the government to overseas countries.

Victoria Street passes the VICTORIA PALACE THEATRE, built in 1911 by Frank Matcham, and runs north of VICTORIA STATION (VIII, C, D1), rebuilt in 1909 and altered after 1923, the principal West End terminus of the Southern Region of British Railways. A passenger terminal used by British Caledonian Airways was built on 'stilts' over the western platforms in 1962, and the station buildings are being extended upwards in 1985 by new offices (the Victoria Plaza). Victoria Street ends at Buckingham Palace Road opposite Grosvenor Gardens.

Opposite the Victoria Palace Theatre stands 'Little Ben', a pedestal street-clock, 30 ft high, modelled on the Clock Tower of the Houses of Parliament. It stood hereabouts from 1892 until 1964 and was brought back, after restoration, in 1981.

GROSVENOR GARDENS (VII, C3), traversed by the road to Hyde Park Corner (compare Route 9), consists of two connected triangles. At its south end is a bronze equestrian statue of Marshal Foch (d. 1929), by Georges Malissard, a replica of one at Cassel in northern France. At No. 32 Lord Birkenhead, the statesman, died in 1930. In Beeston Place, on the right, is the GORING HOTEL, built in 1910, with a pleasant garden at the back. At the north end of Grosvenor Gardens is the RIFLE BRIGADE WAR MEMORIAL, by John Tweed (1925), and in Hobart Place, on the left, No. 4 is the COUNCIL FOR THE PROTECTION OF RURAL ENGLAND, founded in 1926.

5 From Charing Cross to Hyde Park Corner or Victoria via St James's Park and Buckingham Palace

Plan VIII, A3–VII, C3

STATIONS: CHARING CROSS (Plan III, F3), on the Bakerloo, Jubilee, and Northern lines; EMBANKMENT (VIII, A3), on the Bakerloo, Circle, District, and Northern lines; ST JAMES'S PARK (VIII, C2), on the Circle and District lines; VICTORIA (VIII, C1), on the Circle, District, and Victoria lines; GREEN PARK (VIII, A1), on the Jubilee, Piccadilly, and Victoria lines; HYDE PARK CORNER (VII, B2), on the Piccadilly line. — BUSES to Charing Cross, compare Route 1; to Victoria, see Route 8; to Piccadilly and Hyde Park Corner, see Route 7.

ST JAMES'S PARK is open daily until midnight, the GREEN PARK until 7 p.m. — BANDS play in St James's Park, June to August; weekdays, 12.30 to 2 and 5.30 to 7; Sundays, 3 to 4.30 and 6.30 to 8. — Light Refreshments at the Cakehouse, near the lake (east end, north side).

For CHARING CROSS, see Route 1. St James's Park is reached by passing under the ADMIRALTY ARCH (VIII, A2) to the south-west, a triumphal arch designed by Sir Aston Webb and erected in 1910 as part of the national memorial to Queen Victoria. From it a noble vista opens, to the Queen Victoria Memorial and Buckingham Palace, down THE MALL (VIII, B1–A2), first laid out about 1660. A wide boulevard planted with double rows of plane trees in 1911 and forming an admirable processional avenue for State pageants, it takes its name from the game of 'paille-maille', played here during the reign of Charles II. On the left, west of Admiralty Arch, is a bronze statue of Captain James Cook (d. 1779), the explorer, by Brock. The structure next to the Admiralty, known as the Citadel, was built in 1940 as a repository; its grimly functional shape is now obscured by Virginia creeper.

Overlooking the Mall on the right are the once-aristocratic mansions of Carlton House Terrace, intercepted by the Duke of York's Steps, which ascend to Waterloo Place at the foot of Regent Street (see Route 6). Opposite are a road leading to the Horse Guards Parade (Route 2) and an entrance to ST JAMES'S PARK (VIII, B 1,2), the most attractive park in London, with an area of ninety-three acres. It is bounded on the north by the Mall and on the south by Birdcage Walk, and stretches from the Horse Guards Parade on the east towards Buckingham Palace on the west.

Once a marshy meadow belonging to the hospital of St James the Less, it was drained by Henry VIII and converted into a deer park adjoining his new palace, which under the first two Stuarts became a favourite resort of the court. Charles I walked across the park from St James's Palace to his execution in Whitehall (1649). After the Restoration it was laid out as pleasure grounds for Charles II by the French landscape gardener Le Nôtre, and it remained a fashionable rendezvous for over a century. The park was remodelled in 1829 for George IV by the architect John Nash, who created the lake and made other improvements.

Facing the park and the Mall on the north are the memorial to George VI (see Route 6) and the gardens of Marlborough House and St James's Palace. From the gate opposite the road between these two mansions a path descends to the bridge over the lake, the views from which are among the most enchanting in London: in one direction to Buckingham Palace, in the other to the buildings in Whitehall. The lake, which extends almost the whole length of the park, is a haunt of numerous varieties of waterfowl, for whom the island at the east end is preserved as a breeding-place. The pelicans to be found hereabouts are great favourites with Londoners. The path running southward from the bridge leads to Birdcage Walk and Queen Anne's Gate (see Route 4).

In the broad semicircular open space in front of Buckingham Palace, at the south-west end of the Mall, is the conspicuous QUEEN VICTORIA MEMORIAL, sculptured by Sir Thomas Brock, with Sir Aston Webb as architect, and completed in 1911.

From a platform embellished with marble water-basins rises a pedestal surmounted by a gilt-bronze figure of Victory, at whose feet sit Courage and Constancy. At the base, facing the Mall, is the seated figure of Queen Victoria (1819–1901), 13 ft high, carved from a solid block of white marble, and on the other sides of the pedestal are marble groups representing Truth (on the south). Motherhood (west), and Justice (north). Around the memorial are further groups in bronze symbolizing Science and Art (north), Peace and Progress (east), Naval and Military Power (south), and Industry and Agriculture (west), while the garden round the open space is enclosed by a balustrade with piers supporting sculpture including the heraldic shields of countries in the British Commonwealth.

BUCKINGHAM PALACE (VIII, B1), the principal residence of the sovereign, faces the west end of St James's Park and is backed by a private garden of forty acres. The dignified classical façade, 360 ft long, reconstructed in 1913 by Sir Aston Webb, overlooks a large forecourt patrolled by sentries of the Guards' Division in full dress uniform (see below), and the colourful ceremony of Changing the Guard is performed, usually daily (on alternate mornings in October–March), in the forecourt at 11.30 a.m. When the Queen is in residence, the Royal Standard is flown at the mast-head. The wrought-iron screen and gates (with their delightful cherubs), enclosing the forecourt, were the gift of the Dominion countries (1906).

The palace takes its name from Buckingham House, built in 1702–5 by William Winde for John Sheffield, Duke of Buckingham, and purchased in 1761 for George III. Here in 1767 the famous interview between the king and Dr Johnson took place. The house was settled in 1775 on Queen Charlotte, from whom it passed to her son, George IV, and he in 1824 commissioned John Nash, the court architect, to remodel it. Though its name was changed to Buckingham Palace the new mansion (altered by Edward Blore from 1830 on) was little used until the accession of Queen Victoria in 1837, after which it became the permanent London residence of the court. Edward VII was born in the palace in 1841 and died here in 1910, and here Charles, Prince of Wales, was born in 1948, Prince Andrew in 1960, and Prince Edward in 1964. An east wing added in 1847 by Blore gave the palace the form of a quadrangle, and it was the unimposing front of this that was rebuilt, in Portland stone, by Webb.

The interior of the palace, never open to the public, contains many splendid apartments, some decorated under the direction of Queen Mary. The state apartments include the Throne Room, with thrones used at the coronations of George V (1911) and George VI (1937) and their consorts; the Picture Gallery, 155 ft long; and the State Ballroom, 123 ft long (added in 1854 by Sir James Pennethorne), now used for investitures and state banquets. Mendelssohn played the organ in the Music Room in 1842, Prince Albert manipulating the stops, and Queen Victoria and the Prince Consort sang Mendelssohn songs. The Chapel, bombed in 1940, was rebuilt in 1961 and opened as the Queen's Gallery (see below). The apartments of the royal family are in the north wing.

To the north of the palace is GREEN PARK (VII, B3–VIII, B1), a triangular expanse of tree-studded grassland, fifty-three acres in extent, stretching up to Piccadilly. Originally added to the royal parks by Charles II, it succeeded St James's Park as the fashionable resort of society. The Queen's Walk, on its east side, probably named after Caroline, queen of George II, is overlooked by the Ritz Hotel and former palatial mansions of the aristocracy. A passage near the south end of it leads to Lancaster House and St James's Palace (Route 6). CONSTITUTION HILL, between Green Park and the Buckingham Palace gardens, ascends to the Wellington Arch at Hyde Park Corner (Route 7). Three attempts on the life of Queen Victoria were made in this road, in 1840, 1842, and 1849, and here in 1850 Sir Robert Peel was fatally injured by being thrown from his horse.

BIRDCAGE WALK, recalling an aviary established here by Charles II, skirts the south side of St James's Park as it leads towards Westminster. Near its west end are the WELLINGTON BARRACKS (VIII, C1), built in 1833 in a Regency style by Philip Hardwick and partly reconstructed in 1979–82. These are the headquarters of the GUARDS' DIVISION (formerly the Brigade of Guards). which comprises the Grenadier, Coldstream, Scots, Irish, and Welsh Guards. All these regiments wear scarlet tunics with dark blue facings, but they may be distinguished by their cap-bands, the Grenadier Guards (originally the 1st Regiment of Foot Guards, formed in 1656) having a scarlet cap-band, while the Coldstream Guards (raised in 1659 by General Monck at Coldstream on the Tweed) wear white, the Irish Guards (formed in 1902) green, the Welsh Guards (founded 1915) black, and the Scots Guards (the oldest of the regiments, formed in 1642) a red, white, and blue chequered cap-band. All the foot regiments likewise don the high bearskin 'cap' when in full dress uniform, but the Grenadiers may be distinguished by the white plume on the left of the bearskin, the Coldstreams by the scarlet plume on the right, the Irish Guards by a pale blue plume on the right, and the Welsh Guards by a white and green plume on the left, while the bearskins of the Scots Guards carry no plume at all. These regiments of Foot Guards, together with the Household Cavalry, formerly made up the Household Brigade.

The ROYAL MILITARY CHAPEL (adm., p. 34), or Guards' Chapel, opened in 1838, at the east end of the barracks, was almost completely destroyed, with appalling loss of life, when it was hit by a flying-bomb during a Sunday morning service in 1944. It was rebuilt in 1963 to the designs of George, Trew, and Dunn, incorporating the surviving apse, by Street (1878). A war-memorial cloister, by H. S. Goodhart-Rendel (1956), leading from Birdcage Walk to the narthex of the chapel, contains cases with seven books of remembrance, one for each of the regiments of the Household Brigade. The chapel has metal screens by Geoffrey Clarke and the pulpit is a gift of the royal family. On the south wall of the narthex is a memorial to guardsmen who fell in the Falklands Campaign (1982).

On the parade ground to the west is a statue (by James Butler, 1985) of Field-Marshal the Earl Alexander (d. 1969). To the east of the chapel is an entrance to Queen Anne's Gate (Route 4). From the south-east corner of St James's Park, Great George Street goes on to Parliament Square (Route 3).

BUCKINGHAM GATE, skirting the south side of the palace, passes the entrance to the QUEEN'S GALLERY (adm., p. 34), formerly the private chapel of Buckingham Palace (see above), but converted to show a selection (changed from time to time) of the finest paintings, drawings, furniture, and other works of art drawn from all parts of the royal collections.

In Buckingham Gate, No. 10 is the office of the DUCHY OF CORNWALL, instituted in 1337 by Edward III for the support of his eldest son, Edward, the Black Prince, and subsequently providing for the eldest son of the sovereign, who succeeds to the dukedom by inheritance. No. 6, farther on, is the AGRICULTURAL ENGINEERS' ASSOCIATION (founded in 1877).

In PALACE STREET, on the left at the south end of Buckingham Gate, is the WESTMINSTER THEATRE, rebuilt by John and Sylvia Reid in 1966. Good 18th-century houses have survived in CATHERINE PLACE and BUCKINGHAM PLACE, north of Palace Street, which goes on to Victoria Street (Route 4).

Buckingham Gate is extended towards Victoria Station by BUCKINGHAM PALACE ROAD. No. 17 is the headquarters of the GIRL GUIDES ASSOCIATION, established in 1910 by Lord Baden-Powell and his sister, Agnes Baden-Powell; it now has over 800,000 members in Britain and more than six million throughout the world. Almost opposite is the entrance to the ROYAL MEWS (VII, C3; adm., p. 34), built by John Nash in 1826, where the Queen's horses are stabled and her coaches kept.

These include the splendid state carriage (used for coronations) designed in 1762 for George III by Sir William Chambers and painted by G. B. Cipriani, a Florentine artist who had settled in England; the Irish state coach bought in 1852 by Queen Victoria and used for the state opening of Parliament; and the so-called glass state coach bought in 1910 by George V and now used for royal weddings, etc.

Lower Grosvenor Place, on the right beyond the mews, leads to the north end of Grosvenor Gardens (Route 9). In VICTORIA SQUARE, a late-Regency backwater on the right farther on, No. 8 was the home in 1840–44 of the poet Thomas Campbell. Buckingham Palace Road goes on past the west end of Victoria Street and the main entrance to VICTORIA STATION (Route 4); for the continuation towards Chelsea, see Route 8.

6 From Charing Cross to Hyde Park Corner via Pall Mall and St James's Street

Plan VIII, A3–VII, B3

STATIONS: CHARING CROSS (Plan III, F3), on the Bakerloo, Jubilee, and Northern lines; EMBANKMENT (VIII, A3) on the Bakerloo, Circle, District, and Northern lines; GREEN PARK (VIII, A1), on the Jubilee, Piccadilly, and Victoria lines; HYDE PARK CORNER (VII, B2), on the Piccadilly line. — BUSES Nos. 3, 6, 9, 12, 13, 15, 23, 53, 88, and 159 in Regent Street (northbound only) and Haymarket (southbound only); in Piccadilly, see Route 7.

For CHARING CROSS, see Route 1. COCKSPUR STREET, lined with offices of noted steamship companies, runs west past the entrance to Spring Gardens to join Pall Mall East, the extension of the north side of Trafalgar Square from the National Gallery. In the angle of the roads is a fine bronze equestrian statue of George III, by M. C. Wyatt (1836).

In SPRING GARDENS, No. 10 is the headquarters of the BRITISH COUNCIL, established in 1934 to promote a wider knowledge abroad of British life, thought, and culture. SUFFOLK STREET, north of George III's statue, was laid out by John Nash (with Suffolk Place; 1820–30), but has been altered since. Richard Cobden, the apostle of free trade, died in 1865 at No. 23 in this street. Beyond the statue the Haymarket (Route 7) opens on the right.

PALL MALL (VIII, A1, 2), which leads westward from the foot of the Haymarket, derives its name from 'paille-maille' (pronounced 'pell-mell'), an old French game resembling croquet, introduced into England during the reign of Charles I. The distinguished street traverses the once-fashionable district of St James's, still the centre of London club life. On the south, at the corner of Waterloo Place, is a building by John Nash (1827; altered by Decimus Burton in 1858), formerly the United Service Club (founded in 1815 by veterans of the Napoleonic wars) and now occupied by the INSTITUTE OF DIRECTORS.

WATERLOO PLACE, given over to large banks and insurance offices, intersects Pall Mall and is extended on the north by the lower section of Regent Street, ascending to Piccadilly Circus.

On the north side of the place is the GUARDS' CRIMEAN MEMORIAL, by John Bell (1859); the figures of guardsmen at the foot were cast from Russian cannon and the guns at the back of the monument were captured from the Russians at Sebastopol in 1855. In front are statues of Sidney Herbert (Lord Herbert of Lea; d. 1861), secretary for war during the Crimean campaign, and of Florence Nightingale (d.

1910), the 'lady with the lamp'. At No. 12, in the north-west corner of Waterloo Place, is the CRAFTS COUNCIL GALLERY (adm., p. 32), which provides information about contemporary crafts and holds exhibitions. In the lower part of REGENT STREET (III, F2), at the corner of Charles II Street, are the head-offices (by Leslie C. Norton and others, 1960), of the UNITED KINGDOM ATOMIC ENERGY AUTHORITY, established in 1954. Varied and interesting exhibitions are held frequently at the CEYLON TEA CENTRE (No. 22; adm., p. 31), at the corner of Jermyn Street.

In the centre of the southern part of Waterloo Place is the NATIONAL MEMORIAL TO EDWARD VII (1841–1910), a fine equestrian statue by Sir Bertram Mackennal. To the left (east) are statues of Captain R. F. Scott (d. 1912), the Antarctic explorer, sculptured by his widow, Lady Scott; of Colin Campbell, Lord Clyde (d. 1863), commander-in-chief during the Indian Mutiny; and of Lord Lawrence (d. 1879), ruler of the Punjab and Viceroy of India. The statues on the west side are of Sir John Burgoyne (d. 1871), the Crimean general, and Sir John Franklin (d. 1847), the Arctic explorer.

At the south end of Waterloo Place are the DUKE OF YORK'S STEPS, descending to the Mall and St James's Park (Route 5), over which there is a view to the towers of Westminster. At the top of the steps rises the DUKE OF YORK'S COLUMN, 124 ft high, designed by Benjamin Wyatt (1833) and surmounted by a bronze statue 14 ft high, by Westmacott, of Frederick, Duke of York (d. 1827), the second son of George III and Commander-in-Chief of the British Army. Though the duke was assiduous in carrying out reforms in the army, he is now chiefly remembered from a nursery rhyme; his impecuniosity was a by-word, and wits declared after the erection of the monument that he was placed so high to keep him away from his creditors. Most of the cost of the memorial was met by stopping one day's pay from every soldier in the army.

The column stands on the site of Carlton House, the residence of George IV after 1783, when Prince of Wales, but pulled down in 1826. Its name survives in CARLTON HOUSE TERRACE, built by John Nash in 1827–32, opulent mansions of the aristocracy now partly occupied by government departments, extending on either side of the southern part of Waterloo Place. No. 11, on the left, was the house of W. E. Gladstone, the Prime Minister, in 1856–75; No. 12, now Nash House, was converted in 1969 as the headquarters of the INSTITUTE OF CONTEMPORARY ARTS (founded in 1947 by Sir Roland Penrose), with an art gallery for loan exhibitions, a theatre, a cinema, and a restaurant; the public entrance (adm., p. 32) is from The Mall (Route 5).

Nos. 13–15 contain the offices of the CROWN ESTATE COMMISSIONERS, who collect the land revenues of the Crown. No. 15 also houses the Library and Archives of the National Portrait Gallery. No. 17, THE MALL GALLERIES (adm., p. 33), is the home of the FEDERATION OF BRITISH ARTISTS, which includes the ROYAL SOCIETY OF BRITISH ARTISTS, founded in 1823, the ROYAL INSTITUTE OF PAINTERS IN WATER-COLOURS, founded in 1831, the ROYAL INSTITUTE OF OIL PAINTERS, founded in 1882, and the ROYAL SOCIETY OF PORTRAIT PAINTERS, founded in 1891. At No. 17 also are the offices of the CIVIC TRUST, founded in 1957 to inspire an improvement in landscaping and architecture, and the TOWN AND COUNTRY PLANNING ASSOCIATION, established in 1899.

No. 6, to the right in Carlton House Terrace, is the home of THE ROYAL SOCIETY, one of the most important scientific bodies in the world, founded in 1660 to discuss ideas on 'natural knowledge'.

The society now numbers over 1,000 Fellows (F.R.S.), with the addition of eighty-five foreign members. Among the original Fellows were Christopher Wren (in whose rooms the first meeting was held) and John Evelyn, the diarist, and famous presidents have included Wren (elected in 1680), Samuel Pepys (1684), Sir Isaac Newton (1703), Sir Hans Sloane (1727), Sir Joseph Banks (1778; for forty-two years), and Sir Humphry Davy (1820). The rooms (admission by a Fellow's introduction only) contain a fine collection of portraits of men of science, and such interesting relics as Newton's telescope. The Royal Society now has two main functions: to further the development of science through grants, publications, meetings, and advice to the government, and to maintain links with other countries in joint scientific programmes and the free flow of scientific knowledge.

No. 5 in Carlton House Terrace is now the TURF CLUB, established in 1868. No. 3 is the office of the INDUSTRIAL SOCIETY, founded in 1919 to improve business relations and efficiency. No. 1 (now the METALS SOCIETY, formed in 1974 by the amalgamation of the Institute of Metals and the Iron and Steel Institute) was the town house from 1894 until his death in 1925 of the Marquess Curzon, Viceroy of India, a statue of whom, by Mackennal, stands at the corner of Carlton Gardens, which leads to the right back to Pall Mall. WOOL HOUSE (by David Hodges, 1965), on the west side, is the headquarters of the International Wool Secretariat.

Another branch of CARLTON GARDENS prolongs Carlton House Terrace. No. 4 here, rebuilt in 1933, was the headquarters of General de Gaulle, as leader of the Free French movement, from 18 June 1940. Louis Napoleon (later Napoleon III) lived in 1839–40 at No. 1, opposite on the west (now the official residence of the Foreign Secretary), and Lord Kitchener occupied No. 2 in 1914–15. This is now the office of the ROYAL FINE ART COMMISSION, appointed in 1924. At the south end of the open space adjoining these buildings, and facing over the Mall, is the NATIONAL MEMORIAL TO GEORGE VI (1895–1952), an excellent bronze statue by William McMillan, showing the king in the robes he customarily wore for the ceremonies of the Knights of the Garter. It stands in an architectural setting by Louis de Soissons (1955).

At the south-west corner of Waterloo Place and Pall Mall is the ATHENAEUM CLUB, the leading literary club of London, founded in 1824, with a famous library in which Thackeray wrote many of his works. The building, by Decimus Burton (1830), has a frieze below the cornice reproducing that of the Parthenon at Athens. Adjoining it in Pall Mall are the TRAVELLERS' CLUB, founded in 1819 for gentlemen who had travelled not less than 500 miles in a direct line from London (and outside Britain), and the REFORM CLUB, the premier Liberal club, established in 1832. The buildings (1832 and 1840) were modelled by Sir Charles Barry on Italian palazzi.

The short street opposite leads to ST JAMES'S SQUARE (VIII, A2), laid out after 1660 by Henry Jermyn, first Earl of St Albans, as a fashionable residential quarter. Most of the houses have been rebuilt at one time or another, and are now occupied for various other purposes. In the centre of the gardens is a good bronze equestrian statue of William III, by John Bacon the Younger (1808).

NORFOLK HOUSE (No. 31), at the south-east corner, the town house of the Dukes of Norfolk from 1723 until 1938, was rebuilt in 1939, and from it the allied commanders under General Eisenhower launched the invasions of North Africa (1942) and North-West Europe (1944). The first house on this site, lent in 1737–41 to Frederick, Prince of Wales, after he had been turned out of St James's Palace by his father, was the birthplace of George III in 1738. No. 32, rebuilt in 1792 by S. P. Cockerell, was the residence of the Bishops of London from 1771 until 1919. No. 4, in the north-east corner, is a fine Georgian house designed in 1725, probably by Edward Shepherd. On the north-east of the gardens is a memorial to Policewoman Yvonne Fletcher, who was shot nearby in 1984 during the siege of the Libyan People's Bureau.

On the north side of the Square (at No. 10) is CHATHAM HOUSE, built in 1736 by Henry Flitcroft and the residence of three Prime Ministers: the Earl of Chatham (1759–61), the Earl of Derby (1837–54), and W. E. Gladstone (1890). In 1923 it was presented by two Canadian citizens to the ROYAL INSTITUTE OF INTERNATIONAL AFFAIRS, founded in 1920 for the study of foreign affairs. On either side of the steps to the house are pillars carrying the original torch extinguishers. Nos. 11 and 12 are the headquarters of ACAS (the Advisory, Conciliation and Arbitration Service), an independent organization set up in 1975.

No. 14, in the north-west corner, houses the LONDON LIBRARY, the best-known subscription library in England, founded in 1841 by Thomas Carlyle and now containing about one million volumes. No. 15, with a fine classical façade by 'Athenian' Stuart (1763), was originally the home of the Duchess of Richmond ('La Belle Stuart'), who sat as model for the 'Britannia' on copper coins. Nos. 16–17 are occupied by the EAST INDIA, DEVONSHIRE, SPORTS AND PUBLIC SCHOOLS CLUB (founded originally in 1849); at No. 17 Queen Caroline resided while the bill to dissolve her marriage to George IV was brought before the House of Lords, while Lord Castlereagh, the Foreign Secretary involved in the case, lived next door at No. 18 (since rebuilt). The design of No. 20, built in 1775 by Robert Adam, has been reproduced at No. 21.

The road from the south-west corner of St James's Square returns to Pall Mall. To the west here No. 36 (rebuilt by T. P. Bennett and Son, 1963) is the ARMY AND NAVY CLUB, founded in 1837 and familiarly known as 'The Rag'. Opposite is the long façade of the ROYAL AUTOMOBILE CLUB, founded in 1897; the building (by Mewès and Davis, 1911) occupies the site of the old War Office, which had incorporated SCHOMBERG HOUSE, built about 1698. The west wing of this survives as No. 82, and here Thomas Gainsborough, the artist, lived from 1774 until his death in 1788; the east wing has been reproduced in exactly the same style. No. 79 stands on the site of a house that belonged to Nell Gwyn from 1671 until her death in 1687. Here, according to the diarist Evelyn, the former orange-seller used to talk over the garden wall to Charles II as he strolled in the park. No. 71, built by the brothers Smirke (1837), houses the UNITED OXFORD AND CAMBRIDGE UNIVERSITY CLUB, founded in 1830 and re-formed in 1972, while Nos. 48–9, on the right, are the headquarters of the ROYAL BRITISH LEGION, the organization of ex-servicemen formed in 1921 under Field-Marshal Earl Haig.

On the south side of Pall Mall is the inconspicuous entrance to MARLBOROUGH HOUSE (VIII, A2; pronounced 'Mawl-'), built by Sir Christopher Wren in 1709–11, but subsequently heightened and enlarged, to its detriment. It was the home of Queen Mary (the consort of George V) from 1936 until her death here in 1953, and in 1962 it was renovated as a Commonwealth conference and research centre (adm., p. 33). This has a reference library of books on Commonwealth subjects and a public information office on the ground floor.

The house was built for the first Duke of Marlborough, the victor of Blenheim, and his Duchess, the redoubtable Sarah, who after the death of the duke in 1722 until her own death in 1744 lived here in such magnificent style as to overshadow the court of George II ('Neighbour George') at St James's. Later occupants were Leopold I of Belgium (until his accession in 1831) and Queen Adelaide (d. 1849), and in 1850 the house was made the official residence of the Prince of Wales. George V was born here in 1865, and after his accession in 1910 the house became the home of Queen Alexandra, the widow of Edward VII.

On the north of the garden is a brick screen wall designed by Wren, now dwarfed by the buildings in Pall Mall; on the west is the Queen's Chapel (see below). The entrance to the house is from a porte-cochère or carriage porch, part of the extensions made by Sir James Pennethorne for Edward, Prince of Wales, between 1850 and 1863. Beyond the vestibule and a passage is the Saloon, rising two storeys to the original height of the house. Above the cornice are paintings of the Battle of Blenheim, part of a series by Louis Laguerre portraying the Duke of Marlborough's campaigns. The elaborate ceiling paintings, representing the Arts and Sciences, are the work of Orazio Gentileschi (1616) and were originally in the Queen's House at Greenwich. The chimneypiece of coloured marbles was probably inserted by Sir William Chambers when he heightened the building about 1700. Beyond the Saloon is the former State Drawing Room, remodelled by Pennethorne and now the main conference room. The handsome marble chimneypieces at each end date from the mid 18th century. To the right is the Prime Ministers' conference room, to the left the former State Dining Room, containing portraits from the royal collection, including the Family of Frederick, Prince of Wales, by Knapton (1751). The room beyond, formerly the Household Dining Room, retains its original arrangements. On the staircases to the first floor (no access) are large murals by Laguerre of the Battles of Ramillies (on the west) and Malplaquet.

The NATIONAL MEMORIAL TO QUEEN ALEXANDRA (1844–1925), designed by Sir Alfred Gilbert (1932), is in Marlborough Road, facing St James's Palace, and here also is the QUEEN'S CHAPEL, designed by Inigo Jones (1623–7) and intended as the private chapel of the Infanta Maria of Spain, a Roman Catholic, whom Prince Charles (later Charles I) was expected to marry. It was completed for Henrietta Maria, whom he did marry (1625), and refurnished for Catherine of Braganza on her marriage to Charles II in 1661. George III was married here in 1761 to Charlotte Sophia of Mecklenburg-Strelitz. The chapel is notable for its royal pews, its Carolean panelling and its elaborate coffered ceiling. Visitors are admitted to the services held on Sundays at 8.30 and 11.15 a.m. from Easter Day to the end of July and the chapel is included in the weekday tours of Marlborough House.

Pall Mall ends at the foot of St James's Street (see below). Nos. 1–2, on the right in this street, a Gothic brick building with stone surrounds by R. Norman Shaw (1882), contrasts with No. 88, by Shaw and Ernest Newton (1903), a stone building with ironwork balconies, on the opposite corner, facing down Pall Mall.

ST JAMES'S PALACE (VIII, A, B 1; no general adm.), facing up St James's Street, is a rambling and picturesque brick mansion of Tudor origin built round several courtyards. It was long the official London residence of the sovereign and the scene of all important court functions, and foreign ambassadors are still accredited 'to the Court of St James's'.

The palace takes its name from a leper hospital dedicated to St James the Less mentioned as early as the 12th century. This was dissolved in 1532 and in its place

Henry VIII built a royal palace, traditionally to the designs of Holbein, in which Mary I died in 1558. After the fall of Wolsey in 1529, Henry transferred his affections to Whitehall Palace, and although Charles II (1630), James II (1633), Mary II (1662), and Queen Anne (1665) were all born at St James's, it became the official residence of the sovereign only after Whitehall was burned down in 1698. George IV was born here in 1762, but in 1809 the south-east wing was destroyed by fire, and on her accession in 1837 Queen Victoria moved the court to Buckingham Palace. The Royal Levees, for gentlemen (discontinued in 1939), have been resumed here, but after 1861 the Drawing Rooms or Courts (for ladies) were transferred to Buckingham Palace.

The chief relic of the Tudor palace is the picturesque four-storeyed GATEHOUSE, or Clock Tower, retaining its original doors with linenfold panelling. It admits to the private Colour Court, which has a late-17th-century colonnade. Sentries, usually of the Guards' Division, patrol in front of the gatehouse and of the gate of Marlborough House. The approach to the State Apartments is on the east, through the open FRIARY COURT, from the balcony overlooking which the official proclamation of a new sovereign is made by the Heralds. To the west of the gatehouse is the entrance to the AMBASSADORS COURT, on the east side of which is the CHAPEL ROYAL, built about 1532 for Henry VIII, but much altered from time to time.

Visitors are admitted to the services held on Sundays at 8.30 and 11.15 a.m. (from the first Sunday in October until Palm Sunday, and on Good Friday) and to the choral service (at 11.30) on the Feast of the Epiphany (6 January), when royal gifts of gold, frankincense, and myrrh are offered. The gem of the chapel is the magnificent coffered ceiling painted in 1540 and attributed to Holbein. Charles I attended service in this chapel on the morning of his execution (1649) and many royal marriages have been celebrated here, including those of William III and Mary II (1677), Queen Anne (1683), George IV (1795), Queen Victoria (1840), and George V (1893). The choristers wear a Tudor costume of scarlet and gold; among former choristers or organists were the composers Thomas Tallis, William Byrd, John Bull, Orlando Gibbons, Henry Lawes, Henry Purcell, William Boyce, and Sir Arthur Sullivan.

St James's Palace is the headquarters of the Honourable Corps of GENTLEMEN AT ARMS, founded in 1509 by Henry VIII and now consisting of about thirty army officers with distinguished service records, under a captain (always a peer) whose appointment is political. The gentlemen, who form a personal bodyguard for the sovereign at royal levees, wear a resplendent uniform composed of scarlet tail-coats with gold epaulettes and white gauntlets, dark blue pantaloons and Wellington boots, and white plumed helmets. The palace is also the home of the Queen's Bodyguard of the YEOMEN OF THE GUARD, the oldest of the household corps, formed by Henry VII in 1485 (traditionally on the battlefield of Bosworth). The yeomen, who are not to be confused with the Yeomen Warders at the Tower, wear a picturesque royal red uniform of Tudor origin with purple and gold ornaments. Their familiar nickname of 'Beefeaters', popularly claimed to be derived from their fine physique or from the rations formerly served to them, is more probably a corruption of 'buffetiers du roy'. Together with the Gentlemen at Arms, they form the sovereign's dismounted bodyguard at state ceremonies.

Cleveland Row runs past the north side of St James's Palace and of YORK HOUSE, an extension of the palace occupied by Lord Kitchener in 1915–16, the Duke of Windsor (when Prince of Wales) in 1919–30, and the Duke of Gloucester (d. 1974), uncle of the Queen. On the left at the end of the street is STABLE YARD, facing which is the Lord Chamberlain's Office. To the south of this is CLARENCE HOUSE, one of the less successful designs of Nash, carried out in 1829 for William IV, then Duke of Clarence. The interior, much altered since, was restored in 1949 for Princess Elizabeth, who occupied the house until her accession in 1952. Princess Anne was born here in 1950, and Clarence House is now the home of Queen Elizabeth, the Queen Mother.

On the south side of Stable Yard rises LANCASTER HOUSE (VIII, B1; adm., p. 33), begun in 1825 by Benjamin Wyatt for the 'grand old' Duke of York, who died in 1827 before he could either pay for it or occupy it. Originally named York House, it was purchased by one of the Duke's creditors, the Marquess of Stafford (afterwards Duke of Sutherland), and completed by Sir Robert Smirke in 1840, Sir Charles Barry being responsible for much of the lavish decoration.

Under the second Duke of Sutherland, the house (renamed Stafford House) became a gathering point for liberal causes as well as a fashionable social and artistic centre. Queen Victoria often visited her friend the Duchess, saying 'I have come from my house to your palace'. The third Duke, a friend of Giuseppe Garibaldi, was visited by the Italian patriot here in 1864. In 1912 the house was bought by the first Viscount Leverhulme, who changed its name and presented it to the nation, and it became the home of the London Museum until 1941. After restoration from war damage the house is now used for international conferences and for banquets and other forms of government hospitality.

The entrance from Stable Yard is through a two-storeyed portico, leading to a low vestibule. The corridor to the left of this ends at the Garibaldi Room, which has a grey marble fireplace with a fine Italian mirror above. To the left is the East Dining Room, with notable console-tables, and to the right is the State Dining Room, which has decorated pelmets, carved fireplaces, and an unusual 18th-century clock supposed to have belonged to Napoleon. On the other side of this room are the Red Room and the Gold Room, the latter an ante-room to the Duke of Sutherland's Library (entered by a concealed doorway). The corridor on this side of the house gives access to the magnificent Staircase Hall, in the centre, rising to the full height of the building, with a huge lantern the richly decorated ceiling of which is supported by massive black caryatids. The coffered coving below this rests at the ends on fluted Corinthian columns supported by balconies. The walls of imitation marble have good copies by Lorenzi of paintings by Veronese.

The Grand Staircase, with a rococo-style balustrade, ascends to the main staterooms. The corridor on the west leads to an ante-room on the right of which is the West Drawing Room, formerly the Duchess's boudoir, with a ceiling painting representing the solar system, and on the left the State Drawing Room, which has a beautiful coffered ceiling and elaborate fireplaces. Beyond another ante-room is the Great Gallery, over 120 ft long, notable for its decoration, which includes a painting on the ceiling of the lantern by Guercino, previously in a church at Rome. The mantelpiece of the ornate marble fireplace supports a fine 18th-century French clock. On the north side of the building are the Veronese Room, which has a small ceiling painting by that master, and the Music Room, with another finely decorated ceiling. It was probably in this room that Chopin played before Queen Victoria in 1848, and here the Nine-Power Conference held its plenary meetings in 1954.

A passage from the west side of Stable Yard leads to GREEN PARK (Route 5), across which paths go on to Buckingham Palace and to Hyde Park Corner (Route 7). The arcade on the north of Stable Yard was added by Hawksmoor in 1717 to a house of about 1700 (No. 8 Cleveland Row). Overlooking the tiny Cleveland Square, farther north, is the delightful BRIDGEWATER HOUSE, built by Sir Charles Barry in 1845–9 in a rich Renaissance style for the Earl of Ellesmere.

ST JAMES'S STREET (VIII, A1), ascending north from St James's Palace, contains several well-known clubs and some interesting houses. No. 3 (wine merchants) and No. 6 (hatters), on the right, are fine examples of late-18th-century shop fronts. A passage beside No. 3 opens to the charming little court of PICKERING PLACE (1731). Byron House, farther up, replaces the house (No. 8) where Lord Byron 'awoke one morning to find himself famous' in 1811. No. 74, a building by George Basevi and Sydney Smirke (1843) on the other side of the street, stands on the site of the house in which Edward Gibbon, the historian, died in 1794. Nos. 69–70, built by Thomas Hopper about 1826, are now the CARLTON CLUB, the foremost Conservative club, founded by the Duke of Wellington in 1832, and moved here after its original home in Pall Mall had been bombed in 1941.

The narrow ST JAMES'S PLACE, opening on the west here, has a variety of pleasant old houses. Chopin stayed at No. 4 in 1848, on his return from Scotland. SPENCER HOUSE, on the left facing Green Park, is a large mansion in a classical style built in 1765 by John Vardy and restored in 1957 after war damage. No. 26, next to it, is a distinctive block of flats by Denys Lasdun (1959). No. 20 is the ROYAL OCEAN RACING CLUB, founded in 1925.

At No. 8 in KING STREET, on the other side of St James's Street, is CHRISTIE'S, the famous auction rooms, founded in 1766 and specializing in works of art. Louis Napoleon, later emperor of France, lived at No. 1c, also on the north side, in 1846–8.

No. 60 St James's Street, at the corner of Park Place, is BROOKS'S CLUB, founded by Charles James Fox and the Duke of Portland in 1764 and occupying a building by Henry Holland (1778). This was the leading club of the Whigs in the 18th century. At the farther end of Park Place are the headquarters and club of the ROYAL OVER-SEAS LEAGUE, founded in 1910 by Sir Evelyn Wrench to 'promote friendship and understanding amongst British subjects and Commonwealth citizens all over the world' and to encourage individual service to the Commonwealth. It now has over 50,000 members.

Opposite Park Place are the striking publishing offices of THE ECONOMIST, by Alison and Peter Smithson (1966), and beyond, in Ryder Street, are the offices of the CHARITY COMMISSION, constituted in 1853. At No. 28 in St James's Street is BOODLE'S CLUB, founded in 1762, in a building by John Crunden (1765). Farther up (at No. 37) is WHITE'S CLUB, the oldest club in London, evolved in 1693 from a coffee-house of the same name. This was the chief Tory club, the rival of Brooks's, and like both Brooks's and Boodle's was famous in the 18th century as the resort of men of fashion and wealthy gamblers. No. 50, a building by Benjamin Wyatt (1827) on the other side of the street, was formerly the DEVONSHIRE CLUB, established in 1875 in succession to 'Crockford's', a notorious 'gambling-hell'. St James's Street ends on the north at PICCADILLY, which runs east to Piccadilly Circus and west to Hyde Park Corner (see Route 7).

7 From Charing Cross to Hyde Park Corner via the Haymarket and Piccadilly

Plan III, F3–VII, B3

STATIONS: CHARING CROSS (Plan III, F3), on the Bakerloo, Jubilee, and Northern lines; EMBANKMENT (VIII, A3), on the Bakerloo, Circle, District, and Northern lines; PICCADILLY CIRCUS (III, F2), on the Bakerloo and Piccadilly lines; GREEN PARK (VIII, A1), on the Jubilee, Piccadilly, and Victoria lines;

HYDE PARK CORNER (VII, B2), on the Piccadilly line. — BUSES Nos. 9, 14, 19, 22, 25, 38, and 55 all ply along Piccadilly (No. 25 from Berkeley Street). For other buses in Regent Street (lower part) or Haymarket, see Route 6; to Piccadilly Circus, see Routes 15, 18; to Hyde Park Corner, see Routes 9, 10.

From CHARING CROSS to the foot of the HAYMARKET (III, F2), see Route 6. This street, the site of a market removed in 1830, ascends to the junction of Coventry Street and Piccadilly near Piccadilly Circus. On the left, at the corner of Pall Mall, is NEW ZEALAND HOUSE, the headquarters of the High Commissioner for New Zealand, a successful design by Sir Robert Matthew and Johnson-Marshall (1957–63), with a library, information and exhibition rooms, etc., for visitors, and other offices in a tower 225 ft high. On the north is HER MAJESTY'S THEATRE, built in 1897 in a flamboyant style by C. J. Phipps for Sir Herbert Beerbohm Tree, who was manager until his death in 1917.

The theatre stands on the site of the KING'S THEATRE, first opened in 1705 (as the Queen's Theatre), with William Congreve as manager, and renamed in 1714. From the outset it became the home of Italian opera, and *Rinaldo*, the first opera by Handel produced in England, was given here in 1711. Handel's operas continued to be staged (twenty-four in all) until 1734, and from 1729 he acted as his own impresario, in partnership with his early friend, John Jacob Heidegger. Handel's *Esther*, the first oratorio to be heard in England, was produced here in 1732. The theatre was rebuilt in 1791, after a fire, as the Opera House. Haydn conducted at concerts in 1795 (when his last three symphonies, Nos. 102–4, were first performed), but Italian opera continued to be the main attraction. The theatre was partly reconstructed in 1818, by John Nash and G. S. Repton, and of this building the ROYAL OPERA ARCADE survives (entered from Charles II Street, on the north). The name was changed in 1837 to its present form, and Jenny Lind, the 'Swedish nightingale', made her London debut in 1847. The theatre was rebuilt again, after another fire, in 1869, and Wagner's opera cycle, *The Ring*, received its first London production here in 1882.

On the east side of the road is the HAYMARKET THEATRE (officially the Theatre Royal, Haymarket), built in 1820 by John Nash and retaining its distinctive classical portico, though the interior was rebuilt in 1905 by C. Stanley Peach.

The theatre was first opened in 1720 as the LITTLE THEATRE. Susannah Maria Cibber, sister of the composer Thomas Arne, made her debut as a singer in 1733, in which year her husband, Theophilus Cibber (son of Colley Cibber, the actor), flouting the licensing laws, became the manager. Henry Fielding, the first of whose comedies, *Tom Thumb*, had been produced here in 1730, took over as manager in 1735. In 1742 the actor Samuel Foote became lessee and he got round the licensing laws (which required a royal patent) by selling tea and chocolate and offering the theatre tickets free. The building was renamed the THEATRE ROYAL in 1766 and Foote remained here until 1776. In Nash's new theatre of 1820, Samuel Phelps made his debut, in 1837, as Shylock in *The Merchant of Venice*, and Ellen Terry appeared here in 1863, at the age of fifteen. Sir Herbert Beerbohm Tree, the actor-manager, played at this theatre from 1887 to 1896.

Panton Street on the right, beyond the Haymarket Theatre, contains the COMEDY THEATRE, built in 1881 (by Thomas Verity) and restored in 1955. At Haymarket House (No. 28), farther up, is the DESIGN CENTRE (adm., p. 32), opened in 1956 by the Council of Industrial Design (founded in 1944; now the Design Council) for the display of the most recent designs in British furnishings and other products. The picturesque bow windows of the shop (formerly a tobacconist's) at No. 34 Haymarket, near the upper end, are a relic of late-18th-century London.

Immediately to the left at the top of the Haymarket is PICCADILLY CIRCUS (III, F2), one of the busiest traffic points in London, invariably crowded with jostling throngs of vehicles and people. The centre of London for the pleasure-seeker, it is at its most characteristic in the evening, when the electric signs all round are lit up.

Laid out in the late 19th century, the circus stands at the junction of five important streets: Piccadilly on the west; Regent Street (Route 15) running north-west to Oxford Street and Regent's Park, and south to Waterloo Place (Pall Mall; Route 6); Shaftesbury Avenue (Route 18) on the north-east, leading to Soho and Holborn; and Coventry Street (Route 20) on the east, giving access to Leicester Square.

In the centre of the circus is the SHAFTESBURY MEMORIAL, a bronze fountain in the form of a pyramid, designed by Sir Alfred Gilbert and topped by the figure in cast aluminium of a winged archer and his bow. Intended to represent the Angel of Christian Charity, but popularly known as 'Eros' (the Greek god of Love), it was erected in 1893 to the seventh Earl of Shaftesbury (d. 1885), the philanthropist. The figure, restored in 1985, is to be returned from a temporary home in the Royal Festival Hall early in 1986, when the south side of Piccadilly Circus, east of the lower part of Regent Street, will be laid out as a pedestrian precinct, with access to the memorial.

The characteristic block of Victorian buildings on the south of the circus includes the CRITERION THEATRE (by Thomas Verity, 1874), originally the wine cellar to a restaurant. Beneath the roadway, with entrances from every side, is PICCADILLY CIRCUS STATION, the largest underground station in London, designed by Charles Holden and opened in 1928. The Piccadilly 'tube', the busiest in London, was first opened in 1906 from Hammersmith to Finsbury Park as the Great Northern, Piccadilly, and Brompton Railway.

PICCADILLY (III, F2–VII, B3), which runs west for about a mile to Hyde Park Corner, is one of the fashionable shopping streets of London. It is said to derive its name from 'Piccadilly Hall', the popular name given to a house (since demolished) in what is now Great Windmill Street, built for himself in the 17th century by a retired tailor and maker of 'piccadils' (high collars or ruffs with laced or perforated edges), popular at the time. On the north side of the street is the NEW PICCADILLY HOTEL, by R. Norman Shaw (1908), with another frontage on Regent Street. The hotel was partly rebuilt behind its façades in 1985. Messrs SIMPSON'S, the men's outfitters, opposite in Piccadilly, by Joseph Emberton (1935), was a pioneer of large store design.

On the south of Piccadilly are the modern wrought-iron entrance gates of ST JAMES'S CHURCH (III, F1), which was designed by Sir Christopher Wren and built in 1676–84. Gutted by incendiary bombs in 1940, it was beautifully restored in 1954 by Sir Albert Richardson, and a new spire (of reinforced plastic) was added in 1968. The church was the most fashionable in London in the 18th century, and three of its rectors (Tenison, Wake, and Secker) became archbishops of Canterbury. It has galleries in the aisles and a decorated barrel vault covering the combined nave and chancel, supported by piers with Corinthian capitals. The white marble font (at which Lord Chesterfield, the Earl of Chatham, and William Blake, 'artist, poet, visionary', were baptized), the carved limewood altarpiece, and the organ case, salvaged from the bombing, are all by Grinling Gibbons. The organ, built by Renatus Harris in 1685 for Whitehall Palace and given to the church by Mary II, has been restored after war damage. The stained glass in the east windows is the work of Christopher Webb.

Among celebrities buried in the vaults are Charles Cotton (d. 1687), the angler, friend of Izaak Walton, and the Marquess of Queensberry (d. 1810), better known as 'Old Q'. The churchyard has been laid out in memory of the fortitude of Londoners during the Second World War, at the charge of Viscount Southwood (d. 1946), the newspaper proprietor, who is himself commemorated by a fountain by A. F. Hardiman. In the Church House, to the east, is the LONDON BRASS RUBBING CENTRE, with a collection of over sixty brasses and woodcuts. Admission is free (see p. 86), but a charge is made for rubbing which includes materials and assistance. The elegant MIDLAND BANK building on the north-west corner of the churchyard is by Sir Edwin Lutyens (1922).

SACKVILLE STREET, on the right farther on, is the first of several streets with pleasing Georgian houses in a modest style. Beyond it, set back behind a courtyard, is ALBANY (not The Albany), built in 1770 by Sir William Chambers, but converted in 1802 by Henry Holland into 'residential chambers for bachelor gentlemen'. It consists of suites of chambers flanking a covered passage running north to Burlington Gardens, but is not open to the public. Famous residents have included George Canning, Lord Byron, Bulwer Lytton, Lord Macaulay, and W. E. Gladstone.

BURLINGTON HOUSE (III, F1), the rather heavy Renaissance-style façade of which overshadows Piccadilly on the north, is the headquarters of the Royal Academy of Arts, as well as of the Society of Antiquaries and other learned societies, most of whose private rooms are normally open only by invitation. An imposing archway admits to a quadrangle in the centre of which is a statue of Sir Joshua Reynolds (d. 1792), by Alfred Drury. On the north side is Old Burlington House, redesigned in 1715 by the third Earl of Burlington, architect and patron of arts, who was assisted by Colen Campbell.

Handel occupied rooms at the back in 1715–18. In 1854 the building was sold for £140,000 to the government, who in 1866–9 added the upper storey and the entrance loggia, and built the wings on the east and west of the courtyard. The south wing, with the Piccadilly frontage, was added in 1874 by R. R. Banks and E. M. Barry.

Old Burlington House is the home of the ROYAL ACADEMY OF ARTS, founded in Pall Mall in 1768, with Sir Joshua Reynolds as its first president, moved in 1780 to Somerset House in the Strand, then in 1837 to the National Gallery, and finally in 1869 to its present quarters. It comprises about fifty Academicians (R.A.) and thirty Associates (A.R.A.), and vacancies are filled by the vote of all the members. In addition there are a number of Senior Academicians (over seventy-five years of age), while distinguished foreign artists may be elected Honorary Academicians. The Summer Exhibition of the Royal Academy, held regularly since 1769, is open from May usually until August (adm., p. 85) and consists of paintings, sculptures, engravings, and architectural designs by living artists not exhibited before in London. The private view of the exhibition and the Academy Dinner are fashionable and exclusive functions. Special loan exhibitions of outstanding interest are often held at which many works of art not otherwise accessible may be seen.

From the Front Hall in Old Burlington House a staircase ascends to the exhibition galleries, added in 1869 by Sydney Smirke, then goes on up to the Private Rooms of the Royal Academy, which contain diploma works presented on their election by Academicians; portraits of members, including self portraits by Reynolds and Gainsborough, and of royal patrons; sketchbooks of Romney and others; and a collection of historical relics (Reynolds' easel and painting-table, Queen Victoria's paint box, etc.). Here too is the 'Michelangelo Tondo', a relief of the Virgin and Child, the only sculpture by Michelangelo in Britain. Also housed in Burlington House are the ROYAL ACADEMY SCHOOLS, founded in 1768, and providing free tuition to students of approved ability. Famous pupils have included Constable, Lawrence, Turner, and Millais.

In the east wing of Burlington House are the headquarters of the GEOLOGICAL SOCIETY, founded in 1807, and the ROYAL SOCIETY OF CHEMISTRY, established in 1841 (as the Chemical Society). The west wing accommodates the SOCIETY OF ANTIQUARIES of London, the oldest society of its kind, founded in 1707 and incorporated in 1751. Its private rooms contain an important collection of early paintings (Tudor monarchs, etc.) and portraits of distinguished Fellows. Also in this wing are the ROYAL ASTRONOMICAL SOCIETY, incorporated in 1820, and the LINNEAN SOCIETY (for natural history), established in 1788 and named in honour of Carl von Linné (Linnaeus; d. 1778), the great Swedish botanist, whose library, manuscripts, and collection of biological specimens are preserved here.

To the west of Burlington House is the BURLINGTON ARCADE, a covered promenade with exclusive shops, running north to Burlington Gardens, which may be approached also from Regent Street (see Route 15). This privately owned arcade, the first shopping precinct of its kind in England, was built in 1819 by Samuel Ware for Lord George Cavendish, and still retains its Regency atmosphere. Beadles (ex-soldiers of the 10th Hussars) are on duty to enforce the rules. The arcade, 585 ft long, contains seventy-two shops whose original rents were £18 a year (£34 for a double shop). Over the Piccadilly entrance (recast by Beresford Pite in 1930) are the arms of the Chesham family, who sold the arcade in 1926 for £333,000. The PICCADILLY ARCADE, almost opposite, with its graceful bow-fronted shops, was built in 1910 by Thrale Jell.

Parallel to the Burlington Arcade is BOND STREET (II, E3–III, F1), which leads north to Oxford Street (Route 14) and is divided into Old Bond Street (the southern part, as far as Burlington Gardens) and New Bond Street. This 'High Street of Mayfair' is renowned for its highly fashionable costumiers and jewellers, and also contains many picture-dealers' galleries at which exhibitions are frequently held. At the corner of Bruton Street, which diverges left to Berkeley Square (Route 13), is the TIME AND LIFE BUILDING, designed by Michael Rosenauer (1952), with a balustrade including carving by Henry Moore. On the opposite corner of Conduit Street, which leads to Regent Street (Route 15), is the WESTBURY HOTEL, by the same architect (1955). At No. 34, higher up, is SOTHEBY'S (founded in 1744), the well-known auction rooms, and farther on New Bond Street crosses Brook Street, which runs left to Grosvenor Square (see Route 13) and right to Hanover Square (Route 15).

St James's Street, on the left of Piccadilly, descends to St James's Palace and Pall Mall (see Route 6). Albemarle Street, opposite, has some pleasant 18th-century houses. No. 21 is a classical building housing the Royal Institution of Great Britain (III, F1), founded in 1799 for the 'promotion, diffusion and extension of science and useful knowledge'. Among the most popular of its lectures are those for children given during the Christmas holidays. The work of two of its most famous members, Sir Humphry Davy, appointed professor of chemistry in 1802, and Michael Faraday, his assistant after 1813 and professor in 1833, is commemorated in the Faraday Museum (adm., p. 34), in the basement, which contains historic apparatus and a reconstruction of a research laboratory.

In Grafton Street, to the left at the end of Albemarle Street, Sir Henry Irving, the actor, lived in 1872–99 at No. 15a, on the corner, and Lord Brougham (d. 1868), who defended Queen Caroline at her trial, resided for thirty years at No. 4, one of a row of mansions built about 1750, probably by Sir Robert Taylor. The return to Piccadilly may be made by Dover Street, in which No. 40, rebuilt in 1957 after war damage, is the Arts Club, founded in 1863, while No. 37, now a publishing office, with a fine stone façade of about 1772 by Taylor, incorporates part of Ely House, the town house of the bishops of Ely until 1909.

The palatial Ritz Hotel (VIII, A1) on the south side of Piccadilly, designed by Mewès and Davis (1906) with an arcade over the pavement, was one of the first steel-framed buildings to be put up in London, though the exterior stonework obscures this fact.

In Arlington Street, on the east of the Ritz, Sir Robert Walpole, the Prime Minister, lived at No. 5 from 1742 until his death in 1745, while Wimborne House (No. 22), on the other side of the street, replaces another house of his in which his son, Horace Walpole, the author, was born in 1717.

Berkeley Street, on the opposite side of Piccadilly, leads north to Berkeley Square (Route 13), passing the May Fair Hotel (1927), incorporating a small theatre opened in 1963. Beyond Devonshire House, a huge block of flats and shops (1926), on the site of the London mansion of the Dukes of Devonshire, Piccadilly has Green Park (Route 5) on its south side. The wrought-iron gates into the park, attributed to Inigo Jones, were moved here from the old Devonshire House in 1921.

In Bolton Street, on the north, Fanny Burney (d. 1840), the novelist and diarist, lived at No. 11, and in Clarges Street, farther west, Charles James Fox (d. 1806), the politician, lived at No. 46. In Half Moon Street (at No. 42) is the Portland Club, established in 1816.

No. 94 in Piccadilly, a mid-18th-century mansion damaged by bombing, was the home of Lord Palmerston from 1855 until his death in 1865 and is occupied by the NAVAL AND MILITARY CLUB, founded in 1862, which has absorbed the COWDRAY CLUB for nurses and professional women (founded in 1922). No. 95 houses the AMERICAN CLUB, founded in 1919 for Americans in London, and the AMERICAN WOMEN'S CLUB, founded in 1899. White Horse Street, beyond this, gives access to Shepherd Market and Curzon Street (Route 13).

No. 105 in Piccadilly is the headquarters of the ARTS COUNCIL of Great Britain, established in 1946 to encourage the appreciation of the fine arts. Its Poetry Library is freely accessible to visitors (adm., see p. 77). No. 106 is a fine late-18th-century building with decoration by the brothers Adam. No. 127 is the CAVALRY AND GUARDS CLUB; the Cavalry Club, established in 1890 for officers of the mounted services, merged in 1976 with the Guards Club, founded in 1813. No. 128 houses the ROYAL AIR FORCE CLUB, established in 1918. Old Park Lane, leading to Park Lane (Route 13), opens on the right, and farther on, at the corner of Hamilton Place, is the HOTEL INTER-CONTINENTAL, an impressive building in the modern style by Sir Frederick Gibberd (1975).

Piccadilly ends on the west at Wellington Place, better known as HYDE PARK CORNER (VII, B2, 3), the busiest traffic centre in London, with well over 100 vehicles passing every minute during the day. Knightsbridge (Route 10), connected to Piccadilly by an underground motorway built in 1959–62, leads west towards Kensington, and Grosvenor Place runs south to Victoria Station (see Route 9). To the south-east, now isolated on an island in the traffic, rises the WELLINGTON ARCH, a triumphal arch designed by Decimus Burton (1828), surmounted by a large bronze quadriga or four-horse chariot with a figure of Peace by Adrian Jones (1912). It stands opposite the top of Constitution Hill (Route 5), which descends to Buckingham Palace. On the north side of the roadway, beyond Apsley House (see below), is the principal entrance to HYDE PARK (Route 12), which has a fine screen by Decimus Burton (1828), with a triple archway and notable ironwork gates; the reliefs over the centre arch (by John Henning) are copied from the Parthenon frieze at Athens.

On the island in the roadway opposite Apsley House is a bronze equestrian statue of the Duke of Wellington (see below), by Boehm, on a pedestal at the corners of which are a Grenadier Guard, a Highlander, a Welch Fusilier, and an Inniskilling

Dragoon. To the south-west of the monument is the ROYAL ARTILLERY WAR MEMORIAL for both World Wars, by C. S. Jagger (1928), and to the east is the MACHINE GUN CORPS MEMORIAL for 1914–18, by F. Derwent Wood (1925), with a fine if inappropriate figure of David ('Saul has slain his thousands, but David his tens of thousands'). On the west side of the road is a rather austere building of 1829 by William Wilkins (since enlarged), formerly the ST GEORGE'S HOSPITAL, founded in 1733. The hospital, with the medical school established at least as early as 1756, was rehoused in 1980 at Tooting, in south London, and a new use is yet to be found for the building.

APSLEY HOUSE (VII, B3), the last house in Piccadilly ('No. 1, London'), next to the Hyde Park entrance, was long the residence of the great Duke of Wellington (1769–1852). Pesented to the nation in 1947 by the seventh duke, it was opened in 1952 as the WELLINGTON MUSEUM (adm., p. 35). The house contains numerous relics of the 'Iron Duke' and valuable paintings, silver plate, and porcelain collected by him.

The house, built in 1771–8 by the brothers Adam for Henry Bathurst, Baron Apsley and Earl Bathurst, was bought in 1805 by the Marquess Wellesley, eldest brother of the Duke of Wellington, and sold by him in 1817 to the duke, who had lived here since the previous year. In 1828–9 the house was altered by Benjamin Wyatt, who added the Corinthian portico and the west wing, including the Waterloo Gallery, and re-faced the whole of the brick exterior with Bath stone. The Duke of Wellington made Apsley House his permanent London home, quitting the army for politics and becoming Prime Minister in 1828–30. For his opposition to the Reform Bill brought in by Lord Grey he suffered a period of unpopularity; after the windows of his house had been broken by rioters in 1831, iron shutters had to be put up, but these were removed in 1856. After his appointment as Lord Warden of the Cinque Ports (1829) he lived much at Walmer Castle (Kent) and he died there in 1852 at the age of eighty-three.

The Entrance Hall has portraits and robes of the Duke. To the left is the Plate and China Room (formerly the Muniment Room), which contains a notable collection of orders and decorations conferred on him, as well as his swords, batons, and many other personal relics, and beautiful silver and services of Sèvres, Meissen, and other porcelain given to him by British and foreign royalty. Remarkable are the silver-gilt Wellington Shield of 1821–2, with scenes from the Duke's campaigns; the Wellington Vase, presented in 1825; and two candelabra presented in 1816 by the merchants and bankers of the City of London. The Inner Hall, on the right of the Entrance Hall, has busts of the Duke by Chantrey (1823) and Sir John Steell (1846) and his uniform as a colonel of the Grenadier Guards.

From the Vestibule beyond, which has a heroic marble statue of Napoleon by Canova, the staircase (by Benjamin Wyatt, 1828) ascends to the First Floor, where the rooms contain numerous fine paintings by Flemish, Dutch, and Spanish masters. The Piccadilly Drawing Room, a finely decorated room by Adam (1774) on the left of the landing, has paintings of the Chelsea and Greenwich Pensioners by Sir David Wilkie and John Burnet. The Portico Room, beyond, was remodelled by Wyatt. The Waterloo Gallery, 90 ft long, is named from the Waterloo Banquets held here annually from 1830 until the Duke's death, and attended by his senior officers who took part in the great victory over the French. The two large candelabra of Siberian porphyry were given by the Emperor Nicholas I of Russia. In this room also are some of the finest paintings, including works by Correggio ('Agony in the Garden'), Rubens, Ribera, Velazquez, Murillo, and Sassoferrato, many of which were captured after the Battle of Vitoria (1813) from Joseph Bonaparte (by whom they had been looted from the Spanish royal collections) and afterwards bestowed on the Duke by Ferdinand VII. Here also is an equestrian portrait of the Duke by Goya (1812).

The Yellow Drawing Room, beyond, has a portrait of William IV, by Wilkie, and in the Striped Drawing Room are a fine portrait of the Duke by Lawrence (1814) and others of his companions in arms, and a painting of the Battle of Waterloo done in 1843 by Sir William Allan. The Dining Room contains part of the elaborate Portuguese Service, presented to the Duke in 1816 by the Prince Regent of Portugal, and portraits of contemporary monarchs, including George IV (in Highland costume) by Wilkie. The Waterloo Banquets were held in this room from 1820 to 1829. In the Slip Corridor are displayed part of a silver-gilt service made in London in 1807–15, Meissen, Sèvres, and Viennese porcelain, and another part of the Portuguese Service. In the Basement are caricatures, maps of the Duke's campaigns, etc., and the museum's extensive reference collection.

8 From Victoria to Battersea Bridge (Chelsea)

Plan VII, C3 — beyond VI, F3.
STATIONS: VICTORIA (Plan VIII, C1), on the Southern Region and the Circle, District, and Victoria lines; SLOANE SQUARE (VII, D2), on the Circle and District lines. — BUSES Nos. 2, 10, 11, 16, 24, 25, 29, 36, 38, 39, 52, 55, 70, 76, 149, 185, 500, and 507 to Victoria Station (others in Grosvenor Place, see Route 9); No. 137 (from Knightsbridge) in Chelsea Bridge Road; Nos. 19, 39, 45, and 49 across Battersea Bridge (45 and 49 from South Kensington); and Nos. 11, 19, and 22 in King's Road.

For VICTORIA STATION, see Route 4. BUCKINGHAM PALACE ROAD, leaving Grosvenor Gardens (Route 4) on the right, runs southward alongside the station.

On the left is ECCLESTON BRIDGE (VII, D3), a principal changing-point for Green Line services, from which Belgrave Road (compare Route 3) goes on past ECCLESTON SQUARE, well laid out for Thomas Cubitt in 1835. No. 25, on the north side, is the INSTITUTION OF MUNICIPAL ENGINEERS, founded in 1873.

In ECCLESTON STREET, which starts opposite Eccleston Bridge, No. 39 is the office of the NATIONAL FEDERATION OF WOMEN'S INSTITUTES, founded in 1915. The road crosses EBURY STREET, a long thoroughfare leading to the right to Grosvenor Gardens. George Moore, the novelist ('the sage of Ebury Street'), died in 1933 at No. 121, to the left, and Mozart composed his first symphony in 1764 (at the age of eight) at No. 180, near the south end.

In Buckingham Palace Road, farther on, at the corner of Elizabeth Street, is the large VICTORIA COACH STATION (VII, D3), designed by Wallis, Gilbert & Partners and opened in 1932. Buckingham Palace Road ends beyond AIRWAYS HOUSE (1939; extended 1960 and 1965), built as the headquarters of the British Overseas Airways Corporation, founded in 1939 and now part of British Airways, established in 1972. The sculpture over the entrance is by E. R. Broadbent.

PIMLICO ROAD, branching to the right here, passes the south end of Ebury Street (see above) and near ST BARNABAS' CHURCH, a pioneer church of the Anglo-Catholic movement, designed by Thomas Cundy (1847–9). It is prolonged beyond Chelsea Bridge Road by ROYAL HOSPITAL ROAD, which passes the main entrance to the **Chelsea Royal Hospital**, and the NATIONAL ARMY MUSEUM (adm., p. 354. In Chelsea Bridge Road are the CHELSEA BARRACKS, rebuilt in 1962 in a modern style (by Tripe and Wakeham) and quartering regiments of the Guards' Division. The road is extended on the north by Lower Sloane Street, leading to Sloane Square (Route 9).

EBURY BRIDGE ROAD, bearing left past characteristic blocks of flats, goes on south of Chelsea Barracks (see above) to Chelsea Bridge Road, which leads left to CHELSEA BRIDGE (VII, F3), a suspension bridge 700 ft long, rebuilt in 1934–7 by G. Topham Forrest and E. P. Wheeler, crossing the Thames to Battersea Park. Grosvenor Road (see Route 4) leads east along the river from this point to Vauxhall Bridge.

CHELSEA EMBANKMENT (VII, F1–3), a fine esplanade laid out by Sir Joseph Bazalgette in 1874, extends for just over a mile from

Chelsea Bridge to Battersea Bridge, with a view of Battersea Park on the opposite bank of the Thames. On the right the embankment skirts the CHELSEA HOSPITAL GARDENS, from which there is a noble prospect of the delightful brick buildings of the Royal Hospital. The gardens are the setting in May of the colourful Chelsea Flower Show, first held in 1913.

TITE STREET, to the west of the gardens, was once greatly favoured by artists. Augustus John lived for a time at No. 33 and J. S. Sargent, the American painter, occupied No. 31 for twenty-four years until his death here in 1925. James McNeill Whistler lived at No. 46 in 1888 and Oscar Wilde lived at No. 34 after his marriage (1884) until his trial in 1895, writing several of his best-known plays.

On the Embankment is a group of interesting Victorian houses: No. 3, by Bodley and Garner (1876), Nos. 4–6, by Edward Godwin (1880), and Nos. 8–11, by R. Norman Shaw (after 1880). Beyond is the charming old-world CHELSEA PHYSIC GARDEN (VII, F1; adm. p. 31). In the centre is a statue by Rysbrack (1737) of Sir Hans Sloane, who purchased the manor of Chelsea in 1712. In 1723 he presented the garden (for an annual rent of £5) to the Society of Apothecaries, who had leased it in 1673. Towards the end of the 19th century the garden became neglected and in 1899 responsibility for its upkeep was undertaken by the Trustees of the London Parochial Charities. Cotton seed was first sent from the garden to America in 1732, and seeds and specimens of plants are exchanged today with research workers all over the world. The garden is entered on the east from SWAN WALK, which has some good 18th-century houses.

SWAN HOUSE, No. 17 in Chelsea Embankment, is a characteristic design by Norman Shaw (1875–7). To the west of the point where it is joined by Royal Hospital Road (see above), the Embankment is separated by a line of public gardens from CHEYNE WALK (VII, F1; pronounced 'Chainy'), a delightful row of early Georgian dwellings (1718), though with some Victorian insertions. Many of the houses retain their excellent wrought-iron gates, railings, and balconies. No. 4 was the home of the painter Daniel Maclise in 1861–70, and 'George Eliot' (Mary Ann Evans) died here in 1880 after a residence of less than three weeks. No. 16 (the Queen's House), the best of the row, was occupied in 1862–82 by D. G. Rossetti, who maintained his menagerie in the garden. Swinburne and Meredith also lived here for a time.

Farther on is the ALBERT BRIDGE (beyond VII, F1), a combined cantilever and suspension bridge by R. W. Ordish (1873), crossing the river to the west end of Battersea Park. Immediately west of the approach is a figure of Atalanta by F. Derwent Wood (d. 1926), set up as a memorial to the sculptor. In OAKLEY STREET, which leads north from the bridge to King's Road, No. 56 was the home of Captain R. F. Scott (d. 1912), the Antarctic explorer.

Nos. 46–9 in Cheyne Walk, west of the Albert Bridge, are a charming group of early-18th-century houses, and in the gardens just beyond is a good bronze statue by Boehm of the author Thomas Carlyle (1882). It stands opposite the entrance to CHEYNE ROW, a quiet street running north from the river, with a terrace of modest brick houses built in 1708. In one of these (No. 24; formerly No. 5), now called CARLYLE'S HOUSE (VI, F3; adm., p. 31), Thomas Carlyle (1795–1881) and his wife Jane Welsh (1801–66) lived from 1834 until the end of their lives. *The French Revolution* (1834–7), *Heroes and Hero-Worship* (1840), *Past and Present* (1843), and *Frederick the Great* (1853–65) were all written here. The small but dignified house, purchased through the efforts of a group of admirers in 1895 and presented to the National Trust in 1936, remains very much as it was in the time of the Carlyles, with the furniture, etc., used by them. Cases contain books and letters of the 'Sage of Chelsea', as well as many personal relics, and on the walls hang portraits of the Carlyles and photographs and drawings of places with which they are associated. On the topmost floor is the Attic Study, with the large skylight and double walls added by Carlyle in 1853 in a vain attempt to find light and quiet. Visitors may also see the Kitchen in the basement, where Carlyle and Tennyson used to smoke until a late hour, and the little Garden, where Mrs Carlyle's favourite dog, 'Nero', is buried.

Cheyne Row ends at UPPER CHEYNE ROW, where Leigh Hunt, the essayist, lived in 1833–40 at No. 22, one of a number of houses of about 1716. Tobias Smollett, the novelist, lived in 1750–62 at No. 16 in LAWRENCE STREET (to the west), one of several mid-18th-century houses. In this street the famous Chelsea porcelain works flourished from about 1745 until 1784, when they were removed to Derby. In CARLYLE MANSIONS, a block of flats facing the Embankment to the west of Cheyne Row, Henry James, the American novelist, died in 1916 at No. 21.

CHELSEA OLD CHURCH (beyond VI, F3), on the Embankment, founded at least as early as the 12th century but rebuilt at various times, was devastated by a land mine in 1941, when the tower, nave, and aisles were destroyed and the chancel and north chapel gravely damaged. The south chapel, rebuilt in 1528 by Sir Thomas More, fortunately survived the explosion, as did the single arch with its two Renaissance capitals (wrongly attributed to Holbein) opening to the chancel. In the More Chapel are monuments to Sir Robert Stanley (d. 1632) and Lady Jane Guildford, Duchess of Northumberland (d.

1556), and a tablet to Henry James (see above). The chancel, well restored in 1954 by Walter H. Godfrey, has in its south wall a 16th-century monument to Sir Thomas More, who settled in Chelsea about 1524 and counted Erasmus and Holbein among his famous visitors. His first wife was buried here in 1532 and More intended this to be the resting place of himself and his second wife. After his execution in 1535, his head (now at Canterbury) was fixed on London Bridge; his body was buried in St Peter's in the Tower, but may have been moved here later by his daughter Margaret.

In the north or Lawrence Chapel, Henry VIII is thought to have been secretly married to Jane Seymour on 20 May 1536, several days before their official marriage. This chapel, likewise restored, contains a monument to Sara Colvile (d. 1631), with an unusual effigy (a demi-figure rising in a shroud), and a tablet to William de Morgan, perhaps best known as a novelist, who had a pottery in Cheyne Row in 1872–82. The nave and tower were rebuilt in their former (17th-century) style by W. H. Godfrey and the whole church was reconsecrated in 1958. The 17th-century font and pulpit have been replaced. On the north wall is a monument to Lady Jane Cheyne (d. 1669), attributed to Bernini, and on the south is an altar-tomb with effigies of Lord Dacre of the South and his wife (1595). Here also are chained books given to the church by Sir Hans Sloane (d. 1753), whose collections formed the nucleus of the British Museum and whose tomb is in the south-east corner of the churchyard. On the Embankment, close by, is a statue of Sir Thomas More (by L. Cubitt Bevis, 1969).

Farther west is CROSBY HALL (adm., p. 32), an international hall of residence of the British Federation of University Women, founded in 1907. Built in 1927 by Walter H. Godfrey, it incorporates (on the east side) the great hall of Crosby Place, a sumptuous mansion erected in Bishopsgate in 1466–75 by Sir John Crosby, a London alderman and wool merchant, and later supposed to have been occupied by the Duke of Gloucester, afterwards Richard III.

The hall escaped destruction when the house was burned down in the 17th century, and in 1910 it was brought from Bishopsgate and re-erected on its present site. Now used as a dining hall, it retains its fine oak roof and a lofty oriel window with the crest of Sir John Crosby in the vaulting. Behind the Jacobean high table is one of the three copies of Holbein's painting of Sir Thomas More and his family made by the artist for More's three daughters. In DANVERS STREET, to the east of Crosby Hall, Sir Alexander Fleming (d. 1955), the discoverer of penicillin, lived at No. 20, one of a row of mid-19th-century houses.

The Embankment ends at BATTERSEA BRIDGE (beyond VI, F3), an ugly iron structure of 1887–90 by Bazalgette replacing the picturesque wooden bridge of 1772, a favourite subject of Whistler, Turner, and other artists. BEAUFORT STREET, crossing the site of Beaufort House, the manor house (pulled down in 1740) of Sir Thomas More and later of Sir Hans Sloane, runs north from the bridge to King's Road (see below), the main thoroughfare of Chelsea.

There are some interesting old houses in that part of CHEYNE WALK extending west of the bridge. Nos. 91–2, on the corner of Beaufort Street, are notable houses of about 1771. Elizabeth Stevenson (Mrs Gaskell, the novelist) was born in 1810 at No. 93, another 18th-century house, and J. McN. Whistler lived in 1868–78 at No. 96. LINDSEY HOUSE (N.T.; no adm.) was built in 1674 by the third Earl of Lindsey and retains its original façade, but it was altered internally in 1752 (when it became the London headquarters of the Moravian brotherhood) and was subdivided into several houses in 1774. Notable residents have included Sir Marc Brunel and his son Isambard, the civil engineers (in 1811–26). No. 101 was the first London home of Whistler (1863–6), Walter Greaves (in 1855–97) and Hilaire Belloc (in 1900–5) lived at No. 104, P. Wilson Steer died in 1942 at No. 109, and J. M. W. Turner lived anonymously at No. 119 (restored after war damage) from 1846 until his death in 1851. The road goes on to the huge LOTS ROAD POWER STATION, built in 1905 to provide electricity for the underground railways, while Cremorne Road turns away from the river for King's Road and Fulham (see Suburban London).

The return towards Victoria may be made by KING'S ROAD (VI, F2–VII, D2), which runs north-east to Sloane Square (Route 9). PARK WALK, on the north, west of Beaufort Street (see above), retains a fine Regency terrace. PAULTON'S SQUARE, on the right east of Beaufort Street, and CARLYLE SQUARE, on the left farther on, are characteristic squares of 1830–40.

OLD CHURCH STREET, to the west of Carlyle Square, has good early-19th-century terraces, No. 127 in which was the home of William de Morgan (d. 1917), potter and novelist. Bolton Lodge (No. 143) houses the CHELSEA ARTS CLUB (founded in 1891), of which Whistler and Wilson Steer were early members. Two pioneer examples of housing in the modern style are No. 64 (by Erich Mendelsohn and Serge Chermayeff) and No. 66 (by Walter Gropius and Maxwell Fry); both were built in 1936. MULBERRY WALK, farther west, has early-20th-century houses in a modified Dutch style. In MALLORD STREET, south of this, A. A. Milne (d. 1956), the author, lived at No. 13, and Augustus John (d. 1961) lived in a house built for him in 1908–12 and said to be a copy of Rembrandt's house in Amsterdam.

On the left of King's Road, to the east (and partly in Manresa Road), is CHELSEA COLLEGE (VI, E, F3), founded in 1891 (as the Chelsea Polytechnic) and since 1966 a school of London University. It has faculties in branches of education, engineering, medicine, and science, and a library of over 130,000 volumes. GLEBE PLACE, opposite Manresa Road, has many interesting studio houses of about 1850–70, among them No. 48, which belonged to Charles Rennie Mackintosh, the architect. Thomas Augustine Arne, the composer, lived at No. 215 King's Road, a house of 1720, and a later occupant (in 1904–20) was Ellen Terry, the actress. ARGYLL HOUSE, just beyond, at the corner of Oakley Street, was built in 1723 by Giacomo Leoni, the Venetian architect. CHELSEA LIBRARY, farther on, formerly the Town Hall, was built by J. M. Brydon (1887), but has a façade added in 1908 by Leonard Stokes.

Sydney Street, opposite the library, leads to ST LUKE'S CHURCH (VI, E3), the parish church of Chelsea, built in 1820–24 by James Savage and the earliest stone-vaulted church of the Gothic Revival. Charles Dickens was married here in 1836 to Catherine Hogarth, and the father of the novelists Charles and Henry Kingsley was rector in 1836–60, Charles serving as his curate for a time. Sydney Street ends on the north at Fulham Road (see Route 9).

ROYAL AVENUE, on the right of King's Road farther east, was laid out in 1694 and affords a glimpse of the Royal Hospital as it leads to ST LEONARD'S TERRACE, on the north side of Burton's Court, where Nos. 14–32 are among the best 18th-century houses in Chelsea. 'Mark Twain' lived in 1896–7 at No. 23 in TEDWORTH SQUARE, to the south-west. The main road, passing the DUKE OF YORK'S HEADQUARTERS, built in 1801 by John Sanders for the Duke of York's School (moved to Dover in 1909) and now the headquarters of the Greater London Territorial Auxiliary Forces, leads to Sloane Square (Route 9).

9 From Hyde Park Corner to South Kensington via Belgravia

Plan VII, B2 – beyond VI, D1

STATIONS: HYDE PARK CORNER (Plan VII, B2), on the Piccadilly line; SLOANE SQUARE (VII, D2), on the Circle and District lines; SOUTH KENSINGTON (VI, D3) and GLOUCESTER ROAD (VI, D2), on the Circle, District, and Piccadilly lines; EARLS COURT (beyond VI, D1), on the District and Piccadilly lines. — BUSES to Hyde Park Corner, see Routes 7, 10; Nos. 2, 16, 25, 36, 38, 52, 55, and 500 in Grosvenor Place; Nos. 11, 19, 22, and 137 to Sloane Square; Nos. 14 and 45 in Fulham Road; No. 30 in Old Brompton Road; Nos. 31 and 74 in Earls Court Road or Warwick Road.

For HYDE PARK CORNER, see Route 7. An alternative route thence to South Kensington runs via Knightsbridge and Brompton Road (Route 10). The route described below, starting via Grosvenor

Place, goes through the district of BELGRAVIA, which superseded Mayfair as the most fashionable residential quarter in London. With its spacious squares and aristocratic mansions, it was laid out in 1825 and onwards by Thomas Cubitt, who employed George Basevi, the pupil of Sir John Soane, as his principal architect.

GROSVENOR PLACE (VII, B, C3) runs south-east from Hyde Park Corner. In HALKIN STREET, on the right, No. 9 is the CALEDONIAN CLUB, founded in 1891 for Scotsmen. No. 13 in Grosvenor Place is the ROYAL SOCIETY OF HEALTH, formerly the Royal Sanitary Institute, founded in 1876, and No. 17 is the IRISH EMBASSY. Hobart House, farther on, contains the offices of the NATIONAL COAL BOARD, constituted in 1946. Grosvenor Place is extended by Grosvenor Gardens (see Route 4) towards Victoria Station.

GROSVENOR CRESCENT (VII, B2), on the right of Grosvenor Place south of Hyde Park Corner, leads to the north end of Belgrave Square.

Nos. 9–10 in the crescent are the headquarters of the BRITISH RED CROSS SOCIETY, founded in 1908, and No. 1 is the head-office of the ST JOHN AMBULANCE ASSOCIATION AND BRIGADE (compare Route 29). At No. 17, on the other side, is the INSTITUTION OF GAS ENGINEERS, founded in 1863.

BELGRAVE SQUARE (VII, C2), perhaps the most notable of London's many squares, has on each side an exceptionally fine range of buildings in a classical style designed by Basevi (1825–7), while three of the corners are occupied by large handsome mansions. SEAFORD HOUSE, on the east corner, designed by Philip Hardwick, was the residence of Lord John Russell, the statesman, in 1841–70, and is now the Royal College of Defence Studies. No. 24, on the south, built by Henry E. Kendall for Thomas Kemp, the creator of Kemp Town at Brighton, is occupied by the SPANISH EMBASSY, and several other embassies have houses in the square.

No. 3, in the north-west range, was the residence of the Duke of Kent (d. 1942), uncle of the Queen, and the philanthropic Earl of Shaftesbury died in 1885 at No. 5. Henry Hallam, the historian, died in 1859 at No. 24 in WILTON CRESCENT, which is north-west of Belgrave Square, and in a later and more restrained style. Hence, Wilton Place (Route 10) goes on to Knightsbridge.

Nos. 14–15, on the south-west side of Belgrave Square, house the SOCIETY OF CHEMICAL INDUSTRY. No. 14 was formerly the residence of the Duke of Norfolk, while Nos. 15–16 were occupied by the Duke of Bedford. No. 17 is the ROYAL COLLEGE OF PSYCHIATRISTS, refounded in 1971, and Nos. 19–20 are the headquarters of the NATURE CONSERVANCY, incorporated in 1949. No. 32, on the south-east side, is the ROYAL COLLEGE OF VETERINARY SURGEONS, founded in 1844. No. 39, on the north-east, is the ITALIAN INSTITUTE OF CULTURE and No. 47 houses the INSTITUTE OF PHYSICS, founded in 1874. In the gardens is a statue, by Hugo Daini (1974), of Simón Bolívar (d. 1830), the liberator.

Cadogan Place (see below) may be reached direct from Belgrave Square by following CHESHAM PLACE to the south-west (from the south corner) and bearing right into Pont Street. Lord John Russell (d. 1878), the statesman, lived from 1870 at No. 36, on the south side. No. 1 (on the north) is the office of KING GEORGE'S FUND FOR SAILORS, instituted in 1917.

UPPER BELGRAVE STREET leads south-east from Belgrave Square to Eaton Square. Nos. 10–11, in a Regency terrace (left), house the ROYAL INSTITUTION OF NAVAL ARCHITECTS, founded in 1860, and the INSTITUTION OF STRUCTURAL ENGINEERS, established in 1908. Walter Bagehot, the political economist, lived in 1862–70 at No. 12, now the INSTITUTE OF HOUSING.

CHESTER STREET and WILTON STREET, on the same side, have good early-19-century terraces in a modest style. In EATON PLACE, on the right, Lord Kelvin, the scientist, lived at No. 15 and Lord Avebury (Sir John Lubbock) was born in 1834 at No. 29. Field-Marshal Sir Henry Wilson was shot on the doorstep of his house (No. 36) by members of Sinn Fein in 1922. Chopin gave his first London recital in 1848 at No. 99.

The long EATON SQUARE (VII, D2–C3), laid out by Thomas Cubitt in about 1840, has pleasant gardens traversed by the eastward extension of King's Road, with distinguished terraces on both sides. Facing the north-east end, at the corner of Hobart Place, which leads to Grosvenor Gardens (compare above), is the church of ST PETER'S, EATON SQUARE, rebuilt in a classical style by Sir Arthur Blomfield (1875) and the setting for many fashionable weddings.

Lower Belgrave Street goes on from the church to Buckingham Palace Road (Route 8). CHESTER SQUARE, on the right, was laid out in about 1836 by Joseph Cundy. Matthew Arnold (d. 1888), the poet and critic, lived at No. 2, and Mary Wollstonecraft Godwin, second wife of the poet Shelley, died in 1851 at No. 24.

Thomas Cubitt (d. 1855), builder and town planner, lived at No. 3 in LYALL STREET, on the right of Eaton Square. George Peabody, the American philanthropist, died in 1869 at No. 80, near the west end of the square, and Viscount Cecil (d. 1958), a principal creator of the League of Nations, lived at No. 16 in SOUTH EATON PLACE, to the left.

King's Road is extended by Eaton Gate and Cliveden Place south-west to SLOANE SQUARE (VII, D2), which is chiefly notable for the department store of PETER JONES, one of the most striking in London, designed by William Crabtree (in association with Slater and

Moberley and Sir Charles Reilly) and built in 1936–9. In the shady centre of the square is a fountain with sculpture by Gilbert Ledward (1953), and on the east side is the ROYAL COURT THEATRE, built in 1888 (by Walter Emden and W. R. Crewe) and remodelled in 1965. The earlier plays of Bernard Shaw were produced here (in 1904–7) by Harley Granville-Barker. A second and smaller auditorium (1969) is called The Theatre Upstairs.

From Sloane Square, King's Road goes on south-west through Chelsea (see Route 8), while the long SLOANE STREET runs north, passing HOLY TRINITY CHURCH, an 'Arts and Crafts' church by J. D. Sedding (1890), with decoration by Harry Wilson and others and magnificent stained glass by Burne-Jones. The Gothic vault, damaged by bombing, was reconstructed in 1960. In CADOGAN PLACE, farther on, enclosing the largest square in London, William Wilberforce, the abolitionist, died at No. 44 in 1833. On the west side, north of Pont Street, is the DANISH EMBASSY, designed by Arne Jacobsen, with Dissing and Weitling (1975). On the north side is the CARLTON TOWER HOTEL, designed by Michael Rosenauer and opened by an American company in 1961.

Sloane Street goes on to Knightsbridge station (Route 10), while PONT STREET runs west from Cadogan Place through a district formerly known as Hans Town (and named, like Sloane Street, in honour of Sir Hans Sloane). It was laid out about 1780 by Henry Holland, but much of it was rebuilt in the late 19th century in a hideously ornate style satirized by Sir Osbert Lancaster as 'Pont Street Dutch'. Lillie Langtry (d. 1929), the actress, friend of Edward VII, lived in Pont Street at No. 21 (now a hotel).

In HANS PLACE, north of Pont Street, there survive some 18th-century houses. Sir George Alexander (d. 1918), the actor-manager, lived at No. 57 Pont Street, and Arnold Bennett (d. 1931), the novelist, spent the latter part of his life at No. 75 in CADOGAN SQUARE, to the south.

ST COLUMBA'S CHURCH of Scotland (VII, C1), facing Pont Street at its west end, was founded in 1884, destroyed by bombing in 1941, and rebuilt in 1950–55, by Sir Edward Maufe, in an austere but satisfying style. Over the west door is a figure of the saint, and the circular window in the east gable (by Moira Forsyth) shows the cross of St Andrew. The south chapel was dedicated in 1956 as a memorial to the fallen of the London Scottish Regiment.

Beyond the church, Pont Street is extended to Brompton Road by

Beauchamp Place (see Route 10), from which WALTON STREET, with long brick and stucco-fronted terraces of about 1840, runs south-west to Draycott Avenue, which also leads (to the right) to Brompton Road. OVINGTON STREET, Hasker Street, and First Street, on the south of Walton Street, all have unspoiled terraces of the same period.

BROMPTON ROAD (VI, C, D3), from which Pelham Street goes on west to South Kensington station, is extended by the long FULHAM ROAD, passing PELHAM CRESCENT (on the right) and PELHAM PLACE, laid out by George Basevi in 1820–30. On the left are SYDNEY STREET, with good early-19th-century terraces, leading past St Luke's Church (Route 8), and the ROYAL MARSDEN HOSPITAL (formerly the Royal Cancer Hospital), established in 1815 by William Marsden and occupying buildings of 1859–85. It now deals with the treatment of many forms of malignant disease.

Associated with the hospital (in buildings of 1936 and later) is the INSTITUTE OF CANCER RESEARCH, incorporating the Chester Beatty Research Institute (founded in 1909) and 'recognized' by London University. Farther on is the large BROMPTON HOSPITAL for Diseases of the Chest, founded in 1841 by Sir Philip Rose and housed in buildings mainly of 1844–54 (by F. J. Francis; north side) and 1879–82 (by T. H. Wyatt).

Sumner Place, opposite the Royal Marsden Hospital, leads to ONSLOW SQUARE (VI, D3), an unspoiled layout of about 1850. W. M. Thackeray lived at No. 36 in 1854–62, the period of *The Rose and the Ring* (1855), *The Virginians* (1857), and the founding of *The Cornhill Magazine*, with Thackeray as editor (1860). Sumner Place goes on to reach Old Brompton Road (compare below) south-west of South Kensington station (Route 10).

In ONSLOW GARDENS, to the south-west from Onslow Square, James Anthony Froude (d. 1894), the historian, lived at No. 5, and Andrew Bonar Law (d. 1923), the Conservative statesman, at No. 24; and W. E. H. Lecky, the historian, died in 1903 at No. 38. In QUEEN'S GATE, to the north, leading across Cromwell Road (Route 10), is ST AUGUSTINE'S CHURCH, a gaunt brick structure by William Butterfield (1865–71), restored in 1975.

No. 108 in OLD BROMPTON ROAD houses the ROYAL SOCIETY OF BRITISH SCULPTORS, founded in 1904. GLOUCESTER ROAD, farther west, also leads to Cromwell Road, via HEREFORD SQUARE (VI, D2), where George Borrow (d. 1881) lived at No. 22. Sir Herbert Beerbohm Tree (d. 1917), the actor-manager, lived at No. 31 in ROSARY GARDENS, west of Hereford Square, and Field-Marshal Viscount Allenby lived from 1928 until his death in 1936 at No. 24 in WETHERBY

GARDENS, farther west. In HARRINGTON GARDENS, parallel to this road on the north (and leading back to Gloucester Road), Sir William S. Gilbert occupied a grandiose house (No. 39) built for him (by Sir Ernest George and Harold Peto) in 1881.

Jenny Lind, the 'Swedish nightingale', lived for a time at No. 189 in OLD BROMPTON ROAD, at the north end of THE BOLTONS (VI, E 1, 2), part of a layout of 1840–65, with a Gothic church of 1850 (by George Godwin) in the centre of a double crescent of opulent semi-detached villas. BOUSFIELD SCHOOL, near the north end, in contrast, is an early example of the modern style (by Chamberlin, Powell, and Bon, 1955).

On the right of Old Brompton Road, farther west, is EARLS COURT ROAD, which runs north to Kensington High Street (Route 11). It passes BOLTON GARDENS, where Beatrix Potter, author and illustrator of the Peter Rabbit books, lived as a girl at No. 2, and EARLS COURT SQUARE, No. 21 in which is the NATIONAL POETRY CENTRE, the home of the Poetry Society, founded in 1909. Farther north is BARKSTON GARDENS, where Ellen Terry (d. 1928), the actress, lived at No. 22. In WARWICK ROAD, to the west of Earls Court Road, is the EARLS COURT EXHIBITION CENTRE, by C. Howard Crane, the largest reinforced concrete building in Europe when it was opened in 1937. Farther west is the huge EMPRESS STATE BUILDING, twenty-eight storeys and over 300 ft high, designed by Stone, Toms & Partners (1962) and now government offices. Warwick Road passes the ends of Philbeach Gardens, a crescent containing ST CUTHBERT'S CHURCH, an elaborate Gothic church by H. R. Gough (1884), with remarkable ironwork furnishings by Bainbridge Reynolds (1887 on). Warwick Road goes on over West Cromwell Road to the junction of Kensington High Street with Hammersmith Road (see Suburban London).

10 From Hyde Park Corner to the South Kensington Museums via Brompton

Plan VII, B 2–VI, D 3

STATIONS: HYDE PARK CORNER (Plan VII, B2) and KNIGHTSBRIDGE (VII, B 1), on the Piccadilly line; SOUTH KENSINGTON (VI, D 3), on the Circle, District, and Piccadilly lines. — BUSES Nos. 9, 14, 19, 22, 30, 52, 73, 74, and 137 in Knightsbridge (for others to Hyde Park Corner, see Routes 7 and 9); Nos. 14, 30, and 74 in Brompton Road; No. 74 in Cromwell Road (others to South Kensington, see Routes 8 and 9).

For HYDE PARK CORNER, see Route 7. KNIGHTSBRIDGE (VII, B 1, 2), continuing the line of Piccadilly westward, has Hyde Park on its north side at first. AGRICULTURE HOUSE, on the left, was built in 1956 (by R. Ward and Partners) for the National Farmers' Union. The

BERKELEY HOTEL (VII, B2), farther on, was transferred from Piccadilly in 1972 to a new building by Brian O'Rorke, at the corner of Wilton Place.

To the left in WILTON PLACE, which has a fine 18th-century terrace on its west side, is ST PAUL'S, KNIGHTSBRIDGE, a Gothic church by Thomas Cundy (1843) noted for its music. On the north wall outside is a memorial to fifty-two women of the Women's Transport Service (F.A.N.Y.) who died in the Second World War. Wilton Place leads to Wilton Crescent (Route 9).

No. 58 Knightsbridge, with No. 1 Albert Gate adjoining, is the FRENCH EMBASSY (VII, B2); a tablet in the wall commemorates the fiftieth anniversary of the *Entente Cordiale* (1954). No. 60 is the ROYAL THAMES YACHT CLUB, founded in 1775. On the left is SHERATON PARK TOWER, a circular hotel designed by Richard Seifert & Partners (1973). Beyond the north end of Sloane Street (Route 9) and KNIGHTSBRIDGE STATION (VII, B1), Brompton Road branches left from the continuation of Knightsbridge (Route 11). Under the huge BOWATER HOUSE (by Guy Morgan and Partners, 1959) opens an entrance to Hyde Park through which a vigorous bronze group, 'Pan', the last work of Epstein (1959), can be seen.

BROMPTON ROAD (VI, D3–VII, B1), a busy thoroughfare, runs south-west towards the South Kensington museums, passing HARRODS, one of the largest department stores in London, by Stevens and Munt (1901–5).

At the side, in HANS CRESCENT, is a plaque to three police officers killed here by a terrorist bomb in 1983. No. 70 in Brompton Road, on the right, contains the headquarters of the INDEPENDENT BROADCASTING AUTHORITY, created in 1954 (as the Independent Television Authority), and guided tours of the Broadcasting Gallery are arranged (adm., p. 31).

BEAUCHAMP PLACE, with interesting shop fronts, on the left, leads to Pont Street (compare Route 9). YEOMAN'S ROW, farther on, has some good, if small, late-18th-century houses, while BROMPTON SQUARE, on the other side, has terraces of the earlier part of the 19th century. A little beyond is an avenue leading to HOLY TRINITY CHURCH, the parish church of Brompton, built in the Gothic style by T. L. Donaldson in 1829, but given a new chancel before 1899.

BROMPTON ORATORY (VI, C3), or the London Oratory of St Philip Neri, is a Roman Catholic church served by a congregation of secular priests of the Institute of the Oratory, founded by St Philip Neri at Rome in the late 16th century. The institute, introduced into

England in 1847 by Cardinal Newman, was first established in London in 1849 and moved to Brompton in 1854. The church, designed by Herbert Gribble and completed in 1884, is a spacious structure in the Italian baroque style, well proportioned, but perhaps rather too ornate in its decoration for English tastes. The dome, rising 200 ft above the floor to the top of the cross, was added in 1896 by George Sherrin. To the west is a statue (by Bodley and Brindley) of Cardinal Newman (d. 1890).

Services on weekdays at 7, 7.30, and 10 a.m. and at 6 p.m.; Mondays–Fridays at 12.30 (Thursdays also at 8 p.m.); Sundays at 7, 8, 9, 10, 11 (High Mass), 12.30, 3.30 (Vespers), 4.30 and 7.

The entrance to the church is through a lofty portico supported by double columns with the bases of unfinished towers on either side. The interior is notable for the width of the nave (51 ft) and the large side chapels taking the place of aisles. The arches opening into these, supported on each side by double piers of Devonshire marble, carry the arms of Popes and sculptured figures representing the principal virtues. Above the cornice are mosaics of saints connected with St Philip and windows containing the arms of notable benefactors. Between the pilasters (also of Devonshire marble) on either side of the nave are huge Carrara marble statues of the Apostles, by Mazzotti (late 17th century), which previously stood in Siena Cathedral. These, combined with the other decoration (by C. T. G. Formilli), give the nave a somewhat heavy Italianate appearance. The decoration of the chapels also follows Italian models and is notable for its use of coloured marbles. Under the altar in the chapel of St Philip, in the west transept, is preserved a relic of the saint, exposed on Tuesdays. The Sanctuary has carved walnut stalls and a marquetry floor, and altar-rails of Sicilian marble. The Lady Chapel in the east transept has a magnificent Italian altarpiece of 1693 from the former Dominican church at Brescia, while the chapel of St Wilfrid, which opens on the north of the transept, contains an altarpiece of about 1710 from the cathedral of Maastricht (Holland). The organ, above a Calvary of 1952, was redesigned in 1954 by Ralph Downes. The last chapel on this side, with walls of Irish marble, contains as a war memorial a sculptured Pietà by Louis Berra.

Brompton Road (see below) bears to the left opposite the Oratory, while Thurloe Place is extended by Cromwell Gardens and CROMWELL ROAD past the south front of the **Victoria and Albert Museum** (adm., p. 447), opposite which is the striking ISMAILI CULTURAL CENTRE, a religious, social, and cultural centre designed by Casson, Conder & Partners for the Aga Khan Foundation and completed in 1985. It incorporates an art gallery and reading rooms, a prayer hall capable of accommodating 1,200 people, and a roof-top garden. To the south is THURLOE SQUARE, laid out in 1843 by George Basevi. In the central gardens is the Yalta Victims Memorial (by Angela Conner, 1982) to those forcibly repatriated to the Soviet Union and Yugoslavia in 1944–7. Cromwell Road goes on past the **Natural History Museum** (adm., p. 399).

ALEXANDER SQUARE, on the right of Brompton Road, farther on, is one of the best squares in Kensington, with houses of about 1830. Fine houses are to be seen also in ALEXANDER PLACE, to the west, and in EGERTON GARDENS (about 1840) and other streets to the east of Brompton Road, for the continuation of which see Route 9.

In CROMWELL PLACE, opposite the Natural History Museum, Sir John Lavery, the painter, lived in 1899–1940 at No. 5 and Sir J. E. Millais in 1862–78 at No. 7. In Cromwell Road, farther west, is the LYCÉE FRANÇAIS DE LONDRES (No. 35), and in QUEENSBERRY PLACE, on the left, No. 20 is the INSTITUTE OF BIOLOGY. BADEN-POWELL HOUSE, on the corner of Queen's Gate, to the right, is the headquarters of the SCOUT ASSOCIATION, founded in 1907 (as the Boy Scouts) by Lieut.-General Sir Robert (later Lord) Baden-Powell and now numbering over 620,000 in Britain and over sixteen million in more than 100 countries of the world. The building, designed by Ralph Tubbs and opened in 1961 as a centre for scouting and a hostel for visiting scouts, is also a memorial to Lord Baden-Powell (1857–1941). Outside is a statue in granite of B.-P., by Don Potter, and inside can be seen his numerous trophies and mementoes.

CROMWELL ROAD, a broad thoroughfare with substantial residences, goes on beyond Gloucester Road (see Route 9) to the WEST LONDON AIR TERMINAL, a passenger centre for British Airways, opened above the District line railway tracks in 1957 (for British European Airways) and rebuilt by Sir John Burnet, Tait and Partners (1963). Charles Booth (d. 1916), a pioneer of social research, lived at No. 6 in GRENVILLE PLACE, to the east.

EXHIBITION ROAD, starting near South Kensington station (VI, D3) and skirting the Victoria and Albert Museum on the west, ascends to Kensington Road (Route 11). It gives access to a number of important public and academic buildings, occupying a site purchased out of the proceeds of the Great Exhibition of 1851. On the left is a new building (1975) for the Palaeontology Department of the Natural History Museum, with over seven million fossils (no public access), and farther up are the **Geological Museum** and the **Science Museum** (adm., p. 414). Opposite these are an entrance to the Victoria and Albert Museum (see above) and the Henry Cole Wing of the museum (p. 464). Farther up, on this side, is the HYDE PARK CHAPEL, the first chapel of the Mormons, or Latter-Day Saints, to be built in London, designed by Sir Thomas Bennett and opened in 1961, with a fine organ. On the left are the main buildings of the IMPERIAL COLLEGE OF SCIENCE AND TECHNOLOGY (VI, C2, 3).

The Imperial College was established in 1907 'for the most advanced training and research in science, especially in its application to industry'. It has faculties of science, engineering, and economics, and comprises a group of associated colleges (the Royal College of Science, the City and Guilds College, and the Royal School of Mines), and became a school of the University of London in 1908. Most of the Imperial College has been rebuilt since 1953 (by Norman and Dawbarn). The QUEEN'S TOWER, a tall Renaissance-style tower (280 ft high, with a fine peal of bells), designed by T. E. Collcutt, is all that remains of the original buildings of the Commonwealth Institute, opened here in 1893 (as the Imperial Institute) and moved in 1962 to a new site in Holland Park (Route 11).

The former Imperial Institute Road (closed to public traffic), on the left, traverses the main academic precinct of the Imperial College. On the south side are the departments of Chemistry and Biochemistry of the ROYAL COLLEGE OF SCIENCE, founded in 1845, and on the north are the Civil and Electrical Engineering Departments of the CITY AND GUILDS COLLEGE, founded in 1884. Farther west are the chief administrative block of the Imperial College and the new buildings (1969) of the SCIENCE MUSEUM LIBRARY. No. 170 in QUEEN'S GATE, at the end of the road, is a classical building by R. Norman Shaw (1889).

On the left of Exhibition Road, farther up, is the main entrance to the City and Guilds College, with the Mechanical Engineering, Management Science, and other departments. In PRINCE CONSORT ROAD, beyond, is the entrance to the ROYAL SCHOOL OF MINES, founded in 1851, in a building by Sir Aston Webb (1909–13), embellished with statuary. On the south side also is the ROYAL COLLEGE OF MUSIC (VI, C2), founded in 1883 and occupying an elaborate building by Sir Arthur Blomfield opened in 1894.

The college has a good concert hall, and contains a valuable library and (in the Donaldson Museum; adm., p. 34) an exceptionally fine collection of over 300 old musical instruments, including Handel's spinet, Haydn's clavichord, and a guitar said to have belonged to Rizzio, the music master of Mary, Queen of Scots. Sir George Grove was the first director of the college (until 1894), followed by Sir Hubert Parry (until his death in 1918), and famous professors and teachers have included Jenny Lind, Sir Charles Stanford (from 1883 to 1924), Gustav Holst, Ralph Vaughan Williams, Arthur Benjamin, and Sir Adrian Boult. The building of a new Opera Theatre was begun in 1984.

Farther west are the departments of Aeronautics and Chemical Engineering and Technology of the City and Guilds College, and the departments of Physics, Mathematics, etc., of the Royal College of Science, with another entrance in Queen's Gate. On the north side of Prince Consort Road are the IMPERIAL

COLLEGE STUDENTS' UNION, further academic departments, and a hall of residence (Beit Quadrangle, 1910–30). Beyond is HOLY TRINITY CHURCH (VI, C2), a tall Gothic building by G. F. Bodley (1901–4); the west window, a war memorial, includes the arms of the Commonwealth countries and colonies. Prince Consort Road ends at QUEEN'S GATE (compare Route 11), with ornate stuccoed terraces of 1860 and after, No. 41 in which houses the ROYAL ENTOMOLOGICAL SOCIETY of London (founded in 1833) and the MINERALOGICAL SOCIETY (founded 1876).

On the east side of Exhibition Road is the large square of PRINCES GARDENS, where new halls of residence for the Imperial College, designed by Richard Sheppard, Robson & Partners, were completed in 1969, together with a sports centre (on the north side). Nos. 50–51 Princes Gate, on the same side of Exhibition Road, are now the GOETHE INSTITUTE, with a library, reading room, etc., open to visitors.

11 From Hyde Park Corner to Kensington

Plan VII, B 2–beyond VI, B 1

STATIONS: HYDE PARK CORNER (Plan VII, B2) and KNIGHTSBRIDGE (VII, B1), on the Piccadilly line; HIGH STREET KENSINGTON (beyond VI, B1), on the Circle and District lines. — BUSES Nos. 9, 52 and 73 in Knightsbridge and Kensington Road; Nos. 9, 27, 28, 31, 33, 49, and 73 in Kensington High Street; and Nos. 27, 28, 31, and 52 in Kensington Church Street. No. 31 runs south to Earls Court and Chelsea, No. 49 to South Kensington and Chelsea.

From HYDE PARK CORNER to Knightsbridge station, see Route 10. Knightsbridge, keeping to the right here, passes HYDE PARK BARRACKS, the headquarters of the Household Cavalry, rebuilt in 1967–70 (to the designs of Sir Basil Spence), with a huge towerblock overlooking Hyde Park.

The HOUSEHOLD CAVALRY comprises two separate regiments, the LIFE GUARDS, formed originally by the followers of Charles II during his exile, and the BLUES AND ROYALS. This regiment combines the Royal Horse Guards ('The Blues'), which began as a Cromwellian troop of horse, and the 1st Dragoons ('The Royals'). The regiments share the honour of providing a personal bodyguard for the sovereign on state occasions. The Life Guards wear scarlet tunics with blue collars and cuffs and white plumed helmets, while the Blues and Royals wear blue tunics with scarlet collars and cuffs and red plumed helmets. In full dress, white buckskin pantaloons and long knee-boots are worn, as well as the steel cuirasses revived for the coronation of George IV.

TREVOR STREET, on the left of Knightsbridge, leads to TREVOR SQUARE (1818) and MONTPELIER SQUARE (1837), part of a layout of modest but unspoiled early-19th-century terraces.

KENSINGTON ROAD (VI, B1–3), the continuation of Knightsbridge, begins at Rutland Gardens and has Hyde Park on its right. In RUTLAND GATE, to the left, Sir Francis Galton (d. 1911), the founder of eugenics, lived for fifty years at No. 42, and Lord Lugard, the colonial administrator, lived in 1912–19 at No. 51. No. 14 PRINCES GATE, the first house in a long and stately terrace of the mid 19th century, facing the park, was presented to the United States by J. Pierpont Morgan as the official residence of the U.S. Ambassador (hence the Red Indian heads over the windows). John F. Kennedy lived here in 1938–40, when his father was ambassador, but the house is now the ROYAL COLLEGE OF GENERAL PRACTITIONERS, founded in 1952. Field-Marshal Earl Haig died in 1928 at No. 21 Princes Gate; No. 25 is the ROYAL SCHOOL OF NEEDLEWORK, founded in 1872, and containing a notable collection of needlework, both old and new (adm., p. 34).

Exhibition Road, starting opposite the Alexandra Gate of Hyde Park, leads to the South Kensington museums (see Route 10). The next part of the main road is known as KENSINGTON GORE; on the corner is the ROYAL GEOGRAPHICAL SOCIETY (VI, B3), founded in 1830 and housed since 1913 in a building (formerly Lowther Lodge) by R. Norman Shaw (1873–5). Outside are statues of David Livingstone (d. 1873) and Sir Ernest Shackleton (d. 1922), and in the forecourt is a bust of Sir Clements Markham (d. 1916), the historian of Peru.

The small but interesting museum (no public admission) contains a model of Mount Everest, Lord Hunt's Everest diary, and relics of Livingstone, Stanley, Shackleton, Captain Scott, Franklin, and other famous explorers. The map room has a collection of over 500,000 maps and atlases which may be consulted without formality by visitors (Mondays–Fridays, 9.30 to 5.30). ALBERT HALL MANSIONS beyond, also by Shaw (1879), was the first block of flats built in London. At No. 29 in Exhibition Road is the NATIONAL SOUND ARCHIVE (adm., p. 33), founded (as the British Institute of Recorded Sound) in 1948 and now administered by the British Library.

The ROYAL ALBERT HALL (VI, B2), built in 1867–71 to the designs of Captain Francis Fowke, is in the form of an immense oval amphitheatre, 273 ft across and 155 ft high, covered by a glass dome. The terracotta frieze illustrates the Triumphs of Art and Science. Capable of seating about 8,000 people, the hall is much used for concerts (of which the most famous are the Promenade Concerts, founded by Sir Henry Wood in 1895), as well as balls, boxing, public meetings, and other events. The vast interior, which has three tiers of boxes with a balcony and gallery above, is open to visitors when not in use. The organ, by 'Father' Willis, with nearly 10,000 pipes, is one of the largest in Britain.

Facing the hall, in Kensington Gardens, is the ALBERT MEMORIAL, designed by Sir George Gilbert Scott and erected in 1863–76 (at a cost of £120,000) as the national monument to Prince Albert of Saxe-Coburg-Gotha (1819–61), the consort of Queen Victoria. Under an ornate and lofty Gothic canopy, 175 ft high, is a seated gilt-bronze figure of the prince (15 ft high) by J. H. Foley, holding the catalogue of the Great Exhibition of 1851. Around the pedestal are fine marble reliefs of artists and men of letters of every period, 178 in all, by H. H. Armstead and J. B. Philip. At the angles of the pedestal are groups representing Agriculture, Manufactures, Commerce, and Engineering, and at the outer corners of the steps are further groups symbolizing the continents of Europe, Asia, Africa, and America.

The Albert Hall stands on the site of Gore House, famous as the residence in 1836–49 of Lady Blessington, whose salon attracted many eminent men of letters, art, and science. Behind the hall, facing the Royal College of Music (Route 10), is the MEMORIAL TO THE 1851 EXHIBITION, with a poor statue of the Prince Consort by Joseph Durham (1863). On the west of the hall are the ROYAL COLLEGE OF ORGANISTS, founded in 1864 and housed in an exotically decorated building by H. H. Cole (1875), and the ROYAL COLLEGE OF ART (600 students), founded in 1837 for training in the fine arts and industrial design, and created a university in 1967, with the power to grant degrees in art and design. It occupies a rather severe building by H. T. Cadbury-Brown, Sir Hugh Casson, and R. Y. Goodden (1962), with an exhibition hall.

At the junction of Kensington Road and the broad QUEEN'S GATE (see Route 10) is an equestrian statue by Boehm of Field-Marshal Lord Napier of Magdala (d. 1890). In HYDE PARK GATE, farther on, Lord Baden-Powell (d. 1941) lived at No. 9; Sir Jacob Epstein, the sculptor, died in 1959 at his home at No. 18; Sir Leslie Stephen, scholar and mountaineer (father of Virginia Woolf), died in 1904 at No. 22 (then No. 11); and Sir Winston Churchill died in 1965 at his London home, No. 28, which he had bought in 1945. Farther west are PALACE GATE (see below), where Sir John Millais died in 1896 at No. 2, a house designed for him by Philip Hardwick (1878), and DE VERE GARDENS, where No. 29 was the last home (1887–9) of Robert Browning (d. at Venice) and Henry James lived in 1886–1902 at No.

34. The Broad Walk of Kensington Gardens (Route 12) opens on the right beyond Palace Gate, and farther on there is a view through the trees of **Kensington Palace**.

Palace Gate and De Vere Gardens lead to CANNING PLACE (at the north end of Gloucester Road), which, with VICTORIA GROVE and LAUNCESTON PLACE to the south-west, forms the nucleus of a charming early Victorian 'urban village' (1830–45). In DOURO PLACE, north-west of Victoria Grove, No. 6 was the home in 1851–61 of Samuel Palmer, the artist. In PRINCE OF WALES TERRACE, west of De Vere Gardens, No. 5 is the head-office of the DUKE OF EDINBURGH'S AWARD SCHEME, instituted in 1956 to encourage young people in certain leisure-time activities.

Kensington Road is extended by KENSINGTON HIGH STREET (VI, B1), the bustling shopping centre of the royal borough of Kensington. On the right are the prominent ROYAL GARDEN HOTEL (by R. Seifert and Partners, 1965) and the gate of KENSINGTON PALACE GARDENS, an attractive private road shaded by plane trees and lined with opulent mansions. No. 1 Palace Green, at the south end, was built by Philip Webb in 1868–72 for the Earl of Carlisle, and No. 2 was designed by Frederick Hering (1860–62) for W. M. Thackeray, who died here in 1863.

Thackeray wrote *Vanity Fair*, *Pendennis*, and *Henry Esmond* and began *The Newcomes* at No. 16 (then No. 13) YOUNG STREET, on the other side of the High Street, where he lived in 1846–54. Young Street opens into KENSINGTON SQUARE, built after 1690 and a fashionable quarter when the court was at the nearby Kensington Palace. On all sides except the east there survives a variety of old houses, though some are much altered: notable are Nos. 11–12 (originally one house), where Talleyrand, the French statesman, lived in 1792–4. John Richard Green (d. 1883), the historian, lived at No. 14; Sir Hubert Parry (d. 1918), the composer, at No. 17; and John Stuart Mill, the philosopher, at No. 18 (in 1837–51). All these are on the south side. No. 33 (N.T.: no adm.), built in 1695 on the west side, was the home of Mrs Patrick Campbell (d. 1940), the actress and friend of Bernard Shaw, and Sir John Simon (d. 1904), a pioneer of public health, lived at No. 40.

At the corner of Church Street is the parish church of ST MARY ABBOTS (VI, B1), so called from its connection with the abbey of Abingdon (Berkshire), which owned the manor of Kensington in 1260. A church stood on this site before 1100; the present church in the Decorated style, one of the best designs of Sir George Gilbert Scott, was built in 1869–72. The lofty spire, 278 ft high, was completed in 1879 and the cloistral approach in 1893, and the church, well restored in 1956 after war damage, retains a pulpit of 1697 and some old monuments. James Mill (d. 1836), the Utilitarian philosopher, father of J. S. Mill, is buried near the west end.

KENSINGTON CHURCH STREET, which leads north to Notting Hill (Route 12), is well known for its antique shops. Muzio Clementi (d. 1832), the composer, who first came to England in 1766, lived at No. 128. Several terraces of 18th-century houses will be found in the streets to the left, particularly in HOLLAND STREET, where Walter Crane (d. 1915), the artist, lived at No. 13. Church Walk, with a quiet garden, leads back to Kensington High Street.

On the south side of the High Street are several large department stores. The topmost floor of one of them is the KENSINGTON EXHIBITION CENTRE (adm., p. 33), a display area for special exhibitions (entrance from Derry Street, at the side). Above this is a roof-garden with a terrace commanding a wide view over south-west London. To the west is the entrance to High Street Kensington station.

A new group of municipal buildings, between Hornton Street and Campden Hill Road, to the north-west, includes the KENSINGTON CENTRAL LIBRARY, by E. Vincent Harris (1960). A new TOWN HALL for the borough of Kensington and Chelsea, to the designs of Sir Basil Spence, was completed in 1977. Sir Henry Newbolt, the poet, died in 1938 at No. 29, and Ford Madox Ford (d. 1939), the novelist, lived at No. 80 in CAMPDEN HILL ROAD, which ascends to the QUEEN ELIZABETH COLLEGE for women, founded in 1908, moved in 1915 to a new building, by Adams, Holden, and Pearson, and since 1928 part of London University, with a faculty of science. Campden Hill, a road farther up, leads west to HOLLAND PARK SCHOOL, a characteristic example of modern school design, by the L.C.C. architects (1956–9). HOLLAND WALK, beyond this, skirting Holland Park on the east and passing an entrance to Holland House (see below), descends to the main road.

From Argyll Road, west of Campden Hill Road, STAFFORD TERRACE runs parallel to Kensington High Street. No. 18, one of a row of houses built after 1868, is now called LINLEY SAMBOURNE HOUSE (adm., p. 33). The home of Edward Linley Sambourne (d. 1910), the artist, and his successors, from 1874 until 1978, it was bought in 1980 by the G.L.C. and is maintained by the Victorian Society (founded here in 1958) as a characteristic upper-middle-class late-Victorian dwelling. The interior has wallpapers by William Morris, furniture, fittings, and paintings of the period, and Sambourne's drawings for *Punch*. In PHILLIMORE PLACE, to the north, Kenneth Grahame, the author of *The Wind in the Willows*, lived in 1901–8 at No. 16.

HOLLAND PARK, opening on the right of Kensington High Street, is a sylvan retreat on the slope of a hill. In the middle are the east wing and other remains of HOLLAND HOUSE, a historic Jacobean mansion unhappily damaged by bombing in 1941 and then left derelict.

Begun in 1605 for Sir Walter Cope, Chamberlain of the Exchequer, and doubtfully attributed to John Thorpe, the house passed by marriage to Sir Henry Rich, created Earl of Holland (a district of Lincolnshire) in 1624, but executed in 1649. The second earl became in 1673 the fifth Earl of Warwick. The widow of the third earl was married in 1716 to Joseph Addison, the essayist, who has described the then rural setting in his letters and who died here in 1719. The house was sold in 1768 to Henry Fox, first Baron Holland, the father of Charles James Fox, and under the third Lord Holland (1773–1840), the politician's nephew, it became famous as the 'favourite resort of wits and beauties, of painters and poets, of scholars, philosophers, and statesmen', as described by Macaulay. The estate was sold to the L.C.C. in 1952.

The restored east wing of the house, dating from about 1640, has been incorporated in the King George VI Memorial Youth Hostel, new buildings for which were designed by Sir Hugh Casson and Neville Conder (1959). The surviving lower storey and arcades of the centre section, restored in 1964, form the backcloth in summer for an open-air theatre. The original stone gateway piers (1629), attributed to Inigo Jones, survived the bombing and were re-erected here in 1963. To the west are the attractive gardens, with the Ice House (used for exhibitions), to the south, and the Orangery, to the west (used for exhibitions and concerts). The former Garden Ballroom, to the south-west, was converted in 1965 into the Belvedere Restaurant.

At the south end of Holland Park is the COMMONWEALTH INSTITUTE (adm., p. 31), founded in 1887 (as the Imperial Institute) to commemorate Queen Victoria's Golden Jubilee, and moved from Imperial Institute Road in 1962 to a striking new building by Sir Robert Matthew and Johnson-Marshall, with an ingeniously-shaped copper-covered roof.

The primary objects of the institute are to assist the economic development of the natural resources of the British Commonwealth and to provide an exhibition showing its scenery, life, and industries. The exhibition galleries contain interesting models, dioramas, etc., illustrating the natural features and resources of the Commonwealth, and examples of its products and handicrafts. The building also includes a library and reading room, a restaurant, a spacious art gallery for temporary exhibitions, and a cinema where relevant films are shown daily.

Kensington High Street goes on to EDWARDES SQUARE (to the left, where Leigh Hunt, the essayist, lived at No. 32 in 1840–51) and EARLS TERRACE (on the main road, delightful terraces of the early 19th century. In MELBURY ROAD, on the right, Holman Hunt, the artist, died in 1910 at No. 18. TOWER HOUSE, in this road, was designed in 1875 for himself by William Burges, who died here in 1881. The interior, restored in 1976, is a remarkable example of ornate Victorian decoration.

LEIGHTON HOUSE (adm., p. 33), in Holland Park Road, north of the High Street, was built in 1866 (with the assistance of George Aitchison) by Lord Leighton, the artist, who lived here until his death in 1896. The house, with its contents, was given to the Kensington Borough Council in 1926 and is now a centre for Victorian studies. Loan exhibitions, lectures, etc., are held frequently. The remarkable Arab Hall is decorated with 14th–16th-century Oriental tiles and a mosaic frieze by Walter Crane, and has 18th-century damascene stained glass windows. Parts of the walls elsewhere are faced with tiles by William de Morgan. Visitors may see the studios, containing paintings and drawings by Lord Leighton and other Kensington artists, and the delightfully secluded garden should not be overlooked.

On the left of Kensington High Street, farther west, is WARWICK GARDENS, where G. K. Chesterton (d. 1936), the poet and novelist, lived at No. 11. Charles House, in the main road (No. 375), is the DEPARTMENT FOR NATIONAL SAVINGS, separated from the Post Office in 1969. The High Street is extended beyond Warwick Road (Route 10) by Hammersmith Road, passing OLYMPIA, a huge exhibition building opened in 1886 and extended to the main road in 1930. In ADDISON BRIDGE PLACE, opposite the approach to Olympia station, S. T. Coleridge lived in 1811–12 at No. 7. Sir Edward Elgar lived in 1890–91 at No. 51 in AVONMORE ROAD, just beyond. For the continuation to Hammersmith, see Suburban London.

12 Hyde Park and Kensington Gardens

Plan I, F1–VII, B3

STATIONS: HYDE PARK CORNER (Plan VII, B2) and KNIGHTSBRIDGE (VII, B1), on the Piccadilly line, and HIGH STREET KENSINGTON (beyond VI, B1), on the Circle and District lines, for the south side; MARBLE ARCH (II, E2), LANCASTER GATE (I, E3) and QUEENSWAY (I, F1), on the Central line, and BAYSWATER (I, E1), on the Circle and District lines, for the north side. — BUSES in Knightsbridge and Kensington Road, see Routes 10, 11; in Park Lane, see Route 13; Nos. 12 and 88 in Bayswater Road.

HYDE PARK and KENSINGTON GARDENS are open daily, but the gates of the Gardens are closed at dusk and the Park is closed at midnight — CARS and Cycles are allowed on all the roads in Hyde Park except that on the north side of the Serpentine; the speed limit is 30 m.p.h.

RESTAURANTS in Hyde Park: DELL, open daily in summer; SERPENTINE, open all the year. — BANDS play at the bandstand in Hyde Park on Sundays and Bank Holidays from late May to the end of August, from 3 to 4.30 and 6 to 7.30.

BOATING (rowing boats, canoes, and kayaks) on the Serpentine, daily from 10 a.m.

(March–October; Saturdays and Sundays only in winter). Motor Boat trips round the lake. — BATHING in the Serpentine, east of the bridge, daily, all the year round. — BOWLING and putting greens in Hyde Park (May–September; near Alexandra Gate). — TENNIS Courts open all the year.

HYDE PARK, with an area of 360 acres, is bounded on the north by Bayswater Road, which stretches from Marble Arch to Notting Hill Gate, on the east by the once-fashionable Park Lane, and on the south by Knightsbridge and Kensington Road, leading from Hyde Park Corner to the Alexandra Gate. On the west it is conterminous with KENSINGTON GARDENS (275 acres), once the private domain of Kensington Palace, but now equally accessible to the public, so that the two form one continuous open space, the largest in London. Both parks have many fine trees and are the haunt of a surprising variety of birds, natural sanctuaries for which are provided by some of the shrubberies. The complete perambulation of the parks involves a rural walk of about four miles.

Curving diagonally across both parks is THE SERPENTINE, an artificial lake of about forty acres formed by damming the West Bourne, a stream that has now practically disappeared. The lake is the home of numerous waterfowl and is frequented every morning of the year by hardy bathers; the part within Kensington Gardens is known as the Long Water. The motor-road from the Victoria Gate (on the north) to the Alexandra Gate, crossing the Serpentine and following the boundary between the two parks, forms a pleasant and convenient method of reaching Kensington and the South Kensington museums from Paddington and north-west London. On the south side of Kensington Gardens is the Albert Memorial (Route 11) and on the west is Kensington Palace.

The manor of Hyde was the possession of Westminster Abbey from the Norman Conquest until the Dissolution (1536), when it was taken by Henry VIII and converted into a royal deer-park. In 1635 Charles I threw this open to the public and it quickly became a fashionable rendezvous; the Ring, a drive and racecourse laid out, was much frequented by the carriages of society. Later the park became the resort of duellists, while the roads across it were infested with robbers, but under the earlier Georges it was taken in hand again, and in 1730–31 Caroline of Anspach, the queen of George II, had a series of ponds converted into the Serpentine. Harriet Westbrook, first wife of the poet Shelley, committed suicide in this lake in 1816. The park was the scene in 1851 of the Great Exhibition, inspired by the Prince Consort, which occupied a site of about twenty acres between Rotten Row and Knightsbridge. The famous exhibition building of glass and iron, designed by Sir Joseph Paxton, was afterwards moved to Sydenham in south London and re-erected as the Crystal Palace.

Kensington Gardens owe their present appearance mainly to Queen Caroline, under whose direction they were laid out and the noble avenues of trees planted by Henry Wise and Charles Bridgman.

From HYDE PARK CORNER (Route 9), the south-east entrance to the park, three roads set out: that on the left (south) leads to the Alexandra Gate and the Albert Memorial, that in the centre to the Serpentine (see below), and that on the right (now the west carriageway of Park Lane) to MARBLE ARCH (see Route 14), skirting the east side of the park, with exits to Park Lane at the Stanhope and Grosvenor Gates (Route 13). On the left of this, facing the entrance to the park, is the ACHILLES STATUE, a colossal bronze figure by Westmacott, cast from captured French cannon and erected in 1822 to the Duke of Wellington and his companions in arms 'by their countrywomen'. The statue, however, is not an Achilles, but an adaptation of one of the antique horse-tamers on the Monte Cavallo at Rome.

Between the two leftward roads is ROTTEN ROW (VI, B3–VII, B2; perhaps originally 'Route du Roi'), a famous sandy track nearly a mile long (laid out in 1690), reserved for horseriders. The paths on either side were long the fashionable rendezvous after church on Sunday mornings. A path opposite the ALBERT GATE (which affords access to Knightsbridge) passes the DELL, a charming glade below the embankment of the Serpentine, and ascends to the DELL RESTAURANT (by Patrick Gwynne, 1965), at the east end of the lake. SERPENTINE ROAD (once called the Ladies' Mile), skirting the north side and passing the Boathouse, leads to the road connecting the Victoria and Alexandra Gates.

In the Dell is a small formal garden (1983) with a memorial stone to the victims of the Nazis during the Second World War.

To the north, beyond the boathouse, is a weathered boulder from Norway, placed here in 1978, 'to thank the British People for friendship and hospitality during the Second World War'. Farther north is a memorial to W. H. Hudson (d. 1922), the naturalist author, comprising a 'bird sanctuary' and an inappropriate sculptured panel by Epstein (1925) representing 'Rima', the Spirit of Nature in Hudson's *Green Mansions*.

The road crosses the lake by the fine SERPENTINE BRIDGE (VI, A3; or Rennie's Bridge), built in 1826 by the brothers Sir John and George Rennie. The enchanting view eastward includes the distant towers of Westminster Abbey and the Houses of Parliament. On the south shore of the lake are the SERPENTINE RESTAURANT (1963) and the Bathing Station. On the west of the road going on to the Alexandra Gate is the new SERPENTINE GALLERY of the Arts Council (adm., p. 35), mainly devoted to exhibitions of contemporary art. The FLOWER WALK, farther south, one of the most attractive parts of Kensington Gardens, runs west to the Broad Walk.

The path on the west shore of the LONG WATER, the extension of the Serpentine, passes the PETER PAN STATUE, a delightful and popular representation by Sir George Frampton (1912) of the hero of Sir James Barrie's play. On the other side of the lake can be seen 'The Arch', a sculpture nineteen feet high, of Roman Travestine marble, by Henry Moore (1978). At the north end of the lake are a paved garden with fountains and a pavilion, and a statue of Edward Jenner (d. 1823), the discoverer of vaccination; and beyond to the north-east is QUEEN ANNE'S ALCOVE, attributed both to Sir Christopher Wren and to William Kent.

The path leading south-west from the fountains, leaving on the right an obelisk to J. H. Speke (d. 1864), the African explorer, ascends to a striking bronze equestrian figure by G. F. Watts (1903) representing PHYSICAL ENERGY. (A replica of this forms part of the memorial to Cecil Rhodes on the slope of Table Mountain, near Cape Town.) From the sculpture an avenue runs west to the ROUND POND (1728), a favourite resort of model yachtsmen, and beyond this is the BROAD WALK (I, F1–VI, B1), running north and south in front of **Kensington Palace** (adm., p. 372). The elms that were once the pride of the walk were felled when they became dangerous and have been replaced by limes. In the gardens on the south of the house is a statue of William III, presented in 1907 to Edward VII by the Emperor William II of Germany, and seen from the path that leads out to Kensington Palace Gardens (Route 11). To the north-east of the palace is an attractive SUNK GARDEN (1909), enclosed by walks of pleached limes, passed by the path leading to the State Apartments of the palace. The ORANGERY, farther north, designed in 1704 and a notable example of the brickwork of the period, is attributed to both Vanbrugh and Hawksmoor.

The avenue running north from Kensington Palace leads to BAYSWATER ROAD (I, F1–II, E2), which skirts Kensington Gardens and Hyde Park on this side. The first tramway in London ran from Marble Arch along Bayswater Road, in 1861. In ORME SQUARE, opposite the gate, Sir Rowland Hill (d. 1879), the postal reformer, lived at No. 1; and Alice Meynell (d. 1922), the poet and essayist, lived at No. 47 in

PALACE COURT, to the west. This road leads to MOSCOW ROAD, where Edith Sitwell lived at No. 22 Pembridge Mansions in 1914–22 and wrote *Façade* (1921), set to music by William Walton, who visited here.

Bayswater Road runs west past the north end of KENSINGTON PALACE GARDENS, with the new building (by Sir Robert Matthew, Johnson-Marshall & Partners, 1969) of the CZECHOSLOVAK EMBASSY, finely decorated by Czech artists, and PALACE GARDENS TERRACE, in which James Clerk Maxwell (d. 1879), the physician, lived at No. 16; Max Beerbohm, author and caricaturist, was born in 1872 at No. 57; and P. Wyndham Lewis (d. 1957), artist and author, lived at No. 61. Bayswater Road is extended west by Notting Hill Gate (see Suburban London).

In the other direction, Bayswater Road leads to Marble Arch. John C. Loudon (d. 1843), the landscape designer, lived at No. 3 (one of a pair of houses designed by him) in PORCHESTER TERRACE, beyond Queensway station. Sir James Barrie lived in 1902–6 at No. 100 Bayswater Road. LANCASTER GATE (I, E2), farther on, consists of imposing blocks of houses built in 1857–65 by Sancton Wood and others. Francis Bret Harte, the American writer, died in 1902 at No. 74. In CRAVEN HILL, parallel on the north, No. 23 houses the LONDON TOY AND MODEL MUSEUM (adm., p. 33), opened in 1982, with a fine collection of model locomotives, aeroplanes, cars, and sailing boats, as well as dolls and dolls' houses, a Victorian nursery, and an electric railway in the garden. LANCASTER TERRACE, at the corner of which is the twenty-storey ROYAL LANCASTER HOTEL (by T. P. Bennett and Son, 1967), leads to Westbourne Terrace and Sussex Gardens, in Paddington (see Suburban London). Lord Baden-Powell, the founder of the Boy Scouts (now the Scout Association), was born in 1857 at No. 11 in STANHOPE TERRACE (formerly No. 6 Stanhope Street), to the east. No. 1 in HYDE PARK GARDENS, parallel to Bayswater Road, is the headquarters of the ROYAL SOCIETY OF LITERATURE, founded in 1923. Clarendon Place, farther east, leads past CLARENDON CLOSE, in which No. 2 is the office of the FRANCO-BRITISH COUNCIL, set up in 1972 to improve the understanding between France and Britain. No. 10 in HYDE PARK PLACE, facing the main road, is claimed to be the smallest house in London. Stanhope Place, beyond, leads to CONNAUGHT SQUARE, with unspoiled terraces built about 1828. Marie Taglioni, the ballet dancer, lived in 1875–6 at No. 14.

13 From Hyde Park Corner to Marble Arch via Mayfair

Plan VII, B3–II, E2

STATIONS: HYDE PARK CORNER (Plan VII, B2), on the Piccadilly line; GREEN PARK (VIII, A1), on the Piccadilly and Victoria lines; MARBLE ARCH (II, E2) and BOND STREET (II, E3), on the Central line. — BUSES Nos. 2, 16, 30, 36, 73, 74, 137, and 500 in Park Lane; No. 25 in Berkeley Street (to Berkeley Square) and in New Bond Street (southbound) or Davies Street; in Oxford Street, see Route 14.

For HYDE PARK CORNER, see Route 7. The roundabout route to Marble Arch described below, starting at the west end of Piccadilly, turns north into the east carriageway of PARK LANE (II, E2–VII, B3), which skirts Hyde Park (Route 12) and was long synonymous with wealth and fashion. The opulent mansions that once bordered its east side, however, have nearly all given way to large hotels and blocks of flats. The LONDON HILTON HOTEL (twenty-four storeys and over 300 ft high), to an unusual design by Lewis Solomon, Kaye & Partners, was completed in 1963.

The hotel stands at the north corner of HERTFORD STREET, in which Bulwer Lytton wrote *The Last Days of Pompeii* and *Rienzi* (1835) at No. 36. Sir George Cayley, a pioneer of aviation, lived in 1840–48 at No. 20, and General John Burgoyne (d. 1792) and R. B. Sheridan (in 1795–1802) lived at No. 10, which has fine ceilings in the style of Robert Adam. No. 4 in HAMILTON PLACE, to the south, houses the ROYAL AERONAUTICAL SOCIETY, founded as long ago as 1866.

PARK LANE goes on direct to Marble Arch (Route 14), passing STANHOPE GATE (on the right), where Lord Raglan (d. 1855), the Crimean War commander, lived at No. 5, and the luxurious DORCHESTER HOTEL, built in 1931 to the designs of W. Curtis Green. SOUTH STREET, beyond, leads across South Audley Street to Farm Street (compare below). Farther north in Park Lane is the huge GROSVENOR HOUSE HOTEL (1929), with a façade by Lutyens, on the site of a mansion of the Grosvenor family, Dukes of Westminster. At No. 93 in Park Lane (then No. 1 Grosvenor Gate), the property of his wife, Benjamin Disraeli, Lord Beaconsfield, lived during the whole of his married life (1839–72). It is the first of a row of interesting houses with bow fronts, built in the mid 18th century but much altered internally since, and others survive at Nos. 129–32. Sir Moses Montefiore, the champion of Jewish rights, lived at No. 99 from 1825 until his death in 1885.

In PARK STREET, which connects South Street with Oxford Street, No. 2 is the BRITISH STANDARDS INSTITUTION, established in 1901. It prepares recommended standards relating to industry and trade, and now has over 14,000 members.

The route turns right into CURZON STREET (VII, A3) to thread its way through MAYFAIR, long the most fashionable part of London, and still of much interest for its associations with the distinguished people who have resided here. Curzon Street is one of several streets that retain some old houses among the modern blocks of offices. At No. 19, on the right, Lord Beaconsfield died in 1881, and Lord Reading, the Liberal statesman, died in 1935 at No. 32. In CHESTERFIELD STREET, on the left, W. Somerset Maugham, the novelist and playwright, lived in 1911–19 at No. 6. CREWE HOUSE, also on the left, is a pleasant though restored Georgian mansion (now an embassy), built in 1735 by Edward Shepherd and later the town house of the Marquess of Crewe.

Hertford Street, opposite, leads to SHEPHERD MARKET (VII, A3), a 'village' quarter of narrow streets and alleys, laid out by Edward Shepherd (1735) on part of the fairground where the popular May Fair that gave its name to the district had been held since 1688. In Curzon Street, to the east, is the imposing THIRD CHURCH OF CHRIST SCIENTIST (by Lanchester and Rickards, 1912).

Queen Street, on the left of Curzon Street, leads to CHARLES STREET, which has several interesting houses. Sydney Smith, the author and wit, lived in 1837–9 at No. 32, to the left; the Earl of Rosebery, Prime Minister, was born in 1847 at No. 20; and William IV lived here for a time when Duke of Clarence. Dartmouth House (No. 37), to the right, is the headquarters of the ENGLISH-SPEAKING UNION, founded in 1918 to draw together the English-speaking peoples in the interest of world peace and offering assistance to American and other overseas visitors. The facilities include a club, library, and information bureau, and lectures, visits, etc., are arranged.

In this direction, Charles Street leads to BERKELEY SQUARE (II, F3; pronounced 'Barkly'), laid out in 1739–47 and named from Berkeley House (later Devonshire House), part of whose grounds it covered. The fine plane trees in the gardens were planted about 1790. The square was long one of the most aristocratic in London, but its character has been despoiled by the building of immense blocks of offices. LANSDOWNE HOUSE, on the south side, stands on the site of the town house of the Earl of Shelburne (later Marquess of Lansdowne), the Prime Minister who recognized the independence of the United States (1783), and BERKELEY SQUARE HOUSE, on the east side, covers the site of the house (No. 17 Bruton Street) where Queen Elizabeth II was born in 1926. Of old houses the best (on the west side) are No. 44, designed by William Kent (1744), and Nos. 45–6, with good 18th-century stone fronts; Lord Clive, founder of the British Empire in India, committed suicide at No. 45 in 1774; George Canning (d. 1827), the statesman, lived at No. 50, also on the west.

BRUTON STREET leads to Bond Street, while Berkeley Street runs from the south-east angle of the square to Piccadilly (see Route 7). In Fitzmaurice Place, south-west of the square, No. 9 houses the LANSDOWNE CLUB, founded in 1935, and the SAVAGE CLUB, established in 1857. In HILL STREET, on the west side of the square, No. 33 is the office of the COMMONWEALTH DEVELOPMENT

CORPORATION, set up to assist the economic development of the Commonwealth countries and those which have achieved independence since 1948. In FARM STREET, which runs parallel on the north, is the rather florid CHURCH OF THE IMMACULATE CONCEPTION (1849; administered by the Jesuit Fathers), noted for its music.

Farm Street is extended to Park Lane by South Street, which crosses SOUTH AUDLEY STREET. No. 71, on the corner, with a portico, is an unusual house of 1744 attributed to Edward Shepherd. No. 74, just below, is the ALPINE CLUB, founded in 1857, and No. 75 has ceiling paintings on canvas by G. B. Tiepolo, discovered in 1965 and restored in 1968. No. 14, on the other side, was the home of Sir Richard Westmacott (d. 1856), the sculptor. In Audley Square, near the south end of the street, No. 2 is the UNIVERSITY WOMEN'S CLUB, founded in 1886. To the north in South Audley Street is the pleasant little GROSVENOR CHAPEL (II, F3), built in 1730 and adopted as their church by the United States Armed Forces in 1939–45. Behind are the secluded ST GEORGE'S GARDENS, laid out about 1890. South Audley Street crosses MOUNT STREET, which has ornate houses of about 1885 by Sir Ernest George and others, and ends at Grosvenor Square.

From the north-west corner of Berkeley Square, Mount Street and Carlos Place (on the right) lead to the large GROSVENOR SQUARE (II, E, F3), laid out during the reign of George II and named after Sir Richard Grosvenor (d. 1732), but almost completely rebuilt in the last forty years. The square has been associated with the United States since John Adams, the first minister to Britain (1785–8) and later President, came to live at No. 9, in the north-east corner. On the west side is the striking building (1960) of the UNITED STATES EMBASSY, designed by Eero Saarinen (an American architect of Finnish extraction) and surmounted by an American eagle with a wing span of 35 ft. On the north side of the gardens is a fine statue by Sir W. Reid Dick (1948) in memory of Franklin D. Roosevelt, President in 1933–45. No. 20, on this side, was the headquarters of General Eisenhower in 1942 and 1944.

In UPPER GROSVENOR STREET, leading west from the south side, Adlai Stevenson, the American statesman, collapsed and died in 1965. In BROOK STREET, which leads from the north-east angle of the square to Bond Street, are the SAVILE CLUB (No. 69), founded in 1868, and the old-established CLARIDGE'S HOTEL, one of London's most famous hôtels-de-luxe. No. 25 (much altered) was the home of Handel for thirty-five years until his death in 1759, and *Messiah* and many other masterpieces were written here. Colen Campbell, the architect, died in 1729 at No. 76.

From the north-west corner of Grosvenor Square, NORTH AUDLEY STREET leads to Oxford Street (Route 14), passing ST

MARK'S CHURCH (II, E2), rebuilt in 1878 by Blomfield in a Victorian Renaissance style, though retaining the porch and narthex of a church of 1828 (by J. P. Gandy-Deering). Sir Hudson Lowe (d. 1844), governor of Elba during the banishment of Napoleon, is buried here. Sydney Smith died in 1845 at No. 59 in GREEN STREET, which starts opposite the church and reaches Park Lane a little south of MARBLE ARCH.

14 From Marble Arch to St Giles Circus (Oxford Street)

Plan II, E2–III, D2
STATIONS: MARBLE ARCH (Plan II, E2), BOND STREET (II, E3), OXFORD CIRCUS (III, E1), and TOTTENHAM COURT ROAD (III, D2), all on the Central line. Bond Street is also on the Jubilee line, Oxford Circus on the Bakerloo and Victoria lines, and Tottenham Court Road on the Northern line. — BUSES Nos. 7, 8, and 73 in Oxford Street from Marble Arch to St Giles Circus; No. 6, 12, 15, 16A, 23, 88, 137, and 500 from Marble Arch to Oxford Circus only; No. 1 from Orchard Street to St Giles Circus; Nos. 13, 113, and 159 from Orchard Street to Oxford Circus; No. 25 from Davies Street to St Giles Circus (returning to Bond Street). For other buses to Marble Arch, see Routes 12, 13, 16; to Portman Square (Baker Street), see Route 16; to Oxford Circus, see Route 15; to St Giles Circus, see Routes 18, 23.

OXFORD STREET (II, E2–III, D2), the busiest shopping street in London, is also one of the principal thoroughfares connecting the West End with the City. It runs from Marble Arch, at its west extremity, to St Giles Circus, at the junction of Charing Cross Road and Tottenham Court Road, from which it is continued by New Oxford Street and High Holborn towards St Paul's Cathedral and the Bank of England (Route 23). The MARBLE ARCH (II, E2) was designed in 1828 by John Nash, who is believed to have been inspired by the Arch of Constantine at Rome. Intended as the main gateway to Buckingham Palace, it is popularly supposed to have been too narrow to admit the state coach and in 1851 it was moved to its present site at the north-east entrance to Hyde Park (Route 12). The reliefs on the south side are by E. H. Baily, those on the north are by Westmacott, and the arch has excellent wrought-iron gates.

In 1908 the park railings were set back to allow room for the traffic to pass on this side, and in 1960 the Marble Arch was further divorced from the park by a new road linking up with the west carriageway of Park Lane (Route 13) to relieve the appalling traffic congestion around the arch and in Park Lane, which runs south to Hyde Park Corner and Piccadilly. An underground car park, with entrances from Park Lane and The Ring (on the north) and room for 1,100 vehicles in an area of about seven acres, was opened in 1962. The open space just inside Hyde Park is well known as SPEAKERS' CORNER, where those with a message or a grievance may exercise their right of free speech unimpeded by the law, if not by hecklers.

Bayswater Road (Route 12) leads west from Marble Arch to North Kensington, and Edgware Road north-west to Paddington and the west end of Marylebone Road (Route 16). The road junction is the site of TYBURN, for nearly 600 years the famous place for public executions, to which the condemned were brought through the gaping crowds from Newgate Prison or the Tower. The first recorded execution took place in 1196, the last in 1783, and among those who suffered here (usually 'hanged, drawn, and quartered') were Perkin Warbeck, the pretender (1499); Elizabeth Barton, the 'holy maid of Kent' (1534); leaders of the Pilgrimage of Grace (1537); Edmund Campion (1581) and other Jesuit martyrs; Oliver Plunket, archbishop of Armagh (1681; canonized in 1975); and the notorious highwaymen, Claude Duval (1670) and Jack Sheppard (1724). In 1661 the bodies of Cromwell, Ireton, and Bradshaw, exhumed from Westminster Abbey, were gibbeted and beheaded here before being buried at the foot of the gallows. A permanent gallows, the 'Tyburn Tree', stood from 1571 to 1759 at the place indicated by a stone on an island in the roadway opposite the foot of Edgware Road.

MARBLE ARCH CORNER, at the junction of Edgware Road with Oxford Street, was rebuilt (by T. P. Bennett and Son) to incorporate offices, shops, and the Odeon Cinema (opened in 1967). In CONNAUGHT PLACE, a cul-de-sac on the west of Edgware Road, Lord Randolph Churchill, the statesman, father of Sir Winston, lived in 1883–92 at No. 2.

Oxford Street is named after Robert Harley, first Earl of Oxford (d. 1724), the statesman whose collections formed part of the nucleus of the British Museum and who held the manor of St Marylebone, to the north. Though famous for its large department stores, it is of little interest otherwise, and a pleasanter route, taking very little longer, may be threaded through the streets to the north (left), as described below (p. 180).

North Audley Street, on the right beyond Selfridges (see below), leads to Grosvenor Square (Route 13). In Duke Street, on the same side, is the former KING'S WEIGH HOUSE CHAPEL, built in brick and terracotta in 1891 by Alfred Waterhouse, and now the Ukrainian Catholic Cathedral. Bond Street underground station (II, E3), farther east, is 200 yds west of New Bond Street (Route 7). Nearly opposite the station entrance is STRATFORD PLACE, a cul-de-sac built originally in 1774 by Richard Edwin in the style of Robert Adam. No. 10 is the home of the ROYAL SOCIETY OF MUSICIANS of Great Britain (founded in 1738) and the ROYAL PHILHARMONIC SOCIETY (founded in 1813), and has a British Music Information Centre. STRATFORD HOUSE, at the north end, still unspoiled, was formerly Derby House, a town house of the Earls of Derby, and is now the ORIENTAL CLUB, founded in 1824, mainly for those engaged in the East Indian trade. From Davies Street, on the south of Oxford Street, opens SOUTH MOLTON STREET, in which William Blake, the poet and artist, lived for seventeen years until 1821 at No. 17, his only surviving London home. Vere Street, opposite New Bond Street, leads to ST PETER'S, VERE STREET (II, D, E3), a delightful little church (1721–4) designed by James Gibbs, the architect of St Martin-in-the-Fields, and described by Sir John Summerson as a 'miniature forecast' of that church. HENRIETTA PLACE, on the north of the church, runs east to Cavendish Square (see below).

Portman Street, on the left of Oxford Street west of SELFRIDGES, one of the largest stores in London, founded in 1909 by H. Gordon Selfridge (d. 1947), an American businessman, leads to PORTMAN SQUARE (II, D, E2), a fashionable quarter laid out after 1761 and still retaining some of its fine 18th-century houses. No. 20, on the north side, is HOME HOUSE (adm., p. 32), one of the most pleasing designs of Robert Adam, built in 1773–7 for Elizabeth, Countess of Home, daughter of a West Indian merchant.

The rooms are notable for their exquisite stucco decoration, with small paintings by Antonio Zucci and Angelica Kauffmann, and their carved marble fire-places and inlaid doors. The unusual circular staircase well rises the full height of the building and is covered by a spherical dome with a skylight. The house was carefully restored after 1927 for Samuel Courtauld (d. 1948), the textile manufacturer and a noted art collector, who on the death in 1931 of his wife, Elizabeth, a well-known patron of music, presented it to the University of London for use as the COURTAULD INSTITUTE OF ART, established in 1932 for the teaching of art history in all its aspects. The institute is to move to Somerset House (Route 21). No. 21 Portman Square is the HEINZ GALLERY of the Royal Institute of British Architects, whose special exhibitions here are open to the public (entrance from Gloucester Place; adm., p. 34).

Other good houses will be found in the streets and squares to the west and north-west of Portman Square (Montagu Square, etc.; compare Route 16), and especially in the long GLOUCESTER PLACE, built about 1810 and preserving some of its old lamp-brackets. At No. 57 Dickens wrote part of *Our Mutual Friend* (1864); Wilkie Collins (d. 1889), the novelist, lived at No. 65, farther north, and Elizabeth Barrett Browning at No. 99. No. 102 is now the offices of the BRITISH HEART FOUNDATION, established in 1963.

BAKER STREET is an important thoroughfare leading north from Portman Square to Marylebone Road and Regent's Park (see Route 16). It crosses GEORGE STREET (compare below), in which Thomas Moore, the Irish poet, lived until 1801 at No. 85 (near Gloucester Place), and BLANDFORD STREET, where Michael Faraday was apprenticed in 1804–12 to a bookbinder at No. 48 (now a shop). ORCHARD STREET, running south from the square, is extended beyond Oxford Street by North Audley

Street, which leads to Grosvenor Square (Route 13), while WIGMORE STREET, a long uninteresting thoroughfare, runs east to Cavendish Square (compare below), passing the WIGMORE HALL, opened in 1901 and used for concerts.

Fitzhardinge Street leads east from the north side of the square to the smaller MANCHESTER SQUARE (II, D2, 3), built in 1776–88 and little spoiled. On the north side rises HERTFORD HOUSE, the home of the magnificent **Wallace Collection** (adm., p. 465).

Manchester Street, on the west of the house, crosses GEORGE STREET, in which (to the right) are DURRANT'S HOTEL, a well-restored range of 18th-century buildings, and the Roman Catholic church of ST JAMES'S, SPANISH PLACE, a lofty cathedral-like building in the Early English Style, by Joseph Goldie (1890). It takes its name from its predecessor in Spanish Place (leading back to Manchester Square) in which Captain Marryat (d. 1848), the writer of boy's stories, lived at No. 3. In DUKE STREET, south of the square, Simón Bolívar, the Venezuelan patriot, stayed in 1810 at No. 4.

HINDE STREET, going on east from Manchester Square, is prolonged by Bentinck Street to Welbeck Street. On the right, at the corner of Mandeville Place, is the TRINITY COLLEGE OF MUSIC, founded in 1872, and 'recognized' by London University. WELBECK STREET has many 18th-century houses; in one of these (No. 29, to the left) Thomas Woolner, the sculptor and poet, lived in 1860–92, while Anthony Trollope, the novelist, died in 1882 at No. 34. QUEEN ANNE STREET leads to the right (east), crossing Wimpole Street and Harley Street, well known for the consulting rooms of many leading physicians and surgeons.

No. 56 in Queen Anne Street houses the ROYAL ASIATIC SOCIETY, founded in 1823 and the ROYAL ANTHROPOLOGICAL INSTITUTE (founded 1843). Berlioz stayed at No. 58 in 1851 while judging musical instruments at the Great Exhibition. Henry Hallam, the historian, lived in 1819–40 at No. 67 in WIMPOLE STREET, but the house (No. 50) which Elizabeth Barrett left secretly in 1846 to marry Robert Browning has unfortunately been rebuilt. J. M. W. Turner lived in 1803–12 at No. 64 in HARLEY STREET, which runs south to Cavendish Square, passing QUEEN'S COLLEGE, founded in 1848 by F. D. Maurice and the oldest college in England for women (390 pupils). The many well-known pupils have included Gertrude Bell, Octavia Hill, and Katherine Mansfield. The college now occupies also No. 47, once the home of Florence Nightingale. No. 2, at the corner of Cavendish Square, though partly rebuilt, has a fine doorframe carried up to enclose the window above.

CAVENDISH SQUARE (II, D3) was laid out after 1719 by John Prince for Edward Harley, son of the first Earl of Oxford, and some of its original houses still survive. Lord Nelson lived in 1787 at No. 5, on the east side, later the home of Quintin Hogg (d. 1903), founder of the Polytechnic of Central London. The ROYAL COLLEGE OF NURSING, founded in 1916, now occupies No. 20, a house partly of 1729 at the south-west corner, long the home of the Earl of Oxford and Asquith (d. 1928), the Liberal statesman. Alongside and above the staircase are fine murals painted about 1730 and well restored in 1955. On the south side of the gardens in the square, notable for their fine trees, is a statue of Lord George Bentinck (d. 1848), the politician. Nos. 11–14 on the north side of the square, two noble pairs of houses with classical façades, were built about 1770. They were formerly occupied by the Convent of the Holy Child, and the arch connecting them carries a large bronze Madonna by Sir Jacob Epstein which the sculptor called his 'passport to eternity'.

The houses now accommodate HEYTHROP COLLEGE, which grew out of a college founded in 1614 at Louvain (Belgium) for English Jesuits. The college moved to England and in 1926 to Heythrop (Oxfordshire), and from about 1960 non-Jesuit students were admitted. The college moved again, to its present home, in 1970 and became part of the University of London; it awards degrees in the faculties of theology and arts (philosophy).

In CHANDOS STREET, running north from Cavendish Square, is the unusual building of the MEDICAL SOCIETY OF LONDON, founded in 1773. CHANDOS HOUSE, facing down the street, is a fine stone-fronted mansion by Robert Adam (1771). There are other good 18th-century houses in QUEEN ANNE STREET, which leads to the left (see above), and in MANSFIELD STREET, north of this, where the third Earl Stanhope (1753–1816), 'reformer and inventor', lived at No. 20, and No. 13 (now the BRITISH COMPUTER SOCIETY, founded in 1957) was occupied by the architects, J. L. Pearson (d. 1897) and Sir Edwin Lutyens (d. 1944). In 1957 a new building in the same style was opened next to this for the ROYAL COLLEGE OF MIDWIVES, established in 1881. No. 7 in this street houses the BRITISH VETERINARY ASSOCIATION, founded in 1882.

From the south side of Cavendish Square, HENRIETTA PLACE runs west, passing the ROYAL SOCIETY OF MEDICINE (founded in 1805), in a building of 1912 by Sir John Belcher. Close by is the church of St Peter's, Vere Street (see above). HOLLES STREET leads south from the square to reach Oxford Street opposite the entrance to Hanover Square and a little west of OXFORD CIRCUS (III, D, E1; Route 15). On the west corner of Holles Street is the large store (by Slater and Moberley) of JOHN LEWIS, with a 'Winged Figure' outside by Barbara Hepworth (1963). In John Princes Street, to the east, is the NATIONAL DAIRY CENTRE, opened in 1967.

MARGARET STREET, starting from the south-east corner of Cavendish Square, crosses Regent Street (Route 15) and GREAT

PORTLAND STREET, a long thoroughfare with the shops of many motor-dealers, running north to Euston Road (see Route 16). The rest of the route, through a poorer quarter, is of less interest, though it is always quicker to traverse the side streets rather than face the crowds in Oxford Street. GREAT TITCHFIELD STREET, the next street crossed, is (with the neighbouring streets) the centre for wholesale furriers and costumiers. Farther on in Margaret Street is ALL SAINTS' CHURCH (III, D1), a rather florid Gothic building in dark red brick by William Butterfield, consecrated in 1859, and noted for its music. It has a lofty spire, 227 ft high, and an immense reredos with paintings by Sir Ninian Comper, who restored the east end in 1909.

Wells Street, at the end of Margaret Street, leads left to the parallel MORTIMER STREET, to the right in which is the large MIDDLESEX HOSPITAL (III, D1), founded in 1745 and rebuilt in 1929. Rudyard Kipling died here in 1936.

To the north-east, in CLEVELAND STREET, are the buildings (by Sidney Cusdin, 1959) of the medical school (founded in 1835), part of London University, but to amalgamate with the University College School of Medicine (Route 18). Henry Fuseli, the Swiss artist, lived in 1788–1803 at No. 37 in FOLEY STREET, leading west from Cleveland Street, which itself runs north past the soaring Telecom Tower (Route 16).

Mortimer Street is extended by Goodge Street to Tottenham Court Road, crossing CHARLOTTE STREET, the axis of a neighbourhood popular with artists in the 19th century and now containing many foreign restaurants. John Constable, the landscape painter, died in 1837 at No. 76; the house has been demolished, but others of the 18th century survive at Nos. 66–74. Sir Robert Smirke (d. 1867), architect of the British Museum, lived at No. 81, on the west side. In Scala Street, on the east, is POLLOCK'S TOY MUSEUM (adm., p. 34), an exhibition of toys and dolls of many countries and periods, as well as toy theatres and early experiments in moving pictures. From the south end of Charlotte Street, Rathbone Place goes on to Oxford Street some distance west of ST GILES CIRCUS (III, D2), while PERCY STREET, built in 1764–70 and retaining some of its original doorways, leads left to TOTTENHAM COURT ROAD (Route 18).

15 From Piccadilly Circus to Regent's Park (Regent Street)

Plan III, F2–II, B3

STATIONS: PICCADILLY CIRCUS (Plan III, F2), OXFORD CIRCUS (III, E1), and REGENT'S PARK (II, C3), all on the Bakerloo line. Piccadilly Circus is also on the Piccadilly line, and Oxford Circus on the Central and Victoria lines, while GREAT PORTLAND STREET (III, B, C1), on the Circle and Metropolitan lines, is 200 yds E of Regent's Park station. — BUSES Nos. 3, 6, 12, 13, 15, 23, 53, 88, and 159 in Regent Street; Nos. 3, 53, and 137 in Portland Place (northbound only) and Great Portland Street (southbound only). For other buses to Piccadilly Circus, see Routes 7, 18; to Oxford Circus, see Route 14; in Marylebone Road and Euston Road, see Route 16.

REGENT STREET (III, F2–D1), one of the most favoured shopping streets of London, was laid out in 1813–25 by John Nash as part of a scheme to connect the Prince Regent's residence, Carlton House (Route 6), with his newly acquired property of Regent's Park. Now the main south-to-north thoroughfare of the West End, it begins at Waterloo Place (Route 6), takes a sharp bend to the left at Piccadilly Circus and crosses Oxford Street at Oxford Circus. It ends on the north in Langham Place, which bears left in turn to the foot of Portland Place, a broad street already constructed by the brothers Adam but brought into his scheme by Nash, who finished off its northern end with a fine crescent opening towards Regent's Park.

The buildings in Regent Street have all been redesigned in the present century and it is now of no specific interest, apart from its shops. The curved portion opening on the north-west from Piccadilly Circus (Route 7) and known as the Quadrant maintains the bold sweep intended by Nash, though the façades were recast in 1923, not to their improvement, by Sir Reginald Blomfield and others, who incorporated the north front of Shaw's Piccadilly Hotel.

Beyond the curve VIGO STREET leads to the left to the north entrance to Albany (Route 7) and to BURLINGTON GARDENS, on the south side of which is a large building by Sir James Pennethorne put up in 1869 for the University of London.

The building now contains the MUSEUM OF MANKIND (adm., p. 33), displaying treasures from the rich collections of the Ethnography Department of the British Museum, dealing with the life and culture of the peoples of Africa, America, and the Pacific. The permanent exhibition includes an ivory mask from Benin (West Africa), an Aztec skull made of crystal, African and Oceanic carvings, masks from New Guinea, and pre-Columbian gold work from South and Central America. In addition, special exhibitions are mounted, each lasting for about a year, and relevant films are shown. The large reserve collection of the museum can usually be seen on application, and the extensive library of archaeological and anthropological works is accessible to visitors.

The former QUEENSBERRY HOUSE, at the corner of Savile Row, was built in 1721 by Giacomo Leoni, but was altered later in the century.

SAVILE ROW (III, E, F1), which runs parallel to Regent Street, is well known for its fashionable tailors and has some interesting houses. No. 12 was the residence of George Grote, the historian of Greece, from 1848 until his death in 1871. R. B. Sheridan, the playwright, lived at No. 14, but died in 1816 in the front bedroom of No. 17, a house later occupied by George Basevi (d. 1845), the architect of Belgravia. No. 23 contains the offices of the BRITISH ASSOCIATION for the Advancement of Science (1831) and the NATIONAL MONUMENTS RECORD, set up in 1941. CLIFFORD STREET, on the left, was built about 1720, and Nos. 8, 16 and 18 in particular are excellent survivals of this time. Savile Row emerges into CONDUIT STREET, which leads right to Regent Street and left to Bond Street (Route 7). No. 9, to the right, a fine house by James Wyatt, has one of the earliest stucco fronts in London (1799).

Savile Row is continued by Mill Street to Maddox Street, from the left branch of which St George Street leads north to Hanover Square, passing the church of ST GEORGE'S, HANOVER SQUARE (III, E1), built in 1713–24 by John James, a follower of Wren, with a large Corinthian portico and a baroque tower. The altar painting of the Last Supper is by William Kent, and the east windows of the chancel and aisles contain good Flemish glass of 1520 from Malines (Belgium), inserted in 1843 and representing a Tree of Jesse.

Handel was a frequent worshipper here while living in Brook Street. The church has been noted for its fashionable weddings since the late 18th century, and the registers record the marriages of Sir William Hamilton and Emma Hart (Nelson's 'Dearest Emma') in 1791; Benjamin Disraeli and Mrs Wyndham Lewis in 1839; J. W. Cross, a New York banker, and 'George Eliot' (Mary Ann Evans) in 1880; Theodore Roosevelt and Edith Carow in 1886; and H. H. Asquith and Margaret Tennant in 1894. P. B. Shelley and Harriet Westbrook were remarried here in 1814 in confirmation of their Scottish marriage in 1811.

HANOVER SQUARE (III, E1) was laid out in 1717, but has been largely rebuilt; No. 24, of variegated brick, is an example of the original houses. Mary Somerville, the scientific writer, lived in 1818–27 at No. 12, another old house, and Prince Talleyrand (d. 1838), the French statesman, lived for a time at No. 21. At the south end of the gardens is a bronze statue by Chantrey of William Pitt the Younger (d. 1806).

Brook Street (see Route 13) leads west to Grosvenor Square, and Harewood Place north to Oxford Street opposite Holles Street, the entrance to Cavendish Square (Route 14).

The HANOVER SQUARE ROOMS, the principal concert hall in London during the late 18th century, stood on the east side of the square, at the corner of Hanover Street. Here took place the Hanover Square Concerts (1764–81), promoted by Johann Christian Bach (d. 1782) and Carl Friedrich Abel (d. 1787; both composers died in London), and here Haydn conducted the orchestra in his own music on his visit to London in 1791–2.

In HANOVER STREET (at No. 10) is the LONDON DIAMOND CENTRE (adm., p. 33), with a large collection of precious stones (some of which are for sale) and an exhibition of diamond mining, cutting, and finishing. Hanover Street goes on to Regent Street, which it reaches nearly opposite GREAT MARLBOROUGH STREET. The timber-framed block of LIBERTY's store here (1924) represents the Tudor revival at its most exuberant.

In Argyll Street, to the left of Great Marlborough Street, is the PALLADIUM THEATRE (by Frank Matcham), opened in 1910. CARNABY STREET, to the right, is well known for its many colourful dress and other shops catering for the tastes of young people. At No. 47 Great Marlborough Street, farther on, is the LONDON COLLEGE OF MUSIC, founded in 1887.

Regent Street crosses Oxford Street at OXFORD CIRCUS (III, D, E1), then goes over Margaret Street (compare Route 14). On the left just beyond is THE POLYTECHNIC OF CENTRAL LONDON, an institute founded in 1882 by Quintin Hogg (see below), rebuilt in 1911, and several times extended. The object of the institute, which was the first of its kind, is to provide technical and scientific instruction for both day and evening students, and at the same time to assist the moral and physical development of youth, and it now has over 4,100 students.

In LANGHAM PLACE, which curves to the left to connect Regent Street with Portland Place, is ALL SOULS' CHURCH (III, D1), built in 1822–4 by John Nash, who designed the circular classical portico and needle-like spire surrounded by its ring of free-standing columns to close the vista up Regent Street, which it did most effectively until it became overshadowed in 1958 by a huge office building.

A bust of the architect (d. 1835), by Cecil Thomas, was unveiled under the portico in 1956. The church, a simple but successful basilica with no structural chancel, was badly damaged by bombing in 1940 but well restored in 1951. A new undercroft, designed by Brandt, Potter & Partners and containing a meeting hall, refectory and studio facilities for the B.B.C., was constructed in 1976.

PORTLAND PLACE (II, C, D3), one of the widest streets in London, was built about 1774 by Robert and James Adam, who intended it as a kind of close to be surrounded by the houses of the wealthy. Their intentions, however, were never completely carried out and most of the houses have since been rebuilt. The best of the survivals are Nos. 46–8, a double house by James Adam (1774), on the east side. The street is now favoured by several embassies and various institutes and societies. At the foot rises BROADCASTING HOUSE, the headquarters of the British Broadcasting Corporation (B.B.C.), incorporated in 1927 as successor to the British Broadcasting Company. The huge and rather formless building, designed by George Val Myer and F. J. Watson-Hart (1931), has over the main entrance a sculptured group of Prospero and Ariel, one of the last works of Eric Gill. The first public television transmission took place here, in 1932. The immense and ugly building opposite (the former Langham Hotel, 1864), facing up Portland Place and also utilized by the B.B.C., is to be replaced by a new Broadcasting Centre, to the designs of Norman Foster.

Near the south end of the street is a statue by Sir George Frampton in memory of Quintin Hogg (d. 1903). No. 26, on the right, houses the ROYAL SOCIETY OF TROPICAL MEDICINE AND HYGIENE (founded in 1907) and the ROYAL TOWN PLANNING INSTITUTE (established in 1914), while No. 28 adjoining is the ROYAL INSTITUTE OF PUBLIC HEALTH AND HYGIENE, formed in 1937, with a post-graduate medical school. No. 38 (a building of 1979), beyond New Cavendish Street, is the ROYAL COLLEGE OF RADIOLOGISTS, established in 1934. No. 44 is the INSTITUTION OF MINING AND METALLURGY, founded in 1892. The CHINESE EMBASSY (No. 31), on the left, is being rebuilt (from 1983) with a façade which will be a copy of that of its forerunner (demolished in 1980), dating from 1750. An equestrian statue by Tweed of Sir George White (d. 1912), the defender of Ladysmith, stands opposite No. 47 (now the POLISH EMBASSY), the residence in 1902–6 of Earl Roberts.

In NEW CAVENDISH STREET, to the left, No. 61 is the INSTITUTE OF PETROLEUM, founded in 1913. In DEVONSHIRE STREET, on the same side of Portland Place, No. 18 is the INSTITUTE OF ENERGY (established in 1927) and No. 42 houses the ROYAL SOCIETY FOR ASIAN AFFAIRS (founded in 1901). In the same street, on the other side of Portland Place, No. 4 is the INSTITUTE OF

CONTEMPORARY HISTORY, and also the home of the WIENER LIBRARY, which documents the history of Europe from 1933 onwards.

On the right at the corner of Weymouth Street is the ROYAL INSTITUTE OF BRITISH ARCHITECTS (founded in 1834), in a fine building by Grey Wornum (1934). The reliefs on the façade (by E. Bainbridge Copnall) and the pillars each side of the entrance (with sculpture by James Woodford) have met with some criticism, but the interior, with its fine staircase and ornamental glass, is most satisfying. At No. 76 Portland Place are the headquarters (1959) of the CITY AND GUILDS OF LONDON INSTITUTE, an independent educational organization established in 1878; No. 80 is the CHARTERED INSTITUTE OF TRANSPORT, founded in 1919. Henry Brooks Adams (d. 1918), the American historian, lived at No. 98, which was the United States Embassy in 1863–6.

Near the head of Portland Place is a monument to Lord Lister (d. 1912), the pioneer of antiseptic surgery, who lived in 1877–1909 at No. 12 in PARK CRESCENT (II, C3), an admirable semi-circle of buildings (well restored after war damage) distinguished by Ionic colonnades, designed in 1821 by Nash to provide a formal approach to Regent's Park. No. 12 is now the office of the SPASTICS SOCIETY (founded in 1952), and No. 20 is that of the MEDICAL RESEARCH COUNCIL, established in 1913. The arms of the crescent abut on MARYLEBONE ROAD, which runs to the south of Regent's Park (see Route 16).

16 From Marble Arch to Euston, St Pancras, and King's Cross via Marylebone Road

Plan II, E2–III, A3

STATIONS: MARBLE ARCH (Plan II, E2), on the Central line; EDGWARE ROAD (II, C1), BAKER STREET (II, C2), GREAT PORTLAND STREET (III, B, C1), EUSTON SQUARE (III, B2) and KING'S CROSS & ST PANCRAS (III, A3), all on the Circle and Metropolitan lines; MARYLEBONE (II, C1) and REGENT'S PARK (II, C3), on the Bakerloo line; WARREN STREET (III, B1) and EUSTON (III, A2), on the Northern line. Edgware Road is also on the District line, Baker Street on the Bakerloo and Jubilee lines, and King's Cross & St Pancras on the Northern and Piccadilly lines; and Warren Street, Euston, and King's Cross & St Pancras are on the Victoria line. — BUSES Nos. 6, 7, 8, 15, 16, 23, and 36 in Edgware Road; Nos. 1, 18, 27, 30, and 176 in Marylebone Road; Nos. 1, 2, 13, 30, 74, 113, and 159 in Gloucester

Place (northbound) or Baker Street (southbound); Nos. 18 and 30 in Euston Road to St Pancras and King's Cross; No. 176 to Gower Street only; Nos. 27 and 137 to Hampstead Road; Nos. 14 and 73 from Gower Street; and No. 77A from Upper Woburn Place. For other buses to Marble Arch, see Routes 12, 13, 14; in Tottenham Court Road, see Route 18; in Woburn Place, see Route 19; to King's Cross, see Routes 22, 29; to the Angel, see Routes 29, 30.

GREAT CUMBERLAND PLACE, starting opposite the Marble Arch (Route 14), retains some of its original terraces of 1789. It runs north across SEYMOUR STREET, where Michael Balfe (d. 1870), the composer, lived at No. 12 and Edward Lear (d. 1888), the humorous author and artist, lived for a time at No. 30 (to the right), and UPPER BERKELEY STREET, where Elizabeth Garrett Anderson (d. 1917), the first woman to qualify as a doctor in Britain, lived at No. 20 (to the left). The street emerges into BRYANSTON SQUARE (II, D1, 2), which preserves many façades of about 1810.

Chopin, staying incognito in London in 1837, visited James Broadwood, the piano manufacturer, at his house in Bryanston Square. In MONTAGU SQUARE, to the east, built at the same time, Anthony Trollope, the novelist, lived in 1873–80 at No. 39, on the west side.

From Bryanston Square, WYNDHAM PLACE faces north to the semicircular portico of ST MARY'S CHURCH, built in 1824 by Sir Robert Smirke. YORK STREET, behind the church, preserves a row of early-19th-century shops (Nos. 78–94); from its west end Seymour Place leads north to Marylebone Road.

MARYLEBONE ROAD (II, D1–III, B1), constructed in 1754–6 as part of a 'new road' to connect Paddington to Islington, traverses the former borough of St Marylebone, which stretched from Regent's Park as far south as Oxford Street and took its name from the church of 'St Mary on the bourne' or stream (i.e., the Tyburn, long since vanished).

ST MARYLEBONE GRAMMAR SCHOOL, opposite Seymour Place, founded in 1792 as the Philological School, is housed in typical Victorian buildings of 1856. From here a new section of Marylebone Road runs west to a flyover (1967) crossing Edgware Road and leading to Harrow Road and Paddington (see Suburban London). OLD MARYLEBONE ROAD, leading south-west through a humble district to Edgware Road, is of little interest. In HARCOURT STREET, on the left, is the SWEDISH CHURCH, a tall Gothic building of 1910, well restored in 1956. No. 12 is the headquarters of ST DUNSTAN'S, an organization founded in 1915 to help men and women blinded on war service; it now cares for over 1,300 blind persons.

Marylebone Road, running east, broadens out into a boulevard beyond Enford Street. Behind an ornate late-Victorian building (formerly the Hotel Great Central) is MARYLEBONE STATION (II, B, C1), opened in 1899, a smaller terminus of the Western Region which may become a coach station. The road, lined for the most part by commercial buildings and large blocks of 'mansions', passes the WESTMINSTER COUNCIL HOUSE, built in 1914–20 (as the St Marylebone Town Hall), and the more restrained MARYLEBONE LIBRARY (1938), both by Sir Edwin Cooper. The sixteen-storey MARATHON HOUSE, opposite, designed by Gollins, Melvin, Ward & Partners (1959; as Castrol House), is one of the earlier and more successful examples of the modern style.

The upper part of Gloucester Place, alongside, leads to DORSET SQUARE, with unspoiled terraces of the early 19th century. A plaque was unveiled in 1957 on No. 1, at the south-east corner, to 'commemorate the deeds of the men and women of the Free French Forces and their British comrades who left from this house on special missions to enemy-occupied France'. George Grossmith (d. 1912), the actor and author, lived at No. 28. Michael Sobell House (No. 30) contains the offices of the NATIONAL SOCIETY FOR CANCER RESEARCH, founded in 1911.

Marylebone Road crosses BAKER STREET (II, C, D2), a busy street running north to Regent's Park (Route 17) and south to Portman Square (Route 14). It was laid out about 1790, but the surviving houses of this time (south of Marylebone Road) have been disguised by their conversion into shops. In one of them (No. 120) William Pitt lived in 1803–4, his niece, the eccentric Lady Hester Stanhope, keeping house for him. The fabulous 'Sherlock Holmes' also had rooms in Baker Street. In CHILTERN COURT, the huge block of flats at the junction with Marylebone Road, Arnold Bennett, the novelist, died in 1931 (at No. 97). It stands above BAKER STREET STATION (II, C2), the original terminus of the Bakerloo Railway, which was opened in 1906 from here to Waterloo. The station is also a starting-point of the Metropolitan line trains.

Marylebone Road goes on east past MADAME TUSSAUD'S (II, C2; adm., p. 33), the famous waxworks exhibition first established in Paris in 1770 by Marie Tussaud, who began by modelling the victims of the French Revolution. She opened her museum in the Strand in 1802 and transferred it in 1835 to Baker Street, where she died in 1850. Moved to its present site in 1884, the exhibition was reconstructed (after a fire) in 1928. It contains a wide range of wax models of the famous and the infamous, past and present, and tableaux of notable events, including the Battle of Trafalgar (1805). The Chamber of Horrors, with models and relics of notorious criminals, is not suitable for children. The adjoining LONDON PLANETARIUM (adm., p. 33), the first in Britain, opened in 1958, shows the night sky in both hemispheres or at different periods of history, and illustrates the journeys into space. The projector under the distinctive copper dome comprises over 29,000 parts and weighs over two tons. A new exhibition illustrates the work of eminent astronomers.

Opposite YORK GATE, a characteristic example of the Regency style associated with John Nash (1822), forming an approach to Regent's Park, is ST MARYLEBONE PARISH CHURCH (II, C3), an imposing building by Thomas Hardwick (1813–17) with a large classical portico. The chancel was rebuilt in 1885 in an early baroque style by Thomas Harris. Robert Browning was married to Elizabeth Barrett in 1846 in this church, an event commemorated by a window in the north aisle. The bronze medallion of the poet on the west wall is by Gustave Natorp, an American artist (1887); in the other aisle is a tablet to Richard Cosway, the miniaturist, who died in 1821 in Marylebone.

On the left, just beyond the church, is the ROYAL ACADEMY OF MUSIC, founded in 1822, in a building by Sir Ernest George (1911). The contemporary Duke's Hall next to it is used for concerts. A new library was opened in 1968, and a new opera theatre (by Bickerdike, Allen & Partners) in 1980. Opposite begins MARYLEBONE HIGH STREET (II, C, D3), the nucleus of the old village, but retaining nothing of its original character except its narrow winding shape.

A house on the west corner, unhappily demolished in 1958, was the home in 1839–51 of Charles Dickens, who was visited by H. W. Longfellow, the American poet, in 1841. *The Old Curiosity Shop*, most of *Barnaby Rudge, Martin Chuzzlewit, A Christmas Carol,* and *David Copperfield* were all written here, and characters from these novels are shown on a sculptured panel, on the wall of Ferguson House. *Dombey and Son*, though mostly written during a sojourn in Switzerland, draws many of its scenes from this neighbourhood: the church in which Paul Dombey was christened and Mr Dombey married has been identified as St Marylebone.

On the west of the High Street stood the former parish church, called MARYLEBONE CHAPEL after the new church was completed. The chapel, rebuilt in 1741 and seriously damaged by bombing, was demolished in 1949 and the site is now a formal garden. An obelisk marks the grave of Charles Wesley (d. 1788), the hymn-writer, and his nephew, Samuel Wesley (d. 1837), the composer, and a tablet on the wall opposite records famous persons connected with the church and its predecessor.

ULSTER PLACE, on the left of Marylebone Road, is a range of good Regency building by Nash (1825). Beyond this the road has

PARK CRESCENT (II, C3) on its right, leading to Portland Place (see Route 15). On the east corner is INTERNATIONAL STUDENTS HOUSE (1965), in front of which is a memorial with a bust of President John F. Kennedy (1917–63). On the left of the main road is PARK SQUARE, also by Nash (1823–4) but rather heavier in its detail; the north side is traversed by the Outer Circle (Route 17). A little farther on is HOLY TRINITY CHURCH (III, B, 1), by Sir John Soane (1825), the interior of which was reconstructed in 1956 as the headquarters of the Society for Promoting Christian Knowledge, a body founded in 1698. Visitors are admitted to services and for private prayer. The crypt became the headquarters of Penguin Books when they were founded in 1935 by Sir Allen Lane.

The church stands opposite the entrances to GREAT PORTLAND STREET, which runs south to Oxford Street (compare Route 14). On the left (at No. 224) is the ROYAL NATIONAL INSTITUTE FOR THE BLIND, founded in 1868, with a shop where articles made by the blind are on sale. At No. 160, farther on, is the AGRICULTURAL AND FOOD RESEARCH COUNCIL, set up in 1931; and on the other side of the road is the CENTRAL SYNAGOGUE, destroyed by bombing but rebuilt in 1958.

Marylebone Road is prolonged beyond Great Portland Street station by EUSTON ROAD (III, B1–A3), a commercial thoroughfare widened in 1964–6. On the north side stretches the EUSTON CENTRE, huge blocks of offices and shops (by Sidney Kaye, Eric Firmin & Partners), begun in 1963 and including the Euston Tower, of thirty-seven storeys, the tallest office building in London when it was completed in 1969. Conway Street, on the right, leads to FITZROY SQUARE, which has notable ranges of houses. The east and south sides were built in 1790–94 by Robert Adam, but the north and west sides are later (1825–9).

No. 9, on the east side, is the BRITISH THEATRE ASSOCIATION, founded (as the British Drama League) in 1919 and now incorporating the British Theatre Play Library. The third Marquess of Salisbury (d. 1903), the Prime Minister, lived at No. 21, on the west side; and Bernard Shaw occupied No. 29 in 1887–98, when he was music and drama critic of various papers, and wrote his first seven plays here. Virginia Woolf, the novelist, also lived in this house, in 1907–11. Samuel Morse, the painter and inventor of Morse Code, and C. R. Leslie, the artist and biographer of Constable, lived at No. 141 in CLEVELAND STREET (to the west; see below) when they came from America in 1812.

On the south-east corner of Fitzroy Square is the fine Y.M.C.A. INDIAN STUDENTS' UNION building and hostel (by Ralph Tubbs, 1953), and in GRAFTON

WAY, which leads east to Gower Street, No. 58 was the residence for fourteen years from 1785 of Francisco de Miranda, the Spanish-American adventurer, who was visited here in 1810 by Simón Bolívar, the liberator. W. R. Sickert had his studio in 1911–13 at No. 19 in FITZROY STREET, south of the square, and Captain Matthew Flinders (d. 1814), the explorer, lived at No. 56.

In Maple Street, which runs across Fitzroy Street to Cleveland Street, is the entrance to the TELECOM TOWER (formerly the Post Office Tower), a lighthouse-like structure completed in 1965, for television and radio telephony. The tower, 580ft high, has a 40-ft mast supporting a radar aerial, and near the top is a revolving restaurant (closed until further notice) commanding a view extending to the North Downs, Windsor Castle, and the Chiltern Hills.

Euston Road passes under the junction of Tottenham Court Road (on the right) and Hampstead Road by a motorway (1966). At Euston Square station it crosses GOWER STREET, which leads south to the University of London and the British Museum (see Route 18). In the north section, Giuseppe Mazzini, the Italian patriot, lived at No. 183 in 1837–40. Beyond, in Euston Road, is the WELLCOME FOUNDATION, a flourishing scientific research institution established in 1913 by Sir Henry Wellcome (d. 1936), occupying a large building of 1932 by Septimus Warwick. It contains the Wellcome Institute of the History of Medicine and the Wellcome Museum of Medical Science (accessible to students only), but the excellent Museum of the History of Medicine was transferred to the Science Museum in 1980.

Opposite EUSTON SQUARE (1805), named after the Suffolk estate of the Fitzroy family who owned it, is FRIENDS' HOUSE (III, B2; adm., p. 32), built in 1927 (by Hubert Lidbetter) as the head-offices of the Society of Friends, which has over 18,000 members in Britain (over 204,000 throughout the world). The library contains a fine collection of Quaker literature, including the journal of George Fox, the founder, and documents concerning the foundation of Pennsylvania by William Penn. A statue by Marochetti of Robert Stephenson (d. 1859), the civil engineer, stands in the forecourt (to the left) of EUSTON STATION (III, A2), one of the principal termini of the London Midland Region, completely rebuilt in 1962–8 (by W. F. Beatty and Roy L. Moorcroft), with a parcels section over the platforms. Here also are the head-offices of the BRITISH RAILWAYS BOARD, which in 1962 superseded the British Transport Commission (set up in 1947).

At the corner of Upper Woburn Place, which bears right for Tavistock Square (Route 19), is ST PANCRAS CHURCH (III, B2), built in a Grecian style in 1819–22 by W. and H. W. Inwood, who were inspired by the temple of Erechtheus and other buildings at Athens. The octagonal tower is modelled on the Tower of the Winds, and the church has an impressive classical portico. On either side at the east end are curious extensions with caryatids in terracotta (by Rossi) imitated from the Erechtheion. The successful interior, finely restored in 1953, is a plain rectangle with the addition of an apse remarkable for its huge scagliola columns. The unusual pulpit is contemporary.

The ELIZABETH GARRETT ANDERSON HOSPITAL, on the north side of Euston Road, was founded in 1866 and is one of the only three hospitals in England managed entirely by women. It was reopened in 1984, after restoration, as an obstetrics and gynaecology unit. THE PLACE, in Duke's Road, opposite the hospital, is the home of the LONDON CONTEMPORARY DANCE THEATRE, established in 1967. Mabledon Place, on the right of Euston Road farther on, leads to CARTWRIGHT GARDENS, a good early-19th-century crescent by James Burton. In Tavistock Place, farther south, is the MARY WARD CENTRE (1898; by Smith and Brewer), a rare example of the Art Nouveau influence.

The ST PANCRAS LIBRARY, built in 1971 (by Elidir Davies) on the north side of Euston Road, contains the small SHAW THEATRE, named in honour of Bernard Shaw and utilized by the National Youth Theatre, founded in 1956. A new building for the BRITISH LIBRARY (to the designs of Colin St John Wilson) was begun in 1984 to the west of St Pancras Station.

The enormous ST PANCRAS STATION (III, A3), the other chief terminus of the London Midland Region, was built in 1867–74 by Sir George Gilbert Scott and displays the romantic spirit of the Victorians in its most effusive manner. Its spreading façade embodies details from French and Italian Gothic architecture, and its soaring clock-tower is 300 ft high; the west tower rises to 270 ft. The vault over the platforms behind, severely functional in comparison, was designed by W. H. Barlow and constructed by the Butterley Company of Ripley (Derbyshire). It has a length of 690 ft and an exceptional span of 243 ft. Opposite the station is CAMDEN TOWN HALL, built as St Pancras Town Hall by A. J. Thomas (1937).

Pancras Road, starting on the east of St Pancras Station, leads under the railway to ST PANCRAS OLD CHURCH, largely rebuilt in 1848, but retaining a few 12th–13th-century details. Johann Christian Bach (d. 1782), the composer, and John Flaxman (d. 1826), the sculptor, were buried in the churchyard (now a public garden), which contains a remarkable mausoleum designed by Sir John Soane for his wife (1815), in which the architect himself was buried in 1837. Beyond the church, Crowndale Road runs west past the WORKING MEN'S COLLEGE, established in 1854 in Bloomsbury by F. D. Maurice and moved here in 1905. Early art teachers were John Ruskin and D. G. Rossetti, who was replaced by Ford Madox Brown in 1858. Women were admitted for the first time in 1965. The ROYAL VETERINARY COLLEGE, in a street on the right before this, founded in 1791 and rebuilt in 1937, has been since 1949 a school of London University in the faculty of medicine.

Euston Road ends at KING'S CROSS STATION (III, A3), the main terminus of the Eastern Region, with a frontage designed by Lewis Cubitt (1852) and much praised for its fitness for purpose in comparison with St Pancras Station. The tower (120 ft high) contains a clock which adorned the Crystal Palace during the 1851 Exhibition. A new passenger concourse and travel centre, in front, was opened in 1973.

King's Cross, a bustling centre of traffic, takes its name from a monument to George IV which stood here until 1845. GRAY'S INN ROAD turns south to Holborn (see Route 22), while PENTONVILLE ROAD (IV, A1, 2) goes on east from King's Cross to Islington (Route 31) passing, on the right, the new KING'S CROSS MIDLAND Station of British Rail and (in less than half a mile) the churchyard of the demolished St James's Church. This is to be converted into a park in memory of Joseph Grimaldi, the famous clown, who died penniless in 1837 and is buried here. Claremont Square, on the right farther on, gives access to an excellent layout of late-Regency terraces around MYDDELTON SQUARE (1827), in the centre of which is the Gothic ST MARK'S CHURCH, built in 1828 by W. C. Mylne, damaged during the war, and partly restored in 1963. KING'S CROSS ROAD, starting near the west end of Pentonville Road, runs south-east to Farringdon Road (Route 29).

17 Regent's Park and Neighbourhood

Plan I, A 1–II, B 3

STATIONS: BAKER STREET (Plan II, C2), on the Bakerloo, Circle, Jubilee, and Metropolitan lines; REGENT'S PARK (II, C3), on the Bakerloo line; ST JOHN'S WOOD (½ m. NW of Hanover Gate; beyond II, A1), on the Jubilee line; GREAT PORTLAND STREET (III, B, C1), on the Circle and Metropolitan lines; CAMDEN TOWN (½ m. NE of Gloucester Gate; beyond I, A3), on the Northern line. — BUSES in Marylebone Road and Baker Street, see Route 16; Nos. 2, 13, 74, and 113 in Park Road (W of the park); No. 74 in Prince Albert Road (N); Nos. 3 and 53 in Albany Street (E).

REGENT'S PARK is open daily until dusk. — CARS are allowed on the Outer and Inner Circles (speed limit 30 m.p.h.).

RESTAURANT (Rose Garden) in Queen Mary's Gardens, open all the year. — BANDS play on the Holme Green (near the former Bedford College), June to August; weekdays, 12.30 to 2 and 5.30 to 7; Sundays, 3 to 4.30 and 6.30 to 8. —

BOATING on the lake, Easter to October (boats for hire at the N W end, near which there is a paddle-boat pond for children).

REGENT'S PARK, one of the largest open spaces in London, with an area of 472 acres (including Primrose Hill, on the north), was originally Marylebone Park, a royal hunting-ground until the time of the Commonwealth. It reverted to the Crown in 1811 and was laid out afresh from 1812 onward by John Nash for the Prince Regent, after whom it was named and who contemplated taking one of the country villas to be built here. At the same time Nash also built Regent Street as part of a 'royal mile' connecting the park with the prince's house in St James's (compare Route 6) and began the series of classical terraces, in the style now known as Regency, which enclose the park on all sides but the north. The first of these terraces, whose grandiose façades conceal unpretentious residences, was built in 1820 and the scheme was complete by 1827, several of the terraces being designed by Decimus Burton. Considerably damaged in the Second World War, they have been restored and some are in use as government offices. Only a few of the intended villas were built in the park, and in 1838 it was thrown open to the public.

The park is surrounded by a carriage-drive, over 2¾ m. long, called the Outer Circle. Roads on the south and east connect this with the Inner Circle, nearly ¾ m. long, which encloses the beautiful Queen Mary's Gardens, containing the Open Air Theatre. On the west of the Inner Circle is an attractive boating lake of twenty-two acres, and on the north of the park are the Zoological Gardens, reached by the Outer Circle or by the Broad Walk, an avenue stretching north from Park Square (Route 16). Red squirrels were re-introduced into the park in 1984.

The OUTER CIRCLE may be reached from Marylebone Road, which runs a little south of the park, by York Gate (Route 16) or by the upper section of Baker Street, leading to Park Road and the Clarence Gate.

In PARK ROAD, José de San Martin (d. 1850), the Argentine liberator, stayed at No. 23, in an early-19th-century terrace. At the north end of Glentworth Street, to the left, is ST CYPRIAN'S CHURCH, with a characteristic Gothic interior by Sir Ninian Comper (1903), and farther north, in Park Road, is RUDOLPH STEINER HOUSE (by Montague Wheeler, 1926–37), containing a concert and lecture hall.

Inside CLARENCE GATE (II, B2), the drive bears to the left, passing CLARENCE TERRACE (by Burton, 1823), rebuilt behind its stately façade in 1967. SUSSEX PLACE, one of the most dignified of Nash's terraces (1822), likewise partly rebuilt (1972), houses the

LONDON BUSINESS SCHOOL, founded in 1965 (as the London Graduate School of Business Studies) and 'recognized' by London University. A new extension, the Plowden Building, fronting Park Road, was opened in 1983. The ROYAL COLLEGE OF OBSTETRICIANS and Gynaecologists (founded in 1929), close by, occupies a building of 1960. Farther on is HANOVER TERRACE, also of 1822 and ultraclassical in style. Charles Dickens wrote part of *Great Expectations* while staying in 1861 at No. 3. Ralph Vaughan Williams, the composer, lived from 1953 until his death here in 1958 at No. 11, and H. G. Wells, the novelist, died in 1946 at No. 13.

The road on the left beyond this, opposite a path leading to the boating lake, returns to Park Road at HANOVER GATE, with a lodge built by Nash where Admiral Lord Beatty lived in 1910–25. Regent's Lodge, near by, is now the ISLAMIC CULTURAL CENTRE, and to the north is the CENTRAL LONDON MOSQUE, built in 1978 to the designs of Sir Frederick Gibberd, with a dome 75 ft high and a minaret of 150 ft. KENT TERRACE (1827), fronting Park Road to the south-east, is the only terrace by Nash that faces away from the park.

Facing the north end of Park Road is ST JOHN'S WOOD CHURCH (II, A1), a pleasant small Regency church (now United Reformed) by Thomas Hardwick (1813). J. S. Cotman (d. 1842), the landscape painter, is buried in the churchyard, now a public garden. From the church, the centre of a favoured residential district, WELLINGTON ROAD goes on north-west towards St John's Wood station (nearly ½ m.) and Hampstead. In PRINCE ALBERT ROAD, which runs north-east for Primrose Hill and Camden Town (see below), is NUFFIELD LODGE (formerly Grove House), a fine Regency villa by Decimus Burton (1824), altered in 1877 and since 1953 the headquarters of the NUFFIELD FOUNDATION, established in 1943 by William Morris, Lord Nuffield.

In ST JOHN'S WOOD ROAD, which descends south-west from the church to Maida Vale (Edgware Road; see Suburban London), is the main entrance to LORD'S CRICKET GROUND, the headquarters of the Marylebone Cricket Club (M.C.C.), the governing body of the English summer game since 1788, and the county ground of Middlesex. Thomas Lord (d. 1832) opened the first ground in Dorset Square in 1787, but in 1814 he removed to the present ground, bringing with him the original turf. The gateway (1923) is a memorial to the immortal Dr W. G. Grace (d. 1915); the old racket court contains a museum of interest to cricket enthusiasts (adm., p. 33).

The Outer Circle passes (on the right) WINFIELD HOUSE, built in 1936 and presented to the United States Government in 1946 as a residence for the American Ambassador. The house stands on the site of St Dunstan's Lodge, in which St Dunstan's Hostel for blinded ex-servicemen (now at Brighton) was founded in 1915. The road is followed on the left by the REGENT'S CANAL, a branch of the Grand Union Canal, opened in 1820 to connect the Grand Junction Canal at Paddington with the Thames at Wapping. MACCLESFIELD BRIDGE, built by Nash about 1815, crosses the canal to Prince Albert Road (for Primrose Hill), and farther on the Outer Circle passes the main entrance to the **Zoological Gardens** (adm., p. 492). Beyond this on the left are the offices of the ZOOLOGICAL SOCIETY OF LONDON, founded in 1826; on the right is the northern entrance to the Broad Walk (see below).

The Broad Walk is extended northward over Prince Albert Road (see below) to REGENT'S PARK ROAD, in which No. 2 (to the right) is CECIL SHARP HOUSE (adm., p. 31), the headquarters of the English Folk Dance and Song Society and named in honour of Cecil Sharp (1859–1924), a pioneer in the collection of folk music. Built in 1929 by H. M. Fletcher, it was rebuilt in 1951 after war damage.

Regent's Park Road ascends to the left along the side of PRIMROSE HILL, an open space the top of which (219 ft) affords an extensive view over London, with the Telecom Tower by far the most distinctive feature. To the left of this can be seen the Centre Point offices (at St Giles Circus), St Paul's Cathedral, and St Pancras Station, with Britannic House (in the Barbican) and the National Westminster Bank tower behind; and to the right are distinguished the Houses of Parliament, Millbank Tower, the Westminster Cathedral campanile, Portland House (near Victoria Station), and the London Hilton Hotel. W. B. Yeats (d. 1939), the Irish poet, lived at No. 23 in FITZROY ROAD, on the north side of Regent's Park Road, which itself goes past ST MARY THE VIRGIN, a successful church in the Early English style by W. P. Manning (1885). Friedrich Engels, the Marxist philosopher, lived in 1870–94 at No. 121, near the north end. Primrose Hill Road, on the left of Regent's Park Road, leads to ELSWORTHY ROAD, in which Sir Henry Wood (1869–1943), founder of the Promenade Concerts, lived in 1902–37 at No. 4. His visitors included Sibelius, Delius, Janáček, and Bartók. Dame Clara Butt, the singer, lived in 1901–29 at No. 7 in HARLEY ROAD, farther west.

Prince Albert Road is extended eastward beyond Albany Street and Parkway by PARK VILLAGE EAST, part of an estate of suburban villas begun in 1824 by John Nash as an extension to the Regent's Park estate. Others of the attractive villas are in PARK VILLAGE WEST, on the east side of ALBANY STREET, which runs south to the junction of Marylebone Road and Euston Road (Route 16). Henry Mayhew (d. 1887), the founder of *Punch*, lived at No. 55 in this street.

PARKWAY (I, A3) leads north-east past DELANCEY STREET, where Dylan Thomas (d. 1953), the poet, lived at No. 54, and goes on to CAMDEN HIGH STREET, the main street of the once working-class district of Camden Town. At the south end is a statue (1863) of Richard Cobden (d. 1865), the radical statesman. The High Street runs northward from Camden Town station to the REGENT'S CANAL, which here threads the interesting CAMDEN LOCK, where an artists' colony, with craftsmen's shops and studios, has become established. A pleasant walk of nearly two miles may be taken along the canal towpath through the northern part of Regent's Park, skirting the Zoological Gardens, and thence to Lisson Grove, where the canal enters the Maida Hill Tunnel, built in 1816. The High Street is prolonged towards Hampstead by Chalk Farm Road (see Suburban London).

The Outer Circle turns south, passing GLOUCESTER GATE and another classical terrace by Nash (1827). Just beyond this is ST KATHARINE'S CHAPEL (I, A, B3), built in 1829 in a Gothic style to the designs of Ambrose Poynter.

This was formerly the chapel of the St Katharine's Royal Hospital, established in 1148 by Matilda, wife of King Stephen, near the Tower, and the oldest surviving ecclesiastical foundation in England. In 1825, when St Katharine's Docks were excavated, the hospital was removed to Regent's Park, but in 1950 it returned to the East End of London. The chapel, well restored in 1952 after war damage, is now the church of the Danish community in London. It has a notable coffered ceiling, good modern fittings, and wooden figures of Moses and St John the Baptist by C. G. Cibber, the Danish sculptor (1696), brought from the old Danish church at Limehouse. Below the windows are thirty-nine shields-of-arms of the queens of England from Matilda to Queen Mary, recalling that in 1273 the patronage of St Katharine's Hospital was reserved by Eleanor, wife of Henry III, for the English queens. The chapel is opened for visitors by the caretaker, who lives at St Katharine's Hall (adjoining on the north), now a social centre of the Danes in London. In the garden on the south side of the chapel is a copy of the famous Rune stone at Jelling (Denmark).

The drive goes past CUMBERLAND TERRACE, one of the most notable of Nash's terraces (1826; converted into flats, 1962), and CHESTER TERRACE, also by Nash (1825). Chester Road, on the right, leads to the Inner Circle, crossing the BROAD WALK, the southern part of which is lined with beautiful flower gardens and is noted for its chestnuts, best seen when in blossom. CAMBRIDGE GATE, farther south, is a terrace of 1875. Opposite the south-east corner of the park is a striking building by Sir Denys Lasdun (1964) for the ROYAL COLLEGE OF PHYSICIANS, founded by Thomas Linacre, the humanist, in 1518. ST ANDREW'S PLACE, to the south, is a charming terrace of 1826. At the south end of the Broad Walk is PARK SQUARE (Route 16), from which the Outer Circle runs west via YORK TERRACE, designed by Decimus Burton (1821), and YORK GATE (II, B2), then turns north-west by CORNWALL TERRACE (also by Burton) back to Clarence Gate. No. 20 in the terrace is the headquarters of the BRITISH ACADEMY, founded in 1901 for the advancement of historical, philosophical, and philological studies.

From York Gate a road leads north over an arm of the lake to the INNER CIRCLE. On the left is the former BEDFORD COLLEGE, founded in 1849 (in Bedford Square) to provide a liberal education in secular subjects for women, but merged in 1984 with the Royal Holloway College (near Egham, Surrey).

The buildings, by Basil Champneys (1913), were extended in 1931 by Maxwell Ayrton. The parts damaged by bombing in 1941 were rebuilt by Ayrton and reopened in 1950, but in 1984 the buildings were taken over, as REGENT'S COLLEGE, by Rockford College (Illinois), a private liberal arts college, to become a centre for European studies. THE HOLME, a villa built in 1818 by Decimus Burton (for his father, James Burton) near the left arm of the Inner Circle, was also part of the Bedford College, but is now privately owned. A plaque on the bandstand near the lake commemorates the seven bandsmen killed by an I.R.A. bomb in 1982.

A gate opposite the road from York Gate admits to QUEEN MARY'S GARDENS (II, A, B2), filling the space within the Inner Circle. Leased by the Royal Botanic Society from 1840 until 1932, these are perhaps the most beautiful public grounds in London, with their delightful rose and other gardens, a waterlily pond, and the ROSE GARDEN RESTAURANT, by B. and N. Westwood, Piet & Partners (1966).

On the north-west side is the charming OPEN AIR THEATRE, instituted in 1933, under the direction of Robert Atkins. A new auditorium, with seats for 1,200, was constructed in 1975 by William Howell.

18 From Piccadilly Circus to Euston via Soho and Bloomsbury

Plan III, F2–III, A2

STATIONS: PICCADILLY CIRCUS (Plan III, F2), on the Bakerloo and Piccadilly lines; TOTTENHAM COURT ROAD (III, D2), GOODGE STREET (III, C2; for London University), and EUSTON (III, A2), on the Northern line; EUSTON SQUARE (III, B2), on the Circle and Metropolitan lines. Tottenham Court Road is also on the Central line, and Euston on the Victoria Line. — BUSES Nos. 14, 19, 22, 38, and 55 in Shaftesbury Avenue (W section); Nos. 1, 24, 29, and 176 also in Charing Cross Road (northbound only) and Shaftesbury Avenue (E section; southbound); Nos. 14, 24, 29, 73, 134, and 176 in Tottenham Court Road (northbound only) and Gower Street (southbound). Other buses to Piccadilly Circus, see Routes 7, 15; in Euston Road, see Route 16.

For PICCADILLY CIRCUS, see Route 7. The shortest route thence to Euston Road taken by the buses runs via Shaftesbury Avenue, Charing Cross Road and its continuation Tottenham Court Road (an alternative route is via Shaftesbury Avenue, Bloomsbury Way, and Southampton Row; compare Route 19). SHAFTESBURY AVENUE (III, F2–D3), cut in 1886 through a humble quarter to connect Piccadilly with Holborn, skirts Soho (see below) on the south, and is otherwise best known for its shops and theatres.

On the right is the TROCADERO (open daily from 10 until midnight), rebuilt in 1984, with another entrance from Coventry Street. It has shops and restaurants on the ground and lower ground floors. On the upper floor are the GUINNESS WORLD OF RECORDS (adm., p. 32), an exhibition recreating the more dramatic records in the *Guinness Book of Records*, and the LONDON EXPERIENCE, an audio-visual interpretation of some of the events in London's history (performances every forty minutes).

On the left in Shaftesbury Avenue are the LYRIC THEATRE (by C. J. Phipps, 1888), at which Eleanore Duse, the great Italian actress, made her first London appearance in 1893, the APOLLO THEATRE (by Lewen Sharp, 1901), and the GLOBE THEATRE (by W. G. R. Sprague, 1906). The QUEEN'S THEATRE, on the same side, was built in 1907, but reconstructed (by Bryan Westwood) after war damage and reopened in 1959. WINGATE HOUSE, on the same side farther up, designed by Sir John Burnet, Tait, & Partners (1958), has a car park on the first floor and a cinema below ground. For CAMBRIDGE CIRCUS, where Charing Cross Road is crossed, and the continuation of Shaftesbury Avenue thence to New Oxford Street, see Route 19.

In GERRARD STREET, which runs south of Shaftesbury Avenue beyond Wardour Street and is now the centre of a Chinese quarter, John Dryden, the dramatist, lived at No. 43 (largely rebuilt) from 1686 until his death in 1700. Dr Johnson and Sir Joshua Reynolds founded their famous 'Literary Club' in 1764 in this street at the 'Turk's Head', a tavern long since vanished. Mr Jaggers, in Dickens's *Great Expectations*, had a 'rather stately' house on the south side.

A route of greater interest than the main road threads the congested and once squalid streets of SOHO, which extends north to Oxford Street and became the chief foreign quarter of London after the revocation of the Edict of Nantes (1685) caused thousands of French Protestant refugees to flee across the Channel. Soho is noted for its numerous foreign shops and restaurants and for its cosmopolitan atmosphere: the inhabitants include a proportion of French, Italian, and Swiss, but there is a growing number of other nationalities, especially the Chinese.

From GLASSHOUSE STREET, which leaves Piccadilly Circus on

the north (between Regent Street and Shaftesbury Avenue), Sherwood Street, passing the PICCADILLY THEATRE (by Bertie Crewe and E. A. Stone, 1928), ascends on the right towards GOLDEN SQUARE (III, E1), once a fashionable address, but now the London home of the woollen cloth trade. Ralph Nickleby, the avaricious uncle of Nicholas, lived in a 'spacious house' in the square. No. 11, at the south-east corner, has a fine carved doorway of the late 18th century. The statue in the centre of the square, of George II in Roman costume (1753), is by John van Nost.

BEAK STREET, farther north, where Antonio Canaletto, the Venetian painter, lodged in 1749–51 at No. 41 (now a restaurant), leads west to Kingly Street, with ST THOMAS'S CHURCH (1702), retaining its original fittings. Beak Street ends on the east at Lexington Street and this extends left to BROADWICK STREET, which has a terrace of early-18th-century houses (Nos. 48–58) on the north side (restored in 1980). To the right this street leads to Berwick Street, which (with Rupert Street, farther south) is the scene of a lively market. Kemp House here (by Riches and Blythin, 1961) was the first example of 'mixed development' in central London, with shops, offices, and flats in a 170-ft towerblock. Broadwick Street goes on east to WARDOUR STREET, the centre of the film industry in London. Thomas Sheraton (d. 1806), the furniture designer, lived at No. 163 and Willy Clarkson (d. 1934), the theatrical wig-maker, at Nos. 41–3.

Wardour Street runs south to Shaftesbury Avenue, passing the tower (by S. P. Cockerell, 1806) of ST ANNE'S, SOHO (III, E2), a church gutted by bombing in 1941 and not restored. On the tower are memorials to William Hazlitt (see below), the essayist, buried 'on the north side of this ground', and to Theodore, king of Corsica (who died in 1756 in poverty in Soho), with an epitaph by Horace Walpole.

Leading east on the north side of St Anne's is OLD COMPTON STREET, one of the most characteristic streets of Soho, with many foreign restaurants. From it DEAN STREET runs north, passing (on the left) MEARD STREET, which has a row of good if modest houses of 1732. In Dean Street, No. 28 was the birthplace of Joseph Nollekens, the sculptor, in 1737, but has been much altered since; in 1850–56 it was the home of Karl Marx, who began *Das Kapital* here. No. 88, a stationer's, preserves a late-18th-century shop front.

Carlisle Street, on the right of Dean Street, admits to SOHO SQUARE (III, D,E2), laid out in the reign of Charles II, of whom there is a statue (by C. G. Cibber) in the gardens. His natural son, the Duke of Monmouth, who owned a mansion here, chose 'Soho' as his watchword at the Battle of Sedgemoor (1685). In the 18th century the square was one of the most favoured places of residence in London, and after Sir Joseph Banks came to live here in 1777 it became the centre for scientific gatherings, the first meeting of the Royal Institution being held here. The houses have almost wholly been rebuilt since that time, but No. 36, on the west side, and No. 21a, on the east, are good survivals. On the north side is a FRENCH PROTESTANT CHURCH, built in terracotta by Sir Aston Webb (1893), with a carved tympanum of 1950 in memory of Edward VI 'who by his charter of 1550 granted asylum to the Huguenots from France'. The Roman Catholic ST PATRICK'S CHURCH, on the east side, was opened in 1792 and rebuilt in a classical style (by Kelly and Birchall) in 1893.

In FRITH STREET, which leads south from the square to Shaftesbury Avenue, William Hazlitt died in 1830 at No. 6, one of a pair of 18th-century houses, and Mozart stayed with his father and sister in 1764 at No. 20 (much rebuilt). At No. 22 John Logie Baird gave his first demonstration of television in 1926, in the attic, to members of the Royal Institution. GREEK STREET, the parallel street on the east and likewise noted for its foreign restaurants, is named after the colony of Greeks who settled here. De Quincey lodged in poor circumstances at No. 61 in 1802, after running away from Manchester Grammar School.

On the east corner of Greek Street and Soho Square is the HOUSE OF ST BARNABAS (adm., p. 32), a charity founded in 1846 to help the destitute and homeless poor in London, and occupying a mid-18th-century mansion with an interior (restored after war damage) notable for its carved woodwork, rococo plasterwork, and staircase with a wrought-iron balustrade. The French Gothic chapel was designed in 1863.

From the square, Soho Street goes north to Oxford Street (Route 14) and Sutton Row east to CHARING CROSS ROAD (compare Route 19), which it reaches just below ST GILES CIRCUS (III, D2), on the south-east side of which rises CENTRE POINT, a soaring office building, thirty-three storeys and 350 ft high, by Richard Seifert and Partners (1965). It contains the offices of the CONFEDERATION OF BRITISH INDUSTRY, founded in 1965 and representing some 250,000 companies, but is used partly as a night shelter by the young homeless. The road to the south leads to St Giles High Street (Route 23), while TOTTENHAM COURT ROAD (III, D2–B1), noted for its furniture-dealers and electrical suppliers, goes on northward to Euston Road, skirting the district of BLOOMSBURY, with its many squares, mostly developed in the early 18th century. At first an aristocratic quarter, it became in the late 19th century an intellectual and literary centre, but is now better known as the home of the British Museum and the University of London.

In GREAT RUSSELL STREET, at the corner of Tottenham Court Road, is the LONDON CENTRAL Y.M.C.A., a building (by the Elsworth Sykes Partnership, 1976) replacing the memorial building to Sir George Williams, who in 1844 founded the Young Men's Christian Association as a club and recreation centre in which young men could also seek to improve themselves spiritually. The new building contains 764 bedrooms, a large sports and recreation complex, and a conference centre. The World Alliance of Y.M.C.A.s now numbers more than four million members representing over eighty nationalities.

Farther east, on the other side of Great Russell Street, is the central club of the similar YOUNG WOMEN'S CHRISTIAN ASSOCIATION, established in 1887 by the amalgamation of two organizations, both started in 1855, and occupying a building by Sir Edwin Lutyens (1931). CONGRESS HOUSE (by David du R. Aberdeen, 1956) is the headquarters and training college of the TRADES UNION CONGRESS, a voluntary association of trades unions established in 1866 and now numbering ninety-eight unions with over ten million members. In the forecourt is a striking war-memorial sculpture, by Jacob Epstein (1958).

Great Russell Street goes on past the main entrance of the **British Museum** (adm., p. 336), while Bloomsbury Street, on the left, leads to BEDFORD SQUARE (III, D2), the finest of the squares of Bloomsbury, surviving quite unspoiled. It was built about 1775, probably by Thomas Leverton, and named after the landowner, the Duke of Bedford; the middle houses of the ranges on each side are good examples of the style made popular by the brothers Adam.

The Earl of Oxford and Asquith (d. 1928), the Liberal statesman, lived in 1921–4 at No. 44, on the south side of the square, and William Butterfield (d. 1900), the architect, lived at No. 42. Nos. 34–6, on the west, house the ARCHITECTURAL ASSOCIATION, incorporated in 1847, with a school of architecture, and No. 26, on the north, is the NATIONAL COUNCIL FOR VOLUNTARY ORGANISATIONS. No. 22 was the home of Sir Johnson Forbes-Robertson (d. 1937), the actor. At No. 11, in the north-east corner, Henry Cavendish, the natural philosopher, lived from 1786 until his death in 1810; at No. 2 Gower Street (see below), next door, Millicent Fawcett, a champion of women's rights, died in 1929. No. 6, a large house on the east side of Bedford Square, was the residence in 1798–1815 of the Earl of Eldon, Lord Chancellor.

From the north-east angle of the square, MONTAGUE PLACE leads right to Russell Square (Route 19), passing the north entrance of the British Museum, and GOWER STREET (III, B, C2), a long thoroughfare with regular if uninspired terraces of 1796 and after, runs northward to Euston Road. At No. 7, the home of John Millais, the Pre-Raphaelite Brotherhood held its first meeting, in 1848.

In Store Street, on the left, a building of 1966 now houses the Department of Oriental Manuscripts and Books of the BRITISH LIBRARY (see p. 338). At No. 7 in Ridgmount Street, adjacent, is the LIBRARY ASSOCIATION (founded in 1877), whose own library is now administered by the British Library. On the south side of Store Street is the BUILDING CENTRE (adm., p. 31), opened in 1931 as a 'permanent exhibition and information service for all interested in building'. Excellent temporary exhibitions of architecture and allied subjects are held here.

At the corner of Gower Street and Keppel Street is the LONDON SCHOOL OF HYGIENE AND TROPICAL MEDICINE, founded in 1924, incorporating the London School of Tropical Medicine established in 1899 and admitted as part of London University in 1905. The school, which has faculties of medicine and science, is in a fine building by P. Morley Horder and O. Verner Rees (1929). Farther on in Gower Street is the ROYAL ACADEMY OF DRAMATIC ART, founded in 1904 by Sir Herbert Beerbohm Tree, the actor-manager, and occupying a building of 1931. The Vanbrugh Theatre, the private theatre of the academy, with an entrance in Malet Street (see below), was named in honour of the sister-actresses Irene and Violet Vanbrugh. Designed by Alister MacDonald, it was opened in 1954. William de Morgan, potter and novelist, was born in 1839 at No. 69 Gower Street, the continuation of which is described below.

Keppel Street leads to the main entrance (in Malet Street) to the UNIVERSITY OF LONDON (III, C2,3), founded by royal charter in 1836 as a purely examining organization, and consisting mainly of a number of federated schools and colleges. In 1878 it became the first university in Britain to admit women as candidates for degrees, on equal terms with men, but was created a teaching university only in 1900. Many of its departments have been brought together in new buildings begun in 1933.

The university, the last to be established in any great European capital, was constituted to grant academic degrees without religious bias, at first to students of University College, King's College, and certain other institutions which became affiliated, but after 1858 to all students without restriction. In 1900 it was reorganized as a teaching body, the instruction being given in the schools and colleges already existing. Under statutes made in 1926, London University is governed by the Senate, which controls all academic matters, and the Court, which controls the finances; the Senate includes the heads of the principal schools, representatives of the academic staff, and members elected by Convocation, which comprises graduates of the university.

The university has faculties of theology, arts, law, music, medicine, science, engineering, education, and economics (including sociology, etc.). Students attending the affiliated schools and institutes (which have their own governing bodies) are registered as 'internal students', while those presenting themselves for examination only are known as 'external students'. The total number of teachers is about 6,000, of internal students more than 40,000.

The schools of the university include *Birkbeck College* (see below), the *British Postgraduate Medical Federation*, *Chelsea College*, *Heythrop College*, the *Imperial College of Science & Technology*, the *Institute of Education*, *King's College*, the *London School of Economics & Political Science*, the *London School of Hygiene & Tropical Medicine* (see above), *Queen Elizabeth College*, *Queen Mary College*, *Royal Holloway & Bedford New College* (near Egham, Surrey), the *Royal Postgraduate Medical School*, the *Royal Veterinary College*, the *School of Oriental & African Studies* (see below), the *School of Pharmacy*, *University College* (see below), *Westfield College*, and *Wye College* (near Ashford, Kent). In addition, there are medical schools attached to the principal hospitals, while specialist institutes established by the university include the *Courtauld Institute of Art*, the *Institutes of Advanced Legal Studies*, *of Archaeology*, *of Classical Studies*, *of Commonwealth Studies*, *of Germanic Studies*, *of Historical Research* (see below), *of Latin American Studies*, and *of United States Studies*, the *School of Slavonic & East European Studies* (see below), the *Warburg Institute*, and the *British Institute in Paris*, first established in 1894, renamed in 1927, and incorporated in the university in 1969.

The principal building of the university, designed by Charles Holden with a massive tower 210 ft high, is the SENATE HOUSE. This contains the administrative offices and the University Library, which holds about one million volumes and 4,500 current periodicals and includes special collections of Elizabethan literature, economics, and music. It houses also the SCHOOL OF SLAVONIC AND EAST EUROPEAN STUDIES (founded in 1932) and the INSTITUTE OF HISTORICAL RESEARCH (founded 1921). To the north of this building is BIRKBECK COLLEGE, founded in 1823 as a scientific and technical institute, and admitted to the university in 1920. It has faculties of arts, science, and economics, and its students (all evening or part-time) are catered for in buildings opened in 1951. To the north of the college, and also entered from Malet Street, is the STUDENTS' UNION building, opened in 1955, with a dining-hall, library, gymnasium, etc. Both buildings were likewise designed by Charles Holden.

COLLEGE HALL (1931), on the other side of Malet Street, is a hall of residence for women students. Some institutes of the university are accommodated in Russell

Square, Gordon Square, and Tavistock Square (Route 19), while other schools and departments are being housed in this area as space becomes available.

Malet Street ends on the north at TORRINGTON PLACE, which leads to the right towards Gordon Square (Route 19) and left across Gower Street (compare above) to Tottenham Court Road.

In Gower Street, to the north, George Dance the Younger (d. 1825), the architect, lived at No. 91. No. 105 is the ROYAL NATIONAL INSTITUTE FOR THE DEAF, established in 1911. In Tottenham Court Road, almost facing Torrington Place, is the WHITEFIELD MEMORIAL CHAPEL, designed by Edward C. Butler (1958) and now the American Church in London. It stands on the site of Whitefield's Tabernacle, a chapel built originally in 1756 by George Whitefield (d. 1770), the evangelist, but destroyed by bombing in 1945. Goodge Street station is a little to the south.

Gower Street leads northward past the main entrance to UNIVERSITY COLLEGE (III, B2), founded in 1826 through the efforts of Lord Brougham, Thomas Campbell, James Mill, and other lovers of religious toleration for the purpose of providing, on a non-sectarian basis, 'adequate opportunities for obtaining literary and scientific education at a moderate expense'. It received its first charter in 1836 and was incorporated in the University of London in 1907. The college provides courses in the faculties of arts, laws, science, engineering, and environmental studies, as well as medical and clinical sciences. The main building (adm., p. 35), in a classical style by William Wilkins (1828), has a fine Corinthian portico approached by flights of steps. Considerable extensions and additions have been made from time to time, and restoration from severe war damage was completed in 1954. The front quadrangle was completed in 1985 with classical additions by Sir Hugh Casson, a former student.

Beneath the dome, recast by T. L. Donaldson in 1848, is the FLAXMAN GALLERY, containing casts by John Flaxman (d. 1826), the sculptor, acquired in 1851. In the ground-floor Cloisters on both sides are prints and drawings from the college collection, and (on the south) the 'Marmor Homericum', a design in marble showing Homeric subjects by Baron Triqueti (1865), presented by George Grote, the historian, one of the founders of the college. Interested visitors may also see the clothed skeleton of Jeremy Bentham (d. 1832), preserved (in the South Cloister) under the terms of his will, and the EGYPTOLOGY COLLECTION formed by Sir Flinders Petrie (d. 1942).

Incorporated in the college are the SLADE SCHOOL OF FINE ART, established in 1871 by the bequest of Sir Felix Slade (d. 1868), the art-collector; the GALTON LABORATORY, set up by Sir Francis Galton (d. 1911), the founder of eugenics; and the SCHOOL OF LIBRARY, ARCHIVE AND INFORMATION STUDIES, founded in 1919 and reconstituted in 1977. The college's own library contains about 900,000 books and pamphlets. Sir William Jenner, the physician, W. S. Jevons, the economist, Sir William Ramsay, the chemist, A. E. Housman, the poet, J. B. S. Haldane, the biologist, and Marie Stopes, the advocate of birth control, were all teachers at the College. Walter Bagehot, the economist, Lord Lister, the founder of antiseptic surgery, and Alexander Graham Bell, the inventor of the telephone, worked as undergraduates here; and Sir Ambrose Fleming was professor of electrical technology for forty-one years (1885–1926). Walter Sickert, Sir William Orpen, and Augustus John were students at the Slade School. In the south wing is the building (by Sir Albert Richardson, 1954) housing the valuable MOCATTA LIBRARY AND MUSEUM of the Jewish Historical Society, presented to the college in 1906, and built up again after its destruction in the war. The fine GUSTAVE TUCK LECTURE THEATRE here is also by Richardson. At the south end are buildings (by H. O. Corfiato; from 1960) for the Faculties of Engineering and Science.

Other buildings, on the east and reached from Gordon Street, include the BLOOMSBURY THEATRE, opened in 1968, as well as WATES HOUSE and a Chemistry Building (also of 1968), both by A. Cox. Wates House accommodates the BARTLETT SCHOOL OF ARCHITECTURE AND PLANNING, likewise reconstituted in 1977.

A wall monument in Gower Street to Richard Trevithick (d. 1833) recalls that 'close to this place' he built the first railway on which a steam locomotive drew carriages for passengers (1808).

Opposite the college, in Gower Street, is UNIVERSITY COLLEGE HOSPITAL, opened in 1834, but largely rebuilt in 1897–1906 by Alfred Waterhouse and several times extended, with a new building (1967) on the north. In 1846 Robert Liston performed here the first operation in Europe under anaesthetic. The School of Medicine (founded in 1828 and reconstituted in 1980) occupies a building of 1907 to the south. Grafton Way, starting between the hospital buildings, leads across Tottenham Court Road to Fitzroy Square (Route 16), while Gower Street goes on to EUSTON ROAD (III, B2).

19 From Charing Cross to Euston via Holborn

Plan III, F3–III, A2

STATIONS: CHARING CROSS (Plan III, F3), on the Bakerloo and Jubilee lines; EMBANKMENT (VIII, A3), on the Bakerloo, Circle, District, and Northern lines; LEICESTER SQUARE (III, F2, 3), on the Northern and Piccadilly lines; TOTTENHAM COURT ROAD (III, D2), on the Central and Northern lines;

HOLBORN (IV, D1), on the Central and Piccadilly lines; RUSSELL SQUARE (III, C3), on the Piccadilly line; EUSTON SQUARE (III, B2), on the Circle and Metropolitan lines; EUSTON (III, A2), on the Northern and Victoria lines. — BUSES Nos. 1, 24, 29, and 176 in the lower part of Charing Cross Road; Nos. 14, 19, 22, 38, and 55 in the upper parts of Charing Cross Road (northbound only) and Shaftesbury Avenue (southbound only); Nos. 7, 8, 19, 22, 25, 38, and 55 in Bloomsbury Way (eastbound only) and Nos. 7, 8, and 25 in New Oxford Street (westbound only); Nos. 8, 22, 25, and 501 in High Holborn; Nos. 68, 77A, and 188 in Southampton Row and Woburn Place. Other buses to Trafalgar Square, see Routes 2, 6, 21; in Euston Road, see Route 16.

For CHARING CROSS and TRAFALGAR SQUARE, see Route 1. Opening off the north-east angle of the square, between St Martin-in-the-Fields and the National Gallery, is ST MARTIN'S PLACE, No. 6 in which is a survival of about 1830. Also on the right is the TRAFALGAR SQUARE POST OFFICE, and in the centre of the road is a monument by Sir George Frampton (1920) to Edith Cavell, the nurse who was shot by the Germans at Brussels in 1915. On the left is the **National Portrait Gallery** (adm., p. 391), and on the north side of this is a statue of Sir Henry Irving (d. 1905), the actor, occupying approximately the site of the 'Old Curiosity Shop' immortalized by Dickens. Hence the short Irving Street leads to Leicester Square (Route 20). On the other side, near the foot of Charing Cross Road, is the GARRICK THEATRE, built in 1889 (by Walter Emden and C. J. Phipps) for Sir William S. Gilbert.

CHARING CROSS ROAD (III, F3–D2), an unprepossessing thoroughfare opened in 1887 and well known for its second-hand booksellers, runs north to St Giles Circus, at the junction of Oxford Street and Tottenham Court Road. On the right is WYNDHAM'S THEATRE (by W. G. R. Sprague, 1899), just beyond which Cranbourn Street (Route 20) is crossed. In CAMBRIDGE CIRCUS, where Shaftesbury Avenue crosses (see below), is the PALACE THEATRE, built in 1888–91 (by T. E. Collcutt and G. H. Holloway) for Richard D'Oyly Carte as the English Opera House. Farther on are the PHOENIX THEATRE (1930), designed by Sir Giles G. Scott, Crewe, and Masey, and the ST MARTIN'S SCHOOL OF ART, founded in 1854 and occupying a building of 1936 by E. P. Wheeler. No. 127 is the BRITISH FILM INSTITUTE, founded in 1933.

ST MARTIN'S LANE (III, E, F3), an older and more interesting street, also known for its theatres, starts from the north-east corner of St Martin's Place. The COLISEUM THEATRE, on the right, one of London's largest theatres (by Frank Matcham; 1904) and the first in the world to have a revolving stage, became in 1968 the home of the English National Opera Company, formerly the Sadler's Wells Opera

Company (see Route 29). On the left are the charming DUKE OF YORK'S THEATRE (by Walter Emden; 1892) and the ALBERY THEATRE, built by W. G. R. Sprague in 1903 (as the New Theatre) for Sir Charles Wyndham. On the other side of the road between these opens GOODWIN'S COURT, containing a complete row of shops of the late 18th century. A tablet almost opposite the Albery Theatre recalls that the Chippendales had their furniture workshop near this site (1753–1813). Beyond the junction of Cranbourn Street, Long Acre, and Garrick Street (see Route 20) extends UPPER ST MARTIN'S LANE, on the left of which rises the huge THORN HOUSE (1960), designed by Sir Basil Spence, with an abstract bronze sculpture by Geoffrey Clarke on its flat wall.

In West Street, which leads beyond this to Cambridge Circus, are the ST MARTIN'S THEATRE (1916) and the AMBASSADORS THEATRE (1913), both designed by W. G. R. Sprague. Adjoining the latter is the former ST GILES'S MISSION CHURCH, built originally in 1700 as a chapel for Huguenot refugees, but much altered later in the 18th century for the Methodists. John and Charles Wesley (from 1743), George Whitefield, and John Fletcher all preached here.

Upper St Martin's Lane is prolonged by MONMOUTH STREET, which leads to Shaftesbury Avenue, crossing SEVEN DIALS, the junction of seven dingy streets and once notorious as the centre of a thieves' quarter. It takes its name from a column with seven dials which stood here until 1773 and is now at Weybridge (Surrey). On the right is the former CAMBRIDGE THEATRE, built by Wimperis, Simpson and Guthrie (1930), with interior decoration by Serge Chermayeff. Renamed the Magic Castle, in 1984, it is the first permanent theatre in Britain devoted to magic and illusion.

To the right in Earlham Street (in an old warehouse) are the showrooms (adm., p. 31) of the BRITISH CRAFTS CENTRE, devoted to the promotion of fine craftsmanship in Britain, and providing an exhibition of craftsmen's work of all kinds (normally changed about every six weeks). Next door is the DONMAR WAREHOUSE THEATRE, in another converted warehouse (of about 1850).

Shaftesbury Avenue, leaving St Giles High Street with its church on the left and High Holborn on the right (see Route 23), goes on past the SHAFTESBURY THEATRE, built in 1911, as the Princes Theatre, by Bertie Crewe, and bought in 1984 by the Theatre of Comedy. Nearly opposite is the BLOOMSBURY CENTRAL BAPTIST CHURCH, opened in 1848 and partly rebuilt internally in 1964. Coptic Street, opposite the junction of Shaftesbury Avenue and New Oxford Street, is an approach to the **British Museum** (compare Route 18), while BLOOMSBURY WAY (formerly Hart Street) inclines to the right to Bloomsbury Square and Southampton Row (Route 22), passing ST GEORGE'S, BLOOMSBURY (III, D3), a fine church of 1720–31 by Nicholas Hawksmoor, a pupil of Wren. Square in plan and in the classical style favoured by Hawksmoor, it has a grand display of Corinthian columns inside and out. The stepped spire, inspired by Pliny's description of the tomb of Mausolus at Halicarnassus, is topped by an incongruous statue of George I that was a butt for the wits of the period.

BLOOMSBURY SQUARE (III, D3), once a fashionable address, was laid out in 1661 by Thomas Wriothesley, fourth Earl of Southampton, and was the first open space in London to be called a 'square'. The original mansions of this time have all disappeared, but houses on the north side by James Burton (1800–14) have survived. The gardens were planted about 1807 by Humphry Repton; at the north end is a statue of Charles James Fox (d. 1806), the politician, by Westmacott.

SOUTHAMPTON PLACE, which runs south to High Holborn, has good houses of about 1750, in one of which (No. 17, now the NATIONAL LIBRARY FOR THE BLIND), Cardinal Newman spent part of his early life. No. 45 Bloomsbury Square, at the corner of the Place, was the town house of the Earls of Chesterfield; and No. 6, on the west side, was the home of Isaac D'Israeli (d. 1848), father of Lord Beaconsfield. At the north-east corner stood the house of the Earl of Mansfield, Lord Chief Justice, burned in 1780 by the Gordon Rioters, as described by Dickens in *Barnaby Rudge*.

Great Russell Street leads west from Bloomsbury Square to the main entrance of the British Museum, while BEDFORD PLACE, well built (like Montague Street farther west) by James Burton after 1800, runs north to the large RUSSELL SQUARE (III, C3), which began to be laid out by him about the same time and became a favourite residence of merchants and professional men. On the south side of the gardens is an elaborate monument by Westmacott to the fifth Duke of Bedford (d. 1805), the landowner.

Readers of Thackeray's *Vanity Fair* will recall that the Osbornes and Sedleys occupied houses in this square. The RUSSELL HOTEL (1898), on the east side, is an example of the ostentatious style beloved by the late Victorians. STEWART HOUSE, a building of 1983 on the west side, contains the SCHOOL EXAMINATIONS BOARD of the University, reconstituted in 1984. No. 30 (by Sir John J. Burnet, 1915), the ROYAL INSTITUTE OF CHEMISTRY, has a seated figure of Joseph Priestley (d. 1804) over the entrance in an approach to the Senate House of LONDON

UNIVERSITY (see Route 18). Nos. 25–9, among the few surviving houses by Burton in the square (about 1814), now contain the INSTITUTES OF COMMON-WEALTH STUDIES (1949) and OF GERMANIC STUDIES (1950), branches of the university. Sir Samuel Romilly (d. 1818), the law reformer, lived at No. 21, on the north side.

To the north-west of Russell Square is the SCHOOL OF ORIENTAL AND AFRICAN STUDIES of the university, founded in 1916 and moved to a new building here (by Charles Holden) in 1941–4. It has faculties of arts, laws, music (ethnomusicology), science (geography), and economics and political science. On the west of BEDFORD WAY, which leads north from the square, is a striking building by Denys Lasdun & Partners (1976) for the INSTITUTE OF ADVANCED LEGAL STUDIES (founded in 1948) of London University and the INSTITUTE OF EDUCATION, founded in 1932 and now a school of the university.

Bedford Way ends at the south-west corner of Tavistock Square (see below), from which Torrington Place leads left to the narrow WOBURN SQUARE, built in 1828, but now mostly demolished to provide further space for London University, a fate which has already befallen Torrington Square, farther west, of which only the grassy centre survives. At the north-west corner of Woburn Square, in a building by Charles Holden (1958), is the WARBURG INSTITUTE, founded in 1944 for 'research on the character and history of the classical tradition' (and part of the university). The topmost floor is occupied by the COURTAULD INSTITUTE GALLERIES (III, C2; adm., p. 31), with an outstanding collection of paintings and other works of art bequeathed by Samuel Courtauld (see p. 180) and Lord Lee of Fareham (d. 1947), to which was added (in 1981) the Princes Gate Collection, a bequest of about 400 paintings and drawings by Count Antoine Seilern (d. 1978). The galleries are quite inadequate for the display of the many masterpieces and the collections are to be transferred to Somerset House (Route 21) in late 1986.

The Lee Collection includes fine examples of *Botticelli* (Altarpiece of the Trinity, about 1490), *Giovanni Bellini*, *Bernardino Luini*, *Veronese*, *Lucas Cranach the Elder*, *Hans Eworth* ('Sir John Luttrell', 1550), *Rubens* ('Descent from the Cross'), and *Goya*, and of British 17th–19th-century portraits. Among the Courtauld French Impressionist and Post-Impressionist paintings are excellent works by *Manet* ('Bar at the Folies-Bergère', etc.), *Degas*, *Monet* ('Antibes', etc.), *Renoir* ('La Loge', etc.), *Seurat*, *Sisley*, *Pissarro*, *Gauguin*,

Cézanne ('Montagne Ste-Victoire', 'Lake of Annecy', etc.), and *Van Gogh* ('Self Portrait', etc.).

The Princes Gate Collection includes splendid works by *Rubens* ('The Family of Jan Brueghel the Elder', 'The Entombment', 'Landscape by Moonlight', 'Scenes from the Life of Achilles', etc.) and others by *Bernardo Daddi* (Triptych, 1338), the *Master of Flémalle* (Triptych, about 1420), *Palma Vecchio* ('Venus in a Landscape'), *Quinten Massys* ('Madonna'), *Parmigianino* ('Holy Family', and 'Virgin and Child'), *Lorenzo Lotto* ('Holy Family with St Anne'), *Pieter Brueghel the Elder* ('Flight into Egypt', and 'Woman Taken in Adultery'), *Van Dyck* ('Adoration of the Shepherds', etc.), *G. B. Tiepolo* ('Immaculate Conception', etc.), *Degas* ('Lady with a Parasol') and *Cézanne* ('Route Tournante', a late work).

In the galleries also are the Roger Fry bequest of British and French Paintings (of the late 19th and 20th centuries), the Witt Collection of Old Master drawings, and the remarkable Gambier-Parry bequest of early Italian paintings, as well as sculptures, ivories, and other treasures.

To the north of Woburn Square is GORDON SQUARE (III, B, C2), laid out by Thomas Cubitt about 1820, but mostly rebuilt at various times. At its south-west angle is the cathedral-like Gothic church of CHRIST THE KING, now the principal Anglican church serving London University. It was built in 1853 by Raphael Brandon for a sect (known as 'Irvingites') that had its origin in the teaching of Edward Irving (d. 1834), the Scottish divine.

Next to it is UNIVERSITY HALL, opened in 1848 as a hall of residence for Unitarians studying at University College, and now housing the Royal Institute of Philosophy and DR WILLIAMS'S LIBRARY (adm., p. 32) of philosophy, theology, and the history of Nonconformity, founded in 1716 under the bequest of Daniel Williams, the Presbyterian minister. Lytton Strachey (d. 1932), biographer and critic, lived at No. 42, on the east side of the square, and Virginia Woolf, the novelist, and later John Maynard Keynes (d. 1946), lived at No. 46.

No. 53, at the south-east corner of Gordon Square, contains the PERCIVAL DAVID FOUNDATION OF CHINESE ART (adm., p. 34), comprising the unrivalled collection of ceramics made by Sir Percival David and given by him in 1950, together with his library dealing with Chinese art and culture, to the University of London.

The collection consists of about 1,500 pieces covering the Sung, Yüan, Ming and Ch'ing dynasties (from A.D. 960 onwards), some of which came from the former Imperial Collection in Peking and are inscribed with poems, etc., from the brush of the Emperor Ch'ien Lung (1735–95). Notable also are the 'blue and white' porcelain of Ching-tê-chên, and representative enamel decoration of the Ch'êng Hua period.

A building of 1958 on the north side of Gordon Square houses the INSTITUTES OF ARCHAEOLOGY (founded in 1937) and OF CLASSICAL STUDIES (1953) of the University. ENDSLEIGH PLACE, to the north-east, has good houses of about 1850.

TAVISTOCK SQUARE (III, B2, 3), to the east, is also by Cubitt, a range of whose building (1826) survives on the west side (see below). In Woburn House, built in 1932, on the north, is a thriving Jewish Communal Centre which accommodates also the JEWISH MUSEUM (entered from Upper Woburn Place; adm., p. 32), an interesting assembly of antiquities and of domestic and ritual art. Opposite on the east is the large building (by Sir Edwin Lutyens, 1925) of the BRITISH MEDICAL ASSOCIATION, established in 1832. The fountain memorial in the courtyard, by James Woodford and S. Rowland Pierce, was dedicated in 1954 to medical men and women who died in the Second World War.

Woburn House occupies the site of Tavistock House, where Dickens lived in 1851–60, writing *Bleak House*, *Hard Times*, *Little Dorrit*, *A Tale of Two Cities*, and part of *Great Expectations*. A description of the Dickens household has been left by Hans Andersen, who visited the novelist here in 1857. In the old houses on the west side (Nos. 30–45) are the INSTITUTES OF UNITED STATES and OF LATIN AMERICAN STUDIES (both formed in 1965), branches of London University. In the centre of the square is a seated figure of the Mahatma Gandhi (d. 1948), by Fredda Brilliant, and in the south-east corner is a memorial by Lutyens to Dame Louisa Aldrich-Blake (d. 1925), the surgeon. WOBURN PLACE goes on thence to Russell Square (see above), while Tavistock Place runs east towards Regent Square (Route 22).

UPPER WOBURN PLACE, leading north from Tavistock Square, passes the end of WOBURN WALK, whose early-19th-century houses have picturesque shop fronts. W. B. Yeats, the poet, lived at No. 5 here in 1895–1919. The upper floors on the north side are now incorporated in the NEW AMBASSADORS HOTEL (1963), in Upper Woburn Place, which reaches EUSTON ROAD beside St Pancras Church (see Route 16).

20 From Piccadilly Circus to Fleet Street via Covent Garden and Lincoln's Inn

Plan III, F2–IV, E2
STATIONS: PICCADILLY CIRCUS (Plan III, F2), LEICESTER SQUARE (III, F2, 3), COVENT GARDEN (III, E3), HOLBORN (IV, D1), and ALDWYCH (IV, E1), all on the Piccadilly line; CHANCERY LANE (IV, D2), on the Central line. Piccadilly Circus is also on the Bakerloo line, Leicester Square on the Northern line, and Holborn on the Central line; Chancery Lane is closed on Sundays. — BUSES to Piccadilly Circus, see Routes 7, 15, 18; to Charing Cross Road, see Route 19; to the Strand and Fleet Street, see Route 21; to Kingsway, see Route 22; to Chancery Lane, see Route 24.

For PICCADILLY CIRCUS, see Route 7. COVENTRY STREET, extending Piccadilly eastward from the upper end of the Haymarket, leads past the TROCADERO (see Route 18), the PRINCE OF WALES THEATRE, opened in 1884 as the Prince's Theatre and rebuilt in 1937 by Robert Cromie, and the impressive SWISS CENTRE (by David du R. Aberdeen), built in 1967 as a 'shop window' for Swiss trade and industry. Beyond is LEICESTER SQUARE (III, F2), named after the second Earl of Leicester, who built a house near by in 1637 (pulled down in 1790). The square, laid out in about 1665 and once a favourite resort of duellists, was converted in 1874 into a public garden, an oasis in London's traffic, by Baron Grant, the company promoter. The marble statue of William Shakespeare, in the centre, is a copy of that in Westminster Abbey; around the garden are busts of Reynolds, Newton, Hogarth, and John Hunter, all of whom lived in or near the square, which is now best known for its large cinemas and as a gathering place for young people.

At the south-west corner is a bronze statue of Charlie Chaplin (d. 1977), in characteristic pose, by John Doubleday (1981). The square was called by Thomas Pennant the 'pouting-place of princes', for in 1718 George II, when Prince of Wales, moved to Leicester House on quarrelling with his father, and in 1741 Frederick, Prince of Wales (son of George II), did the same. On the south side, beside the road leading to St Martin's Place and Trafalgar Square (Route 19), is the ROYAL DENTAL HOSPITAL founded in 1858, with a school of dental surgery (now part of the United Medical and Dental Schools) attached to London University.

In Leicester Place, north-east of the square, is the church of NOTRE DAME DE FRANCE, a circular building acquired by French Roman Catholics in 1865, bombed in 1940, and reconstructed in a fine modern style in 1955 by H. O. Corfiato. The circular wall is in fact a survival from an 18th-century 'panorama'. Over the entrance is a striking sculpture of the Virgin and Child, by Saupique; above the altar is a rich

Aubusson tapestry woven by a Benedictine monk; and in the Lady Chapel are murals by Jean Cocteau (1959). Farther up is the PRINCE CHARLES THEATRE, designed by Carl Fisher (1962), and now used as a cinema.

Coventry Street is prolonged eastward beyond Leicester Square by CRANBOURN STREET, which crosses Charing Cross Road (Route 19) at the former HIPPODROME THEATRE (by Frank Matcham, 1900; now given over to cabaret), close to Leicester Square station. It meets St Martin's Lane at the junction of several streets, in one of which, Great Newport Street (on the left), is the ARTS THEATRE, the best-known theatre club in London, founded in 1927, in a building by P. Morley Horder. On either side are the two parts of the new PHOTOGRAPHERS' GALLERY (adm., p. 34), which arranges interesting and varied exhibitions.

LONG ACRE (III, E3), which continues Cranbourn Street towards Bow Street (see below), was a favoured address in the 17th century: Oliver Cromwell and John Dryden had houses here. Later it was given over to coachbuilders, but later still it was absorbed in the wholesale fruit trade of Covent Garden.

Garrick Street, which starts to the right of Long Acre, takes its name from the GARRICK CLUB (No. 15), founded in 1831 and favoured by the dramatic and literary professions. Its collection of theatrical paintings is said to be the best in Britain. From the farther end of the street, Bedford Street descends to the Strand (Route 21). In KING STREET, to the left, No. 37, a building of 1975, houses the ROYAL SCOTTISH CORPORATION, founded in 1611 to assist Scots in London. No. 38, the AFRICA CENTRE, is the headquarters of the INTERNATIONAL AFRICAN INSTITUTE, established in 1926. Farther on is a well-restored late-17th-century house by Thomas Archer, the home after 1696 of Admiral Lord Orford (d. 1727) and later famous as Evans's Supper Rooms, the entertainments at which were visited by the Newcomes in Thackeray's novel.

King Street leads to COVENT GARDEN (III, E3), long the site of the principal market in London for vegetables, fruit, and flowers, moved in 1974 to Nine Elms, near Vauxhall (Route 35).

The name of the place was originally Convent Garden, from an old garden of the monks of Westminster Abbey which stretched from Long Acre to the Strand. After the Dissolution the site was claimed by the Crown and in 1552 it was sold to the first Earl of Bedford, who built himself a house facing the Strand. In 1631–5 the area behind this was laid out for the fourth Earl as a select residential quarter by Inigo Jones. The central square was enclosed on two sides by terraces with arcades (miscalled 'piazzas'); these have now vanished, though the eastern block on the north side has been recast in a style approaching the original. The south side of the square was formed by the gardens of Bedford House, the west side largely by St Paul's Church (see below). In 1661 the Duke of Bedford established a small market here under royal charter, the original of the fruit and vegetable market, which was sold in 1913 by a later Duke and again in 1918 for £2¼ million (the annual value of the site in 1552 had been about six guineas).

On the west side of the market square is the 'actors' church' of ST PAUL'S, COVENT GARDEN (III, E, F3), a curious barn-like building, but the 'handsomest barn in Europe' in the words of its original designer, Inigo Jones (1633). Rebuilt and made plainer by Thomas Hardwick in 1798, after a fire, it preserves Jones's east portico with its large Tuscan columns, used as a background by Shaw in the first scene of *Pygmalion*. The entrance is actually at the other end, reached through a gate on the north side of the church, or approached from King Street (see above).

A silver casket on the south wall contains the ashes of Dame Ellen Terry (d. 1928), the actress. Near by is a memorial to Charles Macklin (d. 1797), the actor; on the north wall are others to John Bellamy (d. 1794), founder of the Whig Club, and Thomas Arne (d. 1778), the composer of *Rule Britannia*; and a limewood wreath carved by Grinling Gibbons (d. 1721) was placed beside the west door in 1965 in his memory (all are buried here). At the west end are numerous plaques to persons connected with the theatre.

The vaults and precincts of the church are said to contain the remains of more famous people than any other church in London, excepting Westminster Abbey and St Paul's Cathedral. Among these are Samuel Butler (d. 1680), the author of *Hudibras*; Sir Peter Lely (d. 1680), the artist; William Wycherley (d. 1715), the dramatist; and Thomas Girtin (d. 1802), the watercolourist. Most of the gravestones, however, were moved when the churchyard was levelled. J. M. W. Turner, born in 1775 in Maiden Lane (to the south; house demolished), was baptized in this church.

The former market buildings in the centre of Covent Garden, designed by Charles Fowler (1831–3), were restored in 1980 as a pedestrian precinct, with shops (which keep open on weekdays until 8 p.m.), cafés, bars, etc. To the south of this is the Jubilee Market (1977), where a crafts market is held on Saturdays. The old Flower Market (1872), to the south-east of the square, now contains the LONDON TRANSPORT MUSEUM (adm., p. 33), opened in 1980. The representative collection of road vehicles includes a reconstruction of George Shillibeer's original omnibus (1829) and more up-to-date motor-buses and trolley-buses, trams and coaches. Among the rail vehicles are a steam locomotive of 1872, built for the Duke of Buckingham's private railway, a locomotive of 1866 used on the Circle line, and a windowless coach from the City and South London Railway, the first 'deep tube' railway in the world, opened in 1872. The working displays (many of which can be operated by visitors) include a section of an underground tunnel (with a set of points), an underground train controller, and a signal cabin. Other exhibits show the impact of the railways on London and how the city grew with the expansion of the railway system.

Another of the market's old buildings, to the north-east of the square, is being converted to house the new THEATRE MUSEUM, to be opened in 1986. In SOUTHAMPTON STREET, which descends from the Jubilee Market to the Strand (Route 21), David Garrick, the actor, lived in 1750–72 at No. 27.

RUSSELL STREET, east of Covent Garden, was well known in the late 17th and 18th centuries for its coffee-houses, frequented by Dryden, Pope, Swift, Fielding, Smollett, Johnson, and other literary lions. Boswell first met Johnson in 1763 at No. 8, then a bookshop, but considerably altered since. The street leads past the north front of the Drury Lane Theatre (see Route 22), crossing, before this, the junction of Wellington Street, which descends to the Strand, and BOW STREET, running north 'in the shape of a bent bow'.

On the left in this street is the ROYAL OPERA HOUSE (III, E3), better known as the COVENT GARDEN THEATRE, the principal home of opera and ballet in London. The huge building, by Edward M. Barry (1856–8), has seats for about 2,000 and is well known for its excellent acoustics. Under the impressive Corinthian portico are a sculptured frieze and panels by Flaxman and Rossi salvaged from the previous theatre.

The first theatre on this site was built in 1732 by John Rich, the 'father of English pantomime'. Handel took over in 1735 and produced six of his operas here; *Messiah* was given its first English performance in 1743 and *Samson* and all Handel's later oratorios were produced at this theatre. Peg Woffington, the actress, made her first London appearance at Covent Garden in 1740 and David Garrick played here from 1746. John Beard, who had been one of Handel's leading singers, became lessee in 1761, and in 1767 a pianoforte was heard for the first time in public in England. The theatre increased its fame under the managership of George Colman (from 1767); it was reconstructed in 1792 (by Henry Holland), but was burned down in 1808 and rebuilt in the following year, when the manager was John Philip Kemble. Mrs Sarah Siddons made her farewell appearance in 1812 at Covent Garden, and Edmund Kean made his last appearance in 1833 (when he was taken ill on the stage). William

Charles Macready made his debut here in 1816 and became manager in 1837, when he introduced 'limelight' on the English stage for the first time. In 1847 the name was changed to the Royal Italian Opera, but the theatre was burned down again in 1856.

The present theatre, opened in 1858, became the chief opera house in England. The innumerable famous singers who have been heard here include Jenny Lind and Dame Nellie Melba, Caruso and Chaliapin. In 1911 the Russian Ballet company of Sergei Diaghilev gave its first performance in England. Renamed the Royal Opera House in 1939, the theatre was reopened in 1946, after the war, with a visit by the Sadler's Wells Ballet, who moved here permanently as the Royal Ballet in 1956, in which year the Covent Garden Opera Company, founded in 1946, was renamed the Royal Opera Company. The building was extended on the west in 1982 to provide much-needed rehearsal studios and dressing rooms.

Opposite the theatre is BOW STREET POLICE COURT, built in 1881 and the chief of the eighteen Inner London magistrates' courts. The first courthouse was opened in 1748, with Henry Fielding and his blind half-brother, Sir John Fielding, as the magistrates. The novelist wrote part of *Tom Jones* while living in Sir John's house close by, damaged in the Gordon Riots (1780). The 'Bow Street Runners' (nicknamed 'Robin Redbreasts' from their scarlet waistcoats) were the predecessors of the present-day detective force.

LONG ACRE runs west from the north end of Bow Street to St Martin's Lane (see above) and in the other direction to DRURY LANE (III, D, E3) which connects High Holborn with Aldwych. Sir John Barbirolli, the conductor, lived as a boy at No. 37. To the left in the 'lane' is the NEW LONDON THEATRE (formerly the Winter Garden Theatre), rebuilt in 1973 by Michael Percival as part of a comprehensive scheme incorporating flats, shops, and an underground car park. Long Acre is continued by GREAT QUEEN STREET, built about 1640 and named in honour of Henrietta Maria, queen of Charles I. Once a fashionable street, it still retains a few of its fine old houses (above more recent shop-fronts). On the right is the imposing FREEMASONS' HALL, the headquarters of the United Grand Lodge of England, rebuilt in 1927–33 as a war memorial to masons by H. V. Ashley and Winton Newman. The massive central tower rises to 200 ft above the pavement.

Great Queen Street is extended beyond the broad Kingsway (Route 22) by the short Remnant Street, which ends at the north-west angle of LINCOLN'S INN FIELDS (IV, D, E1), the largest square in central London. The rows of houses facing the square were planned in 1640 by William Newton. The gardens, with their noble plane trees and their tennis-courts, etc., are a favourite lunchtime promenade for city workers.

Before their enclosure in 1735 the 'fields' were the haunt of thieves and duellists, and an occasional place of execution. The north walk is named CANADA WALK to commemorate the setting up in the square of the Royal Canadian Air Force headquarters in 1940, and a memorial maple tree, the gift of the City of Ottawa, was planted in 1945. Farther west in this walk is a memorial (with bronze figures by R. R. Goulden) to Margaret MacDonald (wife of the Prime Minister and noted for her philanthropic work), who died in 1911 at No. 3 Lincoln's Inn Fields.

On the north side of the square, at No. 13, is SIR JOHN SOANE'S MUSEUM (IV, D1; adm., p. 35), with the antiquities and works of art gathered together by Sir John Soane (1753–1837), the architect, in the house which he designed for himself in 1812 and where he lived until his death. He had previously lived next door at No. 12, which he designed in 1792, and these houses, together with No. 14, likewise by Soane, make a balanced composition. The collections have been left as far as possible as the architect arranged them, and features of the museum are the ingenious arrangements for enhancing the effect of space by the use of mirrors and for increasing the room available in the picture gallery by means of hinged shutters. Soane, a bold follower of the classical tradition, exercised a great influence on architecture, and the museum remains a valuable record of the taste of his time.

On the right of the entrance hall are the Dining Room and Library, thrown into one, with Soane's furniture and many of his books, and a portrait of the architect at the age of seventy-five, by Lawrence. Beyond the small Study and Dressing Room, containing antique marbles, etc., is a corridor which leads right to the Picture Room. This is chiefly notable for the two famous series of paintings by William Hogarth: *The Election*, four scenes executed in 1754–7, and *The Rake's Progress*, a series of eight painted in 1735 (beginning in the bottom left-hand corner). They are superb examples of the robust humour and harmonious composition of Hogarth. Also here are landscapes by Turner, Callcott, and others, 18th-century architectural drawings by Piranesi and Clérisseau, and large pictorial drawings of Soane's own compositions. A stair close by leads down to the 'Crypt', with the Monk's Parlour (left), described as a 'Gothick fantasy', and the Sepulchral Chamber, which contains the remarkable sarcophagus of Seti I, king of Egypt in 1303–1290 B.C. and father of Ramesses the Great. This was discovered in 1817 and purchased by Soane for £2,000 after it had been declined by the British Museum. Made from a monolithic block of alabaster, it is ornamented inside and out by scenes and texts from the 'Book of the Gates', while inside, on the bottom, is a figure of the goddess Nut into whose keeping the deceased king was committed. Recesses around the chamber contain Roman funerary urns and other antiquities, and models by the sculptors Flaxman and Banks.

On the ground floor a colonnade, above which is a gallery with models of Soane's buildings (shown on application to the curator), leads to the central Dome, a kind of 'grotto of antiquities' with original sculptures and casts, the former including a bust of Soane by Chantrey. The New Picture Room at the end (replacing the architect's study) and the adjacent ante-room were added in 1889, and contain sculptures, and paintings by Turner and Canaletto (three fine Venetian scenes). The Breakfast Room, reached from the ante-room, has a shallow domed ceiling, and terracotta busts by Flaxman on the black marble mantelpiece. The staircase beyond ascends, passing the Shakespeare Niche (with a model of the poet's bust at Stratford), to the Drawing Rooms, the principal rooms of the house in Soane's time, restored in 1971 and containing more of Soane's furniture, some of it designed by the architect himself.

No. 12, reached from the South Drawing Room, contains architectural models that belonged to Soane, as well as his collection of architectural books and over 30,000 drawings, from the Elizabethan plans of John Thorpe to work by Wren, Chambers, Robert Adam, and Soane himself.

The varied doorways of Nos. 10, 15, 16, and 26, on the north side of Lincoln's Inn Fields, are worth notice. NEWCASTLE HOUSE, on the west side (No. 66), built in 1684–9 for the Marquess of Powis, was rebuilt in the same style in 1930 by Sir Edwin Lutyens. No. 65 is a house of 1772 by Thomas Leverton. LINDSEY HOUSE (now Nos. 59–60), built about 1640 for the Earl of Lindsey, is a fine mansion designed most probably by Inigo Jones and the only survival of the original layout. Nos. 57–8 were built in the same style in the 18th century by Henry Joynes. No. 60 was the residence in 1790–1807 of Spencer Perceval, the Prime Minister, and No. 58, the home in 1834–56 of John Forster, the biographer of Dickens, is described as the abode of Mr Tulkinghorn in *Bleak House*. Nell Gwyn lived in lodgings in the square while an actress and here her first son, later the Duke of St Albans, was born. From the south end of the west range Sardinia Street (see Route 22) leads back to Kingsway, while Portsmouth Street runs south towards the Strand.

On the south side of the square are the research centre (1960) of the IMPERIAL CANCER RESEARCH FUND (founded in 1902) and the large building, with a pronounced Ionic portico, of the ROYAL COLLEGE OF SURGEONS of England (IV, E1), founded in 1800 and rebuilt in 1835 by Sir Charles Barry, but much altered since.

The building contains also the college's library and museum, the nucleus of which is the collection of anatomical preparations formed by John Hunter (d. 1793) and bought by the government in 1799. The museum (adm., p. 32) was gravely damaged by bombing, but new collections have been added as a result of a gift from the

Wellcome Trust. A large building on the west (by Alner W. Hall, 1957) houses the NUFFIELD COLLEGE OF SURGICAL SCIENCES. The last building on this side (by Sir Henry Tanner, 1906–13) is the LAND REGISTRY, established in 1862 and reconstituted in 1966.

To the south of Lincoln's Inn Fields stood the DUKE OF YORK'S THEATRE (or Playhouse), opened in 1660 in the house of the Duke of York (later James II), who granted a licence to Sir William Davenant (d. 1668) and his players (the Duke's Men). Pepys, an enthusiastic playgoer, records several visits, but in 1671 the company moved to Dorset Gardens, south of Fleet Street, taking the name of their theatre with them. This theatre, rebuilt in 1673 on a lavish scale by Wren, is last heard of in 1706. The parent playhouse, renamed the LINCOLN'S INN THEATRE, was taken over in about 1717 by John Rich, who here created pantomime in England, with himself as a famous Harlequin, and in 1728 he first staged *The Beggar's Opera*, John Gay's popular play with music. Thomas Arne's first opera, a setting of Joseph Addison's libretto, *Rosamund*, was produced in 1733. Handel took over the theatre in 1739, but few of his works were performed here and her gave up the venture in 1741. The theatre declined in popularity and was pulled down in 1848.

The archway at the south-east corner of the Fields admits to LINCOLN'S INN (IV, D1, 2), one of the four great Inns of Court (compare Route 24). The main entrance is in Chancery Lane (adm. to halls, etc., see p. 33). The quiet precincts are freely accessible to the public (except on Ascension Day).

Lincoln's Inn may have taken its name from Henry de Lacy, Earl of Lincoln (d. 1311), Edward I's legal adviser, who had a house not far away in Holborn. His crest of a lion appears in the society's arms and he was probably an early patron. Later in the 14th century, however, the inn occupied a site in Holborn that belonged to Thomas de Lincoln, described as the King's Serjeant. Between 1412 and 1422 (when the existing records begin) the society moved to its present site, where it took over the town house of the bishops of Chichester, built after 1227 by Ralph Nevill, also chancellor of England, from whom Chancery Lane (formerly 'Chancellor's Lane') derived its name. The rolls of the inn contain many famous names, among them those of Sir Thomas More, John Donne, William Penn, William Murray (later Earl of Mansfield), Horace Walpole, William Pitt, George Canning, Cardinal Newman, Disraeli, and Gladstone.

On the left of the west entrance is the NEW HALL AND LIBRARY, a building in the Tudor Gothic style by Philip Hardwick (1843). The hall has fine heraldic glass (1954) and is decorated with a huge mural painting, 45 ft high, by G. F. Watts ('Justice, a Hemicycle of Law-givers'), completed in 1859 and restored in 1955. The library, founded in 1497, is the oldest in London and comprises the most complete collection of law-books in England (over 80,000 volumes). On the north-east are the gardens, and beyond are the attractive STONE BUILDINGS, a classical range by Sir Robert Taylor (1756) chiefly occupied by practising barristers.

NEW SQUARE, south of the road through the inn, is a charming and well-preserved quadrangle of the late 17th century, now mainly occupied by solicitors. Dickens, at the age of fourteen, served as a clerk in a solicitor's office here for a short time. On the north of the gardens is a fine ironwork gate dated 1863. Farther east are the picturesque OLD BUILDINGS, dating mainly from the 16th and early 17th centuries. An archway opens to a small courtyard, on the west side of which is the OLD HALL, built in 1491, extended on the south by one bay in 1624, and carefully restored in 1928. It has a fine open roof, a carved oak screen of 1671, and a painting by Hogarth of St Paul before Felix (1748). The hall served as the Court of Chancery from 1737 until 1883, and the case of Jarndyce v. Jarndyce (in *Bleak House*) was heard here.

The CHAPEL, on the north of the courtyard, built in a Gothic style (1620–23), and attributed both to Inigo Jones and to John Clarke, was restored in 1685 by Wren and lengthened westward in 1883, and has been otherwise repaired. The foundation stone was laid by John Donne, the poet, who also preached the first sermon here. The chapel has old oak pews, an 18th-century pulpit, and 17th-century Flemish glass (by Bernard van Linge), restored after being shattered by a Zeppelin bomb in 1915. The east window contains the arms of treasurers from 1680 to 1908. In the open undercroft below, long used (like the Temple Church) as a meeting-place for barristers and their clients, is buried John Thurloe (d. 1668), Cromwell's secretary of state, who had chambers in Old Buildings (at No. 24) in 1645–59. On the east side of the courtyard is the noble GATEHOUSE, facing Chancery Lane and bearing the arms of Sir Thomas Lovell, who built it in 1518. Below the archway is the porter's lodge, and rooms above are said to have been occupied by Oliver Cromwell as a law student.

Cursitor Street, nearly opposite the gatehouse, leads to TOOK'S COURT, in which Nos. 14 and 15 are distinctive houses of about 1720. Field House, in BREAM'S BUILDINGS, a street off Chancery Lane to the south, contains the OFFICE OF FAIR TRADING, a government department set up in 1973 for the protection of the consumer.

CHANCERY LANE, with the offices of stationers, patent agents, and others connected with the law, runs north to High Holborn (see Route 23) and south to Fleet Street. On the left, in this direction, is the PUBLIC RECORD OFFICE (IV, E2), an elaborate building in a Tudor Gothic style, begun in 1851 by Sir James Pennethorne and completed in 1902 by Sir John Taylor. This is the chief repository for the national archives and legal records, from the Norman Conquest onwards, brought together from various courts of law and government departments, but most of the records were moved in 1977 to a new building at Kew, in Surrey.

During office hours (Mondays–Fridays, 9.30 to 5) the Search Rooms, containing records more than thirty years old, are open to holders of readers' tickets, obtainable on written application to the secretary, and photographic copies of records may be ordered. The Keeper of the Records was formerly the Master of the Rolls, a judge who ranks immediately below the Lord Chief Justice.

On the left under the archway is the entrance to the Public Record Office Museum (closed until late 1986). It occupies the exact site of the chapel of a house founded in 1232 by Henry III for converted Jews, but assigned in 1377 by Edward III to the Keeper (later the Master) of the Rolls, who adapted it for his private use. The chapel was pulled down in 1896 to make way for the present buildings, but the 13th-century chancel arch, which came to light then, has been re-erected against a wall beyond the archway (on the right). The museum preserves three monuments in their original positions on the north wall: on the left, to Richard Alington (d. 1561) and his wife; in the centre, to Edward, Lord Bruce of Kinloss (d. 1611), Masters of the Rolls; and on the right, to Dr John Yong (d. 1516), another Master, a splendid Renaissance work confidently attributed to Torrigiani. The windows contain heraldic glass, mostly modern, showing the arms of Keepers and Masters of the Rolls. The most famous of the museum's many interesting documents are the two vellum volumes of *Domesday Book*, a statistical survey of thirty-four counties of England made by order of William the Conqueror (1086). The arrangement of the exhibits when the museum reopens had not been decided at the time of this revision.

Opposite the Record Office is the classical building (by Lewis Vulliamy, 1832) of the LAW SOCIETY, founded in 1825 and controlling the education and examination of articled clerks in England and Wales and the admission of solicitors; it has over 40,000 members. The Library, containing more than 60,000 volumes, occupies a neo-classical building by Charles Holden (1902) at the corner of Carey Street. Chancery Lane ends at FLEET STREET near Temple Bar: thence to Charing Cross, see below; to St Paul's Cathedral and the Bank, see Route 24.

21 From Charing Cross to Fleet Street via the Strand

Plan III, F3–IV, E2

STATIONS: CHARING CROSS (Plan III, F3), on the Bakerloo, Jubilee, and Northern lines; EMBANKMENT (VIII, A3), on the Bakerloo, Circle, District, and Northern lines; ALDWYCH (IV, E1), on the Piccadilly line (open during rush hours only); TEMPLE (IV, F1; closed on Sundays), on the Circle and District lines. — BUSES Nos. 1, 6, 9, 11, 13, 15, 23, 77, 77A, 170, 172, and 176 in the Strand (eastbound buses follow Aldwych); Nos. 1, 4, 5, 68, 171, 176, 188, 501, 502, and 513 cross Waterloo Bridge and Nos. 5, 68, 77, 77A, 170, 172, 188, and 501 turn up Kingsway. For other buses to Charing Cross, see Routes 2, 6, and 19.

For CHARING CROSS and TRAFALGAR SQUARE, see Route 1. The STRAND (III, F3–IV, E2), which runs eastward from the square, was so named because it skirted the bank of the Thames, but this has receded in the course of time and is now hidden by intervening buildings. In Tudor and Stuart times the road was bordered by aristocratic mansions whose gardens sloped down to the river. It is still, as it was then, the principal thoroughfare between the West End and the City, and in consequence is one of the busiest streets in London, apart from its many shops, hotels, and theatres. CHARING CROSS STATION (III, F3), on the right, is a terminus of the Southern Region, built in 1864 (for the South Eastern Railway Company) by Sir John Hawkshaw; the large hotel above it was designed by E. M. Barry. In the station yard stands an 'Eleanor Cross', likewise designed by Barry (1865), a memorial, though not a copy, of the one that stood at Charing Cross. Craven Street and Villiers Street (see below), on either side of the station, go down towards the Victoria Embankment (Route 26) and the Embankment underground station.

The Southern Region station occupies the site of Hungerford Market and Hungerford Stairs, which descended beside the blacking factory in which Charles Dickens worked as a boy. Heinrich Heine, the German poet, lodged at No. 32 in CRAVEN STREET in 1827, and Benjamin Franklin, the American statesman, scientist, and author, lived in 1757–62 and 1764–72 at No. 36. VILLIERS STREET (see below), like Buckingham Street, parallel on the east, is named after George Villiers, Duke of Buckingham, who rebuilt York House on this site (compare Route 26). Rudyard Kipling made his first London home (in 1889–91) at No. 43 Villiers Street. No. 8 in BUCKINGHAM STREET is the head-office of KING GEORGE'S JUBILEE TRUST, set up in 1935 to aid the physical and spiritual welfare of young people. Samuel Pepys lived in this street in 1679–88 at No. 12 (much altered since), then at No. 14 until 1701. The painters William Etty (in 1824–49) and Clarkson Stanfield (in 1826–31) also lived at No. 14. Dickens lived at No. 15 (since rebuilt), where also Miss Betsey

Trotwood took rooms for David Copperfield. Nos. 17 and 18 are good houses with notable doorways.

Opposite Villiers Street, in the Strand, is a block of buildings of 1830, attributed to John Nash. The centrepiece is COUTTS' BANK, the bank of the royal family, founded in 1692 and moved here in 1904. The bank was rebuilt in a modern style, by Sir Frederick Gibberd & Partners, in 1979, when also the older part of the block was restored behind its façades. Beyond, but lying back from the corner of Agar Street, is the former CHARING CROSS HOSPITAL, established in 1818 and rebuilt in 1831 by Decimus Burton, but moved in 1973 to Fulham. The building is now used as a shelter for the homeless. On the other corner of Agar Street is ZIMBABWE HOUSE (formerly Rhodesia House), built in 1908 by Charles Holden for the British Medical Association. The contemporary sculptures by Epstein (mutilated in 1935) were his first major work in Britain. On the south side of the Strand is a glimpse of the north front (by Sir Aston Webb, 1927) of the Royal Society of Arts building (see below). The office of the NEW SOUTH WALES GOVERNMENT, beyond, is a successful example of modern commercial architecture by Sir Denys Lasdun (1959). Farther on, Adam Street (see below) comes in on the right.

JOHN ADAM STREET, which runs east from Villiers Street and parallel to the Strand, traverses a region formerly known as THE ADELPHI (Greek 'adelphoi', the brothers) from the four brothers Adam, who laid it out in 1768–74. The character of the neighbourhood has been destroyed by modern building, but a delightful example of the work of Robert Adam survives in No. 8 John Adam Street, built in 1772–4 and occupied by the ROYAL SOCIETY OF ARTS (III, F3), founded in 1754 for the promotion of science in art, manufactures, and commerce. The fine hall (adm., p. 34) is decorated with six large murals by James Barry (1777–83) illustrating the progress of civilization. Opposite is the huge ADELPHI, a grandiose block of offices built in 1938. It takes the place of Adelphi Terrace, the forefront of the Adam design and the residence of David Garrick, the actor (who died here in 1779), Thomas Hardy, and Bernard Shaw. In ROBERT STREET, close by, Nos. 1–3 were occupied at one time or another by Robert Adam (d. 1792), Thomas Hood, John Galsworthy, and Sir James Barrie. ADAM STREET leads back from the east end of John Adam Street to the Strand. No. 7 retains the original decorative scheme of the Adams; Sir Richard Arkwright (d. 1792), the pioneer of textile manufacture, lived at No. 8.

On the north side of the Strand are the ADELPHI THEATRE, built originally in 1806 but reconstructed in 1930 (by Ernest Schaufelberg), and the VAUDEVILLE THEATRE, opened in 1870 and rebuilt in 1926. Nearly opposite this is the huge SHELL-MEX HOUSE, better seen from the Embankment (Route 26). Southampton Street, on the north side of the Strand, leads to Covent Garden (see Route 20). On the right of the Strand (and entered from a forecourt) are the SAVOY HOTEL, built in 1903–10 by T. E. Collcutt and A. H. Mackmurdo, and the SAVOY THEATRE (rebuilt in 1929 by Frank A. Tugwell), at which most of the Gilbert and Sullivan operas were produced from 1881 onwards under the direction of Richard D'Oyly Carte.

Savoy Street, on the same side farther on, descends to the Victoria Embankment (Route 26), passing the QUEEN'S CHAPEL OF THE SAVOY (IV, F1; adm., p. 34), built in 1505 in the late-Perpendicular fashion and largely rebuilt in the same style after a fire in 1864. The private chapel of the ruling monarch as Duke of Lancaster, it has been since 1937 also the Chapel of the Royal Victorian Order, the youngest order of chivalry in Britain (1896), of which the Queen is sovereign. At the west end are the royal pews, and on the panelling at the sides are small copper plates emblazoned with the arms of the members of the order. The window over the door displays the arms of masters and chaplains of the Savoy and others connected with the chapel, including Gavin Douglas (d. 1522), the poet, bishop of Dunkeld, who is buried here.

The window next to this is in memory of Richard D'Oyly Carte (d. 1901; see above), while a window in the opposite wall with heraldic glass by Joan Howson (1956) commemorates Queen Mary (d. 1953). The window over the altar, designed in part by George VI, has heraldic glass relating to the Royal Victorian Order, and other windows were inserted in memory of the King and the Duke of Kent (d. 1942).

The chapel stands on part of the site of the Savoy Palace, built by Henry III and granted in 1246 to Peter, Count of Savoy, his wife's uncle. Subsequently it passed to John of Gaunt, Duke of Lancaster, whose son Henry IV annexed the Lancastrian estates (including the manor of the Savoy) to the Crown (1399). King John of France, taken prisoner in 1356 at the Battle of Poitiers, died in the palace in 1364, and Geoffrey Chaucer, the poet, is thought to have been married here (in 1366 or before). John Wyclif, the propagator of the Reformation, preached here under the patronage of John of Gaunt. Burned down during the Peasants' Rising of 1381, the palace was rebuilt by Henry VII in 1505 as a hospital, but of this only the chapel has survived. The Independents drew up their 'Confession of Faith' here during the Commonwealth (1658), and the important Savoy Conference on the revision of the Prayer Book took place here in 1661. Samuel Pepys has described several visits to hear the sermons of Thomas Fuller, author of *The Worthies of England*, who died in 1661 after being seized with a fever in the chapel. The ancient ceremony of beating the bounds of the Liberty of the Savoy takes place annually, usually in July.

In SAVOY HILL, below the chapel, the British Broadcasting Company (see below) opened its well-known studio in 1923. Its successor, the B.B.C., incorporated in 1927, remained here until 1931.

LANCASTER PLACE (IV, F1), on the right beyond the Savoy, runs past the west front of Somerset House to Waterloo Bridge (Route 26). On the other side of the street is the office of the DUCHY OF LANCASTER, a possession of the Crown since 1399, when Henry Bolingbroke (son of John of Gaunt, Duke of Lancaster) became king as Henry IV. Brettenham House, beyond, contains the office of the ROYAL HUMANE SOCIETY, founded in 1774 to reward those who save life. WELLINGTON STREET ascends on the left from the Strand to Bow Street and the Covent Garden Theatre.

In this street is the LYCEUM THEATRE, built by Samuel Beazley in 1834, but rebuilt behind its façade in 1904 (and now a dance hall). In the previous building Sir Henry Irving experienced many of his greatest triumphs; he began his long connection with the theatre in 1871 and took over the management in 1878, with Ellen Terry as his leading lady, a partnership that lasted until 1902. At No. 26, on the corner of Tavistock Street, Dickens edited his weekly journal, *All the Year Round* (1859–60), in which *A Tale of Two Cities*, *Great Expectations*, and *The Uncommercial Traveller* appeared.

The crescent of ALDWYCH (IV, E1), followed by all eastbound traffic, bears to the left for Kingsway (see Route 22). CITIBANK HOUSE (by Adams, Holden, and Pearson, 1960), at the corner, stands on the site of the Gaiety Theatre, first opened in 1868 and famous for its musical comedies. Beyond, in the Strand, is MARCONI HOUSE, in which the Marconi Wireless Telegraph Company set up the first public broadcasting station in Britain in May 1922. In November it was taken over by the British Broadcasting Company, who, however, moved in 1923 to Savoy Hill (see above).

On the other side of the Strand is the classical north front of SOMERSET HOUSE (IV, E, F1), a vast quadrangular building of 1776–86 designed by Sir William Chambers, with additional wings on the east by Smirke (1835; occupied by King's College) and on the west by Sir J. Pennethorne (1856). Its principal façade is on the south, facing the Thames. In the quadrangle is a notable bronze fountain-group by John Bacon the Elder (1778).

Somerset House occupies the site of a palace begun for himself in 1547 by the Duke of Somerset, Lord Protector of Edward VI, but still unfinished at his execution in 1552, when it passed to the Crown. Elizabeth I occupied the palace for part of the reign of her sister Mary, and later it became the residence of the queens of James I and Charles I and II. Inigo Jones, the architect, is believed to have died here in 1652, and Oliver Cromwell lay in state here in 1658. In the present building rooms were occupied at first by the Admiralty (to which some of the decorations in the quadrangle refer), the Royal Academy, the Royal Society, and the Society of Antiquaries.

The building is now mainly occupied by public offices. In the west wing is the BOARD OF INLAND REVENUE, inaugurated in 1849 and dealing mainly with death duties, stamps, and taxes. In the south wing is the PROBATE AND DIVORCE REGISTRY, containing a register of wills and testaments dating back to 1382. On Mondays–Fridays (10 to 4.30) a copy of any will may be inspected for a small fee. Among the interesting wills kept here are those of Van Dyck, William Penn, Lord Nelson, the Duke of Wellington, and Charles Dickens, but the wills of Shakespeare, Sir Isaac Newton, Dr Johnson, and others have been transferred to the Public Record Office. Elegant rooms on the upper floors, reached by remarkable spiral staircases, are to become the home of the treasures from the Courtauld Institute Galleries (see Route 19).

KING'S COLLEGE, founded in 1829, primarily for members of the Church of England, and incorporated in 1910 in the University of London, is housed mainly in the east wing of Somerset House and in new buildings of 1971–5 farther east. It provides courses in the faculties of theology, arts, laws, music, medicine, science, engineering, and education, and has a library of 450,000 volumes, particularly strong in ecclesiastical history. A separate theological department was established in 1846 with the object of training candidates for holy orders in the Church of England, and the teaching now embraces all the theological degrees of the university.

In the middle of the Strand rises the charming baroque church of ST MARY-LE-STRAND (IV, E1), a masterpiece of James Gibbs (1714–17), beautifully proportioned and with a graceful steeple and an unusual coffered ceiling to the nave. This was the first of the 'Fifty Churches' designed by the order of Queen Anne. Prince Charles Edward Stuart, the 'Young Pretender', a Roman Catholic, is claimed to have been secretly received into the Church of England here in 1750. The most famous rector of the previous church on this site was Thomas Becket, archbishop of Canterbury. In 1983 St Mary's became the official church of the Women's Royal Naval Service, and a major restoration was completed in 1984.

In STRAND LANE, an alley reached from Surrey Street, on the right beyond the church, by an archway, is the so-called ROMAN BATH (N.T.; no adm., but visible from the alley), a brick bath or reservoir of unknown date, probably Tudor, but certainly not Roman, as is now generally recognized. Measuring 15 ft 6 in. long, it is fed by a spring with a rate of flow of about 2,000 gallons a day. Here also is a second bath or reservoir perhaps installed by Thomas Howard, Earl of Arundel, Surrey, and Norfolk (d. 1646), whose town house stood near by and is, like that of Robert

Devereux, Earl of Essex (d. 1601), remembered in the names of the neighbouring streets (compare below).

To the north of St Mary's towers the huge BUSH HOUSE, the main entrance to which faces Kingsway (see Route 22). Farther east is the imposing AUSTRALIA HOUSE (IV, E1), built in 1911–18 by A. Marshall Mackenzie and A. G. R. Mackenzie as the headquarters in London of the Commonwealth of Australia. Flanking the entrance are groups representing Exploration and Agriculture, and above the cornice are the Horses of the Sun, by Mackennal. The interior, embellished with Australian wood and marble, contains a reading room and reference library open to visitors. Opposite, on the south, is ARUNDEL GREAT COURT, a large rectangular building by Sir Frederick Gibberd & Partners (1975) extending towards the river. It contains a hotel, offices, and shops, and encloses a public garden. During excavation of the foundations a Roman marble head of the 2nd century A.D. was discovered.

In the middle of the roadway where the Strand is rejoined by Aldwych is the national memorial to W. E. Gladstone, by Sir Hamo Thornycroft (1905), showing the statesman robed as Chancellor of the Exchequer, with groups at the foot representing Brotherhood, Education, Aspiration, and Courage. In the roadway to the east stands the church of ST CLEMENT DANES (IV, E1; adm., p. 34), built in 1680–81 by Sir Christopher Wren, gutted by bombing in 1941, but beautifully restored in its original style in 1958 by W. A. S. Lloyd as the headquarters church of the Royal Air Force, formed in 1918. The steeple (115 ft high), added by Gibbs in 1720, happily escaped damage, though the 17th-century bells of the famous peal ('Oranges and lemons, say the bells of St Clement's') were all cracked by falling to the ground. They were recast in 1957 from the old metal by Messrs Mears and Stainbank, who in 1588 cast the sanctus bell, the only one that escaped injury.

Let into the floor are the 735 crests, carved in Welsh slate, of all the units in the R.A.F., and rolls of honour contain the names of 125,000 men and women of the R.A.F. and associated services who died in the World Wars. On the piers are the crests of the R.A.F. Commands. The pulpit was pieced together from fragments, salvaged from the bombing, of the original, attributed to Grinling Gibbons. The reredos was painted by Ruskin Spear; the stained glass windows in the sanctuary are by Carl Edwards. The organ was subscribed for by members of the United States Air Forces. Under the west gallery is a United States Air Force shrine, and let into the floor here are the crests of the Commonwealth air forces. The Crypt, constructed in

1691 and now converted into a chapel, has an altar and sanctuary given by the Royal Netherlands Air Force and a fine black marble font, the gift of the Royal Norwegian Air Force. A stone in the floor at the head of the staircase commemorates pilots of the R.A.F. who trained in Georgia in 1941–2.

A previous church on this site is said to have derived its name from a settlement of Danes here before the Norman Conquest, and to have been the burial-place of Harold I (Harold Harefoot; d. 1040) and other Danish leaders. Oranges and lemons are distributed among the children of the former parish after a special service held in March. Dr Samuel Johnson (d. 1784), who worshipped regularly in the church, is commemorated by a statue (by Percy Fitzgerald, 1910) outside the east end.

CLEMENT'S INN, north of the church, survives in name only as one of the nine Inns of Chancery (compare Route 23). Justice Shallow, in Shakespeare's *Henry IV*, Part II, was 'once of Clement's Inn'. No. 3 was the headquarters of the Women's Social and Political Union (the Suffragette Movement), founded by Emmeline Pankhurst in 1903. ESSEX STREET, on the right beyond the church, was laid out on the grounds of Essex House in 1675, but has been rebuilt since. ESSEX HALL, destroyed in 1944 and rebuilt (by Kenneth Tayler) in 1958, is the headquarters of the Unitarian and Free Christian Churches and stands on the site of the original Unitarian church, established in 1774.

On the north of the Strand just beyond rises the elaborate Gothic edifice of the LAW COURTS (IV, E1, 2), officially the ROYAL COURTS OF JUSTICE, the central office of the Supreme Court of Judicature for England and Wales, established in 1873. This rambling and unrealistic pile of buildings, with a frontage of 514 ft to the Strand, was begun in 1874 by G. E. Street and completed in 1882 after the architect's death by Sir Arthur Blomfield and A. E. Street. The lofty Central Hall, 238 ft long and 80 ft high, has a mosaic floor by Street and statues of the architect (d. 1881), of Sir William Blackstone (d. 1780), presented by the American Bar Association in 1924, and of Lord Russell of Killowen (d. 1890). The various courts, entered by way of the hall, serve the Court of Appeal and the three divisions of Chancery, Queen's Bench, and Probate, Divorce and Admiralty. When the courts are sitting (Mondays–Fridays 10.30 to 1 and 2 to 4, during the legal terms), the public is admitted to the galleries, approached on either side of the main entrance.

The entrances for the judges, barristers, and solicitors are in Carey Street, on the north, and here also is the Bankruptcy Court, part of a new wing opened in 1968. On or about 23 October the historic ceremony of paying Quit Rents (to which visitors are admitted) takes place at the Law Courts. The payment is for the rent of two pieces of land whose whereabouts have been forgotten: the 'Moors' in Shropshire and the 'Forge' at St Clement Danes. For the first the Corporation of London offers two faggots cut with a bill-hook and a hatchet, and for the second six horseshoes and sixty-one nails, and the rents are collected by the Queen's Remembrancer on behalf of the Crown.

The shop of Messrs TWINING'S, the tea merchants, opposite the main entrance of the Law Courts, is probably the smallest in London. Near the east end of the Law Courts and the foot of Chancery Lane is the ineffectual TEMPLE BAR MEMORIAL, denoting the end of the Strand and the beginning of Fleet Street, as well as the boundary between Westminster and the City. Designed by J. E. Boehm and set up in 1880, with statues of Queen Victoria and Edward VII (as Prince of Wales) on either side and a bronze 'griffin' (by C. B. Birch), the unofficial badge of the City, on the top, it marks the site of Temple Bar, a triple gateway built by Wren in 1672, taken down in 1878, and re-erected ten years later at Theobald's Park (Hertfordshire).

A gateway of one kind or another marking the entrance to the City is thought to have stood on this spot as early as the 12th century. On spikes at the top the heads of executed traitors and felons were exposed, while Titus Oates (in 1685) and Daniel Defoe (1703) were among those stood in the pillory here. When the sovereign visits the City on state occasions the custom (dating back to the reign of Elizabeth I, if not earlier) of 'asking permission' to pass Temple Bar is still observed. The sovereign is met here by the Lord Mayor of London, who surrenders the Sword of State; this is immediately returned to him and is henceforth carried before the Queen as a symbol that he is responsible for her protection in the City.

For FLEET STREET, and thence to St Paul's Cathedral and the Bank, see Route 24; for CHANCERY LANE, etc., see Route 20.

22 From the Strand to King's Cross via Kingsway and Coram's Fields

Plan IV, E I–III, A3

STATIONS: ALDWYCH (Plan IV, E1), on the Piccadilly line (open during rush hours only); HOLBORN (IV, D1), on the Central and Piccadilly lines; CHANCERY LANE (IV, D2), on the Central line (closed on Sundays); RUSSELL SQUARE (III, C3), on the Piccadilly line; KING'S CROSS & ST PANCRAS (III, A3), on the Circle, Metropolitan, Northern, Piccadilly, and Victoria lines. — BUSES Nos. 5, 68, 77A, 172, 188, and 501 in Kingsway; Nos. 68, 77A, and 188 in Southampton Row; Nos. 5, 19, 38, 55, and 172 in Theobalds Road; Nos. 18, 45, 46, 172, and 259 in Gray's Inn Road. For buses in the Strand and Aldwych, see Route 21; in New Oxford Street and High Holborn, see Route 23; to King's Cross, see Routes 16, 29.

From Charing Cross to Lancaster Place, the approach to Waterloo Bridge, see Route 21. ALDWYCH, which curves to the north from the Strand at this point, is said to take its name from an old settlement ('ald wic') of the Danes in this neighbourhood. The façade of INVERESK HOUSE (by Mewès and Davis, 1907), on the left corner, conceals one of the earliest steel-framed buildings in London.

CATHERINE STREET, the first street on the left, leads past the DUCHESS THEATRE (by Ewen Barr, 1929) and the main entrance of the DRURY LANE THEATRE (IV, E1; officially the Theatre Royal, Drury Lane), the largest (3,000 seats) and one of the most famous theatres in London, long noted for spectacular drama and pantomime, but now better known for its lavish musical shows. The theatre, the fourth on this site, was built in 1809–12 by Benjamin Wyatt; the massive Ionic colonnade in Russell Street on the north was added by Samuel Beazley in 1832 and the auditorium was reconstructed in 1922, but Wyatt's vestibule, rotunda, and staircases remain intact and are the only interior parts of a Georgian theatre surviving in London.

In the foyer is a statue of Shakespeare by John Cheere (d. 1787), while the rotunda beyond contains statues of Edmund Kean (as Hamlet), Michael Balfe, the composer, David Garrick, and Shakespeare, and a plaque with a portrait of Sir Henry Irving, 'from the dramatic artistes of Italy'. The first theatre on the site was built in 1663 for Thomas Killigrew and the 'King's Company', who received a charter from Charles II, and Nell Gwyn, said to have been born in an alley off Drury Lane, traditionally sold oranges here before she became an actress (in 1665). The theatre was rebuilt in 1674 (after a fire) by Wren, and John Dryden became its principal playwright. In 1711 Colley Cibber, the actor and Poet Laureate, became part controller of the theatre. Thomas Arne was appointed resident composer in 1744, but gave up his post in 1760, after a quarrel with David Garrick.

Garrick, who first appeared here in 1742, became manager in 1746, acquired the theatre in the following year, and installed his own company. His management began with a prologue by Dr Johnson that included the famous line, 'We that live to please must please to live'. Sarah Siddons made her London debut here in 1775, playing Portia in *The Merchant of Venice*, at £5 a week (she was a failure). In the same year, the theatre, after being damaged in a riot, was restored (by Robert Adam) for David Garrick, who, however, resigned as manager in 1776. He was replaced by R. B. Sheridan, for whom the theatre was rebuilt again, in 1794, by Henry Holland. Sheridan here produced his delightful comedies and he remained as manager until 1816, but the theatre was burned down in 1809. Others connected with Drury Lane were Charles Macklin, John Kemble, and Edmund Kean, who made his first appearance in London here, in 1814 (as Shylock in *The Merchant of Venice*). The prologue for the opening of the present building was written by Lord Byron.

RUSSELL STREET (see Route 20) leads west from the theatre to Bow Street and

Covent Garden and east to Drury Lane. On the north side are the FORTUNE THEATRE (by Ernest Schaufelberg, 1924) and an alley admitting to the CROWN COURT CHURCH OF SCOTLAND, opened in 1718 and rebuilt in 1909. DRURY LANE ascends from Aldwych past the back of the Theatre Royal on its way to Long Acre and High Holborn (see Route 20). At No. 9 in KEAN STREET, on the right, is the ALDWYCH READING ROOM of the Science Reference Library, part of the British Library.

On the north-west side of the wide crescent of Aldwych are the STRAND THEATRE and the ALDWYCH THEATRE, which with the WALDORF HOTEL between them form a single composite design by A. Marshall Mackenzie and A. G. R. Mackenzie (1905). Ivor Novello (d. 1951), the composer, lived in a flat above the Strand Theatre. The interiors of both theatres were designed by W. G. R. Sprague.

On the other side of the road is INDIA HOUSE (IV, E1), the office of the High Commissioner for the Republic of India, built in 1928–30 by Sir Herbert Baker. The interior, decorated in the Indian style with carving and paintings by artists of that country, includes a reference library, reading room, and cinema, and exhibitions of Indian arts and crafts are held. Facing up Kingsway is BUSH HOUSE, a massive block of office buildings completed in 1931 to the designs of Helmle, Corbett, and Harrison of New York, and named after Irving T. Bush, the American business executive. The B.B.C.'s Overseas Services are broadcast from here. Over the main entrance is a colossal sculpture, 'Youth' (by Malvina Hoffman, 1925), 'to the friendship of English-speaking peoples'.

Aldwych makes a wide sweep down again to the Strand (Route 21), with a good view of St Clement Danes. In Houghton Street, on the left, is the LONDON SCHOOL OF ECONOMICS AND POLITICAL SCIENCE, founded in 1895 and since 1900 a branch of London University. It has faculties of arts, laws, science (anthropology and geography), and economics (including commerce). The buildings date mainly from 1902 and 1920–28. Attached to the school is the British Library of Political and Economic Science, established in 1896 and rehoused in 1978. The largest of its kind in the world, the library comprises about two million books, tracts, and pamphlets.

KINGSWAY (IV, D, E1), a fine boulevard 100 ft wide opened in 1906, runs northward from Aldwych to High Holborn and Southampton Row, lined mainly by large office buildings. The tram subway nearly three-quarters of a mile long beneath the street, connecting the Victoria Embankment with Southampton Row, was closed in 1952, when London's last tram ran, but was converted in 1963 into a road underpass for northbound traffic from the Embankment. ST

CATHERINE'S HOUSE, at the east corner, was the principal office of the Royal Air Force in 1919–55.

It now contains the OFFICE OF POPULATION CENSUSES AND SURVEYS, created in 1970 and incorporating the GENERAL REGISTER OFFICE for the registration of births, marriages, and deaths, an office thought to have been established in 1522 by Thomas Cromwell, though it was not until 1836 that a system of civil registration was instituted. The office is open to the public on Mondays–Fridays (8.30 to 4.30).

The site of the Stoll Theatre, farther up Kingsway, is occupied by an office building, by Lewis Solomon, Kaye & Partners (1960), with the ROYALTY THEATRE in its basement. This is entered on the south side, from Portugal Street, which leads to CLARE MARKET, formerly notorious as a thieves' quarter, and PORTSMOUTH STREET. A 16th-century antique shop here claims to be the original of Dickens's 'Old Curiosity Shop' (but see p. 209).

On the left in Kingsway (at Nos. 45–59) are the head-offices of the CIVIL AVIATION AUTHORITY, and farther up (at Nos. 65–71) is the GALLAHER BUILDING (formerly Kodak House), a pioneer of modern office building by Sir John Burnet (1911). KINGSWAY HALL, also on the left, is now used for lectures, concerts, and gramophone recordings. SARDINIA STREET, on the right, leading to Lincoln's Inn Fields (Route 20), takes its name from a chapel of the Sardinian embassy (see below). On the north side of the street is the PUBLIC TRUSTEE OFFICE, a government office opened in 1908 and rehoused in 1916.

Great Queen Street, on the left of Kingsway, leads to Drury Lane and Long Acre (Route 20). On the east in Kingsway is the Roman Catholic church of SS. ANSELM AND CECILIA, built in 1909 by Frederick Walters to take the place of the Sardinian chapel, the first building to be burned in the 'No Popery' riots of 1780. In Parker Street, to the left, is the BRITISH INSTITUTE OF MANAGEMENT, with an information office. HOLY TRINITY CHURCH (IV, D1), on the west in Kingsway, was built in 1910 by Sir John Belcher and J. J. Joass and stands on the site of the house in which Mary Lamb killed her mother in a fit of insanity in 1796.

Kingsway is prolonged beyond High Holborn (with Holborn station; Route 23) by SOUTHAMPTON ROW (III, C,D3), which goes on to Russell Square (Route 19). On the right are the BAPTIST CHURCH HOUSE (1903), with a statue of John Bunyan at the Catton Street angle, and the CENTRAL SCHOOL OF ART AND DESIGN of the G.L.C., founded in 1896, with W. R. Lethaby, the architect, as the first principal (until 1911). The building (by W. E. Riley, 1908), has a large extension on the north, containing the JEANNETTA COCHRANE THEATRE, opened in 1963.

In THEOBALDS ROAD, to the right, are several huge blocks of office building, including MERCURY HOUSE (1955), the headquarters of CABLE AND WIRELESS, formed in 1929 to bring together the telecommunication services of the British possessions. ADASTRAL HOUSE (1950), next to it, became in 1955 the headquarters of the AIR MINISTRY (now part of the Ministry of Defence), who brought with them the name of their previous home in Kingsway, adapted from the R.A.F. motto, *Per ardua ad astra*.

Drake Street, a new road on the right, near the beginning of Theobalds Road, admits to RED LION SQUARE (IV, D1), laid out in 1684 by Nicholas Barbon, a notorious speculative builder, but almost entirely rebuilt since. No. 17, on the south side, was occupied by D. G. Rossetti in 1851 and by William Morris and Sir Edward Burne-Jones in 1856–9. Among the plane trees is a bust of Bertrand Russell (d. 1970), the philosopher, by Marcelle Quinton (1980). At the north-east angle is CONWAY HALL (1929), the headquarters of the South Place Ethical Society, a liberal religious body founded originally in 1793. Princeton Street leads east from the square to BEDFORD ROW (IV, C, D1), an exceptionally wide street with characteristic examples of early-18th-century architecture. Well restored after bomb damage, it is mainly occupied by solicitors and accountants.

The street is extended north beyond Theobalds Road by GREAT JAMES STREET, with unspoiled terraces of about 1720–30. In MILLMAN STREET, which has unusual terraces of 1888, farther north, No. 33 is the BRITISH POSTGRADUATE MEDICAL FEDERATION, founded in 1945, comprising thirteen institutes specializing in medicine and now a school of the University of London.

In THEOBALDS ROAD farther east is the HOLBORN CENTRAL LIBRARY (1960). Benjamin Disraeli was born in 1804 at No. 22, one of a row of mid-18th-century houses.

The line of Theobalds Road is continued eastward beyond Gray's Inn Road by Clerkenwell Road (passing near St John's Gate and Church, Route 29) and Old Street, which ends at Shoreditch (Route 32).

JOHN STREET, starting opposite the gardens of Gray's Inn (Route 23), has rows of houses of about 1760. It is prolonged by DOUGHTY STREET, which has early-19th-century terraces. Sydney Smith, the clerical wit, lived at No. 14 in 1803–6. No. 48, now THE DICKENS HOUSE (IV, C1; adm., p. 32), was the home of Charles Dickens from April 1837 until December 1839, and is the only permanent residence of the novelist in London to have survived. Here the *Pickwick Papers* were completed, *Oliver Twist* and *Nicholas Nickleby* were written, and *Barnaby Rudge* was started (though the last did not begin to appear in print until 1841). Mary Hogarth, Dickens's sister-in-law, died in this house in 1837, and here his daughters Mamie and Kate were born. The house was purchased in 1924 by the Dickens Fellowship and now contains a wealth of portraits, illustrations, autograph letters, and furniture and relics of Dickens, as well as the most complete library in the world appertaining to him. In the basement is the 'Dingley Dell' kitchen, a reproduction of that in which the Pickwickians made merry.

LONDON HOUSE, at the corner of Doughty Street and Guilford Street, was designed by Sir Herbert Baker in 1937 (and extended in 1948) as a hall of residence for male university students from the Commonwealth.

In Gray's Inn Road, to the east (compare below), is NEW PRINTING HOUSE SQUARE (IV, B1), built in 1974, with the offices of *The Times*, founded in 1785 by John Walter as the *Daily Universal Register* and given its present title in 1788. To the south is the building (formerly Thomson House) of the associated newspaper, the *Sunday Times*.

Doughty Street ends on the north at MECKLENBURGH SQUARE, the east side of which (restored after bombing) was built as a formal design about 1812 by Joseph Kay. R. H. Tawney (d. 1962), the social historian, lived at No. 21. On the north side is WILLIAM GOODENOUGH HOUSE (1957), a hall of residence for American and Commonwealth students. A footpath connects the north side of the square with Brunswick Square, emerging beside the offices of the Thomas Coram Foundation (see below).

GUILFORD STREET skirts the south side of CORAM'S FIELDS (III, B3–IV, B1), a large playground laid out over the grounds of the FOUNDLING HOSPITAL. Established in 1739 by Captain Thomas Coram (d. 1751) for the care of destitute children, the hospital enjoyed the support of the composer Handel (who trained the choir) and the painter Hogarth, who persuaded artists to give their works to raise funds for the charity. Dickens, in *Little Dorrit*, made Tattycoram a 'foundling'. The hospital school was moved in 1926 to Berkhamsted and the buildings were then demolished, except for the colonnades (1745) bordering the grounds. In 1954 the school was sold to the Hertfordshire County Council, and the work (consisting of the care and upbringing of the first children of unmarried mothers) was concentrated here, the name of the charity being changed to the Thomas Coram Foundation.

From Lamb's Conduit Street, opposite Coram's Fields on the south, GREAT ORMOND STREET, with many 18th-century houses, leads west. No. 23 was the home of John Howard, the prison reformer, from 1777 until his death in 1790. On the north side is the HOSPITAL FOR SICK CHILDREN (IV, C1), the first and perhaps the largest hospital of its kind, founded in 1852 by Dr Charles West, and occupying buildings of 1872–90, with a new wing in memory of Viscount Southwood (d. 1946), the newspaper proprietor, a former chairman of the hospital. The large bronze figures of SS. Nicholas and Christopher are by Gilbert Ledward (1952–5).

At the west end of the street is the ROYAL LONDON HOMOEOPATHIC HOSPITAL (founded in 1849), in a building of 1895 with an extension of 1909 in QUEEN SQUARE (III, C3), probably named after Queen Anne, though the lead statue of about 1775 in the garden may well represent Queen Charlotte. At the north-east corner is the NATIONAL HOSPITAL for Nervous Diseases (founded in 1859), in buildings of 1884 and 1937; and on the south side are the ITALIAN HOSPITAL (1899) and the church of ST GEORGE THE MARTYR, built in 1706–23, altered inside in 1827, and restored in 1952. A footway from the south-west corner of the square goes on to Southampton Row.

Guilford Street leads to BRUNSWICK SQUARE (III, B3), laid out with Mecklenburgh Square, on the other side of the Fields, as a balanced composition by S. P. Cockerell (1790). On the west is the imposing BRUNSWICK CENTRE, with terraced housing on either side of a shopping precinct, designed by Patrick Hodgkinson (1965–73). On the north is the large SCHOOL OF PHARMACY of London University, founded in 1842 and rebuilt in 1939–60 to designs by Herbert J. Rowse. The school has faculties of medicine (pharmacy) and science (toxicology and pharmacology). Adjoining are the offices (1937) of the THOMAS CORAM FOUNDATION (see above; adm., p. 35).

In the handsome Court Room here, an exact copy of the original in the Foundling Hospital, the old woodwork and plasterwork have been installed, and this room, the landing, and the fine Picture Gallery contain notable paintings by Hogarth ('Captain Coram', etc.), Reynolds, Richard Wilson, Allan Ramsay, and Benjamin West (all governors of the hospital), a cartoon by Raphael, and a bust of Handel by Roubiliac. Other mementoes include Hogarth's punch-bowl, the keyboard of Handel's organ, and an original score of *Messiah*. Outside the offices is a statue of Thomas Coram (1963), by William McMillan, who used Hogarth's portrait for the likeness.

To the west from the square, BERNARD STREET, with early-19th-century houses, leads to Russell Square station (Route 19).

HUNTER STREET, running north from Brunswick Square, is extended by Judd Street towards St Pancras Station (Route 16). From the junction of these streets, TAVISTOCK PLACE leads west to Tavistock Square (Route 19) and east to REGENT SQUARE (III, B3), of which only the south side survives from the Regency.

REGENT SQUARE CHURCH (now a United Reformed church), on this side, was built in 1965, after the gutting by bombing of the Presbyterian Church of England, established in 1827 by Edward Irving, the Scottish Presbyterian minister. Here took place the 'speaking with unknown tongues', as described by his friend Carlyle, before Irving's expulsion for his heterodox views in 1832.

Sidmouth Street runs east from Regent Square to GRAY'S INN ROAD (IV, A1–D2), a long dismal thoroughfare leading southward to Holborn (Route 23). In this direction is the EASTMAN DENTAL HOSPITAL, the gift of an American citizen. It occupies buildings by Burnet, Tait, and Lorne (1930) which also contain the INSTITUTE OF DENTAL SURGERY of London University, established in 1948. In AMPTON STREET, the extension of Sidmouth Street, the Carlyles lodged for nearly four months in 1831–2 at No. 33 (then No. 4). It is one of several streets in this neighbourhood with early-19th-century houses. The northward end of Gray's Inn Road is at KING'S CROSS (Route 16).

23 From St Giles Circus to St Paul's Cathedral via Holborn and Newgate Street

Plan III, D2–IV, E3

STATIONS: TOTTENHAM COURT ROAD (Plan III, D2), HOLBORN (IV, D1), CHANCERY LANE (IV, D2), and ST PAUL'S (IV, E3), all on the Central line. Tottenham Court Road is also on the Northern line (Charing Cross section) and Holborn on the Piccadilly line; Chancery Lane is closed on Sundays. HOLBORN VIADUCT (IV, D3) is a terminus of the Southern Region. — BUSES Nos. 8 and 25 ply from St Giles Circus to the Bank, and Nos. 22 and 501 from High Holborn (Kingsway) to the Bank; No. 171 in Chancery Lane (northbound) and New Fetter Lane (southbound); Nos. 18, 45, 46, 171, 243 and 259 in Gray's Inn Road; Nos. 18, 45, and 46 in Shoe Lane (northbound) and Farringdon Street (southbound), for Ludgate Circus. For other buses to St Giles Circus, see Routes 14, 18; for buses in Shaftesbury Avenue, High Holborn, and Bloomsbury Way, see Route 19; in Kingsway and Southampton Row, see Route 22; in Cheapside and St Martin's-le-Grand, see Route 29.

For ST GILES CIRCUS, where Oxford Street meets Tottenham Court Road and Charing Cross Road, see Route 14. NEW OXFORD STREET (III, D2, 3), which extends Oxford Street eastward to join High Holborn, was cut through a slum quarter in 1847. ST GILES HIGH STREET, the older thoroughfare, starting south of the prominent office block of Centre Point, leads to the beginning of High Holborn. It passes ST GILES-IN-THE-FIELDS (III, E3), rebuilt in 1731–3 by Henry Flitcroft, with a noble baroque steeple 150 ft high. The church is the third on the site, the first having been a royal foundation of Matilda, queen of Henry I (1101). The fine interior, well restored in 1953, has columns of Tuscan red marble, a decorative stucco barrel vault, and the original wrought-iron altar-rails.

David Garrick, the actor-manager, was married here in 1749. At the Regency font Clara Allegra Byron, daughter of Lord Byron and Miss Clairmont, was baptized in 1818, and Shelley had his two children baptized (possibly on the same day), three days before he left England for the last time. In the north-west corner of the church is a tombstone to the memory of George Chapman (d. 1634), translator of Homer, and on the north wall is a memorial tablet to Andrew Marvell (d. 1678). Both poets are buried in the church, as are Lord Herbert (d. 1648), the poet, and James Shirley (d. 1666), the dramatist. In the vestibule is a monument erected in 1930 to John Flaxman (d. 1826), with a sculpture by his own hand.

The gateway on the west side of the churchyard has a curious relief of the Day of Judgement in the tympanum, dating from 1687. Opposite the south-east corner of the church is the restored table-tomb of Richard Penderel, 'unparallel'd Pendrell' (d. 1672), who helped Charles II to escape after the Battle of Worcester. The inscription (original in the church) is worth reading. Sir John Oldcastle, the Lollard leader and supposed original of Shakespeare's Falstaff, was 'hung and burnt hanging' in St Giles's Fields in 1417. The Great Plague of London (1665) began in this area, later spreading to the City.

HIGH HOLBORN (III, D3–IV, D2), starting beyond Shaftesbury Avenue (Route 19), passes south of the Shaftesbury Theatre. In Endell Street, on the right, is the SWISS PROTESTANT CHURCH, founded in 1762 and rebuilt in 1854 (by George Vulliamy). Services are held on Sundays in French. Drury Lane (see Route 20) diverges on the right beyond the Westminster branch of the MOORFIELDS EYE HOSPITAL, formerly the Westminster Ophthalmic Hospital (founded in 1816 by George Guthrie, the military surgeon, and rehoused in 1928). Farther on are the KODAK GALLERY (adm., p. 33), whose photograph exhibitions are held from time to time, and the former HOLBORN TOWN HALL, a flamboyant building of 1906 by Warwick and Hall.

High Holborn, joined on the left by New Oxford Street, goes on to cross the north end of Kingsway (Route 22). Little and Great Turnstile, two passages on the right, lead to Lincoln's Inn Fields and the Soane Museum (Route 20). Farther on are the heavily ornate buildings of the PEARL ASSURANCE COMPANY, erected in 1914–30 and extended in 1956–62. On the left rises the sixteen-storey STATE HOUSE, by Trehearne and Norman Preston & Partners (1960; now government offices), with a huge abstract bronze, 'Meridian' (15 ft high and weighing four tons), by Barbara Hepworth, in a courtyard. Opposite is PENDEREL HOUSE, containing the London Weather Centre of the Meteorological Office (1965).

CHANCERY LANE (Route 20) bears to the right farther on for Lincoln's Inn and Fleet Street. Below No. 53 are the LONDON SILVER VAULTS (adm., p. 35), established in 1885, underground strongrooms with a vast assembly of old silver, Sheffield plate, etc. In Southampton Buildings, the next turning off High Holborn, is the PATENT OFFICE (IV, D2), now part of the Department of Trade and Industry, which grants patents for new inventions and registers designs and trade-marks. It has well over two million patent specifications. The library, now called the SCIENCE REFERENCE LIBRARY (and administered by the British Library) has about 170,000 books and monographs, the finest collection of scientific and technical works in England.

On the north side of High Holborn (at No. 21) is a late-17th-century entrance gateway to GRAY'S INN (IV, C1–D2), one of the four Inns of Court (compare Route 24), known to have existed as a school of law in the 14th century, and named after the landowners, the Lords de Gray. The buildings (adm., p. 32) were much damaged by bombing. The LIBRARY (41,000 volumes), rebuilt by Sir Edward Maufe (1958), is on the east side of South Square, which contains a statue (by F. W. Pomeroy, 1912) of Francis Bacon, the philosopher and statesman, who was treasurer of the inn and retained his chambers here from 1576 until his death in 1626. On the north side of the square is the fine HALL, built in 1556–60, bombed in 1941, and rebuilt in 1951 largely in its original style, though with an additional oriel window, the gift of the American Bar Association. The late-16th-century carved screen and 16th–17th-century heraldic glass survived the bombing and have been replaced, and plaques on the walls bear the arms of treasurers since 1775. Shakespeare's *The Comedy of Errors* was first acted in the hall in 1594, and the Court of Exchequer met here in the 18th century.

To the north of this range of building is the delightful late-17th-century GRAY'S INN SQUARE (restored after war damage), from which there are exits to Gray's Inn Road. The contemporary CHAPEL, on the south, altered about 1840, was gutted by bombing but restored in 1960. To the west are the charming GARDENS, laid out about 1600, where Pepys and Addison walked, the 'best gardens of the Inns of Court' (Charles Lamb). The older of the catalpa trees here is reputed to have been planted by Bacon from slips brought home from America by Sir Walter Raleigh.

Famous members of the inn include Sir Nicholas Bacon, the statesman, father of Francis Bacon; Sir William Gascoigne, the Chief Justice who is credited with committing the Prince of Wales (later Henry V) to prison; Thomas Cromwell, the minister of Henry VIII; Lord Burghley and Sir Francis Walsingham, the Elizabethan statesmen; Sir Thomas Gresham, founder of the Royal Exchange; Archbishop Laud; John Bradshaw, the regicide; Sir Samuel Romilly, the legal reformer, who occupied chambers at No. 6 Gray's Inn Square in 1778–91; Lord Macaulay, the historian; and Lord Birkenhead, the Conservative statesman. No. 11 South Square is now the SENATE OF THE INNS OF COURT, the governing body of the barristers, established in 1974.

High Holborn ends at the foot of Gray's Inn Road (Route 22), and HOLBORN (IV, D2) begins here. This broad thoroughfare takes its name from the 'Hole Bourne', the upper part of the Fleet River (compare Route 24), which flowed through a deep hollow or valley. Stone obelisks topped by silver 'griffins' (or dragons) on either side of the road (Holborn Bars) mark the entrance to the City of London. Opposite is STAPLE INN, with its picturesque timber-framed façade of overhanging gables, built in 1586 and the only survival of Elizabethan domestic architecture in London (last restored in 1950).

The inn, reputed to have been in the 14th century a hostel of the wool merchants ('merchants of the staple'), became in the reign of Henry V (1413–22) one of the nine INNS OF CHANCERY in London. These were subordinate to the Inns of Court (compare Route 24) and the custom was for students of law to enter an inn of chancery before passing on to an inn of court, but since the 18th century they have had no connection with the law and have mostly disappeared or been rebuilt. Staple Inn was arranged round two courtyards, erected in 1545–89 and largely rebuilt in the 18th century. In 1886, after it had ceased to be an inn of chancery, it was acquired by the Prudential Assurance Company, who later leased it to the INSTITUTE OF ACTUARIES, founded in 1848. Devastated in 1944 by a flying-bomb, the inn was largely restored in its former style by 1954. The Hall, on the south side of the first court, was rebuilt in 1955 incorporating material salved from the bombed 16th-century hall. Dr Johnson occupied No. 2 in the court in 1759–60, when he is said to have written *Rasselas* in the evenings of a week to pay for his mother's funeral. Mr Grewgious, in *Edwin Drood*, had chambers in the second court, which has been partly rebuilt.

In the roadway is the ROYAL FUSILIERS WAR MEMORIAL, by Albert Toft (1922). Brooke Street, to the left, leads to ST ALBAN'S CHURCH, built in 1863 by Butterfield, greatly damaged in 1941, and well restored in 1961 by Adrian Scott. It contains a striking bronze of Christ rising from the dead, by Hans Feibusch (1985). To the left in Holborn are the offices of the PRUDENTIAL ASSURANCE COMPANY, grandiose Gothic buildings in red brick and terracotta by Alfred Waterhouse, built in 1879 and extended in 1899–1906. Under the arch to the inner court is a bust (by Percy Fitzgerald) of Charles Dickens, who lived in 1834–7 (and began the *Pickwick Papers*) at Furnival's Inn, a former inn of chancery on this site. On the south side of Holborn is the entrance to BARNARD'S INN, incorporating remains of another inn of chancery, where Pip and Herbert Pocket shared rooms in *Great Expectations*. The restored 14th-century hall (with 16th-century panelling and heraldic glass) was from 1894 the hall of Mercers' School, founded in 1447 and controlled by the Mercers' Company from 1542 until it closed in 1958. Beyond Fetter Lane and the tall offices of the *Daily Mirror* group (by Anderson, Forster, and Wilcox; 1961), remarkable for the use of colour, is HOLBORN CIRCUS (IV, D2), with an inferior equestrian statue of Prince Albert (1874).

St Andrew Street, to the right here, leads to SHOE LANE, in which No. 76 is the INTERNATIONAL PRESS CENTRE, containing also the PRESS CLUB for journalists, founded in 1882. On the north of the Circus begins HATTON GARDEN, long known as the street of diamond merchants. Giuseppe Mazzini, the Italian patriot, lived in exile at No. 5 (which has a bas-relief portrait) in 1841–2, while inspiring his young countrymen in their struggle for political freedom.

Charterhouse Street runs north-east from Holborn Circus towards Smithfield and Charterhouse (Route 29). On the left at the outset is ELY PLACE (IV, D2), a private cul-de-sac, lined by charming late-18th-century houses with 'Adam' doorways. Still outside the jurisdiction of the police, it is watched over day and night by a beadle who before the war called the hours from 10 p.m. to 5 a.m. The street derives its name from a town house of the bishops of Ely (pulled down in 1772), in which John of Gaunt died in 1399. The famous garden, referred to in *Richard III* (iii, 4), was granted in 1576 to Sir Christopher Hatton, Lord Chancellor of Elizabeth I, for the annual rent of £10, ten loads of hay, and a red rose plucked at midsummer. The only survival from the bishop's house is ELY CHAPEL, called ST ETHELDREDA'S CHURCH since it was purchased in 1874 by the Roman Catholics (the first pre-Reformation church in England to be so returned). Built about 1290, it is a masterpiece of the Geometrical or early-Decorated style, restored in 1935 by Sir Giles G. Scott and again in 1952 after damage to its fine chestnut roof. The splendid windows at the east and west ends show interesting tracery; the east window has striking glass by Joseph E. Nuttgens (1953); the west window (about 1300) is one of the largest in London. Notable also are the carved corbels for statues, with crocketed gables above, between the side windows. The moulded doorway on the south-west is the original entrance from the palace, and the small cloister on this side is planted with fig trees. Below the church is a large undercroft, built in 1251 incorporating stout walls, possibly of an older structure. The wooden piers here were introduced during a restoration in 1875.

Charterhouse Street crosses, farther on, the junction of Farringdon Street (compare below) and Farringdon Road. In Cowcross Street, on the right of the latter, is the entrance to FARRINGDON STATION (formerly Farringdon Street station), from which the first public passenger-carrying underground railway in the world was opened in 1863 to Paddington. Part of the original building remains. Greville Street, extending Cowcross Street to the west, crosses SAFFRON HILL, in which No. 67 is the NATIONAL SOCIETY FOR THE PREVENTION OF CRUELTY TO CHILDREN, founded in 1884.

HOLBORN VIADUCT (IV, D2, 3), about a quarter of a mile long, was built in 1867–9 by William Haywood over the valley of the 'Hole Bourne' to connect Holborn Circus with Newgate Street. On the right is ST ANDREW'S CHURCH (adm., p. 34), rebuilt in 1684–90 by Wren (who in 1704 refaced and heightened the medieval tower), but bombed in 1941 and restored in 1961 in its former style by Lord Mottistone, who also designed the tomb of Captain Thomas Coram (d. 1751). The font, pulpit, and part of the organ were originally in the Foundling Hospital, as were the two figures of children on the tower.

The registers record the burial in 1770 of Thomas Chatterton, the youthful poet (who poisoned himself at his lodgings at No. 39 Brooke Street, since rebuilt), and the baptism in 1817 (at the age of 12) of Benjamin Disraeli, born into the Jewish faith. William Hazlitt was married here in 1808, with Charles Lamb as the best man and his sister Mary as the bridesmaid.

The CITY TEMPLE just beyond, a Congregational church opened in 1874 under Dr Joseph Parker, the famous preacher, was destroyed in an air-raid in 1941. Rebuilt in 1958 to the designs of Lord Mottistone and Paul Paget, but embodying the façade of the old building, it has seats for 1,400 and a theatre beneath seating 800 people. ATLANTIC HOUSE (1951), opposite, is the London regional headquarters of H. M. STATIONERY OFFICE, the government printing and publishing organization, established in 1786.

Beyond the middle section of the viaduct, which bridges Farringdon Street (Route 24; reached by steps), is the HOLBORN VIADUCT STATION (IV, D3) of the Southern Region, rebuilt in 1962 by Ronald Ward and Partners. On the left farther on is the HOLY SEPULCHRE CHURCH, one of the largest of the City churches (sometimes called St Sepulchre's). A foundation of the 12th-century Crusaders, it was rebuilt in the 15th century and greatly repaired in 1670–77 by Wren, after damage in the Great Fire. The medieval tower and three-storey fan-vaulted porch have survived; the church was restored, in poor fashion, in 1878 and redecorated in 1967. The south aisle is now the memorial chapel of the Royal Fusiliers and the east window here contains heraldic glass by Gerald Smith, who also designed the east window of the chancel (both 1950). At the east end of the south aisle is a wall tablet (a copy of the original) to Captain John Smith (d. 1631), 'sometime Governour of Virginia and Admiral of New England', who was rescued by Pocahontas, the Indian chieftain's daughter, and who is buried near by. At the east end of the north aisle is an organ by Renatus Harris (1677). The two pulpits, the font, and the fine altarpiece all date from the 17th century.

The north chapel was dedicated in 1955 as the musicians' memorial chapel and has panelled walls and a book of remembrance. A window of 1946 (by Gerald Smith), on the north, commemorates Sir Henry Wood (d. 1943), founder of the Promenade Concerts, who deputized for the organist here at the age of twelve, and whose ashes are buried below. Other windows, by Brian Thomas (1962–3), commemorate Dame Nellie Melba (d. 1931), the Australian opera singer, and John Ireland (d. 1962), the composer. The bells ('of Old Bailey' in the nursery rhyme) were repaired in 1983.

The church is well known for its musical activities, and special services are held, e.g., on St Cecilia's Day (22 November). At the west end of the north aisle is a bell of 1605 which used to be rung at midnight outside the condemned cell at Newgate Prison (see below) before an execution. Here also is a charred oak beam from the prison chapel, burned in 1780. Until the late 18th century a nosegay was presented to every condemned criminal as he passed the church on his way to Tyburn, and it remained the custom to toll the church bells for each execution until 1890.

Adjoining the church in Giltspur Street is the former Watch House, built in 1791, destroyed in 1941, and rebuilt in 1962, when a bust (1935) of Charles Lamb, a pupil of Christ's Hospital, was moved here from Christ Church (see below).

Giltspur Street, east of the church, leads to St Bartholomew's Hospital and Church (Route 29). On the other side of the road is the CENTRAL CRIMINAL COURT (IV, D, E3; adm. p. 31), the chief court for crimes committed in Greater London, popularly called the OLD BAILEY from the street at whose corner it stands. Built in

1902–7 by E. W. Mountford (and restored after heavy war damage), it embodies part of the wall of the notorious Newgate Prison which stood on this site. The copper dome, 195 ft above the ground, is surmounted by a large bronze figure of Justice (not blindfolded as is usually the case), by F. W. Pomeroy.

When the courts are sitting (Mondays–Fridays at 10.15 and 1.45) the public is admitted to the galleries. On the first two days of each session the judges carry posies of flowers and sweet herbs are strewn round the courts, a survival from the time when these were necessary to overcome the noxious smells from the prison. The main hall is decorated with frescoes by G. Moira (1954) and contains a statute (by Drury, 1913) of Elizabeth Fry (see below). Excavations in 1966 for a large extension to the Central Criminal Court, on the east (by McMorran and Whitby), revealed a section of the Roman and medieval City Wall.

NEWGATE PRISON, the principal prison of London from the 13th century, began to be rebuilt in 1770, but was fired during the Gordon Riots (1780) and not finally completed until 1782. Public executions, previously carried out at Tyburn (see Route 14), took place in front of the prison from 1783 to 1867, and then within its walls until 1901. Among famous prisoners who were confined at Newgate were William Penn, the Quaker; Titus Oates, the perjurer; Daniel Defoe (in 1702–4); Jonathan Wild, hanged in 1725 (compare Fielding's novel); and Lord George Gordon, leader of the Gordon Rioters, who died of gaol fever in 1793. The appalling conditions in the prison were greatly alleviated through the efforts of Elizabeth Fry (d. 1845), and the prison was pulled down in 1902.

In Old Bailey, which descends to Ludgate Hill (Route 24), Milton's *Tenure of Kings and Magistrates*, a defence of the execution of Charles I, and other political writings were burned by the common hangman in 1660.

The line of Holborn is continued by NEWGATE STREET (IV, D, E3), named from one of the City gates (demolished in 1767). WARWICK LANE, on the right, passing CUTLERS' HALL (1887), with its terracotta frieze by George Tinworth, leads to Stationers' Hall and Ludgate Hill (see Route 24). On the other side of the road is the shell of CHRIST CHURCH, built by Wren in 1677–87, but burnt out in 1941 (the interior is now a lawned garden). It stands on the site of the choir of a great church of the Franciscans, used after the Dissolution by the boys of Christ's Hospital (see below). The fine steeple, also by Wren (1704), survived the bombing and was restored in 1960.

In King Edward Street, beyond the steeple, are the principal entrances to the POST OFFICE (IV, D3), formerly the General Post Office (and colloquially the 'G.P.O.'). On the left, in the King Edward Building (1910), is the London Chief Office, with a counter

150 ft long. In the same building is the NATIONAL POSTAL MUSEUM (adm., p. 33), opened in 1966 and extended in 1969, with an unrivalled collection of stamps, drawings, documents, etc., and a philatelic library. Opposite on the east is the Postal Headquarters Building (1895), the principal administrative building, and the former headquarters of the Postmaster-General (an office created by Oliver Cromwell in 1657). Between the buildings is a statue of Sir Rowland Hill (d. 1879), who introduced the penny post in 1840, and on the north-east is the Postmen's Park (see Route 29).

Beneath the Post Office is the unique POST OFFICE RAILWAY, 6½ m. long, which runs underground from Whitechapel to Paddington, via Liverpool Street Station, the King Edward Building and Mount Pleasant (Route 29). Electrically driven and automatically controlled, the trains transmit about 40,000 mailbags a day at a speed of 35 m.p.h. The railway was completed in 1926 and carries over thirty trains an hour during rush hours. Under the loading-yard of the Post Office, west of the King Edward Building, is a well-preserved bastion of the Roman wall.

The King Edward Building occupies part of the site of a monastery of the Franciscans, or Grey Friars, established here early in the 14th century. The conventual buildings were replaced after the Dissolution by Christ's Hospital, the famous 'Bluecoat School', founded in 1552 by Edward VI and moved in 1902 to Sussex.

Newgate Street, skirting the north side of the St Paul's precinct (Route 24), is joined by the street of St Martin's-le-Grand (Route 29). At the junction is a new BRITISH TELECOM CENTRE, completed in 1985. Opposite is St Paul's underground station, to the right of which is PANYER ALLEY, named from its having been inhabited by basketmakers. A relief of 1688 showing a boy seated on a pannier, supposed to mark the highest ground in the City, was removed during the bombing and replaced in 1964 on Panyer Alley Steps, close by. Cheapside (Route 29) goes on eastward to the Bank, while ST PAUL'S CHURCHYARD (IV, E3), enclosing **St Paul's Cathedral** (adm., p. 404), opens on the right.

24 From Fleet Street to St Paul's Cathedral (The Temple)

Plan IV, E2–IV, E3.

STATIONS: ALDWYCH (Plan IV, E1), on the Piccadilly line (open in rush hours only); ST PAUL'S (IV, E3), on the Central line; TEMPLE (IV, F1; closed on Sundays), BLACKFRIARS (IV, E3), and MANSION HOUSE (V, E1), on the Circle and District lines. Blackfriars is also a terminus of the Southern Region. — BUSES

Nos. 4, 6, 9, 11, 15, 23, 502, and 513 in Fleet Street and Ludgate Hill, passing St Paul's Cathedral; No. 18 in Shoe Lane (from Holborn) and Ludgate Hill. For other buses in Shoe Lane, and in Farringdon Street, see Route 23; in Chancery Lane and Fetter Lane (New Fetter Lane), see Route 23; in New Bridge Street, see Route 26.

From Charing Cross via the Strand to Temple Bar, the beginning of FLEET STREET (IV, E2, 3), see Route 21. The street, mentioned as early as the 13th century, takes its name from the Fleet River, which rises at Hampstead and flows down the valley from Holborn to enter the Thames at Blackfriars Bridge. The stream was covered over in 1765 and is now conveyed through a sewer under Farringdon Street and New Bridge Street. Fleet Street, long famous as the 'street of ink', still contains the publishing offices of some of the national newspapers, as well as the London offices of many of the larger provincial newspapers. As it slopes steeply down to Ludgate Circus, it affords one of the most striking views of St Paul's Cathedral.

Fleet Street has been associated with printing since about 1500, when Wynkyn de Worde, the assistant of William Caxton, set up his press 'in Fletestrete at the signe of the Swane'. The newspapers are mostly printed in the narrow streets, courts, and alleys that cluster round Fleet Street, particularly on the south side. This neighbourhood is busiest between 9 p.m. and midnight, when most of the daily papers are printed, in time to catch the night trains from the London termini to the provinces. 'Late London' editions, however, continue to be printed until about 4 a.m., after which the presses are silent until the first editions of the evening papers are called for. These appear at about 10 a.m. and new editions continue to be published throughout the day until 6 p.m. or later. Visitors can often arrange to see the papers being printed, on written application to one or other of the newspaper offices.

On the south side of Fleet Street, at No. 1, opposite the Temple Bar Memorial, is CHILD'S BANK (now part of the Royal Bank of Scotland), established in 1671 and the oldest bank in London. Charles II, the Duke of Marlborough, Prince Rupert, Nell Gwyn, Pepys, and Dryden were among the early customers of the bank, which is generally agreed to be the original of Tellson's Bank in Dickens's *A Tale of Two Cities*.

A gateway just beyond, built in 1684 by Roger North, admits to MIDDLE TEMPLE LANE, which descends to the Victoria Embankment and bisects THE TEMPLE (IV, E2), a name which covers both the Inner and the Middle Temple, two of the great Inns of Court. (For the continuation of Fleet Street, see p. 252.)

The Temple was originally the headquarters in England of the Knights Templars, an order of military crusaders founded in 1119 at Jerusalem with the object of protecting the Holy Sepulchre and recovering Palestine from the Saracens. They were established in Holborn in about 1130 and moved here in the reign of Henry II (1154–89). In 1312, on the dissolution of the Order, the Temple passed to the Crown, and in 1324 it was granted to the Knights Hospitallers of St John, who in the reign of Edward III leased it to a number of professors of the common law. These shortly began to take in students to reside with them, thus establishing the beginnings of the legal community that has persisted at the Temple ever since. The Temple is first known to be mentioned as an Inn of Court in 1449; at the Dissolution of the Monasteries (1540) it reverted to the Crown, but in 1608 the two societies were confirmed in their possessions by James I.

The four INNS OF COURT (Lincoln's Inn and Gray's Inn are the others) originated in the reign of Edward I, by which time the clergy no longer practised in the courts of justice, their place being taken by professional students of law. By long custom the inns enjoy the exclusive privilege of admitting law students to practise as advocates in the courts of England and Wales. Students may pursue their legal studies elsewhere, but they must pass the examinations of one of the inns and must 'keep terms' (usually twelve) by dining in hall a certain number of days in each term before they can be 'called to the Bar', after which they are entitled to plead for others in a court of law. Barristers remain outside the bar (originally the division in hall between the senior members, called 'benchers', and the barristers) until they are elected Queen's Counsellors, when they 'take silk', i.e., don silk gowns (other barristers wear 'stuff' gowns). Women have been called to the Bar since 1922. The four inns remain independent of each other, and each is governed by its 'benchers' under the presidency (usually honorary) of a 'treasurer'.

The Inner and Middle Temple were named from their proximity to the City and in relation to the Outer Temple. This last, however, was never more than a piece of land that belonged to the Templars and later became the site of Essex House, the mansion of the Earl of Essex, favourite of Elizabeth I. The name is now given to an office building in the Strand. Buildings belonging to the Inner Temple bear the device of the Winged Horse, those of the Middle Temple bear the Lamb and Flag. The buildings of both inns suffered severely from bombing during the war, but they have been restored, partly in their original style. The secluded precincts are accessible to the public, except on Ascension Day.

The buildings of the Middle Temple lie mainly to the west of Middle Temple Lane. On the right, about half-way down, is MIDDLE TEMPLE HALL (adm., p. 33), with a noble assembly chamber, over 100 ft long, opened by Elizabeth I in 1576. It was considerably damaged by bombing, but has been restored using the original materials as far as possible. The elaborate double hammerbeam roof is one of the most splendid in England; the walls are covered with panelling bearing the arms of Readers (or principal lecturers) of the Inn since 1597. At the east end is a heavily carved oak screen with doors added in 1671, and on the dais are portraits of Charles I and other monarchs. The serving table is said to have been made from the timbers of Drake's ship, the *Golden Hind.* Shakespeare's own company is believed to have acted *Twelfth Night* in this hall on 2 February 1602.

The many famous members of the Middle Temple include Sir Walter Raleigh; John Pym, the Parliamentarian; the Earl of Clarendon, the Royalist statesman and historian; John Evelyn; William Congreve; Henry Fielding; Sir William Blackstone, the famous jurist; Edmund Burke; William Cowper; R. B. Sheridan; the Earl of Eldon, Lord Chancellor; Thomas Moore, the Irish poet; Thomas de Quincey; and W. M. Thackeray. Oliver Goldsmith, though not a member, lived at No. 2 Brick Court (since rebuilt) from 1768 until his death in 1774, during which time Blackstone, who occupied the rooms below, often complained of the noise made by his 'revelling neighbour'.

FOUNTAIN COURT, on the north of Middle Temple Hall, was the trysting place of Ruth Pinch with her brother Tom (in *Martin Chuzzlewit*). From the fountain, steps lead down to Garden Court, beyond which a gate opens towards the Embankment. On the right of Middle Temple Lane, farther down, is the new building, by Sir Edward Maufe (1958), of the MIDDLE TEMPLE LIBRARY, which grew out of a bequest of Robert Ashley (d. 1641), a barrister, and now contains over 90,000 volumes (including the most comprehensive collection of American legal textbooks and law reports in Britain). Some 65,000 volumes were lost when the old library (farther west) was bombed. Between the old and new libraries, and bounded on the south by the Embankment, are the MIDDLE TEMPLE GARDENS (no adm.).

An opening on the east of Middle Temple Lane opposite Brick Court admits to PUMP COURT, the north and west sides of which survive from about 1680; the south side with the ranges of building beyond was rebuilt in 1949–51 after war damage. The east side is now enclosed by an arcade, to the south-east of which rises INNER TEMPLE HALL (adm., p. 32), destroyed by bombing in 1941 and newly built in 1952–5 by Sir Hubert Worthington, who adopted a modified Georgian style. It has a marble floor (heated from underneath) and windows containing heraldic glass by Hugh Easton that includes the arms of former benchers of the inn who have become Lord Chancellors. The vaulted chamber called the buttery at the west end, with the crypt below, survives from the 14th century. The INNER TEMPLE LIBRARY, to the east, founded before 1507 but destroyed in the bombing, was rebuilt in 1958 by Sir Hubert Worthington and now holds over 100,000 books.

Among famous members of the Inner Temple are John Hampden, the statesman; William Wycherley; the notorious Judge Jeffreys; Lord Chancellor Thurlow; James Boswell; and the historian, Henry Hallam. Samuel Johnson (not a member) had rooms in the Inner Temple in 1760–65.

Farther east is KING'S BENCH WALK, with delightful chambers, Nos. 4–6 of which were built in the late 17th century. Mitre Court, on the north side, opens to Fleet Street, and a gate on the east admits to Bouverie Street (see below).

To the south-west are PAPER BUILDINGS, built in 1848, and beyond are the large INNER TEMPLE GARDENS (no adm.), fronting the Embankment. The fountain-figure of a child here is in memory of Charles Lamb, the essayist, who was born in 1775 in Crown Office Row (facing the gardens on the north, but recast after war damage) and who lived in the Temple until 1817. In one or other of the Temple Gardens were traditionally plucked the white and red roses that became the badges of the Houses of York and Lancaster (compare *Henry VI*, Part I, ii, 4).

To the north of Inner Temple Hall is the TEMPLE CHURCH (IV, E2; adm., p. 35), which serves both inns of court and is exempt from episcopal jurisdiction. It consists of a circular nave (the 'Round'), completed in 1185 on the model of the Church of the Holy Sepulchre at Jerusalem and one of the only five medieval round churches surviving in England, and a large chancel (the 'Oblong'), a splendid example of the Early English style, added in 1240. The church was very badly damaged in 1941, but the fan-vaulted chancel, with its wide nave and aisles, and triplets of lancet windows, was carefully restored by Walter H. Godfrey in 1954, when the reredos of 1682 (designed by Wren and carved by William Emmett) was brought back and new clustered columns of Purbeck marble were introduced. In the south aisle are the old double piscina and a fine 13th-century effigy of a bishop; through a panel of glass let into the floor at the west end can be seen the grave-slab of John Selden (d. 1654), the great jurist and antiquary, who is buried in the 13th-century undercroft below. The round church, which has an elaborate late-Norman doorway, protected by a porch, was rededicated, after its restoration by W. H. Godfrey, in 1958. The Purbeck marble for the clustered columns (which have richly carved capitals) and for the shafts of the excellent triforium arcading was obtained from the original quarries. Almost all of the fine 12th–13th-century military effigies of Associates of the Temple in the nave were severely damaged in the bombing, but have been carefully repaired (1961).

Lawyers used to await their clients in the 'Round', each occupying a particular place like the merchants on the Stock Exchange. Christopher Wren was married in the church in 1669 to his first wife, Faith Coghill, and Charles Lamb was baptized here in 1775. On the north, in the former churchyard, a stone slab marks the approximate whereabouts of the grave of Oliver Goldsmith (d. 1774). To the north-east is the MASTER'S HOUSE, the residence of the incumbent of the church; attributed to Wren, it was destroyed in 1941 but has been rebuilt in its former style.

INNER TEMPLE LANE leads north from the church porch to FLEET STREET, which it reaches through a gateway opposite Chancery Lane (Route 20). Above the gate is a restored timbered building of 1610–11 with an overhanging upper storey. PRINCE HENRY'S ROOM (adm., p. 34), on the first floor, with its original 17th-century plaster ceiling and carved oak panelling, is supposed to have been the council chamber of the Duchy of Cornwall under Prince Henry, the elder son of James I. It now contains an exhibition relating to Samuel Pepys, the diarist. Farther on is the COCK TAVERN, built in 1887 to replace the 16th-century tavern, frequented by Tennyson and Dickens, which stood on the other side of the road. It preserves some of the fittings of its predecessor, including the gilded sign of the cock carved by Grinling Gibbons.

On the north side of Fleet Street is the octagonal church of ST DUNSTAN-IN-THE-WEST (IV, E2), of 13th-century foundation, but rebuilt in 1829–33 by John Shaw and repaired in 1950. The noble tower has an open-work lantern inspired by that of All Saints' Pavement at York. Over the east or vestry porch is a contemporary statue of Elizabeth I (1586) and inside are figures of 'King Lud' and his sons, all of which were brought from Ludgate when it was demolished. The clock of 1671 with its 'striking jacks', removed when the former church was pulled down, was returned in 1936.

The north bay of the octagon serves as the chancel and has a window by Gerald Smith replacing one destroyed in 1940. The north-west window (by Kempe) shows Izaak Walton, the angler, a vestryman of the church in 1629–44, and the subjects of his *Lives*. The *Compleat Angler* was first published in St Dunstan's churchyard in 1653. Thomas White, the founder of Sion College, was vicar here in 1575–1624 and was followed by John Donne, the poet, vicar until his death in 1631.

FETTER LANE (IV, D, E2), on the left farther on, leading to Holborn, is said to derive its name from the 'faitours' or vagrants that once infested it, but more likely takes it from a colony of 'feutriers' or felt-makers. Clifford's Inn, a block of flats on its west side, occupies the site of the oldest inn of chancery (compare Route 23). Opposite the lane is Mitre Court, admitting to the Inner Temple (see above), and just beyond on the same side opens SERJEANTS' INN, originally one of the two independent societies of serjeants-at-law ('servientes ad legem'), the highest order of barristers, dissolved in 1877. Now an insurance building, the north side was partly restored (after war damage) in 1955 in a style intended to maintain its traditional character.

On the north side of Fleet Street are numerous little courts and alleys noted for their literary associations, though wholly rebuilt in recent years. CRANE COURT was the headquarters of the Royal Society in 1710–80 and later the home of the Philosophical Society, before whom Coleridge gave his famous lectures on Shakespeare (1810–13). Dr Johnson lived in JOHNSON'S COURT (not named after him) in 1765–76 and then in BOLT COURT, farther on, until his death in 1784.

Johnson's Court, reached under the wing of No. 166 Fleet Street, gives access to GOUGH SQUARE, on the west side of which is DR JOHNSON'S HOUSE (IV, E2; adm., p. 32), the charming late-17th-century building in which the great lexicographer lived from 1747 to 1759 and where his wife Tetty died in 1752. The famous *Dictionary* (published in 1755) was compiled here and *The Rambler*, which appeared twice weekly for two years, was written, as were the earlier numbers of *The Idler*. The kitchen, the old staircase and panelling, and the quaint cupboards are worth inspection, but the most interesting room is the attic, where Johnson laboured at the dictionary, assisted by six amanuenses. The house contains his chair and other relics, engravings and autograph letters, and an early edition of the dictionary. In WINE OFFICE COURT, on the left of Fleet Street farther east, is the OLD CHESHIRE CHEESE, a delightful tavern rebuilt in 1667, which claims to have been frequented by Johnson, Boswell, and Goldsmith (though it is not mentioned by Boswell).

BOUVERIE STREET and WHITEFRIARS STREET, with the offices of well-known papers, lead south from Fleet Street to the Embankment. The latter street takes its name from a monastery of Carmelites or White Friars, founded about 1241 and dissolved in 1538. The privilege of sanctuary attached to the precincts of the monastery survived until 1697 and in consequence it became the haunt of lawless characters (under the name of Alsatia; compare Scott's *The Fortunes of Nigel*). Both streets end at TUDOR STREET, in which are the offices of *Punch*, the humorous magazine first published in 1841.

On the north side of Fleet Street are the huge offices (by Elcock and Sutcliffe, 1930) of the *Daily Telegraph*, the first London daily penny paper, founded in 1855, and farther down is the prominent *Daily Express* office (by Ellis and Clarke, 1931), with its facing of black tiles. Shoe Lane, beside it, leads towards Holborn Circus (Route 23), and opposite are the headquarters (in a building of 1935 by Sir Edwin Lutyens) of REUTER'S, the famous international news agency, established as a world-wide service in 1858, and of the PRESS ASSOCIATION, founded in 1868.

Beside this opens an entrance to ST BRIDE'S CHURCH (IV, E2; adm., p. 34), dedicated to Bridget, a 6th-century Irish saint, and the 'parish church of the Press'. Rebuilt in 1670–84 by Wren, it was burnt out in an air-raid in 1940, except for the beautiful steeple of 1701, called by W. E. Henley a 'madrigal in stone'. This was originally 234 ft high, but after it was struck by lightning in 1764 it was reconstructed 8 ft shorter, though still the loftiest of the City's steeples. The church was restored in 1957 by W. Godfrey Allen in a style following closely the original intentions of Wren (one of his handsomest designs), but with a fresco (by Glyn Jones) on the flat east wall of the sanctuary to give it the appearance of an apse. In front of this is a carved oak reredos (a memorial to the Pilgrim Fathers and in particular to Governor Winslow, who was an apprentice printer in Fleet Street), and the graceful font of 1615, saved from the bombing, has been replaced. Samuel Pepys, born in 1633 in Salisbury Court close by (on the site of the *White Swan*), was baptized at this font. The statues of St Bride and St Paul (1957) are the work of David McFall.

Samuel Richardson (d. 1761), the novelist, who had a printing business in Salisbury Square, was buried in the church. Excavations below the building in 1952–6 revealed the lower parts of a sequence of earlier churches, the oldest showing early Saxon work. Beneath the churchyard and partly underlying the church, remains were discovered in 1952 of a Roman building, the earliest known in London outside the City wall. An interesting museum illustrating the history of St Bride's has been opened in the crypt, where also the excavated remains and Richardson's lead coffin (damaged in the bombing) can be seen. No. 1 in SALISBURY SQUARE, to the west of the church, is the office of PRESS COUNCIL, set up in 1953 to preserve the freedom and maintain the character of the British Press.

Fleet Street finishes at LUDGATE CIRCUS (IV, E3), on the north-west side of which is a tablet to Edgar Wallace (d. 1932), the crime novelist and journalist. New Bridge Street (Route 26) leads south from the circus to Blackfriars Bridge, and FARRINGDON STREET, following the course of the Fleet River, runs north under Holborn Viaduct (see Route 23).

Caroone House (1972), on the right in this street, incorporates a new CONGREGATIONAL MEMORIAL HALL, commemorating the 'fidelity to conscience' shown by the ministers ejected in 1662 from the Church of England under the Act of Uniformity of Charles II. In the previous building the Labour Representation Committee, the forerunner of the Labour Party, was founded in 1900. The hall stands partly on the site of the FLEET PRISON, a notorious debtors' prison that is depicted in Hogarth's *The Rake's Progress* and described in Dickens's *Pickwick Papers*. William Penn was among those unfortunate enough to be incarcerated here. The prison, rebuilt after the Great Fire of 1666 and again after its destruction in the Gordon Riots (1780), was finally demolished in 1846.

LUDGATE HILL (IV, E3), a short but busy thoroughfare, ascends briskly from Ludgate Circus to St Paul's Cathedral. EXPORT HOUSE (beyond the railway), designed by Theo H. Birks (1962), is occupied by the Department of Trade and Industry. A good 'surprise' view opens of St Bride's steeple before Old Bailey (Route 23) bears left for Newgate Street and Smithfield. Farther up, adjoining the site of Ludgate, one of the City gates (pulled down in 1760), is the church of ST MARTIN-WITHIN-LUDGATE (adm., p. 35), rebuilt by Wren in 1677–87 and now pleasantly restored. It has notable doorways and a font of 1673 with a Greek palindromic inscription, and is secluded from the noisy street by vestibules between which rises the tower, with an elegant spire forming an effective foil to the twin towers of St Paul's.

Ave Maria Lane, leaving Ludgate Hill farther up, is continued by Warwick Lane (see Route 23) to Newgate Street, skirting the St Paul's precinct (see below). On the left is an approach to STATIONERS' HALL (IV, E3), the hall of the Stationers' and Newspaper Makers' Company, founded in 1403 and incorporated in 1557 (the newspaper makers were first included in the title in 1933). The company, long restricted to those engaged in printing, publishing, and allied trades, maintained a monopoly of printing during the latter part of the 16th century, and until the passing of the Copyright Bill of 1911 every work published in Britain had to be registered at Stationers' Hall. The registers, which date from the foundation of the company, are of the highest interest and contain such entries as the First Folio of Shakespeare (1623), Milton's *Paradise Lost* (1667), and Dr Johnson's *Dictionary* (1755). Rebuilt in 1670 after the Great Fire, the Hall was given a new east front in 1800 by Robert Mylne and extended by a wing on the north-east in 1887. The great hall, restored after war damage, has a fine 17th-century screen and oak panelling; the Court Room, also badly damaged by bombing, was rebuilt in its former style in 1956.

A gateway on the left, farther north, admits to AMEN COURT, a quiet precinct containing the houses, partly of the 17th century, of the Canons Residentiary of St Paul's. The Rev. Richard Harris Barham, author of *The Ingoldsby Legends*, died in 1845 at No. 1.

Ludgate Hill ends at ST PAUL'S CHURCHYARD (IV, E3), the road that surrounds **St Paul's Cathedral** (adm., p. 404). JUXON HOUSE (1967), built over the pavement and partly enclosing the entrance to the churchyard, has a public viewing-gallery on its topmost floor, 90 ft up. It stands at the south-west corner of PATERNOSTER SQUARE, a pedestrian precinct (1966) with a large 'piazza' and blocks of office buildings arranged to allow new vistas of the cathedral, laid out in accordance with the plan for the surroundings of St Paul's drawn up by Lord Holford and approved in 1956. To the north of the cathedral is the CHAPTER HOUSE, a charming brick building by Sir Christopher Wren (1714), altered in the 19th century, gutted by bombing in 1940, and restored to Wren's original design in 1957.

In the precinct is a sculpture by Elizabeth Frink ('Paternoster'; 1975), and in the newer precinct of OLD CHANGE COURT, south of the cathedral, is a sculpture by Michael Ayrton ('Icarus'; 1973). DEAN'S COURT, to the south-west of the cathedral, leads past the DEANERY, another delightful work by Wren, built in 1672. The former CHOIR HOUSE adjoining (entered from Carter Lane and now a youth hostel) was built about 1874. WARDROBE PLACE, off Carter Lane to the west, is a peaceful oasis with houses of the 17th and 18th centuries.

25 From St Paul's Cathedral to the Bank or London Bridge

Plan IV, E3–V, F2

STATIONS: ST PAUL'S (Plan IV, E3), on the Central line; MANSION HOUSE (V, E1), CANNON STREET (V, F1), and MONUMENT (V, F2), all on the Circle and District lines; LONDON BRIDGE (IX, E2), on the Northern line. Monument station is connected by an escalator with Bank station (compare Route 28); Cannon Street and London Bridge are termini also of the Southern Region. — BUSES Nos. 6, 9, 11, 15, 18, 23, 76, and 513 in the west part of Cannon Street (only Nos. 23 and 513 pass Cannon Street station); and Nos. 8A, 10, 21, 35, 40, 43, 44, 47, 48, 133, 501, and 513 across London Bridge. For buses in Queen Victoria Street and across Southwark Bridge, see Route 27; in King William Street and Gracechurch Street, see Route 34.

To ST PAUL'S CHURCHYARD from Holborn via Newgate Street, see Route 23; from Fleet Street via Ludgate Hill, see Route 24; for the route from St Paul's to the Bank via Cheapside, see Route 29. CANNON STREET (IV, E3–V, F2), the shortest way from St Paul's to London Bridge or the Tower, runs eastward from the south side of the cathedral. The west part was constructed in 1854; the older section beyond Walbrook was formerly Candlewick Street, the street of the wax-chandlers. The whole street is now lined by large blocks of office buildings. ST PAUL'S GARDEN, a formal garden on the left, marks the site of Cordwainers' Hall (i.e., shoemakers', from Cordovan leather), burned down in 1941. On the north is the tower of ST AUGUSTINE'S, built by Wren in 1696; the church of 1680–87, likewise damaged by bombing, has been demolished, and the tower now forms an entrance to the chapel of the remarkable CHOIR SCHOOL of St Paul's Cathedral (by Architects' Co-Partnership, 1967). To the east of the garden rises a dignified office building designed by Trehearne and Norman Preston & Partners (1956), now containing the London headquarters of the BANK OF AMERICA. The south front was recessed so as not to impede the view of St Paul's from Cannon Street. In the main vestibule is a stone from a foot-postern of 1663, formerly part of the City gateway to Aldgate. On the outside wall (to the south-east) is a memorial of 1932 (salvaged from the demolished church of St Mildred) to Admiral Arthur Phillip (born nearby in 1738), the founder and first governor of Australia.

On the right of Cannon Street are the brick buildings, by Sir Albert Richardson (1959), of THE FINANCIAL TIMES. While excavating for the foundations, slight remains of two timber huts of the Saxon period (about A.D. 900) were discovered. On the same side, farther on, are the London headquarters of the CRÉDIT LYONNAIS BANK, by Whinney, Son, and Austen Hall (1978), the first major building in the world to be clad in glass-reinforced cement, both outside and inside.

Cannon Street crosses Queen Victoria Street, which leads right to Blackfriars Bridge and left to the Bank (see Route 27). At the junction is the entrance to the Mansion House underground station, and to the left is the church of St Mary Aldermary. QUEEN STREET (V, E, F1), farther east, runs north to Cheapside (Route 29) and south to Southwark Bridge (Route 26).

At the corner is the LONDON CHAMBER OF COMMERCE and Industry, with over 8,500 members, founded in 1881 and moved here in 1934. Below in Queen Street is a notable late-18th-century house (No. 28), one of the few surviving in the City. COLLEGE HILL, the next turning on the right of Cannon Street, takes its name from a college established here in 1422 by Richard Whittington.

DOWGATE HILL, the next side-street, contains TALLOW CHANDLERS' HALL (No. 4), largely remodelled about 1880, and SKINNERS' HALL (No. 8), rebuilt after the Great Fire of 1666, but with a façade of about 1790 (by William Jupp) and later alterations. The restored hall is decorated with large panel paintings commissioned in 1902 from Sir Frank Brangwyn, while a fine staircase of about 1670 ascends to the 17th-century Court Room, panelled with fragrant Virginian cedar. The Skinners'

Company, which alternates in precedence with the Merchant Taylors', has met on this site at least since 1295. At No. 10 is DYERS' HALL, built in 1840 (by Charles Dyer), but altered since.

CANNON STREET STATION (V, F1), a terminus of the Southern Region, was built in 1866 by Sir John Hawkshaw and J. W. Barry, but partly reconstructed in 1955–61 by Charles Poulson.

The OVERSEA-CHINESE BANKING CORPORATION, opposite, occupies the site of St Swithun's, a church probably of Saxon foundation, but rebuilt by Wren and demolished in 1962 after war damage. In the wall has been set the LONDON STONE, of unknown origin, though claimed by Camden and later writers to have been the *milliarium* of Roman London from which distances were measured. In Shakespeare's *Henry VI*, Part II (iv, 6), the rebel Jack Cade strikes the stone with his staff, exclaiming 'Now is Mortimer lord of this City' (1405). Originally much larger, the stone formerly stood on the other side of the street and it was moved to the church wall in 1798. In St Swithin's Lane, to the east, is FOUNDERS' HALL (No. 13), rebuilt in 1877 and restored in 1967. BUSH LANE HOUSE, beyond the station, is an unusual office building, by Arup Associates (1976), with an external structure of stainless steel tubes.

In the narrow LAURENCE POUNTNEY HILL, on the right of Cannon Street, are two fine Queen Anne houses with carved doorways. Abchurch Lane, farther on to the left, passes the church of ST MARY ABCHURCH (adm., p. 35), rebuilt by Wren in 1681–7, with an internal dome painted in 1708 by William Snow. Damaged in 1940, this was restored in 1953; the splendid reredos by Grinling Gibbons (1686), the largest in the City, has likewise been restored, the canopied pulpit and other fine woodwork have been brought back, and the church was reopened in 1957. The 14th-century crypt of the original church, revealed by the bombing, has been opened up.

Cannon Street ends at a busy junction of roads from which King William Street leads north-west to the Bank (Route 34), Gracechurch Street north-east to Bishopsgate (Route 32), and Eastcheap east towards the Tower (Route 34). KING WILLIAM STREET also runs south to London Bridge, passing the end of the street, on the left, in which rises THE MONUMENT (V, F2; adm., p. 33), the 'loftiest isolated stone column in the world', a prominent fluted Doric column, 202 ft high, designed by Sir Christopher Wren in collaboration with Robert Hooke. It was erected in 1671–7 to commemorate the Great Fire of London, which broke out on 2 September 1666 at a point in Pudding Lane said to be exactly 202 ft east of the column. The fire, which raged for five days, devasted 436 acres of the City, destroying about 460 streets with some eighty-nine churches and more than 13,000 houses. A further inscription on the pedestal, ascribing the fire to the 'Popish faction', was removed in 1831. The relief on the west side of the pedestal is by C. G. Cibber, the Danish sculptor; the top of the column is surmounted by an urn with a gilt flaming ball, 42 ft high. The platform, reached by an internal spiral staircase with 311 steps, commands a view over the City and the river that is now restricted by the many tall new office blocks.

King William Street crosses Thames Street (Route 27) by a viaduct. On the right, at the approach to London Bridge, is FISHMONGERS' HALL (V, F2), one of the noblest of the halls of the City livery companies, rebuilt in a classical style in 1832–4 by Henry Roberts.

The Fishmongers' Company, one of the oldest and wealthiest of the twelve great livery companies, and fourth in order of precedence, was already in existence before 1154 and received its first charter from Edward I. The hall, originally built on this site in 1504, was the first of the City halls to catch alight during the Great Fire of 1666, and was again the first to be set on fire in the air-raids of September 1940. The interior, finely restored in 1951 by Austen Hall, contains a beautifully embroidered 15th–16th-century pall, a wooden statue of Sir William Walworth, Mayor in 1374 and a Prime Warden of the company, and the dagger with which he slew the rebel Wat Tyler in 1381. The paintings include two fine portraits by Romney, charming river scenes by Samuel Scott and others, and a delightful study in tempera of Queen Elizabeth II (1955) by Pietro Annigoni.

ADELAIDE HOUSE, on the other side of the bridge approach, is a huge block of shipping offices by Sir John J. Burnet (1924). In SWAN LANE, west of Fishmongers' Hall, remains of the Roman timber waterfront (of the late 1st or early 2nd century) were discovered in 1972; and at NEW FRESH WHARF, east of London Bridge, remains of a unique boat, of the 12th century or earlier (later used as a revetment for the waterfront), were excavated in 1974.

LONDON BRIDGE (V, F2), the most famous of all the bridges across the Thames, connects the City with Southwark, and until 1749 was the only bridge over the river in London. The previous bridge was rebuilt in 1824–31 by John Rennie and his sons, Sir John and George Rennie, and widened in 1904. It was demolished in 1968–71 to make way for a new bridge, of pre-stressed concrete, 105 ft wide and with a central span of 340 ft, completed in 1972 to the designs of Harold K. King. During the morning and evening rush-hours, some 20,000 pedestrians cross the bridge.

The first bridge across the Thames was built by the Romans, probably in the 1st century A.D. It stood a little downstream from the present bridge and remains of abutments have been located under the former Billingsgate Market (Route 27). The Roman bridge was replaced by a timber bridge in the time of King Edgar (973–5) and this in turn by a stone bridge, built to the order of Henry II, begun in 1176 by Peter, chaplain of St Mary Colechurch in Cheapside, and not completed until 1209. This likewise stood downstream, opposite the church of St Magnus the Martyr (compare p. 272). Houses and shops came to be built on either side of the roadway, with a chapel in the middle dedicated to St Thomas of Canterbury. The bridge had nineteen narrow arches, which made the passage by river dangerous, and at each end was a fortified gate, on the spikes of which it became the custom to expose the heads of traitors. The houses were pulled down in 1758–62, when the bridge was widened, and the bridge itself was finally demolished in 1832. The Rennies' bridge has been re-erected at Lake Havasu City, Arizona.

London Bridge is the highest point on the Thames that can be reached by ships of any size. The reach below is known as the POOL OF LONDON, while that above was named the KING'S REACH in 1935. The view downstream includes the White Tower and Tower Bridge, with H.M.S. *Belfast* in front, the heights of Greenwich beyond, and the Custom House to the left. Upstream there is a fine panorama encompassing Shell-Mex House, Somerset House, and other buildings lining the river, Unilever House with the Telecom Tower and the steeple of St Bride's to the right of it, and the dome of St Paul's over Cannon Street Station, while huge new office blocks continue to appear above the City skyline.

Near the south end of the bridge are **Southwark Cathedral** (adm., p. 422) and the approach to LONDON BRIDGE STATION (see Route 35).

26 From Westminster Bridge to Blackfriars Bridge (for London Bridge or the Bank)

Plan VIII, B3–IV, F2

STATIONS: WESTMINSTER (Plan VIII, B3), EMBANKMENT (VIII, A3), TEMPLE (IV, F1; closed on Sundays), and BLACKFRIARS (IV, E3), all on the Circle and District lines. Embankment station is also on the Bakerloo and Northern lines; and Blackfriars is a terminus of the Southern Region. — BUSES Nos. 12, 53, 70, 76, 77, 109, 155, 159, 170, 172, and 184 across Westminster Bridge; Nos. 76, 109, 155, and 184 along Victoria Embankment to Blackfriars Bridge; Nos. 1, 4, 5, 68, 171, 176, 188, 501, 502, and 513 across Waterloo Bridge; Nos. 45, 63, 76, 109, 141, and 155 across Blackfriars Bridge; Nos. 45, 63, 76, and 141 in New Bridge Street.

WESTMINSTER BRIDGE (VIII, B3), reached from Parliament Square (Route 3) by the short Bridge Street, is a graceful cast-iron structure, 810 ft long, built in 1854–62 by Thomas Page. Crossing the

Thames from Westminster to Lambeth, it replaces the earlier stone bridge of 1749 (the first to be built over the river after London Bridge), the prospect from which inspired Wordsworth's famous sonnet, 'Earth has not anything to show more fair', written in 1802.

The view today includes the long river façade of the Houses of Parliament, with Millbank Tower rising beyond, St Thomas's Hospital and Lambeth Palace on the opposite bank, and the tall towers of New Covent Garden Market farther off, above Lambeth Bridge. Below the bridge on the right bank is County Hall, with the huge Shell building beyond, and the Royal Festival Hall to the left. Somerset House is seen above the Charing Cross Railway Bridge, with Shell-Mex House and other large buildings standing above the Embankment gardens.

At the Westminster end of the bridge is a large bronze group of Boudicca (Boadicea; d. A.D. 62), the British patriot, in her chariot, by Thomas Thornycroft (1902). Thence the VICTORIA EMBANKMENT (VIII, B3–IV, F2), built in 1864–70 by Sir Joseph Bazalgette, makes a wide sweep following the left bank of the river as far as Blackfriars Bridge, a distance of over a mile and a quarter. Its construction involved the reclamation of an area regularly covered by the tide and the provision of a protecting wall 8 ft thick. The broad roadway, lined for the most part with attractive gardens, affords the shortest, most convenient, and pleasantest route from Westminster to the City.

On the right, just below the bridge, is WESTMINSTER PIER, the chief starting-point of the river steamers. On the other side of the road is NORMAN SHAW HOUSE, a building by Shaw (1891) extended in 1912 and 1940, and until 1967 the headquarters of the Metropolitan Police (New Scotland Yard; see Route 2), but now utilized by Parliament. Beyond rises a colossal building by E. Vincent Harris (1957), the head-office of the MINISTRY OF DEFENCE, created in 1964, incorporating the Admiralty, the War Office, and the Air Ministry. The main entrance, flanked by huge sculptures representing Earth and Water (by Wheeler, 1953), is on the north side, in Horse Guards Avenue.

Under the building is HENRY VIII'S WINE CELLAR, one of the few surviving parts of Whitehall Palace (compare Route 2), a vaulted chamber, 56 ft long, which had to be moved when the foundations were constructed. In the garden on the river side of the building is QUEEN MARY'S TERRACE, part of the river quay with a flight of steps, built in front of the palace in 1691 by Wren for Mary II, and rediscovered in 1939.

In front of the building are statues of General Gordon (d. 1885), by Sir Hamo Thornycroft; Lord Portal (d. 1971), Chief of Air Staff in 1940–45; and Lord

Trenchard (d. 1956), the first Marshal of the Royal Air Force, by William McMillan (1961). On the Embankment is the ROYAL AIR FORCE MEMORIAL, by Sir Reginald Blomfield and Sir W. Reid Dick (1923). In the garden north of Horse Guards Avenue are statues of William Tyndale (d. 1536), translator of the New Testament, by Boehm (1884); of Sir Bartle Frere (d. 1884), the first High Commissioner for South Africa; and of Sir James Outram (d. 1863), the 'Bayard of India'. In front of the garden is a bust of Samuel Plimsoll (d. 1898), the social reformer and 'seamen's friend', and behind rises WHITEHALL COURT, a large Gothic building by Archer and Green (1884), containing suites of apartments, the FARMERS' CLUB, founded in 1842, and the UNITED NATIONS ASSOCIATION of Great Britain and Northern Ireland, founded in 1945. On the wall of the Embankment opposite Northumberland Avenue is a monument to Sir Joseph Bazalgette (d. 1891).

The broad NORTHUMBERLAND AVENUE (VIII, A3), starting north of the garden, leads west to Charing Cross (Route 1). It took its name from Northumberland House here, the town mansion of the Dukes of Northumberland, pulled down in 1874. On the right is the PLAYHOUSE THEATRE (closed), with a façade of 1882 and an interior of 1907. Craven Street (Route 21), starting beside it, ascends to the Strand. Farther up in Northumberland Avenue is the ROYAL COMMONWEALTH SOCIETY, founded in 1868 as the Royal Colonial Institute and now numbering 21,000 members. The library (introduction from a Fellow necessary) contains over 250,000 volumes, specializing in Commonwealth subjects. The building, restored in 1957 after bomb damage, has rooms panelled in woods from many parts of the Commonwealth. Farther up (at No. 18) are the VICTORIA LEAGUE for Commonwealth Friendship and the ROYAL AFRICAN SOCIETY, both founded in 1901. In WHITEHALL PLACE, leading left to Whitehall (Route 2), are the MINISTRY OF AGRICULTURE, FISHERIES, AND FOOD, in a building of 1935, and the NATIONAL LIBERAL CLUB, founded in 1882.

The Victoria Embankment passes under CHARING CROSS RAILWAY BRIDGE, erected in 1860–4 to replace the Hungerford Suspension Bridge, parts of which were used for the Clifton Suspension Bridge over the Avon at Bristol. The separate footway alongside on the north (giving access to the South Bank and Waterloo Station) is still known as HUNGERFORD BRIDGE. To the north of the bridge is the CHARING CROSS PIER (VIII, A3) of the river steamers, and opposite this is the Embankment underground station, with the lower end of Villiers Street (Route 21) beyond.

The course of the river now bends sharply from north to east. Across it there is a fine view of the South Bank and the Royal Festival Hall, with the monstrous Shell building to the right, while ahead is Waterloo Bridge with the dome of St Paul's rising above it. To the left is a delightful section of the VICTORIA EMBANKMENT GARDENS (III, F3–IV, F1), above which soar three huge buildings, the Adelphi

(Route 21) to the left, the Savoy Hotel to the right, and in the centre SHELL-MEX HOUSE (by Messrs Joseph), opened in 1933, with a tower rising to over 200 ft and containing the largest clock in London. In the west corner of the gardens is the charming YORK WATER GATE, sculptured by Nicholas Stone.

This is the only surviving part of York House, begun in 1625 for the Duke of Buckingham, the favourite of James I and Charles I, on the site of a mansion of the archbishops of York, the birthplace in 1561 of Francis Bacon. The position of the gate indicates the former extent of the river.

In the gardens are a refreshment place and a bandstand, and an open-air art exhibition is usually held early in summer. The gardens contain a small memorial to the IMPERIAL CAMEL CORPS (1921); statues of Robert Burns (d. 1796), a fine work by Sir John Steell (1884); Sir Wilfrid Lawson (d. 1906), the temperance advocate; and Robert Raikes (d. 1811), the founder in 1780 of Sunday schools; a wall-fountain to Henry Fawcett (d. 1884), the blind statesman; and a bust of Sir Arthur Sullivan (d. 1900), the composer, with a line by Sir William S. Gilbert (d. 1911), who is himself commemorated by a bronze medallion near Charing Cross Pier.

On the right of the Embankment rises CLEOPATRA'S NEEDLE (IV, F1), an obelisk of pink granite 68 ft 6 in. high and weighing 180 tons. It has not the slightest connection with Cleopatra, but was one of a pair erected about 1500 B.C. by Thothmes III at Heliopolis, the ancient Egyptian centre of sun-worship on the edge of the Nile delta. Presented to Britain in 1819 by Mohammed Ali, the Egyptian viceroy, it was brought to London and set up here in 1878. The inscriptions on the sides record the deeds of Thothmes III and of Ramesses II (the Great), who acquired the obelisks in the 13th century B.C. The companion obelisk is now in Central Park, New York. The bronze sphinxes flanking the base, designed by George Vulliamy, have been left as scarred by a bomb in 1917.

Opposite the needle is the BELGIAN WAR MEMORIAL, by Sir Reginald Blomfield, with sculptures by Victor Rousseau, erected by the people of Belgium in 1920 in gratitude for British aid in 1914–18. In Savoy Place, farther on to the left, is the INSTITUTION OF ELECTRICAL ENGINEERS, founded in 1871. Savoy Street, just beyond this, ascends past the Savoy Chapel (Route 21) to the Strand.

The Embankment passes under WATERLOO BRIDGE (IV, F1), designed by Sir Giles Gilbert Scott and completed in 1939, though not opened officially until 1945. Built of steel and concrete in a clean functional style, it has five graceful arches each about 240 ft wide. Replacing the famous bridge of 1817 by John Rennie, it crosses the river to the South Bank and Waterloo Station (Route 36). On the right beyond the bridge is the floating station of the RIVER THAMES POLICE, while to the left rises the noble south façade, nearly 600 ft long, of SOMERSET HOUSE (see Route 21). The terrace is raised 50 ft above the level of the roadway, and the lower arcade originally stood in the river, the middle arch forming a water-gate. At the corner of TEMPLE PLACE is a statue of Isambard Brunel (d. 1859), the civil engineer.

Downstream are the *Wellington*, once a naval sloop, now serving as the livery hall of the Honourable Company of Master Mariners, and the *President* and *Chrysanthemum*, training ships of the London Division of the Royal Naval Volunteer Reserve. In the garden east of the Temple station are statues of W. E. Forster (d. 1886), the Liberal statesman who secured the passing of the Education Act, and John Stuart Mill (d. 1873), the philosopher and economist. In the parapet of the Embankment is a memorial to W. T. Stead (d. 1912), the journalist, and farther east is the SUBMARINE WAR MEMORIAL for both wars.

The Embankment skirts the TEMPLE GARDENS (IV, E, F2; see Route 24), outside which are two cast-iron griffins (1849) brought from the old Coal Exchange (demolished in 1963) and marking the boundary of the City. Beyond Middle Temple Lane a fine view opens of Inner Temple Hall and other buildings, while ahead Blackfriars Bridge is seen, with a huge power-station rising beyond it. Hamilton House, at the corner of Temple Avenue, is the headquarters of the ECONOMIC AND SOCIAL RESEARCH COUNCIL, which in 1984 replaced the Social Science Research Council, set up in 1965. On the left farther on is SION COLLEGE, founded under the bequest of Dr Thomas White (d. 1624) for the Anglican clergy of London and neighbourhood, and housed in Gothic buildings by Sir Arthur Blomfield (1886). The theological library of over 100,000 volumes includes many rare printed books and manuscripts of interest and beauty. The CITY OF LONDON SCHOOL (780 boys), just beyond, was established in 1834 in succession to a foundation of 1442 by John Carpenter, a town clerk of London, for 'foure poore men's children'. The new buildings (by Davis and Emanuel) opened here in 1883 have been several times extended.

Noted Old Citizens include Sir John Seeley, the historian; Sir William Henry Perkin, the discoverer of aniline dyes; Lord Oxford and Asquith, the statesman; Bramwell Booth of the Salvation Army; Sir Frederick Gowland Hopkins, a pioneer in the discovery of vitamins; and C. E. Montague, the journalist and author.

The Victoria Embankment finishes at the approach to BLACKFRIARS BRIDGE (IV, F3), which crosses the river for Southwark and Bankside (Route 36). First built in 1760, the bridge was rebuilt in 1865–9 by Joseph Cubitt and widened in 1904. Opposite the approach, with a distinctive curved façade, is the large UNILEVER HOUSE, designed by J. L. Simpson and Sir John Burnet and completed in 1932. An underpass beneath the bridge approach, emerging in Queen Victoria Street (Route 27), was opened in 1967. During the excavations (in 1962), part of the hull of a Roman wooden ship of the late 2nd century A.D. was discovered (it is now in the Museum of London). A RIVERSIDE WALKWAY (1981), passing under the bridge and the railway from Holborn Viaduct and Blackfriars stations, connects the Victoria Embankment with Upper Thames Street (Route 27); it is accessible from Blackfriars Bridge, but not from the underpass.

NEW BRIDGE STREET (IV, E3) leads north from the bridge approach to Ludgate Circus (Route 24). No. 14, on the left (now offices), stands on part of the site of the medieval palace of BRIDEWELL, named from a well near by dedicated to St Bride or Bridget. Rebuilt in 1523 by Henry VIII, the palace was granted by Edward VI to the City to house the Bridewell Royal Hospital founded in 1553. This subsequently became a place of detention and correction for vagrants and immoral women. Burned down in the Great Fire, the building was reconstructed in 1802 and again in 1862, incorporating the previous court room. Excavations in 1978 in Bridewell Place, behind, revealed the foundations (with unusual brickwork) of the Tudor palace. In Bride Lane, farther north, is the ST BRIDE FOUNDATION INSTITUTE, established in 1894, mainly for printers, with the ST BRIDE PRINTING LIBRARY, containing over 30,000 books and pamphlets.

27 From Blackfriars Bridge to the Bank or to the Tower via Thames Street

Plan IV, F3–V, F3
STATIONS: BLACKFRIARS (Plan IV, E3), MANSION HOUSE (V, E1), CANNON STREET (V, F1; closed on Saturdays and Sundays), MONUMENT (V, F2), and TOWER HILL (V, F3), all on the Circle and District lines; BANK (V, E1), see Route 28. — BUSES to Blackfriars Bridge, see Route 26; Nos. 18, 95, 149, and 184 across Southwark Bridge; No. 76 in Queen Victoria Street to the Bank (also Nos. 6, 9, 11, 15, and 149 from Cannon Street to the Bank); across London Bridge, see Route 25; to the Tower, see Route 34.

QUEEN VICTORIA STREET (IV, E3–V, E1), opened in 1871 to connect the Embankment and Blackfriars Bridge with the Bank, runs eastward from the foot of New Bridge Street (Route 26), passing the main entrance to the BLACKFRIARS STATION of the Southern Region, rebuilt in 1977.

The district it cuts through at first was named from a monastery of the Dominicans or Black Friars founded in the 13th century and laid waste at the Dissolution. Blackfriars Lane, on the left beyond the railway bridge, ascends past APOTHECARIES' HALL (No. 12), a building partly of 1670, partly of 1786, enclosing a quiet courtyard. The society, one of the City livery companies, separated from the Grocers' Company and incorporated in 1617, is still an examining body in medicine and surgery. The charming interior includes a hall and court room with 17th-century panelling, a bust of Gideon de Laune (apothecary to Anne of Denmark), and portraits of James I, Charles I, and the surgeon, John Hunter (the last a sketch by Reynolds). John Keats became a licentiate of the society in 1816. The name of PLAYHOUSE YARD, just below the hall, recalls the Blackfriars Playhouse, first opened in 1576 and reopened in 1596 by James Burbage, the friend of Shakespeare (who had a house near by and probably acted here).

On the left in Queen Victoria Street, opposite the new station buildings, is CONTINENTAL BANK HOUSE, formerly the offices of *The Times* (see Route 22), rebuilt in 1965 by Llewelyn-Davies, Weeks & Partners. It stands on the site of PRINTING HOUSE SQUARE, so called from the King's Printing House established in the locality in 1627 by Charles I, from which was published in 1665 the first issue of the *London Gazette*, the official government newspaper. John Walter II installed in 1814 the first steam printing press in England. The *Observer*, a weekly paper founded in 1791, moved its offices in 1965 to an adjacent building by the same architects.

PUDDLE DOCK, the road on the right beyond the station buildings, forms one end of the exit from the Blackfriars Underpass (compare Route 26). To the east is a building (by Richard Seifert and Partners, 1978–81) incorporating the new MERMAID THEATRE (IV, F3), replacing the theatre opened in 1959. The first theatre to be built in London since the war and in the City since the 16th century, the Mermaid was the inspiration of Sir Bernard (now Lord) Miles, the actor-manager. The new building includes a restaurant overlooking the river, a cafeteria, and a small theatre (250 seats) for children, and it is connected by a high-level walkway with Blackfriars Station.

Farther up, on the north side of Queen Victoria Street, is the church of ST ANDREW-BY-THE-WARDROBE (adm., p. 34), rebuilt by

Wren in 1685–95, gutted by bombing in 1940, and restored in 1961, with furnishings from other bombed churches. Its name was derived from the proximity of the King's Great Wardrobe or storehouse established by Edward III. The church is now occupied by the Syrian Orthodox Church of southern India. The Rectory, in St Andrew's Hill, on the north, is a good 18th-century brick house. Next to the church are the headquarters (1868) of the BRITISH AND FOREIGN BIBLE SOCIETY, founded in 1804 'to encourage a wider circulation of the Holy Scriptures, without note or comment'. Since its inception the society has published or circulated the whole or parts of the Bible in over 1,700 languages, and it distributes over two million copies every year. The library (adm., p. 31) contains an unrivalled collection of versions of the Scriptures, including rare editions of early English, Hebrew, Greek, and other Bibles.

BAYNARD HOUSE, on the opposite side of the road, completed in 1981, is the chief London station for long-distance telecommunication services. It contains also the TELECOM TECHNOLOGY SHOWCASE (adm., p. 35), an exhibition that includes early telegraphs and telephones, as well as the latest communication equipment, with many displays and working models. In the forecourt of the building is a 'totem pole' illustrating Shakespeare's 'Seven Ages of Man', sculptured by Richard Kindersley (1980).

Beyond WHITE LION HILL, the other exit on Queen Victoria Street from the Blackfriars Underpass, is ST BENET'S CHURCH, a pleasant small church rebuilt by Wren in 1677–85 and used by Welsh Episcopalians since 1879. The exterior has good brickwork and carved festoons over the windows; the interior is notable for its carved woodwork (galleries, altar-table, etc.). Henry Fielding, the novelist, was married here to his second wife in 1747, and Inigo Jones (d. 1652), the architect, was buried in the previous church.

On the other side of the road just above is the COLLEGE OF ARMS (IV, E3), sometimes called the Heralds' Office, the official authority in England, Wales, Northern Ireland, and the Commonwealth in all matters appertaining to armorial bearings and pedigrees. It received its first charter from Richard III in 1484; its present charter was granted by Mary Tudor in 1555, two years after it had acquired Derby Place, the town house of the Earls of Derby. This mansion, burned down in the Great Fire, was rebuilt in brick in 1671–7, under the direction of Francis Sandford, the Lancaster Herald, and is one of the few surviving secular buildings erected immediately after the fire. It was restored in 1953–6, when the fine 18th-century wrought-iron entrance gates (previously at Goodrich Court, Herefordshire) were given by an American benefactor.

The library of the college is the most extensive of its kind in the world, while the heraldic and genealogical records and collections are unparalleled. The corporation comprises three Kings of Arms (Garter, who presides, Clarenceux, and Norroy & Ulster), assisted by six Heralds (York, Richmond, Windsor, Somerset, Lancaster, and Chester) and four Pursuivants (Portcullis, Rouge Dragon, Rouge Croix, and Bluemantle). The chief functions of these officers of arms are to assist the Earl Marshal in arranging certain State ceremonies, such as coronations, royal proclamations, and the opening of Parliament, and to confirm and preserve pedigrees and armorial bearings. The office of Earl Marshal has been hereditary in the person of the Duke of Norfolk since 1672. Though he is not a member of the corporation, that body cannot act in any important matter without his approval. Members of the public who have particular questions to ask may visit the college between 10 and 4 on Mondays–Fridays, and arrangements can sometimes be made for showing the college to parties, after these hours (on application to the Secretary). The college contains fine woodwork by William Emmett, whose brother Maurice was the builder and may also have had a hand in its design.

On the left beyond the College of Arms a fine view of St Paul's has been opened up. On the right are the international headquarters (by H. and M. Lidbetter, 1963) of the SALVATION ARMY, founded by William Booth in the East End of London in 1865. LAMBETH HILL, on the east, leads to Upper Thames Street (see p. 270). Higher up, on the left, is the church of ST NICHOLAS COLE ABBEY, founded in the 12th century, rebuilt by Wren in 1671–81, burnt out in 1941, and restored in 1962. The name of the church was formerly 'Cold Abbey', probably from 'Cold Harbour' (a shelter for travellers). The font and much of the woodwork were saved from the bombing; the east windows have striking glass by Keith New (1963). The tower bears the weathervane, a fine sailing-ship model, of the vanished church of St Michael Queenhithe (1677). The church is now used by the presbyterian congregation of the Free Church of Scotland.

In Great Trinity Lane, to the right, is BEAVER HOUSE, the head-office (1926) of the Hudson's Bay Company, founded in 1670 by Prince Rupert to trade in furs with the North American Indians and still the most important Canadian fur company. The surrounding streets are now the centre of the London fur market. On the west in Little Trinity Lane (at No. 9) is PAINTER-STAINERS' HALL, rebuilt in 1668 and much altered in 1880 (new wing) and 1915. To the south of this, near the foot of HUGGIN HILL, a complete Roman bath system, perhaps enlarged for Hadrian in about A.D. 122 and demolished in the late 2nd century, was excavated in 1969.

Queen Victoria Street crosses Cannon Street (Route 25) and Queen Street, the latter leading north to Cheapside, beyond which can be seen the south façade of Guildhall (Route 30). On the left is the church of ST MARY ALDERMARY (adm., p. 35), so named, according to Stow, because 'elder than any church of St Marie in the Citie'. First mentioned in the 11th century, it was rebuilt by Wren in 1679–82, incorporating some part of the 16th-century walls. Of the tower, 135 ft high, completed in 1629, the upper stage was refashioned in 1711 by Wren. Rebuilt under a bequest made by Henry Rogers on the condition that the church be a copy of the previous building, it is the finest of Wren's few excursions into the Gothic style. The plaster fan-vaulting, repaired after war damage, is particularly remarkable. The pulpit and west doorway have been attributed to Grinling Gibbons, and a sword-rest (dated 1682) against a pier of the south arcade is also said to be his. New stained-glass windows have been inserted to the designs of Crawford and Lee, that at the west end commemorating the defence of London against air attack in 1939–45.

John Milton married his third wife, Elizabeth Minshull, in the church in 1663. The St Antholin Lectures, established in 1559 at a church of that name near by (pulled down in 1875), are now given here (Wednesdays in January at 1.5). In BOW LANE, west of the church, a group of early Roman town houses, destroyed by a fire in about A.D. 130, was discovered in 1979.

On the right of Queen Victoria Street is the colossal BUCKLERSBURY HOUSE, a block of offices designed by O. Campbell-Jones and completed in 1962. It stands over the site of the Roman TEMPLE OF MITHRAS, revealed in 1954 during excavations for the foundations of the building and laid bare under the direction of W. F. Grimes, then director of the London Museum. The remains have been rebuilt in the forecourt of the adjacent Temple Court and are accessible to visitors. The temple, which was in use from about A.D. 90 to 350, was on the plan of a basilica, about 60 ft long by 20 ft broad. The entrance, at the east end, led directly into the nave, which was separated on either side from narrow aisles by arcades of circular columns, the bases of which survive, supported by sleeper walls. The west end, a raised sanctuary terminating in a triple apse, lay on the bank of the Walbrook.

The basilica was an architectural form used originally for pagan temples, but adopted also for the earliest Christian churches. The important discoveries within the temple made clear that it had been dedicated to the worship of Mithras, a sun-god of Persian provenance, whose cult was introduced to Rome from Asia Minor. The god came to be worshipped throughout the Roman Empire in the 1st–3rd centuries and specially venerated by soldiers, officials, and merchants. Mithraism, in fact, was a personal religion for men only, with progressive grades of initiation, to which admission could be gained only through a series of rigorous ordeals. The beautiful head of Mithras and other finds from the site are in the Museum of London.

Queen Victoria Street is joined by Poultry immediately before reaching the open space in front of the BANK OF ENGLAND (Route 28).

The short street of LAMBETH HILL (see p. 268) descends to UPPER THAMES STREET, which runs east at no great distance from the river. Once a narrow and congested thoroughfare, it has been much widened in recent years, and many new commercial buildings have sprung up. Lambeth Hill reaches the street beside the fine tower (all that remains) of ST MARY SOMERSET, built by Wren about 1694 and topped by curious obelisks and urns (the body of the church was pulled down in 1871).

Upper Thames Street formerly ran west to reach Queen Victoria Street near Blackfriars station, but a new road has been built which joins the eastern exit from the Blackfriars Underpass instead, and the old road now ends in a cul-de-sac. To the left from this begins the RIVERSIDE WALKWAY that passes under Blackfriars Bridge to meet the Victoria Embankment (see Route 26).

Excavations for the new roads and for new buildings have created several opportunities for achaeological 'digs' and many important finds of the Roman and medieval periods have been made. To the east of the Mermaid Theatre is the site of BAYNARD'S CASTLE, built originally by Ralph Baynard, a follower of William the Conqueror, but rebuilt about 1428 by Humphrey, Duke of Gloucester, and destroyed in the Great Fire. Part of a corner turret has been located and in 1973 a 14th-century dock was discovered close by. Objects of the 14th and 15th centuries, perhaps originally in the King's Great Wardrobe (see above), include remains of garments, leatherwork and pottery, as well as many pilgrims' tokens. A long section of the Roman riverside wall, built in the 2nd or 3rd century (but reinforced in the 4th century), was excavated in 1976; it had been used partly as a foundation for the castle. Sculptured Roman stones discovered in 1975 on the site of the castle have been identified as part of a massive public monument. Farther east, the timbers of a mid-14th-century building were discovered in 1974 and remains of a 14th-century building with chalk walls. Further excavation in 1981 revealed the south-east tower of Baynard's Castle, together with a length of wall and an earlier timber wall, but the remains are now covered by a school playground. All the removable objects are now in the Museum of London.

Queenhithe, on the right of Upper Thames Street as it proceeds eastward, opens to QUEENHITHE DOCK, first mentioned in 899 and the site of the earliest fishmarket in London. On the left is the church of ST JAMES GARLICKHITHE (adm., p. 34), 'consumed by the late dreadful conflagration' (1666), rebuilt in 1676–83 by Wren and restored in 1959 after war damage. It has a charming steeple (added in 1714–17 by Hawksmoor) resembling those of St Stephen Walbrook and St Michael, Paternoster Royal, and the interior has good woodwork and iron hat-racks and sword-rests, etc. Parts of a timber building of the 1st century A.D. were discovered in GARLICK HILL, near the church, in 1984.

On the right in Upper Thames Street is VINTNERS' HALL (V, F1), rebuilt in 1671 after the Fire, which, however, spared its court room of about 1450, panelled in the 17th century. The exterior of the building was remodelled in 1908–10. The Vintners' Company, one of the twelve great City livery companies, was incorporated in 1437, and possesses rich 15th–16th-century tapestries, a painting of St Martin of Tours, possibly by Rubens, and fine collections of plate and 18th-century English wine-glasses.

The company enjoys the royal prerogative (with the Dyers' Company) of keeping swans on the Thames, and in July each year a voyage is made up river from Temple Stairs, above Blackfriars Bridge, to Henley for the purpose of counting and marking swans ('swan upping'). Geoffrey Chaucer, whose father was a vintner, was probably born (about 1340) in the Vintry, as the neighbourhood was formerly called.

Upper Thames Street reaches Queen Street, which ascends on the left to Cannon Street (Route 25). In the other direction Queen Street Place leads to SOUTHWARK BRIDGE (V, F1), rebuilt in 1913–21 by Sir Ernest George.

Farther east is the church of ST MICHAEL, PATERNOSTER ROYAL (adm., p. 35), one part of whose name comes from the paternosters or rosaries made near by, while the 'royal' shows the connection of the district with La Réole, the centre of a wine-producing region near Bordeaux. The church was rebuilt in 1686–94 by Wren and the steeple added in 1713; shattered by flying-bombs in 1944, it was restored in 1967 for THE MISSIONS TO SEAMEN, a charitable body founded in 1856. Richard Whittington (d. 1423), four times Mayor of London, who was buried in the previous church, had a house in COLLEGE HILL, above, where Nos. 21–2 have splendid late-17th-century doorways.

Beyond Dowgate Hill the main roadway passes under the large CANNON STREET STATION (see Route 25). On the right farther on is MONDIAL HOUSE, a prominent white-clad building (1978), partly occupied by British Telecom.

To the east of and partly under Cannon Street station, the remains of a Roman palace, probably the official residence of the Governor of *Londinium* and dating from the late 1st or early 2nd century, was excavated in 1960–66. Another Roman building, possibly the Governor's private house, was discovered in 1969 in SUFFOLK LANE, farther east; and excavations in 1955 in ARTHUR STREET, yet farther east, revealed the tessellated floor and hypocaust of a building of the 1st–3rd centuries (now in the Museum of London).

Upper Thames Street passes Fishmongers' Hall (Route 25) and goes under LONDON BRIDGE (reached by steps), beyond which it is continued by LOWER THAMES STREET (V, F2–IX, D3). Excavations in 1981 on the east side of Fish Street Hill, which ascends to the Monument (Route 25), located the road leading north from the Roman bridge. On the river side is the church of ST MAGNUS THE MARTYR (adm., p. 35), rebuilt in 1671–87 by Wren, with one of his very finest steeples, 185 ft high, added in 1705. After 1760 the passage beneath this formed part of the footway to Old London Bridge. The interior, restored in 1951 after war damage, has a handsome organ, by Abraham Jordan (1712), and other good woodwork. Henry Yevele (d. 1400), architect of the nave of Westminster Abbey, was buried in the previous church; Miles Coverdale (d. 1569), publisher of the first complete English Bible (1535), was rector in 1563–6 and is buried here. The dedication is a mystery; it may be to Magnus of Orkney, canonized in 1135, though the church was already in existence in the 11th century.

To the east of the church is the large International Branch of the MIDLAND BANK, by Richard Seifert & Partners (1981). Excavations in the vicinity in 1982–3 revealed the existence of four successive waterfronts: a Roman timber quay of about A.D. 220; a Saxon quay of perhaps the 9th century (with evidence of a gateway), altered after 959; a Norman quay of about 1090; and a 12th-century waterfront.

Farther east is the former BILLINGSGATE MARKET, long the principal market in London for fish of all kinds, named after a river gate in the City wall and that in turn probably from a Saxon family. The fishmarket was moved to the Isle of Dogs (see Suburban London) in 1982, and the buildings are to be restored to contain offices and shops. A free fishmarket was established by statute here in 1699, but until the early 18th century it was used also for coal, corn, and provisions. The market hall, rebuilt in 1874 by Sir Horace Jones, was extended in 1961.

WATERMEN'S HALL, on the left of Lower Thames Street, in St Mary-at-Hill, has a late-18th-century front. A Roman house, occupied from the late 2nd century A.D. until the early 5th century, together with its adjoining private bath-house (of the 3rd century), was uncovered in 1968–70 on the opposite corner of St Mary-at-Hill.

Adjoining the former fishmarket is the CUSTOM HOUSE (V, F2) of the Board of Customs and Excise (compare Route 34), built in 1814–17 by David Laing, though the centre portion was recast in 1826–8 by Sir Robert Smirke. It has an impressive frontage, 490 ft long, towards the Thames (best seen from London Bridge).

A custom house has stood on this site since the 14th century. Remains of it were discovered in 1973, as well as of the Roman waterfront (probably of the late 2nd century) and a fine 13th-century ship. St Dunstan's Hill, opposite, ascends to the church of ST DUNSTAN-IN-THE-EAST, with a tower and lantern-steeple by Wren (1698) perhaps inspired by that of Newcastle Cathedral. The church, of Saxon origin, was rebuilt in 1817–21 by David Laing; it was gutted by bombing in 1941 and the interior has been laid out as a garden. A small temple-like building of the 3rd century was excavated in 1967 at the foot of St Dunstan's Hill. In Harp Lane, leading off Lower Thames Street farther east, is BAKERS' HALL (by Trehearne and Norman Preston & Partners, 1960), the fourth hall to stand on this site. The first was built in 1506 and the previous hall was bombed in 1940.

Lower Thames Street, passing the huge office building of Tower Place, ends at the foot of TOWER HILL (Route 34), near the entrances to Tower Pier and the **Tower of London** (adm., p. 434).

28 The Bank of England and its Neighbourhood

Plan V, E1, 2
STATION: BANK (Plan V, E1), on the Central and Northern lines, and the terminus of the Waterloo and City line of the Southern Region, is connected by escalator with Monument station (V, F2), on the Circle and District lines. — BUSES in Queen Victoria Street, see Route 26; in Cheapside, see Route 29; in Princes Street, see Route 30; in Threadneedle Street, see Route 32; in Cornhill, see Route 33; in King William Street, see Route 34.

The triangular open space familiarly known as 'the Bank' is the commercial pulse of the City of London and one of the most congested points in the metropolis. From it radiate seven important streets, and it is estimated that some 500 buses pass it during the business day. On the north side rises the Bank of England, on the east is the Royal Exchange, and to the south-west is the Mansion House.

Under the centre of the cross-roads is BANK STATION, reached from the pavements on all sides by subways, and connected by a 'travolator' (completed in

1960 and running at 180 ft per minute) to the terminal platforms of the Waterloo and City Railway, the oldest surviving 'tube' (1894–8). The first part of the Central Line, from the Bank to Shepherd's Bush, was opened in 1900. The Mansion House station is nearly ¼ m. south-west, at the junction of Cannon Street and Queen Victoria Street.

The BANK OF ENGLAND (V, E1, 2) is a huge building seven storeys high, with three further storeys below the ground, and covers an area of over four acres. Over the main entrance, in Threadneedle Street (on the south), are sculptures by Sir Charles Wheeler; in the pediment of the lofty portico can be seen the 'Old Lady of Threadneedle Street', a popular nickname for the Bank. The massive external blank wall, relieved by fluted mock-Corinthian columns, is the work of Sir John Soane, appointed architect of the Bank in 1788. The Lothbury façade (on the north) was begun in 1795, the Threadneedle Street frontage in 1825, and the Bank was completed in 1833. The buildings within the wall were reconstructed in 1924–39 by Sir Herbert Baker, who retained but modified the Court Room by Sir Robert Taylor (1773). From the entrance hall (adm., see below) can be seen the central courtyard (on the site of the burial-ground of a vanished church) containing sculptures of Charles Montague (d. 1715; see below), and Lord Norman, governor in 1920–44, the latter by Wheeler.

The idea for a national bank was first mooted by William Paterson, a wealthy City merchant, but the bill for its establishment was introduced by Charles Montague, later Earl of Halifax, who was rewarded with the chancellorship of the exchequer. Incorporated by Royal Charter in 1694, it was the first joint stock bank in England (and the only one until 1834), its original capital being £1,200,000. In 1946 the capital stock, then amounting to £14,553,000, was transferred to the Treasury. The Bank of England is the Government's banker and is the only bank in England and Wales with the right of issuing paper money, the profits on which are paid to the Exchequer. It manages the National Debt, administers the Exchange Control Regulations, and acts as the banker of British banks and of most overseas banks, though no new commercial business is now undertaken. It is controlled by a governor, a deputy governor, and sixteen directors appointed by the sovereign for a limited term of years. The vaults of the Bank hold the nation's gold reserve. From 1780, when it was threatened in the Gordon Riots, until 1973 the Bank was protected nightly by a detachment of Guards, but these have now been superseded by electronic equipment. The gate-keepers and messengers have long-tailed pink coats and scarlet waistcoats, said to be modelled on the livery of the first governor's servants.

A conducted tour of parts of the Bank may be arranged by writing to the Information Division (Threadneedle Street, EC2) or by telephoning 601–4444, extension 3832, though a wait of several months can be expected. The tour, which lasts about one and a half hours, includes a small museum, illustrating the history of the Bank, but not the vaults.

To the south-west of the Bank, near the junction of Queen Victoria Street and Poultry, is the MANSION HOUSE (V, E1), the official residence of the Lord Mayor of London, a classical building by George Dance the Elder (1739–53), rather spoiled by its shallow Corinthian portico. The tympanum is filled with allegorical reliefs by Sir Robert Taylor.

The mayoralty was established in 1191 or 1192 after the recognition by Prince John of the corporate unity of the citizens of London. The first mayor was Henry FitzAilwyn, who held office for twenty-one years, but in 1215 a new charter was granted by John (now king) under which the mayor was to be elected annually. The same individual, however, was not debarred from holding office more than once, the most famous instance being that of 'Dick' Whittington, four times mayor (in 1397, 1398, 1406 and 1419). The phrase 'Lord Mayor' is first found (in English) in 1414 and became general from the early 16th century onwards. The Lord Mayor for the ensuing year is now chosen on Michaelmas Day (29 September) from two Aldermen who have served as Sheriff and who are nominated by the Liverymen of the City guilds. He is installed on the Friday preceding the second Saturday in November, and on the Saturday rides in the State coach of 1756 to the Law Courts, where he is received by the Lord Chief Justice, part of a popular pageant (the Lord Mayor's Show) that dates back to the 14th century, when the Mayor rode to Westminster to present himself to the sovereign.

Visitors enter the Mansion House (see p. 33) on the west by the door in Walbrook. The principal room is the Egyptian Hall, 90 ft long, used for banquets, receptions, and similar functions, and said to be modelled on the hall of that name described by Vitruvius though by no means Egyptian in style. Other rooms shown are the Conference Room, with a notable stucco ceiling; the Salon, which has good 19th-century tapestries and a Waterford glass chandelier with 8,000 pieces; the Drawing Rooms, containing portraits by Lely and Kneller; and the small Court of Justice, which has cells beneath. The corporation plate includes notable 16th–18th-century pieces.

WALBROOK, the short street leading south from the Mansion House to Cannon Street station, lies a little to the east of the course of a stream of that name navigable in medieval times but now conveyed through a sewer. The church of ST STEPHEN, WALBROOK, immediately behind the Mansion House, has an interior that is one of the masterpieces of Sir Christopher Wren (1672–7). The beautiful circular dome, 63 ft high, carried by eight arches supported on Corinthian columns, was wrecked by bombs in 1941, but finely restored in 1954.

The stone font with its carved wood cover, the fine carved pulpit and elaborate sounding-board, and the altar-rails are of Wren's time, but the combined organ and doorcase at the west end were introduced in 1765. On the north wall is a painting of the Martyrdom of St Stephen by Benjamin West, the American artist.

Of the first church, built about 1100 on the west side of the Walbrook, Henry Chichele (pronounced 'Chich-ly'), afterwards archbishop of Canterbury, was rector in 1396–7; it was rebuilt on its present site in 1429–39. John Dunstable (d. 1453), the 'father of English harmony', and Sir John Vanbrugh (d. 1726), the architect and playwright, were buried here. A major restoration of the church was under way in 1985.

To the south-east of the Bank, in the angle between Threadneedle Street and Cornhill, is the ROYAL EXCHANGE (V, E2), the third building of its kind on this site. The first exchange, founded in 1565 by Sir Thomas Gresham, was destroyed in the Great Fire, and the second was burned down in 1838. The present building, erected in 1842–4 by Sir William Tite, is a classical structure with a Corinthian portico, approached by a broad flight of steps from which it is the custom to proclaim a new sovereign. The group in the tympanum, by Sir Richard Westmacott, depicts Commerce with the charter of the Exchange, attended by the Lord Mayor, British merchants, and representatives of foreign nations. In front of the building are an equestrian statue of the Duke of Wellington, by Chantrey (1844), and a war memorial by Sir Aston Webb (with figures by Alfred Drury; 1920) to Londoners who served in the armed forces in 1914–19 and 1939–45. The campanile, rising to 180 ft on the east side of the exchange, has a statue of Sir Thomas Gresham on one face and is surmounted by a gilded vane (perhaps the original) shaped like a grasshopper, the crest of Gresham.

The interior of the building (no general adm.) is partly occupied by the London International Financial Futures Exchange, a money market opened in 1982 and providing facilities for dealing in contracts covering interest rates and currencies. The large central court, in a Renaissance style, has a pavement of Turkish honestone, a survival from Gresham's exchange. The panels of the wall arcades carry large paintings, mostly of episodes in the history of London, by Lord Leighton, Frank O. Salisbury, Stanhope Forbes, Sir Frank Brangwyn, and others (1897–1922). At the corners of the court are statues of Elizabeth I (by M. L. Watson), Charles II (by John Spiller), Queen Victoria (by Sir Hamo Thornycroft), and Prince Albert (by J. G. Lough), and a striking bust of Abraham Lincoln (1930), carved from Indiana limestone by Andrew O'Connor, the American sculptor. The carillon of the exchange plays English, Scottish, Welsh, Irish, Canadian, and Australian tunes daily (at 9 a.m., 12 noon, and 3 and 6 p.m.).

In the open space behind the Royal Exchange are a seated bronze figure of George Peabody (d. 1869), the American merchant and philanthropist, and a charming bronze group of Maternity by Dalou (1878).

In the angle between Threadneedle Street and Throgmorton Street, on the north, is the STOCK EXCHANGE (V, E2), colloquially 'the House', the institution for the buying and selling of stocks and shares, founded in 1773. The previous exchange on this site, opened in 1802, was demolished from 1966 on to make way for a fine new building, by Llewelyn-Davies, Weeks, and Fitzroy Robinson. The first part of this, a prominent twenty-six-storey towerblock, 321 ft high, was completed in 1970; the second part, with a new trading floor, a cinema, and a viewing gallery, 142 ft long (entrance from the corner of Threadneedle Street and Old Broad Street; adm., p. 35), was opened in 1973.

The London Stock Exchange is owned by a private company, with about 4,200 members, governed by a council of thirty-six, one-third of whom are elected every year by ballot. Members are elected on the nomination of a retiring member, pay an entrance fee of 600 guineas and an annual subscription of 100 guineas. They are required to find three sureties of £500 each for the first four years and must purchase at least three shares in the Stock Exchange company. Applicants who have served for four years as clerks are usually admitted if they pay half the fee and subscription and find only two sureties. Members are divided into 'jobbers', or dealers, and 'brokers'. The former, as a rule, deal only with other members, confining their activities to particular classes of securities; the broker acts as intermediary between the jobber and the public, buying and selling on commission. Bargains are made 'on the nod', no documents being signed and no written pledges being given; members who cannot comply with their bargains, however, are expelled, or 'hammered'. Speculators who buy anticipating a rise in prices are called 'bulls', while those who sell believing they will fall are known as 'bears'. The Stock Exchange Official List, published daily, is compiled from the day's transactions. After closing hours (3.30 p.m.) an animated 'street market' in securities is carried on in Throgmorton Street and the neighbouring courts. The CITY COMMUNICATIONS CENTRE, established in 1976, on the seventh floor of the Stock Exchange, provides information about the financial and business aspects of the City.

Also in Throgmorton Street (No. 28) is DRAPERS' HALL, rebuilt after the Great Fire, but largely reconstructed in 1866 by Herbert Williams, who gave it a new front, and restored in 1949 after war damage. The hall contains valuable plate, including the Elizabethan Lambard Cup (1578), and some notable portraits, including a double portrait by Zucchero supposed to represent Mary, Queen of Scots, and James I. In the gardens is a mulberry tree believed to have been planted during the reign of that king. The company, which ranks third in order of civic precedence among the City livery companies, was incorporated in 1364.

OLD BROAD STREET runs north-east from Threadneedle Street past the end of Throgmorton Street. In Austin Friars, starting to the north at the junction, is the DUTCH CHURCH (V, E2), originally the nave of an Augustinian friary founded in 1253 and granted in 1550 by Edward VI to Dutch and other foreign Protestant refugees. This building, which became the church of the Dutch community in London, was completely destroyed by a bomb in 1940, and a fine new church, designed by Arthur Bailey, was built on part of the site in 1950–54. It has a large west window with stained glass by Max Nauta of Amsterdam telling the story of the churches, and other windows by Hugh Easton and William Wilson.

Old Broad Street goes on past the east end of London Wall (Route 31) to Broad Street and Liverpool Street stations (Route 32). No. 19, on the right, is the CITY OF LONDON CLUB, built in 1832 by Philip Hardwick. It occupies the site of the South Sea Company's office, where Charles Lamb was a clerk in 1789–92.

29 From the Bank to King's Cross via Cheapside and Smithfield (Charterhouse)

Plan V, E1–III, A3

STATIONS: BANK (Plan V, E1), see Route 28; ST PAUL'S (IV, E3), on the Central line; BARBICAN (IV, C3; closed on Sundays), FARRINGDON (IV, C2), and KING'S CROSS & ST PANCRAS (III, A3), on the Circle and Metropolitan lines. King's Cross & St Pancras is also on the Piccadilly, Northern and Victoria lines. — BUSES Nos. 8, 22, 25, and 501 in Poultry and Cheapside; Nos. 4, 141, and 502 in Aldersgate Street; Nos. 141, 279A and 502 in London Wall (from Aldersgate Street to Moorgate); Nos. 277 and 279 in St John Street; Nos. 63, 221, and 259 in Farringdon Road and King's Cross Road; Nos. 5, 55, 243, and 259 in Clerkenwell Road; Nos. 19, 38, 171, 172, and 259 in Rosebery Avenue.

POULTRY (V, E1), a short street named from its medieval occupation by poulterers, runs west from the Mansion House (Route 28), leaving Queen Victoria Street on the left. On the right, at the corner of Princes Street, is the old Union Bank branch (by Sir Edwin Cooper, 1931) of the NATIONAL WESTMINISTER BANK. Next is the ornate head-office of the MIDLAND BANK (founded in 1836), by Gotch and Saunders with Sir Edwin Lutyens (1925–8).

The name of OLD JEWRY, farther on, recalls that this was the quarter occupied by the Jews before their expulsion by Edward I in 1290. Some restored Georgian houses of 1776 (by the brothers Adam) survive in FREDERICK'S PLACE, opening on the left of the street.

Poultry is extended beyond Bucklersbury by CHEAPSIDE (IV, E3–V, E1), once known as the Chepe or West Chepe (from the Old English 'ceap', to barter) and in the Middle Ages the chief market of London. The names of side-streets probably indicate the positions of the various traders' stalls. BECKET HOUSE, on the right, built by Noel Clifton (1958), incorporates a new MERCERS' HALL, replacing that on the same site destroyed by bombing in 1941.

The Mercers' Company, first mentioned as a fraternity in the 12th century and incorporated in 1393, is the richest of the City livery companies and the first in order of civic precedence. The hall stood on the site of a hospital of St Thomas of Acon, founded about 1190 by the sister of Thomas Becket, traditionally on the site of the house where the archbishop was born about 1118. The hospital was placed under the patronage of the Mercers, and after the Dissolution its chapel became the chapel of the company. Under the floor an early-16th-century recumbent figure of the dead Christ, of outstanding beauty, was discovered in 1954 (it is now in the Museum of London). Sir Thomas Gresham, the founder of the Royal Exchange, was a member of the company, which possesses some valuable plate.

The tower of ST OLAVE'S JEWRY, in Ironmonger Lane, on the north, is the only survival of a Wren church built in 1670–79 and pulled down in 1888. Under No. 11 in this street is a Roman pavement (sometimes shown to visitors on application).

King Street and Queen Street, named after Charles II and his consort, lead respectively right to Guildhall (Route 30) and left to Southwark Bridge (Route 27). On the left beyond the road junction rises the famous steeple of ST MARY-LE-BOW (V, E1; often called Bow Church), a beautiful campanile 221 ft high, designed by Sir Christopher Wren and completed in 1683, with a spire surmounted by a weathervane in the form of griffin nearly 9 ft long. The church itself (adm., p. 35), rebuilt by Wren in 1670–83, was severely damaged by bombing in 1941, but finely restored (1964) to the designs of Laurence King. It has stained-glass windows by John Hayward (that on the north-east showing the Virgin holding St Mary's in her arms and surrounded by other City churches), a rood presented by the German Federal Republic, and a bronze relief (1966) commemorating the Norwegian resistance movement of 1940–45.

The church stands above an early Norman crypt (approached from outside, on the south-west) of about 1080–90 (the oldest ecclesiastical work in London, except the Tower chapel). This is supposed to have given the medieval church its name of St Maria-de-Arcubus, because it was the first in London to be built on arches (or bows) of stone. The crypt, restored in its original style as far as possible, incorporates some Roman brick and has aisles separated from the nave by monolithic columns. Its south aisle, converted into a chapel, has an etched glass screen by John Hayward.

The church was at one time the chief 'peculiar' in the City, coming directly under the jurisdiction of the archbishop of Canterbury. The Court of Arches, the principal ecclesiastical court, named from the church, was held here at least as early as 1272 (but now sits in the Sanctuary at Westminister). True Londoners, or 'cockneys', are those born within the sound of Bow Bells. The bells in the old story that called back Dick Whittington to be 'Lord Mayor of London' perished in the Great Fire; fragments of their successors, similarly destroyed in 1941, are incorporated in twelve new bells, rung for the first time in 1961.

In the former churchyard is a statue of Captain John Smith, a replica of one in Jamestown (Virginia), unveiled in 1960. On the west wall of the church, outside, is a tablet (with lines by Dryden) to John Milton, the poet, son of a scrivener, who was born in 1608 in BREAD STREET, to the west. Sir Thomas More, the statesman, was born in 1478 in MILK STREET, on the right beyond the church, but his birthplace has likewise disappeared. Excavations in 1977 at the corner of Milk Street and Russia Row revealed a Roman mosaic of the 2nd century A.D. (inside a timber building), a Saxon cottage, and a medieval house (probably burned in the Great Fire of 1666).

In Wood Street, on the right of Cheapside, farther west, is an old plane tree protected in the leases of adjacent buildings and said to be that in which the thrush sang loud in Wordsworth's *Poor Susan*. SADDLERS' HALL, on the same side, was destroyed by fire in 1940, but a new hall (by L. Sylvester Sullivan) just north of Cheapside was opened in 1958. The company, claiming to be the oldest of the City livery companies, is believed to have received a charter from Edward I. Foster Lane, just beyond, contains ST VEDAST'S CHURCH (adm., p. 35), the only church in England (apart from Tathwell in Lincolnshire) dedicated to this saint, who was bishop of Arras and died in 540. Rebuilt by Wren in 1670–73, it was sadly bombed in 1940, but restoration (by S. E. Dykes Bower) was completed in 1962. The interior has a richly carved ceiling, a fine organ by Renatus Harris (1731), a 17th-century pulpit attributed to Grinling Gibbons, and windows illustrating the life of St Vedast, by Brian Thomas. The graceful steeple, one of Wren's finest (1697), escaped destruction. Robert Herrick, the poet, son of a goldsmith of Cheapside, was baptised in 1591 in the previous church here. On the south side of Cheapside are additional buildings for the BANK OF ENGLAND, completed in 1963, in a modified Georgian style by Victor Heal.

At the head of Cheapside, St Paul's Churchyard opens to the left, with a fine view of the cathedral. Newgate Street keeps on to Holborn, while ST MARTIN'S-LE-GRAND (IV, D, E3) leads to the right past the London Post Office (Route 23). This short street takes its name from a college of secular canons established before the Norman Conquest and demolished in 1548. The site is partly occupied by ST MARTIN'S HOUSE, a building by L. Sylvester Sullivan (1927). Just beyond Gresham Street (Route 30) is the site of Aldersgate ('Aldred's Gate'), pulled down in 1761. The church of ST BOTOLPH ALDERSGATE is one of three (originally four) churches dedicated to the 7th-century Saxon saint and standing by City gates of London. It escaped the Great Fire, but was rebuilt in 1754 and the interior was recast in 1788 by Nathaniel Wright. In the south aisle are stained-glass windows by M. C. Farrar Bell of historical subjects (1955).

The small churchyard, on the south, has been converted into the secluded POSTMEN'S PARK, with a statue of Sir Robert Peel (d. 1850) and a cloister given by G. F. Watts (1880) containing tablets recording acts of heroism in everyday life. The bronze minotaur (1973) is by Michael Ayrton.

Aldersgate Street goes on to Clerkenwell Road and Old Street (compare Route 30), but the route bears left beyond St Botolph's, following LITTLE BRITAIN, in which Mr Jaggers had his forbidding office in *Great Expectations*. The name is said by Stow to be taken from a house of the Duke of Brittany. The narrow street turns sharply right, passing St Bartholomew's Hospital, and ends at WEST SMITHFIELD (i.e., 'smooth field'), a large open space that was once a tournament ground outside the City walls, and is now best known for its meat market.

From the reign of Henry I (1100–35) until 1840 the great St Bartholomew's Fair was held here around Bartholomew Tide (24 August). The most important cloth fair in England (lasting three days) during the later Middle Ages, when the country's wealth expanded with its growing exports of wool and cloth, it became from the 16th century a pleasure fair lasting a fortnight, with dramatic and other entertainments (compare Ben Jonson's *Bartholomew Fair*). Smithfield was also the principal horse and cattle market from about 1150 until 1855, and in the 12th century it became the chief place of execution. Sir William Wallace (in 1305) and Anne Askew (1546) are among those who suffered here, and in the reign of Mary Tudor no fewer than 270 Protestants were burned at the stake. Wat Tyler, the rebel leader, was slain here in 1381 by Sir William Walworth, the mayor, in the presence of Richard II.

To the south-east of Smithfield are the extensive buildings of ST BARTHOLOMEW'S HOSPITAL (IV, D3), the oldest hospital in London on its original site, founded in 1123, together with an Augustinian priory (see below), by Rahere, a courtier of Henry I, as the result of a pilgrimage to Rome. On the outer wall are memorials to Sir William Wallace, the Scottish patriot (unveiled in 1956), and to several of the Protestant martyrs (see above). The hospital was refounded by Henry VIII in 1546 after the suppression of the priory. The fine gatehouse, with a statue of the king, was erected in 1702; the Great Hall and other buildings in the quadrangle are to the designs of James Gibbs (1730–34), and later additions (from 1808) were made by Thomas Hardwick. Yet further additions were made between 1878 and 1923. Within the gates to the left (visitors admitted) is the small church of ST BARTHOLOMEW THE LESS, largely rebuilt (except for the 15th-century tower) in 1823 by Hardwick, who preserved the octagonal form of the previous church of 1789 by the younger Dance. It was restored in 1950, when new memorial windows by Hugh Easton were inserted. In the floor of the vestibule is a brass of 1439 to William Markeby and his wife. Inigo Jones, the architect, was christened in the medieval church in 1573.

The Great Hall (no general adm.), farther east, is a noble work by Gibbs with a gilded and decorated ceiling, and the so-called Charter window of the 17th century showing Henry VIII presenting a document to the Lord Mayor. It contains portraits by Reynolds, Lawrence, and others, and on the staircase are two large paintings by Hogarth given in 1737 by the artist to the hospital, of which he became a governor.

William Harvey, the discoverer of the circulation of the blood, was chief physician of the hospital in 1609–43. The famous medical college ('Bart's'), the oldest in London, was founded in 1662, and John Abernethy was lecturer here from 1791 until 1815, when he was elected principal surgeon of the hospital. The college, now affiliated to the University of London, has a faculty of medicine, a valuable library, and a museum of 12,000 anatomical specimens. It is partly housed in new buildings close to Charterhouse.

GILTSPUR STREET leads from the south corner of Smithfield to the junction of Holborn Viaduct and Newgate Street (Route 23). In Cock Lane, on the right, is a gilt figure of a naked boy marking PYE CORNER, where the Great Fire of 1666, which started at Pudding Lane, is popularly (but incorrectly) supposed to have stopped.

On the east side of Smithfield is the entrance to the Norman church of ST BARTHOLOMEW THE GREAT (IV, D3; adm., p. 34), the oldest in London (after the chapel in the Tower) and the most interesting. The present building consists of little more than the choir of the great priory-church founded in 1123 for Augustinian canons (compare above). The churchyard occupies the site of the nave, and the 13th-century entrance gate (restored in 1932) was originally the west entrance to the south aisle. Above the gateway is an Elizabethan house with a timber-framed front (1595), revealed in 1915 by the explosion of a Zeppelin bomb loosening the tiles that concealed it. At the Reformation most of the church and the conventual buildings were destroyed or alienated. There survives, apart from Rahere's choir and vaulted ambulatories, the crossing and one bay of the nave, built before 1170; the transepts, shortened by Sir Aston Webb, who began a successful restoration in 1863; and the Lady Chapel, of 14th-century origin.

The Choir has massive piers and round arches in the mature Romanesque style; the triforium is also Norman work, but the clerestory was rebuilt early in the 15th century. On the south side the triforium is broken by a beautiful oriel introduced by Prior William Bolton (1506–32) and formerly communicating with the prior's house. It bears his rebus, a bolt (or arrow) piercing a tun (or cask). The apsidal east end of the choir, with its attenuated columns, was built in 1863–85 by Webb, but probably recaptures the style of the original apse, demolished in the 15th century in favour of a square end. On the north side of the sanctuary is the beautiful canopied tomb (late 15th or early 16th century) with an effigy of the founder (d. 1143), a prebendary of St Paul's Cathedral and the first prior of St Bartholomew's. The South Transept contains the 15th-century font (the only medieval font in the City) at which William Hogarth (see below) was baptized. In the South Ambulatory is the alabaster tomb of Sir Walter Mildmay (d. 1589), founder of Emmanuel College, Cambridge, and Chancellor of the Exchequer under Elizabeth I. The Lady Chapel, divided from the east end of the choir by a fine modern iron screen, was largely rebuilt after 1885. In the 18th century it was used as a printing office and Benjamin Franklin was employed here (1725). Below it is a small Crypt, probably once a charnel-house. In the North Ambulatory are the entrances to former chapels; the North Transept, restored in 1893 after long occupation by a blacksmith's forge, is separated from the crossing by a 15th-century open stone screen.

A Norman doorway with 15th-century wooden doors, west of the south transept, opens to the east walk of the Cloisters (key with the verger), built about 1405 but largely reconstructed in its original style in 1905–28. Arches in the east wall indicate the entrance to the vanished chapter house. On Good Friday, in continuance of a custom begun in 1686, twenty-one poor widows each receive a mint coin at St Bartholomew's. The money (now supplemented by gifts of hot-cross buns and a proportion of the collection at the service) is laid out on a tombstone in the churchyard.

Inigo Jones was the son of a clothworker of CLOTH FAIR, north of the church, which preserves a charming house of about 1640 (No. 41), one of the very few surviving in the City from before the Great Fire. The painter Hogarth was born in 1697 in BARTHOLOMEW CLOSE, south-east of the church, and Milton went into hiding here for a time after the Restoration in 1660. No. 87, near Little Britain, is BUTCHERS' HALL (1959).

On the north side of West Smithfield is the CENTRAL MEAT MARKET (IV, C, D3), the largest in the world, built in 1867–86 by Sir Horace Jones and covering about ten acres with an extension on the west towards Farringdon Road. The market is at its busiest between 5 and 9 o'clock in the morning, and there are sections for poultry (rebuilt in 1962 after a fire), provisions, etc. Long Lane leads to the right for Barbican station (Route 30), while the roadway through the middle of the market from Smithfield gives access to CHARTERHOUSE STREET, running west to Holborn Circus (Route 23) and east to St John Street and Charterhouse Square.

On the north side of the square is CHARTERHOUSE (IV, C3; adm., p. 31), an interesting institution founded in the 14th century as a Carthusian priory, but re-established in 1611 by Thomas Sutton as a school and a hospital for poor gentlemen. The buildings, mostly of the 16th century, were greatly damaged by incendiary bombs, but have been carefully restored in their former style by Lord Mottistone and Paul Paget (1956).

The priory, founded in 1371 by Sir Walter de Manny, a distinguished soldier who fought under Edward III, owed allegiance to the great French monastery of the Grande-Chartreuse, of which name Charterhouse is a corruption. After its suppression in 1537 the buildings were granted to Lord North, who in 1545 constructed himself a mansion out of them. This passed to John Dudley, Duke of Northumberland (beheaded in 1553), and later to Thomas Howard, Duke of Norfolk (executed in 1572), who made considerable alterations. Elizabeth I was entertained here, as was James I after his arrival from Scotland in 1603 for his coronation. By this time the property had passed to another Thomas Howard, later Earl of Suffolk, but in 1611 he sold it for £13,000 to Thomas Sutton, a wealthy coal-owner, who established a hospital for eighty poor 'brethren' and a school for forty poor boys.

The school, which grew into one of the foremost public schools in England, was transferred in 1872 to Godalming in Surrey. W. M. Thackeray, who was a pupil, has described Charterhouse (under the name of Greyfriars) in *The Newcomes*, Colonel Newcome being both an ex-pupil of the school and a poor brother. In 1875 the Merchant Taylors' School, founded in 1561, was accommodated here, but in 1933 this school moved in turn, to Moor Park (Hertfordshire). The Master's Court and neighbouring buildings were gravely damaged during an air-raid in 1941; the first stage of the restoration was completed in 1951, when thirteen brethren returned from temporary quarters at Godalming. Owing to a decline in the revenues of the charity the number of these will probably never rise much above forty. The brethren must be bachelors or widowers over sixty years of age and members of the Church of England.

The modernized 15th-century Gatehouse gives access to the MASTER'S COURT, where restoration after war damage has revealed the old stone walls, parts of which belonged to the monastic church, on the east. This was pulled down by Lord North to make way for his house, but in 1947 the lead coffin of the founder, Sir Walter de Manny (d. 1372), was found near the site of the altar. The present CHAPEL, farther north-east, was formerly the chapter-house of the priory, and the south and east walls survive from the 14th century. The ante-chapel was added in 1512 as the lay-brothers' choir; the north arcade and aisle were built in 1614 and the outer aisle in 1824. The chapel has a notable pulpit and screen, and contains the ornate tomb of Thomas Sutton (d. 1611), by Bernard Jansen, with a fine effigy by Nicholas Stone, and monuments by Chantrey to Lord Ellenborough (d. 1818) and by Flaxman to Dr Raine (d. 1811), headmaster of the school. A small fragment of the tomb of Sir Walter de Manny is also preserved.

On the north of the Master's Court is the magnificent GREAT HALL, erected in the 16th century by Lord North, largely with stonework from the monastic buildings. Restored after war damage, it is again used as a dining hall by the brethren. It has a beautiful 16th-century fireplace and screen, and a 17th-century gallery, and incorporates the original hammerbeams of the roof. Next to it is the 17th-century LIBRARY, and above this is the GREAT CHAMBER, one of the finest Elizabethan rooms in England before the bombing, and now restored to its former splendour, with a rich gilded plaster ceiling, an elaborate fireplace, and handsome Flemish tapestries.

On the site of Brooke Hall, to the north-east of the court, a muniment room has been erected. The 16th-century WASH HOUSE COURT, to the west, has been rebuilt after war damage to provide new quarters for the brethren. To the north-east of this is the GREAT CLOISTER, originally surrounded by the cells of the monks, but later occupied by both Charterhouse and Merchant Taylors' Schools.

ST BARTHOLOMEW'S MEDICAL COLLEGE is partly accommodated in new buildings by Easton and Robertson begun in 1949 and approached from Rutland Place, north-east of CHARTERHOUSE SQUARE, in which Nos. 4 and 5, on the east side, are a pair of houses of about 1700, with later doorcases.

St John's Lane, branching to the left from St John Street (which goes on to Islington; see Route 30), is spanned by ST JOHN'S GATE (IV, C3; adm., p. 35), once the main entrance to an influential priory of the Order of the Hospital of St John of Jerusalem, better known as the Knights Hospitallers, an order of chivalry founded late in the 11th century at Jerusalem. Its headquarters were later moved to the island of Rhodes and then to Malta (1530–1798). The priory, built about 1148, soon after the establishment of the order in England, was burned down by Wat Tyler's rebels (1381) and the gatehouse was rebuilt in 1504 by Prior Thomas Docwra, whose arms, with those of the order, are on the north side.

After the suppression of the order in England the priory buildings were appropriated by the Crown (1559), and by the 19th century they had become the 'Old Jerusalem Tavern'. The order was revived in 1831, and in 1873 the English members purchased St John's Gate, practically all that survived of the priory, and began to develop the ambulance work for which they are now best known. In 1888 they were established as the Venerable Order of the Hospital of St John of Jerusalem, an entirely British royal order of chivalry.

On the ground floor of the gatehouse is an interesting AMBULANCE MUSEUM (adm., p. 35), opened in 1984 and illustrating the work of two organizations that merged in 1968: the St John Ambulance Association, founded in 1877 to train people in first-aid, and the St John Ambulance Brigade, formed in 1887 to provide a body of volunteers to assist the medical services. The brigade now has a world-wide membership of 250,000. The room over the gate was once occupied by Edward Cave, the founder in 1731 of the *Gentleman's Magazine*, to which Johnson and Garrick contributed. Now known as the Council Chamber, it contains interesting relics of the Knights Hospitallers. The annexe on the south-east of the gateway was added in 1903 by J. Oldrid Scott.

ST JOHN'S SQUARE, cut through by Clerkenwell Road, occupies the site of the courtyard of the priory. On its north-east side is ST JOHN'S CHURCH (IV, C3; adm., p. 35), rebuilt in 1721–3 on the site of the priory church consecrated in 1185. Parts of the choir walls were incorporated in the 18th-century building; the original church had a round nave (as usual with the Order of St John) the outline of which is marked on the ground in the Square. In 1931 the church reverted to the order, but it was severely damaged in 1941 by incendiary bombs. Rebuilding was completed in 1958 to designs by Lord Mottistone. The 15th-century altar-paintings, given by Grand Prior John Weston to commemorate the order's victory at the siege of Rhodes, were looted from the church at the Dissolution but rediscovered in 1915. Below the chancel survives the original Crypt, the three west bays of which are pure Norman work of about 1140, while the two east bays and the side chapels were completed about 1170.

CLERKENWELL ROAD (IV, C1–3; pronounced 'Clark-') leads west across Farringdon Road to Gray's Inn Road (Route 22). CLERKENWELL GREEN, opening on the right, was long a centre of radical reform and noted for its political gatherings. Nos. 37–8, on the north side, built in 1738 as a Welsh charity school, now contain the MARX MEMORIAL LIBRARY, founded in 1933 and containing over 100,000 books, etc., devoted to working-class history. The building was from 1893 to 1922 the publishing house of the Social Democratic Federation, and here Lenin printed his newspaper *Iskra* on thin paper for smuggling into Imperial Russia. On the west of the Green is the CLERKENWELL CONFERENCE CENTRE (formerly the Middlesex Sessions House), a classical building of 1782, much altered since. On a slope to the north rises ST JAMES'S CHURCH (IV, C2), the parish church of Clerkenwell, built in 1788–92 by James Carr and renovated in 1882 by Blomfield, with a baroque steeple rebuilt in its former style in 1849. In FARRINGDON LANE, to the north-west of the Green, behind the offices of THE NEW STATESMAN, a socialist weekly founded in 1913 under the influence of Sidney Webb and Bernard Shaw, can be seen the medieval CLERKS' WELL, discovered in 1924 and since restored.

FARRINGDON ROAD, the continuation of Farringdon Street (compare Route 23), goes on north-west from Clerkenwell Road. At No. 119, on the left, are the head-offices of the GUARDIAN, formerly the *Manchester Guardian*, founded as a weekly newspaper in 1821, and a daily paper since 1855. In Pine Street, a parallel street on the right, is the FINSBURY HEALTH CENTRE, a fine example of modern architecture by Lubetkin and Tecton (1938). Beyond the crossing of Rosebery Avenue is the huge MOUNT PLEASANT PARCEL POST OFFICE (IV, B1, 2), built in 1900–34 and damaged in 1943. It is the largest of its kind in the world, with nine and a half acres of floor space, and about a million parcels are handled every week. Lloyd Baker Street, on the right at the beginning of King's Cross Road, ascends to LLOYD SQUARE, on three sides of which are unusual semi-detached houses of 1819. King's Cross Road joins Pentonville Road a little east of KING'S CROSS STATION; thence to Euston, etc., and to the Angel at Islington, see Route 16.

ROSEBERY AVENUE, starting from Clerkenwell Road near Gray's Inn Road, was cut through a squalid district and leads north-east to St John Street (Route 30) short of the Angel. It passes the former FINSBURY TOWN HALL (by C. Evans Vaughan, 1895) and the offices (1920) of the THAMES WATER AUTHORITY (formerly the Metropolitan Water Board), incorporating a room, with notable woodcarving and plasterwork, from the Water House of 1693. The fine Research Building to the north-east was added by Howard Robertson in 1938. The surrounding reservoirs are on the site of the New River Head, the end of the water-supply brought to London from the Lea Valley by Sir Hugh Myddelton in 1613. Opposite is the SPA GREEN ESTATE, with characteristic examples of post-war blocks of flats (by Lubetkin and Tecton, 1950).

Beyond is the SADLER'S WELLS THEATRE (IV, A2), rebuilt in 1931 by

F. G. M. Chancellor as a home of popular opera in north London, under the management of Lilian Baylis. Its ballet company, formed in 1931, first achieved an international reputation under the direction of Ninette de Valois, but the principal company was transferred to the Royal Opera House in 1956. The principal opera company moved in 1968 to the Coliseum Theatre and the second company was re-formed, as the New Sadler's Wells Opera Company, in 1982. The first theatre was built by Thomas Sadler, who in 1683 discovered an old well in the garden of his house and developed it as a popular 'spa'. This theatre was rebuilt in 1765 and here Joseph Grimaldi, the famous clown, played from 1781 to 1805, and Samuel Phelps produced thirty-four of Shakespeare's plays in 1844–63.

30 From the Bank to the Angel (Islington) via Guildhall and the Barbican

Plan V, E1–IV, A2

STATIONS: BANK (Plan V, E1), see Route 28; ST PAUL'S (IV, E3), on the Central line; BARBICAN (IV, C3; closed on Sundays), on the Circle and Metropolitan lines; ANGEL (IV, A3), on the Northern line. — BUSES Nos. 9, 11, 21, 43, 76, and 133 in Princes Street; Nos. 4, 141, 279A, and 502 in Aldersgate Street; Nos. 141, 279A, and 502 in London Wall; Nos. 4, 277, and 279A in Goswell Road and No. 279 in St John Street (Nos. 277 and 279 from Smithfield); in Cheapside, see Route 29; others to the Angel, see Routes 16, 29.

From the open space fronting the Mansion House (Route 28), PRINCES STREET (V, E1) runs north-west, with the Bank of England on its right. On the left are entrances to GROCERS' HALL, the fourth on this site, completed in 1892 and restored after its partial demolition by a flying-bomb in 1944. Seriously damaged by fire in 1965, when many treasures were lost, it was restored again in 1967. The guild of 'pepperers', the forerunners of the grocers, first heard of in 1180, lapsed in the reign of Edward III, but was revived as a fraternity in 1345 and received its first charter as the Grocers' Company in 1428. The company is the second in precedence of the twelve great City livery companies.

In Lothbury, on the north side of the Bank, is the church of ST MARGARET LOTHBURY (adm., p. 35), rebuilt in 1686–95 by Wren (the last of his churches to be completed, except St Paul's) and containing an unusual 17th-century chancel screen, probably of Hanseatic origin. In the north aisle is a bronze bust of Sir Peter le Maire (d. 1631), perhaps by Hubert Le Sueur; and in the south aisle (now a chapel) is the charming font, which, like the splendid pulpit and sounding board, is attributed to Grinling Gibbons.

In a niche of the wall opposite the church is a statue of Sir John Soane (d. 1837), architect of the Bank. No. 41 Lothbury (a building of 1932) was the head-office of the WESTMINSTER BANK, founded in 1834 and amalgamated in 1968 with the National Provincial Bank to form the National Westminster Bank (see Route 32). The street is extended eastward by Throgmorton Street, passing the Stock Exchange (see Route 28). In Drapers Gardens, near Throgmorton Avenue, on the north, is a thirty-storey building (by Richard Seifert & Partners, 1967), formerly the headquarters of the NATIONAL PROVINCIAL BANK, founded in 1833, and now housing departments of the National Westminster Bank.

GRESHAM STREET (V, D, E1), starting opposite Lothbury at the foot of Moorgate (Route 31), leads west to Aldersgate Street. On the right, at the junction of Basinghall Street, is GRESHAM COLLEGE, established in 1579 under a bequest of Sir Thomas Gresham, the founder of the Royal Exchange, for the delivery of free public lectures in Latin and English in divinity, astronomy, music, geometry, physics, law, and rhetoric.

Christopher Wren was professor of astronomy here in 1657–61. The present college, by Dendy Watney (1913), is now part of the Graduate Business Centre of The City University (Route 30), and the lectures are given in the Barbican Centre (p. 295).

Farther west, at the corner of King Street, is the church of ST LAWRENCE JEWRY (adm., p. 35), rebuilt by Wren in 1670–81, but gutted by bombing in 1940, and restored in 1954–7, largely in its former style, by Cecil Brown. The classical tower and spire, rebuilt to their old design, are surmounted by the original weathervane in the form of a gridiron, recalling the martyrdom of St Lawrence. In the nave and the Commonwealth chapel are stained-glass windows by Christopher Webb, and the reredos has a painting by the restorer. A new vicarage has been provided in the north-west corner of the church, which is the official church of the City Corporation. The retiring Lord Mayor attends service here before the election of his successor on Michaelmas Day.

The Spital Sermon, preached originally at the priory of St Mary Spital, and at Christ Church (Newgate Street) before its destruction, is now given here on the second Wednesday after Easter, when the Lord Mayor and Aldermen attend in state.

King Street ends on the north in the yard of GUILDHALL (V, D, E1; adm., p. 32), the Hall of the Corporation of the City of London, rebuilt in the early 15th century, but given a new south front in the Gothick fashion in 1789 by George Dance the Younger, and altered and extended at various other times.

Guildhall, the seat of municipal government in the City and the principal place of civic assembly, replaces an earlier hall of great but unknown age which stood farther west in Aldermanbury. The present hall was built in 1411–25, and of this period there survives the porch of the gatehouse, part of the Great Hall and a double crypt. The building was seriously damaged in the Great Fire of 1666, but was immediately repaired, perhaps by Wren. Further rebuildings and restorations were carried out, particularly by Sir Horace Jones (1864–84) and by Sydney Perks, who rebuilt the east wing (1909). Guildhall was damaged again during the great fire of 29 December 1940, but was partly restored by Sir Giles Gilbert Scott in 1954, and large new extensions have been built.

Visitors are admitted to the Court of Common Council which meets in Guildhall every third Thursday (holidays excepted) at 1 p.m.

High over the porch is the coat-of-arms of the City, with its motto, *Domine dirige nos* (Lord, direct us). The porch, which retains its fine 15th-century vaulting, leads direct into the GREAT HALL, the principal chamber, 152 ft long, 49½ ft wide, and 89 ft high. Though preserving part of its original walls, it was largely rebuilt after the Great Fire, and considerably restored in 1864–6 by Sir Horace Jones. The roof, destroyed in 1940, was reconstructed by Sir Giles G. Scott, who provided stone arches with a flat panelled ceiling between, giving an effect of extra height. He also introduced new panelling at the east end of the hall, and new stained-glass windows whose design incorporates scrolls bearing the names and dates of 663 Mayors and Lord Mayors. Around the cornice are painted shields of the livery companies, and embroidered banners with the arms of the twelve 'great' companies were hung here in 1957.

The large monuments by the north wall commemorate Lord Nelson (by James Smith, with an inscription by Sheridan), the Duke of Wellington (by John Bell), and the Earl of Chatham (by John Bacon the Elder; inscription attributed to Burke); those on the south wall are to William Pitt the Younger (by J. G. Bubb; inscription by Canning) and William Beckford, Lord Mayor in 1762 and 1769 (by F. J. Moore). The inscription on this last, said to have been a speech made by Beckford to George III, is worth reading. At the west end is a timber screen and gallery (1972), above which are figures of Gog and

Magog, carved in limewood by David Evans (1953), replacing the 18th-century figures lost in the bombing and themselves said to have been inspired by effigies carried in medieval pageants. To the right of the screen is a fine bronze seated statue of Sir Winston Churchill (1959), by Oscar Nemon; to the left survives an unusual 15th-century window.

The hall is used for municipal and public meetings, and for civic receptions and banquets, among the most notable being those given to visiting royalty and State officials. On Midsummer Day (24 June) the 'Common Hall' of the mayor and aldermen with the liverymen of the City guilds is held here, a colourful ceremony at which the Sheriffs for the ensuing year are elected (visitors usually admitted on previous application). On the second Saturday in November the new Lord Mayor, admitted to office here on the preceding day, gives a banquet to members of the Cabinet and other distinguished citizens. The hall was formerly used for important trials, and Anne Askew, the Protestant martyr (1546), Henry Howard, the poet Earl of Surrey (1547), and Lady Jane Grey and Archbishop Cranmer (both in 1554) were among those condemned here. Chopin played in the hall in 1848 in aid of Polish refugees.

Beneath the hall is a spacious early-15th-century CRYPT (restored in 1961), part of the original building. It is divided by a wall into two sections, the eastern of which, nearly 77 ft long, has six clustered columns of Purbeck marble supporting a groined vault with carved bosses. The western section, much altered after the Great Fire, was restored in 1972, when parts of the previous Guildhall (of before 1400) were revealed. The LIVERY HALL, by Sir Giles G. Scott (1957), north of the Great Hall, provides a meeting place for those livery companies that have no halls of their own.

A corridor opening on the east of the porch, with paintings of events in the City's history, gives access to a spacious Hall of 1872 in the Tudor Gothic style (formerly the Guildhall Library; now used for receptions). The timber ceiling bears the arms of fourteen of the City livery companies. On the landing are statues by Arnold Quellin of Charles II and Sir John Cutler (d. 1693), a City merchant and benefactor.

On the east of Guildhall Yard is the GUILDHALL ART GALLERY, established in 1886 on the site of the Guildhall Chapel (demolished in 1822). Its large collection consists mainly of British paintings of the 19th century; only a small part can be shown, but some of the City's pictures are usually on view in the Barbican Centre. Loan exhibitions of the work of London art societies are held frequently in the gallery.

Opposite the gallery to the south is the IRISH CHAMBER (1825), the headquarters of the Honourable the Irish Society, incorporated in 1613 to manage the estates allotted to the corporation after the plantation of Ulster in 1609. In Guildhall Buildings, the adjacent street, is the MAYOR'S AND CITY OF LONDON COURT (1893).

On the west of Guildhall Yard, in an extension of 1974 (by Sir Giles G. Scott, Son & Partners) are the Town Clerk's Office and the GUILDHALL LIBRARY (entrance from Aldermanbury; see below). The library, founded originally in 1425 and re-established in 1828, contains over 140,000 volumes (though it lost many in the bombing) and is particularly notable for its works on every aspect of London; it also has numerous manuscripts and an unrivalled collection of London prints.

Among the many valuable possessions may be noted Ralph or Radulph Agas's plan of Elizabethan London (about 1591); a rare plan of London by John Ogilby (1676); the deed of purchase of a house in Blackfriars bearing Shakespeare's signature (1613); the first, second, and fourth folios of Shakespeare's plays; the Great Chronicle of London, used by John Stow, the Elizabethan topographer; an illuminated English missal of the early 15th century from St Botolph Aldersgate; and a remarkable modern manuscript register (in four volumes) containing representations of the monuments, coats-of-arms, etc., in the City churches. The library displays a fine collection of old clocks, watches, and chronometers, the property of the Clockmakers' Company.

Also in this building is the CITY RECORDS OFFICE, containing the most complete and extensive municipal records in the country (open Mondays–Fridays, 9.30 to 4.45). Calendars of many of the records are published by the corporation.

To the west of Guildhall is ALDERMANBURY, a street (named from a 'bury' or court of an alderman) leading north from Gresham Street past the site (now a garden) of ST MARY ALDERMANBURY, a church rebuilt by Wren in 1680–87, but bombed in 1940. The walls and tower have been incorporated in a new chapel and library (1964–7) built at Westminster College, Fulton (Missouri), as a memorial to Sir Winston Churchill. A 19th-century monument remains to John Heming and Henry Condell, Shakespeare's fellow-actors and editors of the First Folio (1623).

On the right opens a paved square with a sculpture, 'Beyond Tomorrow', by Karin Junzen (1972). To the north of this are the City of London EXHIBITION HALL, for special municipal exhibitions, and the GUILDHALL JUSTICE ROOM (1969). In Aldermanbury are the CHARTERED INSURANCE INSTITUTE (founded in 1897), in a building of 1934, with a museum of fire-fighting equipment (adm., p. 31), and (on the left) Aldermanbury House, containing the office of the EXPORT CREDITS GUARANTEE DEPARTMENT, established under an act of 1975. In the quiet ALDERMANBURY SQUARE, at the end of the street, are Royex House, which contains the NATIONAL INVESTMENT AND LOANS OFFICE, established in 1980, and BREWERS' HALL, rebuilt in 1960 by Sir Hubert Worthington and T. W. Sutcliffe. On the north-east side, near the end of Basinghall Street, is the approach to the CITY BUSINESS LIBRARY (adm., p. 77), specializing in company information and market research, and with extensive collections of directories and periodicals, English and foreign newspapers, and books on various aspects of commerce.

Gresham Street continues west past Wood Street (see below), on the corner of which is GARRARD HOUSE, a large block of offices designed by Arthur S. Ash (1956). It incorporates HABERDASHERS' HALL, the third on the site, the first (built in 1448) having been burned down in the Great Fire and the next destroyed during the Second World War. The company is one of the twelve senior livery companies. The entrance to the hall is in Staining Lane, at the north end of which is PEWTERERS' HALL, built by David Evelyn Nye and Partners (1960). The court room contains oak panelling and fittings salved from the bombed hall in Lime Street. On the right of Gresham Street, farther on, is the church of ST ANNE AND ST AGNES, a small but attractive building by Wren (1676–87), damaged in 1940 and restored in 1966. Lutheran services in English are now held here.

At the corner of Foster Lane, to the left, is GOLDSMITHS' HALL (V, D1), an elaborate building in the Renaissance style by Philip Hardwick (1835).

The rich interior contains some notable portraits and a very fine collection of plate. The company, ranking fifth in order of precedence among the great livery companies, was incorporated in 1327 and still has the duty of assaying and stamping precious metals, its hallmark being the leopard's head. The 'Trial of the Pyx', i.e., the testing of the coinage issued from the Royal Mint, has been the prerogative of the company since medieval times, and the test is still carried out every March, samples of coins, each value in its own box (called a 'pyx'), being sent to the hall for the purpose.

From the end of Gresham Street, St Martin's-le-Grand and ALDERSGATE STREET lead right past St Botolph's Church (see Route 29) and the approach (by steps at the roundabout) to the **Museum of London** (adm., p. 374). On the podium walk in front of the museum is a bronze memorial to John Wesley, who in 1738 attended a meeting nearby which led to his conversion and the birth of the Methodist movement. A covered podium walk connects the museum with the Barbican Centre (p. 295), with an exit to Aldersgate Street opposite Barbican station.

On the right of Aldersgate Street, just beyond the roundabout, is the entrance to IRONMONGERS' HALL, by Sydney Tatchell (1925). The company is the smallest of the twelve great livery companies. Farther on is BARBICAN STATION, beyond which the short Carthusian Street leads left to Charterhouse Square, for Charterhouse (Route 29). On the opposite side of Aldersgate Street, farther on, is the GOLDEN LANE ESTATE, a spacious layout with blocks of flats of varying sizes by Chamberlin, Powell, and Bon (from 1960 on). The former CRIPPLEGATE INSTITUTE, on its south-east side, founded in 1894, is now mainly occupied by a school, but also has a small theatre. Aldersgate Street is extended by Goswell Road (p. 296) to the Angel at Islington.

On the right at the roundabout begins LONDON WALL (V, D1), a wide thoroughfare cut through to Moorgate in 1959. It traverses an area that was sadly devastated by the bombing but has now been largely rebuilt as the BARBICAN. This adventurous scheme, evolved by the City of London (within whose boundaries most of the area lies) and begun in 1962, comprises a commercial zone, on the south, planned by Sir Leslie Martin (the county council architect) and his successor Sir Hubert Bennett (in conjunction with H. A. Mealand and E. G. Chandler, the city planning officer and architect), and a residential and cultural area, on the north, designed by Chamberlin, Powell, and Bon.

London Wall, running between eighteen-storey blocks of offices rising above podia connected by elevated walkways, passes above the remains of the west gate of a ROMAN FORT (adm., p. 34) dating from the late 1st or early 2nd century A.D., and hence older than the City wall. Its existence was discovered only in 1950, on the clearance of bomb damage.

London Wall crosses WOOD STREET, which leads south to Gresham Street, passing the barrack-like CITY OF LONDON POLICE STATION, by Donald McMorran and George Whitby (1966). In the centre of the road opposite this is the solitary tower of ST ALBAN'S (now converted into offices), the only survival of a Gothic church by Wren (1687) demolished by bombing.

Wood Street, following more or less a Roman predecessor, runs north across the site of the fort to Fore Street, passing (on the right) the end of a road inside the line of the City wall (see below), a section of which, showing Roman and medieval work, can be seen in the former churchyard of ST ALPHEGE (now a public garden).

The junction of Wood Street with the wall marks the probable site of Cripplegate (perhaps from the old English 'crepelgeat', a covered way). Nearly opposite St Alphege's garden, and almost hidden by new office blocks, is the 14th-century tower-porch of the chapel of ELSING SPITAL (a priory founded in 1329), incorporated in St Alphege's church at the Reformation. On the right in Wood Street is

ROMAN HOUSE, by Owen Campbell-Jones (1957), covering the spot where the first bomb fell on London, at 12.15 a.m. on 25 August 1940.

Opposite the angle between Wood Street and Fore Street is an approach to the large church of ST GILES CRIPPLEGATE (V, D1; adm., p. 34), rebuilt after a fire in 1545 and altered several times since, badly damaged (except for the 15th-century tower, heightened in 1683) in the first air-raid on London, and restored in 1959.

Oliver Cromwell was married in this church in 1620; and among those buried here are John Foxe (d. 1587), author of the *Book of Martyrs*; Sir Martin Frobisher (d. 1594), the explorer; John Speed (d. 1629), the map-maker; and John Milton (d. 1674), whose supposed burial-place is marked by a stone west of the chancel. Lancelot Andrewes, one of the translators of the Bible, was vicar of St Giles in 1589–1605. Some of the furnishings have been moved here from the closed church of St Luke's, Clerkenwell, including the fine 18th-century organ, restored by Noel Mander in 1970.

To the south of the church, bounded by a modern 'moat', is a fine length of the CITY WALL, with a half-round bastion. The wall was built about A.D. 190, of Kentish ragstone, and is 7 to 8 ft thick. It originally stood 15 ft or more high, but the upper part was rebuilt in medieval times, when it was heightened to about 32 ft. The wall was reinforced with at least twenty-one external bastions, 18 to 30 ft across and projecting some 6 to 10 ft from the surface, and these were made solid after A.D. 367. To the south-west of St Giles is a circular bastion and to the south of this are two further half-round bastions with another length of wall, revealed by bombing and now facing the east side of the Museum of London. The two lengths of wall originally formed the north and west boundaries of the Roman fort (see above).

To the north-west of St Giles a new building was completed in 1969 for the CITY OF LONDON SCHOOL FOR GIRLS (550 pupils), founded in 1894. The school is surrounded by large new blocks of flats, the first of which was occupied in 1968. The scheme includes over 2,000 flats, and some of these are in three towerblocks each about 400 ft high, the tallest residential blocks in Europe when they were built. To the north of the girls' school is an ornamental lake, and a walkway over this gives access to the BARBICAN CENTRE for Arts and Conferences, (V, C1), designed by Chamberlin, Powell, and Bon, begun in 1971 and completed in 1982. The centre includes a splendid concert hall, with 2,000 seats, the home of the London Symphony Orchestra; a spacious theatre, with 1,150 seats, and a smaller theatre (The Pit), both occupied by the Royal Shakespeare Company; three cinemas, an art gallery (adm., see p. 31), a library, conference rooms and two restaurants.

The interesting but complicated interior is arranged on nine floors or levels. The walkway (see above) is on Level 7, the terrace foyer fronting the lake on Level 5, and the entrance to the car park from Silk Street and Whitecross Street (see below) on Level 3. The art gallery is on Level 8, and here also are a sculpture court, a conservatory, and the approach to two exhibition halls on the north side of Beech Street. Also in Silk Street is the GUILDHALL SCHOOL OF MUSIC AND DRAMA of the City Corporation, founded in 1880 and moved in 1977 to a new building by Chamberlin, Powell, and Bon.

In FORE STREET (compare above), on the right, is SALTERS' HALL, the headquarters (1977) of one of the twelve great City livery companies. MOOR LANE, on the left beyond this, runs north past BRITANNIC HOUSE, one of the tallest buildings in London, thirty-five storeys and 395 ft high, designed for the British Petroleum Company by Joseph F. Milton, Cashmore & Partners (1966). Opposite is the entrance to Silk Street.

Moor Lane ends on the north at CHISWELL STREET, which leads to the right to Finsbury Square (Route 31) and left past the head-offices of WHITBREAD'S BREWERY, with a pleasant courtyard enclosed by 18th-century buildings (no general adm.). Brewing was carried on here by Samuel Whitbread and his successors from 1749 until 1976.

In the main building are portraits of the first three Samuel Whitbreads (by Reynolds, Gainsborough, and George Richmond) and the ornate Speaker's Coach, designed in Holland in 1698 for William III and afterwards presented to the Speaker of the House of Commons by the king or Queen Anne. The Porter Tun Room, to the east, and the room above, which has a massive king-post roof, 60 ft wide, may be hired for receptions and banquets. Opposite the brewery offices is a well-restored row of 18th-century houses.

From the west end of Chiswell Street, BEECH STREET goes on as an underpass to Aldersgate Street, emerging opposite Barbican station. Whitecross Street leads north, starting west of the brewery offices, to OLD STREET, which runs west to the junction of Clerkenwell Road (Route 29) and GOSWELL ROAD, the northward continuation of Aldersgate Street. No. 14 in Charterhouse Buildings, on the left at the junction, contains the SOCIETY OF GENEALOGISTS, founded in 1911. No. 137 Goswell Road, farther north, is the EARLY MUSIC CENTRE, established in 1978 to facilitate the performance of music of the 18th century and before. In King Square, on the right, is ST BARNABAS'S CHURCH (IV, B3), built in 1826 by Thomas Hardwick and pleasantly restored after war damage.

To the left of Goswell Road is Northampton Square, with THE CITY UNIVERSITY (IV, B3), founded in 1891 as the Northampton Institute, later a college of advanced technology, and in 1966 created one of the new technological universities; it now has over 3,000 students. The older buildings (by E. W. Mountford, 1894–6) face St John Street, to the west, but extensions were made in 1953–6 (by O. Campbell-Jones) and in 1966–70 (by Richard Sheppard, Robson & Partners), including a library, refectory, and assembly hall. Goswell Road joins City Road just before it reaches the ANGEL (see Route 31).

31 From the Bank to the Angel via Moorgate and City Road

Plan V, E1–IV, A2
STATIONS: BANK (Plan V, E1), see Route 28; MOORGATE (V, D1), on the Circle, Metropolitan, and Northern lines; OLD STREET (V, B2) and ANGEL (IV, A3), on the Northern line. — BUSES in Moorgate: Nos. 9, 11, and 133 to London Wall and Broad Street station; No. 21 to Finsbury Square; No. 76 to Old Street; No. 43 to City Road and the Angel; Nos. 104 and 214 from Finsbury Square to the Angel (Nos. 5, 55, and 243 traverse Old Street).

From the BANK to the north end of Princes Street, see Route 30. MOORGATE (V, E1–D2), a busy street lined by banks and insurance offices, goes on northward. Moorgate Place, on the right, gives access to the INSTITUTE OF CHARTERED ACCOUNTANTS, founded in 1880, with a decorative hall built in 1893 by Sir John Belcher, extended in 1930, and altered internally in 1970. The reliefs on the front are by Sir Hamo Thornycroft and Harry Bates. Moorgate crosses LONDON WALL, which runs west through the Barbican (see Route 30) and east to Old Broad Street. On the left, at the head of Coleman Street, is ARMOURERS' AND BRASIERS' HALL, first built about 1450, but rebuilt in 1840 by J. H. Good, Junior.

In the east branch of London Wall is CARPENTERS' HALL (V, D2), dating from 1876–80, though the Carpenters, among the wealthiest of the City livery companies, have occupied this site for over 500 years. The hall was destroyed by bombs in 1941, but rebuilding began in 1956 (when also a commemoration stone was unveiled) and was completed in 1960. Near the junction with Old Broad Street (Route 28) is the church of ALL HALLOWS, LONDON WALL, rebuilt in 1765–7 by George Dance the Younger, severely damaged in 1941, restored in its original style in 1962, and now a guild church. A short section of the City wall bounds the churchyard, on the west.

Immediately beyond London Wall stood the Moor Gate, one of the City gates, pulled down in 1762. The name, like that of Finsbury, which lies beyond it, preserves the memory of the moor or fen which lay outside the City wall until it was drained in the 16th century. To the left is the approach to MOORGATE STATION on the underground railway, now also a terminus of the London Midland Region of British Rail. John Keats, the poet, was born in 1795 at the sign of the 'Swan and Hoop' in Moorgate, then occupied as livery stables in which his father was an ostler (No. 85, on the left, now stands on the site). On the right is the School of Business Studies of the CITY OF LONDON POLYTECHNIC (founded in 1970). This was formerly the City of London College, established in 1848 and moved here after its building in Ropemaker Street (to the north-west) was burned down in 1940. Sidney Webb, the Fabian sociologist, was a student. Farther on opens the oval FINSBURY CIRCUS, laid out in 1815, its centre a shady oasis with mulberry and other trees. LUTYENS HOUSE on the north-west side (formerly Britannic House), built in 1924–7 by Sir Edwin Lutyens, is now occupied by British Telecom.

Beyond South Place, Moorgate is extended by the short Finsbury Pavement to FINSBURY SQUARE (V, C2), laid out in 1777–90 and now overshadowed by great blocks of commercial buildings. The square was the first place where gas was employed for public lighting. In WORSHIP STREET, to the north, is a row of shops and houses (Nos. 91–101), built by Philip Webb (1863). The long CITY ROAD continues northward, passing the entrance to the parade-ground and headquarters (V, C1, 2) of the HONOURABLE ARTILLERY COMPANY of the City of London, the oldest military body in Britain.

The first origins of the company are unknown, but it was incorporated in 1537 by Henry VIII as the Guild or Fraternity of St George and from it were chosen the officers of the City Trained Bands. Milton, Wren, and Pepys are among the famous men who have served in its ranks. The company has been established on its present ground since 1642; the centre block of its headquarters (Armoury House) dates from 1735, but extensions were made in 1828 (the wings) and in 1857 (the fortress-like front). Since 1660 the captain-general has usually been either the Sovereign or the Prince of Wales. The H.A.C., though a territorial regiment, provided many officers for the regular army in the two World Wars, and it is one of the few regiments privileged to march through the City with 'bayonets fixed, drums beating, and colours flying'. The H.A.C. also fires all salutes from the Tower of London and claims the right of furnishing a guard of honour when royalty visits the City, and its veterans provide a company of pikemen and musketeers as a bodyguard to the Lord Mayor on ceremonial occasions. The regiment now consists of four squadrons mobilizing for the British Army of the Rhine, and it continues to train officers for other units. The Ancient and Honorable Artillery Company of Boston, the oldest military body in the United States, was founded in 1638 by Captain Robert Keayne and other emigrant members of the H.A.C.

On the other side of City Road (No. 47) is WESLEY'S HOUSE (V, C2; adm., p. 35), a characteristic dwelling of about 1770, the home of John Wesley (1703–91) for the last years of his life. Among the rooms shown are Wesley's study, the bedroom where he died, and the small adjoining room used by him for private prayer. These contain much of his furniture, his books, and many personal mementoes. Next to the house on the north is WESLEY'S CHAPEL (adm., p. 35), the 'cathedral of Methodism', opened by the founder in 1778, rebuilt in 1899 after a fire, and restored in 1978. It retains its original pulpit and font. John Wesley is buried in the small graveyard behind the chapel and commemorated by a statue (by J. A. Acton, 1891) in front. A library of nearly 5,000 volumes on the history of Methodism, opened in the crypt in 1959, is administered by the Wesley Historical Society, formed in 1893.

Opposite is the entrance to BUNHILL FIELDS (V, B1–C2), the chief burial-place of the Nonconformists from 1685, but disused since 1852. Its name is said to be a corruption of 'bonehill', so called from its being the repository for the bones disinterred from the charnel-house of St Paul's by Protector Somerset in 1547. On the right of the main walk are the altar-tomb of Isaac Watts (d. 1748), the hymn-writer, and the graves of Daniel Defoe (d. 1731), with an obelisk erected in 1870 by boys and girls of England, and William Blake (d. 1827), 20 yds north-west of Defoe. On the left is the tomb of John Bunyan (d. 1688), with an effigy of 1862 by E. C. Papworth; and about 50 yds west of this is the grave of Susannah Wesley (d. 1742), mother of John Wesley.

Defoe died in lodgings in Ropemaker Street, in an area west of Moorgate laid waste by bombing that affected also Bunhill Row, west of the cemetery, where John Milton lived from 1662 until his death in 1674, completing *Paradise Lost* (1664) and writing *Paradise Regained* (1671). The area has been rebuilt under the Barbican plan. In Roscoe Street, on the left of Bunhill Row near its north end, is the former FRIENDS' BURIAL GROUND, opened in 1661 and converted into a garden in 1952. George Fox (d. 1691), founder of the Society of Friends, was buried here.

OLD STREET (IV, C3–V, B3) runs west to Goswell Road (Route 30) and east to Shoreditch (Route 32), while CITY ROAD, bearing left from East Road (for Highgate, etc.), runs north-west to Islington, passing the MOORFIELDS EYE HOSPITAL, formerly the Royal London Ophthalmic Hospital, the earliest of its kind in Britain (1804), rehoused in 1899. New buildings in the neighbourhood include the laboratories of the INSTITUTE OF OPHTHALMOLOGY of London University. Opposite the point where the road is joined by Goswell Road are COLEBROOKE ROW and DUNCAN TERRACE, two long streets with terraces of the late 18th century, facing each other across a garden on the site of the New River (now carried underground). Charles Lamb lived in 1823–7 in a cottage (No. 64) at the farther end of Duncan Terrace. City Road ends at the ANGEL (IV, A2), a road junction named from a former coaching inn (see also Suburban London), from which Pentonville Road goes on to King's Cross (see Route 16).

32 From the Bank to Shoreditch via Bishopsgate

Plan V, E2–V, A3

STATIONS: BANK (Plan V, E1), see Route 28; LIVERPOOL STREET (V, D2), on the Central, Circle, and Metropolitan lines. — BUSES Nos. 6, 8, 22, and 149 in Threadneedle Street; Nos. 5, 6, 8, 8A, 22, 22A, 35, 47, 48, 78, 149, and 243A in Bishopsgate and Shoreditch High Street (Nos. 8A, 35, 47, and 48 from Gracechurch Street; Nos. 5, 22A, and 78 in Houndsditch and Middlesex Street, to and from Aldgate; Nos. 8 and 8A turn into Bethnal Green Road).

From the BANK the route, skirting the north side of the Royal Exchange (Route 28), follows the curiously named THREADNEEDLE STREET (V, E2), almost wholly given over to banking. On the left opens Old Broad Street, leading to Throgmorton Street and the Stock Exchange (see Route 28). On the right (at No. 30) is the entrance to MERCHANT TAYLORS' HALL, the largest of the City livery companies' halls, dating originally from 1345, but partly rebuilt after the Great Fire. Gutted by bombing in 1940, it was restored in 1959 by Sir Albert Richardson. The company, the largest in the number of liveries of the twelve great companies, received its earliest known charter in 1327.

Threadneedle Street ends at BISHOPSGATE (V, E2–C3), starting on the south at the east end of Cornhill, from which it is extended by Gracechurch Street towards London Bridge (see Route 34). On the left is the old head-office of the NATIONAL PROVINCIAL BANK (see p. 289), a classical building by John Gibson (1866). GRESHAM HOUSE, beyond, occupies the site of the residence of Sir Thomas Gresham (see below), founder of the Royal Exchange and Gresham College. Farther on are the new offices of the NATIONAL WESTMINSTER BANK, designed by Richard Seifert & Partners and completed in 1981, with a towerblock over 600 ft high, the tallest commercial building in Britain.

Great St Helen's, opening on the right, admits to ST HELEN'S CHURCH (V, E2; adm., p. 34), one of the largest and finest of the old London churches, often called the 'Westminster Abbey of the City' from the number and interest of its monuments to City dignitaries. The church, dedicated to the Empress Helena (d. 327), mother of Constantine the Great, may be of Saxon foundation, but its first known mention is in the mid 12th century. It became the church of a Benedictine nunnery founded about 1212, and in consequence has two parallel naves, that on the north used by the nuns (mostly daughters of City merchants) and that on the south by the parishioners. The church dates mainly from the 13th century, but the single arcade, which has clustered piers and tall arches, was recast in 1475. A south transept, with a double chapel on the east having niches for statues, was added about 1374.

The entrance on the west to the parochial choir is through a fine 17th-century doorcase, and an even finer doorcase covers a door dated 1633 on the south side. On the south wall is the excellent monument (recoloured) of Sir John Spencer (d. 1608). The pulpit is Jacobean work, and in the chancel is an unusual wooden sword-rest of 1665, perhaps the oldest in the City. On the north of the chancel is the finest monument in the church, the canopied tomb of Sir William Pickering (d. 1574), ambassador to France, and on the south is the table-tomb with effigies of Sir John Crosby (d. 1475), builder of Crosby Hall, and his first wife. The south chapels contain the table-tomb of John Otteswich (about 1400) and other monuments brought from St Martin Outwich in Threadneedle Street, pulled down in 1874. In the nuns' choir are the table-tombs of Sir Thomas Gresham (d. 1579; see above) and Sir Julius Caesar (d. 1636), Master of the Rolls and Chancellor of the Exchequer to James I, the latter carved by Nicholas Stone.

On the east wall there is a monument to Sir Andrew Judd (d. 1558), the founder of Tonbridge School, and on the north wall is a 16th-century Easter Sepulchre, the apertures below which allowed a view of the altar from the sacristy. Blocked squints and a doorway and a wall-stairway (perhaps the night stairs) formerly opened to the conventual buildings on the north side of the church. The foundations of these and of the Norman or Saxon church were discovered during excavations in St Helen's Place in 1922.

In St Helen's Place, farther north, is LEATHERSELLERS' HALL, rebuilt in 1878 and extended by the addition of a court room, etc., in 1926. The hall was seriously damaged by fire in an air-raid in 1941, but was again rebuilt (by Kenneth Peacock) in 1960. The Leathersellers, first mentioned in the 14th century and incorporated in 1444, are among the wealthiest of the City livery companies.

The small ST ETHELBURGA'S CHURCH, abutting on Bishopsgate north of St Helen's Place, is one of the oldest in London, though much restored from time to time. The dedication to Ethelburga, abbess of Barking and sister of St Erconwald, bishop of London in 675, implies a Saxon foundation. The church was rebuilt about 1430, but practically the only work of this time is in the arcade and the west gable, above which rises a charming belfry of the late 17th or 18th century. Three windows in the nave (by Leonard Walker, 1928–30) commemorate Henry Hudson (d. 1611), who made his Communion here in 1607 with his crew before setting out on his first voyage in search of the North-West Passage. In the chancel are panels of 17th-century heraldic glass. The parish of St Ethelburga is the smallest in London (three acres).

The site of the Bishop's Gate (demolished in 1760) is at the junction with Camomile Street (leading to Bevis Marks, Route 33) and Wormwood Street. On the south-west corner is the HONGKONG BANK GROUP, in a building 300 ft high by Ley Colbeck & Partners and Richard Seifert & Partners (1975). Just beyond is the church of ST BOTOLPH BISHOPSGATE, rebuilt in 1725–9 by James Gold and altered internally in the 19th century. In the south aisle is the roll of honour of the London Rifle Brigade. Edward Alleyn, the actor and founder of Dulwich College, was baptized in the previous church (1566) and John Keats, the poet, in the present building (1795). In the churchyard, on the west, is the former church school, a building of 1861 with figures of a boy and girl in Coade stone.

Houndsditch, on the right, and Middlesex Street, farther on, lead to Aldgate High Street (see Route 33). Liverpool Street, on the left, passes the south side of the large LIVERPOOL STREET STATION (V, D2, 3), a terminus of the Eastern Region, built in 1875 over a burial-ground used as a plague pit in 1665, but to be rebuilt (1985). Adjacent on the west is BROAD STREET STATION (V, D2), a terminus of the London Midland Region, built in 1866 and likewise to be rebuilt.

Devonshire Row, opposite Liverpool Street Station on the east, leads to DEVONSHIRE SQUARE, laid out about 1740. Two of the original houses survive on the north side (No. 13 is now Coopers' Hall); on the north-east is a former warehouse, restored in 1982 as offices, one of the few remaining parts of the large Port of London Authority Warehouses. In ARTILLERY LANE, to the right from Bishopsgate farther north, No. 56 preserves a rare mid-18th-century shop front.

On the right in Bishopsgate is the BISHOPSGATE INSTITUTE, by C. H. Townsend (1894), with a façade showing Art Nouveau decoration. Concerts, organ recitals, and lectures are given, and the reference library includes some 120,000 volumes on the history and topography of London. The institute also has a lending library and a worthy collection of maps, prints, and watercolours of old London. In SPITAL SQUARE, beyond, No. 37, an 18th-century house restored by the Spitalfields Trust, became in 1981 the headquarters of the SOCIETY FOR THE PROTECTION OF ANCIENT BUILDINGS, founded in 1877 by William Morris.

Bishopsgate is extended by the short Norton Folgate to SHOREDITCH HIGH STREET (V, B, C3), an unattractive commercial thoroughfare. Great Eastern Street, on the left, leads to Old Street (see below), while Commercial Street, starting opposite, runs south-east to Whitechapel High Street (see Route 33). On the same side, a little farther on, is Bethnal Green Road, leading towards the Museum of Childhood (see Suburban London) and Victoria Park. At the junction of Shoreditch High Street with Hackney Road is ST LEONARD'S CHURCH (V, B3), the parish church of Shoreditch, founded as early as 900, rebuilt in 1736–40 by George Dance the Elder, and last restored in 1968. It has a large portico, with Tuscan columns, and an imposing steeple, 192 ft high. In the churchyard, pleasantly laid out as a garden, are the old stocks and whipping-post. James Burbage (d. 1597) and his son Richard (d. 1619; the friend of Shakespeare), who are buried in the church, built the first theatre in London in 1576 or 1577 in Curtain Road, west of the High Street (tablet on Nos. 86–8). In 1598, owing to a difficulty over the lease, The Theatre, as it was called, was pulled down overnight and the materials taken to Southwark to build the Globe Theatre (see Route 36).

OLD STREET, starting west of the church, leads across City Road (Route 31) to Goswell Road, from which it is prolonged by Clerkenwell Road and Theobalds Road (Route 22) towards Holborn, a useful if uninteresting cross-route. At the outset it passes the former SHOREDITCH TOWN HALL, built in 1866 by C. A. Long and enlarged (and the tower added) by William Hunt in 1902. In the long Hoxton Street, starting opposite, is HOXTON HALL, built in 1863 as a music-hall and now a community centre of the Society of Friends. Pitfield Street, on the right farther west, leads towards HOXTON PARISH CHURCH (1826), by Francis Edwards, a pupil of Soane.

Over ¼ m. north of Shoreditch church, in KINGSLAND ROAD, is the interesting GEFFRYE MUSEUM (V, A3; adm., p. 32), occupying the charming Ironmongers' Almshouses, built round a spacious forecourt about 1715 under a bequest of Sir Robert Geffrye, a master of the Ironmongers' Company and Lord Mayor of London in 1685–6. At the time of their erection the almshouses were in rural surroundings, but by the beginning of the present century they had become absorbed in an industrial quarter. In 1912 new almshouses were built at Mottingham (Kent) and the property was taken over by the L.C.C., who opened it as a museum in 1914. Above the entrance is a copy of a statue (by John van Nost) of Sir Robert Geffrye (d. 1704). The almshouses chapel has been restored and the rooms contain a fascinating collection of furniture and woodwork, from Elizabethan times to the 1930s, with panelling, doorways, staircases, etc., from old London houses. In the north wing are children's workrooms and in the south wing is an exhibition hall. The museum, situated in a cabinet-making district, is designed partly to assist students, who may use the reference library and seek technical advice from the staff.

33 From the Bank to Aldgate via Cornhill, returning via Fenchurch Street

Plan V, E1–V, E3

STATIONS: BANK (Plan V, E1), see Route 28; ALDGATE (V, E3), on the Circle and Metropolitan lines; ALDGATE EAST (beyond V, E3), on the District and Metropolitan lines; MONUMENT (V, F2), on the Circle and District lines, connected to Bank by escalator. — BUSES Nos. 15 and 25 in Cornhill and Leadenhall Street, and Nos. 10, 40, and 44 in Fenchurch Street (all these continue along Aldgate High Street); Nos. 8A, 35, 47, and 48 in Gracechurch Street; Nos. 23, 42 and 78 in the Minories and Mansell Street (to and from Tower Hill or Tower Bridge); Nos. 5, 22A, and 78 in Middlesex Street and Houndsditch (to and from Bishopsgate).

CORNHILL (V, E1, 2), a busy centre of commerce named from a former grain-market, leads east from the Bank, passing the Royal Exchange (Route 28) on its south side. Thomas Gray, the poet, was born in 1716 in the house whose site is occupied by No. 39. On the same side is ST MICHAEL'S CORNHILL (adm., p. 35), a church of Saxon foundation, rebuilt by Wren in 1670–72 and greatly restored by Sir George Gilbert Scott in 1857–60. The handsome Gothic tower, 130 ft high, with delicately carved pinnacles, was added in 1718–24 by Nicholas Hawksmoor. The bench-ends, carved about 1850 by W. Gibbs Rogers, are worth notice. William Boyce, the composer, was organist of the church in 1736–68. The first London coffee-house was opened in St Michael's Alley, close by, in 1652.

Farther on is ST PETER'S CORNHILL (adm., p. 35), long thought to be the earliest church in London, on the strength of an old brass tablet in the vestry claiming it to have been founded in A.D. 179 by

'Lucius, the first Christian king of this land, then called Britaine'. The church, rebuilt by Wren in 1677–81, has an Italianate brick tower and an unusual chancel-screen, the only one known to be designed by Wren and still in its place. Memorial windows to the Fifth Army (1916–18) and the Royal Tank Regiment were dedicated in 1960. The organ was originally built by Father Smith, but the manual on which Mendelssohn played in 1840 is preserved in the vestry. George Borrow, the author, was married in this church in 1840.

Cornhill ends at the point from which Bishopsgate leads north, passing Threadneedle Street (Route 32), and Gracechurch Street runs south towards London Bridge (see Route 34). It is extended eastward by LEADENHALL STREET (V, E2, 3), the chief centre of the shipping industry.

An opening on the right gives access to LEADENHALL MARKET, rebuilt in 1881 (by Sir Horace Jones) and dealing mainly in meat, game, and provisions. This site, occupied as a market since the 14th century, was the centre of Roman London, and remains of a basilica, or town hall (of the late 1st century A.D.), and other administrative buildings were discovered in 1881.

Many new office blocks have been built in Leadenhall Street and the neighbouring streets in recent years. On the north of the street is the P. & O. BUILDING (1968) and set back behind an open court is the COMMERCIAL UNION ASSURANCE building (1969), with a tower 387 ft high. Both buildings are by Gollins, Melvin, Ward & Partners.

On the south of Leadenhall Street rises the striking new building of LLOYD'S (V, E2), begun in 1980 to a revolutionary design by Richard Rogers & Partners, with lifts and stairways, pipes and ducts, all on the outside (to be completed in 1986). The building will include a public viewing gallery, with an exhibition on the history of Lloyd's. The present headquarters, on the opposite corner of Lime Street, were designed by Terence Heysham (1952–7). Of the previous headquarters, by Sir Edwin Cooper (1925–8), on the site of the new building, only the entrance archway survives.

The ceiling and fittings in the Committee Room in the older building, with decoration by Robert Adam and Thomas Carter, were brought from the beautiful 18th-century dining room at Bowood, Wiltshire (part of a wing demolished in 1955), but are to be incorporated in the new building.

Lloyd's is an association of underwriters (about 22,000 members) incorporated in 1871 for the promotion of marine insurance and the diffusion of shipping intelligence. It grew out of a gathering of merchants at the coffee-house kept in 1688 in

Tower Street and later in Lombard Street by Edward Lloyd, who posted up shipping information for the benefit of his patrons. These customers formed their own committee in 1771, and in 1774 took rooms at the Royal Exchange. In 1811 a trust deed was adopted giving Lloyd's a 'constitution' and since 1911 all kinds of insurance (except long-term life assurance) have been undertaken. Lloyd's maintain agents in every part of the world who send in a ceaseless flow of marine information. *Lloyd's News*, a single sheet giving shipping information, was first published in 1696 (but ran for nine months only); *Lloyd's List*, started in 1734, is still published. Foreign members were admitted for the first time in 1968, women in 1969.

The Underwriting Room in the older building is an elegant chamber 340 ft long with the caller's rostrum near the centre. Bad news is signalled by one stroke and good news by two strokes on the Lutine Bell, salvaged from a frigate of that name which sank in 1799 while carrying a cargo of gold specie valued at £1,400,000 and insured at Lloyd's. The Nelson Room holds many relics of the great admiral, together with his portrait by Lemuel Abbott and the log-book of the *Euryalus*, his signal-frigate at Trafalgar, containing the only record of his famous message. At the outer corners of the older building are carved panels symbolizing Air, Sea, Fire, and Land, by James Woodford.

The new building of Lloyd's stands on the site (from 1726) of East India House, where Charles Lamb, James Mill, and John Stuart Mill were clerks in the employment of the East India Company, chartered by Elizabeth I in 1600 and dissolved in 1858.

At the foot of St Mary Axe, on the left, is the church of ST ANDREW UNDERSHAFT, rebuilt in 1520–32, except for the lower part of the tower (15th century), and given a new east gable in 1876. The name is apparently derived from a maypole shaft, taller than the church, which until 1517 was set up each May Day outside it. Notable are the door with its knocker in the tower, the beautiful 17th-century pulpit, and the font by Nicholas Stone (1631). The fine nave ceiling was rebuilt in 1950 using the old bosses. Of the several excellent monuments the most interesting is that at the east end of the north aisle to John Stow (d. 1605), author of the *Survey of London* (1598), an alabaster tomb by Nicholas Johnson. The quill in Stow's hand is renewed by the Lord Mayor at a service held annually in April. The monument on the north wall to Sir Hugh Hamersley, Lord Mayor in 1627, is remarkable for the finely sculptured figures of the attendants; that in the chancel to Sir Thomas Offley, Lord Mayor in 1556, is by Gerard Johnson. Hans Holbein, the painter, lived in the parish, as recorded by a tablet in the south aisle, and he may have died here (of the plague, 1543). The west window contains heraldic glass and royal portraits, partly of the 17th century.

On the right in St Mary Axe is the BALTIC EXCHANGE (V, E3), rebuilt in 1903 and enlarged in 1956, the headquarters of merchants and shipping brokers (about 700 companies) who deal in grain, timber, coal, oil and other floating cargoes. It was formed in the early 18th century by the amalgamation of two exchanges, one of which was named from the 'Virginian and Baltick' coffee-house, and hence it has nothing specifically to do with the Baltic. The markets are most active from 12 to 1.30 and from 4 to 4.30. In the same building is the INSTITUTE OF CHARTERED SHIP-BROKERS, founded in 1911. In Bury Court, on the right, beyond, is the CHAMBER OF SHIPPING, by Sir John Burnet, Tait, and Lorne (1939). St Mary Axe ends at Bevis Marks (see below).

Farther on in Leadenhall Street is ST KATHARINE CREECHURCH, i.e., Christchurch (from an Augustinian priory of that name founded in 1108). The tower dates from 1504, but the body of the church was rebuilt in 1628–31 and consecrated by William Laud, then bishop of London, the 'Popish' character of the service later being cited against him at his trial. Near the south-west angle is a pier of the previous church, now projecting only 3 ft above the floor, the level of which has risen some 15 ft in the rebuilding. The 17th-century plaster ceiling has bosses with the arms of the chief City livery companies. The organ is by Father Smith (1686); the font bears the arms of Sir John Gayer, Lord Mayor in 1646, whose escape from a lion in Arabia is commemorated by the 'Lion Sermon' given annually on 16 October. In the south chapel is a monument to Sir Nicholas Throckmorton (d. 1571), ambassador to France, after whom Throgmorton Street is named.

In the south aisle are remarkable Stations of the Cross, painted by Arnold Daghani, an Austrian artist; and a window here, by M. C. Farrar Bell (1963), commemorates the troopship *Lancastria*, sunk in 1940. The east window has 17th-century glass in the form of a Catherine wheel. An extensive restoration was completed in 1962, when the church became the headquarters of the Industrial Christian Fellowship, formed in 1877.

Leadenhall Street is joined by Fenchurch Street (see p. 310) at the quaint ALDGATE PUMP, a 'draught' (draft) on which was long a facetious expression for a worthless bill. Near the corner of Duke's Place stood (until 1760) the Ald Gate, the easternmost of the City gates, the house above which was leased by Geoffrey Chaucer in 1374. ALDGATE and its continuation, ALDGATE HIGH STREET (V, E3), going on eastward, are the approach to a once distinctively Jewish quarter, the beginning of the 'East End' of London.

In JEWRY STREET, running south from Aldgate to Crutched Friars (see below), is the Science and Technology School of the CITY OF LONDON POLYTECHNIC, in a building by A. W. Cooksey (1902), extended by Verner O. Rees (1934). This formerly housed one of the schools of the SIR JOHN CASS FOUNDATION, established in 1710 for poor children by Alderman Sir John Cass (d. 1718), whose Primary School (rebuilt in 1909) is on the north side of Aldgate.

On the north of Aldgate is the approach to DUKE'S PLACE and Houndsditch (see below). Duke's Place is extended by BEVIS MARKS, in which (at No. 12) is the entrance to the SPANISH AND PORTUGUESE SYNAGOGUE, the oldest synagogue in England, founded in Creechurch Lane near by in 1657 and rebuilt here in 1701. Bevis Marks has been widened in recent years and several new office blocks have been built. Outstanding among these is BURY COURT HOUSE, by Lister Drew & Associates (1983), with a glass-panelled façade and a glass canopy over the pavement. HOLLAND HOUSE, in Bury Street alongside, was built in 1914 by H. P. Berlage, the Dutch expressionist architect. Bevis Marks is continued by Camomile Street to Bishopsgate (Route 32).

HOUNDSDITCH, which runs north-west to Bishopsgate, was the centre of Jewish brokers and dealers, and is the scene of an animated street market on Sunday mornings. At its foot is the church of ST BOTOLPH ALDGATE (V, E3), founded in 1125 and rebuilt in 1741–4 by George Dance the Elder, with a prominent steeple. The interior was much altered in the late 19th century, and the south end has been restored after being hit by a bomb in 1941. The lectern, given in 1943, is made of oak from the roof of Guildhall, destroyed in 1940. In the vestry (not usually shown) is preserved a mummified head said to be that of the Duke of Suffolk (father of Lady Jane Grey), beheaded in 1554. J. S. Cotman, the landscape painter, was a churchwarden here, and William Symington (d. 1831), a pioneer of steam navigation, is buried in the churchyard.

Farther up in Houndsditch is the administrative building of the CITY OF LONDON POLYTECHNIC, which has 3,000 full-time and 12,000 part-time students in its four schools. The MINORIES (pronounced 'Minneries'), a street leading south from Aldgate High Street to Tower Hill (Route 34), takes its name from a vanished convent of Minoresses or nuns of St Clare (founded in 1294). In the former precincts the remains of Anne Mowbray, Duchess of York, who died in 1481 at the age of eight, were brought to light in 1964, and she was re-buried in her coffin in Westminster Abbey. On the right beyond the street is the ALDGATE COACH STATION, behind which rises the huge BAIN DAWES HOUSE, by Trehearne and Norman Preston & Partners (1982).

The HOOP AND GRAPES, on the right of Aldgate High Street, is a 17th-century tavern, well restored in 1982. MIDDLESEX STREET, on the left, leading to Liverpool Street Station (Route 32), is better known under its popular name of Petticoat Lane. The cosmopolitan street market held here on Sunday mornings is one of the more curious sights of London. Aldgate High Street is prolonged beyond Middlesex Street by WHITECHAPEL HIGH STREET. On the right is the large SEDGWICK CONFERENCE CENTRE, by Fitzroy Robinson & Partners (1985), containing the Chaucer Theatre, an exhibition area, and conference and seminar rooms. Farther on is the SIR JOHN CASS SCHOOL OF ART of the City of London Polytechnic, and on the other side of the street, adjoining the east exit from Aldgate East station (see below), is the WHITECHAPEL ART GALLERY, built in 1899 by C. H. Townsend under the inspiration of the Art Nouveau style. Loan exhibitions of unusual interest are held at frequent intervals (adm., p. 36).

The High Street goes on to penetrate the district of WHITECHAPEL, once mainly occupied by Jewish traders, whose clothing shops have been taken over by Bangladeshis and Bengalis. COMMERCIAL ROAD, diverging on the right, is a long and busy thoroughfare giving access to the London Docklands (see Suburban London).

COMMERCIAL STREET, starting near the west exit from Aldgate East station, leads northward to Shoreditch (Route 23). On the right in this street is TOYNBEE HALL, the first of the Universities Settlements, a social service centre founded in 1884 by Canon Samuel Barnett and named in honour of Arnold Toynbee (d. 1883), the economist and reformer, who worked in Whitechapel from 1875. The buildings, much damaged in the war (though the hall, with murals by Archibald Ziegler, survived), were reconstructed in 1967–70. ATTLEE HOUSE, part of Toynbee Hall, built in 1972 (by David Manley), is a memorial to Lord Attlee (d. 1967), the Labour Prime Minister, and an experimental 'social workshop'.

Farther on in Commercial Street is CHRIST CHURCH (V, D3), formerly the parish church of Spitalfields, a manufacturing district. It belonged in medieval times to the priory of St Mary Spital, founded in 1197 but long since disappeared. The church, with its heavy portico and wide tower, is a characteristic work of Nicholas Hawksmoor (1714–29), and has a good 18th-century pulpit and a monument of 1794 by Flaxman. Opposite is the LONDON FRUIT EXCHANGE, with an auction room accommodating 400 buyers (sales on Mondays and Wednesdays). Beyond to the left is the large SPITALFIELDS MARKET, the principal East End market for fruit, flowers, and vegetables, founded in about 1680, rebuilt in 1886–93 (the eastern part survives) and again in 1928.

To the north and east of the market is a quarter occupied in the 18th century by silk merchants and weavers, some of whose houses have been well restored by the Spitalfields Trust, set up for this purpose in 1977. Fine houses of 1722–8 survive in FOURNIER STREET, north of Christ Church, including the Rectory (No. 2), designed by Hawksmoor. The GREAT MOSQUE, at the east end, was built in 1743 as a Huguenot chapel and later became a synagogue, but was converted in 1976 for Bangladeshi immigrants. In PRINCELET STREET, to the north, No. 4, built in 1724, was first occupied by Benjamin Truman, the brewer. No. 19, a house of about 1718, has been restored as the Spitalfields Centre for the Study of Minorities. WILKES STREET, linking these two streets, has houses of 1721, among them No. 11, with a rare timber doorcase, and No. 1, which retains its long windows in the attic for throwing light on to silk weavers' looms. No. 106 in COMMERCIAL STREET, north-east of the market, was formerly a horse and carriage repository. Nos. 135–53, farther on, were the first flats (1863–4) built by the Peabody Trust, founded in 1862 by George Peabody, the American philanthropist, to provide working-class housing in London. ELDER STREET, to the west, has houses of 1725–7, including Nos. 5 and 7, with rows of weavers' windows. Mark Gertler, the painter, lived in 1912–15 at No. 28.

FENCHURCH STREET (V, E2, 3), running south-west at first from Aldgate Pump (see p. 307), contains the offices of many shipping companies. On the left is LLOYD'S REGISTER OF SHIPPING, which occupies a decorative building of 1901 by T. E. Collcutt.

This society, which has no connection with Lloyd's, was founded in 1760 for the classification of merchant ships in accordance with their strength and cargo-carrying capacity. A committee of merchants, shipowners, and underwriters supervises the construction of new ships and fixes the load-lines of merchant vessels, while a staff of ship and engine surveyors is maintained in all the chief ports of the world. *Lloyd's Register*, issued annually, gives the particulars of all ships carrying merchandise, British and foreign, of 100 tons or upwards in deadweight. The highest class for iron and steel ships is 100 A 1 and for wooden ships A 1, a symbol that has become a guarantee of good faith in the shipping world ('A 1 at Lloyd's').

Railway Place, on the same side farther west, gives access to FENCHURCH STREET STATION (V, E, F3), a terminus of the Eastern Region, opened in 1853 but now being rebuilt (1985) behind its façade of 1883. At the corner of Mark Lane, just beyond, is the war memorial building (by Ronald Ward and Partners, 1957) of the INSTITUTE OF MARINE ENGINEERS, founded in 1889.

On the right in MARK LANE, which leads south to Great Tower Street (see Route 34), is the restored 15th-century tower of ALL HALLOWS STAINING. The church was demolished in 1870, but two years later a 12th-century crypt chapel, from the hermitage of St James-on-the-Wall near Cripplegate, was re-erected here by the Clothworkers' Company. In HART STREET, starting opposite Dunster House (occupied by shipping companies), is ST OLAVE'S CHURCH (V, F3), dedicated to King Olaf, the patron-saint of Norway, after his martyrdom in 1030, mostly rebuilt in 1450, but sadly wrecked by bombing in 1941. From this ordeal only the tower, heightened in 1732, the vaulted 12th-century crypt, and the panelled vestry of 1662 (on the south) escaped. The church was reopened after its restoration (retaining some of the fire-blackened stones) in 1954. On the north of the chancel is a delightful bust of Elizabeth Pepys (d. 1669), sculptured by John Bushnell and placed here by her husband Samuel Pepys (d. 1703), who was a regular worshipper from the time he became secretary at the Navy Office (see below). Both Pepys and his wife are buried in the vault beneath the chancel, and the diarist is commemorated by a bust of 1883 on the wall of the south aisle (above the Navy Officers' gallery where he had his pew) and an annual service in May. The east window contains striking glass (a war memorial) by A. E. Buss (1954), and other windows by the same artist show the arms of the Port of London Authority, the Clothworkers' Company, and the Corn Exchange. The south aisle is the chapel of the corporation of Trinity House, who attend a service here every Trinity Monday. The finely-carved pulpit (possibly by Gibbons) and the altar-rails date from the 17th century and the communion-table from the 18th century. The skulls above the churchyard gate (1658) in SEETHING LANE, on the east, are referred to by Dickens as 'St Ghastly Grim' in *The Uncommercial Traveller*. Pepys lived in Seething Lane from 1660, when he became Clerk of the Acts to the Navy Board, but later moved into the Navy Office in CRUTCHED FRIARS (i.e., 'Crossed Friars', from a vanished friary of the Holy Cross), the continuation of Hart Street. A garden, with a bust of the diarist, by Karen Jonzen (1983), marks the site of his house. No. 42 in this street (now the regional office of Toc H) is an excellent residence of the early 18th century.

MINCING LANE, farther west, said by Stow to be named from the 'minchens' or nuns of St Helen's (Bishopsgate), is the centre of the colonial tea and wine trades. At the corner of Fenchurch Street a new CLOTHWORKERS' HALL was opened in 1958; the first hall of the company, built in 1482, perished in the Great Fire and the third hall, opened in 1860, was destroyed in an air-raid in 1941. The Clothworkers, one of the twelve great livery companies, were incorporated in 1528, and possess a loving-cup presented by Samuel Pepys, who was Master in 1677. Rood Lane, on the left farther on, leads to St Margaret Pattens church in Eastcheap (Route 34).

Opposite Mincing Lane is FOUNTAIN HOUSE, a fourteen-storey office building by W. H. Rogers and Sir Howard Robertson (1958), one of the first of the new commercial skyscrapers in the City. Between Mincing Lane and Rood Lane is PLANTATION HOUSE, accommodating the LONDON COMMODITY EXCHANGE, which deals in the sales or purchases of cocoa, coffee, rubber, sugar, wool, vegetable oils, and many other commodities, and the LONDON METAL EXCHANGE, moved here in 1980 and dealing in copper, lead, tin, zinc, silver, and aluminium.

Fenchurch Street is continued beyond Gracechurch Street (Route 34) by LOMBARD STREET, (V, E2), the banking and financial centre of London since the Middle Ages. It takes its name from the Lombard merchants from northern Italy who settled here as early as the 12th century and established themselves as money-lenders after the expulsion of the Jews. Some of the numerous banks in the street hang out signs in the medieval fashion. No. 54 is BARCLAYS BANK, founded in 1896; No. 67 is WILLIAMS & GLYN'S (incorporating Glyn, Mills, founded in 1753), now part of the Royal Bank of Scotland. No. 68 was the London office of MARTIN'S BANK (founded in Liverpool in 1563), the oldest bank in England, but merged with Barclays Bank in 1969. No. 71 is LLOYDS BANK (founded in Birmingham in 1765), occupying a building by Sir John J. Burnet (1930).

On the north side of Lombard Street is the church of ST EDMUND THE KING (adm., p. 34), dedicated to the king of East Anglia martyred by the Danes in 870, rebuilt in 1670–79 by Wren, and restored after being hit by a bomb in 1917. It has an unusual steeple, added in 1708, and good woodwork (pulpit, font cover, etc.). Joseph Addison, the author, was married in this church in 1716 to the Dowager Countess of Warwick. In Post Office Court, to the left farther on, is the BANKERS' CLEARING HOUSE, established in 1770 and rebuilt in 1951.

This is an institution through which the claims on each other of certain banks (called 'clearing banks') during each day can be compared and the difference settled by means of a cheque on the Bank of England. The total amount in cheques and bills that changes hands in the course of a day averages £21,800 million. The clearing banks are Barclays, Lloyds, the Midland, and the National Westminster (which formerly made up the 'big five'), together with Coutts' and Williams & Glyn's. In the same building are the influential INSTITUTE OF BANKERS, founded in 1879, and the BRITISH BANKERS' ASSOCIATION, with a membership of nearly 300 banks.

Lombard Street skirts the north side of St Mary Woolnoth church to join King William Street just short of the BANK (see below).

34 From the Bank to London Bridge or to the Tower and Tower Bridge

Plan V, E1–IX, E3

STATIONS: BANK (Plan V, E1), see Route 28; MONUMENT (V, F2; escalator connection to Bank) and TOWER HILL (V, F3), on the Circle and District lines. — BUSES Nos. 21, 43, 133, and 501 in King William Street; Nos. 8A, 10, 35, 40, 44, 47, and 48 in Gracechurch Street; No. 23 in Eastcheap and Tower Hill; Nos. 23, 42, and 78 in the Minories and Mansell Street; Nos. 42 and 78 across Tower Bridge; Nos. 47 and 70 in Tooley Street or Druid Street (to the south); across London Bridge, see Route 25; in Fenchurch Street, see Route 33.

KING WILLIAM STREET (V, E1–F2), named after William IV, runs south-east from the BANK (Route 28) to London Bridge. On the left, at the beginning of Lombard Street (Route 33), is the church of ST MARY WOOLNOTH (open weekdays), the most original work of Nicholas Hawksmoor, a pupil of Wren. Built in 1716–24, it has a rusticated west front with an oblong tower from which rise unusual square turrets. The striking entrance leads into a rich interior, square in plan and with a group of triple Corinthian columns at each corner. The church has a good reredos in the form of a baldacchino, fine ironwork altar-rails, and a carved pulpit with an unusual canopy; against the walls have been set the former fronts of the galleries. On the north wall is a tablet to John Newton (d. 1807), the evangelist, joint author with Cowper of the *Olney Hymns*. He was rector of St Mary Woolnoth from 1779 until his death, but his remains were later removed to Olney (Buckinghamshire). On the south wall is a tablet to Edward Lloyd (d. 1713), the coffee-house proprietor.

In Clement's Lane, on the left farther on, is ST CLEMENT'S EASTCHEAP (adm., p. 34), a church rebuilt by Wren in 1683–7, but restored internally in 1872 by Butterfield and again in 1933 by Sir Ninian Comper. It contains notable 17th-century woodwork (font cover, pulpit with sounding board, and reredos), and tablets commemorate Thomas Fuller (d. 1661), the historian, who lectured here from 1647; John Pearson (d. 1686), later bishop of Chester, who gave his celebrated *Exposition of the Creed* here; and Brian Walton (d. 1661), compiler of the Polyglot Bible and likewise bishop of Chester, who was rector of St Martin Orgars (since pulled down) from 1628.

King William Street reaches an irregular open space formed by the junction of Cannon Street, leading west to St Paul's (Route 25), Gracechurch Street, running north-east to Bishopsgate (Route 32), and Eastcheap, which leads east towards the Tower. On the south is the entrance to the MONUMENT STATION (V, F2), from one side of which King William Street goes to LONDON BRIDGE (see Route 25), while a little to the east Fish Street Hill descends to the Monument (Route 25) and St Magnus the Martyr's Church (Route 27). Gracechurch Street derives its name from the vanished St Benet Gracechurch ('grass church', probably because it stood in a grassy plot), while EASTCHEAP (V, F2) was so called to distinguish it from Cheapside (compare Route 29).

In Lovat Lane, on the right, is an entrance to ST MARY-AT-HILL (adm., p. 35), a medieval church only partly destroyed in the Great Fire. The east end and the interior were rebuilt by Wren in 1670–76, but the old west end and tower survived until 1780 and the north and south walls until about 1830. The organ-case, font, reredos, and box-pews (among the few old pews in the City) all date from the 17th century, but the pulpit and reading-desk and the carvings on the gallery were added in 1849 by W. Gibbs Rogers. Edward Young, author of *Night Thoughts*, was married here in 1731 and Wilson Carlile, founder of the Church Army, was rector from 1891 to 1926. According to Stow, Thomas Becket was at some time 'parson' here. In St Mary-at-Hill, the lane on the east, are a fine projecting clock and a passage (on the south) with a skull and crossbones over the entrance.

On the left, near the beginning of GREAT TOWER STREET, is the church of ST MARGARET PATTENS (adm., p. 35), named, according to Stow, from the pattens (clogs with iron rings on the soles for keeping shoes out of the mud) formerly made in the adjoining Rood Lane (two pairs are preserved in a case on the south wall). The church, founded in 1067, was rebuilt in 1684–7 by Wren, with a simple but effective spire, 199 ft high. At the west end are two canopied pews (unique in London), one of which bears the monogram 'CW 1686' and is most probably that of the architect himself. The alabaster font has been attributed to Grinling Gibbons. The north gallery, converted into conference rooms in 1956, is now used as offices by the College of Preachers.

On the right of Great Tower Street, at No. 26, are the CHRIST'S HOSPITAL OFFICES (compare Route 23), in a building of 1915 by Sir Reginald Blomfield.

MARK LANE (originally 'Mart'), leading on the left to Fenchurch Street (see Route 33), is the centre of the grain trade. King's Beam House, at the corner, is the headquarters (1956) of the BOARD OF CUSTOMS AND EXCISE. The Commissioners of Customs, first appointed by Charles II in 1671, were previously accommodated in Lower Thames Street (Route 27); the Excise Department was divorced from the Inland Revenue Department in 1909. The CORN EXCHANGE, on the right in Mark Lane, founded originally in 1750 and rebuilt in 1880, was seriously damaged in 1941 and reopened in 1953. The principal market is held on Mondays from 12 to 3.

Byward Street leads left from Great Tower Street to Trinity Square, passing the ancient church of ALL HALLOWS BARKING BY THE TOWER (V, F3; adm., p. 31), founded as early as about 675, mostly rebuilt in the 13th–15th centuries, and sadly damaged by bombing in 1940. The north aisle was reopened for service in 1949, and the other work of restoration (by Lord Mottistone and Paul Paget) completed in 1957. The name 'Barking' refers to the early possession of the church by the Abbey of Barking, in Essex. A 7th-century arch can be seen in the lower part of the tower, which escaped the bombing, and during the clearance of damage parts of a Saxon cross of the 11th century were brought to light. The brick tower, erected in 1658, is the only example in London of church building surviving from the Commonwealth; from it Samuel Pepys viewed the devastation caused by the Great Fire (Diary: 5 September 1666). A handsome new steeple was added in 1959. Above the north porch, built on in 1884 by J. L. Pearson, are statues of St Ethelburga, the first abbess of Barking, and Bishop Lancelot Andrewes, who was born in the parish and baptized here (1555). William Penn, the founder of Pennsylvania, born on Tower Hill, was also baptized in the church (1644); and here John Quincy Adams, sixth President of the United States, was married in 1797.

Since 1922 All Hallows has been the guild church of TOC H, an organization for Christian fellowship founded originally at Poperinghe (Belgium) by the Rev. Neville Talbot and the Rev. P. B. Clayton (d. 1972), long vicar of the church, and named Talbot House (the initials of which are 'Toc H' in the army signaller's old alphabet) in memory of Lieut. Gilbert Talbot, killed in action in 1915. The 'Lamp of Maintenance', from which all other Toc H lamps are lit, is kept on the 15th-century altar-tomb at the east end of the North Aisle of All Hallows, and the ashes of many members of the organization are deposited in the vault.

Also in the north aisle are a war-memorial effigy of Alfred Forster (son of the governor-general of Australia), by Cecil Thomas (1926), and part of a 15th-century Flemish triptych (the centre panel is missing) apparently ordered by Sir Robert Tate, Lord Mayor in 1488. In the Nave are 18th-century sword-rests and a pulpit of about 1670 from the demolished church of St Swithun in Cannon Street. The South Aisle, now the Mariners' Chapel, has a 16th-century Spanish crucifix. Under the east end is an interesting 14th-century Crypt, opened out in 1926 and reserved for private prayer, and adjoining this is a small 17th-century vault. A Memorial Chapel constructed beneath the chancel contains the crusading altar originally in Richard I's castle at Athlit in the north of Israel. Under the tower is a Roman tessellated pavement, in its original position. Near the Baptistery at the west end can be seen the Saxon arch mentioned above and a font of 1944 carved from a piece of the Rock of Gibraltar, with an exquisite cover attributed to Grinling Gibbons (saved from the bombing). The church has much heraldic glass, and an extensive series of 14th–17th-century brasses (the finest collection in London).

The sculpture on the east gable of the church, showing the Toc H lamp, is also by Cecil Thomas. The terrace below this, constructed in 1951, affords a characteristic view of the Tower. The west side of Tower Hill is now enclosed by TOWER PLACE, a huge office building designed by George, Trew, and Dunn (1965), with a large coach park underneath. The sculpture of the 'Hammer Thrower', in bronze glass fibre, is by John Robinson (1973). Near the foot of Tower Hill and the end of Lower Thames Street (Route 27) is the TOWER PIER of the river steamers. A ferry crosses the Thames from here to H.M.S. *Belfast*.

TOWER HILL (V, F3), the broad open space to the north-west of the **Tower of London** (adm., p. 434), is a place of great historic interest, the principal scene of the execution of traitors confined in the Tower. No fewer than seventy-five are known to have suffered here, from Sir Simon Burley, the supporter of Richard II (1388), to Simon Fraser, Lord Lovat (1757). The site of the scaffold is marked by a square of pavement, a memorial to the Earl of Kilmarnock and Lord Balmerino, the Jacobites (beheaded in 1746), in the garden of TRINITY SQUARE, on the north-east side. Here also the striking MERCHANT SEAMEN'S WAR MEMORIALS to men of the Merchant Navy, the fishing fleets, and the lighthouse and pilotage services who lost their lives in the two World Wars. That on the south, designed by Sir Edwin Lutyens (1928), commemorates the 12,000 of the mercantile marine who died in 1914–18. The second memorial, unveiled in 1955, was designed by Sir Edward Maufe (with sculptures by Sir Charles Wheeler) in memory of nearly 24,000 merchant seamen who died in 1939–45 and have no grave but the sea. On the north-west side of Trinity Square rises an ornate and massive building, the former headquarters of the PORT OF LONDON AUTHORITY (now at Tilbury, in Essex), designed by Sir Edwin Cooper and completed in 1922, with a prominent tower 170 ft high. The over-large sculptures are by Albert Hodge (on the tower) and C. L. J. Domen.

TRINITY HOUSE (V, F3; adm., p. 35), on the north side of the square, was rebuilt in 1793–5 by Samuel Wyatt for the 'Guild, Fraternity, or Brotherhood of the Trinity', already a body of some importance when it was granted its first charter by Henry VIII in 1514. The building, severely damaged from the air in 1940, was well restored and extended in 1953 by Sir Albert Richardson. On the front are the arms of the corporation and medallions of George III and Queen Charlotte.

The corporation comprises a Master (at present the Duke of Edinburgh), a Deputy Master, and about twenty Elder Brethren (usually including several heads of state and chiefs of the armed forces), as well as a much larger number of Younger Brethren. Trinity House is entrusted with the duty of erecting and maintaining lighthouses, lightships, and other seamarks; it is the chief pilotage authority in

Britain, and it attends to the relief of aged and distressed master mariners. Until 1874 Masters of the Navy were examined by the Elder Brethren, and these still sit with the judges of the Admiralty division in deciding marine causes in the High Court of Justice.

In the Front Hall are models of ships (including the first lightship, 1796) and lead statues of Captain Richard Maples (d. 1680), by Jasper Latham (the oldest in lead by a British sculptor), and Captain Robert Sandes, deputy master in 1719–21, by Scheemakers. The Court Room, upstairs, is hung with royal portraits by Sir William Beechey and others. The new extension, on the east, contains the Library, used also as a banqueting hall.

Several sections of the old CITY WALL have been disclosed in this neighbourhood. Behind the entrance to Tower Hill station, east of Trinity Square, can be seen an impressive stretch of the medieval wall, incorporating re-used Roman material and standing fully 20 ft in height, with some remains of the parapet and sentry walk. A further stretch of Roman wall is preserved in the basement of Talbot House (No. 42) in Trinity Square; visitors are usually admitted by courtesy of the Warden (but not on Saturdays and Sundays, or after 6 p.m.). An impressive third section, about 110 ft long and 32 ft high, showing Roman and medieval work, can be seen behind an office building (Midland House) in Cooper's Row, just to the north.

On a terrace in front of Tower Hill station are a copy of a funerary inscription to Julius Classicianus, Procurator of Britain from A.D. 61 to about 65 (the original is in the British Museum), and a bronze statue believed to be of the Emperor Trajan (98–117). At the other end of a subway leading to TOWER GARDENS are the remains of a medieval postern gate (probably of the late 13th century) of the City wall.

Beyond the City Wall, at the foot of The Minories (Route 33), is the large new building of the SCHOOL OF NAVIGATION of the City of London Polytechnic. The CRESCENT, behind, preserves some houses of 1760–70 by George Dance the Younger, with good doorcases. Beyond Mansell Street, farther east, is a classical building of 1811 (by James Johnson and Sir Robert Smirke), enlarged in 1882, formerly the ROYAL MINT, but a new mint was completed in 1975 at Llantrisant, near Cardiff, and all coins are now minted there.

EAST SMITHFIELD, on the left of Tower Hill at the beginning of the approach to Tower Bridge (see below), leads past EUROPE HOUSE, an old warehouse reconstructed in 1969–72, by Renton, Howard, and Wood, as the main administrative building of the LONDON WORLD TRADE CENTRE, with conference rooms, an exhibition area, accommodation for visitors, and many other facilities. Beyond is the entrance to ST KATHARINE'S DOCKS (IX, D3;

the public car park, farther east, is entered from Thomas More Street). The dock system (the farthest upstream of London's docks), covering an area of twenty-three acres (ten acres of water), was constructed in 1824–8 by Thomas Telford, but the buildings around the three docks were designed by Philip Hardwick. The docks ceased to operate commercially in 1968 and have been converted into a yacht harbour and a floating museum of old craft.

Facing the entrance, and lying between the East and West Docks, is IVORY HOUSE, built in 1854 as an export warehouse, but partly rebuilt and containing shops and luxury flats, the yacht club headquarters, and the yacht haven office. Behind it is the CENTRAL BASIN, a third dock which is linked to the others and to the Thames. The EAST DOCK has a fine collection of old ships (adm., p. 35), the property of the Maritime Trust.

The *Robin*, a steam coaster built in 1890 on the Thames at Blackwall, and the *Lydia Eva*, built in 1930 at King's Lynn (Norfolk) and the only survivor of a steam-powered herring drifter, have both been refitted as museums. Also here are the *Kathleen & May*, a topsail schooner built in 1900 on the Dee near Chester, the *Cambria*, a Thames spritsail barge built in 1906 at Greenhithe (Kent), and the steam tug *Challenge*, built in 1931 in Scotland for work on the Thames. On loan to the trust is the Nore Light Vessel, built in 1931 in the Isle of Wight. H.M.S. *Discovery*, the polar research ship of Captain R. F. Scott, launched at Dundee in 1901, was brought here in 1979 for restoration and refitting, is to be returned to Dundee on the completion of the work.

On shore between the East Dock and the Central Basin is the DICKENS INN, an 18th-century brewery which came to light when the warehouse enclosing it was demolished, and was then moved to its present site. To the south-east are the blocks of flats of a large new G.L.C. housing estate, and to the south-west is THE WAREHOUSE, an old dock building with an information office and a restaurant. A steel bridge of 1974 crosses the outlet from the Central Basin to reach the WEST DOCK, where several Thames spritsail barges and other sailing craft are moored. On the north side is Europe House (see above); the warehouses on the west were rebuilt in 1982, by Watkins Gray Woodgate International, as INTERNATIONAL HOUSE, a second building for the World Trade Centre. On the south side of the dock is the TOWER HOTEL, built in the modern style in 1973 by Renton Howard Wood Associates.

On the riverside promenade west of the dock entrance is a bronze fountain sculpture, 'Girl with a Dolphin', by David Wynne (1973). Steps ascend from the promenade to Tower Bridge, while a footway leads under the bridge to Tower Wharf in front of the Tower of London.

Tower Bridge Approach skirts the east side of the Tower as it leads south to TOWER BRIDGE (IX, E3), the farthest downstream of the bridges over the Thames, as well as the best known and most distinctive. Built in 1886–94 at a cost of £800,000 (£1½ million, including the approaches), it was designed by Sir Horace Jones and Sir John Wolfe Barry. The bridge is about 800 ft long between the abutment towers and 200 ft between the massive Gothic towers that rise from the river and are connected near the top by two walkways standing 142 ft above high-water level. The central span of the carriageway, reaching 29½ ft above high-water, consists of twin bascules or drawbridges, each weighing about 1,000 tons, which can be raised in a few minutes to allow the passage of large vessels, an operation that has been accomplished more than 500,000 times since the bridge was built. It is estimated that over 10,000 vehicles cross the bridge daily; the speed limit is 20 m.p.h.

The walkways (adm., p. 35), reopened in 1982, are reached by lifts and flights of 128 steps each in the towers (disabled visitors may ascend all the way by lift). They afford a panoramic view of the river and its neighbourhood. Upstream can be seen Guy's Hospital (above London Bridge station); the Victoria Tower of the Houses of Parliament; Southwark Cathedral, above Hay's Wharf; H.M.S. *Belfast*, with London Bridge behind; Centre Point, above Unilever House; the Telecom Tower; the dome of St Paul's; glimpses of the City steeples; the Monument; the church of All Hallows by the Tower; the soaring tower of the National Westminster Bank; and the old Port of London Authority building, behind the Tower of London, in which the White Tower is a prominent feature. The view downstream includes part of St Katharine's Docks, the heights of Greenwich Park, and the television masts at Crystal Palace, with the distant North Downs between. In the base of the south tower are the controls for raising the bascules. Below the bridge approach on the south, and reached by steps, is a museum (adm. as above) illustrating the history of the bridge, with a working model. Also to be seen here are the original boilers and the two steam pumping engines (built by Sir W. G. Armstrong & Company, 1894) that used to raise the bascules (raised by electrically-driven machinery since 1977).

The canyon-like street of SHAD THAMES, to the east of the bridge approach, conveys a good impression of the ranks of warehouses that once lined the Thames on both sides. A riverside walk leads westward past an Ecological Park to the wharf opposite H.M.S. *Belfast* (see below). The whole of the south bank between Tower Bridge and London Bridge is being replanned as a business centre, to be called LONDON BRIDGE CITY, incorporating some of the more historic buildings, such as Hay's Wharf (1857).

Some eight square miles of the LONDON DOCKLANDS, from Tower Bridge downstream to Woolwich, mostly on the north side of the Thames, but including the site of the Surrey Commercial Docks on the south side, are being developed under an ambitious plan formulated in 1976. Work began in 1979, the London Docklands Development Corporation was set up in 1981, and an Enterprise Zone on the Isle of Dogs (see Suburban London) was designated in 1982. New roads are being constructed, new industrial sites are being laid out, housing estates, shopping centres, and schools are being built, and open spaces and sports facilities are being provided. A light railway (to be completed in 1986) is being built from Tower Hill to the Isle of Dogs and Stratford, with connections to the underground system and to British Railways. Over £200 million is being invested by the Government in the ten years up to 1992.

On the south side of the river is the former borough of BERMONDSEY, an industrial region long inhabited by leatherworkers. Tower Bridge Road leads south across TOOLEY STREET (a corruption of St Olave's Street), the main east-to-west thoroughfare (compare Suburban London). A little west of the junction is a memorial bust of Ernest Bevin (d. 1951), the Labour statesman and 'the dockers' K.C.' Vine Lane, on the right farther on, leads to a wharf off which is moored H.M.S. BELFAST (adm., p. 31), a cruiser of 11,500 tons displacement. Commissioned in 1939, she escorted the Arctic convoys, took a leading part in the Battle of the North Cape (when the German battle cruiser 'Scharnhorst' was sunk), and opened the bombardment of the Normandy coast on 'D Day' (1944). The ship can be reached also by ferry from Tower Pier. At Nos 28–34 in Tooley Street is the LONDON DUNGEON MUSEUM (adm., p. 33), designed to illustrate the more macabre events and legends of British history (not suitable for children). Duke Street Hill bears left near the west end of the street to reach the Borough High Street beside the approach to London Bridge station (see below).

35 From London Bridge to Lambeth Bridge via the Borough High Street and Lambeth Road

Plan IX, D2–VIII, D3

STATIONS: LONDON BRIDGE (Plan IX, E2), BOROUGH (IX, F1), and ELEPHANT & CASTLE (IX, D3), all on the Northern line; the Elephant & Castle is also the terminus of the Bakerloo line, on which LAMBETH NORTH (IX, C2) is the nearest station to Lambeth Palace and Bridge; VAUXHALL (VIII, F3), on the Victoria line. London Bridge, Elephant & Castle, and Vauxhall all have stations on the Southern Region. — BUSES across London Bridge, see Route 25; Nos. 10 and 44 from London Bridge to Lambeth Bridge, via Borough Road or Elephant & Castle and Lambeth Road; also Nos. 35, 40, 95, and 133 in Borough High Street; and Nos. 3 and 159 in Lambeth Road. Nos. 44, 77, and 170 ply along the Albert Embankment.

For LONDON BRIDGE, see Route 25. The BOROUGH HIGH STREET (IX, E1–F1), which runs southward from the bridge, is the beginning of one of the great highways of England, the main approach to the Continent, as it has been since the Middle Ages. Kings and statesmen, prelates, ambassadors, and armies set out along this road, not to mention the bulk of the pilgrims bound for the shrine of St Thomas Becket at Canterbury (as related by Chaucer in *The Canterbury Tales*). The hostelries that lined the street in those and in the later coaching days, however, survive only in the names of yards.

Excavations since 1969 have located the positions of two Roman roads, built before A.D. 70 and converging at the southern bridgehead on the Thames below the present bridge (compare Route 25). One road followed more or less the course of the Borough High Street, the other probably came from a crossing of the river between Lambeth and Westminster Bridges.

Below the south end of London Bridge, on the west side, are Nancy's Steps, claimed to be those immortalized by Dickens in *Oliver Twist*, but lost to view when the bridge was rebuilt. On the left are the approaches to Tooley Street (Route 34) and to LONDON BRIDGE STATION (IX, E2), a terminus of the Southern Region. The first station to be opened in London (in connection with the London and Greenwich Railway, 1836), it was almost completely rebuilt in 1978, with two tall towerblocks rising above it. NEW LONDON BRIDGE HOUSE, facing the station, is a large office block (by Richard Seifert & Partners, 1973), with a viewing gallery overlooking the Pool of London. On the west side of the High Street rises **Southwark Cathedral** (adm., p. 422), with an approach to Bankside south of the churchyard (see Route 36).

St Thomas Street, on the left beyond the railway, leads past ST THOMAS'S CHURCH, built in 1703 as the chapel of St Thomas's Hospital (moved in 1868 to Lambeth) and now used as the chapter house of Southwark Cathedral. It incorporates the only semicircular OPERATING THEATRE in Britain, in use in 1821–62 and restored as a museum (adm., p. 34). On the right, beyond, is GUY'S HOSPITAL (IX, E1, 2), founded in 1721 by Thomas Guy, a City bookseller who made a fortune from South Sea stock. The older part, opened in 1726, is built round a forecourt and two inner quadrangles (partly damaged by bombing), and the iron gates and railings of the entrance are the originals. In the forecourt is a statue by Scheemakers of the founder (d. 1724), who is commemorated also by a fine marble monument (1779) by John Bacon the Elder in the chapel, in the west wing, which was completed in 1777. The sculpture on the centre wing (altered in 1774) is also by Bacon. In one of the quadrangles (to which visitors are usually admitted) is an alcove from old London

Bridge (1762), and in the other a statue of Lord Nuffield by Maurice Lambert (1949). Remains of a Roman boat were discovered in 1959 when digging the foundations for an eleven-storey surgical block (New Guy's House), completed in 1961. A large towerblock (Guy's Tower), 480 ft high, built by Watkins Gray Woodgate International in 1968–76, contains the dental school and hospital (established in 1892) and the children's hospital (with a school). Wolfson House, built by Architects' Co-Partnership (1975), is a hostel for medical students. John Keats was a student in 1814–16 at the medical school, founded about 1769. The medical and dental schools of Guy's and St Thomas's Hospitals were amalgamated in 1983 with the School of Dental Surgery of the Royal Dental Hospital to form the UNITED MEDICAL AND DENTAL HOSPITALS, affiliated to London University.

On the right in the Borough High Street is the BOROUGH MARKET, claiming to be the oldest municipal fruit and vegetable market in London, the successor of a market held on London Bridge in the 13th century and moved to its present site in 1756. In a courtyard on the left is the picturesque GEORGE INN (N.T.), the last remaining galleried tavern in London, rebuilt in 1677 after a fire which laid Southwark waste. In the 18th and early 19th centuries it became well known as a coaching terminus, and it is mentioned in Dickens's *Little Dorrit*, but the north wing was demolished in 1889.

In SOUTHWARK STREET, on the right, leading towards Blackfriars Bridge (Route 36), are CENTRAL BUILDINGS, formerly the Hop Exchange, built in 1866 by R. H. Moore, with iron columns on the façade, an imposing entrance, and galleries supported by iron structures round the exchange hall, which is 75 ft high (now a warehouse). The upper storeys were demolished after a fire in 1920. WHITE HART YARD, opposite the junction with Southwark Street, occupies the site of the White Hart Inn, referred to in Shakespeare's *Henry VI* and Dickens's *Pickwick Papers*. A little beyond is TALBOT YARD, on the site of the Tabard Inn, the most famous of the hostelries, from which Chaucer's Canterbury pilgrims set out on their celebrated journey.

On this side of the street stood the notorious MARSHALSEA PRISON, first heard of in the 14th century and moved farther south in 1813. Edmund Bonner, bishop of London, the adherent of Mary Tudor, died here in 1569. Adjoining it on the south was the KING'S BENCH, so called because prisoners committed by the Court of the King's Bench were incarcerated here. This is the prison to which Judge Gascoigne is said (without foundation) to have committed the Prince of Wales (later Henry V). Tobias Smollett and John Wilkes were among the many famous prisoners confined here, as was Mr Micawber in *David Copperfield*, something having failed to 'turn up'. In 1758 the prison was moved to Newington Causeway and used also for debtors, some of whom were permitted to live in lodgings close by (see Dickens's *Nicholas Nickleby*). The King's Bench was burned in 1780 during the Gordon Riots (compare *Barnaby Rudge*) and finally closed in 1860, when imprisonment for debt was abolished. The White Lion Prison, farther south, the Surrey county gaol from the 16th century, later became the site of the NEW MARSHALSEA PRISON (closed in 1849), where 'Roderick Random' and Dickens's father (in 1824) were confined for debt, and 'Little Dorrit' was born and brought up. The county gaol was established from 1798 until 1879 in UNION STREET (formerly Horsemonger Lane) and here Leigh Hunt was committed in 1812 for two years for libelling the Prince Regent as 'a fat Adonis of fifty'. In TABARD STREET, on the left farther south, No. 21 is the NATIONAL COUNCIL FOR CIVIL LIBERTIES, founded in 1934.

Great Dover Street (leading to the Old Kent Road; see Suburban London) branches left from the Borough High Street by the classical church of ST GEORGE THE MARTYR (IX, F1), rebuilt in 1734–6 (on the site of a Norman church) by John Price and restored in 1952 after its damage by bombing. Bishop Bonner (see above) and many others who died in the neighbouring prisons were buried here. General Monck was married in the church in 1652 and 'Little Dorrit' was both christened and married here. Trinity Street, on the left farther on, leads to TRINITY CHURCH SQUARE, with unspoiled early-19th-century terraces. Holy Trinity Church (by Francis Bedford, 1824), in the centre, was restored in 1975, as the HENRY WOOD HALL, and is used for orchestral rehearsals by the London Philharmonic and other orchestras. In front of the building is a 14th-century statue formerly in Westminster Hall and supposed (with no certainty) to represent King Alfred. At its south end the Borough High Street divides into two.

NEWINGTON CAUSEWAY, the left branch, leads past the INNER LONDON SESSIONS HOUSE (1921; restored in 1958) to the Elephant and Castle (see Suburban London).

BOROUGH ROAD leads right from the Borough High Street past the POLYTECHNIC OF THE SOUTH BANK (formerly the Borough Polytechnic), enlarged in 1953–76, then goes on to ST GEORGE'S CIRCUS (IX, C2, 3), an important traffic point, from which Blackfriars Road (Route 36) runs north to Blackfriars Bridge, and Westminster Bridge Road west towards County Hall (compare below). Waterloo Road, bearing right from this in a few yards, runs north-west to Waterloo Station and Bridge (Route 36).

LAMBETH ROAD (IX, C2–D1) runs south-west to Lambeth Palace and Bridge. At its junction with St George's Road is ST GEORGE'S CATHEDRAL, the principal church of the Roman Catholic diocese of Southwark, built in 1840–48 in the Decorated Gothic style by A. W. Pugin, but severely damaged during an air-raid in 1941. It was well restored and improved by Romilly B. Craze in 1953–8, with the addition of a clerestory and other new features, and a fine Lady Chapel was added on the north-west in 1963. In St George's Road, opposite, is a long terrace of early-19th-century houses.

On the south corner of Lambeth Road is a milestone in the form of an obelisk erected in 1771 in honour of the mayoralty of Brass Crosby and moved here in 1905 from St George's Circus. Lambeth Road passes the entrance to the **Imperial War Museum** (adm., p. 368), in the surviving part of the former Bethlem Hospital. The grounds, purchased in 1926 by Lord Rothermere, were converted into the GERALDINE MARY HARMSWORTH PARK in memory of his mother. Lambeth Road retains some late-Georgian houses, in one of which (No. 100) Admiral Bligh of the *Bounty* (d. 1817) lived from 1794.

Lambeth Road crosses KENNINGTON ROAD, which leads south to Kennington Park Road (see Suburban London). No. 112 is the COUNCIL FOR BRITISH ARCHAEOLOGY, founded in 1944. Houses of 1760 and later, with fine doorcases, iron balconies, etc., survive (between Nos. 125 and 143). Kennington Road ends on the north at Westminster Bridge Road. At the junction here, opposite Lambeth North station, is a large office-block (1960) incorporating CHRIST CHURCH (IX, C2), a combined Baptist and United Reformed church, built in 1876 as the successor to the old Surrey Chapel in Blackfriars Road where Rowland Hill (d. 1833 and buried here) was minister. Of the Victorian church, only the spire, erected mainly with American contributions as a memorial to Abraham Lincoln (and ringed with the stars and stripes), survived the bombing. To the south-west, in Hercules Road, in a building of 1958, is the CENTRAL OFFICE OF INFORMATION, which produces information and supplies publicity services for other government departments.

To the east of Christ Church in Westminster Bridge Road is MORLEY COLLEGE (8,000 students), founded in 1882 for working men and women, and known especially for its musical activities. Noted music directors have included Gustav Holst (from 1907) and Sir Michael Tippett (in 1940–51). The building (1924) was enlarged in 1937 (by Edward Maufe) and again in 1973 (by John Winter). Murals by John Piper, Edward Bawden, and others (1958–63) decorate the common room, the refectory, and the Emma Cons Hall; and the college has two concerts halls, a studio theatre, and an art gallery. A new Art Centre was opened in 1969 in a converted public house on the east.

On the left of Lambeth Road, farther west, is LAMBETH WALK, long known for its street market and made famous by a song and dance, but now completely rebuilt as part of a new estate. A mission church of 1910 has been converted into the Henry Moore Sculpture Studio of Morley College. Sir Philip Ben Greet (d. 1936), the actor-manager, lived at No. 160, on the right in Lambeth Road, and at No.

202, beyond the railway bridge, is the MARINE SOCIETY, founded in 1756. On the left, at the beginning of the narrow Lambeth High Street, is the large new building (by David Hodges, 1977) of the PHARMACEUTICAL SOCIETY of Great Britain, founded in 1841.

On the right, at the end of Lambeth Road, is ST MARY'S CHURCH (IX, D1), the former parish church of Lambeth, restored in 1979–83 by the Tradescant Trust (founded in 1977) as the first MUSEUM OF GARDEN HISTORY (adm., p. 33). The churchyard is planted with trees, shrubs, and plants of the kind brought to England by John Tradescant (d. 1638) and his son, also John (d. 1662), and planted in their garden at Lambeth. Both were royal gardeners and their tomb is in the churchyard, east of the church. Also buried here is Admiral William Bligh (d. 1817), in a tomb made of Coade stone.

Of Saxon foundation, the church was rebuilt in 1851 by Philip Hardwick, except for the 14th-century tower. In the north chapel is the brass of Lady Katherine Howard (d. 1535), and on either side of the sanctuary are the fine Tudor Gothic table-tombs, with canopies, of Hugh Peyntwin (d. 1504), archdeacon of Canterbury (on the north), and John Mompesson (d. 1524), master of the registry to the archbishop. The east window, restored after war damage, has stained glass by Francis Stephens (1953) and the church was re-roofed in 1979. New windows by Lawrence Lee (1981) commemorate the Tradescants.

The small 'Pedlar's Window' in the south chapel perpetuates the tradition of a bequest to the parish of the 'Pedlar's Acre', which was valued at 2/8d a year in 1504, but brought in £81,000 when it was sold to the L.C.C. in 1906 as part of the site for the new County Hall. Elias Ashmole (d. 1692), founder of the Ashmolean Museum at Oxford; Cuthbert Tunstall (d. 1559), bishop of London and Durham; and five archbishops are buried in the church. The baptistery (for total immersion), at the west end of the south aisle, is a memorial to Edward White Benson, Primate in 1882–96.

On the left of the church, facing Lambeth Bridge (Route 3), is the entrance to LAMBETH PALACE (IX, D1), the London residence of the archbishops of Canterbury for nearly 800 years. The buildings were begun by Archbishop Hubert Walter (1193–1205), though Stephen Langton (1207–28) was the first archbishop to live here. The palace has been extensively altered and added to by many of his successors, but it still retains to a large extent its medieval atmosphere.

The palace occupies the site of a Saxon manor house that seems to have belonged before the Conquest to the sister of Edward the Confessor. The manor, given by William the Conqueror to the Benedictine monks of Rochester, was acquired about

1190 by Archbishop Baldwin, whose successor began the palace. This was attacked in 1381 by Wat Tyler's rebels, who forced Archbishop Simon of Sudbury to seek refuge in the Tower of London. The palace has been restored after the heavy damage it received from the air in 1941. The Lambeth Conference of Anglican bishops under the presidency of the archbishop of Canterbury, instituted in 1867, is now held every ten years (last in 1978), with over 300 representatives from Britain, the Commonwealth, and the United States. The Library (entered from Lambeth Palace Road) is open to students and accredited readers on application to the librarian.

The entrance (adm., p. 33) is through a red brick Tudor gateway, usually called MORTON'S TOWER after Cardinal Morton, who built it about 1495 and had his audience chamber over the vaulted archway. Thence visitors turn to the right into the courtyard, in the centre of which is a memorial to Archbishop Lord Davidson (d. 1930). The residential part of the palace, forming a Gothic wing on the north, was added in 1828–33 by Edward Blore for Archbishop Howley. The fig trees on the west of the courtyard are believed to have stemmed from those planted in the 16th century by Cardinal Pole. Behind them rises the GREAT HALL, a noble chamber 93 ft long, of medieval origin but greatly damaged during the Commonwealth and rebuilt after 1660 by Archbishop William Juxon, whose arms are over the door inside. The magnificent hammerbeam roof, 70 ft high, in a Gothic style resembling that of Westminster Hall, has been carefully restored after war damage. The windows contain panels and shields of 16th–17th-century glass. The hall, the scene of the Lambeth Conferences, houses part of the valuable Library built up round the collection bequeathed to the see in 1610 by Archbishop Bancroft. The many treasures include beautiful illuminated manuscripts, the medieval registers of archbishops, twenty-five volumes of Elizabethan manuscripts, and early printed books, including a Latin grammar prepared in 1540 for the young Prince Edward.

A corridor on the site of the medieval cloisters leads to the CRYPT below the chapel, the oldest part of the palace, a vaulted chamber with Purbeck marble pillars built about 1200, probably by Archbishop Walter. From an ante-chamber (formerly called the Post Room) on the floor above, an exquisite 13th-century doorway, resembling that of the chapter-house of Westminster Abbey, admits to the CHAPEL, built by Archbishop Boniface (1245–73) but much restored and unhappily gutted in the bombing, from which only parts of the 17th-century gallery and bench-ends survived. Rebuilt in its former style by Lord Mottistone and Paul Paget, the chapel was rededicated in 1955. The new stained-glass windows, by Edwards and Powell, are likewise in the style of their forerunners, inserted by Matthew Parker (d. 1575;

archbishop under Elizabeth I), who is buried in the sanctuary. The second trial of John Wyclif, the reformer (1378), was held in the chapel, in which also many English bishops have been consecrated.

The former Post Room, which contains a richly carved 17th-century screen with the arms of Archbishop Laud, is in the LOLLARDS' TOWER, built as a water-tower by Archbishop Chichele (1414–43), and named from the supposition that the Lollards, followers of Wyclif, were imprisoned here. Opening off the staircase on the north is a turret called the 'Lollards' Prison'. Adjoining the tower on the south is the smaller LAUD'S TOWER, added about 1635 by that archbishop. Hence another corridor leads to the GUARD CHAMBER, rebuilt by Blore, who retained the unusual 14th-century timber roof. Around the walls are many fine portraits of archbishops, including works by Holbein ('Archbishop Warham'), Van Dyck ('Archbishop Laud'), Kneller, Hogarth, Reynolds, Romney, Lawrence, and Sargent.

The ALBERT EMBANKMENT (VIII, D3–F3) runs south from Lambeth Bridge to Vauxhall station, following the bank of the Thames at first. At the corner is LAMBETH BRIDGE HOUSE (1940), offices of the Departments of Transport and the Environment. DOULTON HOUSE (No. 4), a building of 1983, is the headquarters of the INTERNATIONAL MARITIME ORGANIZATION, an agency of the United Nations established in 1958 to provide the means for cooperation between governments on technical matters related to international shipping; it now has a membership of 125 nations. No. 8 is the headquarters of the LONDON FIRE BRIGADE, established in 1866 as the Metropolitan Fire Brigade, and moved to new buildings here (by E. P. Wheeler) in 1937. During the Second World War the brigade was considerably augmented and incorporated in the National Fire Service, but in 1948 it was returned to the L.C.C., who had first assumed control in 1889. In 1965 it was again enlarged, to serve Greater London, and the force, which now numbers over 7,060, maintains 114 stations (including two on the river). No. 9 houses the BRITISH STEEL CORPORATION, established in 1967. Of other characteristic examples of modern commercial architecture on the Embankment, the NATIONAL DOCK LABOUR BOARD office was designed by Sir Frederick Gibberd (1956). Across the river are seen the Tate Gallery and the tall Millbank Tower, and upstream are Vauxhall Bridge and the Battersea power station. ALEMBIC HOUSE (by Oscar Garry and Partners, 1964), on the right farther on, contains the CHEMICAL INDUSTRIES ASSOCIATION and other institutions. The road turns away from the river, crossing the site of Vauxhall Gardens, a celebrated pleasure resort which flourished from 1661 until 1859 and is described by Pepys and by Thackeray (in *Vanity Fair*).

From the end of the road, beside VAUXHALL STATION (VIII, F3), Bridgefoot leads right to VAUXHALL BRIDGE (Route 3), while WANDSWORTH ROAD goes on south-west from the station to the vast NEW COVENT GARDEN MARKET at Nine Elms, built to designs by the Gollins, Melvin, Ward Partnership, and opened in 1974, replacing the old Covent Garden Market (Route 20). The stressed steel skin roof is probably the largest in Europe; the administrative offices, adjoining the flower market, are in two towerblocks, sixteen and twenty-one storeys high, rising from a podium base. The market handles about 4,000 tons of fruit and vegetables daily, as well some 14,000 packages of flowers and plants.

From Kennington Lane, east of Vauxhall station, HARLEYFORD ROAD runs south-east to The Oval (see Suburban London). KENNINGTON LANE, on its way to Kennington Road, passes ST PETER'S CHURCH (1864), designed, with early-Gothic features, by J. L. Pearson, who was also responsible for the neighbouring school and the former orphanage.

36 From Lambeth Bridge to London Bridge via the South Bank, Waterloo, and Bankside

Plan VIII, D3–IX, D2

STATIONS: LAMBETH NORTH (Plan IX, C2), on the Bakerloo line; WATERLOO (IX, B1), on the Bakerloo line and the Northern line (Charing Cross branch); and LONDON BRIDGE (IX, E2), on the Northern line (Bank branch). Waterloo and London Bridge are served also by the Southern Region, and the former is the terminus of the short Waterloo & City Railway to Bank.—BUSES Nos. 77, 149, 159, 170, and 507 in Lambeth Palace Road; Nos. 70, 76, 149, 171, and 507 in York Road; Nos. 70, 76, and 149 in Stamford Street; and No. 70 in Southwark Street (to London Bridge). Nos. 1, 4, 5, 68, 171, 176, 188, 501, 502, and 513 across Waterloo Bridge to Waterloo station; Nos. 45, 63, 109, 141, and 155 in Blackfriars Road; Nos. 44 and 184 in Southwark Bridge Road (to London Bridge station). For buses across Westminster Bridge and Blackfriars Bridge, see Route 26; across Southwark Bridge, see Route 27.

From LAMBETH BRIDGE (Route 3), Lambeth Palace Road runs northward, skirting the wall of the archbishop of Canterbury's palace (see Route 35) and passing behind St Thomas's Hospital. On the right is the approach to ARCHBISHOP'S PARK, part of the palace grounds, opened to the public in 1900. The ALBERT EMBANKMENT (VIII, C, D3), following the river, is a broad footwalk constructed by Sir Joseph Bazalgette in 1866–9 and leading to Westminster Bridge. It affords a fine view of the Houses of Parliament on the opposite bank, with the towers of Westminster Abbey behind. The decorative lamp standards, of entwined dolphins (1870), match those on Westminster Bridge. ST THOMAS'S HOSPITAL (IX, C1), founded at Southwark in 1552, is the successor of a hospital established by the Augustinians there in 1173 and dedicated to St Thomas Becket. The dedication was changed by Edward VI to St Thomas the Apostle, and the hospital was moved in 1868 to new buildings here, damaged by bombing. An entirely new hospital, to the designs of Yorke, Rosenberg, and

Mardall, was begun in 1963, and the first part (on the north) was completed in 1976. The associated medical school, affiliated to London University, is incorporated in the buildings.

At the east end of WESTMINSTER BRIDGE (Route 26) is a monumental lion (1837) moved here from the South Bank near Waterloo Station in 1966. Formerly the trade-mark of a brewery, its principal interest is that it is made of Coade stone, an artificial stone practically impervious to weather, first manufactured by Richard Holt in 1722 and developed commercially in her factory at Lambeth by Eleanor Coade after about 1769. The stone, a kind of terracotta, was extensively used for the decoration of London buildings in the late 18th and early 19th centuries, but the secret of its composition has been lost.

On the north side of the approach to Westminster Bridge stands COUNTY HALL (IX, B1), the imposing headquarters of the Greater London Council, designed by Ralph Knott (with the assistance of W. E. Riley, the former L.C.C.'s architect) in a free Renaissance style. Begun in 1912, the building, opened in 1922 and finally completed in 1933, has nine floors and about 1,500 rooms. Constructed partly on ground recovered from the river, the foundations, covering about six and a half acres, are supported by a concrete raft 5 ft thick. The exterior, faced with Portland stone, has sculptures by Ernest Cole and A. F. Hardiman. Its most notable features are the steep-pitched roofs and the curved colonnade in the centre of the river façade, which is 750 ft long and faces a terrace (open to the public). The central part of a new extension, to the designs of E. P. Wheeler and F. R. Hiorns (with Sir Giles G. Scott as consultant), was opened in 1939; a new wing on the north of this was completed in 1957 and the south block in 1963. A fourth building, designed to provide open landscaped offices and completed in 1974, stands on an island site linked to the other buildings by an enclosed bridge over York Road and by subways.

The G.L.C., which had its first meeting at County Hall in 1965, superseded the L.C.C., constituted under an act of 1888. It now consists of ninety-two councillors, elected directly by the public for four years, presided over by a chairman, who is elected from within the council. The council, the ruling authority for Greater London, controls, or shares control with the borough councils in, such matters as planning, traffic arrangements, housing and street improvements, main drainage, the fire and ambulance services, certain of the courts and judicial services, the maintenance of parks and open spaces, and historic and certain other buildings, such as the Royal Festival Hall. The meetings of the council, usually held every three weeks, on Tuesdays at 2.30 p.m. (except during holidays), are open to the public.

The principal entrance for visitors is in Belvedere Road, on the east of the main building. The Entrance Hall and the Ceremonial Staircase, ascending to the first floor, are decorated with Italian, Belgian, and Ashburton marbles and the numerous committee rooms are panelled in English oak. Other finely decorated rooms include the Conference Hall, an elliptical chamber at the north end; the Voting Lobbies, decorated with Indian laurel; the handsome octagonal Council Chamber, with monolithic columns of veine dorée, a marble quarried in the Italian Alps; and the Members' Reading Room, affording a view of the terrace and colonnade. The excellent Members' Library, containing over 90,000 books on local government and the history and topography of London, is accessible to the public on weekdays on application to the Librarian. The fine collections of London prints, watercolours, maps, and photographs are also available for reference, and reproductions of some of the prints and maps are on sale.

A Roman boat of the 3rd century, discovered in 1910 during the excavations for the foundations of County Hall, is now in the Museum of London. Outside the Hall, to the north, is a memorial (by Ian Walters, 1985) to over 2,100 volunteers who went to Spain in 1936–9 to fight against Fascism.

The area to the north of County Hall, extending to Waterloo Bridge and now known as the SOUTH BANK (IX, A, B1), was the site of the Festival of Britain held in 1951. The embankment has been laid out as a promenade. The open space south of the railway bridge has been known as JUBILEE GARDENS since 1977. To the east of Belvedere Road rises the SHELL CENTRE, two vast ranges of office building, erected in 1957–62 for the Royal Dutch/Shell group of companies (the largest manufacturing organization in Britain) and including an enormous skyscraper, twenty-six storeys and 351 ft high, designed by Sir Howard Robertson and R. Maynard Smith.

In the main courtyard is a bronze fountain, 30 ft high, by Franta Belsky, and the building contains a theatre (or cinema; with a mural by Sir Osbert Lancaster) and a swimming pool of international standard. At the top is a public viewing gallery (closed at present) from which opens a widespread view over London, of the Thames in both directions, and from the hills of Hampstead and Highgate to Crystal Palace.

On the north side of the Charing Cross Railway Bridge (see Route 26) is the ROYAL FESTIVAL HALL (IX, A1), one of the most successful examples of modern architecture in London, designed by Sir Robert Matthew and Sir Leslie Martin for the L.C.C. and opened in 1951. The river frontage was rebuilt and enlarged, to include the main entrance, by Sir Hubert Bennett (1962–5). The building is of reinforced concrete faced with Portland stone. The concert hall, praiseworthy for its decorative scheme and its acoustics, has seats for 3,400 and a platform that will accommodate a choir of 250. The splendid organ (1954) was built by Harrison and Harrison of Durham, with Ralph Downes, the organist, as consultant. The hall is effectively insulated against the noise of passing trains. The terrace in front of the Festival Hall commands a fine view across the Thames.

The FESTIVAL PIER, built out from the terrace in 1983, is connected by ferry every five to ten minutes with Westminster Pier (Route 26) and is the stopping point for river cruises to Tower Pier and Greenwich. Facing the railway bridge is a colossal bust (by Ian Walters, 1985) of Nelson Mandela, the opponent of apartheid in South Africa, gaoled in 1962.

Outside the Royal Festival Hall, on the north, is a memorial sculpture to Fryderyk Chopin (d. 1849), by Marian Kubica (1975). Between the Festival Hall and Waterloo Bridge (Route 26) is a rather stark building (by the G.L.C. architects, 1967) containing the QUEEN ELIZABETH HALL (a concert hall with seats for 1,100) and the PURCELL ROOM (a recital hall accommodating 370). The adjoining HAYWARD GALLERY (adm., p. 32), opened in 1968, is used by the Arts Council for loan exhibitions. Under the southern arch abutment of the bridge is the NATIONAL FILM THEATRE, first opened in 1951 but rebuilt here in 1957. Designed by the architects of the L.C.C., the theatre is capable of seating 500. A second cinema (seating 165) was opened in 1970. A Museum of the Moving Image, designed by Brian Avery, is being built to the south in 1985.

On the downstream side of the Waterloo Bridge approach is the NATIONAL THEATRE (IX, A1), begun in 1969, to the designs of Sir Denys Lasdun (who was advised by theatrical experts), and opened in 1976. The building, replacing the Old Vic (see below), includes two main theatres, the Olivier Theatre (1,160 seats), named in honour of Sir Laurence (now Lord) Olivier, the actor-manager, first director of the National Theatre Company (1962–73), and with an open stage projecting into the auditorium, and the Lyttelton Theatre (890 seats), with a conventional proscenium stage (partly for productions from regional theatres). The smaller Cottesloe Theatre (up to 400 seats), on the east side, is designed for more experimental productions.

The theatre incorporates a restaurant, buffets and bars, as well as rehearsal rooms and a large workshop. Musical events are held and poetry readings are given, and conducted tours of the building are arranged (see p. 34). In the foyer is displayed the fine collection of theatrical paintings given to the National Theatre by W. Somerset Maugham, the novelist and playwright, before his death in 1965. Terraces overlook the river and link the theatre with the bridge and with the Queen Elizabeth and Royal Festival Halls.

Downstream, and reached from UPPER GROUND, the shortest route to Stamford Street (see below) and Blackfriars Bridge, are the IBM CENTRAL MARKETING CENTRE (by Sir Denys Lasdun & Partners, 1983) and the impressive KENT HOUSE (by C. H. Elsom, Pack, and Roberts, 1972), the headquarters of London Weekend Television.

On the other side of York Road, behind the Shell Centre, is WATERLOO STATION (IX, B1, 2), a principal terminus of the Southern Region, first opened in 1848 by the London and South Western Railway Company and rebuilt in 1907–22. The largest station in Britain, it receives about 180,000 passengers every working day. The main entrance, on the north-west, with sculptured groups, is by J. R. Scott. Another entrance is in WATERLOO ROAD (IX, A1–C2), which leads south-east from Waterloo Bridge. On the left, north of the railway bridge, is ST JOHN'S CHURCH, a classical building by Francis Bedford (1824), damaged by bombing in 1940 but restored in 1951 as the 'Festival Church'. Over the altar is a painting by Hans Feibusch.

Elizabeth House, in York Road (to the south-west), is the head office of the DEPARTMENT OF EDUCATION AND SCIENCE, formed in 1964. STAMFORD STREET (IX, A1, 2), which leaves Waterloo Road north of St John's Church and leads to Blackfriars Road (see below), retains some formal Regency terraces (Nos. 63–89 and 95–121). Also on the right are the LONDON NAUTICAL SCHOOL, in a building erected in 1820 as a school for Irish children, and the portico (rebuilt in 1823 in a severe Greek style) of the former UNITARIAN CHAPEL, founded in 1666. On the left is the forecourt of KING'S REACH TOWER (by Derek Stephenson & Partners, 1976), the headquarters of the International Publishing Corporation, with a towerblock 380 ft high.

Waterloo Road leads to St George's Circus (Route 35), passing (beyond the railway) the UNION JACK CLUB for soldiers, sailors, and airmen, opened in 1907 and rebuilt in 1976 (by Fitzroy Robinson & Partners), with accommodation for service and ex-service men and women. Farther on is THE CUT, at the corner of which is the OLD VIC (IX, B2), officially the Royal Victoria Theatre, and long famous for its productions of Shakespeare.

Founded in 1816 as the Royal Coburg Theatre, it was at first notorious for melodrama; the name was changed in 1833 and in 1880 the theatre was remodelled and taken over by Emma Cons, who made it a home for opera and classical plays at popular prices. After the death of Miss Cons in 1912 the work was ably carried on by her niece, Lilian Baylis (d. 1937), who in 1914 formed a permanent Shakespearian company, but after the rebuilding of Sadler's Wells (Route 29) the opera productions were transferred there. The Old Vic suffered considerable bomb damage in the war, when the company was transferred to the New Theatre, but the players returned to their old home in 1950. In 1963–76 it was the home of the National Theatre Company (see above). In 1983 the theatre was bought by a Canadian businessman and was restored (by the Renton, Howard, Wood, Levin Partnership) to its appearance in 1880.

In The Cut, opposite the Old Vic, is the YOUNG VIC, a small theatre (450 seats) for young playgoers, opened in 1970 (to designs by Howell, Killick, Partridge & Amis), with its foyer in a Victorian butcher's shop. In Waterloo Road, farther south, No. 157 is the office of the CHURCH MISSIONARY SOCIETY, founded in 1799, and of SHELTER, the National Campaign for the Homeless.

The Cut leads eastward to BLACKFRIARS ROAD (IX, A3–C3), which connects St George's Circus with Blackfriars Bridge (Route 26). Orbit House (No. 197), on the right, houses the INDIA OFFICE LIBRARY AND RECORDS, administered since 1982 by the British Library. The Records, dating back to 1600, were originally those of the Honourable East India Company and comprise over 190,000 volumes of records, manuscripts, private papers, etc. The Library, founded in 1801 by the East India Company, is the oldest, largest, and finest Orientalist library in the world. It contains about 390,000 printed books and 28,000 manuscripts. Both the Library and the Records are accessible to holders of British Library tickets and to students on application to the Keeper.

On the left, farther north, is CHRIST CHURCH, rebuilt in 1741, but set on fire from the air in 1941 and subsequently demolished except for the chancel, added in 1901. The nave was rebuilt in 1959. PARIS GARDEN, the street on the west, occupies the site of the 14th-century manor house of Robert de Paris; the manor later became a fashionable amusement place and the Swan Theatre, at which Shakespeare was employed, stood here from 1595 until 1633.

SOUTHWARK STREET, a long dismal thoroughfare, continues from Stamford Street (see above) to the Borough High Street (Route 35), passing, on the south (at No. 99), the former KIRKALDY'S TESTING WORKS, built in 1877 and renovated in 1984 as an engineering research centre. On the ground floor is a machine capable of testing the strength of materials up to a force of 350 tons, made in Leeds in 1864 for David Kirkaldy, a pioneer in the scientific testing of materials used in civil engineering. On the left, farther on, is ST CHRISTOPHER HOUSE, the large offices built in 1960 (by Morris de Metz) for the Department of Transport.

A more interesting route turns to the left from Southwark Street (beyond the railway) into Hopton Street, passing the pleasant HOPTON ALMSHOUSES, built in 1752 and restored after war damage. Beyond these a small house of the early 18th century (No. 61) has managed to survive. At the end of the street is FALCON POINT, blocks of flats (by Fitzroy Robinson & Partners, 1980) incorporating the BANKSIDE GALLERY (adm., p. 31) of the ROYAL SOCIETY OF PAINTERS IN WATER COLOURS (founded in 1804), famous members of which have included J. S. Cotman, David Cox, and Peter de Wint. Here also is the ROYAL SOCIETY OF PAINTER-ETCHERS and Engravers (founded in 1880). A passage and steps to the left of the flats lead up to Blackfriars Bridge, and behind the flats begins BANKSIDE REACH, a walkway opened in 1980, with a new pub (the Founders' Arms) and a splendid view (best at sunset) across the Thames to the dome and towers of St Paul's Cathedral, once seen to be surrounded by the City spires (now almost all obscured by large blocks of office building).

The walkway, passing the huge Bankside power station (designed by Sir Giles G. Scott, 1953), leads out to BANKSIDE (IX, D1), which goes on close to the river. The street, once lined by large warehouses (now mostly demolished), traverses historic ground, the site of amusement gardens and theatres in the 16th–17th centuries. At CARDINAL CAP ALLEY, near the end of the walkway, are some early-18th-century dwellings, restored after war damage. Sir Christopher Wren is supposed to have lived at No. 49 during the building of St Paul's. BEAR GARDENS, a lane farther on, leads away from the river to Park Street. The small square towards the farther end is the site of the bear pit in the Elizabethan garden (later described by Pepys and Evelyn), and close by in 1614–56 stood the Hope Theatre. A late Georgian warehouse here contains the small BEAR GARDENS MUSEUM (adm., p. 31), with an exhibition of Elizabethan theatrical history.

PARK STREET runs east past ROSE ALLEY, a name recalling the Rose Theatre (opened by Philip Henslowe in 1587), where Shakespeare is believed to have played. A building on the right beyond the approach to Southwark Bridge (Route 27) covers the site of the GLOBE THEATRE ('this wooden O'), erected by Richard and Cuthbert Burbage late in 1598 (or early in 1599) and burned down in 1613. Shakespeare acted here until 1612 with the King's Company, and here *Hamlet* (1602), *Othello* (1604), *Macbeth* (1606), *King Lear* (1606), and others of his plays were produced. A plaque on the wall shows Southwark at that time, with the theatre.

Bankend turns north from Park Street to reach the east end of Bankside at the picturesque ANCHOR INN, rebuilt in 1775. CLINK STREET goes on eastward, passing under the Cannon Street Railway Bridge (by Sir John Hawkshaw, 1866) and hemmed in by lofty warehouses and newer buildings. Among these are some remains (difficult to see) of WINCHESTER PALACE, a 13th-century and later residence of the bishops of Winchester (whose diocese included South London), occupied by them until 1649, but mostly burned down in 1814. The most notable feature is a splendid rose-window of about 1370, in the west gable of the great hall. Attached to the palace was the Liberty of the Clink, a manor outside the jurisdiction of the City and later, because of this, the chief pleasure quarter of London, with theatres, bear-gardens, and 'stews' (brothels). The Clink Prison, in which Bishops Bradford and Hooper, the opponents of Mary Tudor, were confined, survives only in the name of Clink Street and the expression 'the clink' for imprisonment.

The ravine-like street goes on to WINCHESTER SQUARE, perhaps originally a courtyard of the palace, then bears left past ST MARY OVERIE'S DOCK (where parishioners of St Saviour's were entitled to land goods free of toll) to Cathedral Street, which skirts the west side of **Southwark Cathedral** (adm., p. 422). Remains of the Roman road from Lambeth (see Route 35) were discovered in 1969 in MONTAGUE CLOSE, north of the cathedral. Farther north is a terrace with a view of the river; MINERVA HOUSE, to the west, a large office building in camel-coloured brick, is by Michael Twigg, Brown & Partners (1983). A foot-passage on the south side of the cathedral graveyard leads out to the BOROUGH HIGH STREET (IX, E1), opposite the approach to London Bridge station (Route 35).

PLACES OF INTEREST

BRITISH MUSEUM Plan III, C, D3

STATIONS: TOTTENHAM COURT ROAD, ¼ m. SW, on the Central and Northern lines; HOLBORN, ¼ m. SE, on the Central and Piccadilly lines; GOODGE STREET, ½ m. NW, on the Northern line; and RUSSELL SQUARE, ½ m. NE, on the Piccadilly line. — BUSES in Tottenham Court Road or Gower Street, see Route 18; in New Oxford Street, see Route 23; in Bloomsbury Way or High Holborn, and in Southampton Row, see Route 19.

ADMISSION Mondays–Saturdays 10 to 5, Sundays 2.30 to 6 (free). Closed on New Year's Day, Good Friday, May Day Monday, Christmas Eve and Day, and Boxing Day. — LECTURE TOURS Mondays–Saturdays at 11.30, starting in the Entrance Hall; lectures in the LECTURE THEATRE on Tuesdays–Saturdays at 1.15. Films in the Lecture Theatre, Tuesdays–Fridays at 3.30. Lecture Tours and Films are arranged also by the British Library. — REFRESHMENT ROOM (see Ground Floor plan), open 10.30 to 4.15 (Sundays 3 to 5.15).

The STUDENTS' ROOMS of the various departments (Prints and Drawings, Coins and Medals, etc.) are accessible on weekdays on previous application only. — INFORMATION may be obtained by telephoning 580–1788 or (for the British Library) 636–1544, extension 333.

The READING ROOM of the British Library may be viewed on weekdays, on the hour, from 11 to 4, on application at the entrance. The Library itself is open to holders of Readers' Passes (free), for which personal application should be made at the Library. The Students' Rooms of the Departments of MANUSCRIPTS, of ORIENTAL MANUSCRIPTS AND PRINTED BOOKS, and of PRINTED BOOKS are all open under the same conditions.

The BRITISH MUSEUM, comprising the national museum of archaeology and ethnography and the national library (now called the BRITISH LIBRARY), is the largest and richest of its kind in the world. Built in 1823–52 to the designs of Sir Robert Smirke, it is situated in Bloomsbury, in the angle between Tottenham Court Road and New Oxford Street. The main entrance is on the south side, from Great Russell Street, but there is another entrance on the north, in Montague Place, to the King Edward VII Building, added in 1907–14 by Sir John J. Burnet. The main façade, 370 ft long, is in a severe classical style, with heavy projecting wings and a ponderous colonnade of forty-four Ionic columns. The pediment above the entrance portico has allegorical sculptures by Sir Richard Westmacott.

The museum was founded in 1753, its nucleus being the Cottonian Library of state papers and other manuscripts, collected by Sir Robert Cotton (d. 1631) and presented to the nation in 1702. To this were added the natural history collection, antiquities, and works of art bequeathed to the nation for £20,000 by Sir Hans Sloane (d. 1753) and the collection of manuscripts formed by Robert Harley, first Earl of Oxford (d. 1724), and his son, and bought for £10,000. Montague House in Bloomsbury was purchased in 1755, after a public lottery had raised £300,000, the Royal Library presented by George II was incorporated in 1757, and the collections were opened to the public in 1759. By gift, bequest, and purchase the museum grew rapidly, and in the early 19th century new buildings had to be provided to accommodate the Egyptian sculptures, the Towneley Marbles, and the Elgin Marbles. With the gift by George IV in 1823 of the splendid library collected by his father, Montague House proved quite inadequate, and a new and larger building was begun on the same site.

The first wing completed was the fine gallery called the King's Library (1826) and the classical south front was finished in 1852. The building, however, was already too small, partly owing to the growth of the library, and in 1857 the famous domed Reading Room was constructed by Sydney Smirke to a plan by Sir Anthony Panizzi, the principal librarian, in what had been the interior courtyard. With the acquisition of the Grenville Library and the material from excavations in Assyria and Asia Minor, accommodation once more became a problem, and in 1881 the natural history collections were transferred to their present home in South Kensington. New wings were added on the south-east and south-west in 1882–4, and in 1914 the fine King Edward VII Building was opened on the north side. The North Library was reconstructed in 1937, and a new gallery on the west, the gift of Lord Duveen, was built in 1938 for the magnificent sculptures of the Parthenon. The Ethnographical collections were transferred in 1970 to the new Museum of Mankind in Burlington Gardens (Route 15).

The vast treasures of the museum cannot be absorbed in a single visit. Visitors with limited time at their disposal are advised to begin with the Greek, Roman, Egyptian, and Assyrian sculptures (in the west wing) and the Printed Books and Manuscripts (east wing), then to ascend the main stairs to the Prehistoric and Romano-British galleries, the order followed in this guide. The Medieval and Later collections are in the south-east part of the museum, the Asiatic and Oriental collections are mainly in the north part. The most interesting or important exhibits in the museum have been indicated below by an asterisk (*).

The main doorway opens direct into a large ENTRANCE HALL which contains an information desk and the museum shop. On the left is the approach to the Publications Gallery and the collections of Greek, Roman, and Egyptian sculptures, and beyond is the main staircase, ascending to the Prehistoric, Roman, and Medieval

Rooms. Opposite the staircase is the entrance to the exhibition of Books and Manuscripts, and straight ahead is the Reading Room. To the right of the entrance to this are the cloakroom and a lift to the upper floor.

The BRITISH LIBRARY READING ROOM is a huge circular hall, accommodating about 420 readers, covered by a dome 106 ft high and with a diameter of 140 ft, only 2 ft less than that of the Pantheon at Rome, the widest hemispherical dome in the world. In the centre is the raised desk of the officials, and round this are two circular desks containing the General Catalogue (of books, etc., published before 1970), which runs to 2,110 large volumes of about 500 pages each, the most extensive publication in the world. A cabinet contains a card index of books published from 1970 onwards, and maps and music are entered in separate catalogues. From the central desks those at which readers sit spread out like the spokes of a wheel. The ground-floor shelves around the room hold a large selection of reference books (dictionaries, encyclopedias, histories, and standard works) which may be consulted directly by readers; other books are obtained by filling in application slips.

The BRITISH LIBRARY was formed in 1973 by combining the Library of the British Museum (now the Reference Division of the new library) with the National Library of Science and Invention, which itself included the former Patent Office Library, now part of the SCIENCE REFERENCE LIBRARY (see p. 241). It also incorporates the India Office Library (p. 333) and the Library Association Library (p. 205). The address of the Director General of the Reference Division is Great Russell Street, London WC1B 3DG. A new library is being built near St Pancras Station to house all the divisions, apart from the Lending Division, the headquarters of which will remain at Boston Spa (Yorkshire).

The REFERENCE DIVISION, which contains over ten million items, is rivalled only by the Bibliothèque Nationale at Paris as the largest library in the world. Foreign Books (of which it has much the finest collection) and older books are obtained through a Treasury grant or by donation, while publishers are legally bound to deposit a copy of every book, pamphlet, periodical, and newspaper produced in the United Kingdom at the library, where it must be accepted and preserved. The NORTH LIBRARY, under the jurisdiction of the Department of Printed Books, is reserved for special research and the study of rare books, and Students' Rooms are available in the other Library Departments. Newspapers and periodicals (with the exception of London newspapers earlier than 1801) may be consulted at the NEWSPAPER LIBRARY at Colindale, NW9 (opposite the underground station); passes to the Reading Room are valid also at the Newspaper Library (open weekdays, 10 to 5). Duplicate copies of *The Times* (from 1809) and a few periodicals are kept in the Reference Division. About fifteen per cent of the books in the

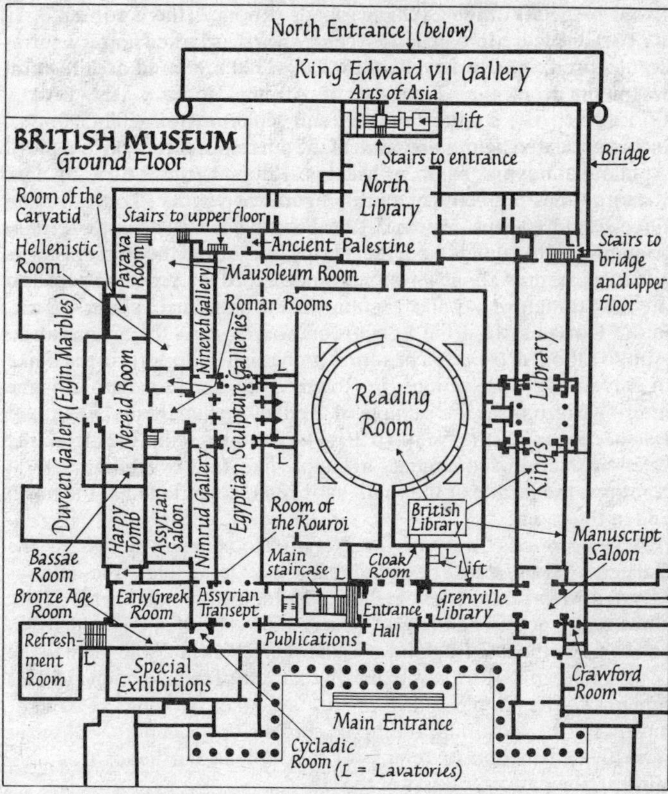

Reference Division are at present kept in a repository at Woolwich, and at least a day's notice is required for these.

Beyond the PUBLICATIONS GALLERY on the west of the Entrance Hall are rooms devoted principally to *GREEK AND ROMAN ANTIQUITIES. Flanking the entrance are two half-columns from the miscalled Treasury of Atreus at Mycenae (in reality a royal tomb of about 1300 B.C.). The first room, the CYCLADIC ROOM, contains marble idols and vessels from the 3rd millennium B.C., illustrating the

Bronze Age art of the Cycladic islands. Room 2 (the BRONZE AGE ROOM) displays Minoan and Mycenaean art, including pottery, terracottas, bronzes, and jewellery of 3000–1100 B.C., and architectural fragments from the 'Treasury' of Atreus. Room 3 (the EARLY GREEK ROOM) contains pottery and sculptures of 1100–500 B.C., including seated figures and lions of the 6th century from the temple of Apollo at Didyma, south of Miletus. Room 4 (the ROOM OF THE KOUROI) has 6th-century marble figures of youths ('kouroi') from Greece and Cyprus. Room 5 (the ROOM OF THE HARPY TOMB) contains marble reliefs from the 'Harpy Tomb' and the frieze of cocks and hens, both of about 480 B.C., from Xanthos in Lycia, and here also are the Strangford 'Apollo', a statue of a young man of about 490 B.C. in the Dorian style, from Lemnos or Anaphe, and the 'Chatsworth' Apollo (about 460 B.C.), a beautiful bronze head formerly in the Duke of Devonshire's collections. In Room 6 (the BASSAE ROOM) is the interior frieze from the Temple of Apollo, begun about 450 B.C., at Bassae. Room 7 (the NEREID ROOM) contains sculptures from the splendid Nereid monument, a temple-like tomb of about 400 at Xanthos; the façade of the tomb has been reconstructed at the north end of the room.

A door on the west of the Nereid Room gives access to the DUVEEN GALLERY, designed expressly to display the famous *ELGIN MARBLES. These are named after the seventh Earl of Elgin, ambassador at Constantinople, who in 1802–12 collected the marbles and brought them to England at a cost of £75,000, and sold them to the government in 1816 for less than half that sum. The collection includes remains of the temple of Erechtheus and other buildings in Athens, but by far the most important part consists of the superb sculptures from the Parthenon or temple of the Athena Parthenos (i.e., the Virgin), the patron goddess of the city.

The temple, which crowned the rocky hill of the Acropolis, was built between 447 and 432 B.C., at a time when Athens was flourishing under the brilliant leadership of Pericles. The principal architect was Ictinus and the decorations were most probably executed under the supervision of the great sculptor Pheidias. A statue of Athena, 40 ft high, made of gold and ivory by Pheidias, was raised in the temple, which remained dedicated to the goddess until about A.D. 450, after which it was converted for Christian worship. At the fall of Athens to the Turks in 1458 it became a Mohammedan mosque. In 1687 the Parthenon was gravely damaged by an explosion during the siege of Athens by the Venetians, and after the restoration of the city to the Turks in 1688 it suffered further injury. A series of drawings made in 1674 by a

French draughtsman, however, has served as a valuable record of the sculptures before their damage.

Models, drawings, and photographs in rooms beside the entrance to the gallery illustrate the history and structure of the Parthenon. The sculptures, generally agreed to be the finest in the world, consist of the Pediment Groups, which filled the east and west gables of the temple and each contained more than twenty statues ranging from just over life-size to 11 ft in height; the Metopes, square panels in high relief set into the outside of the building above the colonnade; and the Frieze, a band of low relief over 500 ft long which ran round the outer walls of the inner chamber.

Around the walls of the central part of the gallery is the FRIEZE, which was long thought to portray the procession up to the Acropolis at the end of the Panathenaic Festival, the greatest of all Athenian festivals, but is now claimed to show the presentation of the heroes of the Battle of Marathon (490 B.C.) to the gods of Olympus. The representation started at the south-west corner of the building with a parade of horsemen, which increases in numbers and artistic virility as it moves towards the left (mostly from the north frieze); the leading horsemen (on slab XXIV, at the north-east angle of the room) are particularly notable. The procession is joined by chariots and citizens, by animals being led to sacrifice (south frieze), and by girls carrying vessels for use in sacrifice, and magistrates and other officials, and culminates (according to the older theory) in the presentation of a sacred peplos or robe to the image of Athena (Nos. 34–6, east frieze; almost facing the door).

In the raised alcove at the north end of the gallery are the sculptures from the EAST PEDIMENT group, symbolizing the Birth of Athena, who is supposed to have sprung from the head of Zeus in complete armour and fully grown. The remains of the group begin on the left with a fragment of Helios, the sun-god, who rises from the sea in his four-horse chariot at daybreak, and ends with one of the horses of Selene, goddess of the moon, sinking into the waves. The male figure facing the surviving horse of Helios is probably either Heracles, a hero famous for his strength, or Dionysus, the youthful god of wine; the two seated female figures to the right of him are Demeter, the goddess of the grain-bearing earth, and her daughter Persephone, while the maiden apparently running towards them is most likely Hebe, the cup-bearer of the gods. The identity of the three other figures has not been definitely agreed on.

In the alcove at the south end of the gallery are the sculptures of the WEST PEDIMENT, which represent the contest between Athena and Poseidon, ruler of the sea, for Attica, the region containing Athens. The object of the contest was to produce the gift most useful to man: Poseidon struck the ground with his trident and a horse appeared, but Athena caused the first olive to grow and was awarded the verdict by the gods. The surviving sculptures have been considerably mutilated; the fine figure in the left angle, however, is recognized as Kephisus or Ilissus, a river god of Athens, and the figures on either side of the centre are Hermes and Iris, the supporters of Athena and Poseidon. To the right of Iris is the driver of Poseidon's chariot, while the figure to the extreme right was probably a sea-nymph.

On the walls of the alcoves are fifteen of the original ninety-two METOPES that alternated with the triglyphs (tablets ornamented with three vertical bands) on the outside of the Parthenon. Forty-one still survive in a decayed condition on the temple and one is in the Louvre at Paris. The museum's panels depict the lively battle between the Lapiths, a mythical Thessalian people, and the Centaurs, half horses and half men, who had attempted to carry off the bride of Peirithous, the Lapith king, and other women from the wedding feast. The myth, a favourite subject in Greek art, represents the triumph of civilization over barbarism.

Room 9 (the ROOM OF THE CARYATID), north of the Nereid Room, contains a beautiful caryatid (the figure of a woman serving as a pillar), from the 5th-century temple of Erechtheus on the Acropolis (see above), as well as an Ionic column from the east porch and bronzes, reliefs, vases, etc. (430–330 B.C.). In Room 10 (the PAYAVA ROOM) is a reconstruction of the Tomb of Payava (of the early 4th century B.C.) from Xanthos, standing 20 ft high, with a remarkable carved roof. The cases hold pottery, terracottas, and bronzes made in the Greek cities of southern Italy. Room 11, above, which affords a closer view of the tomb, contains Etruscan sculptures, bronzes, pottery, and jewellery.

Room 12 (the MAUSOLEUM ROOM), on the right of Room 10, holds the sculptures from the tomb built at Halicarnassus for Mausolus (d. 353 B.C.), a prince of Caria in Asia Minor, by his wife Artemisia, and one of the seven wonders of the ancient world. Here also is part of a sculptured column from the great temple in honour of Artemis at Ephesus ('Diana of the Ephesians'; see the *Acts of the Apostles*, XIX), a centre of Ionian Greeks in Asia Minor, rebuilt after 356 B.C. and another of the seven wonders of the world.

Room 13 (the HELLENISTIC ROOM), south of Room 12, is devoted to Greek art of the Hellenistic period and includes the beautiful statue of the goddess Demeter, of about 330 B.C., from Cnidus, a Dorian city on the south-west coast of Asia Minor; the head of a goddess, perhaps Aphrodite (2nd century B.C.); a bronze head of Sophocles (d. 406 B.C.); the seated figure of Dionysus from the choragic monument of Thrasyllos at Athens; and the Apotheosis of Homer, a white marble relief of about 150 B.C. signed by Archelaos of Priene, found at Bovillae on the Appian Way near Rome. In Room 14 (the FIRST ROMAN ROOM) is the famous Portland Vase, a Roman work of the 2nd century B.C. in the Greek style, consisting of two layers of opaque glass, the white which forms the design being cut away to reveal the blue background. It was smashed by an insane person in 1845, but has been carefully repaired. Here also are a bronze head of Hypnos, the Greek god of sleep (late 4th century B.C.), Apollo playing the lyre (1st century A.D.), and a fine marble bust of a lady, perhaps Antonia (d. about A.D. 38), daughter of Mark Antony and mother of the Emperor Claudius. Room 15 (the SECOND ROMAN ROOM) contains Roman copies of Greek statues, a remarkable head in porphyry (probably of Constantius Chlorus, father of Constantine the Great), and a mosaic of the 2nd century A.D. from Saint-Romain-en-Gal, France.

From Room 16, beyond, stairs lead down to a vestibule, on the south of which is the Assyrian Basement (see below) and on the north the LECTURE THEATRE. On the west are the WOLFSON GALLERIES (Rooms 77–85), opened in 1984–5 and containing a large collection of Greek and Roman sculptures, inscriptions, etc. These include finds excavated from the ruined city of Ephesus, on the west coast of Asia Minor (Room 82); a colossal foot of the Egyptian god, Serapis (2nd century A.D.), in Room 83 (on the left); marbles from the magnificent Towneley gift (Room 84); portrait busts (Room 85, left); other characteristic examples of Greek sculpture (Rooms 80–81, north of Room 82); Greek and Latin inscriptions, among them the dedication of a temple at Priene, on the coast of Asia Minor, by Alexander the Great (Room 78); and many fragments of famous buildings from Greece and other parts of the ancient world (Room 77). Stairs ascend from this room to Room 12.

Parallel to the Greek and Roman rooms are the *ASSYRIAN ANTIQUITIES, displaying the vigorous art of the northern part of the old Babylonian kingdom. The KHORSABAD ENTRANCE (Room 16; south of the Second Roman Room) contains the colossal winged and human-headed bulls that stood at the entrances to the palace of Sargon II (722–705 B.C.), the father of Sennacherib, at Khorsabad, near Nineveh, as well as slabs portraying Sargon II and other sculpture. The LACHISH ROOM, to the south, has wall-slabs illustrating the siege of the city of Lachish, in Palestine, by Sennacherib. The ASSYRIAN SALOON (Room 17), to the west of these, has other sculptures of the time of Sennacherib (704–681 B.C.) and his grandson, Ashurbanipal (668–627 B.C.), including a series of lively wall reliefs showing the lion hunts of Ashurbanipal.

The ASSYRIAN BASEMENT (Room 89), below, has reliefs mainly of scenes from the wars of Ashurbanipal. Room 90, on the left beyond this, contains sculptures from the temple of the goddess Ishtar (the Biblical Ashtorath) at Beth Shan in northern Palestine.

The NIMRUD GALLERY (Room 19), to the east of the Assyrian Saloon, contains sculptures from the palace of Ashurnasirpal II (883–859 B.C.) at Calah (the modern Nimrud), including reliefs of battles and hunting scenes. The ASSYRIAN TRANSEPT (Room 26), at the south end, contains the colossal winged and human-headed lions from the palace of Ashurnasirpal II and other sculptures, and the gates of Ashurnasirpal and Shalmaneser III (858–824 B.C.) from a temple at Balawat. The black obelisk here records the exploits of Shalmaneser III. The NIMRUD CENTRAL SALOON (Room 20), north of the Nimrud Gallery, holds sculptures mostly of the time of Tiglath-pileser III (745–727 B.C.). The NINEVEH GALLERY (Room 21), at the north end, contains reliefs from the palace built at Nineveh, the capital of Assyria, by Sennacherib.

The staircase starting to the north-east of this room ascends to the upper floor, where mummies and smaller Egyptian objects are exhibited. Room 24, opposite the foot of the staircase, is devoted to ANCIENT PALESTINE, and contains a reconstruction of a tomb near Jericho, originally cut into the solid rock about 2200 B.C.

To the east of the Assyrian galleries are the EGYPTIAN ANTIQUITIES, which are mostly arranged chronologically, starting at the north end of the main gallery (Room 25). The NORTH GALLERY contains statues of Sesostriss (or Senusret) III, a king of the 12th Dynasty (about 1850 B.C.), and remains from earlier dynasties, but the most notable sculptures are those of the 18th Dynasty, mainly from Thebes, on the upper Nile, which became the capital of the New Empire about 1600 B.C. They include the colossal red granite head and the arm of a statue, probably of Thothmes III (about 1450 B.C.), and two seated statues and three huge heads of Amenophis (or

Amenhetep) III (about 1400 B.C.), whose name is inscribed on a pair of red granite lions. THE CENTRAL SALOON is devoted to sculptures of the New Kingdom (1567–1085 B.C.), among them the black granite sarcophagus of Merimes, who was viceroy of Nubia under Amenophis III, and two red granite statues of Ramesses II (about 1250 B.C.), whose names and titles are inscribed on two monolithic columns. The colossal green granite scarab of about 550 B.C. is an emblem of the sun-god and was a symbol of creative power among the Egyptians. The SOUTH GALLERY contains sarcophagi and other monuments from the later dynasties. Near the centre is the * 'Rosetta Stone', a slab of black basalt dated 196 B.C., inscribed with a trilingual decree – twice in Egyptian (first in hieroglyphs, the classical writing of the priests, and again in demotic or secular characters) and once in a Greek translation. The stone, which was found near Rosetta, in the Nile delta, in 1799, gave scholars the key, through the Greek, to the Egyptian language.

A new extension on the south-west of the museum, designed by Colin St John Wilson, was opened in 1980. It contains a large gallery (Room 76) for SPECIAL EXHIBITIONS and a pleasant REFRESHMENT ROOM, on the walls of which is a reproduction of part of the Parthenon frieze.

In the east wing of the museum is the British Library's unrivalled collection of PRINTED BOOKS AND MANUSCRIPTS. The wall-cases in the first room hold the GRENVILLE LIBRARY of over 20,000 volumes bequeathed by Thomas Grenville (d. 1846). The centre cases contain a fine collection of beautiful *Illuminated Manuscripts of the 9th–16th centuries, mostly of English, Flemish, French, and Italian origin.

They include Bibles, psalters, books of hours, breviaries, etc., notable being the *Harley Gospels*, written entirely in gold at the court of the Emperor Charlemagne (about 800), the *St Ethelwold Benedictional* (10th century; formerly at Chatsworth, Derbyshire), a *Winchester Psalter* of about 1060, Bede's *Life of St Cuthbert* (of the 12th century, from Durham Cathedral), the *Luttrell Psalter* (made before 1340 for Sir Geoffrey Luttrell, a Lincolnshire landowner), the *Bedford Hours* and *Psalter*, written and illuminated for John, Duke of Bedford, brother of Henry V (English work), the *Bedford Hours* executed for the same duke in Paris (about 1423), and the *Breviary* of Queen Isabella of Spain, probably made at Bruges (about 1490).

The *MANUSCRIPT SALOON, beyond, contains some of the library's most famous treasures, among them numerous manuscripts, autographs, etc., of outstanding literary and historical interest. Cases hold the **Codex Sinaiticus*, a 4th-century Greek manuscript of the Bible, purchased from the Soviet Government in 1933 for £100,000; the **Codex Alexandrinus*, a 5th-century Greek manuscript of the Bible; the **Lindisfarne Gospels*, an exquisite illuminated manuscript believed to have been written about A.D. 700 by Eadfrith, bishop of Lindisfarne; and the 'Stonyhurst' Gospel from Northumbria, found in the coffin of St Cuthbert when it was opened at Durham in 1104. Of the first importance also are a Bull of Pope Innocent III accepting the grant by King John of the kingdoms of England and Ireland to the Holy Roman Church (1214), the original articles of the Barons accepted by John as the basis of *Magna Carta* (1215), and two of the four surviving original copies of the *Great Charter itself. Other cases contain a *Deed of Mortgage bearing the signature of William Shakespeare (1613) and *Sumer Is Icumen In*, the oldest piece of music extant with English words (composed at Reading Abbey in the 13th century). The musical manuscripts include also scores by Purcell, J. S. Bach, Handel (*Water Music*), Haydn, Mozart, Beethoven, Brahms, and Elgar (*Enigma Variations*).

Only a few of the other treasures can be mentioned. The English Literary Autographs include the *Booke of Sir Thomas More*, believed to be partly in Shakespeare's handwriting, and the manuscript of 'Alice's Adventures Under Ground', the original of *Alice in Wonderland*. Historical Autographs: Death warrant of the Earl of Essex, signed by Elizabeth I (1601); letters and documents of Cromwell, Wellington, General Gordon, Mary, Queen of Scots, and many other famous persons; Nelson's memorandum on naval tactics at Trafalgar (1805), and two log-books of his flagship, the *Victory*; and documents concerning the Antarctic Expedition of Captain Scott (1910–12). Chronicles of England: late-8th-century manuscript of Bede's *Ecclesiastical History*; 11th-century manuscript of the *Anglo-Saxon Chronicle*; and the History of Matthew Paris (d. 1259), a monk of St Albans. Medieval Charters and Manuscripts: the *Bosworth Psalter*, probably written at St Augustine's Abbey, Canterbury (late 10th century); unique MS. of *Beowulf* (about A.D. 1000); and an early-15th-century MS. of Chaucer's *Canterbury Tales*. Medieval Biblical Manuscripts: the *Alcuin Bible*, a 9th-century copy of a Latin Bible revised in 796–800 by Alcuin of York, abbot of Tours; the *Wyclif Bible*, the first to be written in English (about 1380). Royal books: the prayer book of Lady Jane Grey; and 15th-century Books of Heraldry.

Foreign Literary Autographs: sketch-books of Leonardo da Vinci and Dürer. Foreign Manuscripts: illuminated Bible prepared at the Benedictine abbey of St Martin at Tours (mid 9th century); early-12th-century illuminated copy of the *Commentary on the Apocalypse* by Beatus, an 8th-century Spanish theologian and geographer; the Gospels of Tsar Ivan Alexander of Bulgaria (1355–6); 15th-century illuminated French MS. of Froissart's *Chronicle*. Greek Papyri: the unique MS. of the *Odes of Bacchylides*, and the *Constitution of Athens* of Aristotle. Greek and Latin Manuscripts: 14th–15th-century Greek copy of the Geography of Ptolemy (about A.D. 90–168), and commentaries on the *Book of Job* composed by Pope Gregory the Great (8th century).

The CRAWFORD ROOM, on the right at the end of the Manuscript Saloon, is mainly used for special exhibitions.

On the left of the Manuscript Saloon is the KING'S LIBRARY, a fine hall built to house the magnificent library of George III, the 65,000 volumes of which are in the cases ranged round the walls. The floor cases contain a fine selection of Oriental Manuscripts and *Early Printed Books. Notable among these are a Chinese translation of the *Diamond Sutra* in the form of a long scroll, the earliest known printed work (A.D. 868), the *Gutenberg Bible* (printed in 1455–6), the first printed edition of Chaucer (1478), the first printed English Bible (by Miles Coverdale, 1535), a first edition of Cranmer's Bible (1540), and the first folio edition of Shakespeare's plays (1623).

The manuscripts include Hebrew, Persian, Turkish, and Indian Mughal works. In the centre of the hall is a statue of Shakespeare by Roubiliac (1758), bequeathed to the museum by the actor David Garrick, and at the north end are interesting collections of POSTAGE STAMPS. Flanking the north doorway are busts of Sir Hans Sloane (in terracotta, by Rysbrack) and Sir Joseph Banks, a benefactor of the museum (by Anne Seymour Damer), and beside the south doorway are busts of Sir Robert Cotton (in terracotta, by Roubiliac) and Dr Charles Burney, the historian of music (by Nollekens).

The staircase beyond the north doorway ascends to the upper Egyptian Rooms, etc., and to the Bridge leading to the King Edward VII Gallery. On the walls of the staircase are Roman mosaic pavements (chiefly from Asia Minor and north Africa), and on the Bridge is displayed a selection of maps, including Christopher Saxton's atlas of England and Wales (1579).

From the west side of the Entrance Hall the main staircase ascends to the UPPER FLOOR. The first rooms here are devoted to *PREHISTORY AND ROMAN BRITAIN. The Central Saloon (Room 35) contains a unique mosaic pavement of the 4th century A.D., with early Christian symbols, discovered in 1963 at Hinton St Mary (Dorset). Here also are a gold cup from Rollaton (Cornwall), a gold neck ornament from Mangerton (Ireland), and a jet necklace from Melfort (Scotland), all of the Early Bronze Age. The FIRST PREHISTORY ROOM (36), on the left, is confined to Early Man and includes flint handaxes of the Palaeolithic period (one found near Gray's Inn in 1690), sculptures made from reindeer antlers,

Mesolithic head-dresses made from the skulls and antlers of red deer, from Star Carr (Yorkshire), and Neolithic pottery and other products of the earliest farming communities. Here too are a burial of about 1800 B.C. from Barnack (Huntingdonshire) and the Folkton 'Drums', chalk cylinders found in a child's grave of the Bronze Age in North Yorkshire.

The LATER PREHISTORY ROOMS (37–9), opening on the south of the Central Saloon, are devoted to the Bronze and Iron Ages (from about 2000 B.C.). Among the relics are dug-out coffins of the early Bronze Age, found in a burial-chamber at Loose Howe (Yorkshire), Bronze Age weapons, etc., including a decorated shield from Aberystwyth (Wales), a large dish of the late Bronze Age (Hallstadt period: 7th–6th century B.C.), from Germany, and a fine painted urn from France of the later Iron Age (about 300 B.C.). In Room 39 are part of the Snettisham Theatre, a hoard of pre-Roman coins and metalwork (torcs or necklaces, bracelets, etc.) found near Sandringham (Norfolk); bronze wine flagons from Lorraine, of about 400 B.C. (early Celtic or La Tène period); an early Iron Age bronze disc from Ireland; a bronze shield of the early Iron Age from the Witham (Lincolnshire); a bronze helmet of before 25 B.C. dredged out of the Thames near Waterloo Bridge; a fine Iron Age mirror found at Desborough (Northamptonshire); Celtic wrought-iron furniture from burials of the 1st century B.C. at Welwyn (Hertfordshire); and remarkable glass gaming pieces from a grave at Welwyn Garden City, of which there is a reconstruction.

Room 40, east of the Central Saloon, is confined to ROMAN BRITAIN (from A.D. 43). Outstanding are the beautiful *MILDENHALL TREASURE, a hoard of 4th-century Roman silver tableware from Mildenhall (Suffolk), ploughed up in 1942, including a large embossed dish of exquisite workmanship, and the *WATER NEWTON TREASURE, the earliest known Roman ecclesiastical silverware, hidden in Huntingdonshire in the 4th century and discovered in 1975. Here also are painted wall-plaster from the Roman villa at Lullingstone (Kent); tablets from the fort of Vindolanda (about a mile south of Hadrian's Wall), the earliest written records in Britain; a bronze head of the Emperor Claudius (d. A.D. 54), found in the river Alde near Saxmundham (Suffolk); a bronze statue of the Emperor Nero (also from Suffolk); a bronze head of the Emperor Hadrian (about A.D. 122) found in the Thames near London Bridge; a cavalry parade helmet from Ribchester (Lancashire; about A.D. 100);

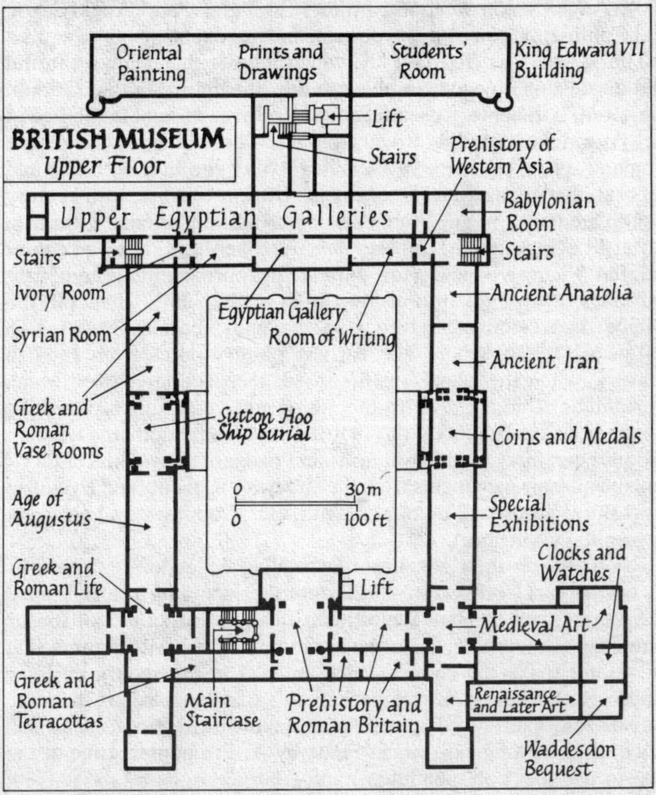

and a magnificent treasure brought to light at Thetford (Norfolk).

Room 41, east of the Roman Britain Room, is devoted to EARLY MEDIEVAL ART, from the later Roman Empire onwards (under rearrangement). Of the greatest interest are a *Silver treasure of the late 4th century A.D. from the Esquiline Hill at Rome; the Lycurgus Cup, an exquisite glass vessel of about 400; an early Byzantine ivory plaque showing the Archangel Michael (early 6th century); a Frankish glass drinking-horn, of the kind exported to Britain; the Franks Casket of carved whale's bone (Northumbrian; about A.D.

700); Anglo-Saxon weapons, pottery, and glass; and Anglo-Saxon and Continental jewellery, brooches, and pendants.

The MEDIEVAL ROOM (42), which follows, has many beautiful and interesting objects. Notable are the 9th-century Lothar Crystal, the set of 12th-century chessmen in walrus ivory found in the Isle of Lewis, and the splendid *Royal Gold Cup of the kings of France and England, probably made in Paris in 1380 for the Duc de Berry and decorated with translucent enamels. Here too are a 13th-century bishop's crosier, in gilt-bronze; a unique carved wooden gittern (a guitar-like instrument) of the late 13th century; a 15th-century painted Flemish shield (for parade at tournaments); and wall-paintings of the mid 16th century from St Stephen's Chapel in the Palace of Westminster. Room 43, beyond, contains MEDIEVAL TILES AND POTTERY. The earliest pottery dates from the 7th century, when the wheel was first used; the decorative tiles, which were made from the 13th to the 16th century, include a pavement from a house in Bristol (about 1450); a floor from Southam Delabere (Gloucestershire), with royal arms and badges (early 16th century); and fine mosaic pavements from the abbeys of Rievaulx and Byland in Yorkshire. Steps lead up to a tile-kiln, etc., from the royal palace at Clarendon (Wiltshire).

Room 44, on the right, has a fascinating collection of *CLOCKS AND WATCHES of the 15th–19th centuries, including a clock shaped like a ship, made by Hans Schlottheim of Augsburg about 1580 for the Emperor Rudolph II; an ornate standing-clock, with figures that move and strike the chimes, made in 1589 at Strasbourg by Isaac Habrecht, it is believed for Pope Sixtus V; a clock made in 1676 for the Royal Observatory by Thomas Tompion, the most famous of British clock makers; long-case clocks made by A. Fromanteel (one of the first to use the 'bob'-pendulum) and George Graham (about 1730; using the 'dead-beat' mechanism); and a remarkable rolling-ball clock to the design of Sir William Congreve (about 1810). The watches include a splendid French gold watch set with diamonds and enamelled with coloured flowers, with a movement made in London by Bouquet (about 1650). Room 45, beyond, contains the WADDESDON BEQUEST of Baron Ferdinand de Rothschild (d. 1898) of Waddesdon Manor (Buckinghamshire). This fine bequest consists mainly of miscellaneous works of art of European origin and of the 15th–17th centuries (pendants, cups, vases, caskets, enamels etc.).

Room 46, on the right, has RENAISSANCE AND LATER exhibits. On display are examples of English metalwork, including a Tudor silver-gilt tazza from Rochester Castle (Kent; about 1530); Continental silver and other metalwork (painted enamel triptych of about 1510 from Limoges, and a silver-gilt ewer and basin made by Pierre Harache in 1697 for the 1st Duke of Devonshire); a stoneware bust of Prince Rupert by John Dwight of Fulham (about 1675); and coins and medals, including examples by Pisanello, Benvenuto Cellini, and Hans Reinhardt. Room 47 contains an excellent collection of jewellery, enamels, and goldsmiths' work; 15th–18th-century European glass (Venetian, etc.); and *English and Continental pottery and porcelain, including a fine selection of Italian majolica, Spanish and other earthenware (Delft, etc.), Lambeth 'Delft', Fulham stoneware, Bow porcelain, Staffordshire slipware and salt-glaze, and Wedgwood ware (medallions, etc.).

Room 49, to the north of the Early Medieval Room, is reserved for SPECIAL EXHIBITIONS, which are held several times a year, usually for a few months each.

From the south side of the Prehistory rooms, access is gained to the TERRACOTTA AND BRONZE ROOM (68), containing Greek, Roman, and Etruscan terracottas and bronzes. Beyond opens the delightful room (69) devoted to *GREEK AND ROMAN LIFE, with cases illustrating home life, agriculture, industry, transport, weapons and armour, religion, music and drama, etc. The room also contains the museum's splendid collections of classical jewellery, silver (including the Roman Chaourse treasure of the 3rd century A.D.), and glassware. Room 70, beyond, is devoted to the AGE OF AUGUSTUS, with images of the Emperor Augustus (27 B.C.–A.D. 14) and related exhibits.

The GREEK AND ROMAN VASE ROOMS (72–3), farther on, contain a wonderful collection of *Greek, Etruscan and Roman vases from the 10th century B.C. onward, including white-ground and black-figured amphorae or wine-vessels presented as prizes at the Panathenaic games, Greek wine bowls and cups of the black-glazed and red-figured design, and Greek and Phoenician perfume-pots and toilet vessels (7th–6th centuries B.C.).

Room 71 contains (at present) the beautiful objects worked in gold, bronze, and enamel from the *SUTTON HOO SHIP BURIAL, the relics of an East Anglian chieftain of about A.D. 625, including his weapons, armour, and jewellery (discovered in 1939).

On the landing of the north-west staircase beyond Room 73 are antiquities from SOUTH ARABIA. To the right is the IVORY ROOM (58), with ivories mostly from the palaces at Nimrud (9th–7th centuries B.C.). Room 57, beyond, contains finds from ANCIENT SYRIA, among them tomb portraits from Palmyra.

On the north of the landing is an entrance to the UPPER EGYPTIAN ROOMS. The first two rooms (60–61) contain a large collection of mummies and mummy cases, the earliest of about 4500 B.C., as well as mummies of sacred animals (including the Bull of Apis, perhaps the 'Golden Calf' of the Bible), wooden coffins, and canopic jars and boxes. Room 62 is divided into two compartments, that on the left containing other funerary furniture, and papyri of 'Books of the Dead', and that on the right the Rhind Mathematical Papyrus of about 1600 B.C. and other papyri. The central passage is hung with copies of tomb-paintings. Room 63 is devoted to objects in everyday use among the ancient Egyptians, and Room 64 (on the right) contains early Egyptian objects, including a granite statue of a boat-builder, ivory figures and other sculpture, decorative pottery and glassware, and an inscribed slab from the royal tomb of Peribsen at Abydos (about 2700 B.C.). Room 65, east of Room 63, contains artistic work (small sculptures, gold figures of gods, seals and scarabs, jewellery, and glassware).

At the east end of this range of rooms is the BABYLONIAN ROOM (54), containing the outstanding collection of *Sumerian Antiquities from Ur of the Chaldees, dating from about 3500–1500 B.C. and largely excavated in 1919–34 by Sir Leonard Woolley. Among the many beautiful and interesting objects may be mentioned the reconstructed harp and silver lyre, and a shell and lapis lazuli mosaic showing a Sumerian king in peace and war. On the east wall is a copper relief of a lion-headed eagle. Also in this room are early painted pottery, seals, tools, and weapons from Western Asia and Babylonian writing tablets with cuneiform inscriptions.

The HITTITE LANDING, at the head of the north-east staircase, has sculptures from Carchemish (see below). Room 55, to the right, is confined to the PREHISTORY OF WESTERN ASIA (pottery, stone stamp-seals, plaster heads modelled over human skulls, etc.) The ROOM OF WRITING (56), next to it, contains Mesopotamian cylinder seals and illustrates the development of writing.

To the south of the landing is Room 52, devoted to ANCIENT ANATOLIA or Asia Minor, part of what is now Turkey. It contains miniature figures of gods and dignitaries made of lapis lazuli, steatite, and gold, and other sculptures from Carchemish, on the Euphrates, the capital of the Hittite Empire, which lasted until about 1200 B.C., as well as Urartian bronzes showing Assyrian influence. Room 51, beyond, is confined to ANCIENT IRAN, formerly Persia, with carvings from Persepolis, the capital of the Archaemenid (Old Persian) Empire; the Oxus Treasure, buried about 200 B.C.; gold masks of the Parthian dynasty (150 B.C. to A.D. 224) from Nineveh; and silver dishes of the Sassanian dynasty (A.D. 224 to 642) showing hunting scenes.

Room 50, farther on, contains a selection from the Department of COINS AND MEDALS' vast collection of coins, etc., of all ages and countries.

From Room 63 a corridor, containing Coptic sculpture and remarkable mummy-portraits of the Roman period in Egypt, leads north to the KING EDWARD VII BUILDING, where a staircase goes up to the exhibition of Prints and Drawings and the Oriental Paintings, and down to the rooms illustrating the Arts of Islam and of South and East Asia.

The collection of *PRINTS AND DRAWINGS, one of the largest and finest in the world, includes watercolours, woodcuts, engravings, and etchings. It is representative of every European school from the 15th century onward, and is particularly rich in British works. Only a small selection can be put on view in the gallery (Room 67; the bulk of the collection is kept in the Students' Room, at the east end); changes are frequent, and special exhibitions are held from time to time.

The west end of the gallery (Room 74) is devoted to an exhibition of ORIENTAL PAINTINGS, prints and sculptures, changed regularly to illustrate the range and variety of the collections, which cover almost every aspect of Eastern art and are especially rich in Chinese and Japanese painting and Buddhist objects, and Persian and Indian miniatures.

The Lower Gallery of the King Edward VII Building is concerned with the civilizations of Asia from the Neolithic period to the 19th century. The exhibits are mostly arranged chronologically, in a clockwise direction. In the western arm of Room 34 are those illustrating the ART OF ISLAM, with rich collections of pottery, glassware, metalwork, ivories, etc.; notable are the Turkish faience and the enamelled glass lamps. Next come the collections illustrating the ART OF INDIA and of Central and South-East Asia, including a fine assembly of Buddhist and Hindu bronzes and sculpture, intricately carved, textiles and antiquities from Central Asia, and weapons, textiles, ivories, wood-carvings, etc., from Indonesia, Vietnam, Burma, and Sri Lanka.

The central part of the gallery is devoted to the ART OF CHINA and Korea, and includes *Chinese pottery, porcelain, bronzes, silver, ivories, glassware, and jade, from Neolithic times (about 5000 B.C. onward) to the Ch'ing dynasty, which ended in

1912. Here are magnificent collections of ritual bronze vessels of the early Shang and Chou dynasties, glazed pottery of the Han dynasty, pottery tomb figures and furniture of the Six Dynasties and the T'ang period, beautiful ceramics of the Sung, Yüan, and Ming dynasties, and Korean pottery (funerary vases, etc.). In the eastern arm of the gallery are the collections illustrating the ART OF JAPAN. Notable are the pottery and porcelain, including funerary vases and tea-ceremony pottery, the small ivories and lacquer work, and the exotic 18th–19th-century armour. The reserve collections of Oriental antiquities are accessible to holders of tickets of admission to the Students' Room.

The staircase from the central entrance to the gallery descends to Room 75, continuing the Japanese art, and to the NORTH ENTRANCE LOBBY, which has an information desk and a bookstall.

CHELSEA ROYAL HOSPITAL Plan VII, F2

STATION: SLOANE SQUARE, about ¼ mile NE, on the Circle and District lines.—BUSES No. 39 in Royal Hospital Road, on the N; Nos. 11 and 137 in Lower Sloane Street, to the NE.

ADMISSION TO THE GROUNDS (free), daily, 10 to dusk; to the MUSEUM, CHAPEL, and GREAT HALL, Mondays–Saturdays 10 to 12 and 2 to 4 (Sundays 2 to 4 only; the Great Hall is closed on also on Saturday mornings); to the COUNCIL CHAMBER, Mondays–Saturdays, 10 to 12; to the NATIONAL ARMY MUSEUM, Mondays– Saturdays 10 to 5.30, Sundays 2 to 5.30 (free).—SERVICES in the Chapel on Sundays at 8.30, 11 (Parade Service), and 12; visitors are admitted, but seats are often filled early.

THE ROYAL HOSPITAL, Chelsea, more familiarly known as Chelsea Hospital, is an institution for veteran and invalid soldiers founded in 1682 by Charles II. The establishment of a standing army during the Commonwealth had made the provision of a hospital, rather than a system of pensions or poor relief, imperative; the inspiration for the idea, however, came from the Hôtel des Invalides in Paris (founded by Louis XIV in 1670), and not from the king's mistress, Nell Gwyn, as was long popularly supposed. The buildings, mainly of brick, were designed by Sir Christopher Wren and consist of three ranges enclosing a quadrangle open towards the river Thames, with wings extending on the east and west. Here the in-pensioners, who at present number about 450, are lodged, boarded, and clothed; invalid pensioners are cared for in the infirmary (rebuilt in 1961 and extended in 1971). Pensioner guides can be provided on previous application to the Adjutant (two weeks' notice required; a tip of 25p is customary).

Built on the site of an unsuccessful theological college founded by James I in 1609, the hospital owes its inception largely to Sir Stephen Fox, the former paymaster-general, who contributed the bulk of the funds and undertook the responsibility for its management. The scheme was supported by John Evelyn, the diarist, and the site was chosen by Wren. The buildings were first opened in 1692, when nearly 500 pensioners were admitted, armed, clothed, and organized under a Governor and other officers. Under William III nearly one-third of the extensive hospital grounds was granted to the Earl of Ranelagh, the treasurer. Some alterations and additions to the buildings were made by Robert Adam in 1765–82 and again later by Sir John Soane, but the main block has remained practically unchanged. The hospital was struck by bombs several times during the war, when the fatal casualties included one centenarian pensioner.

The pensioners wear a uniform dating from the Duke of Marlborough's time: scarlet frock coats in the summer and dark blue overcoats in the winter. Forage caps are normally worn, but these are exchanged for three-cornered cocked hats on special occasions, such as Oak Apple Day (29 May), when the pensioners receive double rations in honour of their founder's birthday. Military duties are now practically confined to attendance at church and pay parades. Pensioners must be of good character and at least sixty-five years of age, unless they are unable to earn their own living, when they must be fifty-five (younger only if disabled during their term of service). On entering the hospital they surrender their out-pensions, but in return are provided with board, accommodation, and clothing, a daily ration of beer or tobacco, and, if necessary, a small weekly allowance. Each year in December is celebrated the Ceremony of the Cheeses (first performed in 1691) and before Christmas the pensioners are presented with a large cake by Australian comrades.

The usual entrance is from Royal Hospital Road by the LONDON GATE, on the north-east. On the left is the OLD BURIAL GROUND, consecrated in 1691 and closed in 1855. Dr Charles Burney (d. 1814), historian of music, organist of the hospital from 1783 until his death, is buried here. The buildings on the east of the road, apart from the guardhouses of Wren, were mainly designed by Sir John Soane (1819); they include the SECRETARY'S OFFICE, with mementoes of the great Duke of Wellington, and a MUSEUM containing an interesting collection illustrating the history of the Royal Hospital, its pensioners and staff, and including over 2,100 medals. Opposite the Office is the LIGHT HORSE COURT, named from the old cavalrymen who formerly occupied the southern of the two projecting wings added by Wren in 1688. The northern wing, destroyed by bombing in 1945, was rebuilt to accommodate further pensioners in 1965. In the centre of the court is a well-head protected by a fine wrought-iron cage with a lantern.

A passage at the north end of the main east range admits to the delightful FIGURE COURT, the central quadrangle (1682), in the middle of which is a fine bronze statue of Charles II in Roman costume, by Grinling Gibbons. This is decorated with oak boughs on Oak Apple Day to commemorate the escape of the king from the Parliamentarians after the Battle of Worcester (1651) by hiding in an oak tree. The north range of building is adorned with a cupola, and on the side facing the Figure Court has a Doric portico flanked by low colonnades with pairs of columns. Between this portico and the main entrance, with its original massive doors, is an octagonal VESTIBULE, steps on either side of which ascend to the Chapel, on the east, and the Great Hall.

The CHAPEL, which has panelled walls and a barrel vault, was completed by Wren in 1687 and has survived almost untouched since, except for the addition in 1920 of carved choir stalls, arranged unusually in the centre on either side of the nave. The older carving (including the fine reredos and altar-rails) is by William Emmett and William Morgan, the plasterwork by Henry Margetts. The spirited painting of the Resurrection, in the dome of the apse, is by Sebastiano Ricci (an Italian who lived in England about 1710–15) and was last restored in 1948. The notable plate bears the hallmark for 1687–8; the altar cross was made to harmonize with it by Leslie Durbin (1953).

The panelled GREAT HALL, serving its original purpose as a dining hall, has royal portraits and copies of flags captured in 1793–1815 in France and the Netherlands and in 1812–15 from the Americans. Over the dais at the west end is a large mural painting of Charles II on horseback, begun by Antonio Verrio but completed by Henry Cooke; and on the tables are six 'blackjacks', great leather jugs from which beer was formerly served. The Duke of Wellington lay in state in this hall before his burial in St Paul's (1852).

In the main east and west ranges are the chief quarters of the pensioners, occupying the whole of the four floors. Each floor in both ranges is divided into two galleries or Long Wards, containing twenty-six berths or cubicles, one for each pensioner. At the south end of the east range is the GOVERNOR'S HOUSE, which includes a COUNCIL CHAMBER beautifully decorated by Wren, with additions by Robert Adam, and hung with fine portraits of Charles I and his family (attributed to Van Dyck), Charles II (by Lely), William III (by

Kneller), and others. From the SOUTH TERRACE, between the ends of the ranges, there is a good prospect of the hospital and the gardens stretching down to the Embankment in which the annual Chelsea Flower Show is held (compare Route 8). The guns displayed below the terrace include a battery captured at Waterloo.

The COLLEGE COURT, formerly the Infirmary Court, added in 1688 on the west of the hospital, is similar in design to the eastern court. Its northern wing has been converted into recreation rooms and a pensioners' club. The buildings on the farther side of the west road (which leads to the Chelsea Gate) are mainly by Soane (1809–22), but his Infirmary, which lay behind the Stable Yard, was destroyed in 1941 by a land mine, with much loss of life. Near the south end of the road is a former greenhouse or orangery built by Vanbrugh about 1725, but remodelled (1963) as a Roman Catholic chapel and library. The house behind, built in 1809 by Thomas Leverton, a pupil of Adam, has since been enlarged and converted into officers' quarters.

Entered from the east road of the hospital and now included in its grounds are the RANELAGH GARDENS (open to visitors), which formed part of the estate of the Earl of Ranelagh (d. 1712), and afterwards became a fashionable place of entertainment. The gardens were laid out afresh about 1860, and of the famous Rotunda and other 18th-century buildings no trace remains. On the north side of Royal Hospital Road is a large open space known as BURTON'S COURT (now a playing-field), on the farther side of which is the old main entrance to the hospital, with notable wrought-iron gates. The avenue across the court was intended as the beginning of a grand avenue leading direct to Kensington Palace (compare Route 8).

In Royal Hospital Road, to the west, is the NATIONAL ARMY MUSEUM, founded in 1960 and moved in 1971 from Sandhurst (Berkshire) to a new building by Lord Holford. Its collections illustrate the histories of the armies of Britain, the Empire, and the Commonwealth from the time of Henry VII to the Falklands Campaign of 1982. They include uniforms, equipment, and weapons, orders and decorations, and personal relics, as well as many military paintings, among them portraits by Reynolds, Romney, Raeburn, Lawrence, and others. Displays show the development of weapons and the evolution of transport and communications in war. A new extension opened in 1983 has reconstructions illustrating the life of the soldier since 1914.

The Library has over 30,000 books on British military history, as well as an important collection of manuscripts, prints, and photographs from 1840 onward. The Reading Room is open on Tuesdays–Saturdays, 10 to 4.30, to holders of readers' tickets, obtainable on written application to the Director. The Department of Education arranges lectures and films on the campaigns and social history of the army.

HOUSES OF PARLIAMENT Plan VIII, C3

STATION: WESTMINSTER, to the N, on the Circle and District lines. — BUSES in Whitehall, see Route 2; in Victoria Street, see Route 4; along Millbank, see Route 3; across Westminster Bridge and along the Victoria Embankment, see Route 26.

ADMISSION to the Houses of Parliament and Westminster Hall at present (1985) only under the escort of a Member of Parliament (preferably on Monday–Thursday mornings).

The HOUSE OF COMMONS normally meets on Mondays–Thursdays at 2.30 p.m. and on Fridays at 9.30 a.m. Visitors are admitted to the gallery (reached via St Stephen's Porch), by order from a member, between 2.30 and 3 (9.30 and 10 on Fridays), or on application at the Admission Order Office in St Stephen's Hall from about 4.30 (Fridays about 9.30) until the house rises (see p. 365). In the latter case there is often some delay, and Commonwealth and foreign visitors will find it preferable to apply to their representatives in London for an introduction. A programme of the proposed business for the week is displayed outside St Stephen's Porch. The HOUSE OF LORDS usually meets on Mondays–Wednesdays at 2.30 and on Thursdays at 3. Visitors must wait outside St Stephen's Porch (Old Palace Yard side; or in Westminster Hall during inclement weather) and are admitted to the Strangers' Gallery (limited accommodation) at 2.40 or 3.10. They are also admitted by permits obtainable from a member or officer of either house, and when the House of Lords is sitting as a Court of Appeal (usually in the morning).

A repository for the records of Parliament was constructed in the Victoria Tower in 1963. The Search Room here of the HOUSE OF LORDS RECORD OFFICE, which preserves some three million documents, including Acts of Parliament from 1497 onward, is open to visitors on Mondays–Fridays from 9.30 to 5.30.

The HOUSES OF PARLIAMENT, officially the New Palace of Westminster, the seat of the supreme legislature in Great Britain and Northern Ireland, is a rambling but dignified pile of buildings in an elaborate late-Gothic style, bordering the river Thames and close to Westminster Bridge. Designed by Sir Charles Barry (who was assisted in the details by A. W. Pugin), it was begun in 1840 and the first parliament here was opened by Queen Victoria in 1852. After the death of the architect in 1860 the work was continued under the direction of his son, Edward M. Barry, and it was finally completed in 1888. The stone used for the exterior was magnesian limestone from Anston, in Yorkshire, but it has failed to stand up to the exacting London climate and is constantly in need of repair. The building, which cost over £3 million, covers an area of about eight acres and has eleven courtyards, 100 staircases, over 1,000 apartments, and about two miles of passages. Besides the House of Commons, in the northern part, and the House of Lords, in the southern part, it contains innumerable offices, committee rooms, libraries, dining rooms, etc., as well as the residences of the Speaker of the House of Commons, the Serjeant at Arms, and other officers, and incorporates Westminster Hall and the crypt of St Stephen's Chapel, practically the only parts of the former royal palace to survive the fire which destroyed the previous building.

At the south-west corner of the building rises the VICTORIA TOWER, completed in 1858, the largest and tallest square tower in the world, with 75-ft sides and reaching 336 ft to the tops of the pinnacles. The archway, 50 ft high, below the tower is that through which the sovereign enters on the State opening of Parliament (generally the second week in November). In the richly decorated façade fronting Old Palace Yard is the ornate porch of the Peers' Entrance. The CENTRAL SPIRE, which has an open lantern serving as the mouth of a ventilating shaft, rises to 300 ft above the ground. On the north of Old Palace Yard is ST STEPHEN'S PORCH, recast by J. L. Pearson in 1888, and farther north is WESTMINSTER HALL, the only remaining part of the medieval building (except St Stephen's Crypt and the Jewel Tower). The north front of the hall (likewise altered by Pearson) faces NEW PALACE YARD, in which is the members' entrance to the House of Commons. The façade of the main building is embellished with niches containing statues of English monarchs, and the north side of the yard is shaded by old catalpa trees.

At the north end of the building stands the splendid CLOCK TOWER, the finial above the lantern of which rises to 320 ft. A light in the tower by night and a flag on the Victoria Tower by day indicate that the House of Commons is sitting. The clock, famous for the accuracy of its time-keeping, has four dials each 23 ft in diameter, with figures 2 ft high and hands 14 and 9 ft long. The pendulum, which beats once every two seconds, is 13 ft long and weighs 685 lb. The hours are struck on the great bell of 'Big Ben' (a name often misapplied to the clock or even to the tower), cast in 1858 at Whitechapel and weighing over thirteen and a half tons. It was named after Sir Benjamin Hall, First Commissioner of Works at the time it was hung. The short north front of the building carries the statues and shields-of-arms of the Anglo-Saxon kings, while the fine east façade (best viewed from the river) bears the shields-of-arms of English sovereigns from William the Conqueror to Victoria. This front is separated from the river wall by a paved terrace, 700 ft long, between the noble pairs of towers at each end. The total length of the east front of the building is 872 ft.

As their official title suggests, the Houses of Parliament stand on the site of the old royal Palace of Westminster, first known to have been occupied by Edward the Confessor (1042–66) and the principal London residence of the sovereign until Henry VIII helped himself to Whitehall Palace in 1529. The palace was added to by William the Conqueror and by his successor William Rufus, who built Westminster Hall in 1097–9. Henry II gave a feast to 6,000 poor people here on New Year's Day, 1236, but in 1399 the hall was largely rebuilt (after a fire) by Richard II, who introduced the magnificent hammerbeam roof. St Stephen's Chapel, originally founded by King Stephen, was begun anew by Edward I in 1292 and completed in 1346 by Edward III, who founded a college, consisting of a dean and twelve canons, in connection with it. In 1512 the palace was gravely damaged by a fire from which only Westminster Hall and the chapel with its crypt and cloisters escaped. It was never entirely rebuilt, and after Henry VIII transferred his loyalties to Whitehall it ceased to be a residence of the sovereign. The New Palace, however, still ranks as a royal palace, under the charge of the Lord Great Chamberlain, an office hereditary since the reign of Henry I in the family of De Vere, Earls of Oxford.

Westminster Hall, as the great hall of the royal palace, was from an early date the meeting-place of the Great Council, the predecessor of Parliament and the Courts of Justice, and it became the custom to proclaim parliament here, though few in fact actually met in the hall. The palace first became a regular seat of parliament in 1547, when the House of Commons transferred its sittings from the Chapter House of Westminster Abbey to St Stephen's Chapel, which (like other free chapels) had been suppressed by Edward VI. From the 16th century the House of Lords assembled in a chamber at the south end of Old Palace Yard (formerly an inner court of the palace) and in 1605 this was the scene of the Gunpowder Plot, the attempt of a number of Roman Catholics to blow up James I with the Lords and Commons as they assembled for the opening of Parliament on 5 November. The plot was revealed through an anonymous letter sent to Lord Monteagle; the cellars were searched, and Guy Fawkes, discovered ready to set fire to the barrels of gunpowder, was captured. Fawkes and the other chief conspirators were executed. The vaults of the Houses of Parliament are still formally searched by Yeomen of the Guard each year before the State opening of the session by the sovereign.

In 1834 the palace was burned to the ground, with the exception of Westminster Hall, the chapel crypt, part of the cloisters, and the Jewel Tower (Route 3). A new building for the legislature was decided on and in 1836 the design of Charles Barry was selected from ninety-seven entered in open competition. The river wall, built of Aberdeen granite, was completed in 1840, the Lords moved into their new home in 1847, and the 'New Palace' was officially opened with the occupation of the House of Commons in 1852. The building was damaged on fourteen occasions during the Second World War, the most serious attack, on 10 May 1941, resulting in the destruction of the House of Commons. A new chamber, designed by Sir Giles Scott in keeping with the older work, was built in 1948–50.

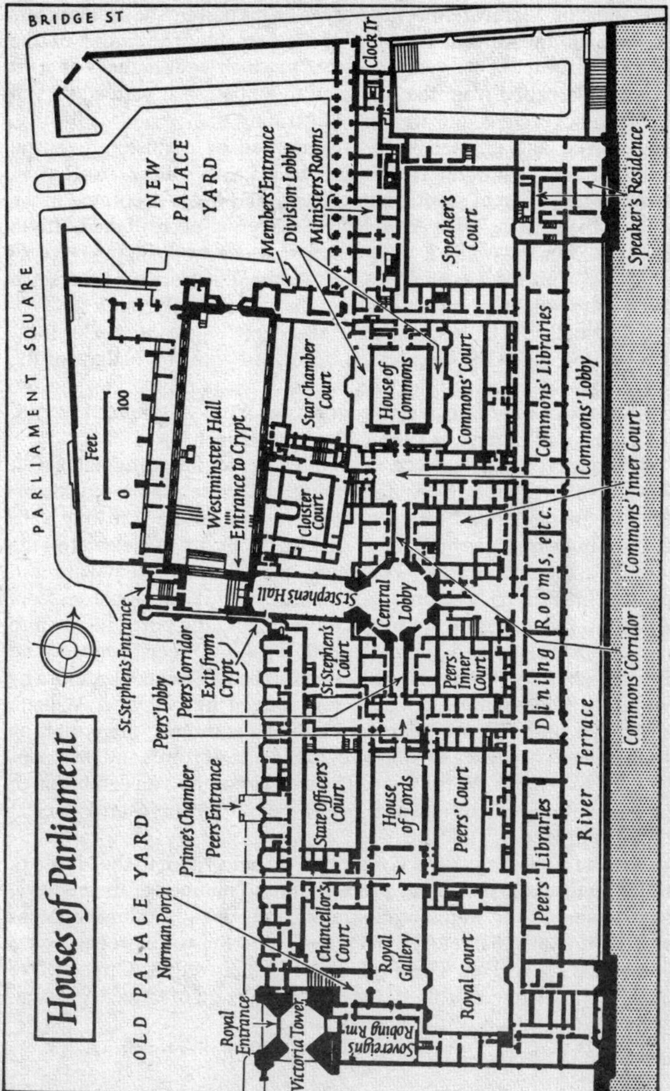
Houses of Parliament
BRIDGE ST
NEW PALACE YARD
PARLIAMENT SQUARE
OLD PALACE YARD
Feet
0
100
Clock Tr
Members' Entrance
Division Lobby
Ministers' Rooms
Speaker's Court
Speaker's Residence
Westminster Hall
Entrance to Crypt
Star Chamber Court
Cloister Court
House of Commons
Commons' Court
Commons' Libraries
Commons' Lobby
Commons' Inner Court
St Stephen's Entrance
St Stephen's Hall
Central Lobby
Peers' Corridor
Exit from Crypt
Peers' Lobby
St Stephen's Court
Peers' Inner Court
Dining Rooms, etc.
Commons' Corridor
Prince's Chamber
Peers' Entrance
State Officers' Court
House of Lords
Peers' Court
Peers' Libraries
River Terrace
Norman Porch
Chancellor's Court
Royal Gallery
Royal Court
Royal Entrance
Victoria Tower
Sovereign's Robing Rm

Under the Victoria Tower the sovereign is met by the high officers of state at the official opening of Parliament. The route of the procession is up the ROYAL STAIRCASE, which leads to the NORMAN PORCH, so called from the intention to embellish it with statues of Norman sovereigns and frescoes illustrating that period of history. The carved and groined vault is supported by a clustered central pillar. On the right is the entrance to the QUEEN'S ROBING ROOM, 54 ft long, the first of several handsome rooms finely decorated in the style of the period. It was adapted as the meeting-place of the Lords in 1941–51. On the walls is a series of frescoes by William Dyce of episodes from the Legend of King Arthur, illustrative of the spirit of chivalry, while around the room runs an oak dado with a series of carved panels, by H. H. Armstead, also depicting Arthurian legends. The ceiling, likewise panelled, is decorated with the badges of the sovereigns of England; the fireplace of variegated marble and the metalwork of the doors are also worthy of note. At the farther end, beneath a rich canopy, is a chair of state of Queen Victoria.

The next room is the ROYAL GALLERY, an imposing hall 110 ft long, with an elaborate ceiling. Around the frieze are the shields-of-arms of the monarchs of England and Scotland, and on the long walls are two huge frescoes by Daniel Maclise: the Death of Nelson (on the left) and the Meeting of Wellington and Blücher after Waterloo, painted in 1858–65. The bronze-gilt statues of English monarchs from Alfred to Queen Anne are by J. B. Philip, and the portraits of more recent sovereigns and their consorts include Queen Victoria and Prince Albert by Winterhalter, Edward VII and Queen Alexandra by Sir Luke Fildes, and George V and Queen Mary by Sir William Llewellyn. In an alcove near the south end is the war memorial, by John Tweed, to peers and officers of the House of Lords and their sons who fell in the two World Wars. The gallery contains an exhibition of Parliamentary records and a model of the old Westminster Palace at the time of Henry VIII.

Beyond is the PRINCE'S CHAMBER, an ante-room to the House of Lords, with dark panelling, probably in the manner of its medieval forerunner. In the wainscoting are portraits of the Tudor monarchs and their royal and noble relatives, and below these are twelve bronze bas-reliefs by William Theed of events in their reigns. Opposite the entrance is a white marble statue by John Gibson of Queen Victoria, enthroned between Justice and Clemency.

The HOUSE OF LORDS is a noble Gothic hall, 80 ft long, elaborately decorated by A. W. Pugin. On both sides are the red leather benches of the peers, who now number over 1,000, and at the south end, raised on a dais and covered by a richly carved and gilded canopy, is the ornate throne of the Queen. When the sovereign is a king, a second throne, slightly lower, stands on the right for his consort. At the opening of Parliament this space sometimes contains the state chair of the Prince of Wales, while the space on the left contains that of the Duke of Edinburgh. In front of the throne is the Woolsack, a plain ottoman stuffed with wool from the British countries and the Commonwealth, occupied during the sitting of the House by the Lord Chancellor, who is its president, with the mace behind him. The woolsack, which by tradition has stood in the house since the time of Edward III, is a reminder of the days when the wealth of England depended to a great extent on its thriving wool trade. The two smaller woolsacks beyond the Chancellor's woolsack are occupied by the judges at the opening of Parliament, and in front of them is the Table of the House, on which motions for discussion are placed ('tabled'). At the north end of the chamber is the Bar, where lawsuits on final appeal are pleaded (see below) and where the Commons, headed by their Speaker, attend on ceremonial occasions. Above the north entrance is the Reporters' Gallery, with the Strangers' Gallery behind; and above the throne on either side are galleries for Distinguished Visitors.

The six recesses behind the galleries are decorated with frescoes that are notable as the first examples of large wall-paintings by British artists. Those on the south, of events in British history, are by C. W. Cope and William Dyce; those at the north end, by Daniel Maclise and J. C. Horsley, symbolize Justice, Religion, and Chivalry. The windows on either side, restored after war damage, contain stained glass by Carl Edwards showing the armorial bearings of peers from 1360 to 1900, while the niches around the chamber are filled with statues of the barons who extorted Magna Carta from King John. The chamber was used by the House of Commons in 1941–50.

Compared with the House of Commons, procedure in the House of Lords is relatively simple and sittings are rarely lengthy. After prayers (conducted by a bishop) and a few questions, the house goes on to the examination of a bill or (if a member has 'moved for papers') to a debate on a topical subject or a matter of policy. Divisions are infrequent, but on these occasions the peers file into the lobbies on either side, where they record a vote of 'Content' or 'Not Content'. The House of Lords is also the final Court of Appeal for all courts in Great Britain and Northern Ireland (except for criminal cases in Scotland).

Beyond the House of Lords, and entered through solid brass gates, is the PEERS' LOBBY, a square chamber with a pavement of fine encaustic tiles. Over the four doors are painted the arms of the six royal lines of England (Saxon, Norman, Plantagenet, Tudor, Stuart, and Hanoverian) with the initial letters of each carved below, and above the south door are the royal arms and motto, and the coats of arms of England, Scotland, and Ireland. The door on the west leads to the Peers' Robing Room, while that on the east gives access to the House of Lords' Library.

The PEERS' CORRIDOR, painted with eight frescoes by C. W. Cope of episodes in the Stuart and Commonwealth periods, leads north to the CENTRAL LOBBY, an elaborately decorated octagonal vestibule, 60 ft across and 75 ft high, with a vaulted stone ceiling that supports the central spire of the palace. The spaces between the embossed ribs of the vault are filled with Venetian glass mosaics showing royal emblems. Over the doors are mosaics of the British patron saints, SS. George and David, designed by Sir Edward Poynter and executed by Salviati (1870–98), and SS. Andrew and Patrick designed by R. Anning Bell and executed by Gertrude Martin (1923–4). The niches round the doors and windows contain statues of the Plantagenet sovereigns and their consorts, and on pedestals are statues of Victorian statesmen. In the pavement of encaustic tiles is the text, in Latin from the Vulgate, 'Except the Lord keep the house, they labour in vain that build it'.

The Central Lobby marks the division between the precincts of the Lords and those of the Commons. Any visitor who has business with a member when Parliament is sitting is admitted to the lobby, where he fills in a 'card' and hands it to one of the policemen on duty.

The COMMONS' CORRIDOR, which has eight paintings by E. M. Ward of incidents in the Commonwealth and Restoration periods, runs north to the COMMONS' LOBBY, a square Gothic chamber with statues of 20th-century statesmen. The door on the east gives access to the House of Commons' Library, etc. On the north is the CHURCHILL ARCH, made from stones damaged in the fire of 1941 and erected here at the suggestion of Sir Winston Churchill in memory of those who 'kept the bridge' during the dark days of the War. Beside the arch are bronze statues of David Lloyd George (d. 1945), by Uli Nimptsch (1963), and Sir Winston (d. 1965), by Oscar Nemon (1969), and a statue of Earl Attlee (d. 1967), the Labour leader, by Ivor Roberts-Jones, was placed in the lobby in 1979.

The door beyond the arch admits to the HOUSE OF COMMONS,

completely destroyed by fire in the air-raid of 10 May 1941, and rebuilt in a free adaptation of the late-Gothic style by Sir Giles Gilbert Scott. The new chamber, opened in 1950, has the same floor length as the old (68 ft), but is longer above the gallery level (now 103 ft). At the north end is the chair of black bean wood (the gift of Australia) of the Speaker, who presides over the House, and in front of it is the Table, of Canadian oak, on which the mace rests while the House is sitting (when the House is 'in Committee', however, the mace is placed under the table and the Speaker vacates his chair). The despatch boxes were presented by New Zealand, the three clerks' chairs by South Africa, and the Serjeant at Arms' chair by Sri Lanka, and many of the other furnishings are gifts also from the Commonwealth; the woodwork around the chamber is of oak from Shropshire. On both sides of the 'floor' of the House are the green hide benches of the members, with seats for 437 (as before), though there are now 650 members. The party in office occupies the benches to the right of the Speaker, the front bench being reserved for cabinet ministers and the Prime Minister taking the seat opposite the despatch box. Facing are the seats of the oppostion, whose leaders likewise occupy the front benches. On the floor before the benches are two red lines (by tradition two sword-lengths apart) across which members must not step while in debate. On the back of the Speaker's chair is a bag in which petitions to Parliament are placed; above it is the Press Gallery and at the other end of the chamber is the Public Gallery. The shields of arms below the galleries are those of members of the House who lost their lives in the two World Wars.

The House is opened each day with a procession in which the Speaker (in his traditional dress of knee breeches and long black gown) is preceded by a messenger (wearing a House of Commons badge, dating from 1755) and the Serjeant at Arms, who carries the mace (the symbol of authority), and is followed by his train-bearer, chaplain, and secretary. On Mondays–Thursdays, after prayers (read by the chaplain) and 'questions' addressed to ministers, public business begins about 3.30 and consists of the presentation of bills and the moving of motions, followed by the 'Orders of the Day', which include the discussion of public bills and certain motions. Visitors should obtain a copy of the official guide, containing the procedure and the agenda of the day's business, from a messenger. If a division is taken, members voting 'aye' file out behind the Speaker's chair into the lobby on his right, while those voting 'no' pass out at the other end of the chamber to the lobby on his left, where they are counted on each side by two members called 'tellers'. The Speaker (unlike the Chancellor in the House of Lords) cannot vote. Business is normally suspended by order at 10 p.m. and a debate of a general nature on a 'motion for the adjournment' then takes place for half an hour, after which the House rises. The sitting of the House may be extended after the 10 o'clock order, however, for business of a special character (financial bills, etc.). Fridays are generally devoted to private members' bills; questions are not usually asked, and the House rises at about 4.30 p.m.

In the No Lobby are three volumes of the journals of the House open to show the record of significant events in parliamentary history: the Commons' protestation of their rights and privileges torn out by James I (1621), the attempted arrest by Charles I in the House of the five members he had impeached of high treason (1642), and the forcible expelling of the Rump Parliament by Oliver Cromwell (1653).

The return is made to the Central Lobby, where the door on the right (west) admits to ST STEPHEN'S HALL, a lofty vaulted chamber, 95 ft long, on the exact site of the royal chapel of St Stephen, and the meeting-place of the House of Commons from 1547 until the fire of 1834. The name 'St Stephen's' is still sometimes used as a synonym for the House of Commons. Over the doors are large mosaics by R. Anning Bell and Gertrude Martin relating to the original founding of the chapel by King Stephen (east end) and the completion of its rebuilding by Edward III. In niches at the angles of the hall are statues of the Norman and Plantagenet kings and queens, and pedestals support statues of British statesmen of the 17th–19th centuries. The windows contain the arms of Parliamentary cities and boroughs, and the panels below them hold paintings, unveiled in 1927, depicting the Building of Britain (877–1707).

Steps lead down to ST STEPHEN'S PORCH, which discloses an impressive view along the length of Westminster Hall. The large window on the left formerly closed the south end of the hall, but it was set back in its present position by Barry. The stained glass of service badges and armorial bearings or monograms of members, by Sir Ninian Comper (1953), together with the sculptured frieze below, by Sir Bertram Mackennal (1922), form the war memorials to members and officers of both Houses of Parliament.

WESTMINSTER HALL, the oldest and chief survival of the medieval palace of Westminster, is a noble and beautiful hall nearly 240 ft long, 68 ft wide, and 92 ft high to the centre of the roof. Built originally in 1097–9 by William II, it was practically rebuilt by Richard II in 1394–9. The architect was Henry Yevele, who designed the naves of Westminster Abbey and Canterbury Cathedral; the splendid hammerbeam roof of twelve bays, the finest of its kind in the world, was largely the work of Hugh Herland, master-carpenter to Edward III.

The oak is believed to have come from Wadhurst, in Sussex, and the delightful angels which form the ends of the beams were carved by Robert Grassington. The lantern was redesigned in 1822 on a smaller scale by Sir John Soane, and the roof, which has the largest unsupported span in the country, was completely restored in 1914–23, using timber from the supposed original source. Four bays of the roof greatly damaged in 1941 have again been restored. In niches and window recesses of the south and east walls are late-14th-century statues of kings, and below the windows is a string-course displaying the chained-hart badge of Richard II.

The chief courts of English law sat in the hall from the late 13th century until 1825 and then in new adjoining buildings until 1882, when the Royal Courts of Justice were opened in the Strand. The 19th-century buildings were then pulled down and the west front was refashioned by J. L. Pearson.

The hall has witnessed many grave and stirring events in English history. Sir William Wallace, the Scottish patriot, was condemned to death in the old hall in 1305, and here Edward II was forced to abdicate in 1327. One of the first events to take place in the new hall of Richard II was, oddly enough, the deposition of that king in 1399 in favour of Henry IV. The hall has been the scene of many important state trials, and among those condemned to death here have been Perkin Warbeck (1498), Sir Thomas More and Bishop Fisher (1535), Lord Protector Somerset (1551), the Earl of Essex (1601), Guy Fawkes and seven of his fellow conspirators (1606), and the Earl of Strafford (1641). The most memorable event was perhaps the condemnation of Charles I in 1649, and a tablet on the steps (actually constructed by Barry) marks approximately the place where the king sat during his trial. Oliver Cromwell was installed as Lord Protector here in 1653, and in 1661, after his body had been exhumed from Westminster Abbey, his head was set up on a pole on the roof of the hall, where it remained until 1684. Titus Oates, the conspirator, was convicted of perjury in the hall in 1685, and here in 1688 the seven bishops who refused to proclaim the declaration of indulgence of James II were acquitted by a jury. The Earl of Derwentwater and others who revolted in 1715 were condemned here, as were Lord Lovat and the Jacobite lords of 1745. Warren Hastings was here acquitted of the charge of impeachment after a trial extending over seven years (1788–95). The last public trial in the hall was that of Viscount Melville in 1806 for the corrupt administration of Navy funds. Feasts preceding their coronations were given in the hall by kings from Stephen to George IV, and until the time of James II it was the custom for the monarch to proceed by river from the Tower for the occasion. Several recent sovereigns and their consorts lay in state in the hall.

From the south-east angle of Westminster Hall a staircase descends to ST STEPHEN'S CRYPT, or the chapel of St Mary Undercroft. This was in fact the crypt of St Stephen's Chapel; completed in 1327, it escaped the fire of 1834. It was rather too elaborately painted and gilded in 1868 by E. M. Barry, but the clustered columns of Purbeck marble, the fine early lierne vault, and the carved bosses depicting the martyrdoms of saints are interesting. The chapel is used for marriages of M.P.s (of whatever persuasion) and the christenings of their children. nother staircase leads up to the west end of Old Palace Yard.

ST STEPHEN'S CLOISTERS, to the east of Westminster Hall, were built in 1526–9 and are remarkable for their fan-vaulted ceiling, rivalling that of Henry VII's Chapel in Westminster Abbey. An oratory opening from the west walk contains a richly-carved mahogany table used in the House of Commons from about 1730 until 1834. The south and east sides of the cloisters, severely damaged in 1940, have been finely restored.

IMPERIAL WAR MUSEUM Plan IX, D2

STATIONS: LAMBETH NORTH, ¼ m. NW, on the Bakerloo line; ELEPHANT & CASTLE, nearly ½ m. E, on the Bakerloo and Northern Lines. — BUSES in Lambeth Road, see Route 35; Nos. 3, 155, 159, and 172 in Kennington Road (W of the museum); Nos. 12, 53, 109, 171, and 184 in St George's Road (E of the museum) or Westminster Bridge Road (farther N). No. 10 from Victoria Station and Nos. 10 and 44 from London Bridge station pass the museum entrance.

ADMISSION Mondays–Saturdays 10 to 5.50, Sundays 2 to 5.50 (free). Closed on New Year's Day, Good Friday, May Day Monday, Christmas Eve and Day, and Boxing Day. The LIBRARY and other reference sections (see below) are open on Mondays–Fridays 10 to 5. FILM SHOWS (free) on Saturdays and Sundays at 3.

The IMPERIAL WAR MUSEUM, established after the First World War and transferred to its present building at Lambeth in 1936, records and illustrates in every aspect all the campaigns in which the armed forces of Britain and the Commonwealth have been engaged since August 1914. Apart from typical examples of the actual material and equipment used by the Royal Navy, the Army, the Royal Air Force, and other services, the museum contains numerous models, paintings, and sculptures, and relics of famous war leaders. In addition, it has valuable reference sections of books, maps, photographs, films, etc., accessible to students. *A considerable rearrangement of the galleries is now taking place, and a programme of reconstruction of the museum, begun in 1985, will result in further changes.*

The creation of a national war museum was approved by the War Cabinet in 1917 and the museum was first opened in 1920 at the Crystal Palace. It was housed in part of the Imperial Institute at South Kensington from 1924 until 1935, and in the following year it was removed to its present home in what was originally the central portion of the Bethlem Royal Hospital for the insane, designed in 1812–15 by James Lewis and given its imposing portico and lofty dome in 1846 by Sydney Smirke. The hospital was transferred to new buildings near Croydon (Surrey) in 1930 and the wings of the old building were subsequently demolished, with the result that the dome now looks top heavy. In addition to its permanent displays, the museum also arranges special temporary exhibitions designed to develop particular themes or mark notable occasions.

In front of the portico are two fifteen-inch naval guns, each weighing 100 tons, from H.M.S. *Ramillies* and *Resolution* (1915–16). From the Entrance Hall a staircase descends to the lower floor, where most of the larger exhibits can be seen. The corridors running east and west of the Entrance Hall give access to a series of smaller rooms, mostly devoted to special exhibits, and lead to the Picture Galleries in each wing.

The centre gallery (Room 21) has been arranged to illustrate the DEVELOPMENT OF MODERN WARFARE since 1775. The exhibits include arms, equipment, and uniforms, drawings, paintings, and photographs. Sections are devoted to the American Revolution (1775–83), the French Revolution (1789–96), the Industrial Revolution as it affected war (1776–1914), the Napoleonic Wars (1796–1815), the American Civil War (1861–5), the growth of Germany (1863–1914), the expansion of the British Empire (1815–1914), and the First World War (1914–18), including a reconstruction of part of a trench. An extensive range of exhibits covers every aspect of the Second World War, including Civil Defence, the Home Guard, the European resistance movements, concentration camps, and the plight of refugees. Also here is part of a Handley Page Halifax bomber of 1941. Other sections deal with modern warfare in Africa, the Middle East, and Vietnam, guerrilla warfare, the nuclear age, and the effect of war on society.

The galleries (Rooms 19 and 22) on either side of the centre gallery and three of those (Rooms 13, 14, and 23) at the farther end of the museum were being rearranged at the time of this revision. The museum has numerous exhibits illustrating modern warfare on land, sea, and in the air, and some of those mentioned below will certainly be on view here.

NAVAL WARFARE: fine collection of models of naval and merchant ships, submarines, and transport and landing craft which have taken part in war at sea since 1914; gun from H.M.S. *Lance* which fired Britain's opening shot at sea in August 1914; the gun which Boy Jack Cornwell was firing when he won the Victoria Cross at the Battle of Jutland in 1916, and the V.C. itself; British twenty-one-inch torpedo of the First World War; the first German magnetic mine recovered intact by the British in 1939; German one-man submarine and an Italian 'human torpedo', both used in the Second World War; arms, equipment, etc., of the Royal Marines; and models of the landing at Walcheren (Holland) and the 'Mulberry' harbour prefabricated for the invasion of Normandy in 1944.

LAND WARFARE: extensive display of field, machine, and anti-aircraft guns, including an Anglo-American M.40 self-propelled gun (1945), and other ordnance and small arms; Mark V tank first used in 1918; French Renault light tank of 1918; a London bus used as a troop-carrier on the Western Front in the First World War and a transport 'jeep' of the Second World War; and models of campaigns and battlefields of 1914–18 and 1939–45, including Gallipoli (1915) and Monte Cassino (1944).

AIR WARFARE: comprehensive collection of aircraft models showing most of the main types used by the combatant powers since 1914; a Bristol F.2.B fighter (1917) and a Sopwith Camel fighter (1918); Fairey Swordfish used by the Fleet Air Arm; Spitfire that flew in the defence of London during the Battle of Britain (1940); De Havilland Mosquito fighter (1945); front fuselage of an Avro Lancaster bomber (1943); cockpit sections of a Hawker Typhoon fighter (1944) and a Japanese 'Zeke'; Rolls-Royce and other aero-engines; German military aircraft (Focke-Wulf FW 190, Heinkel 162, and Messerschmitt 163b); a German V1 flying-bomb (on part of its launching-ramp); and a German V2 rocket.

Rooms 24 and 25, on the north side of the museum, are devoted to TRENCH WARFARE, with uniforms, arms and equipment, etc., another reconstruction of a First World War trench, and a variety of guns, including the thirteen-pounder gun which fired the first British round in France in 1914.

Room 15, in the south-east corner of the museum, contains the Campaign Caravans of Field-Marshal Viscount Montgomery, two of them captured from the Italian forces in 1941 and 1943, and the Map Caravan specially built at Manchester in 1944 for Lord Montgomery, of whom there is a portrait by Sir Oswald Birley (1948).

In Room 16, next to Room 15, is an exhibition concerned with the WAR IN NORTH AFRICA. Room 20, north of Room 15, is devoted to the WAR IN THE FAR EAST. Room 17, to the east of this, is confined to the life and military service of the Duke of Gloucester (d. 1974).

Special sections in the side galleries (under rearrangement) are devoted to armoured warfare; the uniforms of Britain, her allies, and her enemies in both wars; British and foreign decorations and medals (including the Victoria Cross and the George Cross); and flags, badges, and formation signs. Models, maps, photographs, etc., showing the campaigns and battles of the Second World War, include relief maps made for Sir Winston Churchill. Among the many personal relics and souvenirs are the uniforms of Field-Marshals Earl Haig and Viscount Montgomery and Admiral of the Fleet Earl Mountbatten.

The interesting Documents Room, in the west wing, contains the German Surrender Document signed at Luneburg Heath in 1945 (presented by Viscount Montgomery), Hitler's will and the declaration signed by him and Neville Chamberlain after the Munich agreement (1938), Earl Kitchener's Dardanelles directive, and the surrender document prepared after the Easter Rising in Dublin (1916).

The Picture Galleries contain a selection of the museum's 10,000 paintings, drawings, and prints, a remarkable record of the two World Wars as they affected all who were engaged in them. They are the work of the leading British artists, the majority of whom were employed by the government for this purpose. There are important groups of paintings by Sir William Orpen, Sir John Lavery, John S. Sargent, C. R. W. Nevinson, Wyndham Lewis, Paul and John Nash, Dame Laura Knight, and others; drawings by Muirhead Bone, James McBey, Eric Kennington, John Piper, Vivian Pitchforth, Feliks Topolski, etc.; and sculpture by Sir Jacob Epstein (notably a fine head of Sir Winston Churchill), Kathleen Scott (Lloyd George), Sir Charles Wheeler, and others. Beyond the south staircase is the Cinema and Lecture Theatre.

Any painting or sculpture not on view may usually be seen on advance application to the Keeper of the Art Department. The other Reference Departments are also open to the public on previous application (Mondays–Fridays, 10 to 5). The Library comprises a unique collection of about 155,000 books, periodicals, and works in manuscript, in many languages, dealing with the World Wars, not only in their military aspect, but also from the social, economic, and political points of view. The Dome Reading Room, originally designed as a chapel, has been restored after its damage by fire in 1968. The Film Library contains thousands of miles of cinematograph films and the Photograph Library has some four million photographs, both official and unofficial, from allied and enemy sources.

KENSINGTON PALACE Plan VI, A1

Stations: Queensway, nearly ½ m. N, on the Central Line; Bayswater, over ½ m. N, Notting Hill Gate, over ½ m. NW, and High Street Kensington, ¾ m. SW, all on the Circle and District lines. Notting Hill Gate is also on the Central line.— BUSES in Kensington Road, see Route 11; in Bayswater Road, see Route 12.

ADMISSION to the STATE APARTMENTS, Mondays–Saturdays 9 to 5, Sundays 1 to 5. Closed on New Year's Day, Good Friday, Christmas Eve and Day, and Boxing Day.

KENSINGTON PALACE, which stands on the extreme west side of Kensington Gardens (Route 12), was the principal private residence of the sovereign from 1689 until 1760 and the birthplace of Queen Victoria. Partly rebuilt as a country house for William III by Sir Christopher Wren, it was altered and added to by William Benson and William Kent to make a more palatial residence for George I. The palace may be approached by the drive leading south from the Orme Square Gate in Bayswater Road, or from the Palace Gate in Kensington Road by the Broad Walk. The State Apartments on the first floor were reopened to the public, after extensive restoration, in 1975; those on the ground floor were refurbished in 1984 to contain the splendid Court Dress Collection.

Originally named Nottingham House, the palace was built after 1661 by Lord Chancellor Finch, later the first Earl of Nottingham. In 1689 it was purchased from the second Earl by William III, who employed Wren to make many alterations and additions; the south wing, completed by about 1695, is the most notable surviving part of his work. The palace was further enlarged in 1722–6 for George I, and it remained the sovereign's chief residence until the death of George II here in 1760. Mary II (1694), William III (1702), and Queen Anne (1714) also died here, and Princess Victoria, born in the palace in 1819, lived here until the day in 1837 when she was roused from her bed in the early hours to hear the news of her accession. Queen Mary, the wife of George V, was likewise born in the palace (1867), which except for the State Apartments is now occupied by relatives of the royal family and aristocratic pensioners of the Crown. Rooms were prepared in 1981 for the Prince and Princess of Wales.

The STATE APARTMENTS are entered at the north-east corner of the building. The rooms on the Ground Floor include the RED SALOON, in which Queen Victoria held her first Privy Council in 1837; the SALOON, one of the rooms occupied in 1867–83 by the Duke and Duchess of Teck, parents of Queen Mary; and the NORTH DRAWING ROOM, converted into a bedroom (in which Victoria is reputed to have been born), after the Duke and Duchess of Kent, the princess's parents, had taken up residence in 1818. These and other rooms now contain the COURT DRESS COLLECTION, a display of the formal dress worn by men and women at court from 1750 onwards, including that worn by Victoria herself at her Accession Council. The nucleus of the collection was formed by Mr and Mrs Aubrey Bowden and it is on permanent loan to the Queen.

The apartments on the First Floor include some simple but skilful rooms designed by Wren and other more ostentatious rooms by Kent, in which are hung numerous portraits (mostly of the 17th–18th centuries) from the royal collection. The rooms in which Queen Victoria lived before her accession contain many mementoes of her, some of them assembled by Queen Mary.

The QUEEN'S STAIRCASE, designed by Wren in 1691, ascends to the QUEEN'S GALLERY (84 ft long), which is panelled in oak and has two fine carved and gilded mirrors on the chimneypieces by Gerard Johnson and Robert Streeter. The portraits here include Anne Hyde, Duchess of York (by Lely), William III and Mary II, as Prince and Princess of Orange (by Wissing), and a fine Kneller of Peter the Great of Russia. The QUEEN'S CLOSET has portraits of Queen Anne (by Kneller), Prince George of Denmark, her consort (by Mikael Dahl), and Prince William of Gloucester, their son (also by Kneller). This room, the QUEEN'S DINING ROOM, which preserves its original panelling of 1689, and the QUEEN'S DRAWING ROOM, beyond, were used as private apartments by Mary II and Anne. In the QUEEN'S BEDROOM, adjacent, are the state bed of Mary of Modena, the second queen of James II, and an elaborate writing-desk of the mid 17th century that belonged to Mary II, who died in this room at the age of thirty-two. The KING'S PRIVY CHAMBER, farther on, is the first of the rooms rebuilt by William Benson and decorated by Kent (1724). The windows face across the Clock Court to Wren's charming gate-tower in the west wing. The PRESENCE CHAMBER, beyond, has a ceiling painted in the 'antique' fashion by Kent and a fine overmantel carved in limewood by Grinling Gibbons. The KING'S STAIRCASE, to the right, is partly by Wren, but was enlarged for George I and has an iron balustrade by Jean Tijou and walls painted to represent a gallery by Kent, with portraits of court contemporaries.

A short passage on the left admits to KING WILLIAM'S GALLERY, 96 ft long, on the south side of the palace. Designed by Nicholas Hawksmoor, Wren's pupil, in 1695, it has contemporary wood-carving, probably by Grinling Gibbons, and a ceiling painted in 1725 by Kent ('Adventures of Ulysses'). On the walls is a fine selection of paintings from the Queen's private collection, and above the marble chimneypiece is a map of north-west Europe showing William III's possessions (painted in 1694 by Robert Norden), with a compass whose pointer is operated by a wind-vane on the roof. At the east end is the DUCHESS OF KENT'S DRESSING ROOM, with Victorian furnishings from the royal collection and a piano (by Sebastian Erard) that belonged to Albert, consort of Queen Victoria.

Beyond an ANTE-ROOM, containing toys and the dolls' house of Victoria when princess, is QUEEN VICTORIA'S BEDROOM (formerly the King's State Bedroom), furnished in an early-Victorian style and containing many mementoes of the queen, including a cradle made in 1840 and used for all her children. It was from the Bedroom that the young Princess Victoria was called to learn of the death of William IV and of her own accession. The KING'S DRAWING ROOM, which follows, has a ceiling by Kent (1725) and affords a view of Kensington Gardens. It contains 17th-century Italian paintings, part of the Gonzaga collection purchased by Charles I, and in the centre is a remarkable clock, the 'Temple of the Four Monarchies', made about 1730 for the Princess of Wales, mother of George III, with scenes on its four sides showing rulers of Assyria, Persia, Greece, and Rome. Beyond is the KING'S COUNCIL CHAMBER, now containing exhibits from the Great Exhibition of 1851, including an ivory throne presented to Queen Victoria by the Maharajah of Travancore. The CUPOLA ROOM, on the left of the King's Drawing Room, is the most splendid of the rooms decorated by Kent (1722). Princess Victoria was baptized here. It has a coved ceiling painted to simulate a coffered dome, niches with gilded statuary (probably Italian), and a fine bas-relief by Rysbrack (1723), over the fireplace, depicting a Roman marriage. Beyond is the King's Privy Chamber (already visited), from which the staircase at the north end is regained.

MUSEUM OF LONDON Plan V, D1

STATIONS: BARBICAN (closed on Sundays), 300 yds N, on the Circle and Metropolitan lines; ST PAUL'S, ¼ mile S, on the Central line; MOORGATE, nearly ⅜ mile E, on the Circle, Metropolitan, and Northern lines. — BUSES Nos. 4, 141, and 502 in St Martin's-le-Grand (from Cheapside and St Paul's Cathedral); Nos. 4 and 279A in Aldersgate Street; Nos. 141, 279A, and 502 in London Wall.

ADMISSION Tuesdays–Saturdays 10 to 6, Sundays 2 to 6 (free). Closed on New

Year's Day, Christmas Eve and Day, and Boxing Day. — LECTURES on Wednesdays, Thursdays, and Fridays, at 1 p.m. — FOUNTAINS RESTAURANT, to south-west, at street level.

The excellent MUSEUM OF LONDON, opened in 1976, stands in the angle between Aldersgate Street and the broad street of London Wall, in the south-west part of the Barbican (Route 30), and is approached by steps from the roundabout north of St Botolph's church or from the elevated walkway on the north side of London Wall. The museum, built to the designs of Powell and Moya, combines the collections of the former London Museum, illustrating the history and social life of the capital from the earliest times, and those of the Guildhall Museum, devoted specifically to the City of London. The exhibition galleries occupy some 50,000 square feet, on two floors, enclosing an inner courtyard. The exhibits are arranged mainly in chronological order, starting on the upper floor near the main entrance.

The London Museum, founded in 1911 by Viscount Esher and Harcourt, was first accommodated in the state apartments at Kensington Palace. In 1914 it was moved to Lancaster House, but in 1951 it returned to the palace, to the former apartments of Princess Beatrice. The Guildhall Museum, established in 1826, was housed in the Royal Exchange in 1955–68.

On the left of the Entrance Hall adjoining the walkway are the lift to the lower floor and the stairs down to the Lecture Theatre. On the right is the information desk, with the cloakroom beyond, and farther on is the museum shop. The Prehistoric exhibits start beyond this. The museum is not large enough for all its possessions to be put on display at any one time; changes to the arrangement may be made and not all the exhibits mentioned below may be on view. The museum has also an outstanding collection of prints and drawings of old London.

PREHISTORIC ANTIQUITIES. Implements and weapons of the Stone, Bronze, and Iron Ages, from the Thames and the gravel terraces on which much of London is built; especially remarkable are the Palaeolithic flint tools; the Neolithic and Iron Age pottery and tools from the site of Heathrow Airport; leaf-shaped swords and other weapons of the late Bronze Age; bronze scabbards, fine horse-bits, chariot fittings, and a bronze-mounted oak tankard, all dating from the early Iron Age; and pre-Roman gold coins. A model shows the Thames Valley in about 5000 B.C. and a reconstructed section under a City cellar indicates the levels of deposits from Roman to Victorian times.

ROMAN LONDON. Notable pottery, including a jug of the late 1st century found at Southwark and inscribed *Londini*, the earliest known occurrence of this name; tomb figure of a legionary soldier (late 1st or early 2nd century), found in a bastion of the wall near Bishopsgate; tombstone of a Roman centurion (3rd century), from Ludgate Hill; altar from a temple of Isis (3rd century), found at Blackfriars in 1975; and fragments of other sculptures.

Reconstruction of the Roman wharf (late 1st century), with finds from it and the riverside wall; partial reconstruction of a wooden ship found in the Thames near Blackfriars Bridge in 1962; reconstruction of rooms in a Roman house, including a tessellated pavement found 20 ft below the ground, near the Mansion House; the 'Austalis' tile, an inscribed brick found in Warwick Lane near the City wall; complete wooden ladder over 15 ft long, pair of well-preserved leather trunks, and other finds from a 1st-century well near Queen Street, excavated in 1953–5; figurines in bronze, terracotta, etc.; other bronzework, leatherwork (shoes and sandals), glassware, and toilet articles; and a cremation burial (late 1st century) found in Warwick Square in 1966.

Of the first importance are the marble sculptures found in the Temple of Mithras west of Wallbrook (see Route 27), including the head of the sun-god Mithras (late 2nd or early 3rd century), wearing a Phrygian cap and once probably part of a large group showing the god killing a bull; large hand, perhaps of Mithras; head of Minerva; unrivalled head of Serapis, the Graeco-Egyptian god of the underworld, supporting a corn-measure; figure of Mercury; figures of Cautopates, a river god (all these probably of the 2nd century); Mithraic dedication on a marble slab (A.D. 307–8); and a group of Bacchus and his companions (probably 4th century); also a Mithraic group showing a bull-slaying, found in 1889 near the site of the temple.

Also in this section are copies of Roman remains in the British Museum, among them a bronze head of the Emperor Hadrian (about A.D. 122), found in the Thames near London Bridge; the tombstone of a Greek merchant (1st century), found at Tower Hill; and a funerary inscription of the 1st century to Julius Classicianus, Procurator of Britain (also from Tower Hill; Route 34). A window affords a view of part of the City wall that originally bounded the 1st century Roman fort (compare Route 30) and models show the construction of the wall.

SAXON AND VIKING LONDON. Saxon weapons, including swords

and scramasaxes, the large knives from which the Saxons are said to have been named; fine brooches, etc., from Saxon cemeteries on the outskirts of London; large hand-bell of bronze-coated iron, found in the Thames at Mortlake; coins, among them a silver penny minted during Alfred's reign, with a monogram comprising the letters of *Londonia*; axes, spears, and other Viking weapons, and horse-equipment; and a remarkable 11th-century Viking tombstone with a Runic inscription, found in St Paul's Churchyard in 1852.

MEDIEVAL LONDON. Models of the Tower of London, in about 1100, and of St Paul's Cathedral in the 14th century; tree-trunk piles of the medieval London Bridge; part of the wall of the dock at Baynard's Castle, filled in in the 15th century; statues of four Civic Virtues (about 1430), from Guildhall; 13th-century burial slab, with the incised figure of a woman, from the demolished St Swithun's Church; late-15th-century door-frame from the church of St Ethelburga (Bishopsgate); 13th-century coffin-slabs found beneath Guildhall Chapel; 15th-century Gothic cupboard and oak cradle; heraldic panels from the Eleanor Cross in Cheapside (erected about 1294 and destroyed in 1643); the City Common Chest, made entirely of iron, with six locks (early 15th century); fine collection of polychrome jugs and other pottery, some imported from the Continent; 14th-century figure of St Christopher found built into the Tudor wall, and other medieval sculpture; fine leatherwork, horse-equipment, weapons, tools, and implements, metal and wooden vessels, and domestic appliances; medieval dress and ornament, including jewellery; and pilgrim signs and badges, and other religious objects.

TUDOR LODON. Bronze and pottery utensils, and pottery finds from a refuse pit (1490–1525) on the site of the Bank of America, Cannon Street; bronze cannon made at Houndsditch, about 1550 (lent by the Tower); armour made in Henry VIII's royal armoury at Greenwich; bronze head reliquary of about 1550 from northern Italy, found in the Thames at Wapping; remarkable early-16th-century recumbent figure of the dead Christ found under the chapel of the Mercers' Company in 1954; panel with figure of King Stephen from Austin Friars (mid 16th century); glazed tiles, one with a portrait of Elizabeth I; Delft plate of 1600 honouring the queen; typical Elizabethan clothing of the courtier and the merchant, including characteristic woollen caps; the steelyard of Sir Thomas Gresham (1572); copper plate engraved with the earliest known map of London (about 1558); and fine models of 16th-century London.

EARLY STUART LONDON. Stone slab with arms of the City (1623); costumes and clothing of the 17th century; leather 'blackjacks' or beer jugs, and other articles of leather, silver, pewter, and wood; splendid hoard of jewellery discovered in Cheapside in 1912 and thought to be the stock of a Jacobean jeweller; Lambeth 'Delft-ware' and majolica, introduced into England by Flemish immigrants, Fulham stoneware and other London pottery; 'Venetian' and other glassware; pikemen's armour, swords made at Hounslow (Middlesex), and armour made at Greenwich about 1630 and worn by John Dymoke as the hereditary king's champion at the coronation of George III (1761); the silk vest worn by Charles I on the scaffold (1649); bust of Cromwell by Samuel Pierce (1672) and death mask of the Protector (1658); relics of the Civil War; panelled bedroom from Wandsworth (about 1620); models of the Globe Theatre (see Route 36), of London Bridge in about 1600, and of Whitehall Palace (after 1622). Here also is an illuminated model depicting the Great Fire of 1666 (with a spoken commentary taken from Pepys' Diary).

A ramp leads down to steps and the lift descending to the Lower Floor, which contains the later exhibits.

LATE STUART LONDON. Relics of the Great Plague (1665) and the Great Fire; striking contemporary painting of the Great Fire by a Dutch artist; stone slab dated 1681 from a house in Pudding Lane, ascribing the origin of the Fire to a Roman Catholic conspiracy; masonry from Wren's St Paul's Cathedral (removed during repair); iron garden gate from Wren's house in Love Lane; 17th-century stained glass; fine collection of 17th-century glassware; silver-gilt cup made to celebrate the launching of H.M.S. *London*, the ship presented (reluctantly) in 1670 to Charles II by the merchants of London; model of a ship of 100 guns, and other naval relics; inlaid chessboard, with ivory pieces of chess, draughts, and backgammon, given to Samuel Pepys by James II; oak figure of Father Time, from the clock of St Giles Cripplegate; sedan chair of about 1700; reconstruction of a late-Stuart interior, with contemporary chimneypiece and panelling from Poyle Park (Surrey; about 1655), virginals by James White (1656), a longcase clock by Joshua Allsop of East Smithfield (about 1710), and a painted ceiling of about 1676 from No. 15 Buckingham Street, near the Strand.

GEORGIAN LONDON. Paintings, drawings, etc., of 18th-century streets and squares; late-Georgian shop fronts from Cornhill

(Birch's), Greenwich, and Brentford, with contemporary prints; old shop and tavern signs; silver-gilt church plate from St Martin-in-the-Fields; late-18th-century printing press used until 1920 at Bermondsey; dressing table used by David Garrick at the Drury Lane Theatre; caricature of Henry Fielding by Hogarth; bust of James Thomson, the poet, by Roubiliac; a Flora of London and environs published in 1777; fine selection of costumes of the late 18th and early 19th centuries; dolls and dolls' houses, games and toys; reconstruction of a cell from the Debtors' Prison at Wellclose Square (near London Docks), the walls scratched with 18th-century inscriptions; whipping-post and two interior doors from Newgate Prison, demolished in 1902 (in the Old Bailey; see p. 246).

EARLY VICTORIAN LONDON. Gothic Revival woodwork, etc.; reconstruction of a Board School room (the first opened at Whitechapel in 1873); model of the Great Exhibition of 1851 in Hyde Park, and furnishings shown at the exhibition; fireplace of French design, of a kind imported about 1860–70; royal arms from the church of St Botolph Aldgate; 19th-century costumes, including the costermonger's suit of the 'Pearly King of Islington'; horse-drawn fire engine made in 1862 in Long Acre; paintings, cartoons, and models, including one of the massive Euston Arch, built for the London & Birmingham Railway in 1838 and demolished in 1961.

LATER VICTORIAN LONDON, the period of the great expansion of the British Empire. Reconstructions of shop and office interiors, including a bank hall and manager's office (altered by Norman Shaw in 1880), tobacconist's, barber's, draper's, and grocer's shops, a cooper's workshop, and London dock offices; Victorian music-hall scene, and the cast of a balcony front at Wilton's Music Hall in Wellclose Square, opened in 1856 and closed about 1880; Hansom Cab (patented in 1834 by Joseph Hansom), used in the 1890s by Sir Edward Barry.

TWENTIETH-CENTURY LONDON. Exhibits illustrating almost every aspect of life in the capital, with photographs of events; part of the Edwardian façade of a Lyons' teashop; screen and lift interior from Selfridges, installed in 1928; a Woolworth's counter of the 1930s, complete with its goods; one of the first production cars (1936) from the Ford Motor Works at Dagenham (downstream on the Thames); reconstruction of an A.R.P. (Air Raid Precautions) shelter of 1940–41; and a model of the Festival of Britain of 1951 (see Route 36). Part of this section is used for Special Exhibitions. Near the exit is the splendid Lord Mayor's State Coach, made in 1757 by Joseph Berry (with panel paintings by G. B. Cipriani) and used at the Lord Mayor's Show and on other ceremonial occasions.

The ROYAL COLLECTION (not on view at present) includes the robes worn at the coronations of Queen Victoria (1838), Edward VII (1902), and George VI (1937); costumes of Princess Charlotte (daughter of George IV), Queen Victoria, Queen Alexandra, and Queen Mary; a 17th-century Italian cradle and a swing-cot (1840) used for all the children of Queen Victoria; dolls dressed by the queen as a child; Queen Mary's dolls' house and other possessions; the coronation glove of Elizabeth II (1953); and a model of Westminster Abbey during the coronation of George VI.

NATIONAL GALLERY Plan III, F2, 3

STATIONS: CHARING CROSS, on the Bakerloo, Jubilee, and Northern lines; LEICESTER SQUARE, on the Northern and Piccadilly lines; EMBANKMENT, on the Bakerloo, Circle, District, and Northern lines. — BUSES to Trafalgar Square, compare Route 1.

ADMISSION Mondays–Saturdays 10 to 6, Sundays 2 to 6 (free). Closed on New Year's Day, Good Friday, May Day Monday, and Christmas Eve and Day. — LECTURES on Tuesdays–Fridays at 1 p.m., Saturdays at 12; Films on Mondays at 1 p.m.; Guided Tours at 11.30 and (from May to September) at 3.30; Audio-Visual programmes, Mondays–Saturdays 10 to 5 or 5.30, Sundays 2.30 to 5.30. — RESTAURANT in the Basement, open 10 to 5, Sundays 2 to 5.

The NATIONAL GALLERY, comprising one of the richest and most extensive collections of paintings in the world, stands on a terrace overlooking the north side of Trafalgar Square. The older and central portion, with a Grecian portico incorporating columns brought from Carlton House, was designed by William Wilkins and built in 1834–7. The façade, 460 ft long, is too low for the elevation of the building, and the design has been criticized also for its ineffective dome and 'pepper-box' turrets. The view from the portico, however, over Trafalgar Square and down Whitehall to the Houses of Parliament, is one of the finest in London. The collection admirably covers all schools and periods of painting, but is especially notable for its examples of Rembrandt and Rubens and its representation of the Italian schools of the 15th–16th centuries. The British school is only moderately represented, as the national collections are shared with the Tate Gallery, where also the 20th-century European paintings and sculptures will be found. The National Gallery now possesses over 2,000 paintings, all of which are on display in the main galleries and the Lower Floor galleries. The room-to-room arrangement is by the national schools, an order followed in the description below; only the most important works can be mentioned, though almost every picture merits detailed examination.

The National Gallery was founded in 1824 through the purchase by the government of the collection of John Julius Angerstein. The thirty-eight paintings, including five by Claude and the six of Hogarth's *Mariage à la Mode* series, were first exhibited at Angerstein's house at No. 100 Pall Mall. Other paintings were soon acquired, notably Titian's 'Bacchus and Ariadne', Rubens's 'Château de Steen', and Canaletto's 'The Stonemason's Yard', and in 1838 the collection was moved to its present home. Though the first director (Sir Charles Eastlake) was appointed in 1855, the National Gallery had to share its limited quarters with the Royal Academy until 1868. As the collection grew rapidly by purchase, gift, and bequest, further accommodation was needed, and extensions were made in 1876 (the Dome and neighbouring rooms), in 1887 (the central rooms), in 1927 (to house the Mond Bequest), in 1929 (the Duveen Room), and in 1976, on the north-west. Among the principal bequests have been those of J. M. W. Turner (of his own works; 1851), Wynn Ellis (1876), George Salting (1910), Sir Hugh Lane (1917), and Ludwig Mond (1924). A number of masterpieces, including the 'Rokeby Venus' of Velazquez, Holbein's 'Duchess of Milan', Tintoretto's 'Morosini', Rubens's 'Watering Place', and the Leonardo cartoon of the Virgin and Child, have been acquired with the assistance of the National Art-Collections Fund.

On the left of the ENTRANCE HALL is the cloakroom, where umbrellas, etc., must be given up, while to the right is the information desk. Staircases ascend from the hall to Vestibules whose floors are decorated with mosaics by Boris Anrep showing contemporary figures. Farther on is the museum shop, where various reproductions of the paintings may be purchased. The paintings are listed below in alphabetical order of artists, as changes are made from time to time in the arrangement of the rooms.

In Room 1 (see plan) is the exquisite WILTON DIPTYCH, formerly at Wilton House (Wiltshire). Its subject is Richard II presented to the Virgin and Child by his patron saints, SS. John the Baptist, Edward the Confessor, and Edmund, king and martyr, and on the back are the arms and badge of Richard. This is generally agreed to be a work of the late 14th century (about 1395), and by either a French or an English painter.

BRITISH SCHOOL (Rooms 35–39): *John Constable* (d. 1837), 'The

Cornfield', 'The Hay Wain', 'Stoke-by-Nayland', 'Salisbury Cathedral', 'Weymouth Bay', and other masterpieces of landscape painting; *John Crome* (d. 1821), head of the Norwich School, 'Yarmouth Harbour', etc.; *Thomas Gainsborough* (d. 1788), 'Cornard Wood', 'The Watering Place', 'The Morning Walk', 'Mr and Mrs Robert Andrews', 'Dr Ralph Schomberg', 'Mrs Siddons', a famous study, and 'The Painter's Daughters', several delightful portraits at varying ages; *William Hogarth* (d. 1764), *Mariage à la Mode*, a series of six satirical paintings in the artist's well-known manner, and 'The Shrimp Girl'; *John Hoppner* (d. 1810), 'Sir George Beaumont', an instigator of the founding of the National Gallery; *Sir Thomas Lawrence* (d. 1830), 'Queen Charlotte' and 'John Julius Angerstein' (see above); *Sir Joshua Reynolds* (d. 1792), 'The Graces Decorating Hymen', 'Lord Heathfield', 'Colonel Tarleton', 'Lady Cockburn and her Children', 'Lady Albemarle', 'Captain Robert Orme', and other portraits; *George Stubbs* (d. 1806), 'Gentleman Holding a Horse', 'Lady and Gentleman in a Phaeton', and 'The Melbourne and Milbanke Families'; *J. M. W. Turner* (d. 1851), 'Hero and Leander', 'Palestrina', 'Dido Building Carthage', 'Ulysses Deriding Polyphemus', 'Calais Pier', 'Sun Rising in a Mist', 'The Fighting Téméraire', 'Rain, Steam, and Speed', and other characteristic works of the foremost British landscape painter; *Richard Wilson* (d. 1782), 'Holt Bridge' and 'The Valley of the Dee'; *Joseph Wright* (of Derby; d. 1797), 'Mr and Mrs Coltman'; *Johann Zoffany* (d. 1810), 'Mrs Oswald'.

EARLY NETHERLANDISH SCHOOL (Rooms 24 and 25): *Hieronymus Bosch* (d. 1516), 'Christ Crowned with Thorns', a characteristic work; *Dieric Bouts* (d. 1475), 'The Entombment' and 'Virgin and Child'; *Pieter Brueghel the Elder* (d. 1569), 'Adoration of the Kings', in this painter's satirical manner; *Robert Campin* (d. 1444), 'Virgin and Child'; *Petrus Christus* (d. 1472/3), 'Portrait of Edward Grimston'; *Gerard David* (d. 1523), 'Marriage of St Catherine', a fine composition, also 'Deposition' and 'Adoration of the Kings'; *Jan van Eyck* (d. 1441), 'Marriage of Giovanni Arnolfini', a splendid work, also two fine portraits; *Jan Gossaert* (usually called Mabuse; d. 1532), 'Adoration of the Kings', bought from Castle Howard (Yorkshire), also 'Man with a Rosary', etc.; *Lucas van Leyden* (d. 1533), 'A Man Aged 38'; *Marinus van Reymerswaele* (d. after 1567), 'Two Excisemen' (or possibly usurers); *Quinten Massys* (d. 1530), 'Virgin and Child with SS. Barbara and Catherine'; *The Master of St Giles* (active about 1500), 'The Mass of St Giles'; *Hans*

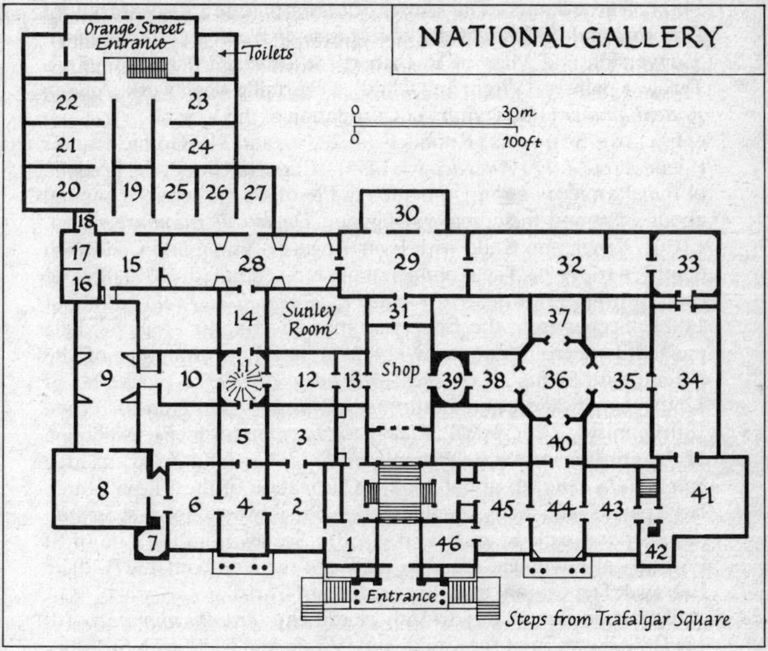

Memling (d. 1494), 'The Donne Triptych' (painted for Sir John Donne about 1468 and previously at Chatsworth, Derbyshire), 'Young Man at Prayer', etc.; *Roger van der Weyden* (d. 1464), 'Pietà', 'The Magdalen Reading', and 'Portrait of a Lady'.

EARLY GERMAN SCHOOL (Room 23): *Albrecht Altdorfer* (d. 1538), 'Landscape with a Footbridge': *Hans Baldung* (d. 1545), 'Portrait of a Senator' and 'Pietà'; *Lucas Cranach the Elder* (d. 1553), 'Cupid Complaining to Venus', 'Portrait of a Young Lady', etc.; *Albrecht Dürer* (d. 1528), 'The Artist's Father'; *Hans Holbein the Younger* (d. 1543), who settled in England in 1527 and became court painter to Henry VIII in 1536, 'The Ambassadors', painted in 1533 (on the floor between them is an elongated skull), and 'Christina of Denmark, Duchess of Milan', painted in 1538 when she was sixteen and Henry VIII was considering her as a bride; *Stefan Lochner* (d.

1451), 'Three Saints'; *The Master of Liesborn* (late 15th century), 'St Dorothy' and 'St Margaret'; *The Master of Werden* (15th century), 'Conversion and Mass of St Hubert'; *Michael Pacher* (d. 1498), a Tyrolese painter, 'Virgin and Child', a charming small work; *Johann Rottenhammer* (16th century), 'Coronation of the Virgin'.

ITALIAN SCHOOLS (Rooms 1–14, 29, 30, and 34). Gothic Schools (Sienese, etc.): *Fra Angelico* (d. 1455), 'Christ in Glory', the predella of the altarpiece of San Domenico di Fiesole, a masterpiece painted about 1430 and including 266 figures; *Duccio di Buoninsegna* (d. 1319), 'Virgin and Child with Four Angels', 'Virgin and Child with Saints', a triptych, 'The Annunciation', etc.; *Giotto* (d. 1337), 'Pentecost', attributed to this early master; *Giovanni di Paolo* (d. about 1482), 'Scenes from the Life of St John the Baptist', four predella panels; *Lorenzo Monaco* (d. 1422 or later), 'Coronation of the Virgin, with Saints', a triptych; *Margarito of Arezzo* (active about 1260), 'Virgin and Child Enthroned'; *Master of San Francesco* (late 13th century), 'Crucifixion'; *Matteo di Giovanni* (d. 1495), 'Madonna of the Girdle' and 'St Sebastian'; *Nardo di Cione* (d. 1365), 'Three Saints'; *Orcagna* (d. about 1368), 'Coronation of the Virgin', three large panels, and many smaller works, possibly by followers; *Stefano di Giovanni* (called Sassetta; d. 1450), 'Scenes from the Life of St Francis', a polyptych; *Ugolino da Siena* (active about 1327), 'The Betrayal, Deposition, and Resurrection of Christ'.

Florentine School (15th–16th centuries): *Fra Bartolommeo* (d. 1517), 'Adoration of the Child' and 'Virgin and Child with St John'; *Alessandro Botticelli* (d. 1510), 'Mars and Venus', 'Adoration of the Kings', 'Mystic Nativity', and 'Life and Miracles of St Zenobius'; *Angelo Bronzino* (d. 1572), 'Holy Family' and 'Venus, Cupid. Folly, and Time'; *Piero di Cosimo* (d. after 1515), 'Mythological Subject' (perhaps the Death of Procris) and 'Battle of the Centaurs and Lapiths' (compare p. 342); *Lorenzo di Credi* (d. 1537), two fine 'Madonnas'; *Benozzo Gozzoli* (d. 1497), 'Virgin and Child among Angels and Saints'.

Leonardo da Vinci (d. 1519), 'The Virgin of the Rocks', a beautiful later version of the subject in the Louvre, and 'Virgin and Child with St John the Baptist and St Anne' (cartoon; purchased from the Royal Academy in 1962 for £800,000, mainly raised by public subscription); *Filippino Lippi* (d. 1504; son of Filippo), 'Virgin and Child with Saints', 'Adoration of the Magi', etc.; *Filippo Lippi* (d. 1469), 'The Annunciation' and 'Seven Saints'; *Masaccio* (d. 1428), 'Virgin and

Child'; *Masolino* (d. after 1432), 'A Pope and St Mathias' and 'SS. John the Baptist and Jerome', two panels of an altarpiece; *Michelangelo* (d. 1564), 'The Entombment' and 'Virgin and Child with St John and Angels', two magnificent if unfinished works attributed to this master; *Antonio Pollaiuolo* (d. 1498), 'The Martyrdom of St Sebastian', a masterpiece of Florentine figure painting, and 'Apollo and Daphne', small but excellent; *Andrea del Sarto* (d. 1531), 'Virgin and Child with St Elizabeth' and 'Portrait of a Sculptor'; *Andrea del Solario* (d. 1524), 'Giovanni Longono' and 'Portrait of a Man'; *Paolo Uccello* (d. 1475), 'The Rout of San Romano' (in 1432, of the Sienese by the Florentines) and 'St George and the Dragon', an important acquisition; *Domenico Veneziano* (d. 1461), 'Heads of Saints'; *Andrea del Verrocchio* (d. 1488), 'Virgin and Child with Angels' (possibly by a follower), and 'Tobias and the Angel', of the School of Verrocchio.

Venetian School (15th–16th centuries): *Gentile Bellini* (d. 1507), 'Man with a Pair of Dividers' and 'The Sultan Mehmet II'; *Giovanni Bellini* (d. 1516), 'Doge Leonardo Loredan', 'Madonna of the Meadow', 'Madonna of the Pomegranate', and 'Pietà', four masterly works; 'The Agony in the Garden', and 'The Circumcision'; and 'Assassination of St Peter Martyr', from the School of Giovanni Bellini; *Vittore Carpaccio* (d. about 1526), 'Adoration of the Kings' and 'Embarkation of St Ursula'; *Vincenzo Catena* (d. 1531), 'St Jerome in his Study', 'Virgin and Child with St John', and 'Warrior Adoring the Infant Christ'; *G. B. Cima* (d. 1517/18), 'Madonnas', 'St Jerome in a Landscape', etc.; *Carlo Crivelli* (d. 1493), 'The Demidoff Altarpiece', with thirteen panels, 'The Annunciation', the artist's acknowledged masterpiece, 'Virgin and Child Enthroned', etc.; *Giorgione* (d. 1510), 'Adoration of the Kings' and 'Sunset Landscape with Saints', also 'Il Tramonte', attributed to Giorgione; *Antonello da Messina* (d. 1479), 'Salvator Mundi', 'Crucifixion', 'St Jerome in his Study', and 'Portrait of a Man'; *Alvise Vivarini* (d. about 1503), 'Virgin and Child'; *Antonio Vivarini* (d. 1476), 'Saints'; *Bartolommeo Vivarini* (d. about 1499), 'Virgin and Child with Saints'.

Schools of Lombardy (Milanese, etc.; 15th–early 16th centuries): *Ambrogio Bergognone* (d. 1523), 'Virgin and Child' and 'Scenes from the Passion'; *Boltraffio* (d. 1516), 'Virgin and Child'; *Bramantino* (d. 1536), 'Adoration of the Magi'; *Gaudenzio Ferrari* (d. 1546), 'The Annunciation', two panels; *Vincenzo Foppa* (d. 1515/16), 'Adoration of the Magi'; *Bernardino Luini* (d. 1532), 'Christ Teaching' and

'Virgin and Child with St John', rich in colour; *Pisanello* (d. about 1455), 'The Virgin and Child with Saints' and 'Vision of St Eustace'; *Ambrogio Preda* (d. after 1508), 'Angels', etc.

Other Northern Schools (Bologna, Ferrara, Verona, etc.): *Antonio Correggio* (d. 1534), 'Madonna of the Basket', 'Venus, Mercury, and Cupid', etc.; *Francesco del Cossa* (d. about 1477), 'St Vincent Ferrer'; *Lorenzo Costa* (d. 1535), 'A Concert'; *Dosso Dossi* (d. 1541), 'Adoration of the Magi'; *Francesco Francia* (d. 1517/18), 'Virgin and Child with Saints, etc.', an altarpiece; *Garofalo* (d. 1559), 'Sacrifice to Ceres'; *Liberale da Verona* (d. about 1529), 'The Death of Dido'; *Gerolamo dai Libri* (d. 1556), 'Virgin and Child with St Anne'; *Andrea Mantegna* (d. 1506), 'Virgin and Child with the Magdalen and St John the Baptist', 'The Agony in the Garden', 'Samson and Delilah', and 'The Triumph of Scipio', in monochrome; *Bartolommeo Montagna* (d. 1523), 'SS. John the Baptist, Zeno, and Catherine of Alexandria'; *Paolo Morando* (d. 1522), 'St Roch and the Angel', part of a triptych; *Francesco Morone* (d. 1529), 'Virgin and Child'; *Parmigianino* (d. 1540), 'Mystic Marriage of St Catherine'; *Cosimo Tura* (d. 1495), 'Virgin and Child', 'Allegorical Figure', and 'St Jerome'; *Marco Zoppo* (d. about 1478), 'The Dead Christ', small but good.

Central Italian Schools (15th–16th centuries): *Piero della Francesca* (d. 1492), 'The Baptism of Christ', 'The Nativity', and 'St Michael and the Dragon'; *Pietro Perugino* (d. 1523), 'Virgin and Child, with SS. Raphael and Michael', a triptych; *Pintoricchio* (d. 1513), 'St Catherine of Alexandria', 'Return of Odysseus', etc.; *Raphael* (d. 1520), 'St Catherine of Alexandria', 'Madonna of the Tower', 'Virgin and Child' (called the 'Ansidei Madonna'), 'Crucifixion', 'Pope Julius II', and other works of this serene master; *Luca Signorelli* (d. 1523), 'Holy Family', 'The Triumph of Chastity', 'The Circumcision', 'Virgin and Child with Saints and Angels', and 'Coriolanus Persuaded to Spare Rome'.

Later 16th-century Venetian School: *Jacopo Bassano* (d. 1592), 'The Way to Calvary'; *Bonifazio* (d. 1553), 'Virgin and Child with Saints'; *Paris Bordone* (d. 1570), 'Portrait of a Lady'; *Lorenzo Lotto* (d. 1556), 'Lucretia', 'Family Group', etc.; *Moretto* (d. 1555), 'St Bernardino of Siena', and other saints, etc.; *G. B. Moroni* (d. 1578), 'Italian Nobleman' and other portraits; *Palma Vecchio* (d. 1528), 'Portrait of a Poet' and 'Flora'; *Sebastiano del Piombo* (d. 1547), 'The Raising of Lazarus', 'Holy Family', and 'Salome'; *Girolamo Romani* (called Il Romanino; d. 1566), 'Virgin and Child' and 'The Nativity', a polyptych; *Tintoretto* (d. 1594), 'Christ Washing Peter's Feet' (a large canvas), 'Vincenzo Morosini', 'St George and the Dragon' and 'The Origin of the Milky Way', notable examples of this master; *Titian* (d. 1576), 'Venus and Adonis', 'Bacchus and Ariadne', 'The Death of Actaeon', 'Noli me Tangere', 'Man in a Blue Sleeve', 'The Vendramin Family', 'Caterina Cornaro', 'Allegory of Prudence', and other masterpieces by this great artist; *Paolo Veronese* (d. 1588), the last of the great Venetians, 'The Adoration of the Magi', 'The Family of Darius before Alexander', two large-scale compositions, 'The Vision of St Helena', 'The Magdalen laying aside her Jewels', 'The Consecration of St Nicholas', and four paintings from a ceiling decoration.

17th-century Italian Schools: *Caravaggio* (d. 1610), 'The Supper at Emmaus', and 'Salome with the Head of St John the Baptist' (painted in Malta); *Annibale Carracci* (d. 1609), 'Landscape with Figures' and 'Pietà'; *Bernardo Cavallino* (d. 1654), 'The Finding of Moses'; *Luca Giordano* (d. 1705), 'Martyrdom of St Januarius' and 'Phineas and his Companions Turned to Stone'; *Guercino* (d. 1666), 'The Incredulity of St Thomas'; *Jan Liss* (or Lys; d. 1629), 'Mercury and Argus' and 'Judith and Holofernes'; *Mattia Preti* (d. 1699), 'The Marriage at Cana'; *Guido Reni* (d. 1642), 'Adoration of the Shepherds by Night', a large altarpiece, 'Susannah and the Elders', 'Ecce Homo', etc.; *Salvator Rosa* (d. 1673), Self Portrait, 'Landscape with Tobias and the Angel' and 'Witches and their Incarnations'; *Sassoferrato* (d. 1685), 'Virgin and Child'; *Bernardo Strozzi* (d. 1644), 'Allegorical Figure of Fame'; *Domenico Zampieri* (Domenichino; d. 1641), 'Landscapes with Figures' and 'St George and the Dragon'.

18th-century Venetian School: *Antonio Canaletto* (d. 1768), 'The Stonemason's Yard', 'View on the Grand Canal', 'The Scuola di San Rocco', 'The Bucentaur at the Piazzetta', and 'Regatta on the Grand Canal', also 'Eton College' and 'Interior of the Rotunda at Ranelagh', examples of his work in England (1747–54); *G. M. Crespi* (d. 1747), 'St Jerome in the Desert'; *Francesco Guardi* (d. 1793), 'Santa Maria della Salute', 'The Doge's Palace', 'The Piazza San Marco', and other delightful scenes by this master; *Pietro Longhi* (d. 1785), 'Masked Visitors at a Menagerie', etc.; *G. A. Pellegrini* (d. 1741), 'Rebecca at the Well'; *G. B. Pittoni* (d. 1767), 'Nativity' (the figure of the Almighty had been painted out); *G. B. Tiepolo* (d. 1754), 'The Trinity Appearing to St Clement', 'The Deposition', and other fine works.

Also *Pompeo Batoni* (worked in Rome; d. 1787), 'Time Destroying Beauty' and 'John Scott of Banks Fee'.

DUTCH SCHOOL (Rooms 15–19 and 26–28): *Hendrik Avercamp* (d. 1634), 'Winter Scene'; *Jan van de Cappelle* (d. 1679), 'River Scenes'; *Aelbert Cuyp* (d. 1691), 'Portrait of a Man', and 'The Large Dort' and other characteristic landscapes with cattle; *Karel Dujardin* (d. 1678), 'Portrait of a Young Man' (perhaps the artist); *Gerbrandt von den Eeckhout* (d. 1674), 'The Wine Contract'; *Carel Fabritius* (d. 1654), 'Man in a Fur Cap'; *Jan van Goyen* (d. 1656), 'Winter Scene'; *Frans Hals* (d. 1666), 'Family Group in a Landscape', 'Man with a Glove', 'Lady with a Fan', and other fine portraits; *Bartholomeus van der Helst* (d. 1670), Portraits; *Meindert Hobbema* (d. 1709), 'The Avenue at Middelharnis', 'The Path through the Wood', and other notable landscapes; *Gerard Honthorst* (d. 1656), 'Christ before the High Priest' and 'St Sebastian'; *Pieter de Hooch* (d. about 1684), Dutch Courtyards and Interiors; *Philips Koninck* (d. 1688), two fine Landscapes; *Nicholas Maes* (d. 1693), 'Card Players'; *Michiel Mierevelt* (d. 1641), 'Portrait of a Lady'; *Aert van der Neer* (d. 1677), 'Canal Scene'.

Rembrandt van Rijn (d. 1669), a superb collection, notable among which are the 'Portrait of an Officer on Horseback' (a large and magnificent work acquired in 1960), 'An Old Man in an Armchair' (from the Duke of Devonshire's collection at Chatsworth), 'Belshazzar's Feast', 'A Jewish Merchant', 'A Capuchin Friar', 'A Jewish Rabbi', 'An Old Man as St Paul', two Self Portraits (1640 and 1669), 'Burgomaster Trip and his Wife', 'Saskia as Flora', 'Hendrickje Stoffels' (his mistress), 'A Woman Bathing', 'The Adoration of the Shepherds', and 'The Woman Taken in Adultery'.

Jacob van Ruisdael (d. 1682), 'Landscape', an exceptionally fine work; *Gerard Terborch* (d. 1681) 'The Peace of Münster' (1648), 'The Guitar Lesson', etc.; *Hendrick Terbrugghen* (d. 1629), 'The Concert' and 'Singing Luteplayer'; *Willem Van de Velde* (the Younger; d. 1707), 'Coast Scene'; *Jan Vermeer* (d. 1675), 'Ladies at the Virginals'; *Jan Wynants* (d. 1682), 'Landscape with Figures and Animals'; and many small landscapes, seascapes, and genre works by these artists and by Jan Both, Gerard Dou, Gabriel Metsu, Isaak and Adriaen van Ostade, Paul Potter, Salomon van Ruysdael, Jan Steen, and Adriaen Van de Velde.

FLEMISH SCHOOL (Rooms 20–22), with many examples illustrating every aspect of the work of *Peter Paul Rubens* (d. 1640) and his pupil, *Anthony Van Dyck* (d. 1641). Rubens was in England as envoy to Charles I in 1629–30, when he painted 'Peace and War'; and Van Dyck, invited to this country in 1632 by the king, became the court painter and died in London. Both painters received knighthoods, Rubens for the ceiling of Whitehall Palace (compare p. 111). Among the many splendid works by Rubens are 'The Château de Steen', a brilliant landscape, 'Le Chapeau de Poil' (often miscalled the Chapeau de Paille), 'The Watering Place', 'The Adoration of the Magi', 'Samson and Delilah', and 'Rape of the Sabines', 'The Brazen Serpent', and 'The Judgement of Paris', three rich canvases of his late period. Van Dyck is represented by 'Charles I on Horseback', a large and thoughtful study, 'George and Francis Villiers', 'Portrait of an Artist', an early work, 'Portrait of a Lady and Child', 'Il Marchese Cattaneo and his Lady', and 'The Abbé Scaglia adoring the Virgin'. The 'First Earl of Denbigh' is also attributed to this artist, and 'The Triumph of Silenus' is a combined work of Rubens and Van Dyck. Also: *Jacob Jordaens* (d. 1678), 'Portrait of a Man and a Woman' (previously at Chatsworth), and two groups of the 'Holy Family' in his characteristic 'peasant' style; and *David Teniers the Younger* (d. 1690), 'The Four Seasons' and two fine Village Scenes.

SPANISH SCHOOL (Rooms 41 and 42): *Goya* (d. 1828), 'Duke of Wellington' (bought for £140,000, stolen in 1961, and returned in 1965), and two characteristic portraits; *El Greco* (d. 1614), 'Christ Expelling the Traders from the Temple', 'The Agony in the Garden', two masterpieces, and 'The Adoration of the Name of Jesus', an enchanting sketch for a painting in the Escorial near Madrid; *Morales* (d. about 1586), 'Virgin and Child'; *Murillo* (d. 1682), 'The Two Trinities', 'Self Portrait', 'Peasant Boy', etc.; *Ribera* (d. 1652), 'The Dead Christ'; *Velazquez* (d. 1660), 'The Rokeby Venus', slashed by militant suffragettes in 1914, 'Christ in the House of Martha', 'Christ after the Flagellation', 'The Immaculate Conception', 'St John on Patmos', and 'Philip IV', a full-length portrait and a brilliant later bust-portrait; *Zurbaran* (d. about 1664), 'St Francis' and 'St Margaret'.

FRENCH SCHOOL (Rooms 32, 33, 40, and 43–46). 17th century: *Philippe de Champaigne* (d. 1674), 'The Dream of St Joseph', a large altarpiece, and 'Cardinal Richelieu'; *Claude Lorraine* (d. 1682), 'Marriage of Isaac and Rebecca', 'Embarkation of St Ursula', and other magnificent examples of his classical landscapes, and 'The Enchanted Castle' (in more romantic vein); *Gaspard Dughet* (d.

1675), Landscapes; *Louis Le Nain* (d. 1648), 'Adoration of the Shepherds'; *Eustache Le Sueur* (d. 1655), 'St Paul at Ephesus'; *Francisque Millet* (d. 1679), 'Mountain Landscape'; *Nicolas Poussin* (d. 1665), 'Adoration of the Shepherds' (formerly owned by Reynolds), 'Cephalus and Aurora', 'The Annunciation', 'The Adoration of the Golden Calf', 'Landscape with a Snake', 'The Triumph of Pan' (commissioned by Cardinal Richelieu), and other examples of this master; *Simon Vouet* (d. 1649), 'Ceres'.

18th century: *Boucher* (d. 1770), 'Pan and Syrinx'; *Chardin* (d. 1779), 'The Lesson' and 'The House of Cards'; *Fragonard* (d. 1806), 'Interior Scene'; *Lancret* (d. 1743), 'The Ages of Man' and 'Family in a Garden'; *Nattier* (d. 1766), 'Manon Balletti' and 'Man in Armour'; *Perronneau* (d. 1783), 'Girl with a Kitten', a pastel; *Quentin de la Tour* (d. 1788), 'Portrait of Henry Dawkins', pastel; *Watteau* (d. 1721), 'La Gamme d'Amour'.

Earlier 19th century: *Corot* (d. 1875), 'Avignon from the West' (*, see below), 'Dardagny', 'La Charrette, Souvenir de Saintry', and other landscapes; *Courbet* (d. 1877), 'Les Demoiselles des Bords de la Seine', *'Snowstorm', and 'Still Life'; *Daumier* (d. 1879), *'Don Quixote and Sancho Panza'; *David* (d. 1825), 'M. Blauw', a Bavarian minister; *Delacroix* (d. 1863), 'Baron Schwiter', 'Crucifixion', and 'Ovid among the Scythians'; *Delaroche* (d. 1856), 'Execution of Lady Jane Grey'; *Géricault* (d. 1824), 'Horse Frightened by Lightning'; *Ingres* (d. 1867), 'M. de Norvins' and 'Madame Moitessier'.

Later 19th century (Impressionists and Post-Impressionists): *Boudin* (d. 1898), 'Harbour at Trouville', and other landscapes; *Cézanne* (d. 1906), 'Les Grandes Baigneuses' (bought for £475,000), 'The Painter's Father', 'Cézanne Chauve', 'La Vieille au Chapelet', 'Dans le Parc du Château Noir', 'Aix, Paysage Rocheux', and other characteristic Provençal landscapes; *Degas* (d. 1917), 'Après le Bain', 'Danseuses', 'La Coiffure', 'Lola at the Cirque Fernando', etc.; *Fantin-Latour* (d. 1904), 'Roses'; *Gauguin* (d. 1903), 'Bouquet de Fleurs'; *Manet* (d. 1883), *'Eva Gonzales', 'La Servante de Bocks', 'Concert at the Tuileries' (with portraits of Baudelaire, Fantin-Latour, Gautier, and Offenbach), and 'The Firing Party', two fragments from a large canvas, 'The Execution of the Emperor Maximilian'; *Monet* (d. 1926), 'La Plage de Trouville', 'Le Bassin aux Nymphéas', 'Nirvana jaune', 'Vétheuil; Sunshine and Snow', 'Gare St Lazare', and 'L'Inondation; Bords de l'Epte' (a snow scene); *Berthe Morisot* (d. 1895), 'Jour d'Été'; *Pissarro* (d. 1903), 'Springtime at Louveciennes', 'Côte des Boeufs', 'The Louvre, Snowy Morning', 'La Route de Sydenham', and 'The Boulevard Montmartre at Night'; *Renoir* (d. 1919), *'Les Parapluies', 'La Source', 'La Première Sortie', 'Portrait of Misia Sert', 'Danseuses', 'Cradle Rock, Guernsey', and 'The Seine at Asnières'; *Henri Rousseau* (d. 1910), 'Tropical Storm with a Tiger'; *Seurat* (d. 1891), 'Une Baignade, Asnières'; *Sisley* (d. 1899), 'L'Abreuvoir de Marly'; *Toulouse-Lautrec* (d. 1901), 'Femme assise dans un Jardin'; *Van Gogh* (d. 1890), 'Landscape with Cypress Trees', 'Sunflowers', and 'L'Herbage aux Papillons'; *Vuillard* (d. 1940), 'Madame Wormser and her Children' (the gift of an officer of the Free French Navy).

*The paintings (nearly all of the French school) bequeathed by Sir Hugh Lane in 1917 were the subject of a lengthy dispute arising out of his will. They have been divided into two groups, to be shown alternately at the National Gallery and in Dublin, an exchange being made every five years (from 1961). The group at present on view (from 1981) includes Manet's 'Concert at the Tuileries', while the second group contains Corot's 'Avignon from the West', Renoir's 'Les Parapluies', and Manet's 'Eva Gonzales'.

NATIONAL PORTRAIT GALLERY Plan III, F3

STATIONS: CHARING CROSS, to the S, on the Bakerloo, Jubilee, and Northern lines; LEICESTER SQUARE, to the N, on the Northern and Piccadilly lines; EMBANKMENT, to the SE, on the Bakerloo, Circle, District, and Northern lines. — BUSES to Trafalgar Square, compare Route 1; in Charing Cross Road, see Route 19.

ADMISSION Mondays–Fridays 10 to 5, Saturdays 10 to 6, Sundays 2 to 6 (free). Closed on New Year's Day, Good Friday, May Day Monday, Christmas Eve and Day and Boxing Day. — LECTURES on Tuesdays and Thursdays at 1.10, Saturdays at 3.

The NATIONAL PORTRAIT GALLERY adjoins the National Gallery on its north-east side and is entered from St Martin's Place, which leads north from Trafalgar Square. The collection was founded in 1856 with the object of illustrating British history, literature, arts, and science by means of portraits of the most eminent men and women. The Italianate building, erected mostly at the charge of W. H. Alexander, was designed by Ewan Christian and completed in 1896, and an extension, the gift of Lord Duveen, was opened in 1933.

The collection now numbers over 7,000 paintings, sculptures, drawings, engravings, and photographs. Though the avowed aim of the gallery is 'to look to the celebrity of the person represented, rather than to the merit of the artist', there are good examples of the work of Lely, Kneller, Reynolds, Romney, Lawrence, Millais, G. F. Watts, and other leading artists. Only about one-third of the collection is on view, but any portrait in storage can usually be shown on request, though advance notice is desirable.

By arrangement with the National Trust, selections from the National Portrait Gallery's paintings are on permanent loan to Montacute House, Somerset (mainly Tudor and early Stuart portraits), and Beningbrough Hall, Yorkshire (later Stuart and early Georgian works), and are on view at these houses from April to October.

To the left of the entrance is the gallery's shop. From the Vestibule, where umbrellas, etc., must be left, stairs go up to a landing from which a lift ascends to the SECOND FLOOR. The gallery's collections are arranged more or less in chronological order, starting at the head of the stairs, facing the lift. Here and on the Upper Mezzanine Floor below are MEDIEVAL PORTRAITS, including Geoffrey Chaucer, Henry V, and Richard III, and a copy of the portrait of Richard II in Westminster Abbey.

The TUDOR PERIOD (Room 1), with portraits of Henry VII (1485–1509), believed to be the oldest from life in the gallery (1505); Sir Thomas More, the statesman and author of *Utopia*, with his family and descendants (a large canvas by Rowland Lockey); Henry VII and Henry VIII together (cartoon by Holbein); Henry VIII (1509–47; after Holbein), his first two queens, Catherine of Aragon and Anne Boleyn, and his last queen, Catherine Parr; his advisers, Cardinal Wolsey and Thomas Cromwell; Archbishops William Warham and Thomas Cranmer, the Protestant martyr; and the poets, Henry Howard, Earl of Surrey, and Sir Thomas Wyatt; Edward VI (1547–53) as Prince of Wales (by a follower of Holbein); Mary I (1553–8; by Hans Eworth) and her husband, Philip II of Spain; Lady Jane Grey (beheaded in 1554); Bishops Latimer and Ridley (burned in 1555); and Cardinal Pole, the last Roman Catholic archbishop.

Elizabeth I (1558–1603) appears in three portraits, one of about 1575, one of about 1592 showing her standing on a map of England and celebrated by a sonnet, and the third a fine portrait previously at Warwick Castle. Here also are her counsellors, Sir Francis Walsingham, Sir Christopher Hatton, and Lord Burghley and his son, Robert Cecil, Earl of Salisbury; her favourites, the Earl of Leicester and the Earl of Essex; Sir Thomas Gresham, the founder of the Royal Exchange; Sir Philip Sidney, poet and man of action; Mary, Queen of

Scots (executed in 1587); and William Shakespeare, by Droeshout, from an early folio and considered to be the best likeness. The miniatures here include Sir Francis Drake, the Elizabethan 'sea-dog' (by Hilliard).

The EARLY STUARTS (Room 2): James I (1603–25; by Mytens); his queen, Anne of Denmark; their eldest son, Henry, Prince of Wales; their daughter Elizabeth (by Honthorst) and her husband, Frederick V of Bohemia; James's favourite, the Duke of Buckingham; the Somerset House Conference, commemorating the treaty with Spain (1604); Sir Walter Raleigh, historian and adventurer; Ben Jonson, the playwright; and John Donne, poet and Dean of St Paul's.

Charles I (1625–49; also by Mytens); his consort, Henrietta Maria; his supporters, Archbishop Laud and the Earl of Strafford; his nephew Prince Rupert, the Cavalier general; and Charles II as Prince of Wales; Sir Anthony Van Dyck; Victoria Stanley, Lady Digby (by Van Dyck); Inigo Jones, the architect (after Van Dyck); and Thomas Howard, Earl of Arundel, patron of the arts (by Rubens; a splendid study). Here also are Oliver Cromwell (by Robert Walker) and his generals, Henry Ireton and John Lambert.

Room 3 is devoted to 17TH-CENTURY ARTS AND SCIENCES. John Evelyn, the diarist (by R. Walker); Izaak Walton, the angler (by Huysmans); William Harvey, discoverer of the circulation of the blood; Sir William Petty, the economist (by Fuller); Robert Boyle, the scientist; the poets, John Dryden (by Kneller), Samuel Butler (by Soest), Andrew Marvell, and John Milton (as a young man); the painter, John Michael Wright; and John Bunyan, author of *Pilgrim's Progress*. The statue of Francis Bacon, statesman and philosopher, is a copy of that at St Albans.

The LATER STUARTS (Room 4): Charles II (1660–85); his queen, Catherine of Braganza; three of his mistresses, Nell Gwyn and the Duchesses of Portsmouth and Cleveland; his statesmen, the Duke of Albemarle and the Earl of Clarendon; and the members of the notorious 'Cabal' ministry (Clifford, Ashley, Buckingham, Arlington, and Lauderdale); Samuel Pepys, the diarist; Sir Christopher Wren (by Kneller); Sir Peter Lely (a self portrait); Abraham Cowley, poet and royalist; and Sir Isaac Newton, the scientist (by Kneller).

James II (1685–8; by Kneller) and his second queen, Mary of Modena (by Wissing); his opponent, the Duke of Monmouth; and the infamous Judge Jeffreys; William III (1688–1702) and Mary II (1688–94); George Savile, Marquess of Halifax, the statesman;

William Wycherley, the playwright; Thomas Betterton, the actor; and Henry Purcell, the composer.

The EARLY EIGHTEENTH CENTURY (Room 5 and adjoining landing): Queen Anne (1702–14); the Duke of Marlborough (an equestrian portrait by Kneller); Robert Harley, Earl of Oxford, the Tory statesman; Archbishop John Tillotson, famous for his sermons; Daniel Finch, Earl of Nottingham, the statesman; George I (1714–27) and the Electress Sophia (a bust); James Stuart, the 'Old Pretender', and with his sister, as children (by Largillière); Henry St John, Viscount Bolingbroke, the Tory statesman; and John Campbell, 2nd Duke of Argyll, promoter of the union between England and Scotland.

Room 6 (east of the landing) is confined to EARLY-18TH-CENTURY ARTS AND SCIENCES. Bishop Berkeley, the philosopher; the artists, Samuel Scott (by Hudson) and Mikael Dahl (a self portrait); Richard Boyle, Earl of Burlington, the Palladian architect; Lady Mary Wortley Montagu, traveller and letter-writer, and her son; Jonathan Swift, Alexander Pope, and others of the great Augustans; Sir Hans Sloane, the physician; Edmond Halley, the astronomer; and Lancelot 'Capability' Brown, the landscape gardener (by Dance). This and the following rooms contain notable busts by Roubiliac: of himself, in marble; terracottas of Handel, Pope, and Hogarth; and a remarkable coloured plaster bust of Colley Cibber, the actor.

Room 7 contains portraits of members of the KIT-CAT CLUB, a political and literary circle of the Whig party that flourished during the first twenty years of the 18th century and was dedicated to securing the Hanoverian succession. The forty-two portraits, all painted by Sir Godfrey Kneller, include a self portrait; Sir Robert Walpole, the Prime Minister; Joseph Addison and Sir Richard Steele, the essayists; William Congreve, the playwright; Sir John Vanbrugh, playwright and architect; Jacob Tonson, the bookseller (in whose rooms the club first met); and the Duke of Newcastle and the Earl of Lincoln, the only double portrait. About half of the portraits are at Beningbrough Hall (see above).

Room 8 is given over to part of the EARLY GEORGIAN PERIOD. George II (1727–60) and Queen Caroline of Anspach; Frederick, Prince of Wales, and his sisters ('The Music Party'; by Mercier); Prince Charles Edward Stuart, the 'Young Pretender', his brother Cardinal York (the 'last of the Stuarts'), and his opponent the Duke of

Cumberland; the composers, George Frideric Handel (by Hudson), William Boyce, and Thomas Arne (a caricature); William Hogarth and Sir James Thornhill (self portraits); Thomas Gray, the poet; Horace Walpole, man of letters; and John Wesley, the founder of Methodism (by Hone).

The 18TH-CENTURY ARTS are further illustrated in Room 9. Thomas Gainsborough, Sir Joshua Reynolds, Allan Ramsay, and Joseph Wright of Derby (all self portraits); David Garrick, the actor (by Gainsborough); Joseph Wilton, the sculptor, and John Stuart, Third Earl of Bute, Prime Minister and botanist (both by Reynolds); Laurence Sterne, a superb study by Reynolds and a bust by Nollekens; the Earl of Chesterfield, statesman and man of letters (by Ramsay); Tobias Smollett, the novelist; and Sir William Hamilton, diplomat and archaeologist.

THE BEGINNINGS OF EMPIRE (Room 10): William Pitt, Earl of Chatham, the statesman; Lord Clive of India; Warren Hastings, later Governor-General of India (an early portrait by Reynolds); James Wolfe, the hero of Quebec; Captain James Cook, the explorer; and Admiral Richard Kempenfelt, who perished at the sinking of the *Royal George*.

THE MID-GEORGIAN PERIOD (Room 11): George III (1760–1820; by Ramsay) and Queen Charlotte; Field-Marshal Lord Amherst (by Gainsborough); General Wolfe (a bust by Wilton); George Washington; General Sir John Burgoyne, soldier and dramatist; Lord North, the Prime Minister who lost the American colonies (by Dance); the Death of the Earl of Chatham (by J. S. Copley); and busts of Fox and the younger Pitt, by Nollekens.

BRITAIN AT WAR, 1793–1815 (Room 12, west of the landing): William Pitt the Younger (by Hoppner) and his rival Charles James Fox; Lord Thurlow (by Philips) and Henry Dundas, Lord Melville (by Lawrence), the Tory statesmen; Lord Grenville, the Prime Minister (by Hoppner), and other Whig statesmen; Edmund Burke, the opponent of the French Revolution; Admirals St Vincent, Hood, and Collingwood; General Sir John Moore; Lord Nelson (by Beechey) and Lady Hamilton (by Romney); and the Duke of Wellington and other men of action.

The ROMANTIC MOVEMENT (Room 13): John Clare, the peasant poet; Robert Burns (by Nasmyth) and Sir Walter Scott (by Landseer); William Wordsworth (a fine study by Haydon), S. T. Coleridge, and Robert Southey; Charles Lamb (by Hazlitt); John Keats (by Severn); P. B. Shelley (the only authentic portrait) and his second wife, Mary Wollstonecraft Shelley; Lord Byron (in Albanian costume); Leigh Hunt, the poet and essayist (by Laurence); George Romney (a self portrait); Henry Fuseli (by Northcote); Thomas Girtin (by Opie); John Constable (by Reinagle); John Opie (a self portrait); J. M. W. Turner (by Linnell); and William Blake (by Philips), as well as a life mask of the poet-visionary.

SCIENCE AND THE INDUSTRIAL REVOLUTION (Room 14): Edward Jenner, the discoverer of vaccination; Erasmus Darwin, physician and naturalist (by Wright of Derby); the engineers, Matthew Boulton, James Watt (by C. F. von Breda), Sir Marc Brunel, John Smeaton, and John Rennie (bust by Chantrey); John L. Macadam, the road builder; Sir Richard Arkwright, inventor of the spinning-frame (by Wright of Derby); Robert Owen, the social reformer; John Wilkinson, the ironmaster (by Abbott); and Adam Walker, scientific lecturer, and his family (by Romney).

THE REGENCY, etc. (Room 15): George IV (1820–30) and Caroline of Brunswick (both by Lawrence); Maria Fitzherbert, the Prince Regent's first wife (by Reynolds); Charlotte, Princess of Wales; Lord Brougham (by Lawrence); and a large group of the House of Lords discussing the bill to divorce Queen Caroline (1820; by Sir George Hayter); the statesmen, Lord Liverpool, Lord Castlereagh, and George Canning (all by Lawrence); R. B. Sheridan, the playwright; J. P. Kemble, the actor (by Gilbert Stuart); the actresses, Dorothea Jordan (by Hoppner), Sarah Siddons (by Beechey), and Elizabeth Farren, later Countess of Derby (by Downham); Sir John Soane, the architect; William IV (1830–37); the reformers, William Cobbett, Elizabeth Fry, and Sir Francis Burdett (by Shee); Earl Grey, promoter of the Reform Bill of 1832; the first Meeting of the House of Commons after the Reform Bill (with 375 figures; by Hayter); and William Wilberforce, the abolitionist, a fine unfinished portrait by Lawrence.

From the landing near Room 12, stairs descend to the FIRST FLOOR, which is devoted to the Victorian Period and the 20th Century. The rooms on the left (west) are used for special exhibitions.

THE EARLY VICTORIANS (Room 16, facing the stairs, and Room 17): Queen Victoria (1837–1901), in her coronation robes (by Hayter); Prince Albert (d. 1861; engraving by F. C. Lewis); and Lord Melbourne, the queen's first Prime Minister; Lord Tennyson (by

Lawrence) and Thomas Hood, the poets; George Borrow, author of *Lavengro*; Charles Dickens (by Maclise) and W. M. Thackeray, the novelists; Charles Kean, the actor; Helena Faucit, the actress (bust by Foley); Jenny Lind, the 'Swedish nightingale'; M. W. Balfe and other Victorian composers; Lord Macaulay, the historian; the Brontë sisters (by their brother, Branwell); and Charlotte Brontë, Elizabeth Gaskell, and Charlotte M. Yonge (pastels, all by Richmond); Sir Charles Barry and A. W. N. Pugin, the architects; Daniel Maclise and William Etty, the painters; D. O. Hill, the early photographer; Michael Faraday, the pioneer of electricity (by Philips); Sir George Cayley, the pioneer of aviation; and Cardinal Newman and John Keble (pastels by Richmond).

THE 1840S, POVERTY AND THE PEOPLE (Room 18), with portraits of Lord George Bentinck, who repealed the Corn Laws; the Prime Ministers, Sir Robert Peel (by Linnell), Lord John Russell (by Watts), Lord Aberdeen, and Lord Derby; the Earl of Shaftesbury, the philanthropist (by Watts); Isambard K. Brunel, the pioneer of railways and shipbuilding; and George Bradshaw, the printer and engraver, famous for his railway timetables.

THE CRIMEA, INDIA, AND THE EMPIRE (Room 19, west part of corridor): group showing Queen Victoria and the Prince Consort; Sir James Brooke, Rajah of Sarawak (by Grant); Sir Herbert Edwardes, the Indian administrator; the generals, Sir James Outram, Sir Henry Havelock (bust by Adams), and Sir Charles Napier; Sidney Herbert, secretary for war during the Crimean campaign (by Grant); Florence Nightingale, a bust by Steel, and at Scutari in the Crimea; Lord Palmerston, the Prime Minister; and the explorers, Sir Richard Burton (by Leighton), David Livingstone (by Bonomi), and Sir John Ross.

VICTORIAN SCIENCE AND TECHNOLOGY (Room 20, south of corridor): Prince Albert, the inspirer of the Great Exhibition of 1851 (by Winterhalter); Sir Joseph Paxton, designer of the 'Crystal Palace'; James Nasmyth and Lord Armstrong, the engineers and inventors; Sir William Siemens, the electrical pioneer; Sir Daniel Gooch, the railway engineer (by Grant); Charles Darwin and T. H. Huxley (both by Collier), and other men of science. Also here are Matthew Arnold, Thomas Carlyle, and John Stuart Mill (all by Watts).

MID-VICTORIAN ART AND LITERATURE (Room 21): G. F. Watts (by himself), and Ellen Terry, at the age of seventeen (by Watts); the poets, Robert and Elizabeth Barrett Browning, and A. C. Swinburne (by Watts); Charles Kingsley, the novelist; Christina

Rossetti and her mother (by D. G. Rossetti); and William Morris, the craftsman and visionary (by Watts).

The LATER VICTORIANS (Room 23, east part of corridor): the Marquess of Salisbury and Lord Randolph Churchill (father of Sir Winston), the politicians; the military leaders, Earl Roberts, Viscount Wolseley, General Gordon (bust by Boehm), and Lord Kitchener; Cecil Rhodes, the South African statesman (by Watts); Robert, Lord Baden-Powell, founder of the Boy Scouts; Colonel Burnaby, the guardsman-balloonist (by Tissot); Thomas Carlyle, W. E. Gladstone, and Benjamin Disraeli (all by Millais); and the explorers, Admiral Parry and Sir John Franklin.

The Later Victorians are continued in Room 24 (north of corridor): Coventry Patmore, the poet (by Sargent); Robert Louis Stevenson (by Richmond); Sir Henry Irving, the actor; Ellen Terry as Lady Macbeth (by Sargent); Adelina Patti, the singer; W. S. Gilbert and Sir Arthur Sullivan (both by Millais); Sir Edward Burne-Jones and James McN. Whistler (by Greaves); busts of Stevenson, Sir John Millais (by Onslow Ford), Lord Leighton (by Brock), and W. E. Henley (a fine bust by Rodin); and a large group of the Private View of the Old Masters Exhibition at the Royal Academy (1888), with leading artists and patrons of the day.

Room 25, at the end, is mainly concerned with the EDWARDIAN PERIOD. Edward VII (1901–10) and Queen Alexandra (both by Fildes); the Marquess Curzon, the statesman (after Sargent); Admiral Lord Fisher, who carried out many reforms in the Navy; Henry James, the novelist (by Sargent); Rupert Brooke, the poet; Lady Colin Campbell, journalist and socialite; Nellie Farren, the actress (by Graham Robertson); Ethel Smyth, the composer (drawing by Sargent), Virginia Woolf (by Duncan Grant), Gwen John (self portrait) and other artists; and the Selecting Jury of the New English Art Club (by Orpen, 1909).

On the landing near Room 25 are ROYAL PORTRAITS, including a group of George V (1910–36) and Queen Mary, with their two eldest children (by Sir John Lavery, 1913); Princess Victoria, daughter of Edward VII (by Philip de Laszlo, 1907); George V (by Sir Oswald Birley, about 1935); and a bust of Queen Mary (by W. Reid Dick, 1938).

Stairs descend to the Lower Mezzanine Floor, which has further royal portraits, among them a group of George VI (1936–52) and his family (by Sir James Gunn, 1950); George VI and Queen Elizabeth (the Queen Mother; both by Sir Gerald Kelly, about 1938–9); a controversial portrait of Queen Elizabeth II, by Pietro Annigoni (1969); the Duke of Edinburgh (1983), the Prince of Wales (1980), and Lady Diana Spencer, now Princess of Wales (1981; all three by Bryan Organ); and bronze heads of George VI (by W. Reid Dick,

1945) and of the Queen (1981) and the Duke of Edinburgh (1979), both by Franta Belsky.

Stairs go on down to the Ground Floor. Room 28, on the right (north) is given over to 20TH-CENTURY PORTRAITS, among them Sir Winston Churchill, striking studies by Sickert (1927) and Graham Sutherland (1954); Ramsay MacDonald (by Lavery), Neville Chamberlain (by Henry Lamb), Harold Macmillan (by Bryan Organ), Harold Wilson (by Ruskin Spear), and other statesmen; Viscount Montgomery (by Frank O. Salisbury); the Earl Mountbatten (by John Ulbricht); Bertrand Russell, the philosopher (by Roger Fry); John Maynard Keynes, the economist, and his wife, the ballerina Lydia Lopokova (by William Roberts); the writers, Dame Edith Sitwell (by Tchelitchew), Wyndham Lewis (self portrait), and T. S. Eliot (by Patrick Heron); the composers, Constant Lambert (by Christopher Wood), Sir Arthur Bliss (by Mark Gertler), and Sir William Walton (by Michael Ayrton); and the artists, Dame Laura Knight (self portrait with model), Vanessa Bell (by Duncan Grant), Sir Stanley Spencer and Graham Sutherland (self portraits).

Among the gallery's more recent sculptures, some of which may be on view here, are bronzes of Joseph Conrad, Bernard Shaw, W. B. Yeats, and Somerset Maugham (all by Epstein), of Sir Edward Elgar, Ralph Vaughan Williams, and Sir Thomas Beecham (with expressive hands), and of Aneurin Bevan, initiator of the National Health Service (by Peter Lambda), and Henry Moore, the sculptor (by Marino Marini). The gallery has also a growing collection of photographs.

The rooms in the BASEMENT are usually reserved for Recent Acquisitions and Special Exhibitions. Lectures are given in Room 22, on the First Floor.

NATURAL HISTORY MUSEUM Plan VI, C2, 3

STATION: SOUTH KENSINGTON, nearly ¼ m. SE, on the Circle, District, and Piccadilly lines, reached by a subway entered from the south-east corner of the gardens. — BUSES in Brompton Road and Cromwell Road, see Route 10; in Kensington Road, see Route 11.

ADMISSION Mondays–Saturdays 10 to 6, Sundays 2.30 to 6 (free). Closed on New Year's Day, Good Friday, May Day Monday, Christmas Eve and Day, and Boxing Day. — LECTURES or films on Tuesdays, Thursdays, and Saturdays at 3, in the Lecture Hall. — CAFETERIA (unlicensed; closed on Sundays) on the First Floor; Snack Bar on the Ground Floor (open daily).

The NATURAL HISTORY MUSEUM, officially the British Museum (Natural History), is one of the group of interesting museums at South Kensington. Reached from Cromwell Road, west of the Victoria and Albert Museum, it is housed in a vast Romanesque palace designed by

Alfred Waterhouse and built in 1873–80. The south front of this has a length of 675 ft and it is flanked by symmetrical towers 192 ft high. The building is faced throughout with terracotta slabs bearing series of animals moulded in relief, and recent cleaning of the façade has revealed the varied colours of the slabs and the fine details of the carvings. Though the public galleries cover nearly four acres of floor-space, only a small proportion of the specimens can be put on show. The museum includes important Reference Libraries and very extensive Study Collections, usually accessible to mature students and research workers on written application to the Director.

The museum was built up round the scientific collections of Sir Hans Sloane, purchased for the nation after his death in 1753 to form part of the nucleus of the British Museum. To this was added the large botanical collection bequeathed in 1820 by Sir Joseph Banks. In 1856, at the suggestion of Sir Richard Owen, the first director, the museum was divided into its present five departments of Zoology, Entomology, Palaeontology, Mineralogy, and Botany, and the collections were removed from Bloomsbury and opened here in 1881.

The museum's collections now amount to about fifty million items. Among the historic specimens are those from Captain James Cook's explorations in the Pacific, Charles Darwin's epic voyage in H.M.S. *Beagle*, and Captain R. F. Scott's ill-fated expedition to the South Pole. The Library, of about 500,000 volumes, has an unsurpassed collection of early natural history manuscripts and drawings. One of the museum's most important activities is in the field of research, not only in collecting and classifying specimens, still an important function, but in examining the detailed structure of organisms and other scientific work (the museum employs about 300 scientists) and in organizing expeditions to many parts of the world. The museum also provides a free service to schools and other educational institutions.

Nearly all the galleries have been rearranged in recent years, to their considerable improvement. The new exhibitions are laid out in accordance with modern ideas of museum display; they concentrate much more on explaining the development of certain themes and ideas than in simply providing cases full of rows of specimens.

The entrance through an ornate Romanesque portal leads direct into the CENTRAL HALL, 170 ft long and 72 ft high, with moulded terracotta decorations on the stairs, pillars, and balconies, and painted and gilded floral designs on the ceiling. The cloakroom is to the right of the vestibule, the bookstall and shop to the left. The Fossil Galleries (described below) open to the right (east); the galleries concerned with birds, insects, whales, etc., are to the left. The Central Hall and the bays on both sides are devoted to an exhibition (1979) about DINOSAURS AND THEIR RELATIVES, investigating the way in which these great prehistoric reptiles are related to each other and to other animals, both living and extinct. The reconstructions include a Diplodocus, based on a skeleton, 84 ft 9 in. long and 11 ft 5 in. high (in the Carnegie Museum at Pittsburgh, U.S.A.), the horned Triceratops, the giant flesh-eating Tyrannosaurus, the only one in western Europe (40 ft long), and Iguadons found in England and Belgium.

The NORTH HALL, behind the grand staircase, is mainly given over to special exhibitions and recent acquisitions, but here and in the corridor beyond are specimens of all the major fish, reptile, and amphibian groups, and including a coelacanth (a fish long believed to be extinct). Here also is the giant panda, Chi-Chi, who lived in the Zoological Gardens from 1958 until his death in 1972 and was then given to the museum. On either side of the entrance to the hall are statues of Charles Darwin (d. 1882) and Thomas Henry Huxley (d. 1895).

The corridor leads to the NORTH BLOCK, completed in 1959, but not open to the public. It contains a general library (with map and reading rooms, etc.) and a splendid Lecture Hall, but is mainly taken up by the museum's vast reference and study collection of mammal specimens, occupying eleven floors.

On the west of the North Hall is the Children's Centre, and on the west of the Central Hall is a small gallery confined to Arachnids (scorpions and spiders).

From the Central Hall the grand staircase, on the landing of which is a statue of Sir Richard Owen (d. 1892), ascends to the FIRST FLOOR. On the east balcony is an exhibition (1980) concerned with MAN'S PLACE IN EVOLUTION, showing how *homo sapiens* developed from his ape-like ancestors through various stages, such as Neanderthal man (here portrayed), and his relation both to fossil animals and living creatures.

The MINERAL GALLERY, in the east wing, contains a remarkable collection of over 9,000 specimens of minerals, arranged according to their chemical composition and crystal structure, as well as examples of most of the rock types. The wall cases on the left of the entrance illustrate crystal structure; those on the right demonstrate the identification of minerals by X-rays, in which much work has been done in recent years. Cases on the right near the door contain specimens from the collection of Sir Hans Sloane and a fine selection of gold, platinum, and precious stones. Cases on the left and round the sides of the gallery serve as an introduction to mineralogy. In the centre of the gallery are cases with models of crystal structures. At the east end is the fine Meteorite Pavilion, containing a variety of specimens, among them an iron meteorite weighing three and a half tons which was found in 1854 near Melbourne.

A staircase from the balconies leads to the SECOND FLOOR, on which are a marble statue by Chantrey of Sir Joseph Banks (d. 1820) and a section of a Giant Sequoia, or Big Tree of California, cut down in 1892, by which time it had attained a height of 276 ft and a girth of 49 ft. The 1,335 rings of annual growth indicate that it started life in A.D. 557. The BOTANICAL GALLERY opened in the east wing in 1963 contains specimens of British and foreign plants, dioramas of natural scenes, and cases illustrating plant physiology, ecology, and the conservation of plant life. On the landing is a herbarium with about 600 examples of British wild flowers.

On the south balcony (and the neighbouring part of the east balcony) are coloured marbles and other ornamental stones, a large jade boulder from Siberia, a gypsum crystal, historic specimens from Antarctica, fluorescent minerals, a large crystal of calcite showing its double refractive properties, and further meteorites, including one that fell in the Argentine and weighs over half a ton.

In the west wing on this floor is a splendid new exhibition (1981) concerned with the ORIGIN OF SPECIES. It traces the arguments of Charles Darwin for natural selection, as set out in his pioneer work, published in 1859, and provides evidence of some of its effects among living species. Specimens, models, and even games with computers are used to illustrate Darwin's ideas and to encourage visitors to test for themselves the validity of his conclusions. At the farther end is the fine ROWLAND WARD PAVILION, showing groups of African mammals in their natural habitat, including the giraffe and its relative the okapi (discovered only in 1901).

The MAMMAL BALCONY, on the west side of the Central Hall, displays a wide selection of mammals from every part of the world, among them the primitive egg-laying platypus and the giant anteater of Australia, and the Alaskan moose, the largest species of deer. The stairs from the north end of the balcony return to the ground floor.

In the west wing, on the ground floor, is the delightful BIRD GALLERY. Bays on the south side, designed as an introduction to the study of birds, include a skeleton and model of the flightless Dodo of Mauritius, which became extinct in the 17th century. In other bays birds are grouped according to families and include some beautiful humming birds from Central America. The pavilion at the farther end shows British birds, partly in their native habitat, and recordings of bird song may be heard.

A corridor on the right of the Bird Gallery, towards the end, leads to the INSECT GALLERY, with exhibits explaining the anatomy, flight, migration, camouflage, etc., of insects and their uses to man, and a splendid collection of butterflies and moths. On the right is a gallery confined to MARINE INVERTEBRATES, including crustacea (crabs, lobsters, shrimps, etc.), starfish, sea urchins, molluscs, and octopuses. Cases at the end illustrate the religious and ornamental use of shells, etc.

To the north of this gallery opens the WHALE HALL, containing skeletons of the blue or rorqual whale, the largest of living mammals (82 ft long; with a model of one 91 ft long); right whales (one 60 ft long) from Greenland and North America; the sperm whale (60 ft long), the largest of the toothed whales; the bottle-nosed whale; and the Californian grey whale (44 ft). Here also are models of other whales, dolphins, and porpoises; and upstairs are cases showing fossils of whales and illustrating their structure.

Another corridor on the north of the Bird Gallery admits to the HALL OF HUMAN BIOLOGY, an interesting exhibition (1977) that explains, with the help of demonstrations and working models, the development of a human being from a living cell and the effects of experience and environment in shaping the individual's perception, thinking, reason, and language.

The east wing of the ground floor is devoted to the extensive FOSSIL COLLECTION, mostly arranged zoologically. On the left at the entrance are cases of British fossils; on the right are fossils from the collection made by William Smith (d. 1839), the 'father of English geology'. The long main gallery traces the evolution of mammals from the earliest known examples to the giant mammoths and elks of the Ice Age. Notable are the 'straight-tusked' elephant, nearly 13 ft high, found near Chatham (Kent) in 1911; the mammoth remains discovered near the Thames at Aveley (Essex) in 1964; the giant Irish deer, which had antlers sometimes over 11 ft in span, and a giant sloth from South America. The pavilion at the end shows modern examples of the larger mammals: elephants, hippopotami, and rhinoceroses.

A corridor near the west end of the gallery, with exhibits illustrating the succession of living things from their earliest origins to the present day, leads to a small room containing FOSSIL PLANTS, including the earliest known plants and fine specimens from the coal measures. On the right opens the gallery of FOSSIL REPTILES, among which are the great sea-lizards, the ichthyosaurs and plesiosaurs, the first of which were discovered at Lyme Regis (Dorset) in 1811 by Mary

Anning. In this gallery also is an exhibition illustrating the ecology of an oak woodland.

Near the west end opens the gallery containing FOSSIL INVERTEBRATES, with specimens of jellyfish and sea lilies, and the earliest known British fossil, a sea fan 800 million years old. At the end is a fossil Portheus, a giant fish 14 ft long. The FOSSIL FISHES gallery, reached from the east end of the Reptile gallery, has interesting dioramas illustrating life in the sea during successive geological ages. The gallery west of this is mainly utilized for a special exhibition concerned with WILDLIFE IN DANGER.

A five-story extension to the museum behind the present building, approved in 1980, will contain new exhibition galleries, a restaurant, and further educational facilities for schools.

St PAUL'S CATHEDRAL Plan IV, E3

STATIONS: ST PAUL'S, to the NE, on the Central line; MANSION HOUSE, ¼ m. SE, on the Circle and District lines. — BUSES Nos. 4, 6, 9, 11, 15, 18, 23, 76, 141, 502, and 513 all pass the cathedral on the S side; Nos. 8, 22, 25, and 501 pass the entrance to St Paul's Churchyard on the NE.

ADMISSION Mondays–Saturdays from 8 a.m. to 7 p.m., Sundays 8 a.m. to 6 p.m. (daily to 5 p.m. in October–March); for Service only on 25 January, Good Friday, Easter Sunday, Ascension Day, and Christmas Day. Visitors are requested not to walk about during Service, which begins on Sundays at 8, 10.30, and 11.30 a.m. and 3.15 p.m., and on Mondays–Saturdays at 7.30 (except Saturdays), 8, and 10 a.m. (Saturdays only), and 12.30 (except Fridays) and 5 p.m. (4 p.m. in winter). Guided Tours on Mondays–Saturdays at 11 and 2. — Tickets for the CRYPT, open on Mondays–Saturdays, 10 (Saturdays at 11) to 4.15 (to 3.15 in winter), are obtainable in the South Transept; for the WHISPERING GALLERY, the STONE GALLERY, and the GOLDEN GALLERY (at the same times) at the E end of the South Aisle; the BALL is closed at present.

ST PAUL'S CATHEDRAL, the seat of the bishop of London and the 'parish church of the British Commonwealth', stands in a commanding position at the top of Ludgate Hill, the spiritual heart of the City of London, as the Bank is its commercial centre. The largest as well as the most famous of the City churches, it stands on the site of the great medieval church of 'Old St Paul's', burned down in the Great Fire of 1666. Built of Portland stone, the new church was begun in 1675, opened for service in 1697, and finally completed in 1710. It is the masterpiece of Sir Christopher Wren (1632–1723), a beautiful and harmonious Renaissance building with twin baroque towers rising above the dignified west façade and dominated by its famous dome, the largest church dome in the world after St Peter's at Rome. The cathedral is 515 ft long outside and 180 ft wide across the west front; internally, it is 463 ft long and 227½ ft wide across the transepts. The nave, 180 ft long, is the widest of any Anglican church in England (125 ft, including the aisles) and 92½ ft high to the vault. The dome is 112 ft in diameter, and the height from the floor of the church to the top of the cross is 365 ft. The west towers are each 212½ ft high. The area of the church (87,400 sq. ft) is the greatest of any cathedral in England, except that of the Anglican cathedral of Liverpool (completed in 1978).

The earliest recorded church on this historic site was endowed by Ethelbert, the first Christian king of Kent, and here Mellitus was consecrated bishop of the East Saxons by St Augustine in 604. His cathedral, rebuilt in stone between 675 and 685 by the saintly Bishop Erconwald, was burned down by Viking raiders in the 9th century. It was raised again in 962, but was destroyed by a fire that swept through the City in 1087, and a new church on a larger and more elaborate plan was begun by the Norman Bishop Maurice. Though the work was delayed by another fire in 1136, the choir was in use by 1148 and the steeple completed in 1221. King John submitted himself to the Papal Legate here in 1213, pledging his kingdom to pay an annual tribute to Rome. By this time the choir was considered inadequate; it was rebuilt by 1240 and later extended eastwards, and in 1315 the church was given a lofty new spire of wood covered with lead, which reached a height of at least 480 ft (and possibly much higher). St Paul's, now attached to a college of secular canons, was the longest cathedral in England (596 ft) and one of the largest in Europe. Here in 1377 John Wyclif, the reformer, was tried for heresy, and in 1527 William Tyndale's translation of the New Testament was publicly burned. Prince Arthur, the elder brother of Henry VIII, was married in the cathedral to Catherine of Aragon in 1501. In the 14th–15th centuries the great church had increased in splendour, but by the middle of the 16th century it began to be seriously neglected, and Henry VIII removed many of its treasures. Lord Protector Somerset demolished the north cloister to provide stones for his new palace in the Strand, and the nave began to be used as a place of business ('Paul's Walk'). In 1561 the great spire was struck by lightning and brought down, causing a fire that damaged much of the church, and though a restoration was undertaken in 1627–42, when Inigo Jones partly rebuilt the west end and added a fine new portico, the church was again in a sadly dilapidated state when it was almost completely destroyed in the Great Fire of 1666.

At first it was thought that the cathedral could be repaired (the ruined nave was patched up and used for service until 1673), but Sir Christopher Wren, Surveyor General of the Works under Charles II, persuaded the Commissioners to accept his plan for a completely new church. He gathered round him some of the finest craftsmen of the time: Nicholas Hawksmoor as clerk of the works, Thomas and Edward Strong as master-masons, Grinling Gibbons and Jonathan Maine as wood-carvers, Jean Tijou as ironworker, and Francis Bird and Caius Gabriel Cibber as sculptors. The first stone was laid in 1675, the choir was opened for service in 1697, and the last stone was placed in position in 1710. Wren had originally planned the church in the form of a Greek cross (one having four equal arms), with a large central dome supported by eight massive pillars, but in response to the demands of the Court party, who hoped for the return of Roman Catholicism, it was given a longer nave and side chapels. Wren had to face much adverse criticism both during the building of the church and after its completion; his salary was withheld with the object of making him finish the building more rapidly, and in 1718 he was dismissed from his post as surveyor. After his death, however, he was buried in the crypt, where many other famous men have since been interred, some of them commemorated by memorials (not always in the best taste) in the cathedral.

St Paul's was miraculously spared during the great fire of 29 December 1940, which devastated a great area around it. During the whole of the war it was guarded by a devoted band of voluntary firewatchers, whose courage and promptness on many occasions saved it from the fate of Old St Paul's. In 1941, however, it received direct hits from high-explosive bombs which wrecked the high altar and the north transept and destroyed most of the glass, now all replaced by clear glass. The cathedral is a favourite venue for society weddings and services of thanksgiving, etc., and in 1981 it was chosen for the wedding of Charles, Prince of Wales, and Lady Diana Spencer.

The cathedral was once so notoriously hemmed in by buildings that it was difficult to obtain a good general impression of the exterior. The open spaces created by aerial bombardment, however, revealed many splendid and sometimes unusual prospects, and the new buildings that have been erected in the vicinity have been designed to allow some of these vistas to remain. The church as a whole is remarkable for the relationship between the Gothic plan of the structure and the classical Renaissance details. The exterior columns and coupled pilasters consist of two orders, the lower Corinthian, the upper Composite. On the north and south sides of the nave and choir aisles the upper part is little more than a screen masking the flying buttresses that help to support the clerestory of the nave. The stone balustrade along the top was one of the features introduced against the wishes of the architect, who declared that 'ladies think nothing well without an edging'. The arms of the transepts are each terminated by a semicircular portico, the pediment above which contains (on the north) the royal arms of the Stuarts, by Grinling Gibbons, and (on the south) a Phoenix, with the inscription *Resurgam*, by C. G. Cibber. The phoenix characterizes the rise of the new St Paul's from the ashes of

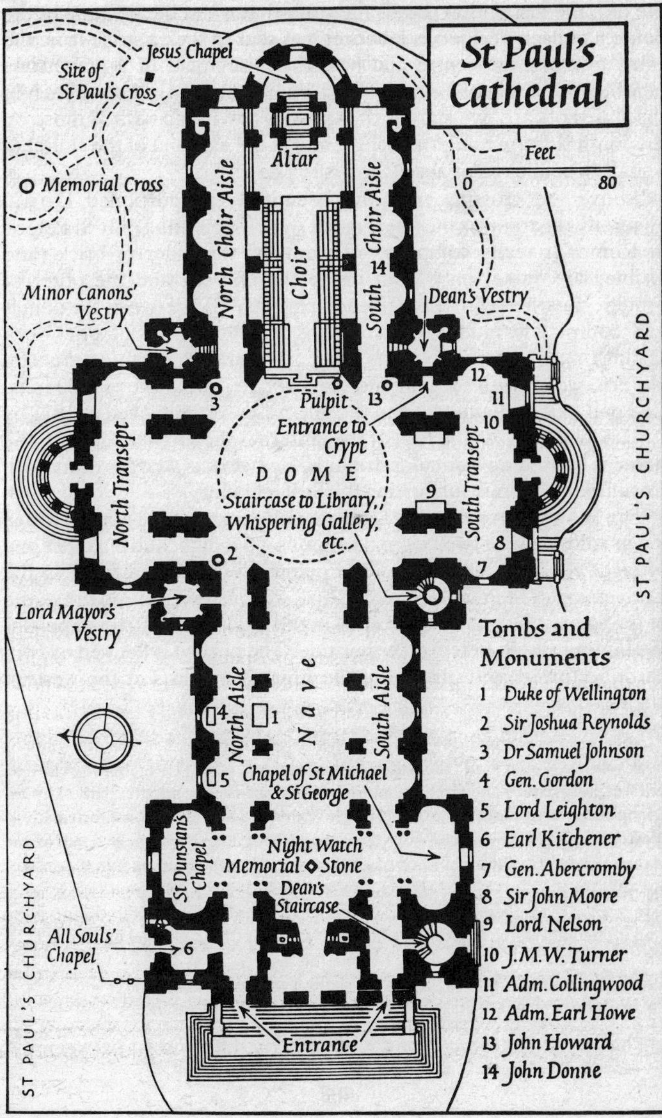

Tombs and Monuments

1 Duke of Wellington
2 Sir Joshua Reynolds
3 Dr Samuel Johnson
4 Gen. Gordon
5 Lord Leighton
6 Earl Kitchener
7 Gen. Abercromby
8 Sir John Moore
9 Lord Nelson
10 J. M. W. Turner
11 Adm. Collingwood
12 Adm. Earl Howe
13 John Howard
14 John Donne

the old; the inscription recalls the story that when the position of the dome had been decided, a labourer was sent to seek a stone from the ruins to mark the centre and brought a fragment of a gravestone bearing only the word *Resurgam* (I shall rise again). Above each of the transepts are five statues of Apostles (by Francis Bird; those on the south side are modern copies), and at the east end of the church is a shallow semicircular apse (the Jesus Chapel).

Above the crossing rises the beautifully proportioned DOME, generally regarded as the finest in the world, excepting only St Peter's at Rome. It really comprises two domes, the inner of brick (and visible, of course, only from inside the church) and the outer of timber, sheathed with lead (releaded in 1965–8). Between the domes and completely hidden from view is a hollow cone of brickwork resting on the outer edge of the inner dome and supporting a graceful lantern, which with the ball and cross above it weighs over 700 tons. The ball (6 ft in diameter) and the gilt cross were replaced in 1821 by C. R. Cockerell. At the foot of the lantern is the Golden Gallery; the dome is carried on a circular drum, while below is a larger drum with Corinthian columns supporting the Stone Gallery.

The WEST FRONT, facing Ludgate Hill, has a double portico with a lower colonnade of twelve great columns, 50 ft high, and an upper one of eight columns, 40 ft high. The pediment contains a relief of the Conversion of St Paul, by Francis Bird, who also sculptured the statue of the saint, 15 ft high, on the apex of the pediment, and the Apostles (St James? and St Peter) on either side. The portico is flanked by twin baroque towers with figures of the four Evangelists at the western angles.

The north tower contains a peal of twelve bells, hung in 1878, and in the south or clock tower is 'Great Paul', the largest bell in England, cast at Loughborough in 1882 and weighing sixteen and three-quarter tons. It is rung for five minutes daily at 1 p.m. Of the three clock bells the largest, 'Great Tom' (five and a half tons), originally at Westminster Palace but recast in 1709 for the cathedral, is tolled on the death of one of the royal family, the archbishop of Canterbury, the bishop of London, the dean of St Paul's, or the Lord Mayor. The clock was built in 1893 by John Smith of Derby.

In front of the cathedral (and with her back to it, as remarked by 18th-century wits) is an ineffectual statue of Queen Anne (1886), a copy of the original by Bird (1712). An inscription in the pavement behind this records that Queen Victoria here returned thanks to the Almighty on the sixtieth anniversary of her accession (1897). Thence a broad flight of marble steps ascends to the West Entrance.

The INTERIOR shows even more clearly the contrast between the

Gothic plan of the church and the classical details. The nave has massive rectangular piers with pilasters on the inner face carried up to the barrel vault, which in each bay is intercepted by a small dome. The aisles, which also have shallow domes, are lower than the nave, a fact not evident from outside the church, as already inferred, and the triforium space above contains the Library and other rooms. The triforium has consquently a blank wall to the nave, the upper part of which is lit by a single large window in each bay of the clerestory.

Visitors are recommended first to walk up the NAVE to the dome space to enjoy the spacious dignity of the cathedral. At the west end are two bronze candelabra by Henry Pegram (1897) and a memorial slab in the floor to the Night Watch that guarded St Paul's during the war. Under the third arch of the north arcade is a colossal monument to the Duke of Wellington (d. 1852), the principal work of Alfred Stevens, begun in 1856 but still unfinished at his death in 1875. The equestrian statue of the duke was added in 1912 to the designs of Stevens by John Tweed. A bronze effigy of Wellington rests on a large sarcophagus, with a marble canopy over it and allegorical sculptures above the pediments.

The great DOME, the inner face of which rises 218 ft above the floor, is supported by eight massive double piers with Corinthian capitals, themselves buttressed at the angles of the crossing by four supports so huge that they contain space in their interiors for vestries and the library staircase. In the spandrels below the Whispering Gallery are mosaics executed by Antonio Salviati and representing (from the north) SS. Matthew and John (designed by G. F. Watts), SS. Mark and Luke (by W. E. F. Britten), and Isaiah, Jeremiah, Ezekiel and Daniel (all by Alfred Stevens). In the quarter-domes below the arches are mosaics of the Crucifixion, the Entombment, the Resurrection, and the Ascension, by Sir William Richmond (d. 1921). In niches above the Whispering Gallery are statues of the Fathers of the Church, while the surface of the dome itself is decorated with eight large paintings in grisaille of scenes in the life of St Paul, by Sir James Thornhill (1715–21). In the floor beneath the dome is a memorial plaque to Sir Winston Churchill (d. 1965), unveiled in 1974.

At the north angles of the dome space, beside the entrances to the transept aisles, are statues of Sir Joshua Reynolds (d. 1792), by John Flaxman, and Dr Samuel Johnson (d. 1784), in a Roman toga, by John Bacon the Elder. The NORTH TRANSEPT, badly damaged in 1941 by a bomb which fell through into the crypt below, bringing down the famous inscription to Wren (see below), was rededicated after its restoration in 1962. Among the memorials that survived in the transept are those to Admiral Lord Rodney (d. 1792), by J. C. F. Rossi, and Sir Arthur Sullivan (d. 1900), with a bronze relief by Sir W. Goscombe John. The classical font here is by Francis Bird (1727).

In the first recess (from the east) of the NORTH AISLE are Two Angels at the Gate of Death, by Marochetti, in memory of Viscount Melbourne (d. 1848), the Prime Minister, and his brother. On the wall beyond is a bust of Earl Roberts (d. 1914), by Tweed, and in the next recess (opposite the Wellington monument) is the sarcophagus of General Gordon (d. 1885), with a bronze effigy by Boehm. The last recess on this side contains the cenotaph of Lord Leighton (d. 1896), the painter, with a bronze figure by Sir Thomas Brock. Beyond is ST DUNSTAN'S CHAPEL (reserved for private prayer), with a 17th-century oak screen by Jonathan Maine and a mosaic by Salviati. At the end of the aisle, beneath the north-west tower, is ALL SOULS' CHAPEL, converted in 1925 into a memorial chapel to Field-Marshal Earl Kitchener (d. 1916). The white marble effigy, the figures of SS. Michael and George, and the altar, with a Pietà, were all sculptured by Sir W. Reid Dick. Behind the grille on the north wall are rolls of honour of Royal Engineers, including Dominion and Indian corps, who fell in the two World Wars.

The south-west tower (usually closed) contains the DEAN'S STAIRCASE, built by William Kempster, with an ironwork balustrade by Jean Tijou. Next to it is the CHAPEL OF ST MICHAEL AND ST GEORGE, an order instituted in 1818 to reward distinguished service in the foreign affairs of the Empire. Above the stalls of the Knights Grand Cross (G.C.M.G.) hang their banners. The oak throne at the west end commemorates Lord Forrest (d. 1918), the first Australian peer; the screen between the chapel and the aisle was carved by Jonathan Maine. The memorials in the SOUTH AISLE are of little interest, but on a pier of the south arcade is Holman Hunt's 'Light of the World', a replica of his painting at Keble College, Oxford. At the east end of the aisle is the entrance to the staircase ascending to the Library and Galleries (see below).

The west aisle of the SOUTH TRANSEPT, once used as the Baptistery, contains monuments to General Sir Ralph Abercromby (d. 1801), by Westmacott, and Sir John Moore of Corunna (d. 1809), by John Bacon the Younger. To the left of the latter is a bronze memorial by Princess Louise (daughter of Queen Victoria) to the 4,300 of the Colonial Troops who fell in the South African War. In the main bay is a monument to Admiral Lord Nelson (d. 1805), a fine work by Flaxman with figures on the pedestal typifying the North Sea, the Baltic, the Nile and the Mediterranean. In the east transept aisle are monuments to J. M. W. Turner (d. 1851), a statue by Patrick Macdowell; Admiral Lord Collingwood (d. 1810), by Westmacott; Admiral Earl Howe (d. 1799), by Flaxman; and Lord Heathfield (d. 1790), the defender of Gibraltar, by Rossi. Under the arch is a monument to Sir Henry Lawrence (d. 1857), the defender of Lucknow, by J. G. Lough, and facing this is the entrance to the Crypt (see below). At the angle of the dome space is a statue of John Howard (d. 1790), the prison reformer, by the younger John Bacon, the first memorial to be admitted to the new St Paul's.

The SOUTH CHOIR AISLE, entered through fine ironwork gates by the French craftsman Jean Tijou, contains monuments to Dean Milman (d. 1868), by F. J. Williamson; Archbishop Frederick Temple (d. 1902), by F. W. Pomeroy; and various bishops. In a niche of the south wall is the unusual monument of John Donne (d. 1631), poet and Dean of St Paul's, a delicately sculptured figure in a shroud, by Nicholas Stone. This was practically the only monument of Old St Paul's to survive the Great Fire. The JESUS CHAPEL, occupying the apse at the east end of the church, was severely damaged by bombing, but has been restored more in keeping with the original intentions of Wren. Consecrated in 1958, this is Britain's memorial to its American allies who lost their lives in military operations based on this country, and it contains a roll of honour of 28,000 names. The chapel has windows by Brian Thomas and an altar-rail designed by S. E. Dykes Bower and made at Mortlake, in Surrey.

The CHOIR is enclosed by a low screen made from the original wrought-iron altar-rails by Tijou. On the right is the pulpit of variegated marble, and on either side of the choir are the two parts of the organ case, richly carved by Grinling Gibbons. The organ, originally built by Father Smith (1697), was reconstructed in 1930 by Henry Willis and Sons. The beautifully carved Choir Stalls are also the work of Gibbons; especially notable are the oblong panels below the canopy, with foliage exquisitely carved in pear-wood. The reredos, damaged beyond repair by the bombing, was replaced in 1958 by a High Altar of marble with a carved oak baldacchino to the designs of W. Godfrey Allen and S. E. Dykes Bower. This is Britain's memorial to more than 324,000 men and women of the Commonwealth who lost their lives in the two World Wars.

The vaulting and walls of the choir are decorated with glass mosaics, designed by Sir William Richmond. Those in the saucer-domes represent (from the west) the Creation of the Beasts, Birds, and Fishes, while the dome of the great eastern apse shows Christ in Majesty, with recording angels on either side.

The CRYPT, entered from the South Transept, extends under the entire cathedral and contains the graves of many famous men. To the right in the South Choir Aisle, at the foot of the staircase, is a bust of Sir John Macdonald (d. 1891), premier of Canada. The second recess contains the tomb of John Rennie (d. 1821), the engineer, and a monument to Sir Edwin Landseer (d. 1873), the painter. In the third recess is the tomb of Sir Christopher Wren (d. 1723) and above it the original tombstone with the famous epitaph, *Lector, si monumentum requiris, circumspice* (Reader, if you seek his monument, look around). This bay is known as the 'Painters' Corner' from the many graves of artists, who include Lord Leighton, Benjamin West (d. 1820), Sir Thomas Lawrence (d. 1830), Sir John Millais (d. 1896), J. M. W. Turner, and Sir Joshua Reynolds. Close by are memorials to Sir Anthony Van Dyck (d. 1641) and William Blake (d. 1827).

The chapel at the east end of the nave, occupying the site of the medieval parish church of St Faith, was redesigned by Lord Mottistone and dedicated in 1960 to the use of the Order of the British Empire, instituted by George V in 1917. In the nave, to the north-east, are the graves of Sir Hubert Parry (d. 1918) and Sir Arthur Sullivan, the composers; and on the walls on the north side are a relief of the Redemption, by J. S. Sargent (d. 1925), memorials to John Constable (d. 1837) and P. Wilson Steer (d. 1942), the artists, and a tablet to Sir Alexander Fleming (d. 1955), the discoverer of penicillin, whose ashes are buried near by. The ashes of Sir Max Beerbohm and Walter de la Mare, both of whom died in 1956, are also buried here, and they are commemorated by plaques on a pier to the south.

The west portion of the crypt contains the huge sarcophagus of the Duke of Wellington, made from a block of Cornish porphyry and resting on a granite base. Farther on to the left are memorials to the Air Transport Auxiliary in 1939–45 and to Florence Nightingale (d. 1910). Below the centre of the dome is the imposing tomb of Admiral Lord Nelson, in which his body is preserved in spirit (the only one so preserved in the cathedral). The tomb consists of a coffin made from the mainmast of the French flagship *L'Orient*, in a 16th-century marble sarcophagus designed by Benedetto da Rovezzano and intended first for Cardinal Wolsey and later for Henry VIII, but occupied by neither.

On the south is a memorial (by David Kindersley, 1985) to 255 servicemen and civilians killed in the Falklands campaign of 1982. The recesses to the south contain the tombs of Admirals Lord Beatty (d. 1936), Lord Jellicoe (d. 1935), and Lord Collingwood, Nelson's successor, and of Lord Napier of Magdala (d. 1890) and a tablet to Admiral Lord Keyes (d. 1945). To the north are the graves of Field-Marshals Viscount Wolseley (d. 1913), Sir Henry Wilson (d. 1922), and Earl Roberts, and of the Earl of Northesk (d. 1831), third in command at Trafalgar, and a bust of Lawrence of Arabia (d. 1935). In the next bay to the left are a memorial to W. E. Henley (d. 1903), the poet, with a fine bust by Rodin, and a bust (after Houdon) of George Washington, presented in 1921 by the American people. On the wall close to this is a tablet to Pilot-Officer William Fiske, who lost his life while flying with the R.A.F. in the Battle of Britain, 'an American citizen who died that England might live'. In the opposite bay are busts of Sir Stafford Cripps (d. 1952), the Labour minister, by Epstein, and R. J. Seddon (d. 1906), prime minister of New Zealand, and memorials to W. M. Hughes (d. 1952), prime minister of Australia, and other Colonial statesmen. The nave contains wall monuments to Charles Reade (d. 1884), the novelist; Sir Walter Besant (d. 1901), the historian of London; Prebendary Wilson Carlile (d. 1942), founder of the Church Army (all on the left); and Sir George Williams (d. 1905), founder of the Y.M.C.A. A new TREASURY was opened in 1981 in a north part of the crypt to display church plate and other treasures from the cathedral and from other churches in the diocese of London. Near the entrance is a memorial (also by David Kindersley, 1985) to Sir Philip Sidney, poet and soldier, who died of his wounds at Zutphen (Holland) in 1586. Farther west are Wren's Great Model of St Paul's (1614) and other models, and on the north is the LECTURE ROOM (1983).

The Upper Parts of the cathedral are approached by the staircase opening off the South Aisle. An easy climb of 143 steps leads to the SOUTH TRIFORIUM GALLERY, which has architectural fragments and other relics (no public access).

At the west end of the gallery is the LIBRARY, notable for its carved woodwork and containing a good collection of manuscripts, books, autographs, etc., the nucleus of which was formed by a bequest of Bishop Compton (1714). The medieval collections were destroyed in the Great Fire or scattered during the Commonwealth.

From the entrance to the Triforium a flight of 116 steps ascends to the WHISPERING GALLERY, at the foot of the drum supporting the inner dome and 100 ft above the floor of the cathedral, of which it offers an unusual survey. It is also the best place from which to see

Thornhill's paintings on the dome. The gallery derives its name from the fact that words whispered against the wall on one side are distinctly audible near the wall on the opposite side, 107 ft away in a straight line. A further climb of 117 steps leads out to the STONE GALLERY, at the base of the outer dome, commanding an extensive prospect over London, most of whose famous buildings are in view, at the same time giving an excellent impression of the great many new buildings that have sprung up all round.

An even more impressive view is obtained from the GOLDEN GALLERY, at the foot of the lantern surmounting the outer dome, and 166 steps higher by a winding staircase between the domes. Thence a further ascent leads into the BALL at the top of the lantern (limited view), 627 steps from the floor of the church.

The churchyard around the cathedral, laid out as a public garden, is still enclosed by railings made of iron smelted at Lamberhurst, in the Kentish Weald. On the south side of the nave are some fragments of the medieval cloisters and chapter house, destroyed in the Great Fire. To the north of the choir a memorial with a figure of St Paul, by Mackennal (1910), marks the approximate site of Paul's Cross, a famous open-air pulpit, taken down by Parliament in 1643. Here the Pope's condemnation of Martin Luther was proclaimed in the presence of Cardinal Wolsey.

SCIENCE & GEOLOGICAL MUSEUMS Plan VI, C3

STATION: SOUTH KENSINGTON, nearly ¼ m. S, on the Circle, District, and Piccadilly lines, reached by a subway entered in Exhibition Road north of the Science Museum. — BUSES in Brompton Road and Cromwell Road, see Route 10; in Kensington Road, see Route 11.

ADMISSION to both museums, Mondays–Saturdays 10 to 6, Sundays 2.30 to 6 (free). Closed on New Year's Day, Good Friday, May Day Monday, Christmas Eve and Day, and Boxing Day. — LECTURES in the Science Museum on Tuesdays and Thursdays at 1 and Saturdays at 3, in the Lecture Theatre (reached from Gallery 5); adm. to other lectures by ticket (obtainable in advance from the Information Office at the museum). Films of general scientific or engineering interest (especially for children), in the Small Theatre (on the Lower Ground Floor). — LECTURES and Films in the Geological Museum on Tuesdays–Thursdays and Saturdays at 2.30 in the Lecture Room. Field Excursions are arranged by the museum. — REFRESHMENT ROOM in the Science Museum (Centre Block, third floor). — The SCIENCE MUSEUM LIBRARY is open (free) on Mondays–Saturdays (except Bank Holidays) from 10 to 5.30; the GEOLOGICAL LIBRARY is open (free) on Mondays–Fridays, 10 to 4.

The SCIENCE MUSEUM and the GEOLOGICAL MUSEUM are adjoining museums in Exhibition Road, South Kensington, close to the Natural History Museum. The Science collections, established in 1857 and divorced from the Victoria and Albert Museum in 1909, occupy a large building (begun by Sir Richard Allison) which will eventually be extended as far as Queen's Gate. The first part, the Eastern Block, was completed in 1928; the first of the new Centre Block galleries was opened in 1963. The museum, covering almost every aspect of science in its application to technology and industry, comprises an unparalleled assembly of machines, industrial plant, and scientific instruments, including many working models and examples of original and historic apparatus. The museum is of great educational value and even the unscientific visitor will find it of much interest.

The Geological Museum (p. 421) is the headquarters of the Geological Survey of Great Britain, the oldest in the world, founded in 1835. The collections, first opened in 1837, were moved in 1935 to a handsome building here by John H. Markham. The museum now forms part of the Institute of Geological Sciences, founded in 1965, mainly for research. A new Lecture Hall, study room, and demonstration laboratory were opened in 1976.

In the ENTRANCE HALL of the Science Museum is a Foucault Pendulum, the apparatus devised in 1851 to demonstrate the rotation of the Earth on its own axis. On the right are the cloakroom and shop, with GALLERY 1 beyond, reserved for special exhibitions.

From the Entrance Hall steps descend to the EAST HALL, which contains most of the larger exhibits illustrating the development of motive power. At the outset is a working model of the Thames Flood Barrier (p. 526). Among the notable and historic steam engines are a beam pumping engine of 1777 and two rotative engines of 1788 and 1797, all by Matthew Boulton and James Watt; an atmospheric beam engine from Pentrich Colliery (Derbyshire; 1791); the high-pressure vertical steam engine and boiler of Richard Trevithick (1803); a cross-compound textile mill engine made in 1903 at Burnley (Lancashire); and a triple-expansion engine designed for the yacht *Glen Strathallan* (1928).

GALLERY 2, on the left of the hall, contains hot air, gas, and oil engines, boilers, and turbines, including the first diesel engine (designed by Rudolf Diesel) to be made in Britain (1897) and the axial-flow turbo-generator designed by Sir Charles Parsons in 1901.

GALLERY 3, on the right, devoted mainly to stationary steam engines, includes models made by Watt in 1765 for his experiments on steam, engines designed by him in partnership with Boulton, and models of beam and horizontal engines; and the steam turbine and dynamo invented by Sir Charles Parsons (1884). Models include windmills at Sprowston (Norfolk) and Cranbrook (Kent), the Pelton wheel (for utilizing the power of waterfalls), Newcomen's atmospheric pumping engine (1740), and Smeaton's mine pumping engine (1772).

The lower part of GALLERY 4 is used for special exhibitions. In an alcove on the north is a reproduction of James Watt's workshop at Heathfield Hall, near Birmingham, where he lived from 1790 until his death in 1819. The upper floor of Gallery 4 is designed as an introduction to the History of Science and Engineering. Gallery 4A, on the right, is the Schools' Reception area. At the end of Gallery 4 are the lifts to the upper floors of the museum; farther west, beyond Gallery 5, is the LARGE LECTURE THEATRE, and facing the stairs is the Information Office:

GALLERY 5 (under rearrangement) is concerned with diesel engines and electric power. Among the museum's exhibits are a reproduction of Faraday's original experiment in the continuous generation of electricity (1831), models of early electric power stations (the first designed by Thomas Edison in New York, 1881), Parsons's original turbo-generator installed at Ackton Hall Colliery (Yorkshire) in 1900, and models of the power station at Castle Donington (Leicestershire), the largest in Britain when it was built (1956).

Gallery 6, farther west, is given over to SCIENTIFIC EXPLORATION. Here are the actual command module from the Apollo 10 space craft, the first in which men circled the moon (in 1969); a full-size model of the landing on the moon by Apollo 11 (1969); a modern diving bell for underwater exploration; and a copy of a Vickers Submersible craft, made (like the original) of plastic material. Other exhibits illustrate the use of infra-red rays and X-rays, as well as radar and other inventions in the furthering of scientific exploration. At the farther end of the gallery, on the right, is a working million-volt impulse generator.

Galleries 7 to 9, beyond, are devoted to RAIL AND ROAD TRANSPORT, with many working models, some of which are arranged to show their internal construction. Here are William Hedley's 'Puffing Billy', the oldest locomotive in the world, built for Wylam Colliery (Northumberland) in 1813, George and Robert Stephenson's 'Rocket' (1829), Timothy Hackworth's 'Sans Pareil' (1829), the Great Western Railway express locomotive 'Caerphilly Castle' (1923), the prototype diesel-electric locomotive 'Deltic' (1955), and a London Transport Underground car of 1929. A reconstructed signal-box shows the development of railway signalling by means of models and actual apparatus, and the full-scale signals near by can be operated. Among other exhibits are a reconstruction of a railway station booking-office of the late 19th century and drawings, photographs, etc., showing the development of railway construction and operation.

The Road Transport collection includes a Glasgow tramcar of 1902, and illustrates the evolution of the mechanically-propelled road vehicle from the steam carriages of Cugnot (1770) and Murdock (about 1784), of which there are models, to the petrol-driven motor-car (Benz, 1888; etc.) and motor-cycle (Wolfmuller, 1894), and thence to a Rolls-Royce 'Silver Ghost' of 1909, the Rover gas-turbine car, the first in the world (1950), and a Wankel rotary-engined car, the NSU Spyder (1965). The bicycles range from the Hobby Horse of 1818 and the Michaux 'Boneshaker' of about 1867 to the Moulton machine of 1962.

Gallery 9A, above on the right, is concerned with Roads, Bridges, and Tunnels. In Gallery 10, at the farther end, is an exhibition of Fire-Fighting Appliances. Stairs descend from here to the Children's Gallery and the Small Lecture Theatre, on the Lower Ground Floor.

The interesting CHILDREN'S GALLERY is designed as an introduction to some important branches of pure and applied science. Models, dioramas, and working demonstrations show the development of transport by land, sea, and air; methods of communication; sources of mechanical and electrical power; the measurement of time; etc. The automatically opening door and the periscope, through which children can see into the Transport gallery above, are popular exhibits.

At the end of the Children's Gallery are reconstructions of a Victorian bathroom and kitchen, and to the right are the collections of Domestic Appliances, Locks and Fastenings (with an 18th-century locksmith's shop front from Piccadilly), and Firemaking.

An escalator from Gallery 6 and stairs from Galleries 9 and 10 ascend to the FIRST FLOOR. Gallery 30 (at the west end): ASTRONOMY, an excellent display outlining its history from the early Egyptians onward, with several terrestrial and celestial globes, copies of early telescopes made by Galileo Galilei (d. 1642), the Italian scientist, and by Sir Isaac Newton; an Orrery of 1716, made for the Earl of Orrery and used to show the movements of the planets; the telescope with which Sir William Herschel discovered the planet Uranus in 1781; the mirror of the great Rosse telescope of 1843, then the largest in the world; quadrants and other instruments; a model (over 21 ft in diameter) of the face of the moon as seen from the earth; and a star dome (demonstrated from time to time). The display is continued in Gallery 29, which is also concerned with MAPMAKING AND SURVEYING (Ramsden's theodolite of about 1790, used in the first scientific mapping of Britain).

Gallery 27: METEOROLOGY, including a wide range of thermometers, barometers, and other measuring instruments, continued in Gallery 28, which also illustrates TIME MEASUREMENT (working 14th-century clock mechanism from Wells Cathedral, etc.). Gallery 26: AGRICULTURAL Implements and Machinery, a fine series of exhibits, among them a working combine harvester, dairy equipment, etc., illustrating every aspect of mechanized farming, and culminating in a Leyland Diesel Synchro Tractor of 1980; and (to the right) GAS MANUFACTURE and Distribution, including a model of Murdock's first factory gas works (1807), part of the retort house from the Fakenham gas works (Norfolk), and a full-size model of a North Sea gas offshore drilling rig.

Gallery 25 (to the east): TELECOMMUNICATIONS (telegraph office of 1850, ship's radio cabin at 1910, etc.) and the Development of MICROELECTRONICS (continued in Gallery 20). Gallery 24: TEXTILE MACHINERY (Arkwright's original spinning machine (1769), copies of Hargreaves's spinning-jenny (1767) and Crompton's mule (1779), early weaving and knitting machines, etc.). Gallery 21: MECHANICAL ENGINEERING (hand tools and early machine tools, the original model of Nasmyth's first steam hammer, etc.). Gallery 23: GLASS TECHNOLOGY. Gallery 22: IRON AND STEEL PRODUCTION (a Bessemer converter of 1864, etc.); P. J. de Loutherbourg's 'Coalbrookdale by Night' shows the pioneer ironworks of Abraham Darby (the first to use coal) in 1801.

On the SECOND FLOOR, Galleries 41–5 are mainly confined to various aspects of Chemistry and Nuclear Science. Gallery 45: INDUSTRIAL CHEMISTRY (the manufacture of soap, dyes, detergents, plastics, man-made fibres, etc.; the refining of petroleum; model of Lindsey oil refinery in Lincolnshire; 1968). Gallery 44: ATOMIC PHYSICS and Nuclear Power (part of Cockcroft and Walton's first apparatus for splitting the atom (1932); cross-section through a nuclear reactor (full-size copy); the first atomic weapons, etc.). Gallery 40: PRINTING AND PAPERMAKING (wooden hand press of about 1700 compared with modern printing presses; early typewriters, etc.). Gallery 41: CHEMISTRY BEFORE 1900 (lighting, weighing and measuring, etc.). Gallery 43: STRUCTURE OF MATTER (periodic table of the elements actuated by push buttons, apparatus and notebooks of John Dalton (who first developed the atomic theory, 1803–8), Michael Faraday, and other British chemists, X-ray crystallography, model of the DNA spiral, and chemistry in the service of human welfare; full-size models show the organs of the body). Gallery 42: PURE CHEMISTRY (reconstructions of laboratories of the 19th century and 1965, etc.) and Chemical Engineering.

Gallery 46 (to the west): the Development of COMPUTING, with early calculating devices, etc., a 'Philosophical Table' of 1762, one of the earliest electronic computers (1950), and a computer terminal which can be operated by visitors. Gallery 47 illustrates AIR AND SEA NAVIGATION, with the cockpit of a De Havilland 'Comet' aircraft and a full-size ship's bridge. Gallery 48: MARINE ENGINES, among them Symington's 'atmospheric' engine of 1788, and Turbines (models for Parsons' *Turbinia*, the first turbine-driven vessel, 1894, and of the turbine installations of the *Queen Elizabeth*, 1938), Boilers, Propellers, and Steering Gear. On two floors in the centre of the block is an outstanding collection of models of SAILING SHIPS (including an early Egyptian boat, a Viking galley, the *Santa Maria* of Christopher Columbus, an Elizabethan galleon, and Nelson's famous flagship, the *Victory*) and of Yachts, fishing vessels, and other small craft, all set against their natural backgrounds; and a tableau of the Admiralty Board in 1677, with Charles II and Secretary Samuel Pepys. Gallery 50: DOCKS AND HARBOURS, including a model of the Port of London (1966–73); and Diving Equipment. Gallery 49: Models of WARSHIPS (H.M.S. *Warrior*, the first sea-going ironclad, 1861), submarines, etc., and of MERCHANT STEAMERS and Motor-Ships (the paddle steamers *Sirius* and *Great Western* that made the first crossings of the Atlantic under power, 1838; the *Great Britain*, 1843, the first screw steamer to cross the Atlantic).

Galleries 68 and 69, on the THIRD FLOOR, are taken up by the fascinating AERONAUTICAL COLLECTION. This includes models of Montgolfier's hot-air balloon (1783) and Lunardi's hydrogen balloon (1784), and of the hot-air balloon that achieved an altitude record of 45,836 ft (1974); a reproduction of the first model glider (1804) of Sir George Cayley, a pioneer of aviation; the model for the first projected aeroplane, made by Henson and Stringfellow (1843); the original glider used successfully in 1895 by Otto Lilienthal; and a replica of the aeroplane built by the Wright brothers in 1903, the first power-driven heavier-than-air machine to make a sustained flight carrying a man. Among early aircraft (best seen from the raised walkway) are the A. V. Roe triplane (1909), the J.A.P.-Harding monoplane (1910), the S. F. Cody biplane (1912), the Fokker E.III monoplane (1916), and the Royal Aircraft Factory's SE5A biplane of 1917. The Vickers-Vimy aeroplane is that in which Alcock and Brown made the first non-stop Transatlantic flight (1919), the De Havilland 'Gipsy Moth' is that flown by Amy Johnson to Australia (1930). The Supermarine S6B seaplane won the Schneider Trophy for Britain in 1931. Exhibits of the Second World War include a Hurricane and Spitfire that took part in the Battle of Britain, the Gloster-Whittle aircraft (the first successful jet-propelled machine, 1941), a rocket-powered Messerschmitt 163 fighter, a German rotating-wing kite (1943), and a V1 flying-bomb, shown in section to display its mechanism. Here also are Frost's 'Ornithopter', a curious but unsuccessful machine with flapping wings (1902); Professor Piccard's stratosphere gondola (1932); the car of the Beta airship, made at Farnborough in 1910 (and models of other airships); the Cierva C30A Autogiro (1934), and models of other autogiros and helicopters; and the Rolls-Royce 'Flying Bedstead', the first jet-propelled machine to take off vertically (1952). A wide range of aero-engines shows their development from Stringfellow's steam engines to modern jet engines, including the Rolls-Royce Olympus engine that powered the prototype Concorde; and a series of over a hundred scale models illustrates the development of aircraft up to the modern civil airliner.

Gallery 67: SPACE EXPLORATION and Rockets, including models of satellites (the Russian Vostok I, the first manned space vehicle, 1961; the American Mercury and Gemini capsules), part of a Blue Streak rocket vehicle (about 1960), and a German V2 rocket engine shown in section. Here also is a working model of a supersonic wind tunnel, and above it is an Astronomical Observatory with a telescope of 1885. The display is continued in Gallery 66, which has a Black Arrow satellite launch vehicle (1969–71) and a model of the Lunar Rover used on Apollo missions. In this gallery also are TELECOMMUNICATIONS, including Marconi's beam transmitter and receiver (1896), J. L. Baird's first television transmitter (1926), and other historic apparatus. On the right is the radio station, GB2SM, where demonstrations are given.

Gallery 65: GEOPHYSICS and Oceanography (continued in Gallery 62, to the right). Gallery 64: MAGNETISM AND ELECTRICITY (reconstruction of a late-19th-century laboratory, etc.). Gallery 60: PHOTOGRAPHY (two of the earliest impressions, made by Niepce in 1826–7; early daguerrotype apparatus; camera with which Fox Talbot in 1835 produced the first photographic negative on paper) and CINEMAPHOTOGRAPHY (apparatus of Le Prince, Edison, and Paul, and examples of the pioneer work of Eadweard Muybridge and William Friese-Greene). Here also is a reconstruction of Baird's studio, the first in Europe, at the Regent Street

Polytechnic. Gallery 61: Optical Instruments (a large and fine collection, including a microscope made in 1675 for Robert Hooke) Gramophones, and Talking Machines. Gallery 63: Early Physics, including the scientific instruments used for the instruction of the children of George III. Gallery 62: Heat and Thermal Instruments (Joule's original apparatus, 1843, etc.).

Stairs from the north ends of Galleries 61 and 65 go up to the Wellcome Museum of the History of Medicine, on two floors, a splendid exhibition based on the collections made by Sir Henry Wellcome (1853–1936) and transferred from the Wellcome Foundation in Euston Road. On the lower floor are models, dioramas, etc., illustrating the history of medicine, surgery, dentistry, and nursing, and many fine reconstructions, among them the ward of Joseph Lister, the pioneer of antiseptic surgery, at Glasgow (1868), Dr Bruce's electrotherapy room (1905), and a chemist's shop from Hexham (Northumberland; 1905). Other reconstructions illustrate, for instance, the development of surgery from an operation in 1895 to a heart operation in 1980. On the upper floor is an exhibition relating to the Science and Art of Medicine, including many objects associated with noted scientists.

The Science Museum Library, in a building on the north side of the former Imperial Institute Road (see Route 10), comprises about 480,000 volumes and about 21,000 sets of periodicals and transactions of learned societies, covering every important branch of pure and applied science (except medicine).

The collections of the Geological Museum are displayed in a large hall with two galleries above. From the Entrance Hall, decorated with British ornamental stones, steps lead up through an arch of beautiful British marbles to the Main Hall. Facing the entrance is a rotating globe, 6 ft in diameter, showing the geology of the Earth. In the centre of the hall are cases containing a splendid collection of precious and ornamental stones. Notable also are the vases of Derbyshire 'blue john' (a kind of fluorspar), Siberian aventurine quartz, and Ashford black marble (a limestone from Derbyshire), and a small piece (128 grams) of the Moon, formed probably over 3,900-million years ago and collected in 1972 by the Apollo 16 astronauts.

On the south side of the museum is an excellent display (starting at the west end) illustrating the Story of the Earth, with dioramas, maps, relief models, and mineral specimens, giving an explanation of the origin of the Earth and tracing the evolution of its main features through the various geological processes. On the north-east side is an exhibition dealing with the geology of BRITAIN BEFORE MAN, and on the mezzanine floor above is a display of BRITISH FOSSILS, seen in a geological context.

A new exhibition of Treasures of the Earth is being constructed (1985) on the north-west side of the museum; the mezzanine floor above this is mainly reserved for temporary exhibitions.

The First Floor Gallery is confined mainly to the REGIONAL GEOLOGY OF BRITAIN, with a comprehensive collection of British minerals and fossils. Cases at the east end, near the top of the main staircase, are devoted to the Wealden district of south-east England, while those to the north of this cover the geology of London and the Thames Valley. The Second Floor Gallery is given over to ECONOMIC MINERALOGY, with interesting maps and dioramas, and mineral specimens. In the south-east bay is a section exhibiting British minerals, and at the west end is a model illustrating the geology of Stonehenge.

The GEOLOGICAL LIBRARY, on the north-west side (ground floor), the principal geological library in the country open for free reference, contains over 70,000 books and 30,000 maps, as well as numerous pamphlets and periodicals, dealing chiefly with the geology of Britain.

SOUTHWARK CATHEDRAL Plan IX, E1

STATION: LONDON BRIDGE, 200 yds E, on the Northern line and a terminus of the Southern Region. — BUSES across London Bridge, see Route 25; in Borough High Street and Southwark Street, see Route 35.

ADMISSION daily, 7.30 a.m. to 6 p.m. Services on Sundays at 9, 10.20, and 11 a.m. and 3 p.m.; on Mondays–Fridays at 12.30 (Matins and Holy Communion) and 5.30 (Evensong; sung on Tuesdays and Fridays); on Saturdays at 12 noon and 4.

SOUTHWARK CATHEDRAL, officially the collegiate and cathedral church of St Saviour and St Mary Overy, is the mother church of the diocese of Southwark, which was created in 1905 and includes most of south London and much of east Surrey. Though often altered and restored, and given a new nave in the late 19th century, the church remains, after Westminster Abbey, the most impressive Gothic building in London. It has associations with Shakespeare and other Elizabethan players of Bankside and with John Harvard, the founder of Harvard University. The cathedral stands near the southern approach to London Bridge, its noble tower a familiar object in views across the river from the City.

The first church on this site was founded, according to tradition, by a community of nuns who settled here about A.D. 606. The dedication until 1540 was to St Mary Overy or Overie, a suffix that has been the subject of much controversy based on no definite evidence. The most probable of the numerous conjectures is that it means 'over the river' (i.e., from the City). In 852, presumably after the nuns had left Southwark, a college of priests declaring allegiance to no particular order was established by St Swithun, bishop of Winchester. This later became a priory for canons regular of the Augustinian order, who in 1106 erected a large church in the Norman style of which some traces survive. The priory enjoyed the patronage of the bishops of Winchester, who built a diocesan palace near by. The Norman church was burned down in 1206, and the new building that rose in its place, under Bishop Peter des Roches, was the first in London to be constructed in the Gothic style. Of this church there survives the crossing, with the lower part of the central tower, the choir with its ambulatories, and the retro-choir. The transepts were added early in the 14th century, but the south transept was recast about 1420 by Cardinal Beaufort. The 13th-century nave, partly rebuilt in 1469, when it was given a timber roof, was declared to be in a dangerous state by 1830. Demolished in 1839, it was replaced at first by an ineffectual 'preaching place' and in 1890–97 by a more satisfactory Gothic nave to the designs of Sir Arthur Blomfield.

The church continued to be the property of the Augustinians until 1540, when the priory was dissolved. A small parish church had been built adjoining the priory church on the south, but at the Dissolution the parishioners took over the larger church, whose dedication they changed to St Saviour, the name of the suppressed abbey of Bermondsey (see Suburban London). The church remained in the diocese of Winchester until 1877, when south London was transferred to that of Rochester (under one of whose bishops, Dr Thorold, the nave was rebuilt), but in 1905 the diocese of Rochester was divided, so that Southwark became an independent see, with St Saviour's as its cathedral. Late Roman objects found in a well below the cathedral are now in the Museum of London.

Almost the only notable feature of the exterior of the cathedral is the fine TOWER, 163 ft high, the lower part of which was built in the early 13th century, while the two upper stages were raised in 1520 (the pinnacles, however, are later). The oldest of the peal of twelve bells dates from 1735. On the south of the choir can be seen some of the paving stones of the old parish church, demolished in 1822. The cathedral is entered by the South Porch, which admits to the west end of the nave.

The NAVE of seven bays, rebuilt in 1890–97 by Sir Arthur Blomfield, follows the medieval choir closely in style (see below). At the west end of the south aisle is a section of 13th-century arcading;

the marble font close by, designed by G. F. Bodley, has an elaborate wooden Gothic cover, 13 ft high, by Walter Hare. At the west end of the north aisle are two relics (restored) from the Norman church: a round-headed doorway and a recess that was once probably part of a tomb. In front of this is a 15th-century 'memento mori', probably from the tomb of one of the canons, and against the west wall are preserved some of the 150 richly-carved and coloured bosses that formed part of the 15th-century roof. Near the east end of the north aisle is the inadequate tomb of John Gower, the friend of Chaucer, with the head of the effigy resting on his three best-known works. The poet lived and died (in 1408) in the precincts of the priory. At the east end of the south aisle is a memorial to William Shakespeare (1912), with a recumbent alabaster figure by Henry McCarthy and a relief depicting Southwark during the poet's time. The stained-glass window above, by Christopher Webb (1954), shows numerous figures from the plays.

The massive piers of the CROSSING are part of the early-13th-century building. Those on the south have clustered shafts that are carried down almost to the floor, but on the north these are stopped at a platform about 12 ft up, perhaps to allow for a screen enclosing the North Transept (see below), which was completed early in the 14th century.

The early-13th-century CHOIR of five bays contains the oldest Gothic work in London. It has massive piers with detached shafts, the inner three of which are carried up to the springing of the vault ribs. The vault itself was remade in the early 19th century, though the bosses are perhaps original. The triforium has an arcaded wall-passage with free-standing columns (the first of its kind in England), and shows interesting detail. The clerestory also has a wall-passage, with a stepped triplet arch, and a single lancet window in each bay. The choir stalls were designed by Blomfield, the bishop's throne and the stalls for the suffragan bishops (north of the sanctuary) are by Bodley and Hare. In the floor between the stalls are slabs commemorating the dramatists, John Fletcher (d. 1625) and Philip Massinger (d. 1639), and Edmund Shakespeare (d. 1607), 'a player', youngest brother of the poet; all are buried in the church, but their graves are unidentified. The splendid altar-screen, in the Perpendicular style, was erected in 1520 by Richard Fox, bishop of Winchester. Mutilated in 1703, it was restored in 1830, when the cornice of angels was added, and in 1912 the niches (divided horizontally by charming rows of angels) were filled with statues mostly representing persons connected with the church or diocese. A new altarpiece was introduced in 1929 by Sir Ninian Comper, who also gilded the lower part of the screen and designed the glass in the 19th-century east window.

On the west wall of the NORTH TRANSEPT is an unusual and much-repaired memorial, by Nicholas Stone (1633), to the Austin family, and close by is an elaborately carved muniment chest of 1588. On the north wall are a blocked aumbry; a wooden sword-rest of 1674 with the arms of the City and Southwark; the tomb of Lyonell Lockyer (d. 1672), a quack doctor of the time of Charles II (the inscription is worth reading); and a good bust of Richard Blisse (d. 1703). On the east of the transept are two much-restored Norman arches.

To the east of the North Transept is the Chapel of St John the Evangelist, entered from the North Ambulatory by a 16th-century studded doorway. It has been called the HARVARD CHAPEL since it was rebuilt in 1907 (by C. R. Blomfield) in memory of John Harvard, the founder of Harvard University, Massachusetts, who was born in the parish (1607) and baptized in the church. The east window, painted by the American artist, John La Farge, was presented by Joseph H. Choate, the United States ambassador, in 1905 and restored in 1948 after war damage. In the north-east corner of the chapel is a Norman shaft, discovered during the rebuilding.

The NORTH AMBULATORY or choir aisle is approached through an unusual moulded arch. On the north side are a memorial to John Trehearne (d. 1618), 'gentleman portar' to James I, and two recessed tombs, perhaps of priors; the second now contains a fine wooden effigy of a cross-legged knight of about 1290, possibly one of the De Warennes who were benefactors of the priory. On the south side is the characteristic Jacobean tomb of Alderman Richard Humble (d. 1616).

At the east end of the church is the delightful LADY CHAPEL, properly a retro-choir, as the original Lady Chapel, farther east, was pulled down in 1830. It consists of four parallel aisles of equal height, separated by graceful clustered columns supporting a low vault and ending in chapels with groups of triple lancets. Here in 1555 Stephen Gardiner, bishop of Winchester, and Edmund Bonner, bishop of London, presided at the courts at which Bishops Hooper and Ferrar and other Marian martyrs were condemned to the stake. The chapel was well restored in 1832–5. On the west side can be seen the tracery of openings blocked by the 16th-century screen. In the north wall is a window by C. E. Kempe with figures of St Thomas Becket, Charles I, and Archbishop Laud; the second chapel from the north contains a beautifully carved 17th-century altar-table (covered, but shown by a verger). In the SOUTH AMBULATORY is seen the fine tomb of Lancelot Andrewes (d. 1626), bishop of Winchester, with a new canopy (1930) replacing that destroyed by fire in 1676, and the arms of dioceses and cathedrals that he served. Next to it is the tomb of Edward Stuart Talbot (d. 1934), the first bishop of Southwark, with a gilded effigy by Cecil Thomas.

A window on the south side contains a panel of Elizabethan glass, the only old glass in the church. Below the arch to the South Transept are Roman tesserae dug up in the churchyard. The quaint inscription on the brass (to the right) of Susanna Barford, who died in 1652 at the age of ten, is worth reading.

The SOUTH TRANSEPT was rebuilt about 1420 by Cardinal Beaufort (half-brother of Henry IV), whose niece, Joan Beaufort, was married to James I of Scotland in the church in 1423. The arms of the cardinal are carved on the pillar to the north of the door. Opposite is a memorial to John Bingham (d. 1625), one of the 'bargainers' who bought the church for the parish in 1612 (it had been rented only since 1540), and below this is a small monument to William Emerson (d. 1575), supposed to be an ancestor of R. W. Emerson, the American essayist. The transepts have no triforium and are otherwise simpler than the choir in architectural form, confirming the fact that the canons completed their church only after overcoming financial difficulties. The unsatisfactory vaulting was raised in 1830, and the large gable windows are both 19th-century insertions.

TATE GALLERY Plan VIII, E3

STATIONS: PIMLICO, ⅜ m. SW, on the Victoria line; WESTMINSTER, ¾ m. N, on the Circle and District lines; VAUXHALL, ½ m. SE, on the Victoria line and the Southern Region. — BUSES along Millbank and in Vauxhall Bridge Road, see below and Route 3.

ADMISSION Mondays–Saturdays 10 to 5.50, Sundays 2 to 5.50 (free). Closed on New Year's Day, Good Friday, May Day Monday, Christmas Eve and Day, and Boxing Day. — LECTURES and Films in the Lecture Room on Tuesdays–Fridays at 11, Saturdays at 3; Lecture Tours on Tuesdays–Fridays at 1, Saturdays at 2.30, Sundays at 3. — LICENSED RESTAURANT, with delightful murals by Rex Whistler (1928), open Mondays–Saturdays 12 to 3; REFRESHMENT ROOM, open Mondays–Saturdays, 10.30 to 5.30; Sundays 2 to 5.15; both on the Lower Floor.

The TATE GALLERY accommodates the greater part of the national collection of British painting, as well as the national collections of modern foreign painting (especially from France) and of modern sculpture. It owes its establishment largely to the munificence of Sir Henry Tate, the sugar refiner, who commissioned the building and gave his own collection of sixty-five paintings. The gallery, designed by Sidney R. J. Smith in a modified classical style and opened in 1897, stands on Millbank, facing the Thames, between Lambeth and Vauxhall Bridges. It is most conveniently reached by bus from Parliament Square (passing the gallery) or from Victoria Station to Vauxhall Bridge, a few minutes' walk from the entrance. The British paintings, though shared with the National Gallery, include almost every important artist since the 17th century, while the sculpture includes notable works by Rodin and other masters.

The idea of a national collection of British art was first mooted by Sir Francis Chantrey, the sculptor, who in 1841 bequeathed his fortune to the Royal Academy for that purpose. Many further bequests were made and eventually Sir Henry Tate (d. 1899) offered to build a gallery, a site for which was found on ground previously occupied by the Millbank Penitentiary, a model prison opened in 1816 in accordance with the ideals of Jeremy Bentham, the legal reformer, and pulled down in 1892. New galleries and a sculpture hall were added in 1899 by the founder, and in 1910 further galleries were built (through the generosity of Sir Joseph Duveen) to house J. M. W. Turner's bequest of a great number of his own paintings, drawings, and sketches (compare p. 381). In 1926 Lord Duveen (son of Sir Joseph) provided for new galleries (partly to house works of the American artist, J. S. Sargent) and in 1937 an enlarged sculpture gallery was opened at his expense. Works purchased under the Chantrey Bequest, which now realizes about £3,000 annually, are presented to the Tate. Most of the better-known French Impressionist and Post-Impressionist paintings have been transferred to the National Gallery.

A new extension on the north-west side of the Tate Gallery, completed in 1979 to the designs of Michael Huckstepp, has created more space for the gallery's extensive and growing collections, which now number about 10,000 works. A further extension, to house all the paintings, etc., of J. M. W. Turner, was begun in 1983 (to the designs of James Stirling) on the north-east of the gallery, and the completion of this will result in some rehanging of the existing rooms showing the British paintings.

To the north of the entrance is a statue of Sir John Millais (d. 1896), by Sir Thomas Brock. Steps ascend to a Vestibule and the CENTRAL HALL, to the right of which is the cloakroom, where umbrellas, etc., must be left, and to the left is the Gallery Shop, where publications and reproductions of paintings may be obtained. The British Paintings of before about 1900 are arranged, for the most part chronologically, on the left of the gallery (Rooms 2 to 17). The Impressionists and Post-Impressionists and the Modern Paintings are on the right (Room 30 onward). Rooms 27 and 28, in the centre of the gallery, are mostly reserved for Special Exhibitions. Beyond the Central Hall is the fine SCULPTURE GALLERY, which often contains a representative selection of British and foreign sculpture.

This usually includes a number of the following works, some of which, however, will be found in the picture galleries. *Rodin*, 'Le Baiser' (marble), 'The Age of Bronze', 'St John the Baptist', and other splendid bronzes; *Reg Butler*, 'Woman' and 'Girl'; *Carpeaux*, 'H. J. and Mrs Turner'; *César*, 'The Man of Saint-Denis'; *Dalou*, 'Alphonse Legros' and 'La Paysanne'; *Degas*, 'La Petite Danseuse' and other bronzes of dancers; *Frank Dobson*, 'Susannah', 'Truth', 'Head of Sir Osbert Sitwell' (in brass); *Epstein*, 'The Visitation', 'Somerset Maugham', 'Professor Einstein', 'Rockdrill' (1913), etc.; *Gaudier-Brzeska*, 'La Chanteuse Triste' and 'Horace Brodzky'; *Giacometti*, 'Standing Woman'; *Eric Gill*, 'Mankind' and 'Prospero and Ariel'; *Barbara Hepworth*, 'Bicentric Form', 'Squares with Two Circles', 'Theme on Electronics (Orpheus)', etc.; *Eric Kennington*, 'Effigy of T. E. Lawrence'; *Kršinic*, 'Study of a Girl'; *Maurice Lambert*, 'Swan'; *Arnold Machin*, 'Spring' (terracotta); *Maillol*, 'The Three Nymphs', 'Torso', and 'Woman with a Necklace'; *Manzù*, 'Susanna' and 'Cardinal'; *Marini*, 'Cavalière'; *Meštrovič*, 'Head of the Artist', 'Strahinič Ban' (14th-century Serbian hero), and 'Woman with a Guitar'; *Carl Milles*, 'Folke Filbyter'; *Henry Moore*, 'Family Group', 'King and Queen', 'Recumbent Figure', etc.; *Nimptsch*, 'Reclining Woman'; *Renoir*, 'La Laveuse' and 'Venus Victrix'; *Alfred Stevens*, Casts for the Wellington monument in St Paul's Cathedral; *J. Havard Thomas*, 'Cassandra', 'Lycidas', 'Thyris', 'Cardinal Manning'; *G. F. Watts*, 'Clytie' and 'Daphne'; *Derwent Wood*, 'Torso'; *Ossip Zadkine*, 'Venus'. On the walls are usually hung some of the gallery's larger paintings.

The paintings are described below in their periods or schools (only the more important works can be mentioned). The BRITISH PAINTINGS start in Room 3.

16TH–17TH-CENTURY PAINTING: *John Bettes*, 'Man in a Black Cap' (the earliest work in the gallery, 1545); *William Dobson* (d. 1646), 'Endymion Porter'; *Hans Eworth* (d. 1573), 'Lady Golding'; *Marc Gheeraerdts* (d. 1635), 'Lady in a Masque Dress' and 'Captain Thomas Lee'; *George Gower* (d. about 1596), 'Sir Thomas and Lady Kytson'; *Cornelius Johnson* (d. 1664), 'Cornelia Veth' and other portraits; *Sir Godfrey Kneller* (d. 1723), 'The Angel Appearing to Tobit', a remarkable early work, 'First Marquess of Tweeddale', 'John Smith, the Engraver', etc.; *Sir Peter Lely* (d. 1680), 'Elizabeth,

Countess of Kildare', 'Frans van Helmont', 'Two Ladies of the Lake Family', etc.; *Daniel Mytens* (d. before 1648), 'James, Third Marquess of Hamilton'; *Jan Siberechts* (d. about 1700), 'Landscape with Rainbow' (Henley-on-Thames) and 'Longleat' (Wiltshire); *Gerard Soest* (d. about 1681), 'Henry Howard, Sixth Duke of Norfolk'; *Paul van Somer* (d. 1622), 'Elizabeth Grey, Countess of Kent'; *Anthony Van Dyck* (d. 1641; see p. 389), 'Lady of the Spencer Family'; *Antonio Verrio* (worked in England from 1671; d. 1707), Sketch for a Ceiling Decoration; *John Michael Wright* (d. about 1700), 'Sir Neill O'Neill'.

18TH-CENTURY PAINTING: *James Barry* (d. 1806), 'King Lear Weeping over the Dead Cordelia'; *Charles Brooking* (d. 1759), 'Fishing Smacks Becalmed'; *Francis Cotes* (d. 1770), 'Paul Sandby'; *Arthur Devis* (d. 1787), 'Dr Clayton's School at Salford', 'The James Family', etc.

THOMAS GAINSBOROUGH (d. 1788), 'James Baillie and Family', 'Gainsborough Dupont', 'Giovanna Baccelli', 'Landscape at Sunset', 'Lord Kilmorey', 'Margaret' and 'Mary', the painter's daughters, 'Sir Benjamin Truman', 'Suffolk Landscape', 'The Market Cart', 'View of Dedham', etc.; *Francis Hayman* (d. 1776), 'Wrestling Scene from *As You Like It*'; *Joseph Highmore* (d. 1780), Illustrations to Richardson's *Pamela*, 'Mr Oldham and Guests', etc.

WILLIAM HOGARTH (d. 1764), 'Bishop Hoadly', 'Calais Gate (the Roast Beef of Old England)', 'Duchess of Bolton', 'Hogarth's Servants', 'James Quin, the Actor', 'Lavinia Fenton', 'Scene from *The Beggar's Opera*', 'Self Portrait, with his Dog', 'The Graham Children', and other fine portraits; *Francis Holman* (d. 1790), 'Shore Scene'; *Thomas Hudson* (d. 1779), 'Mrs Collier'; *Angelica Kauffmann* (d. 1807), 'Self Portrait'; *George Lambert* (d. 1765), Landscapes; *Marcellus Laroon* (d. 1772), 'The Knight and the Beggar Woman'; *P. J. de Loutherbourg* (d. 1812), 'An Avalanche in the Alps' and other romantic landscapes; *William Marlow* (d. 1813), 'Capriccio: St Paul's and a Venetian Canal' and 'View on the Thames'; *Philip Mercier* (d. 1760), 'Hanoverian Party on a Terrace', 'The Music Party', and 'The Young Seamstress'; *George Morland* (d. 1804), 'Stable Interior', etc.; *John Opie* (d. 1807), 'A Peasant's Family', 'Master William Opie', and 'Self Portrait'; *Allan Ramsay* (d. 1784), 'Alexander Boswell, Lord Auchinleck' (father of James Boswell), 'Lady Hall of Dunglass', etc.

SIR JOSHUA REYNOLDS (d. 1792), 'Admiral Keppel', 'Francis and Suzanna Beckford', 'Lady Bamfylde', 'Lord Ligonier', 'Sir

Watkins Williams-Wynn and his Mother', and other portraits, 'Three Ladies Adorning Hymen', and a series of Self Portraits; *George Romney* (d. 1802), 'Jacob Morland of Capplethwaite', 'Lady Hamilton as Circe', 'Lady in a Brown Dress', and 'Mr and Mrs William Lindow'; *Francis Sartorius* (d. 1804), 'Black Horse with Two Dogs'; *Samuel Scott* (d. 1772), 'Admiral Anson's Action off Cape Finisterre' (1747) and 'Arch of Westminster Bridge' (1749); *Gilbert Stuart* (d. 1828), 'Benjamin West, the Artist'; *George Stubbs* (d. 1806), 'Mares and Foals in a Landscape' and other characteristic works; *Sir James Thornhill* (d. 1734), Sketch for a Ceiling Decoration; *Benjamin West* (d. 1820), 'Cleombrotus ordered into Banishment', 'Lady Beauchamp-Proctor', and 'The Golden Age'; *Richard Wilson* (d. 1782), 'Lake Avernus', 'Llyn-y-Cau, Cader Idris', 'The Thames near Twickenham', and other landscapes, 'Francesco Zuccarelli, the painter'; *John Wootton* (d. 1765), 'Members of the Beaufort Hunt'; *Wright of Derby* (d. 1797), 'An Experiment with the Air-Pump', 'Moonlight with Lighthouse, Tuscany', 'Sir Brooke Boothby', and 'Thomas Stainforth'; *Johann Zoffany* (d. 1810), 'Charles Macklin as Shylock', 'The Bradshaw Family', etc.

EARLY-19TH-CENTURY PAINTING: *Thomas Barker* (d. 1847), 'Landscape at Bath'; *Sir William Beechey* (d. 1839), 'Thomas Law Hodges'; *William Blake* (d. 1827), the poet-mystic, Illustrations to Dante's *Divine Comedy*, and other works by him and by his followers (Samuel Palmer, etc.); *R. P. Bonington* (d. 1828), 'Grand Canal' and other Venetian scenes; *William Collins* (d. 1847), 'Prawn Catchers', etc.

JOHN CONSTABLE (d. 1837), many delightful landscapes, including 'Admiral's House, Hampstead', 'Dedham Mill', 'East Bergholt House' (his birthplace), 'Flatford Mill' (his father's corn-mill), 'Hadleigh Castle' (a large sketch), 'Hampstead Heath' (several studies), 'Malvern Hall' (Warwickshire), 'Old Chain Pier, Brighton' (1827), 'Salisbury Cathedral', 'The Glebe Farm', 'The Valley Farm', 'Trees near Hampstead Church', and 'Yarmouth Jetty'; also portraits of 'Golding and Ann Constable' (his parents), 'Maria Bicknell' (his future wife), 'The Bridges Family', etc.; *J. S. Copley* (d. 1815), 'The Death of Major Peirson', 'The Siege of Gibraltar', etc.; *J. S. Cotman* (d. 1842), 'The Drop Gate', etc.; *David Cox* (d. 1859), 'The Welsh Funeral' and 'Windy Day'; *John Crome* (d. 1821), 'Moonlight on the Yare', 'Mousehold Heath', 'Slate Quarries', 'The Poringland Oak', and 'Yarmouth Harbour'; *Francis Danby* (d. 1861), 'The Deluge', a huge canvas; *Sir Charles Eastlake* (d. 1865). 'The Colosseum at Rome'; *William Etty* (d. 1849), 'Hero and Leander', 'The Bather', etc.; *Henry Fuseli* (d. 1825; a Swiss admirer of Blake), 'Lady Macbeth seizing the Daggers', 'Shepherd's Dream from *Paradise Lost*', and 'Titania and Bottom'; *Andrew Geddes* (d. 1844), 'Mrs Greatorex'; *B. R. Haydon* (d. 1846), 'Chairing the Member' and 'Punch, or May Day'; *Sir Edwin Landseer* (d. 1873), 'Duchess of Abercorn', 'John Philip Kemble as Hamlet', 'Lake Scene', 'Scene at Abbotsford', and 'The Hunted Stag'; *Sir Thomas Lawrence* (d. 1830), 'Homer Reciting his Poems', and 'Mrs Siddons' and other portraits; *C. R. Leslie* (d. 1859), 'Uncle Toby and Widow Wadman'; *G. R. Lewis* (d. 1871), 'Harvest Scene, Afternoon', etc.; *John Linnell* (d. 1882), 'Kensington Gravel Pits'; *Daniel Maclise* (d. 1870), 'Scene from *Twelfth Night*'; *John Martin* (d. 1854), 'The Great Day of His Wrath', 'The Last Judgement', and 'The Plains of Heaven', three large canvases; *Sir Henry Raeburn* (d. 1823), 'Lady Dalrymple' and 'Mrs Downey'.

J. M. W. TURNER (d. 1851), an unsurpassed range of paintings, the majority bequeathed by the artist. The many splendid landscapes include 'A Ship Aground', 'Avalanche in the Grisons', 'Buttermere', 'Crossing the Brook', 'Fishermen at Sea', 'Frosty Morning', 'London from Greenwich' (1809), 'Morning among the Coniston Fells', 'Petworth Park' (Sussex) and 'Interiors at Petworth', 'Richmond Hill' (Surrey), 'Snowstorm: Hannibal crossing the Alps', 'Spithead', 'The Arch of Titus and the Campo Vaccino at Rome', 'The Bay of Baiae', 'The Bridge of Sighs' and other Venetian scenes; 'The Old Chain Pier, Brighton', 'The Shipwreck', 'The Tenth Plague of Egypt', and 'The Thames near Walton Bridges'; also a Self Portrait at the age of about twenty-three, and a fine selection of sketches and watercolours; *James Ward* (d. 1859), 'Gordale Scar' (Yorkshire), a large romantic painting, and 'Tabley Park' (Cheshire); *Sir David Wilkie* (d. 1841), 'The Blind Fiddler' and 'Village Holiday'; *Peter de Wint* (d. 1849), 'Harvesters'.

THE PRE-RAPHAELITES: *Ford Madox Brown* (d. 1893), 'Chaucer at the Court of Edward III', 'Christ Washing Peter's Feet', 'Lear and Cordelia'; *Sir Edward Burne-Jones* (d. 1898), 'The Golden Stairs' and 'King Cophetua and the Beggar Maid'; *William Dyce* (d. 1864), 'Pegwell Bay' and 'St John Leading the Virgin from the Tomb'; *Arthur Hughes* (d. 1915), 'April Love' and 'The Eve of St Agnes'; *W. Holman Hunt* (d. 1910), 'Claudio and Isabella', 'Our English Coasts' (usually called 'Strayed Sheep'), 'The Awakening Conscience', and

'Trial of the Innocents'; *Sir John Millais* (d. 1896), 'Christ at the House of His Parents' (often called 'The Carpenter's Shop', painted when the artist was twenty), 'John Ruskin at Glenfinlas', 'Ophelia' (modelled by Elizabeth Siddal), 'The Boyhood of Raleigh', 'The Order of Release', 'The Vale of Rest', etc.; *William Morris* (d. 1896), 'Queen Guinevere'; *D. G. Rossetti* (d. 1882), 'Beata Beatrix' (Elizabeth Siddal), 'Monna Vanna', 'Proserpine' (modelled by Jane Morris), 'The Annunciation', and 'The Girlhood of the Virgin'.

LATE VICTORIAN AND EDWARDIAN SCHOOLS: *Aubrey Beardsley* (d. 1898), 'Caprice' and 'The Front at Hove'; *Charles Condor* (d. 1909), 'Springtime' and 'Windy Day, Brighton'; *Richard Dadd* (d. 1887), 'The Flight out of Egypt'; *Augustus Egg* (d. 1863), 'Past and Present'; *Sir Lukes Fildes* (d. 1927), 'The Doctor'; *Stanhope Forbes* (d. 1948), 'The Health of the Bride'; *W. P. Frith* (d. 1909), 'Derby Day'; *Walter Greaves* (d. 1930), 'Battersea Reach', 'Hammersmith Bridge', 'Self Portrait', etc.; *Edward Lear* (d. 1888), 'View of Reggio'; *Lord Leighton* (d. 1896), 'Bath of Psyche', 'Lieder ohne Worte', etc.; *R. B. Martineau* (d. 1869), 'Kit's Writing Lesson' and 'The Last Day in the Old Home'; *Ambrose McEvoy* (d. 1927), 'Euphemia' and 'The Ferry'; *Albert Moore* (d. 1893), 'A Garden' and 'Blossoms'; *Sir William Nicholson* (d. 1949), 'A Hill above Harlech'; *Sir W. Q. Orchardson* (d. 1910), 'The First Cloud'; *Sir William Orpen* (d. 1931), 'The Mirror'; *Sir Edward Poynter* (d. 1919), 'A Visit to Aesculapius'; *James Pryde* (d. 1941), 'The Doctor' and 'The Grave'; *Charles Ricketts* (d. 1931), 'Deposition'; *David Roberts* (d. 1864), 'A Cathedral Porch'; *Sir William Rothenstein* (d. 1945), 'The Doll's House'.

JOHN S. SARGENT (d. 1925), the American painter, who was born in Florence in 1856 and settled first in Paris and later in London: 'Carnation, Lily, Lily, Rose', 'Claude Monet Painting', 'Lord Ribblesdale', 'Mont Blanc', 'The Misses Hunter', 'W. Graham Robertson', and a series of portraits of the Wertheimer family; *Walter Sickert* (d. 1942), 'Dieppe', 'Ennui', 'Interior of the New Bedford Theatre' (Camden Town), 'George Moore', and 'St Mark's, Venice'; *P. Wilson Steer* (d. 1942), 'Boulogne Sands', 'Chepstow Castle', 'Mrs Cyprian Williams and her daughters', 'The Toilet of Venus', 'Walberswick Pier', etc.; *Alfred Stevens* (d. 1875), 'Mrs Collman', 'Samuel Pegler', and a self portrait at the age of fourteen; *James Tissot* (worked in England in 1871–82), 'Ball on Shipboard', 'Gallery of H.M.S. *Calcutta*', etc.; *Henry Tonks* (d. 1937), 'An Evening in the Vale'; *Henry Wallis* (d. 1916), 'The Death of Chatterton'; *J. W.*

Waterhouse (d. 1917), 'The Lady of Shalott'; *G. F. Watts* (d. 1904), 'Eve Repentant', 'Eve Tempted', 'Hope', and 'Psyche'; *James McNeill Whistler* (d. 1903), the American artist who lived in Chelsea from 1857, 'Miss Cecily Alexander', 'The Little White Girl', 'Valparaiso', and several Nocturnes.

20TH-CENTURY BRITISH PAINTING: *Augustus John* (d. 1961), 'Llyn Treweryn', 'Madame Suggia', 'Sir Matthew Smith', 'Smiling Woman', 'W. B. Yeats', and other fine works; *Gwen John* (d. 1939), 'Portrait of Dorelia'; *Wyndham Lewis* (d. 1957), 'Edith Sitwell', 'Ezra Pound', and 'Workshop'; *Stanley Spencer* (d. 1959), 'Apple Gatherers', 'Christ Bearing the Cross', 'Double Nude Portrait', 'Resurrection' (1926 and 1950), 'Self Portrait', and 'Swan Upping'. Works by the Camden Town group (Mark Gertler, Harold Gilman, Charles Ginner, Spencer Gore, and others), and by Sir Winston Churchill, Duncan Grant, Henry Lamb ('Lytton Strachey'), John and Paul Nash, Sir Matthew Smith, Edward Wadsworth, Ethel Walker, and Christopher Wood. Later works by the Euston Road school (Sir William Coldstream, Rodrigo Moynihan, Victor Pasmore, etc.) and by Francis Bacon, Ivon Hitchens, David Jones, L. S. Lowry ('Industrial Landscape', 1955), Henry Moore, Ben Nicholson, John Piper, Ceri Richards, and Graham Sutherland ('Somerset Maugham').

Some of the 19th-century British paintings are in the Lower Floor rooms and corridors (reached from Rooms 10 and 16), and here also are 19th-century British watercolours and drawings, including fine works by Alexander and J. R. Cozens, Thomas Girtin, J. S. Cotman, David Cox, and Peter de Wint.

THE IMPRESSIONISTS AND POST-IMPRESSIONISTS: *Bonnard* (d. 1947), 'La Table', 'Pont de la Concorde', etc.; *Cézanne* (d. 1906), 'The Gardener', and characteristic Provençal landscapes; *Degas* (d. 1917), 'Carlo Pellegrini', 'La Toilette', etc.; *Fantin-Latour* (d. 1904), 'Mr and Mrs Edwards'; *Forain* (d. 1931), 'Girl Bathing' and 'Le Prétoire'; *Gauguin* (d. 1903), 'Harvesting' and other paintings done in Brittany and Tahiti; *Manet* (d. 1883), 'Madame Manet with a Cat'; *Modigliani* (d. 1920), 'Peasant Boy' and 'Portrait of a Girl'; *Monet* (d. 1926), 'Dans le Parc' and 'Les Peupliers'; *Pissarro* (d. 1903), 'Haymaking', 'Self Portrait', etc.; *Henri Rousseau* (le Douanier; d. 1910), 'Flowers'; *Sisley* (d. 1899), 'Bridge at Sèvres' and 'Small Meadows in Spring'; *Toulouse-Lautrec* (d. 1901), 'Les Deux Amies' and 'Émile Bernard'; *Utrillo* (d. 1955), 'Montmartre', 'Place du Tertre', 'Porte St-Martin'; *Van Gogh* (d. 1890), 'Field at Arles',

'View at Auvers', 'The Yellow Chair'; *Vuillard* (d. 1940), 'Seated Woman', and 'The Mantelpiece'.

MODERN FOREIGN PAINTING: works by Georges Braque (the co-founder with Picasso of Cubism), Marc Chagall (d. 1985; 'The Poet Reclining', etc.), Paul Delvaux, André Derain ('The Pool of London' and 'Portrait of Matisse'), Raoul Dufy, Juan Gris, Paul Klee, Oskar Kokoschka ('View of the Thames'), Fernand Léger, André Masson, Henri Matisse (d. 1954; 'Standing Model', 'Portrait of Derain', etc.), Edvard Munch ('The Sick Child'), Pablo Picasso (d. 1973; 'Flowers', and a series of figures showing the development of his style), Georges Rouault ('La Mariée', etc.), Maurice Vlaminck ('La Carouge'), and others.

The gallery also has a comprehensive and growing collection of contemporary works, both British and foreign, showing the varied development of more recent and mostly abstract styles, such as Surrealism, Constructivism, Abstract Expressionism, and so on.

TOWER OF LONDON Plan V, F3

STATION: TOWER HILL, to the N, on the Circle and District lines. — BUSES Nos. 23, 42, and 78 in the Minories or Mansell Street (No. 23 in Eastcheap and Tower Hill; Nos. 42 and 78 across Tower Bridge); in Fenchurch Street, etc., see Route 33; across London Bridge, see Route 25.

ADMISSION Mondays–Saturdays from 9.30 to 5 (March to October) or 4 (November to February); on Sundays from 2 to 5 in March–October only (the Tower closes from half to three-quarters of an hour after these times). The admission charge varies, according to the season, from £2 to £3; children and pensioners, £1 to £1.50. Closed on New Year's Day, Good Friday, Christmas Eve and Day, and Boxing Day. Tickets cover admission to the Bloody Tower, the Beauchamp Tower, the Museum of Heraldry, the Bowyer Tower, and the White Tower (with the armouries). — Admission to the CROWN JEWELS, March–October, Mondays–Saturdays 9.30 to 5.45, Sundays 2 to 5.30 (a long wait may be expected); November–January, Mondays–Saturdays 9.30 to 4.30 (closed in February). Tickets (80p; children and pensioners 40p) are obtainable at the Jewel House (see plan). — The CHAPEL ROYAL is shown only to parties conducted by a warder. Visitors are also admitted (without ticket) to the services held in the chapel (except in August) on Sundays at 9.15 (Holy Communion) and 11.

The TOWER OF LONDON, one of the most imposing fortresses in England, as well as the most interesting and best known, stands on the north bank of the Thames below London Bridge. Begun by William the Conqueror with the triple object of protecting the city, overawing its citizens, and controlling the approaches to London by river, it has been altered and added to by many succeeding monarchs. Built originally within the south-east angle of the City walls, its boundaries were extended eastward beyond the walls in the 12th century, and it now forms a separate Liberty with an overall area of eighteen acres. The Tower has been in its time a citadel, a royal palace, a state prison, and an arsenal maintained by a garrison, and in the World Wars it was again used as a prison.

The exceptional interest of the Tower depends partly on its close association with many events in English history, partly on the excellence of its medieval fortifications. In the centre rises the Norman keep or White Tower, largely the work of the Conqueror, with a chapel that shows the oldest ecclesiastical architecture in London. The tower is surrounded by the large Inner Ward, enclosed by a massive wall flanked with thirteen towers, and this is surrounded in turn by the narrow Outer Ward, protected by a second wall with six towers facing the river and two (formerly three) bastions on the north front. A broad moat (now dry) encircles the fortifications, which are approached at the south-west angle, as in medieval times, when they were defended by two outer or barbican towers commanding a series of drawbridges.

The commander of the Tower is a high-ranking army officer who bears the title of 'Constable of the Royal Palace and Fortress of London'. He is seconded by a Lieutenant, but neither of these officers now resides in the Tower and their duties are performed in the main by the Major and Resident Governor. This officer is supported by the Yeomen Warders, a body of about forty ex-servicemen, specially selected, who will assist visitors and show them round the Tower. They wear a picturesque blue costume of Tudor origin, changed on ceremonial occasions for an equally old and even more picturesque costume of royal red and gold, almost identical with that of the Yeomen of the Guard (compare p. 136), with whom, however, they have had no connection since 1510.

The Chief Warder of the Tower (formerly called the Yeoman Porter) locks the gates at 9.30 each evening and presents the keys to the Resident Governor, an interesting ceremony nearly 700 years old which may be seen by visitors who obtain permission in writing from the governor. It is the duty of the Yeoman Gaoler to carry the processional axe on ceremonial occasions. Previously, when a prisoner left the Tower to face trial the edge of the axe was turned away from him, but if he were then condemned to death, the edge was turned towards him. Every third year on

Ascension Day (next in 1987), the choirboys of St Peter's Chapel assemble on Tower Green to 'beat the bounds' of the Tower Liberties. Other interesting ceremonies concern the installation of a new Constable and the proclamation of a new sovereign. On 21 May each year a sheaf of white Eton lilies and red roses is laid on the traditional spot where Henry VI, founder of Eton College and the last of the Lancastrian monarchs, was murdered in the Wakefield Tower (1417).

The oldest part of the fortress is the White Tower, begun about 1078 by Gundulf, later bishop of Rochester, under the direction of William I. The work, continued under William Rufus, was probably completed for Henry I by Ranulph Flambard, Bishop of Durham, who was also the first of the long list of celebrated prisoners to be confined here (1101). The inner wall with its towers was mainly built by Henry III (1216–72), who also threw up the outer wall facing the river, but the western section of the inner wall, with the Beauchamp Tower, and the remainder of the outer wall are the work of Edward I (1272–1307). Apart from the Bloody Tower and the Cradle Tower, built in the 14th century, and the outer bastions on the north, added by Henry VIII, who also rebuilt St Peter's Chapel, the Tower experienced little change until the 19th century, when several towers were restored and the barracks for the garrison built. The Tower has maintained a military garrison continuously since the 11th century, and has also been a repository for arms for that length of time. It was regularly occupied as a royal residence by every monarch (except Elizabeth I) down to James I, but the palace, which stood to the south of the White Tower and was probably begun by Henry I, was demolished by Oliver Cromwell and no trace of it survives. Charles II was the last monarch to observe the ancient custom of spending the last night before his coronation in the Tower, from which he rode in procession through the City to Westminster Abbey.

In its function of royal fortress and state prison, the Tower has been intimately connected with the gloomier side of English history. Sir William Wallace (beheaded in 1305), David II of Scotland (1346–57), and King John of France (1356–60) were all imprisoned here during the wars with France and Scotland. Richard II signed his abdication in the Tower (1399) and James I of Scotland was kept here in 1406–7, the first part of his long imprisonment. Charles, Duke of Orléans, and other prisoners taken at Agincourt (1415) were also confined here. The Duke of Clarence, brother of Edward IV (1478), was murdered in the Tower, as Edward V and his brother the Duke of York, the 'little princes in the Tower', were said to have been (1483; by Richard III, if Shakespeare is to be believed). Henry VIII was married in the Tower to Catherine of Aragon (1509), and Anne Boleyn, her successor, was executed here in 1536, as was Catherine Howard, Henry's fifth queen, in 1542. Others who suffered during the bluff king's reign were Sir Thomas More and Bishop John Fisher, both beheaded in 1535; Thomas Cromwell, Earl of Essex, the royal favourite (1540); the Countess of Salisbury, the last of the Plantagenets (1541); and Henry Howard, the poet Earl of Surrey (1547). Lord Protector Somerset was imprisoned here by Edward VI, and subsequently executed (1552). The many victims of Mary Tudor include Lady Jane Grey, who spent her nine days' reign here, her husband Lord Guildford Dudley, and her father the Duke of Suffolk, all beheaded in 1554; and Archbishop

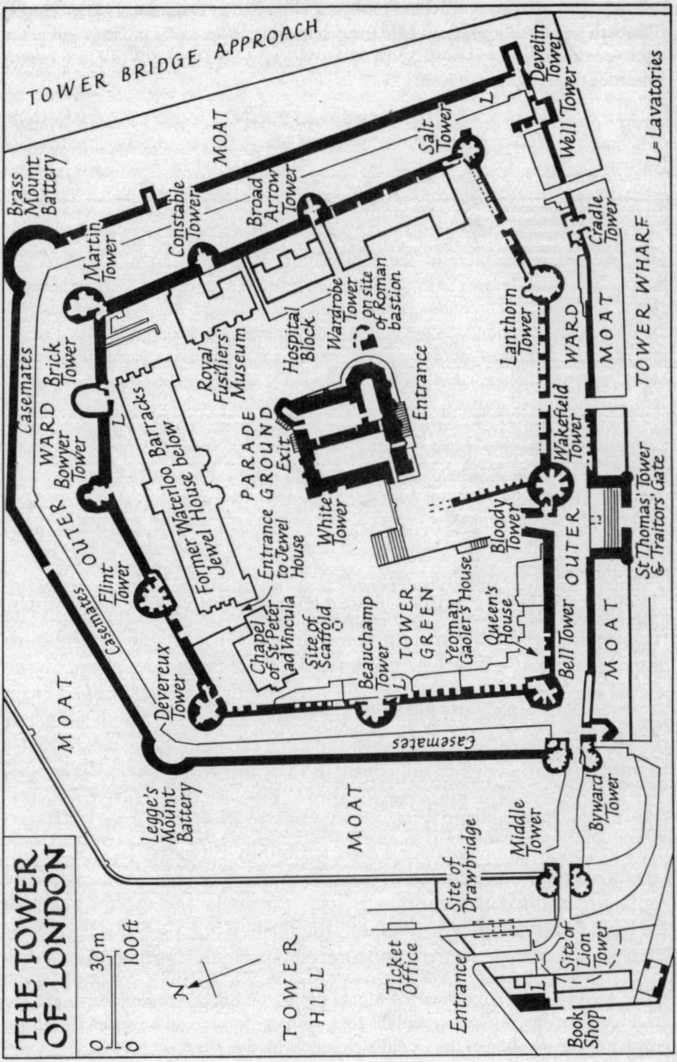
THE TOWER OF LONDON
0 30m
0 100ft
N
TOWER BRIDGE APPROACH
MOAT
Brass Mount Battery
Martin Tower
Constable Tower
Broad Arrow Tower
Salt Tower
Develin Tower
Well Tower
L
L=Lavatories
Cradle Tower
TOWER WHARF
Lanthorn Tower
Wardrobe Tower on site of Roman bastion
Hospital Block
Royal Fusiliers' Museum
Brick Tower
Casemates
WARD
OUTER
Bowyer Tower
Barracks
Former Waterloo Jewel House below
PARADE GROUND
Exit
White Tower
Entrance
Wakefield Tower
St Thomas' Tower & Traitors' Gate
Bloody Tower
Entrance to Jewel House
Flint Tower
Chapel of St Peter ad Vincula
Site of Scaffold
Beauchamp Tower
TOWER GREEN
Yeoman Gaoler's House
Queen's House
Bell Tower
Devereux Tower
Legge's Mount Battery
Byward Tower
Middle Tower
Site of Drawbridge
Site of Lion Tower
Ticket Office
TOWER HILL
Entrance
Book Shop

Cranmer and Bishops Ridley and Latimer (all burned at Oxford in 1553). Princess Elizabeth was closely confined here for two months by her sister in 1554, and in the same year the Tower was subjected to its last siege, by Sir Thomas Wyatt (afterwards beheaded) and his Men of Kent.

The roll of famous prisoners continued under Elizabeth, with the Duke of Norfolk, executed in 1572 for intriguing on behalf of Mary, Queen of Scots; the Earl of Northumberland, found stabbed in 1585; and the Earl of Essex, the queen's favourite, beheaded in 1601. Sir Walter Raleigh was imprisoned three times in the Tower, in 1592, in 1603–16, and in 1618, before his execution at Westminster, and in 1605–6 Guy Fawkes and his fellow conspirators were likewise confined here. Among other illustrious prisoners of the 17th century were the Earl of Strafford and Archbishop Laud (beheaded in 1641 and 1645); George Monck, Duke of Albemarle (1644–7); General John Lambert and other regicides (1660–61); William Penn, the Quaker (1668–9); Samuel Pepys (1679), on an unsuccessful charge of complicity in the Titus Oates plot; Algernon Sidney, charged with being implicated in the Rye House plot and beheaded in 1683; and the Duke of Monmouth, the opponent of James II, beheaded in 1685. The infamous Judge Jeffreys died in the Bloody Tower in 1689. Among the last prisoners who passed through the Tower to their execution were the Jacobites, the Earl of Derwentwater (1716) and Simon Fraser, Lord Lovat (1747), the last man to be beheaded in England. Later prisoners include John Wilkes, the Radical politician (1768), Lord George Gordon, who organized the 'No Popery' riots (1780), and Rudolf Hess (1941), while several spies were shot here during the World Wars.

The main entrance to the Tower is at the south-west angle, from the lower part of Tower Hill, where so many of those confined in the fortress met their doom (compare Route 34). Outside the modern gate is the ticket-office, and on the right inside is the bookshop, on the site of the Lion Tower, where the royal menagerie was lodged from the 14th century until 1834. The tower was defended on all sides but the south by an outer moat (now filled in), crossed on the west side by a causeway with a drawbridge built in 1278 and now partly re-covered. The approach to the main fortifications, taking a sharp turn to the left (to the confusion of attackers), passes over the site of a second drawbridge to the MIDDLE TOWER, built by Edward I (d. 1307), but altered in 1717 and refaced in the 19th century. Beyond it a causeway replacing a third drawbridge crosses the wide MOAT, dug out by Richard I and drained in 1843. On the farther side rises the BYWARD TOWER, built by Edward I and altered later in the 14th century.

On each side of the archway is a guardroom, and in the rooms above are the machinery for the portcullis, a plain 16th-century screen, and a remarkable 14th-century mural painting of the Crucifixion, discovered in 1953.

The Byward (i.e., 'password') Tower admits to the OUTER WARD, between the two lines of walls. On the left is the BELL TOWER, built by Richard I about 1190, but altered in the 13th century. This was the prison of Bishop Fisher, Sir Thomas More, Princess Elizabeth, and the Duke of Monmouth, and curfew is still rung nightly just before 9 p.m. or dusk. Along the top of the rampart leading north to the Beauchamp Tower is 'Princess Elizabeth's Walk'; the late-12th-century wall on the east of the tower encloses the Queen's House. On the right farther east is ST THOMAS'S TOWER, a turreted structure built by Henry III about 1242 and containing an oratory dedicated to St Thomas of Canterbury. Below it is the famous TRAITORS' GATE, with an arch 60 ft wide, formerly the entrance from the river, through which passed many traitors and others opposed to the royal power, after being brought by water from Westminster.

Opposite the gate is the Bloody Tower (see below), the gateway beneath which, the only entrance to the INNER WARD in the Middle Ages, was built by Henry III and still retains its portcullis in working order. On the right (east) of the gate is the massive WAKEFIELD TOWER, likewise the work of Henry III, with a vaulted room on the ground floor where Henry VI is believed to have been murdered in 1471.

The Wakefield Tower contained the public records from 1360 until 1856, and the Crown Jewels (see below) until 1967. The adjoining Great Hall, where Anne Boleyn stood trial in 1536, was pulled down during the Commonwealth. A private entrance stairway, built about 1230 for Henry III, was discovered during excavations adjoining the Wakefield Tower on the east in 1958.

In front of the Wakefield Tower rises the impressive White Tower (see below), approached by a flight of steps. A terrace starting from the top of the steps leads back to the BLOODY TOWER, built during the reign of Richard II and given this name at least as early as 1597. A room on the second floor is said to be that in which the 'Little Princes' were smothered in 1483. Archbishop Cranmer and the Protestant bishops were confined in the tower, and through the small window on the north side Archbishop Laud stretched his hands to bless the Earl of Strafford on his way to the scaffold. Sir Walter Raleigh spent the thirteen years of his second imprisonment here, writing the *History of the World* and taking the air on the terrace along the rampart to the west. Rooms in the tower have been furnished in the style of Raleigh's time.

The rampart formerly ran behind the QUEEN'S HOUSE (properly the King's House), a picturesque timber-framed dwelling built during the reign of Henry VIII (1509–47) and extended on the east in the 17th century. It is the residence of the governor and is not accessible to the public.

In a small room in the west wing Anne Boleyn was incarcerated for the last days of her life, and in the council chamber (in the south wing) Guy Fawkes and his confederates were examined in 1605. The Scottish Jacobite lords were confined in this house (then the residence of the lieutenant) and it was from the doorway here in 1716 that Lord Nithsdale escaped, in the dress of his wife's maid, on the night before he was to have been beheaded. The Queen's House is adjoined on the north by the YEOMAN GAOLER'S HOUSE, rebuilt in the early 17th century. Lady Jane Grey was imprisoned here in 1554 and on the morning of her own execution saw the headless body of her husband brought back from Tower Hill. Rudolf Hess was kept here after landing in Scotland on his abortive mission in 1941.

The west part of the Inner Ward, bounded on the north by the royal chapel, is known as TOWER GREEN. The ravens always to be seen here are perhaps a relic of the menagerie kept in the Lion Tower; they are protected by the Crown under the care of a Raven Master and a special allowance is made for food. Their disappearance is held to presage the fall of the White Tower and the British Empire. A brass plate on the northward part of the green marks the SITE OF THE SCAFFOLD, reserved for those of royal or noble blood. Here were executed Anne Boleyn (1536) and Catherine Howard (1542), the wives of Henry VIII, the aged Countess of Salisbury (1541), Viscountess Rochford (1542), Lady Jane Grey (1554), and the Earl of Essex (1601). All fell by the axe, except Anne Boleyn, who was beheaded with a sword. Lord Hastings was executed near by in 1483 by the order of the Duke of Gloucester (later Richard III), but most other condemned prisoners met their end on Tower Hill.

On the west of the green rises the BEAUCHAMP TOWER (pronounced 'Beecham'), a semicircular three-storeyed bastion built about 1300 and named after Thomas Beauchamp, Earl of Warwick, imprisoned here in 1397–9 by Richard II. The walls of the room on the first floor are covered with inscriptions carved or scratched by prisoners, some of which, however, have been brought from other parts of the Tower.

The inscription over the fireplace was carved by Philip Howard, Earl of Arundel, who was confined here in 1585 and died in custody ten years later; No. 14, on the right of the fireplace, is an elaborate carving by John Dudley (d. 1554), who was

imprisoned here with his father, the Duke of No
Ambrose, Earl of Warwick (represented by
Leicester (oak leaves, from *robur*, an oak), C
(gillyflowers), and Henry (honeysuckle). Th
the room (No. 48) is supposed to refer to th
the room contain Roman tiles, medieval potte

The CHAPEL ROYAL of St Peter ad Vincula,
was founded probably in the reign of Henry I (1100–35) a
name to its being consecrated on the festival of 'St Peter in Cla
Rebuilt in the late 13th century, it was almost completely recon-
structed after a fire in 1512 and has been much repaired since. It was reinstated as a Chapel Royal in 1966. Before the altar are buried Anne Boleyn and Catherine Howard, with the Duke of Northumberland and the Duke of Somerset, 'two dukes between two queens . . . all four beheaded', in the words of Stow. Here also are interred Lady Jane Grey and her husband, the Earl of Essex, and the Duke of Monmouth, and in the crypt lie Bishop Fisher and the Jacobite lords executed in 1746–7.

The body of Sir Thomas More (whose head is at Canterbury) was originally buried here, but may have been removed by his daughter to Chelsea Old Church. Other illustrious victims of the headman's axe lie in unmarked graves in the chapel or th
burial-ground (now part of the green; 'no sadder spot on earth', says Macaulay). T
font of the chapel is Tudor work; the organ was built originally in 1699 by Fat
Smith; the altar frontal is of cloth used at the coronation of Queen Elizabeth II
divided among the royal chapels. In the north aisle is the splendid monument o
Duke of Exeter (d. 1447), formerly in St Katharine's Chapel, Regent's Par
moved here in 1950.

To the east of the chapel, and facing the Parade Ground,
former WATERLOO BARRACKS, built in 1845 and until 1
headquarters of the Royal Fusiliers (see below). From the
floor room, stairs lead down to a stronghold constructed i
house the CROWN JEWELS, or Regalia.

Practically all the regalia of the English monarchy w
melted down during the Commonwealth, and though
recovered at the Restoration (1660), most of the present
from after that time. The oldest crown is *St Edward's C*
from King Edward the Confessor and weighing near
made of gold for the coronation of Charles II (1661)
for the actual coronation ceremony. It is changed im
for the lighter *Imperial State Crown*, made for C

838) and used also when the sovereign appears at the arliament and other State functions. Its gold frame is set ,000 diamonds and other precious stones, including the ge t ruby given to the Black Prince in 1367 by Pedro the Cruel f C and worn by Henry V in his coronet at the Battle of Agi rt, and one of the two 'Stars of Africa' cut from the 'Cullinan' dia d, the largest ever found, presented to Edward VII in 1907. The *perial Indian Crown*, with an emerald of thirty-four carats and ove ,000 diamonds, was worn by George V at the Delhi Durbar in 1911. The *Crown of Queen Elizabeth* (consort of George VI), also made in 1911, is set with the famous 'Koh-i-Noor' diamond of 108 carats presented to Queen Victoria in 1850 by the army of the Punjab. The oldest *Queen Consort's Crown* is that made for Mary of Modena, consort of James II (1685), for whom also the gold *Diadem* or circlet was made. Other crowns are those of Queen Mary (consort of George V) and the Prince of Wales (son of George II; 1728), and the Small Crown of Queen Victoria (1870).

The larger of the *Orbs* (the King's Orb) was made for Charles II, the smaller (the Queen's Orb) for Mary II. *St Edward's Staff*, made of gold and 4 ft 7 in. long, is surmounted by an orb and was also fashioned for Charles II. The *Royal Sceptre* is surmounted by a cross and adorned with gems, including the larger of the 'Stars of Africa' (530 carats), the largest cut diamond in the world. The *Sovereign's Sceptre with the Dove*, also called the Rod of Equity, is held in the sovereign's left hand at the coronation. The *Queen's Sceptre with the Cross* (used by all queens consort at coronations) and the *Ivory Sceptre*, with a dove of white onyx, were both made for Mary of Modena, and the *Queen's Sceptre with the Dove* for Mary II. The *Anointing Spoon*, made in the late 12th century, perhaps for the coronation of King John (1199), and the *Ampulla*, a vessel (shaped like an eagle) to contain the oil for the anointing, probably of the time of Henry IV (1399–1413), are the only survivals of the medieval egalia, but both were restored for the coronation of Charles II. The welled *Sword of State* was made for George IV's coronation (1821).

Other regalia include the *Bracelets* worn at the coronation as emblems of ereignty (two pairs made for Charles II and one pair presented by the Common- lth for the coronation of Queen Elizabeth II) and the *Golden Spurs of St George*, mblem of chivalry, likewise made for Charles II. Also displayed here and in the nd-floor room is a fine selection of royal plate, of which the *Queen Elizabeth Salt* –3) is the oldest piece. The *Exeter Salt*, shaped like a tower, was given to

Charles II by the city of Exeter, and the *Wine Fountain* to the same monarch by the corporation of Plymouth. Cases contain *Maces of Serjeants-at-Arms* of the time of Charles II and James II, a late-17th-century alms-dish used on Maundy Thursday (sometimes in Westminster Abbey, but elsewhere in most years) and a silver-gilt punch-bowl of 1842. Here also are the 'Curtana', or Sword of Mercy, the State Sword used at the opening of Parliament, the Swords of Spiritual Justice (with a blunt point) and Temporal Justice (with a sharp point), the coronation robes of Queen Elizabeth II, mantles and insignia of the Orders of Knighthood, and decorations for valour.

On the north side of the former barracks, and approached round the east end, is the entrance to two interesting exhibitions. On the left is the MUSEUM OF HERALDRY, with rolls of arms, Tudor and later armorials, etc., armorial porcelain, heraldry in gold and silver, and examples of modern heraldic art. In the centre are a mantle of the Knights of the Bath (whose chapel is in Westminster Abbey) and the habit and insignia of the Heralds. The ORIENTAL GALLERY, on the right, has a remarkable collection of arms and armour, etc., from Turkey, India and the Far East. Of particular interest is the only suit of elephant armour in Britain, probably a trophy won at the Battle of Plassey in 1757 and brought home by Lord Clive.

To the north of the barracks, on the curtain wall of the Inner Ward, is the 13th-century BOWYER TOWER, where the Duke of Clarence is supposed to have been drowned in a butt of malmsey wine in 1478 at the instigation of his brother the Duke of Gloucester. The tower now contains a small collection of instruments of torture and punishment, including an execution axe of about 1660 and the block used in 1747 for Lord Lovat, the Jacobite.

To the east of the Parade Ground is the REGIMENTAL MUSEUM of the Royal Fusiliers (City of London Regiment), formed in the Tower in 1685, and amalgamated with other fusilier regiments in 1968. To the south of this are the former Hospital Block and a late-17th-century brick building, restored in 1959 to house the New Armouries, but now used as the offices of the Armouries. To the east of the White Tower is an elaborate bronze cannon of Flemish make (1607) with the arms of the Order of St John of Jerusalem, captured by the French at Malta in 1798 and shortly after by the British, and mounted on a carriage designed at Woolwich in 1827. Near the south-east angle of the tower are the slight remains of the 12th-century WARDROBE TOWER, incorporating the base of one of the bastions of the Roman City wall, and adjoined by the lower courses of a length of the 2nd-century wall. A modern staircase on the south side of the White Tower, approximately on the site of the medieval staircase, ascends to the original entrance at first-floor level (as usual in Norman keeps).

The WHITE TOWER, the oldest part of the whole stronghold, is named from its being built originally of white Caen stone from Normandy. Begun about 1078 for William the Conqueror by Gundulf, afterwards bishop of Rochester and architect of that cathedral, it was completed about 1100 for Henry I. The tower, a characteristic Norman keep, is roughly rectangular in plan, measuring about 118 ft (from east to west) by 107 ft. Of four storeys, it has walls varying from 11 to 15 ft in thickness and extends 90 ft from the floor to the battlements. The corner turrets, which differ from each other in design, are capped by curious cupolas added in the 17th century, when also the exterior was restored by Wren, who replaced the Norman windows (except four on the south side) with others of a classical nature. Under the medieval staircase the bones of two children, conjectured (without any positive evidence) to be the 'Little Princes', were discovered in 1674. The interior, little changed structurally and still conveying something of the atmosphere of a grim Norman fortress, is interesting for its ancient chapel and its extensive collection of arms and armour.

On the First or Gun Floor the first room entered is the SPORTING GALLERY, containing hunting and sporting weapons from the Middle Ages to the 19th century, among them silver-mounted hunting swords, crossbows for hunting and target shooting, and firearms (matchlocks, flintlocks, sporting guns, etc.). The percussion-lock, some early examples of which are shown, was invented in the Tower by the Rev. Alexander Forsyth (d. 1843). The notable Scottish weapons include a silver-decorated sporting gun made in Dundee in 1614 for Louis XIII of France and a gun of engraved brass made for Charles I when a young man. The TOURNAMENT ROOM adjoining has armour used in the joust and tournament in the 15th and 16th centuries, including late-15th-century armour for a German joust, the Scharfrennen; a 15th-century saddle for the Hohenzeuggestech, a joust in which the contestant stood in his stirrups; armour made about 1590 in Germany for the court of the Emperor Maximilian I; and foot-combat armour made in 1591 for Christian I of Saxony. The 15th-century Brocas Helm here is considered to be the finest tilting-helmet in existence. To the south of the room is the CRYPT of St John's Chapel, in the tiny cell opening from which Sir Walter Raleigh is supposed to have spent his last imprisonment.

A staircase from the Sporting Gallery ascends to the second or Banqueting Floor. In the south-east angle is the CHAPEL OF ST JOHN, the oldest church in London (about 1080), a beautiful example of mature Norman architecture, consisting of a nave of four bays with aisles and a clerestory, covered by a barrel vault, and an apse opening by five stilted arches to an ambulatory. The nave arcades have plain arches and massive round piers with square capitals, some of which are carved with an early T-shaped figure. The gallery behind the clerestory is a continuation of the wall passage at the third-floor level.

The old glass in the windows was part of Horace Walpole's collection at Strawberry Hill. In former times aspirants to the knighthood of the Bath kept their vigil here throughout the night before their investiture. Mary I was married by proxy in the chapel to Philip of Spain (1554), and Archbishop Simon of Sudbury was dragged from the altar to his execution on Tower Hill in 1381 by Wat Tyler's rebels.

To the north of the chapel is the MEDIEVAL ROOM, which contains the earliest arms and armour in the Tower's collections. These include medieval swords (among them a fine processional sword of the 15th century), a late-14th-century visored basinet of Italian make from Churburg Castle, and late-15th-century Gothic horse armour probably made for Waldemar VI of Anhalt-Zerbst. This room retains its original fireplace, and garderobes or latrines in the thickness of the wall. The 16TH-CENTURY ROOM, on the west, formerly the Banqueting Hall, has horse and parade armour, pistols and other firearms, and infantry weapons, among them two long-bows from the *Mary Rose* (see below), almost the only survivals of this English weapon. Notable also are the 'Lion' armour embossed with lions' masks and damascened in gold, probably made about 1540 in France, and the German armour made in 1540 for a man nearly 7 ft tall.

A staircase at the north-west angle goes up to the Third or Council Floor. In the TUDOR ROOM, formerly the Council Chamber, much of the armour was made in the royal armouries established at Greenwich by Henry VIII. This includes three suits of foot-armour made for the king himself, one of them weighing 94 lb, and armour made for Robert Dudley, Earl of Leicester, and other famous Elizabethans. The equestrian 'Burgundian Bard' armour, beautifully engraved, the splendid body armour made at Augsburg, and the helmet with curious ram's horns were all presented to Henry VIII by Maximilian I. Among the weapons from the royal arsenal are a spiked club with three pistol-barrels, called 'Henry VIII's walking-stick', and a huge lance used by the Duke of Suffolk, father of Lady Jane Grey. The 17TH-CENTURY ROOM adjoining has gilt armour presented to Charles I by the City of London (but of French make) and armour of Prince Henry (son of James I), of Charles II when prince, and of James II, made in London in 1686 and a late example of the craft. Here also are the armour, arms, and accoutrements of bodyguards, cavalry, and infantry, and armour from the collection of Louis XIV.

A stairway from the north-east of the 17th-Century Room descends to the vaults in the Basement. The MORTAR ROOM, the first room entered, contains several interesting pieces of ordnance, including a large mortar used at the siege of Namur in 1695 and a bronze mortar used for fireworks at the peace of Aix-la-Chapelle in 1748. At the south end is the SUB-CRYPT of St John's Chapel, entered by an archway popularly but erroneously regarded as the cell where Guy Fawkes was confined while being subjected to torture. In the crypt are some fine small cannon and a gilded Lion of St Mark, captured at Corfu in 1809. The CANNON ROOM, on the west, contains arms and armour of the Civil War period and English and foreign guns, some made for the ships of Henry VIII's navy and one salved from the *Mary Rose*, sunk by the French in 1545. Here also is the Norman well, 40 ft deep. The exit from the White Tower is made on the north, to the Parade Ground.

To the south of the White Tower and the Wardrobe Tower (compare above), on the curtain wall of the Inner Ward, is the LANTHORN TOWER, rebuilt in the 19th century. Its predecessor probably occupied the site of a tower at the south-east corner of the Roman city, while the Wakefield, Bell, and Middle Towers may well stand on the foundations of bastions of the Roman river-wall. A section of this wall, dating from about 390, but refaced and thickened in the 13th century, and originally standing about 20 ft high, was revealed by excavation in 1976–7, inside and partly under the 19th-century curtain wall. A HISTORY GALLERY, constructed close by in 1978, illustrates the history of the Tower, with plans at various stages of its development and models of the Tower as it appeared in 1547 and 1856. A modern breach in the curtain wall to the west opens to the Outer Ward.

The parapet walk of the INNER CURTAIN WALL, opened in 1983 and entered to the east of the Wakefield Tower, may be followed west to the Bloody Tower and east and north as far as the Martin Tower. The 13th-century SALT TOWER, at the south-east angle of the wall, has many inscriptions and carvings of prisoners, including a figure cut in 1561 for casting horoscopes. Farther north is the BROAD ARROW TOWER, which (like the wall) is of the 13th century, but has a chamber arranged as it would have appeared in the late 14th century. Beyond is the CONSTABLE TOWER, rebuilt in the 19th century, and at the north-east angle is the MARTIN TOWER (13th century, but modernized), the scene of the daring attempt by Colonel Blood in 1671 to carry off the Crown and other regalia. It contains reproductions of prints and maps of the Tower. Farther west is the BOWYER TOWER (see above), and at the north-west angle is the DEVEREUX TOWER, where the Earl of Essex was confined. The corner bastions on the north of the outer wall were constructed by Henry VIII; a similar bastion between these, added in the 19th century, was destroyed by a bomb in 1940.

An opening in the wall to the east of the Traitors' Gate gives access to the TOWER WHARF, commanding a view of the river and of Tower Bridge. It was originally constructed (before 1228) with soil from the moat and supports a number of 18th–19th-century cannon. The Honourable Artillery Company fires a salute of sixty-two guns here on the anniversaries of the birth, accession, and coronation of the sovereign, and one of forty-one guns on the birth of a prince or princess and other royal occasions. A footway (passing a picnic area) leads under the bridge to the St Katharine's Docks (Route 34).

VICTORIA AND ALBERT MUSEUM Plan VI, C3

STATION: SOUTH KENSINGTON, nearly ¼ m. SW, on the Circle, District, and Piccadilly lines, reached by a subway approached from the west side of Exhibition Road. — BUSES in Brompton Road and Cromwell Road, see Route 10; in Kensington Road, see Route 11.

ADMISSION Mondays–Thursdays and Saturdays, 10 to 5.50, Sundays 2.30 to 5.50. Closed on Fridays and on New Year's Day, May Day Monday, Christmas Eve and Day, and Boxing Day. — LECTURE TOURS on Saturdays at 12 and 3 (assemble at the Main Entrance). Lectures on Tuesdays and Wednesdays at 1.15, Thursdays at 1.15 and 6.45, and Sundays at 3.30, in the Lecture Theatre (approached from Exhibition Road, for the evening lectures).

RESTAURANT (licensed) in Room 39, open until 5.30 — The MUSEUM SHOP is open until 5.30 or 5.45.

The LIBRARY is normally open from 10 to 5.45 on Mondays–Thursdays and Saturdays (except Bank Holidays; closed also 1 to 2 on Saturdays), to holders of tickets (free), obtainable from the Reading Room (78, on First Floor plan). — The PRINT ROOM is open without obligation from 10 to 4.30 on Mondays–Thursdays and Saturdays (except Bank Holidays; closed on Saturdays from 1 to 2). — The TEXTILE STUDY ROOMS are open on Mondays–Thursdays (except Bank Holidays) from 10 to 5, on Saturdays from 10 to 12.30. — The INDIAN DEPARTMENT STUDY ROOMS are open on Mondays–Thursdays (except Bank Holidays) from 10.30 to 5.30. — The telephone number of the INFORMATION OFFICE is 589–6371, extensions 372 and 411.

The HENRY COLE WING (see p. 464) and the BOILERHOUSE PROJECT are open at the same times as the main museum, except that the Boilerhouse Project is closed between exhibitions.

The VICTORIA AND ALBERT MUSEUM, at South Kensington, is the national museum of fine and applied art of all countries and periods. It comprises also the national collections of sculpture (except modern sculpture), watercolours, and miniatures, and the national library of art. The museum has an impressive Renaissance façade designed by Sir Aston Webb and completed in 1909. Over the main entrance in Cromwell Road, on the south, are statues of Queen Victoria and Prince Albert, by Alfred Drury, and flanking it are others by Goscombe John of Edward VII and Queen Alexandra. There is a second entrance in Exhibition Road, on the west; and the niches between the windows on both fronts are occupied by statues of famous British artists and craftsmen. The great central tower, 185 ft high, has a lantern in the shape of an Imperial Crown surmounted by a figure of Fame.

Even the most cursory survey of this vast treasure house will occupy at least a full day, and successive visits are essential to gain a satisfactory knowledge of its contents. The exhibits are arranged in two separate groups: the Primary Collections, in which masterpieces of all the arts are brought together by style, period, or nationality, and the Departmental or Study Collections, in which the objects are grouped within the various classes of sculpture, ceramics, painting, metalwork, etc. In the description below, the Primary Collections are dealt with first. For the benefit of visitors with little time to spare the most interesting or important exhibits have been indicated by an asterisk (*).

The museum, colloquially the 'V. and A.', grew out of the Museum of Manufactures established at Marlborough House in 1852 under the inspiration of the Prince Consort and Sir Henry Cole. It included objects bought at the Great Exhibition of 1851 and collections of the Government School of Design that had been set up in 1837. The original intention was the 'application of fine art to objects of utility', but the museum soon extended its ideals and changed its name to the Museum of Ornamental Art. In 1857, under the inspiration of Prince Albert (who aimed to establish a cultural centre out of the profits of the Great Exhibition), it was moved to its present site and its name again changed, to the South Kensington Museum. Gifts and bequests were heaped on the museum and these with government grants enabled it to expand greatly beyond its original plan, so that its buildings, though frequently added to, became quite inadequate. In 1891 a competition was held for the design of additional buildings facing Cromwell Road and Exhibition Road. It was won by Aston Webb and in 1899 the foundation stone was laid (her last major engagement) by Queen Victoria, who directed that the title be changed once more. When the museum was reopened in 1909 the scientific collections were transferred to the Science Museum.

Beyond the Entrance Hall is the MAIN VESTIBULE (Room 49), on the right of which is the cloakroom, and on the left the museum shop. Room 43, beyond the Vestibule, contains the Primary Collection of *EARLY MEDIEVAL ART, a superb assembly of many treasures. These can be divided into three periods, the first covering Late Antique and Early Christian Art, which developed from the art of Greece and Rome, flourished throughout Europe and the Near East from the late 2nd to the 7th century, and was adapted by the Christian church after A.D. 313. The second period covers Byzantine Art and Christian Art under Islam, illustrating the expansion of the Byzantine style of the Near East from the 8th to the 15th century and its influence on Europe, and the contemporary style that developed in Persia under the Sassanian dynasty (3rd–8th centuries). The third period is

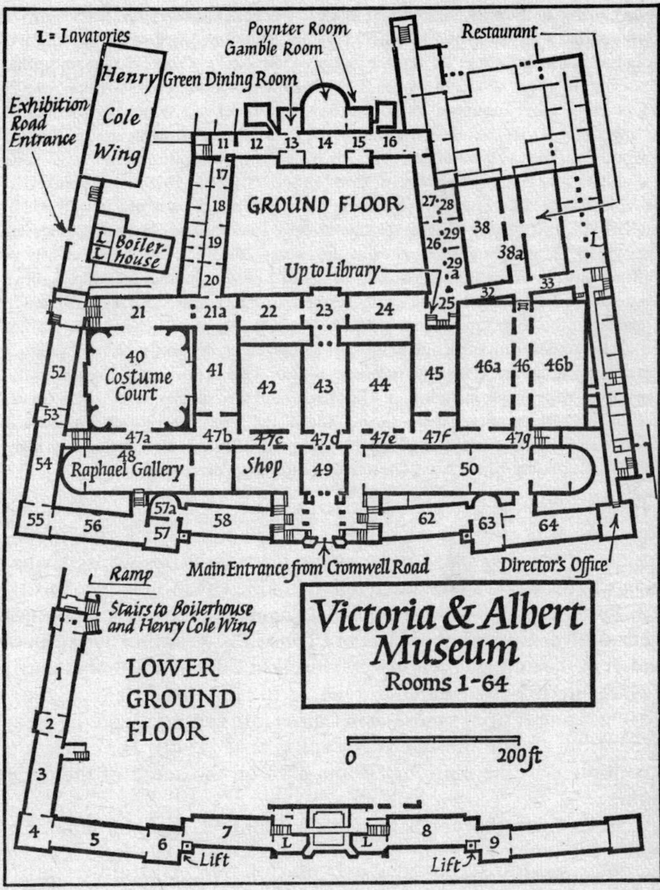

concerned with Early Medieval Art in Western Europe, from the fall of the Roman Empire (4th century) until the early 13th century.

Only a few of the treasures can be mentioned, and they are given in chronological order: among the ivories are the *Symmachi Panel*, the leaf of a diptych in the classical style, made in Rome about A.D. 400, and the *Lorsch Gospel Cover*, Carolingian craftsmanship of the early 9th century, made in Aachen; the *Beresford Hope Cross*, a reliquary that was worn round the neck, is Italo-Byzantine work of the 9th century, probably made in Rome or Southern Italy; the *Easby Cross*, a Northumbrian cross-shaft of about 800, comes from Easby, near Richmond (Yorkshire); a *Crucifix Reliquary* of ivory mounted on gold is Saxon work of the Winchester school of carving, dating from the late 10th century; the *Veroli Casket*, from near Rome, made of wood overlaid with bone and ivory, is of Byzantine inspiration and was made probably in the reign of the Emperor Constantine VIII (976–1028); an *Adoration of the Kings*, a splendid late-11th-century relief in whalebone, was probably made in England; the gilt-bronze *Gloucester Candlestick*, given to the abbey of Gloucester about 1110, is also English work, but the *Alton Towers Triptych*, previously in Staffordshire, is French craftsmanship of about 1150, in enamel on copper-gilt; a plaque of the *Last Judgement*, of enamel on copper-gilt (about 1150), is attributed to Winchester; the elaborate *Eltenberg Reliquary*, in the shape of a church, dates from about 1170 and is from the Rhineland; *Caskets* of walnut, covered with bone plaques portraying saints, are Italian work of the 12th or 13th century; the French craftsmanship in copper-gilt includes an *Altar Cross* and a *Reliquary of the True Cross*, both of the 13th century. At the farther end of the room are 12th-century carved columns and capitals from Italy, France, and Spain, and sculpture, including a head in limestone of about 1230 from Thérouanne cathedral (destroyed in 1553).

Room 42, to the left, is devoted to ISLAMIC ART, with outstanding examples of pottery, ivories, glassware, wood-carvings, and metalwork, and velvets, silks, and carpets, from countries whose civilization was based on Islam, the religion founded by Mohammed in A.D. 622. Particularly notable are the glass hanging-lamps from mosques (12th–13th centuries), the 'Luck of Edenhall', a beautiful Syrian glass beaker of the mid 13th century previously at Edenhall (Cumberland), the large marble basin dated 676 (i.e., A.D. 1277) from Hama (Syria), the inlaid pulpit from a mosque in Cairo (15th century), and the great carpet from a tomb-mosque at Ardabil (Persia; 1540). The collection is continued in the corridor (Room 47C) on the south of the main room.

Room 44 (on the opposite side of Room 43) and the adjoining corridor (Room 47E) are given over to FAR EASTERN ART, a magnificent collection of stoneware and porcelain, metalwork, sculpture, paintings, costumes, and textiles representing Chinese art from prehistoric times to the present day, and including beautiful robes of the Imperial Court and the lacquer throne of the Emperor Ch'ien Lung (1736–95). The Japanese works include fine armour and weapons, lacquered wood, pottery and porcelain, and colour-prints.

Room 45, reached from Room 47E or from Room 24 (see below) is used for temporary exhibitions.

Rooms 22–5, beyond Room 43, are confined to GOTHIC ART, illustrating the style that developed in Europe from about the middle of the 12th century and flourished until the end of the 15th century. Room 22 (on the left) contains majolica and other pottery, ivories, etc., and madonnas and angels carved in stone, wood, and terracotta, showing the richness of Italian Gothic art. Examples are the Angel of the Annunciation carved in wood, ascribed to *Nino Pisano* (about 1350); a relief of the Virgin and Child, in Istrian stone, by the Venetian sculptor, *Bartolommeo Buon* (1451); and a splendid bust of the prophet Haggai, by *Giovanni Pisano*, from the façade of Siena cathedral (about 1290).

Room 23 (which with Room 24 is devoted to *Northern Gothic Art) contains the 14th-century Butler-Bowdon and Syon copes, two fine examples of English embroidery; the 14th-century German Hildesheim cope; an effigy of a knight of the De Lucy family, of about 1330, from Lesnes Abbey (Kent); and (in a case) an early-14th-century diptych of Christ blessing the Virgin and Child, English work in ivory.

Room 24 contains a 15th-century French Angel of the Annunciation, in painted oak; a reliquary believed to have contained the relics of St Boniface (15th-century South German work); and fine reliefs from an altarpiece (English, late 14th century). The altarpieces include an English example, with alabaster panels in an oak framework (the 'Swansea Altarpiece') and a Flemish example, in oak (both of the late 15th century). In the cases are the delicate ivory Soissons diptych, French work of the late 13th century; an early-14th-century ivory statuette of the Virgin and Child, also French; the 14th-century Ramsey Abbey censer, in silver-gilt, an excellent specimen of English metalwork; the late-14th-century Studley Bowl, English work in silver-gilt, chased and enamelled; and the silver-gilt Mérode Cup, French craftsmanship of the early 15th century.

Room 25 (Spanish Gothic Art) contains a processional cross of about 1400, silver and gilt on wood, from Barcelona, and the large retable or altarpiece of the same period from the church of St George at Valencia, with scenes from the life of the saint.

The stairway on the right, with 15th–17th-century Spanish carpets, ascends to the Library (p. 464). The walls of Rooms 32 and 33, the corridor east of Room 25, are hung with Persian, Turkish, and other carpets, and two 16th-century tapestry maps of Warwickshire and Worcestershire. Rooms 46–46B, to the right of the corridor, contain the museum's extensive collection of CASTS of famous sculpture. To the left of the corridor are the Restaurant and another corridor (Room 38A) with an exhibition of Japanese paintings.

Rooms 26–9: LATE-GOTHIC AND EARLY-RENAISSANCE ART, with sculpture, woodwork, metalwork, and textiles, mainly from France, Germany, and the Netherlands, showing the decline of the Gothic style and the advent of the Renaissance. Notable in Room 26 are the St Hubert crosier, Flemish work of the mid 16th century; the German Agate cup of about 1500; the Burghley Nef, a salt-cellar in the form of a ship (French; 1482–3); and the Louis XII triptych of about 1500, in Limoges enamel, with portraits of the king and his wife, Anne of Brittany. The late-15th-century 'palmesel', or wooden figure of Christ on the ass, was used in the Palm Sunday procession in south Germany. Rooms 27 and 28 are given over mainly to German Late-Gothic Art of the early 16th century, including beautiful carved figures in wood by *Veit Stoss* and *Tilman Riemenschneider*, 'hone-stone' reliefs, three stained-glass windows (from Cologne and Bruges), and two carved and painted limewood altarpieces, one showing the legend of St Margaret. Room 29 contains a painted and gilded stone altarpiece of about 1525 from the neighbourhood of Troyes (France), and 15th–16th-century English, Flemish, Italian, and Spanish copes and palls. Room 29A, south of this, has examples of Renaissance art from Spain, notably the wrought-iron screen from Avila and the marble effigies of a grandee and his wife (all of the early 16th century).

Room 38, entered from Room 29, contains a rich assembly of *GOTHIC TAPESTRIES, mostly of the 15th–16th centuries and of Flemish provenance. One depicting the Story of Troy was made in 1472 by Pasquier Grenier of Tournai for the magistrates of Bruges to present to Charles the Bold, Duke of Burgundy, and came from the castle of the Chevalier Bayard, near Grenoble. The three large 'Triumphs' illustrate Petrarch's allegorical poem *I Trionfi* and were woven in Brussels in 1507–10. The four large and magnificent 'Hunting Tapestries', woven between 1425 and 1450, probably at Tournai, were previously in the possession of the Duke of Devonshire at Chatsworth (Derbyshire).

Rooms 11–20: *ITALIAN RENAISSANCE ART, starting in Room 16 (entered from Room 27), an exceptionally fine selection showing well the spirited revival of art that began in Italy in the 15th century, and including a splendid collection of carved and gilded marriage chests ('cassoni') and chest-fronts. Room 16 contains superb examples of the work of *Donatello* (d. 1466), the foremost Florentine sculptor before Michelangelo, including Christ delivering the keys to St Peter (his finest work outside Italy) and the Dead Christ supported by Angels (marble relief), the Virgin and Child with Angels (the Chellini Madonna), the Lamentation over the Dead Christ (both in bronze), and the Virgin and Child (in gilded terracotta); also a bust of Giovanni Chellini, the physician, by *Antonio Rossellino* (d. 1479). The two late-15th-century doorways at the ends of the room are from the palace at Gubbio of Federigo da Montefeltro, Duke of Urbino. In Room 15 are marble reliefs of the Virgin and Child with Angels, by *Agostino di Duccio* (d. 1481), and a fine Lamentation by *Bartolommeo Bellano*, a disciple of Donatello.

Room 14 contains a fine series of enamelled terracotta sculptures by *Luca della Robbia* (d. 1482), his nephew *Andrea*, and the latter's son, *Giovanni*. Of particular note are the Adoration of the Shepherds and the arms of René of Anjou, by Luca, the attractive Boy with the Bagpipes, an Adoration of the Kings, and two Madonnas in relief, by Andrea, and a Bust of Christ and two fine kneeling Angels, by Giovanni. In the centre of the room is a tiled pavement in majolica (tin-glazed earthenware) from the Palazzo Petrucci at Siena. In Room 13 are the carved tomb of Santa Giustina, made about 1476; medals by *Pisanello*, *Matteo de' Pasti*, and others; and a Pietà in bronze once ascribed to *Giovanni Minelli*.

Opening off Room 13 is the GREEN DINING ROOM, decorated and furnished by William Morris, Philip Webb, and Edward Burne-Jones, the first of three refreshment rooms designed from 1866 onward. Next to it is the CENTRAL DINING ROOM, opened in 1868 and recently restored, with lavish decoration by Godfrey Sykes and James Gamble. The ceiling, of enamelled iron plates, and the stained-glass windows (made by Powell & Sons) were designed by Gamble: the marble chimneypiece, by Alfred Stevens (about 1869), came from the dining room at Dorchester House, in Park Lane. The GRILL ROOM, on the east, was designed by Sir Edward Poynter and decorated mainly by students of the Royal College of Art.

Room 12 contains twelve roundels of the Labours of the Months, by *Luca della Robbia*; cases of bronze statuettes by *Bertoldo*, *L'Antico*, *Riccio*, and others; a fine chimneypiece by *Desiderio da Settignano* (d. 1464); and step ends by *Giuliano da Sangallo* from the Palazzo Gondi at Florence. One of the doorways came from the ducal palace at

Gubbio. The staircase ascending from Room 11 was inspired by the neighbouring Della Robbia ware.

Room 17, on the left, has a painted ceiling of about 1500 from Cremona, with figures of Apollo and the Muses; an early-16th-century chimneypiece of Paduan design; and a tempera painting of the Virgin and Child, by *Carlo Crivelli.* Room 18 is mostly devoted to Florentine and Sienese sculpture of the late 15th century, including the lovely Virgin with the laughing Child, in terracotta, of *Antonio Rossellino*; Scenes from the Life of St Francis, terracotta studies by *Benedetto da Majano* for reliefs on the pulpit of Santa Croce in Florence (1474–5); the Allegory of Discord, a stucco study for a bronze relief by *Francesco di Giorgio Martini*; a Virgin and Child in marble by *Domenico Rosselli*; and works by *Andrea del Verrocchio* (d. 1488), the great Florentine master, including a sketch model for the monument of Cardinal Niccolo Forteguerri in the cathedral at Pistoia (1476), and a terracotta statuette of St Jerome. Room 19 contains sculpture from Northern Italy: Venetian works by *Antonio Bregno* (Annunciation), *Pietro Lombardi* (an enchanting Christ Child), *Tullio Lombardi* (Head of Faith), etc., and Milanese sculptures by *Amadeo* (Dead Christ supported by Angels) and *Cristoforo Mantegazza* (Lamentation). Cases hold Venetian glass and North Italian metalwork. In Room 20 are marble statuettes and reliefs by the Milanese sculptor, *Agostino Busti*, called Il Bambaia; a terracotta bust of St Mary Magdalen, attributed to *Giovanni Rustici*; a reliquary bust of St Antigus, in copper, silvered and gilt (about 1500); and a remarkable pearwood altarpiece and predella of the early 16th century, showing a Crucifixion, from Piedmont.

Rooms 21A (beyond Room 20) and 21 (right): CONTINENTAL ART OF THE 16TH CENTURY, mostly in the late-Renaissance style often known as Mannerist. In Room 21A are an elaborate marble altarpiece by *Andrea Ferrucci*, from San Girolamo at Fiesole (about 1495); and stained-glass windows of the 16th century, one from the cathedral at Cortona, by *Guillaume de Marcillat.* Among the objects in the cases are an altar-cross and candlesticks, of rock-crystal mounted in silver-gilt, made by *Valerio Belli* of Vicenza for Francis I of France. In the centre of Room 21 is the celebrated *Samson slaying a Philistine, a marble group by *Giovanni da Bologna* (about 1565), purchased in 1953 from Hovingham Hall (Yorkshire) for £25,000. Also in this room are a bust of Pope Sixtus V in gilt-bronze by *Bastiano Torrigiani*; a head of Cosimo I, Grand Duke of Tuscany, in porphyry on serpentine, by *Francesco del Tadda*; a small model in red wax of a Slave, a sketch for the tomb of Pope Julius II, by *Michelangelo*; and a fine gilt-wax group of the Deposition by *Jacopo Sansovino*, probably for the use of Perugino and other painters. The cases hold beautiful bronze statuettes by *Alessandro Vittoria*, *Giovanni da Bologna*, and others; metalwork, including examples of Milanese damascening; and terracotta sketch-models.

From the west end of Room 21 stairs descend towards the Boilerhouse (p. 465) and the Henry Cole Wing. Other stairs go up to Room 51, which contains NEO-CLASSICAL SCULPTURE, including marbles by *Canova* ('Theseus and the Minotaur' and 'Sleeping Nymph') and *Thorvaldsen* ('Night and Day', and 'Aurora as the Genius of Light'). To the north of this room is the EXHIBITION ROAD VESTIBULE, which displays notable bronzes by Auguste Rodin, among them 'St John the Baptist', 'The Prodigal Son', 'The Age of Bronze', and 'Cybele, the Mother Goddess'.

From Room 21 other stairs go down to Rooms 1–6 on the Lower Ground Floor, devoted to CONTINENTAL ART OF 1570–1825, arranged to show the decorative taste of the period, which covers the transformation from the late-Renaissance style to the baroque. Room 1A contains a bronze relief of the Emperor Rudolph II by *Adriaen de Fries* (1609), a highly-decorated spinet by *Annibale dei Rossi* of Milan (1577), and an unusual North German altarpiece in amber (about 1650), and a splendid astronomical globe with a clock, in gilt-copper and silver, made at Augsburg in 1584. Room 1B has 16th–17th-century French and Italian furniture, and a marble bust of Elizabeth of Bohemia (daughter of James I), by *François Dieussart* (1641). In Room 1C are 17th-century tapestries with scenes from Tasso's epic, *Gerusalemme Liberata*; a magnificent marble bust of Thomas Baker (d. 1658), High Sheriff of Suffolk, by *Gianlorenzo Bernini*; other Italian sculptures by *Giuliano Finelli*, *G. B. Foggini*, *Giuseppe Mazzuoli*, and *Cosimo Fancelli* (Widowed Lady, about 1660). In the centre is a Dying Achilles, by *Veyrier* (1683). A splendid French cabinet of about 1630, formerly at Mentmore Towers (Buckinghamshire), is traditionally associated with Marie de' Medici, queen of Henri IV. The cases hold ivories and terracottas, ebony and silverware.

The small Room 2 contains further sculpture, ivories, majolica, and silverware, including a fine nautilus cup by *Nikolaus van der Kemp* (1613) and a richly-fashioned ewer and basin bearing the town mark of Genoa (1621–2). In Room 3A are bindings and designs for books; the elaborately-embroidered Torah Mantle, made for a synagogue in Amsterdam (1650 or later); and a silver-gilt mace wrought by *G. G. de Forli* in Rome (about 1700). Room 3B consists of a panelled room of the late 17th century brought from a farmhouse near Alençon (Normandy), believed to have been a hunting-lodge of Henri IV.

Room 3C is divided into three sections. The first contains arms (including a fine rapier of about 1660 made in Nuremburg), silverware, glassware, etc.; Hercules in terracotta by *Lucas Faydherbe*, Flemish work of about 1640; and a St Joseph with the Christ Child by *Jose Risueno* (about 1700). The second section is confined to religious art of the Counter Reformation, with French and Italian vestments, altar-frontals, and metalwork, and a characteristic Virgin of the Sorrows, a head in painted wood by *Pedro de Mena* (d. 1688). In the third section are Delft ware, silverware, etc.; the fine Breghtel clock, of silver and enamel, made about 1660 at The Hague; and a rare French harpsichord of japanned and painted wood, made in 1681 by *Jean-Antoine Vaudry*, musical instrument maker to Louis XIV. Room 4 contains 18th-century glassware, faience (pottery with painted designs), and exquisite Meissen and other porcelain, including part of a table-fountain of about 1775 from the Meissen factory.

On the left in Rooms 5–7 is displayed the JONES COLLECTION, an outstanding assembly of works of art, mainly French and of the 17th and 18th centuries, bequeathed in 1882 by John Jones, a retired military tailor of Piccadilly. The collection includes beautiful furniture, silverware, Sèvres and other porcelain, and paintings. Notable in Room 5 are a wardrobe with arabesque decoration in the style of Boulle; a commode of oak veneered with Japanese lacquer, made in Paris about 1755; and a portrait by *François Boucher* (1758) of Madame de Pompadour, the favourite of Louis XV.

On the right in Rooms 5–7 is a display of 18TH-CENTURY EUROPEAN ART (furniture, silverware, ivories, sculptures, etc.). Of note in Room 5 are the elaborate Viennese writing cabinet, dated 1716; a group in ivory and walnut, the Judgement of Solomon (south German work of about 1735); and the ornate bureau, inlaid with mother-of-pearl, brass, and ivory (about 1760), of Frederich Augustus III of Saxony. On the right in Room 6 are a carved altarpiece, together with its terracotta sketch-model, by *Andrea Brustolon* (d. 1732), and (in a wall case) a jewel casket thought to have belonged to the Empress Maria Theresa of Austria. In the centre are terracotta figures (Cupid and Psyche, etc.) by *Claude-Michel*, called Clodion (d. 1814). On the left in this room is a fine bracket clock signed by *Robert Robin* (d. 1799), clockmaker to Louis XV and XVI.

On the left in Room 7 is the boudoir of Madame de Sérilly, from Paris (1778). Among the works of art are a longcase clock, also signed by *Robin*; a commode veneered with mahogany, birch, and other woods, made in Stockholm in 1779 for Gustavus III of Sweden; a marquetry jewel-cabinet made about 1780 for Marie Antoinette by *Jean-Henri Riesener*; a Sèvres-mounted work-table and music-stand (about 1785) that also belonged to Marie Antoinette; and Sèvres porcelain presented in 1788 by Louis XVI to Tippoo Sahib, the notorious ruler of Mysore. On the right in Room 7 are further examples of 18th-century French furniture; a French harpsichord in the 'Chinese' style, by *Pascal Taskin* (1786); sculptures by *Jean-Antoine Houdon* and others, and (in wall cases) French porcelain, including neo-classical Sèvres made in imitation of Wedgwood jasper-ware. The oval neo-classical room here (about 1780) came from a house in Lombardy. The staircase at the end of Room 7 ascends to the Entrance Hall.

Rooms 8 and 9, on the Lower Ground Floor east of the Entrance Hall, are being arranged (1985) to show 19th Century Continental Art.

By passing through the Main Vestibule again and turning left in the corridor (Room 47) the magnificent Primary Collection of *INDIAN ART will be reached. In the principal gallery (Room 41) are cases of Mughal jade and crystal carvings, etc., and (in the centre) a splendid Mughal carpet, made probably at Lahore about 1640 and presented to the East India Company. The bays contain a fine selection of Indian miniature paintings, ranging from the enchanting Rajput and Mughal works of the 16th–18th centuries to Hindu paintings down to the 19th century from the Punjab Hills of northern India. On the walls are hung carpets, bedspreads, embroideries, and temple-hangings, many of great beauty. The first part of the adjoining corridor (Room 47B) holds Gandhara and other early sculpture, bronzes, etc. (from the 3rd millennium B.C. onward); in the western sections (Room 47A) are furniture (inlaid tables and cabinets, etc.), bedspreads and hangings, ivories (including a set of chessmen of about 1790 from Bengal, one side of which represents troops of the East India Company and the other of an Indian army), and paintings done by British artists in India. A curiosity is the large wooden model of a tiger mauling a

British officer, made about 1790 for Tippoo Sahib of Mysore. Inside is a small organ which produces sounds imitating the groans of the unfortunate victim.

As the space available allows for the display of only a relatively small proportion of the treasures of the Indian collection, rooms for the study of paintings and textiles have been arranged in the museum (north of Room 28).

In Room 48, south of the corridor, are hung the celebrated *RAPHAEL CARTOONS, seven of a set of ten commissioned by Pope Leo X as designs for tapestries, and executed by Raphael in 1515–16. The cartoons, painted in sized colours on paper and depicting scenes in the lives of SS. Peter and Paul, are among the finest examples of mature Renaissance art; they were purchased in 1623 for Prince Charles (later Charles I) at a cost of £300 and are now the property of the Queen. The tapestries, woven in Brussels for the Sistine Chapel of the Vatican, are now in the picture gallery there.

The room also contains a 17th-century tapestry, woven at Mortlake (Surrey) from one of the cartoons and lent by the Duke of Buccleuch. In the centre is an elegant Renaissance fountain by *Giovanni Rustici*, the Florentine sculptor, and over the entrance is the singing-gallery from Santa Maria Novella at Florence, designed after 1490 by *Baccio d'Agnolo*. At the west end is *Gianlorenzo Bernini's* splendid *'Neptune and a Triton' (about 1670), which stood in the garden of the Villa Montalto at Rome and later belonged to Reynolds, and on the west wall is a fresco of the Nativity by *Perugino* (d. 1523), transferred to canvas.

The room on the east of the Cartoon Gallery contains a collection of ARCHITECTURAL DETAILS in wood, among them shop fronts, doors and door-cases, balconies, staircases, and furnishings, mostly English (and many from vanished London houses), but including also French and Italian work. Especially notable is a house front of about 1600 built for Sir Paul Pindar in Bishopsgate Without.

Room 40, the large court on the north of the corridor, farther west, holds a fine series of *COSTUMES, mostly English, of the 16th–20th centuries, as well as costume dolls, English and Continental fans, and contemporary fashion plates. Also in the court are a panelled room of about 1620 from Haynes Grange (Bedfordshire) and part of the dining room at Drakelowe Hall (Derbyshire), painted in 1793 by Paul Sandby.

Room 40A, in the upper part of the Costume Court, has a fascinating collection of MUSICAL INSTRUMENTS, from the 16th century onwards, mainly arranged in chronological order, starting to the left of the staircase. Here is one of the earliest known harpsichords, made by Jerome of Bologna in 1521, and other instruments include 16th-century virginals, 16th–17th-century lutes, chittarones (bass lutes), and theorboes (larger bass lutes), a German baroque organ, baroque oboes and flutes, an inlaid guitar, a violin by Antonio Stradivari (d. 1737), and various keyboard instruments of the period, 18th-century viols (forerunners of the violin family), barytons (a kind of bass viol), clavichords and early pianos, a fine collection of French harps (including an early pedal harp of after 1785), late-18th-century English pianos by Broadwood and other masters, and an unusual 19th-century 'Giraffe' piano. The pull-out cases contain further string and wind instruments; and the room also houses 19th-century musical-boxes and the museum's study collection of clocks.

From Room 51 (north-west of the Costume Court) stairs ascend to Rooms 52–8, covering ENGLISH FURNITURE AND DECORATIVE ARTS OF 1500–1750. The first rooms (under rearrangement in 1985) are confined to the Tudors and early Stuarts. Room 52 contains an early-16th-century bust of Henry VII, in painted and gilded terracotta, by Torrigiani (compare p. 480); Queen Elizabeth's virginals, dating from about 1570; and the 'Great Bed of Ware', a celebrated carved and painted Elizabethan bed, 12 ft square, mentioned in 1596 and referred to by Shakespeare and Ben Jonson. Here also are notable silver-gilt plate, including the Mostyn Salt, bearing the hallmark of London (1586–7), and the Vyvyan Salt (London, 1592–3); a table-desk of Henry VIII (about 1525) in painted leather; and bookbindings with the arms of Henry VIII and James I. In the centre is a panelled room of about 1575 from Sizergh Castle (Westmorland), containing a carved and inlaid bedstead of 1593 from Moreton Corbet, near Shrewsbury.

Room 53 has notable table carpets and other embroidery of the late 16th and early 17th centuries. Room 54 has silverware, glassware, furniture, and clocks; and includes part of the Oxburgh Hangings (about 1570), woven by Mary, Queen of Scots, and Elizabeth Hardwick, Countess of Shrewsbury, while the queen was being held in captivity under the Earl. The oak panelling and the plaster ceiling are from the state room of the Old Palace at Bromley-by-Bow, completed about 1606, probably for James I. Here also is the Stoning of St Stephen, a relief in lime and lancewood by Grinling Gibbons, and a cravat carved in limewood by Gibbons.

Rooms 55 and 56 cover the Restoration and William and Mary periods (1660–1700). Room 56 includes a panelled room of 1686–8 from Clifford's Inn; two fine late-17th-century bedsteads; earthenware, silver, etc., and notable furniture, including an elaborate japanned cabinet and mirror, and examples of the newly introduced marquetry. Rooms 57 and 58 deal with the Queen Anne and early Georgian periods (1700–1750). In the former is a room designed by James Gibbs, with an Italian stucco ceiling, from Henrietta Place, Marylebone (about 1725). The latter contains three typical rooms: one of about 1730, panelled in pinewood, from Hatton Garden; the music room from Norfolk House, St James's Square, designed by Matthew Brettingham (1756); and a panelled room of about 1755 from Great George Street, Westminster. The furniture, which shows the advent of the rococo style, includes side-tables, designed by James Moore and by the architect Henry Flitcroft, and a looking-glass by William Kent.

The adjoining staircase ascends to the First Floor, where Rooms 122–25 are devoted to ENGLISH FURNITURE AND DECORATIVE ARTS OF 1750–1830. In the first room (125) are a 'Chinese' bedstead from Badminton (Gloucestershire), made, probably by William Linnell, for the Duke of Beaufort, and a pinewood and marble chimneypiece from Winchester House, Putney (both of the mid 18th century); a mantelpiece and wallpaper from a house at Wotton-under-Edge (Gloucestershire), and panels of wallpaper in the popular 'Chinese' fashion (all about 1750); and part of the drawing-room from Northumberland House, near Charing Cross, with elegant decoration by Robert Adam (1773–4). Room 124, which follows, has notable furniture, including some fine bookcases. Room 123 contains the 'Strawberry Room' from Lee Priory (Kent), a neo-Gothic design by James Wyatt (after 1782); and here also are silver, notably the Newdigate centrepiece, made by Paul de Lamerie (1743–4), and Chelsea porcelain, including the Dudley vases made about 1767 (traditionally for George III) and a tea and coffee service of over forty pieces (about 1765). Room 122 has a ceiling (with paintings by Zucchi) and chimneypiece designed by the brothers Adam, from the drawing-room of David Garrick in the Adelphi (about 1770); furniture by Robert Adam, including the Kimbolton cabinet, made for the Duke of Manchester (1771); the silver tea and coffee service of David Garrick (London, 1774–5); and panels of French wallpaper (about 1775) from Ashburnham Place (Sussex). Room 121, beyond, has REGENCY furniture, silver, and ceramics.

Rooms 118–20 illustrate VICTORIAN FURNITURE AND DECORATIVE ARTS (1830–1900). Room 120 contains furniture, paintings, sculpture, and ceramics of the earlier Victorian period (down to about

1860), including pieces designed by A. W. Pugin, Alfred Stevens, and R. Norman Shaw, and objects shown at the Great Exhibition of 1851. Room 119 illustrates the work of William Morris, the Pre-Raphaelite artist, and his followers. Room 118 is devoted to the late Victorian period and includes examples of designs by William Burges, Alfred Gilbert, C. R. Ashbee, and Charles Rennie Mackintosh, the early exponent of Art Nouveau. The room of 1877 with Gothic Revival panelling is from a house in Birmingham.

The staircase to the north of Room 118 descends to rooms illustrating BRITISH ART AND DESIGN, 1900–1960, arranged chronologically by decades. Room 74 contains furniture, tableware, fabrics, bookbindings, sculpture, pottery, etc., of the period, including a safe designed by Sir Edwin Lutyens (1904) and a furnishing fabric by Graham Sutherland (1948). Room 74A, beyond, covers the period from 1940 to 1960.

Rooms 70–73, north of these rooms, occupied by the THEATRE MUSEUM, are closed pending the transfer of the museum to Covent Garden (Route 20).

The other rooms in the museum are mainly occupied by the Departmental Collections. These should not be disregarded, however, by those who have time to give to them, as many of the exhibits are of great individual interest and beauty. Room 62, on the east of the Entrance Hall, contains English medieval sculpture, with architectural fragments and magnificent 14th–15th-century alabaster images and panels, mostly for altarpieces and originally painted and gilded. The eastern half of the room has European, Near Eastern, and Latin American carvings in ivory. Room 63 is concerned with Continental sculpture, while Room 64 holds Italian bronzes, medals, and plaquettes.

The large room 50, north-east of the Main Vestibule, is divided into three sections. The western part contains a splendid collection of *ENGLISH SCULPTURE, including a fine series of portrait busts and other works extending in date from the 17th to the 19th century, with characteristic examples of *Le Sueur* ('Charles I'), *John van Nost the Younger* ('George III'), *Rysbrack* (model for the monument of Sir Isaac Newton in Westminster Abbey), *Peter Scheemakers* ('Viscount Cobham'), *Roubiliac* ('Handel', a fine sculpture formerly in Vauxhall Gardens; and model for the monument of the Duke of Argyll in Westminster Abbey), *Nollekens* ('Charles James Fox'), *Joseph Wilton* ('Dr Antonio Cocchi', etc.), *Thomas Banks* ('Thetis Dipping Achilles in the River Styx'), *John Flaxman* (plaster model of St Michael for a marble sculpture at Petworth House, in Sussex), *Sir Francis Chantrey*, and *Alfred Stevens* (model for the Wellington monument in St Paul's Cathedral). Here also are medieval and later church monuments, mostly from vanished churches, including the 17th-century Finch monument from Eastwell (Kent), with carving by Nicholas Stone.

The central and eastern parts of Room 50 are devoted to CONTINENTAL ARCHITECTURE AND SCULPTURE, including the larger objects from the Primary Collections for which no space can be found elsewhere. At the west end is a large and handsome rood-screen in marble and alabaster from Hertogenbosch (Bois-le-Duc), dating from 1610–13; the figure of St Peter on the left is attributed to Nicholas Stone, who worked in Holland for a time. Among other notable architectural details in the museum's collections (mostly Italian) are the monument of about 1435 to the Marchese Spinetta Malaspina from Verona; the arch of an altar, possibly by *Giuliano de Majano* (d. 1490); the balcony of the Palazzo Pola at Treviso (in Istrian stone, after 1492); a chimneypiece of about 1500 from Padua, carved with hunting scenes; the great doorway of 1515 from Ghedi (Brescia); two doorways in slate from the workshop at Genoa of *Giovanni Gaggini* (d. 1517); a fine dormer window of about 1523 from a French château; the monument to Gabriele Moro (d. 1546) from Venice; a fountain attributed to *Benedetto da Rovezzano* (d. 1552); and a chimneypiece in the style of *Giorgio Vasari* (d. 1574) from Florence. The eastern apse of the gallery is filled with the chancel chapel from Santa Chiara, Florence, built in 1493 by *Giuliano da Sangallo*.

Rooms 127–30 on the First Floor and 133–45 on the Second Floor are given over to the rich and extensive Study Collection of CERAMICS. Rooms 127–8 contain French earthenware and porcelain of the 16th–18th centuries; 129–30, Chinese glassware, jade carvings, etc., and Japanese netsuke and lacquer-work; 133, Islamic pottery of the Near East; 134–5, Italian and other European tin-glazed earthenware; 136, German stoneware and faience; 137, English earthenware and stoneware, a fine selection, and Continental peasant pottery; 138, Renaissance enamels from France and Italy; 139–40, English pottery, porcelain, and enamels, mainly of the 18th–19th centuries; 141, Northern European tiles and tilework; 142, German, Spanish, and Italian porcelain and enamels; and 143–5, Far Eastern pottery and porcelain. Room 131 and Room 112 (on the floor below) hold the collection of GLASSWARE.

Rooms 65–9, reached from Room 11 (on the Ground Floor), are given over to DOMESTIC SILVER, British work in the first three rooms and Continental work in the others. Notable pieces are the Pusey Horn, of about 1450, the Howard Grace Cup (1525), and the earliest known teapot (1670) and coffeepot (1682); the mace of St Andrew's church, Holborn (1694); and an engraved silver table-top, French work of about 1700. Rooms 81–4 and 87–93 are devoted to METALWORK: Room 81 (left) to Pewter and Cutlery; Room 82, Sheffield Plate, etc.; Room 89, which follows, Enamelled work; Room 83, Continental church plate; Room 84, English church plate, from the Middle Ages to the early 19th century; Room 93 (left), Watches and metal-cased clocks; Rooms 91–2, Jewellery, rings, and gold snuff-boxes, another fine collection; Rooms 88a and 90, European arms and armour; and Rooms 87–8, Islamic armour and other metalwork.

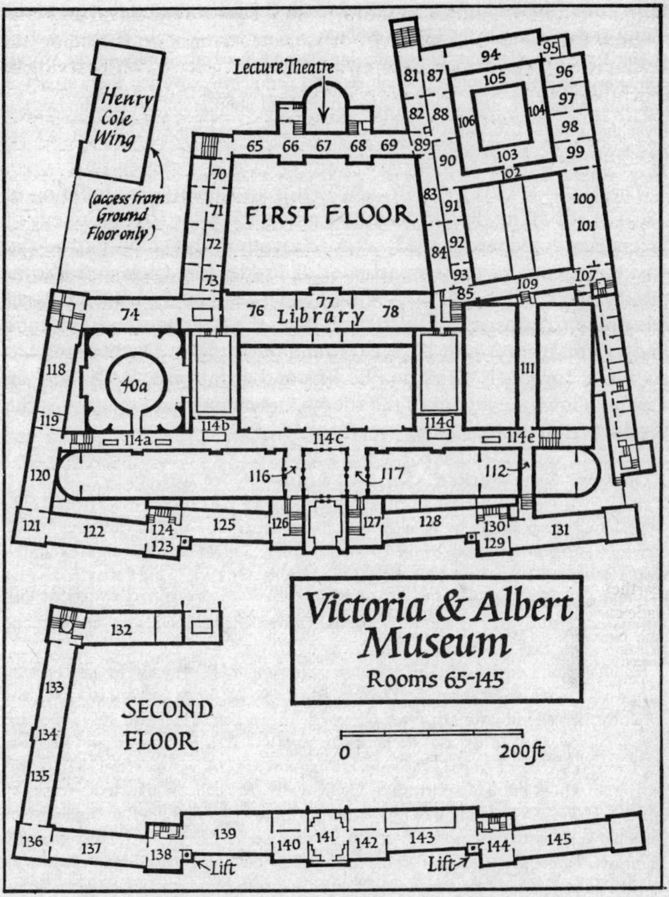

The corridor on the east of Room 90 gives access to the 20TH-CENTURY STUDY COLLECTION in Rooms 103–6. The TEXTILE STUDY ROOMS (94–101 and 109) hold many fine examples of European and Far Eastern woven fabrics, embroideries, etc., including splendid Chinese court robes and silken tapestry pictures. The corridor (111) south of Room 109 is illuminated through fine examples of 13th–19th-century STAINED GLASS, from English and European sources. The long corridor (114) to the right contains an exceptionally comprehensive collection of

IRONWORK. Rooms 116–17, on the left, with German stained glass, lead to the staircases descending to the Main Vestibule.

The LIBRARY (Rooms 77–8), the largest and finest art library in the world, contains over 300,000 books, pamphlets, and periodicals, covering every aspect of fine and applied art, and an extensive collection of photographs. It also houses the Dyce and Forster Libraries, which include the correspondence of Garrick, several novels in manuscript of Dickens, etc.

The HENRY COLE WING is a Victorian Renaissance building of 1867–71 (by Henry Scott) occupied until 1975 by the Royal College of Science and opened in 1983, after renovation, to exhibit part of the vast collections of the Department of Prints, Drawings and Photographs, and Paintings. It is approached via the Exhibition Road Vestibule (compare Route 10) and from the main museum by stairs and a ramp from Room 21 (see Ground Floor plan). The building has six floors (or levels), reached by lifts and a staircase. Room 151 on Level 1 shows the layout of the rooms, but changes are made in some displays from time to time.

On Level 2 are PRINTS AND DRAWINGS (Room 202), PRINT MAKING TECHNIQUES (206–9), and 18TH–19TH CENTURY BRITISH PAINTINGS (217–21), among them works by *Kneller* (self portrait), *Gainsborough* (his daughters), *Reynolds*, *Richard Wilson*, *John Crome*, *Turner*, and *Millais* (his first exhibited work). Room 203 is reserved for special exhibitions. On Level 3 are PHOTOGRAPHS and Photographic Processes (306–9) and BRITISH WATERCOLOURS (302), including characteristic works by Sandby, Cozens, Turner, Girtin, David Cox, and Peter de Wint.

Room 406 on Level 4 contains a superb collection of *PORTRAIT MINIATURES, with works by *Hans Holbein the Younger* (d. 1543), *Nicholas Hilliard* (d. 1619; the foremost British miniaturist), *Isaac Oliver* (d. 1617), *Peter Oliver* (d. 1647; his son), *Samuel Cooper* (d. 1672), and *Richard Cosway* (d. 1821). Rooms 403 and 421 hold the IONIDES COLLECTION, the valuable bequest of C. A. Ionides (d. 1900), the art patron, of whom there is a portrait by G. F. Watts. The collection includes works by *Nardo di Cione* ('Coronation of the Virgin'), *Botticelli* ('Smeralda Bandinelli'; once owned by Rossetti), *Tintoretto* (self portrait), *Louis Le Nain* ('Landscape with Figures'), *Domenico Tiepolo* (sketch for a ceiling painting), *Delacroix* ('Shipwreck of Don Juan'), *Theodore Rousseau* ('Landscape with Stormy Sky'), *Millet* ('Wood Sawyers'), and *Degas* (Scene from Meyerbeer's opera, *Robert le Diable*). On this floor also are 16TH–19TH CENTURY EUROPEAN PAINTINGS, especially from the German, Swiss, and French schools (418–20); a unique panorama of Rome, 44 ft in circumference, painted in 1824 (417); and the transparencies painted by Gainsborough for showing in his 'Exhibition Box' (416). On Level 5 is the PRINT ROOM, accessible on application.

Rooms 603 and 620 on Level 6 contain *Paintings, sketches, and drawings by

John Constable (d. 1837) given by his daughter, including 'Salisbury Cathedral' and other fine landscapes and the full-size oil sketch for 'The Hay Wain'. Room 621 illustrates the Constable tradition in English landscape painting. The descent to Level 1 may be made by the Great North Staircase, a remarkable feature of the building.

The old boiler-house wing of the museum has been converted for the Boiler-house Project, completed in 1982. Sponsored by the Conran Foundation, this is a centre for exhibitions (changed from time to time) of the history and practice of industrial design.

WALLACE COLLECTION Plan II, D2

Stations: Bond Street, ¼ m. SE, on the Central line; Baker Street, ½ m. NW, on the Bakerloo, Circle, and Metropolitan lines. — Buses in Baker Street, see Route 16; in Oxford Street, see Route 14.

Admission Mondays–Saturdays 10 to 5, Sundays 2 to 5 (free). Closed on New Year's Day, Good Friday, May Day Monday, Christmas Eve and Day, and Boxing Day. — Lectures on Tuesdays and Thursdays at 1.

The Wallace Collection, the finest as well as the largest collection of works of art of all kinds presented to any nation by a private individual, was formed mainly by the third and fourth Marquesses of Hertford and the latter's son, Sir Richard Wallace. It was bequeathed by Lady Wallace in 1897 and is maintained in Hertford House, the residence of the Marquesses and Sir Richard, an 18th-century mansion on the north side of Manchester Square, in the angle between Baker Street and Wigmore Street, a little north of Oxford Street. The collection is especially valuable for its 17th–18th-century French paintings, furniture, sculpture, and porcelain, but is remarkable, too, for its European and Oriental arms and armour, its fine gallery of English, Flemish, Dutch, Spanish, and Italian paintings, and its Renaissance terracottas and bronzes, Italian majolica, and other smaller objects of ornamental art. The treasures receive added distinction by being set out as in a private residence.

The collection, begun by the first and second Marquesses of Hertford, was considerably enlarged by the third Marquess (d. 1842), who has been brilliantly pilloried as Lord Steyne by Thackeray in *Vanity Fair*. The main part, however, was formed by the fourth Marquess (d. 1870), who resided for most of his life in Paris and was a connoisseur of 18th-century French art. The collection passed to his son, Sir Richard Wallace (d. 1890), who greatly augmented it by the addition of the armouries and the medieval and Renaissance works, and after the Franco-Prussian War (1871) transferred a large part of it to London. He reopened Manchester House (built in 1776–8 for the fourth Duke of Manchester and later the London residence of the Marquesses of Hertford), renamed it Hertford House in their honour, and extended it northward to contain his now priceless collection. This was bequeathed to the nation by his widow on condition that a home be found for it in central London. The freehold of Hertford House was purchased, and the collection was made accessible to the public in 1900. A major renovation of the interior took place in 1975–82.

From the ENTRANCE HALL, which contains a portrait of Queen Victoria in her robes of state (a study by the American artist, Thomas Sully), the GRAND STAIRCASE ascends to the First Floor, where the more important objects in the collection are displayed. The marble staircase has a balustrade of wrought-iron and gilt-bronze made for Louis XV's Cabinet des Médailles in Paris, now part of the Bibliothèque Nationale. On the landing are a marble group of Cupid and Psyche, by C. A. Cayot (1706), and two 18th-century Gobelins tapestry panels. The fine paintings by François Boucher ('The Rising and the Setting of the Sun', etc.) were designs for tapestries and once in the possession of Madame de Pompadour.

Room 13, on the left of the landing, contains cabinets, clocks, chairs, etc., of the period of Louis XV (1715–74). On the walls are hung characteristic views of 18th-century Venice by Antonio Canaletto and Francesco Guardi. Rooms 15 and 16, beyond, are devoted mainly to Dutch and Flemish paintings of the 17th century, including a fine portrait of the artist, by Rembrandt, and a delightful group of oil sketches by Rubens.

Other works are by J. A. Backer, Pieter de Hooch, Gabriel Metsu, Jan Steen, D. Teniers the Younger, and Gerard Terborch. Here also is a charming Marriage of the Virgin, by Murillo. Rooms 17 and 18, which follow, are hung with 17th-century Dutch landscapes and seascapes, including works by Aelbert Cuyp, M. Hobbema, A. van der Neer, I. van Ostade, Rembrandt, J. van Ruisdael, and W. van de Velde the Younger.

The large PICTURE GALLERY (Room 19) contains the most important paintings in the collection. Among the masterpieces on view here are: *Philippe de Champaigne*, 'The Annunciation' and 'Adoration of the Shepherds'; *Claude*, 'Italian Landscape'; *Dughet*, 'The Falls of Tivoli'; *Gainsborough*, 'Mrs Robinson' ('Perdita', the mistress of George IV); *Frans Hals*, 'The Laughing Cavalier', the best-known picture in the collection; *Hobbema*, 'Stormy Landscape';

Lawrence, 'George IV'; *Murillo*, 'Holy Family', etc.; *Poussin*, 'Dance to the Music of Time'; *Rembrandt*, 'The Artist's Son, Titus', and 'Jean Pellicorne with his Son, and his Wife with their Daughter'; *Reynolds*, 'Mrs Carnac' and 'Nelly O'Brien'; *Romney*, 'Perdita Robinson', a fine study; *Salvator Rosa*, 'Landscape'; *Rubens*, 'Christ's Charge to Peter', 'The Holy Family', and 'The Rainbow Landscape'; *Sassoferrato*, 'Marriage of St Catherine'; *Titian*, 'Perseus and Andromeda', painted in 1554 for Philip II of Spain; *Van Dyck*, 'Philippe le Roy and his wife, Marie de Raet,' and 'Self Portrait as Paris'; *Velazquez*, 'Don Baltasar Carlos' and 'Lady with a Fan'; and *A. van de Velde*, 'Dutch Man of War'.

Room 20, entered from the west of the gallery, contains 19th-century French paintings, including a number of small but detailed works by Meissonier, and others by Corot, Decamps, Prud'hon, Ary Scheffer, and Théodore Rousseau. The cases in the centre hold early-19th-century miniatures, mainly French, including works by J. B. Isabey ('Napoleon', 'Wellington', etc.). Room 21 is devoted to 18th-century French art. On the walls is a delightful series of romantic pastoral scenes ('fêtes champêtres' and 'conversations galantes') by Watteau, Pater, Lancret, Boucher, and Fragonard. The handsome furniture includes chests of drawers by Gaudreau and Cressent, and three secretaires by Riesener known to have belonged to Marie Antoinette. Here also are notable 18th-century clocks and candlesticks, and cases contain a fine collection of miniatures, showing the work of Horenbout (portrait of Holbein), François Clouet, Samuel Cooper, Isaac Oliver, and Richard Cosway (Mrs Fitzherbert), and the Swedish artists, Lanfransen (or Lavreince) and P. A. Hall.

In Room 22 are the so-called marriage commode of Marie Antoinette, by Dubois, a portrait of Madame de Pompadour and other paintings by Boucher, and the splendid Avignon clock, made by Gouthière (1771). Room 23 contains further French furniture, including a writing-table and cartonnier in oak and green lacquer by Dubois that probably belonged to Catherine the Great of Russia. Also in this room are late-18th-century paintings by Greuze and others, and two popular studies of children by Reynolds ('Miss Bowles' and 'The Strawberry Girl').

A passage, with a case containing a silver-gilt service made at Augsburg (in 1767–73), leads left to Room 24, which has a monumental clock attributed to Boulle, a fine cartonnier surmounted by a clock, attributed to Cressent, and paintings by Desportes,

Nattier, Pater, and others. Room 25 contains a magnificent roll-top desk by Riesener (1769), a rich collection of gold boxes, and two fine busts by Houdon, of Madame Victoire de France and Madame de Sérilly. Room 14, beyond, has further Venetian scenes by Canaletto, the large library-cabinet made by Levasseur for the third Marquess of Londonderry, a remarkable régulateur clock in gilt-bronze, with intricate astronomical movements, and cases of exquisite Sèvres porcelain.

The descent is made again to the GROUND FLOOR. Room 1, on the east side of the Entrance Hall, contains 18th-century French furniture, including chairs covered with Beauvais tapestry, and busts of Charles I (by Roubiliac) and Queen Caroline (by Rysbrack). Among the paintings are portraits by Hoppner ('George IV as Prince of Wales'), Lawrence ('The Countess of Blessington'), and Reynolds ('Mrs Hoare and her Son' and 'St John in the Wilderness'). Room 3 is devoted to the late Middle Ages and the Renaissance. Near the entrance is a 16th-century bronze bust of Charles IX, by Germain Pilon. Cases contain a fine collection of miniatures, terracottas, glass, silver, bronzes, enamels, ivories, and boxwood carvings (the last including a beautifully carved miniature shrine, Flemish work of about 1500). On the walls are paintings by Jordaens ('Riches of Autumn') and others, alabaster reliefs from England (15th century) and Denmark (16th century), and a noble head of Christ, carved in marble by Torrigiani. Room 4 continues the medieval and Renaissance collections, with fine Italian majolica, Continental earthenware, coins and medals, and bronze statuettes. Notable are the 7th-century Bell of St Mura, from Ireland, and the 15th-century Horn of St Hubert, in the first of the centre cases, and a large majolica wine-cooler from Urbino, in the centre case.

A corridor (with cases of Hispano-Moresque ware and 15th–16th-century Italian majolica) gives access to Rooms 5–7, which contain the superb collection of EUROPEAN ARMS AND ARMOUR, arranged for the most part in chronological order (beginning in Room 7). Notable pieces are the equestrian armour made at Nuremberg in 1532–6 and bearing the arms of the Palatinate (Room 5), the war harness for man and horse made about 1475–85 for the Von Freyberg family of Upper Bavaria, a richly decorated shield with the arms of Diane de Poitiers, and superb English armour made about 1590 in the royal armouries at Greenwich (all in Room 6). Room 8 (beyond Room 7) has a notable collection of ORIENTAL ARMS AND

ARMOUR, mostly of the 17th–19th centuries, and paintings of Oriental scenes by 19th-century French artists.

Room 9 (now the bookshop), in the south-west corner, contains 19th-century English paintings, including 'The Arab Tent', by Landseer. Room 10, beyond, is hung with oil paintings by Bonington and Delacroix. A passage on the left, with fine watercolours by Bonington and Turner, leads to Room 11, which has notable 18th-century French furniture (some of it from the workshops of Boulle), a painting of Louis XIV and his heirs attributed to François de Troy, and busts by Coysevox of Louis XIV and of Charles Le Brun, the director of his Academy of Fine Arts. Room 12, behind the Grand Staircase, contains 18th-century French decorative art, including fine selections of Sèvres porcelain and gold boxes. Room 2, beyond, the last room visited, has furniture by Boulle and beautiful turquoise and dark blue Sèvres porcelain. Among the paintings are 'The Centurion Cornelius', now attributed to a follower of Rembrandt, 'Isabelle Brandt' (his first wife), by Rubens, 'River Scene at Dordrecht', by Cuyp, and a 'Family Group' by Van der Helst.

WESTMINSTER ABBEY Plan VIII, C3

STATIONS: WESTMINSTER, Bridge Street, to the NE, and ST JAMES'S PARK, Broadway, to the W, both on the Circle and District lines. — BUSES Nos. 3, 11, 24, 29, 70, 76, 77A, 88, and 159 all pass the abbey.

ADMISSION daily from 8 a.m. to 6 p.m. (to 7.45 on Wednesdays), but on Sundays only the nave and its aisles are open. Services are held on Sundays at 8, 10.30, and 11.40 a.m. and 3 and 6.30 p.m.; on weekdays at 7.30 (except Saturdays), 8, 9 (for the pupils of Westminster School), 12.30 (except Saturdays), and 5 (Saturdays at 3). Guided Tours on Mondays–Fridays at 10, 10.30, 11, 2, 2.30, and 3; on Saturdays at 10, 11, and 12.30 (less frequently in November–March). On Ash Wednesday, Good Friday, and Christmas Day the abbey is open for service only.—The CHOIR and its aisles, with the whole east end of the church, are open on Mondays–Fridays, 9 to 4.45 (last adm. at 4), on Wednesdays also 6 to 7.45 (free); on Saturdays, 9 to 2.45 (last adm. at 2) and 3.45 to 5.45 (last adm. at 5); visitors must obtain tickets from a verger at either the north or the south gate of the choir aisles. —The CHAPTER HOUSE and the CHAMBER OF THE PYX are open on Mondays–Saturdays from 10.30 to 12 and 1 to 6 (to 3.30 in October–February; free), and the NORMAN UNDERCROFT, with the abbey museum, daily from 10.30 to 4; all are closed on New Year's Day, Good Friday, Christmas Eve and Day, and Boxing Day. —The ABBEY GARDEN is open on Thursdays from 10 to 6 (October–March, to 4). Band Concerts in August and September, 12.30 to 2.

The usual ENTRANCE to the abbey is from Broad Sanctuary by the West Door.

The Chapter House, the Chamber of the Pyx and the Norman Undercroft may also be approached from Dean's Yard by the South Cloister.

WESTMINSTER ABBEY, officially the Collegiate Church of St Peter, is the premier church of England not of cathedral status. Refounded in the 11th century by Edward the Confessor, it has been the scene of the coronation of the English sovereigns from William the Conqueror in 1066 to Elizabeth II in 1953, and most of the English kings from Henry III to George II, with their consorts, are buried here. No church is more intimately connected with English history (the Chapter House, for instance, was the meeting place of early parliaments), and interment within the abbey walls has for centuries been considered the most fitting honour that a nation can bestow on its illustrious sons. The abbey is crowded with monuments, some to persons long since forgotten and others of doubtful artistic value. Many of the monuments are to men who are buried elsewhere, and as a whole they tend to distract attention from the architecture of the abbey church itself.

The eastern part of the church, built in the 13th century, is the purest example in the country of the Early English style. The nave, rebuilt in the late 14th century by Henry Yevele, called 'the greatest English architect', was designed to correspond with the existing work. The only important additions to the medieval church have been the splendid chapel added at the east end by Henry VII and the twin west towers raised in the 18th century. The abbey is 513 ft long, including Henry VII's Chapel, 75 ft wide across the nave and aisles and 200 ft across the transepts; the nave, 102 ft high to vault, is the loftiest Gothic nave in England (York Minster 99½ ft). The height of the western towers is 225 ft.

Westminster Abbey is not the seat of a bishop, neither is it a parish church. It is a 'royal peculiar', a distinction shared only with St George's Chapel in Windsor Castle. The abbey is under the jurisdiction of a Dean and Chapter who are subject only to the sovereign, and neither the Archbishop of Canterbury nor the Bishop of London has any authority over its affairs.

The abbey occupies a site once known as Thorney Island, a tract of low ground apparently surrounded by water. Here, according to tradition, a church was built by Sebert, king of the East Saxons, and consecrated in 616 by Mellitus, the first bishop of London. The first authentic church is that of a Benedictine abbey founded before 750 and known as 'Westminster' (i.e., 'west monastery') from its position in relation to the City of London. The abbey was rebuilt on a larger scale some time after his

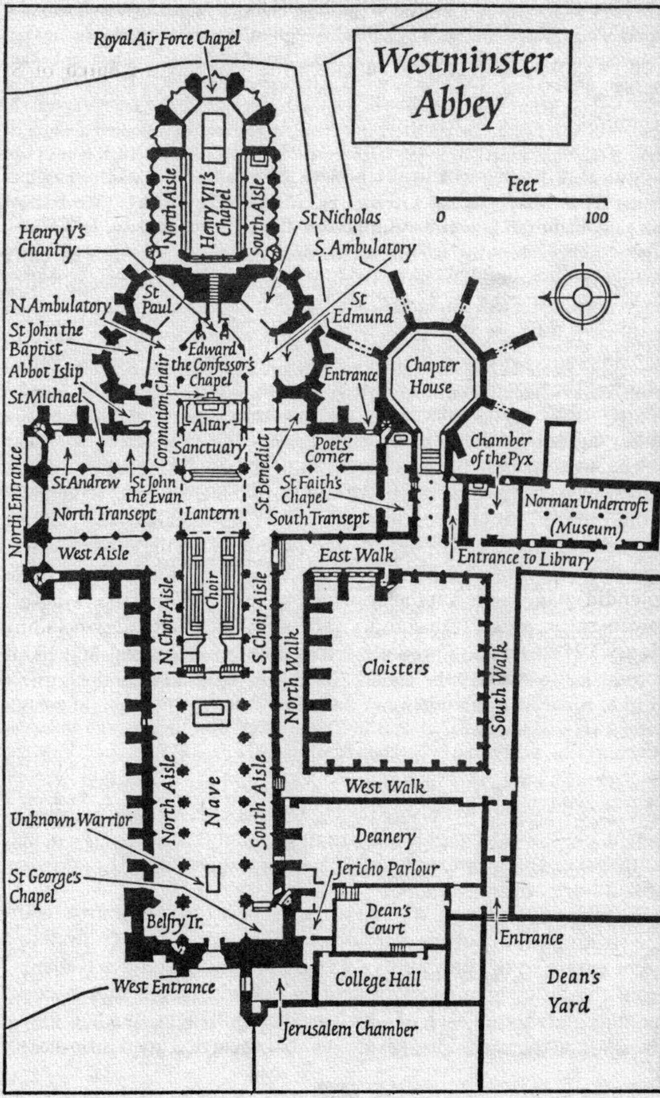

Westminster Abbey
Royal Air Force Chapel
Feet
0
100
North Aisle
Henry VII's Chapel
South Aisle
St Nicholas
S. Ambulatory
Henry V's Chantry
St Paul
N. Ambulatory
St Edmund
St John the Baptist
Edward the Confessor's Chapel
Chapter House
Entrance
Abbot Islip
Coronation Chair
St Michael
Altar
Sanctuary
St Benedict
Poets' Corner
Chamber of the Pyx
North Entrance
St Andrew
St John the Evan
St Faith's Chapel
North Transept
Lantern
South Transept
Norman Undercroft (Museum)
West Aisle
East Walk
Entrance to Library
Choir
N. Choir Aisle
S. Choir Aisle
North Walk
Cloisters
South Walk
North Aisle
Nave
South Aisle
West Walk
Unknown Warrior
Deanery
St George's Chapel
Jericho Parlour
Belfry Tr.
Dean's Court
Entrance
College Hall
Dean's Yard
West Entrance
Jerusalem Chamber

accession in 1042 by Edward the Confessor, and the church, which followed a Norman plan, was consecrated by him in 1065, shortly before his death. In 1163 the Confessor was canonized and his remains transferred to the place of honour behind the high altar. A Lady Chapel was added at the east end in 1220 by Henry III, but in 1245 the king determined to rebuild the entire church on a more magnificent scale in honour of St Edward. The architect was Henry of Reims, who adopted the French style of the time, especially in the arrangement of polygonal chapels radiating from the ambulatory, and by 1269, when the church was rededicated, it was completed as far as the fourth bay of the nave. Henry III was buried in the church in 1272 and from this time (until the 19th century) it became the royal burial place. In 1298 the domestic buildings of the abbey were largely destroyed by fire, and the existing remains date from the 13th–14th centuries, except for the Norman work surviving in the Chamber of the Pyx and the nearby Undercroft.

The western part of the Norman nave was left standing until 1376, when it was rebuilt in the style of the remainder of the church by Henry Yevele, the architect of the nave of Canterbury Cathedral. The work was largely completed by 1388, except for the nave vaulting, raised by Abbot Islip in 1506. The Henry V Chantry was added in 1441, but in 1503 the Lady Chapel was demolished in favour of a splendid new chapel intended by Henry VII as the burial place of the saintly Henry VI, whose canonization he hoped to secure. But the king's body was never transferred from Windsor and in 1509 the chapel (completed in 1519) became the resting-place of Henry VII himself. In 1532 Abbot Islip was buried in the chantry chapel he had built for himself off the north ambulatory.

At the Reformation the abbey suffered the same fate as other religious establishments. In 1540 it became the seat of a bishopric, which lasted, however, only for ten years. The monks returned under the Catholic Mary Tudor, but they were removed again by Elizabeth I, who in 1561 placed the abbey under an independent Dean and Chapter (originally twelve prebendaries, but now five canons residentiary), who still govern it today. The renewal of the outer stonework, begun by Sir Christopher Wren in 1688, has gone on practically ever since, so that the exterior is by no means a faithful copy of the medieval church. The Gothick west towers, with the gable between them, were raised by Nicholas Hawksmoor, a pupil of Wren, in 1734–9, and Henry VII's Chapel was refaced by James Wyatt in 1822. The façade of the north transept was completely recast by Sir George Gilbert Scott and J. L. Pearson in 1875–92, and the west front and south transept restored by J. T. Micklethwaite after 1898. The central tower intended by Wren, however, has never been built. Further extensive restorations of the fabric have been undertaken in recent years.

Entering by the great WEST DOOR the visitor will be impressed by the striking beauty of the interior of the church, an effect owed to a great extent to the harmony of its proportions. The nave is divided from the aisles by arcades of acutely pointed arches supported by circular piers round each of which are grouped eight attached shafts, the shaft on the nave side of every pier being carried up to form a rib of the lofty fan vault. Above the arcade runs the triforium, with its graceful tracery and series of small carved heads, and higher still is the spacious clerestory. The cleaning of the stonework and the gilding of the roof bosses and ribs (1964) has enhanced the beauty of the great church. The chandeliers were presented in 1965.

It is as well to survey the architecture of the church as a whole before studying the numerous monuments (some of the older of which have been effectively recoloured). The north transept has east and west aisles (that on the east once divided into three chapels), but the south transept has an east aisle only (the Poets' Corner), the place of the west aisle being occupied by the cloisters, which abut against the south side of the church. From the choir opens a series of apsidal chapels and, on the east, the great chapel of Henry VII. In the centre is the chapel of St Edward the Confessor, the 'burial-place of kings', with the high altar brought rather far forward on its west side, as a result of which the ritual choir has been extended beyond the transepts into the first three bays of the nave, an arrangement uncommon in England but probably adopted to provide space for coronations and other ceremonies. There is practically no ancient glass in the abbey.

A few yards from the west door is perhaps the best known and in some ways the most moving memorial in the church, the grave of an UNKNOWN WARRIOR, brought from France and buried here on 11 November 1920 as representative of more than a million British who gave their lives in the First World War. He rests in soil brought from the battlefields, under an inscribed slab of black marble quarried in Belgium. On a pillar to the north-east hangs the Padre's Flag, a Union Jack carried in France during the First World War and used to cover the grave during the first twelve months. Below it is the Congressional medal of Honour, the highest military distinction of the United States, bestowed on the Unknown Warrior in 1921. Nearer the west door is a memorial stone to Sir Winston Churchill (d. 1965), who is buried at Bladon (Oxfordshire).

A stone farther east indicates the grave of George Peabody (d. 1869), the only American buried in the abbey before his remains were removed to Massachusetts. Other slabs in the nave mark the graves of the architects, Sir Charles Barry (d. 1860), Sir George Gilbert Scott (d. 1878), G. E. Street (d. 1881), and J. L. Pearson (d. 1897); Sir James Outram (d. 1863), Lord Clyde (d. 1863), and Lord Lawrence (d. 1879), all of Indian Mutiny fame; Thomas Telford (d. 1834) and Robert Stephenson (d. 1859), the engineers; David Livingstone (d. 1873), the African missionary; and the statesmen, Bonar Law (d. 1923) and Neville Chamberlain (d. 1940). Telford's slab was replaced in 1974 by one of cast iron, with brass lettering.

The Old Baptistery, under the South-West Tower, is now ST GEORGE'S CHAPEL, fitted up by Sir Ninian Comper and dedicated in 1932 to those who died in 1914–18. On the wrought-iron screen hangs a trophy presented by the Mayor of Verdun, and slabs in the floor of the chapel mark the graves of Field-Marshals Viscount Plumer (d. 1932) and Viscount Allenby (d. 1936). A case to the right of the entrance contains memorial books with the names of civilians killed in 1939–45, and above this is a tablet in memory of President Franklin D. Roosevelt (d. 1945). On a pillar to the left is a contemporary portrait of Richard II (1377–99), the oldest known portrait of an English monarch, and below this is a memorial (1985) to the Earl and Countess Mountbatten.

All the monuments in the nave aisles date from after the Reformation. In the floor at the west end of the SOUTH AISLE is a stone in memory of Lord Baden-Powell (d. 1941), the founder of the Boy Scouts. On the south wall is the Abbot's Pew, a small oak gallery erected in the 16th century by Abbot Islip and communicating with the adjoining house (now the Deanery) built by him. Below is a monument to William Congreve (d. 1729), the dramatist, by Francis Bird, and in the third bay beyond the cloister door one to Major John André, hanged in 1780 during the American War as a spy; the bas-relief below, designed by Robert Adam and carved by Peter van Gelder, shows George Washington receiving his vain petition for a soldier's death. This and the next bay contain fine 13th-century shields-of-arms.

At the east ends of both nave aisles are desks where tickets for the whole eastern part of the church are obtained. Entrance to this is by the North Choir Aisle or (preferably) by the Ritual Choir.

The south aisle is extended by the SOUTH CHOIR AISLE (no general admission). On the left are the characteristic Elizabethan monument of Thomas Owen (d. 1598), with his effigy in alabaster still showing traces of painting, and a tablet to William Tyndale (d. 1536), translator of the Bible. Farther on is the fine marble monument with effigy of William Thynne (d. 1584). On the right (second bay) are monuments to Dr Isaac Watts (d. 1748), the hymn-writer, John Wesley (d. 1791) and Charles Wesley (d. 1788); all are buried elsewhere. On either side of the over-elaborate monument to Admiral Sir Cloudsley Shovel (d. 1707) are memorials to Lord Clive of India (d. 1774) and Admiral Blake (d. 1657), and above is a bust by Rysbrack of Sir Godfrey Kneller (d. 1723). In the floor near by are slabs to Sybil Thorndike (d. 1976), the actress (whose ashes are buried here), and to Noël Coward (d. 1984), actor and playwright.

On the north side of the nave, against the Choir Screen, is a monument by Rysbrack to Sir Isaac Newton (d. 1727), discoverer of the law of gravity.

Newton is buried in the nave close by, and here also are the graves of the scientists, Lord Kelvin (d. 1907), Lord Rutherford (d. 1937), and Michael Faraday (d. 1867). Floor-slabs in the North Aisle mark the graves of Charles Darwin and Sir John Herschel (d. 1871), the astronomer, while the latter's father, Sir William Herschel (d. 1822), the discoverer of Uranus, and his son, also Sir William (d. 1917), the author of the fingerprint identity system, are also commemorated.

In the floor of the NORTH AISLE is a stone inscribed 'O Rare Ben Johnson', indicating the grave of the poet, Ben Jonson (d. 1637); the original stone is in the wall below the monument to Thomas Banks (d. 1805), the sculptor. In the west bays are floor-slabs to David Lloyd George (d. 1945), buried at Llanystumdwy in North Wales, to Ramsay MacDonald (d. 1937), Ernest Bevin (d. 1951), and Clement Attlee (d. 1967), the Labour statesmen, and to Sidney and Beatrice Webb (d. 1947, 1943), the Fabian sociologists. At the west end is a large monument by Sir Richard Westmacott to Charles James Fox (d. 1806), the Whig politician.

Some of the windows in the aisle commemorate famous engineers, including Sir Charles Parsons (d. 1931) and Sir Henry Royce (d. 1933). The North-West Tower, or BELFREY TOWER, called by Dean Stanley the 'Whig Corner', contains monuments to the third Marquess of Salisbury (d. 1903), with a bronze effigy by W. Goscombe John, and to Viscount Howe (d. 1758), by Scheemakers, given by the province of Massachusetts, at that time still a British colony; and the busts of Lord John Russell (d. 1878), by Tweed of Joseph Chamberlain (d. 1914), and by Onslow Ford of General Gordon of Khartoum (d. 1885). Over the west door are figures of Christ, St Peter, and St Edward the Confessor, carved in teak by Michael Clark (1967), and a large monument to William Pitt the Younger (d. 1806), by Westmacott. The great 15th-century west window is filled with painted glass of 1735.

The CHOIR SCREEN was designed, in the Decorated style, by Edward Blore (1834). The opening in the centre admits to the RITUAL CHOIR of four bays, three of them occupying the eastern part of the nave; the stalls are by Blore (1847). Above the central space between the choir and the sanctuary rises the LANTERN, the roof of which was destroyed by bombing in 1941. From this space there are good views of the great rose windows in the transepts: that on the north was designed by Sir James Thornhill (1722) but altered in the restoration of Scott and Pearson; the window on the south, the largest of its kind in England, was reglazed in 1902.

The SANCTUARY, within the altar-rails, is the impressive setting of coronations; it has a mosaic pavement (usually covered by a carpet) executed by a Roman artist in 1268 for Abbot Ware. On the north are the three finest medieval tombs in the abbey: that on the east is of Edmund Crouchback (d. 1296), Earl of Lancaster, second son of Henry III and founder of the house of Lancaster, and next to this is the tomb of his cousin, Aymer de Valence (d. 1324), Earl of Pembroke. Around the tombs are finely sculptured 'weepers' or statuettes of relatives, while the canopies bear the figures of the earls on horseback. The other and smallest tomb is that of Aveline, Countess of Lancaster (d. 1273), wife of Edmund Crouchback. The Altar and Reredos, designed by Sir George Gilbert Scott (1867), have a glass mosaic of the Last Supper by Salviati and sculptured figures by Armstead. On the south of the Sanctuary are the early-14th-century oak Sedilia, with defaced paintings identified as Sebert, St Peter and King Ethelbert, and the tomb of Anne of Cleves (d. 1557), the fourth queen of Henry VIII, above which is hung a 16th-century Brussels tapestry.

The NORTH TRANSEPT contains the graves and monuments of many famous statesmen. On the east side are statues by John Gibson of Sir Robert Peel (d. 1850); by Brock of W. E. Gladstone (d. 1898; buried in front); by Boehm of Lord Beaconsfield (d. 1881); and by Chantrey of George Canning (d. 1827); and a monument to John Holles, Duke of Newcastle (d. 1711), by James Gibbs and Francis Bird. On the west are a large monument by the elder John Bacon to William Pitt, Earl of Chatham (d. 1778); and statues of Lord Palmerston (d. 1865) and Lord Castlereagh (d. 1822). Beneath the pavement are the graves of Henry Grattan (d. 1820), the Irish patriot, William Wilberforce, C. J. Fox, and the elder and younger Pitts. In the centre of the west aisle of the transept is the large monument by Flaxman to the Earl of Mansfield (d. 1793), Lord Chief Justice, and on the walls are busts of Warren Hastings (d. 1818), Governor-General of India, and Richard Cobden (d. 1865), the apostle of free trade. The north-west window (1911) illustrates Bunyan's *Pilgrim's Progress*.

The NORTH CHOIR AISLE, opening to the west, is often called the 'Musicians' Aisle'. Those commemorated here include (on the south) the composers Orlando Gibbons (d. 1625) and Henry Purcell (d. 1695), who was organist from 1679 (and is buried near by), and (on the north) John Blow (d. 1708) and William Croft (d. 1727), composers and likewise organists, and Dr Charles Burney (d. 1814), the historian of music. Among the floor-slabs to more recent composers can be read the names of Edward Elgar (d. 1934), R. Vaughan Williams (d. 1958), Benjamin Britten (d. 1976), and William Walton (d. 1983).

Also commemorated in the aisle are William Wilberforce (d. 1833), chief opponent of the slave-trade (a good statue by Samuel Joseph), and several scientists, notably Sir Joseph Hooker (d. 1911), the botanist; Lord Lister (d. 1912), the founder of antiseptic surgery; and Alfred Russel Wallace (d. 1913) and Charles Darwin (d. 1882), the scientists who independently formulated the theory of evolution. The painted shields-of-arms date from the 13th century; the window in the third bay was given by J. W. Gerard, American ambassador in Berlin in 1914–17, in memory of British prisoners who died in Germany in the First World War. On the north wall is a monument to Spencer Perceval, assassinated in 1812 in the House of Commons by a madman; the relief, by Westmacott, shows the incident.

The east aisle of the North Transept was formed by combining the CHAPELS OF SS. JOHN THE EVANGELIST, MICHAEL, AND ANDREW. At the entrance is the huge monument by Joseph Wilton to General James Wolfe (d. 1759), the hero of Quebec. On the left in the aisle is a memorial to Sir John Franklin (d. 1847), lost in the search for the North-West Passage, with an inscription by Tennyson. To the right is the unusual monument to Sir Francis Vere (d. 1609), a noted Elizabethan general, with his effigy below and four kneeling warriors supporting a slab with his accoutrements, and in the next chapel is an over-dramatic monument by Roubiliac to Lady Elizabeth Nightingale (d. 1734). In the north chapel is the large cenotaph of Lord Norris (d. 1601), and around the walls are memorials including statues by E. H. Baily of Thomas Telford (d. 1834), the engineer, by Flaxman of John Kemble (d. 1823), the actor, and by Chantrey of Mrs Siddons (d. 1831), the actress, inspired by Reynolds's 'Tragic Muse'; tablets to Sir Humphry Davy (d. 1829), inventor of the safety lamp, and Lord Rayleigh (d. 1919), the physicist; and a bust of Sir James Young Simpson (d. 1870), who introduced the use of chloroform.

On the left of the North Ambulatory is the chantry CHAPEL OF ABBOT ISLIP, which is in two storeys. The lower (adm. on application to a verger), containing the grave of Abbot John Islip (d. 1532), who completed the nave, is separated from the ambulatory by a screen erected by the abbot himself and carved with his rebuses (an eye with a man grasping a slip of a tree, and a man slipping from a branch). The upper storey, fitted up as a memorial chapel to nurses, midwives, and ambulance workers who lost their lives in the Second

World War, has a window by Hugh Easton (1950). In the ambulatory, the backs of the tombs of Edmund Crouchback and Aymer de Valence are worth inspection.

The first of the apsidal chapels opening off the North Ambulatory is the CHAPEL OF ST JOHN THE BAPTIST, entered through the so-called Chapel of St Erasmus, in reality no more than a vestibule. It has 16th-century doors and remains of paintings, and over the entrance is a beautifully carved niche with a triple canopy, brought by Abbot Islip from a vanished chapel. The Chapel of St John contains tombs of 15th-century abbots and, in the centre, the large marble table-tomb of Thomas Cecil, Earl of Exeter (d. 1623), with effigies of himself and his first wife. His second wife declined the less honourable position on his left hand and is buried in Winchester Cathedral. The small tomb of 1305 to the north-east contains the remains of Humphrey and Mary de Bohun, grandchildren of Edward I.

The next chapel opening off the ambulatory is the CHAPEL OF ST PAUL. On the right are the tombs of Lord Bouchier (d. 1431), standard-bearer to Henry V; Francis, Lord Cottington, Chancellor of the Exchequer to Charles I (d. in exile in Spain, 1652); and the Countess of Sussex (d. 1589), founder of Sidney Sussex College at Cambridge. On the left, by the door, is a bust of Sir Rowland Hill (d. 1879), the originator of penny postage. The grille of Queen Eleanor's tomb (see below), fine wrought-iron work of 1294 by Thomas of Leighton (Buzzard), can be seen on the other side of the ambulatory.

Steps lead up from the North Ambulatory to Henry VII's Chapel, with its two side aisles. Under the one-way system now imposed on visitors, the North Aisle is visited first, then the Chapel itself. A bridge (1970) over the steps provides access to the Chantry of Henry V and the Chapel of Edward the Confessor (with its royal tombs), and the return is then made by the bridge to the South Aisle of Henry VII's Chapel.

The NORTH AISLE (or Elizabeth Chapel) is chiefly notable for the elaborate tomb (well restored in 1956) of Elizabeth I (d. 1603), the work of Maximilian Powtrain and John de Critz, with the effigy of the queen in white marble. Below the cornice of the canopy are the arms of monarchs of England beginning with Edward the Confessor and of others of Elizabeth's kin. In a recess is the ring traditionally given as a pledge of clemency by the queen to her favourite, the Earl of Essex, but intercepted by the Countess of Nottingham when he attempted to send it back on his condemnation. Mary I (d. 1558) is buried in the same tomb as her sister and successor. At the foot of the tomb is the

Martyrs' Memorial (1977) to those who 'divided at the Reformation by different convictions, laid down their lives for Christ and conscience sake'. At the east end of the chapel (the 'Innocents' Corner') are the tombs of two infant children of James I who died in 1606–7. The younger is represented in an alabaster cradle, an unusual but delicately carved monument by Maximilian Colt. A small 17th-century sarcophagus close by contains bones generally thought to be those of Edward V and his brother Richard, Duke of York, sons of Edward IV, the princes reputedly murdered in the Tower in 1483. Near by is the grave of Anne Mowbray (d. 1481), the child Duchess of York, who was buried here in 1965 in the lead coffin in which she was found at Stepney.

The Lady Chapel is invariably called the CHAPEL OF HENRY VII after its royal founder, for whom it was built in 1503–19. Attributed to Robert Vertue, the king's master-mason, it is the richest example in England of the late-Perpendicular Gothic style, the beauty of its decoration culminating in the exquisite tracery of the fan vaulting. 'On entering,' writes Washington Irving, 'the eye is astonished by the pomp of architecture and elaborate beauty of sculptured detail. The very walls are wrought into universal ornament, incrusted with tracery, and scooped into niches crowded with statues of saints and martyrs. Stone seems, by the cunning labour of the chisel, to have been robbed of its weight and density, suspended aloft as if by magic, and the fretted roof achieved with the wonderful minuteness and airy security of a cobweb.' The chapel consists of a nave, with five smaller chapels radiating from the eastern apse and north and south aisles entered from outside the 16th-century doors. These are of oak, plated with bronze, carved with heraldic devices referring to the ancestry of Henry VII and Elizabeth of York, whose marriage united the Houses of York and Lancaster and brought to an end the Wars of the Roses.

On each side of the nave are the delicately carved stalls of the Knights of the Bath, an order founded by Henry IV in 1399 and reconstituted by George I in 1725, when the chapel was dedicated as the chapel of the order, with the Dean of Westminster as its dean. No installation of knights took place after 1812, however, until the ceremony was revived by George V in 1913, when the present banners were hung above the beautifully carved canopies of the stalls. Each stall bears copper plates with the arms of the present and former holders; the lower seats are for the esquires, three of whom attend each knight. The carved misericords beneath the seats are worth examination. A case at the west end of the chapel contains the sword used by George VI at the service of installation of Knights of the Bath in 1951.

In a vault beneath the pavement between the door and the altar is the grave (without inscription) of George II (d. 1760), the last monarch buried in the abbey, and his queen, Caroline of Anspach (d. 1737). The grave of Edward VI (d. 1553) is below the altar, which is a copy (1935) of the original by Torrigiani, destroyed by iconoclasts in 1641. Behind the altar is the splendid tomb of Henry VII (d. 1509) and Elizabeth of York (d. 1503), the masterpiece of Pietro Torrigiani of Florence, made in 1512–18. It consists of a black marble sarcophagus with a carved frieze of white marble on which rest the fine gilt-bronze effigies of the king and queen. At the sides are gilt-bronze medallions with the figures of angels and saints, and the tomb is enclosed by a bronze grille of English workmanship. The royal remains actually rest in the vault below, and here also is buried James I (d. 1625).

The north chapel of the apse is filled with the over-ornate tomb of George Villiers, Duke of Buckingham (d. 1628), the favourite of James I and Charles I. In the next chapel is the Roll of Honour of the 1,497 airmen of Britain and her allies who fell in the Battle of Britain (1940). The large monument is to John Sheffield, Duke of Buckingham (d. 1721), and a slab in front of it marks the grave of Anne of Denmark (d. 1619), queen of James I. The east chapel, now the ROYAL AIR FORCE CHAPEL, was dedicated in 1947 to those of the flying forces who lost their lives in the Battle of Britain. The excellent stained-glass window by Hugh Easton includes in its design the badges of the 63 fighter squadrons who took part in the battle, and a line from Shakespeare, 'We few, we happy few, we band of brothers'. A hole in the stonework, caused by a bomb, remains. The ashes of Lord Trenchard (d. 1956), the 'father of the R.A.F.', are buried beneath the floor. In the next chapel is the marble altar-tomb of Dean Stanley (d. 1881), with his effigy by Boehm. The south chapel of the apse is almost filled by an over-elaborate monument to the Duke of Richmond and Lennox (d. 1624), cousin of James I.

Oliver Cromwell, Henry Ireton (his lieutenant and son-in-law), Admiral Robert Blake, and John Bradshaw, the regicide, were originally buried in the east chapel, but at the Restoration their bodies were exhumed and dishonoured. Blake was reinterred in St Margaret's churchyard, but the heads of Cromwell, Ireton, and Bradshaw were struck off and exposed on the roof of Westminster Hall.

The bridge from the top of the steps outside Henry VII's Chapel crosses the ambulatory to the CHANTRY OF HENRY V, built by John of Thirsk (1441). On the tomb of Henry V (d. 1422) rests his wooden effigy, robbed of its silver-gilt plates and its solid silver head in the reign of Henry VIII, but given a new bronze head in 1971. The body of his queen, Catherine of Valois (d. 1437), Shakespeare's 'beautiful Kate', buried in the old Lady Chapel, was disinterred at its demolition and not buried here until 1776.

The chantry forms the entrance to the CHAPEL OF ST EDWARD THE CONFESSOR, the most sacred part of the abbey, built over the apse of the Saxon church and structurally the east end of the choir. In the centre is the large but mutilated Shrine of Edward the Confessor (d. 1066), long a goal of pilgrimage. The Purbeck marble tomb (one of the two in England still containing the body of its saint; the other is in Dorset) was made in 1268 by Peter of Rome at the order of Henry III and still retains traces of its splendid mosaics. The recesses on each side enabled pilgrims to kneel in prayer or in hope of a cure from sickness. The golden feretory decorated with gold images of saints and precious stones, stolen at the Dissolution, was replaced by a wooden superstructure by John Feckenham (1556–60), the last abbot of Westminster, and is usually covered by a pall presented by Edward VII in 1902.

On the north side of the chapel are the magnificent tombs of Henry III (d. 1272), the builder of the abbey, and (right) his daughter-in-law, Eleanor of Castile (d. 1290), the first queen of Edward I. The king's tomb, of Purbeck marble decorated with glass mosaics, was designed by Peter of Rome, while Eleanor's tomb was made by Richard Crundale. Both tombs have splendid gilt-bronze effigies (1291; the earliest in England) by William Torel, a London goldsmith, and both are covered by 15th-century testers or canopies. To the left is the plain altar-tomb of Edward I (d. 1307), with a now illegible 16th-century inscription, *Scottorum malleus*. When the tomb was opened in 1774 his body (6 ft 2 in. long) was in good preservation, clothed in royal robes with a gilt crown. The 15th-century carved stone screen which forms the back of the high altar has scenes on the cornice from the life of the Confessor (worth close inspection). Against it stands the CORONATION CHAIR, made of oak by Walter, the 'king's painter', for Edward I, and attached to this underneath is the famous STONE OF SCONE, a block of sandstone used as the coronation seat of the kings of Scotland at Scone Abbey from about 850 and carried off by

Edward I in 1297 as a token of the subjugation of Scotland. In the chair, which was made to hold it, every English monarch since Edward II (except Edward V, who died young, and Edward VIII, who abdicated) has been crowned, but on these occasions the chair is covered with a cloth of gold and moved into the sanctuary before the high altar. Against the screen are the state sword (7 ft long) and wooden shield of Edward III.

On the south side of the chapel adjacent is the tomb of Richard II (d. 1400) and his first queen, Anne of Bohemia (d. 1394), with gilt-bronze figures (by Nicholas Broker and Godfrey Prest) and a painted tester. Next to this is the elaborate tomb of Edward III (d. 1377), with a gilt-bronze effigy (probably by John Orchard), a finely carved oak tester above, and niches round the sides for statuettes of his twelve children of which only those on the outside survive. Both these tombs are thought to have been designed by Henry Yevele, who was master-mason to Edward III. At the end is the black marble tomb of Philippa of Hainaut (d. 1369), queen of Edward III, with a white marble effigy by Henniquin of Liège.

By re-crossing the bridge from Henry V's Chantry, the SOUTH AISLE of Henry VII's Chapel (sometimes called the Lady Margaret Chapel) is reached. The first of its several fine tombs is that of Margaret, Countess of Lennox (d. 1578), the mother of Henry Darnley (second husband of Mary, Queen of Scots), who is identified as the foremost figure on the south side. Next comes the splendid tomb of Mary, Queen of Scots (d. 1587), who was beheaded by Elizabeth I and buried first in Peterborough Cathedral, but was removed here by Mary's son, James I. This, the last royal tomb erected in the abbey (about 1612), has an effigy in the attitude of prayer under the lofty canopy. The tomb on the east is that of Margaret Beaufort (d. 1509), Countess of Richmond and mother of Henry VII, a patron of learning and foundress of St John's and Christ's Colleges at Cambridge. A great benefactress also of the abbey, she died in the abbot's house (now the deanery). The tomb, another magnificent work by Torrigiani (1511–13), supports a gilt-bronze effigy in which the exquisite modelling of the hands is particularly notable. The grille round the tomb was removed and sold in 1822, but rediscovered and brought back in 1914. At the east end is a large monument, by Kent and Scheemakers, to General Monck, Duke of Albemarle (d. 1670), who helped to restore the Stuarts, and a vault in front contains the graves of Charles II (d. 1685), Mary II

(d. 1694) and her husband William III (d. 1702), and Queen Anne (d. 1714) and her consort Prince George of Denmark (d. 1708). The beautiful carving on the east wall is characteristic of the chapel. At the west end are a medallion by W. Goscombe John to Earl Cromer (d. 1916), the 'regenerator of Egypt', and tablets to the Marquess Curzon (d. 1925) and Cecil Rhodes (d. 1902).

On the left at the foot of the steps from Henry VII's Chapel is the SOUTH AMBULATORY. The first of the apsidal chapels on this side is the CHAPEL OF ST NICHOLAS, which has a good 15th-century stone screen. On the right is the tomb of Philippa, Duchess of York (d. 1431), and next to this is the monument of Elizabeth, Duchess of Northumberland (d. 1776), designed by Robert Adam and sculptured by Nicholas Read. The vault below the chapel is the burial-place of the Percys, Dukes of Northumberland, the only family with the right of interment in the abbey. In the centre of the chapel is the splendid marble tomb of Sir George Villiers (d. 1606) and his wife, parents of the Duke of Buckingham, with effigies by Nicholas Stone. On the east are the characteristic Elizabethan monuments of the wife and daughter of Lord Burghley, Elizabeth I's minister (1589), and of Anne, Duchess of Somerset (d. 1587), widow of the Protector. In the ambulatory opposite is an oak Retable or Altarpiece, late-13th-century French or English work, richly decorated ('the most remarkable example of early medieval painting'), but sadly damaged by misuse.

The CHAPEL OF ST EDMUND, king and martyr, is separated from the ambulatory by a medieval oak screen. On the right, inside, is the remarkable tomb of William de Valence (d. 1296), Earl of Pembroke and half-brother of Henry III. It consists of a stone altar-tomb surmounted by an oak chest on which rests an effigy in oak covered with gilded copper plates and enriched with remains of Limoges enamel. On the left of this is the fine Jacobean monument of Edward Talbot (d. 1618), eighth Earl of Shrewsbury, and his wife, and on the north-east of the chapel is the seated figure in alabaster of Lady Elizabeth Russell (d. 1601), the oldest non-recumbent statue in the abbey. In the centre are the table-tombs of Robert Waldeby (d. 1397), archbishop of York, who accompanied the Black Prince to France, and of Eleanor de Bohun (d. 1399), Duchess of Gloucester, whose brass, showing her in the habit of a nun, is the largest and finest in the abbey. A slab near by marks the grave of Edward Bulwer Lytton (d. 1873), the novelist. On the east of the chapel are an alabaster tomb with the effigy of Frances, Duchess of Suffolk (d. 1559), mother of Lady Jane Grey, and the small alabaster effigies, unfortunately mutilated, of two infant children of Edward III. Beside the screen is a fine alabaster tomb with the effigy in armour of John of Eltham (d. 1337), second son of Edward II. Opposite, in the ambulatory, are the backs of the tombs of Richard II and Edward III, with enamelled coats-of-arms and exquisite little brass statuettes on the latter.

The last chapel on the south is the CHAPEL OF ST BENEDICT (usually closed, and best seen from the transept). Near the railings is an alabaster tomb with the effigy of Simon Langham (d. 1376), abbot of Westminster and later archbishop of Canterbury and Lord Chancellor of Edward III. Between this chapel and the next is a small 13th-century altar-tomb containing the remains of children of Henry III and Edward I. Opposite in the ambulatory is an early-14th-century tomb said to contain the remains of Sebert (d. 616), the reputed founder of the church; on the back of the Sedilia above it are defaced 14th-century paintings.

Part of the SOUTH TRANSEPT and its aisle is known as the POETS' CORNER, to many the most interesting quarter of the abbey. On the east of the aisle are busts of John Dryden (d. 1700), by P. Scheemakers, and Henry Wadsworth Longfellow (d. 1882), by Brock, the latter placed here by English admirers of the American poet. Next comes the fine Purbeck marble altar-tomb, under a canopy, erected in 1556 for Geoffrey Chaucer (d. 1400), the father of English poetry. Beneath the pavement in front are the graves of Robert Browning (d. 1889) and Alfred, Lord Tennyson (d. 1892). Close by are the ashes of T. S. Eliot (d. 1965) and John Masefield (d. 1967), and memorial slabs to Gerard Manley Hopkins (d. 1889), a Roman Catholic (unveiled in 1975), Henry James (d. 1916), the Rev. C. L. Dodgson (Lewis Carroll; d. 1898), W. H. Auden (d. 1973), George Eliot (Mary Ann Evans; d. 1880), and Dylan Thomas (d. 1953). Another memorial (1969) is to Lord Byron (d. 1824), whose body, refused admission to the abbey, is buried at Hucknall Torkard (Nottinghamshire). On the east wall of the aisle outside, near the door providing an exit from the abbey, is a tablet (1954) to William Caxton (d. 1491) who in 1477 set up the first printing press in England in an alley close by.

On the south wall of the aisle, above the door to the Crypt under the Chapter House (closed to visitors), is a medallion of Ben Jonson (d. 1637), and to the right are a monument (restored in 1778) to Edmund

Spenser (d. 1599), author of the *Faerie Queene*, buried near the Chaucer tomb, and a bust by Rysbrack of John Milton (d. 1674), with a monument below to Thomas Gray (d. 1771). On the pier is a bust of Adam Lindsay Gordon (d. 1870), the Australian poet, and a slab in the floor to the north of this marks the grave of Thomas Parr ('Old Parr'; d. 1635), who is said to have lived under ten sovereigns and attained the age of 152 years. On the west side of the screen between the transept and the aisle are monuments to many famous writers. The monument to William Shakespeare (d. 1616), by Peter Scheemakers, was erected in 1740 and is inscribed with lines from *The Tempest*. The carved heads at the corners of the pedestal represent Elizabeth I, Henry V, and Richard III. On the left are a bust of Dr Samuel Johnson (d. 1784), by Nollekens, and statues of William Wordsworth (d. 1850) and Thomas Campbell (d. 1844). Above these are busts of Samuel Taylor Coleridge (d. 1834), by Thornycroft, and Robert Southey (d. 1843), by Weekes, and above Shakespeare are plaques to John Keats (d. 1821) and Percy Bysshe Shelley (d. 1822). On the right are a bust of Robert Burns (d. 1796), by Steell, a statue of James Thomson (d. 1748), author of *The Seasons* and *Rule, Britannia*, and a tablet to the Brontë Sisters with a line from a poem by Emily, 'with courage to endure'.

In the floor in front of these monuments are the graves of Johnson, Garrick, Sir Henry Irving (d. 1905, the actor), R. B. Sheridan (d. 1816, the playwright), Charles Dickens (d. 1870), and Handel. Farther north are the graves of Thomas Hardy (d. 1928) and Rudyard Kipling (d. 1936). On the south wall of the transept are two 13th-century wall-paintings, uncovered in 1936. Here also is the entrance to the 13th-century CHAPEL OF ST FAITH (reserved for private prayer); formerly the revestry, it contains two 16th-century Brussels tapestries.

Over the door to the chapel is a monument to Oliver Goldsmith (d. 1774), with an epitaph by Dr Johnson and a bust by Nollekens, and to the right are a bronze medallion of John Ruskin (d. 1900) and a copy of the fine bust by Chantrey of Sir Walter Scott (d. 1832). On the west wall are a medallion of Jenny Lind (d. 1887), the 'Swedish nightingale', and a monument to the composer, George Frideric Handel (d. 1759), the last work of Roubiliac. A chamber organ by Snetzler, given in 1965, usually stands near by. By the first pier are busts of William Makepeace Thackeray (d. 1863), by Marochetti, and Lord Macaulay (d. 1859), whose grave is near by, and farther on are a statue by Westmacott of Joseph Addison (d. 1719), and a monument to David

Garrick (d. 1779), the actor. Near the innermost pier are memorials to William Camden (d. 1623), the antiquary, and to George Grote (d. 1871) and Bishop Thirlwall (d. 1875), the historians of Greece (who share a single grave); and on the pier east of this is a bronze bust of William Blake (d. 1827), by Epstein (1957).

A door at the east end of the South Choir Aisle, showing rich but much-worn carving, admits to the CLOISTERS. The earliest and finest work, dating from the mid 13th century, is in the north-east corner; the remainder was recast in 1344–86. Opening off the east walk is the vestibule admitting to the CHAPTER HOUSE, a noble octagonal chamber, 60 ft across, built in 1245–55, probably by Henry of Reims, the builder of the church. A slender central pier of clustered shafts supports the lofty vault, a supposed copy of the original and provided by Sir George Gilbert Scott when he restored the chapter house in 1866. Visitors are provided with overshoes to avoid damage to the remarkably well-preserved 13th-century pavement, the finest of its kind in England. The motifs include the arms of Henry III, the legend of St Edward and the pilgrim, heraldic beasts, and a curious fish (the 'Westminster salmon'). The wall arcades were greatly restored by Scott, though in the original style; they were decorated with a series of 14th-century paintings of which little more than a fragment (the Revelation of St John) has survived (restored in 1920). The tracery of the six large windows, each 39 ft high, was restored by Scott, though again to the former design, and it is probably the earliest example of the Geometrical or Early Decorated style in England. In 1941 much of the glass was destroyed by bombing, but in 1951 the windows were reset including some of the old glass (1882), illustrating scenes from the abbey's history (a memorial to Dean Stanley), and quarries of new glass (by Joan Howson and others) showing the arms of persons connected with the abbey. In the head of the noble doorway ('one of the most beautiful things in English art') is a circular tympanum with the figure of Christ in Majesty (introduced by Scott and not part of the original design), and on either side of this are pairs of censing angels and the beautiful figures of the Virgin and the angel of the Annunciation, 13th-century work of the highest order.

The Chapter House, built to the order of Henry III, has been called the 'cradle of all free parliaments', for here the Great Council met in 1257, and here Parliament assembled from 1352 until 1547, when St Stephen's Chapel in the Palace of Westminster became its regular meeting-place. From then until 1866 the chapter house was used as a repository for state papers. Above the steps on the south side of the Vestibule are tablets to James Russell Lowell (1819–91), the American author, minister in Britain in 1880–85, and to Walter Hines Page (1855–1918), American ambassador in 1913–18. On the north side is a Roman sarcophagus, probably of the 3rd century, with a Saxon lid, or possibly the original lid carved with a cross by the Saxons when they used it for a second burial. The coffin was found under the green on the north side of the abbey nave in 1869. The vestibule has a quadripartite vault supported by Purbeck marble columns and wall-shafts; in the tympanum over the entrance from the cloisters are remains of a carving of the Tree of Jesse. The flying buttresses of the chapter house were added in the 14th century, but the pyramidal roof is modern, replacing a flat roof destroyed about 1740.

On the south side of the vestibule is the entrance to the LIBRARY and Muniment Room (adm. by special permission only), in part of the monks' dormitory, and beyond is the CHAMBER OF THE PYX, entered through a restored Norman doorway with two heavy doors secured by seven locks. Originally a sacristy, part of Edward the Confessor's church, it has a massive central pier and the oldest altar in the abbey. Later it became the royal treasury and the repository of the 'pyx' or chest containing the trial-plates of gold and silver used as standards of reference for the coins of the realm.

The East Walk of the cloisters is extended on the south by the 11th-century Dark Cloister, which emerges into the yard of Westminster School. On the left is the door into the NORMAN UNDERCROFT, the only other surviving part of the Confessor's church, consisting of five vaulted bays below the dormitory. It now contains the abbey museum, which includes architectural fragments, old seals and charters, 14th–15th-century chests (one for copes), and the coronation chair made for Mary II. The wax effigies were carried at the funerals of persons buried in the abbey; the oldest is that of Charles II (d. 1685), the one of Elizabeth I being a copy made in 1760, and others are of Mary II (d. 1694), William III (d. 1702), the Duchess of Richmond ('La Belle Stuart'; d. 1702), Queen Anne (d. 1714), and the Duchess of Buckingham (d. 1743) and her two sons. The figures of the Earl of Chatham and Lord Nelson are not funeral effigies, but were made to attract visitors to the abbey. Previously it had been the custom to show the embalmed bodies of royal persons at their funerals, though sometimes these were replaced by effigies of wood, several of which are preserved here. The oldest, of Edward III (d. 1377), is perhaps the oldest wooden effigy in Europe; others represent Anne of Bohemia (queen of Richard II), Henry VII and his wife Elizabeth of York (both realistically carved), Mary I, and Anne of Denmark (queen of James I).

A passage on the left farther on leads to the charming LITTLE CLOISTER, originally part of the monks' infirmary. On the east are some remains of the INFIRMARY CHAPEL, built about 1160 and seen through a doorway inserted in 1372, but ruinous since the dissolution of the abbey in 1540. Many 12th–13th-century bishops were consecrated here. A passage to the south opens to the secluded ABBEY GARDEN, bounded by Great College Street and Westminster School.

The south walk of the main cloisters was the burial-place of the abbots from 1068 to 1214. Beside a former entrance to the Refectory (part of which survives) are 14th-century recesses which served as cupboards for towels. On the wall is a memorial (by Eric Fraser, 1979) commemorating four centuries of English seamanship; and near by are the graveslabs of J. P. Salomon (d. 1815), the virtuoso who brought Haydn to London, and Muzio Clementi (d. 1832), the composer. The large 18th-century recess in the west walk takes the place of the monks' lavatorium or washing-place. On the wall near by are memorials by Gilbert Ledward to those of the submarine branch of the Royal Navy killed in the two World Wars and to Commandos and members of the Airborne Forces and Special Air Service who died in 1939–45. A passage extending the south walk leads out to Dean's Yard (Route 4).

Another passage on the right opens to the picturesque ABBOT'S COURTYARD (no entry). On the east side of this is the DEANERY (once the abbot's lodging), rebuilt after its destruction by bombing, and on the west is COLLEGE HALL, the old dining room of the abbot, now used by Westminster School. The steps on the north side ascend to the JERICHO PARLOUR, built by Abbot Islip, a panelled ante-room to the JERUSALEM CHAMBER, formerly the abbot's retiring room and now the chapter-room. Built about 1370 by Abbot Litlington and restored in 1956, it has an unusual oak ceiling, an elaborate 17th-century overmantel of wood, and 16th–17th-century tapestries. Henry IV died in the chamber in 1413, thus fulfilling the prophecy that he would die in 'Jerusalem' (Shakespeare's *Henry IV*, Part 2, iv, 5).

WESTMINSTER CATHEDRAL Plan VIII, D1

STATION: VICTORIA, ¼ m. W, on the Southern Region and the Circle, District, and Victoria lines. — BUSES in Victoria Street, see Route 4; to Victoria Station, see Route 8.

ADMISSION daily 6.45 a.m. to 8 p.m. (shorter periods on Good Friday, Easter Saturday and Sunday, Christmas Day, and Boxing Day). Services on Sundays at 7, 8, 9 and 10.30 a.m. (High Mass), 12 noon, and 3.30 (Vespers and Benediction), 5.30, and 7 p.m.; on Mondays–Saturdays at 7, 8, 8.30, 9, 10.30 (High Mass on Saturdays), 12.30, 1.05 (except Saturdays), 4.15 (Mondays–Fridays; Vespers), 5.30 (High Mass on Mondays–Fridays, Vespers on Saturdays), and 6 (Saturdays only). Tickets required for the Sacristy and for the Tower lift (Easter–October, 10 to 4).

WESTMINSTER CATHEDRAL is the principal Roman Catholic church in England, the seat of the Archbishop of Westminster, who holds precedence over the other four provinces of England and Wales. It stands near the south-west end of Victoria Street, from which it is approached via Ashley Place. The vast and imposing church, designed by John Francis Bentley (d. 1902), is in an early-Christian Byzantine style, inspired to some extent by St Mark's at Venice, though the exterior strikes a highly original effect by its alternate bands of red brick and Portland stone. The foundation stone was laid in 1895, the fabric was completed and the church opened for service in 1903, and the consecration ceremony took place in 1910. The cathedral is 342 ft long inside, the nave (the widest in England) is 60 ft across, or 149 ft including the aisles and side chapels, and the height of the main arches is 90 ft, while the dome rises to 117 ft above the floor. The nave has room for a congregation of about 2,000 and the whole church covers an area of about 54,000 sq. ft. The singular square campanile (St Edward's Tower) is 284 ft high to the top of the cross.

The site for the cathedral was bought in 1884 by Cardinal Manning (1865–92), who succeeded Cardinal Wiseman, the first archbishop of Westminster (1850). The building was begun under Cardinal Vaughan (1892–1903) and completed under Cardinal Bourne (1903–35). The ninth archbishop, the Most Reverend Basil Cardinal Hume, was appointed in 1976.

The cathedral is orientated from north-west to south-east, but, in the description below, the high altar will be regarded as on the east. Over the main entrance (used only on Sundays) is a tympanum with a mosaic by R. Anning Bell (1916) representing Christ in Majesty with the Virgin and SS. Peter, Joseph, and Edward the Confessor. Above and behind this rises the narthex or vestibule, flanked by domed turrets, and higher still can be seen the west window of the nave. On each side of the great doorway are medallions with the figures of twelve archbishops of Canterbury.

The weekday entrance is by the door on the left of the main entrance. Inside, to the left, is the approach to the tower-lift. From the narthex at the west end of the church a striking impression is obtained of its extent and harmonious proportions, though the brick walls and piers are for the most part still bare. When the scheme of decoration is complete the lower surfaces, to a height of about 30 ft, will be covered with variegated marbles, while the upper parts of the church, including the vaulting and domes, will be faced with mosaics illustrating the doctrines of the Church. Some idea of the intended effect may be obtained from the chapels that have been completed.

At the west end of the NAVE are two monolithic columns of deep red Norwegian granite, symbolic of the Precious Blood of Jesus to which the cathedral is dedicated. The nave itself consists of three wide bays separated by massive piers rising to support large domes. The great rood, 30 ft in length, hanging from the arch at the east end, is by Christian Symons, and is painted with figures of Christ and the Mater Dolorosa. Over the aisles are galleries supported by columns of dark green marble hewn from the quarry in Greece which supplied the marbles for the great basilica of Santa Sophia at Constantinople (A.D. 563). They have beautiful capitals of white Carrara marble, no two of which are carved alike. On the main piers are the fourteen Stations of the Cross, bas-reliefs in Hopton Wood limestone from Derbyshire, carved by Eric Gill. The white marble pulpit was enlarged and redesigned as a memorial to Cardinal Bourne (d. 1935). Cardinal Heenan (d. 1975) is buried beneath the floor, close by. The statue of St Peter at the north-west end of the nave is a copy of that in St Peter's at Rome.

In the south-west corner of the cathedral is the BAPTISTERY, with bronze gates and a large font of coloured marbles designed by J. F. Bentley. The altar here was erected in 1946 by the Royal Canadian Air Force to officers and men who fell in 1939–45. The statue of St John the Baptist is a copy in block tin of that by Thorvaldsen on the cathedral at Copenhagen.

An arcaded marble screen separates the Baptistery from the CHAPEL OF SS. GREGORY AND AUGUSTINE. On and above the altarpiece here (by Henry Holiday) are mosaics illustrating the conversion of England to Christianity. In the aisle east of this chapel is a mosaic by Boris Anrep to St Oliver Plunket, archbishop of Armagh, hanged at Tyburn in 1681. The CHAPEL OF ST PATRICK and the Saints of Ireland is decorated with Irish marbles. In niches round the chapel are the badges of Irish regiments who fought in the First World War, and a casket on the left of the altar holds the roll of honour. In the CHAPEL OF ST ANDREW and the Saints of Scotland, native granite and marble have been extensively used, while on each side of the altar are fine bas-reliefs by Stirling Lee of SS. Ninian, Margaret of Scotland, Bridget, and Columba. In the CHAPEL OF ST PAUL THE APOSTLE (where the crib is set up at Christmas) are mosaics by Justin Vulliamy and Boris Anrep (1965).

Beyond the chapel is the SOUTH TRANSEPT, and from this opens the elaborately decorated LADY CHAPEL, the first part of the church to be completed. Behind the altar is a mosaic by Anning Bell of the Virgin and Child, and other mosaics by Gilbert Pownall include the heads of Isaiah, Ezekiel, Daniel, and Jeremiah.

The outer aisle of the chapel leads to the SACRISTY, and from this a stair descends to the CRYPT (adm. by previous arrangement only), dedicated as the Chapel of St Peter and lined with Greek marble. In its south wall are four recesses in which are preserved some fragments of the True Cross, a mitre of St Thomas Becket, and other relics. On the west (immediately below the high altar) is the small Chapel of St Edmund, with an altar below which a relic of St Edmund Rich, archbishop of Canterbury (d. 1240), is preserved, and the tombs of Cardinal Wiseman (d. 1865) and Cardinal Manning (d. 1892), originally buried at Kensal Green. Cardinal Griffin (d. 1956) and Cardinal Godfrey (d. 1963) are also buried here.

The SANCTUARY is raised 4 ft 6 in. above the nave, so that it is easily visible from every part of the church. The altar table is a single block of Cornish granite, 12 ft long and twelve tons in weight, uncovered only on Maundy Thursday and Good Friday. Above the altar crucifix, which is 7 ft 3 in. high, rises a white marble canopy or baldacchino, supported by eight columns of yellow Verona marble on pedestals of verde antico. The choir stalls are of oak inlaid with ivory and ebony; the archbishop's throne, on the north, is a smaller copy of the papal chair in the basilica of St John Lateran in Rome. The arcaded galleries on either side are of marble. The cathedral ends on the east in a wide apse containing the RETRO-CHOIR, which is raised 13 ft above the floor of the nave. At the top of the steps leading to it is a bas-relief of Christ the King in Hopton Wood stone by Lindsay Clarke, while the mosaic of the great tympanum over the high altar, by Gilbert Pownall, represents Christ in Glory, with the twelve Apostles and the emblems of the Evangelists on either side.

From the NORTH TRANSEPT, on the wall of which is a mosaic of St Joan of Arc, opens the CHAPEL OF THE BLESSED SACRAMENT, reserved for private devotion. It is enclosed by a fine bronze-gilt grille surmounted by a 'pelican in her piety', while the altar-rails of similar metal are adorned with the Instruments of the Passion. The inner veil of the tabernacle is hung from gold wedding rings bequeathed by matrons for the purpose. The mosaics on the walls and ceiling, the work of Boris Anrep, were completed in 1962.

On the north is the small CHAPEL OF THE SACRED HEART and St Michael, and opening off the North Transept is the CHAPEL OF ST THOMAS OF CANTERBURY, or Vaughan Chantry, with a cenotaph supporting the marble effigy of Cardinal

Vaughan (d. 1903), the founder of the cathedral, who is buried at Mill Hill (Middlesex). In the finely decorated CHAPEL OF ST JOSEPH, the easternmost opening off the north aisle, is the tomb of Cardinal Hinsley (d. 1943). The CHAPEL OF ST GEORGE and the English Martyrs has an altarpiece carved in low relief by Eric Gill (1946) and a figure of St George by Lindsay Clarke. The body of John Southworth, the 'parish priest of Westminster', hanged at Tyburn in 1654 and beatified in 1929, was brought here from Douai in France in 1930. The CHAPEL OF THE HOLY SOULS, the last on this side, has beautiful mosaics designed by Christian Symons.

The CAMPANILE is well worth ascending for the extensive prospect over west London. Among the places in view are Westminster Abbey and the Houses of Parliament to the north-east, with County Hall and the new Shell Centre behind them and St Paul's Cathedral farther away. St James's Park and Palace and Buckingham Palace are to the north, with Green Park beyond; and Hyde Park and Kensington Gardens are to the north-west, with the Albert Hall and Brompton Oratory to the left. Immediately west is Victoria Station, which has the Royal Hospital at Chelsea (just in view) to the left of it, while to the south-west can be seen Chelsea Bridge and south-eastward rises the tall Millbank Tower. On the north horizon are the heights of Harrow, Hampstead, and Highgate, and to the south-east is the television mast at Crystal Palace, while in the distance to the south stretches a long length of the North Downs. The campanile, 273 ft high in itself, is 48 ft higher than the west towers of Westminster Abbey, but 63 ft lower than the Victoria Tower of the Houses of Parliament. The cross, 11 ft high, that surmounts it, contains a relic of the True Cross. The lift in the campanile is the third highest in any church, exceeded only by those in the Riverside Church, New York.

ZOOLOGICAL GARDENS Plan I, A2

STATIONS: CAMDEN TOWN, over ½ m. NE, on the Northern line; REGENT'S PARK, over ¾ m. S, on the Bakerloo line; GREAT PORTLAND STREET, over ¾ m. SE, on the Circle and Metropolitan lines; BAKER STREET, 1¼ m. SW, on the Bakerloo, Circle, Jubilee, and Metropolitan lines. — BUSES No. 74 from Camden Town station and from Hyde Park Corner, Marble Arch, and Gloucester Place (near Baker Street station) to Prince Albert Road, N of the Main Entrance; Nos. 3 and 53 from Charing Cross, Oxford Circus, and Great Portland Street station to Gloucester Gate, ¼ m. E of the South Entrance. — WATER-BUSES, see p. 56.

ADMISSION to the gardens daily (except Christmas Day) 9 a.m. (10 in November–February) to 6 p.m. (7 on Sundays and Bank Holidays) or sunset (animal houses closed half an hour earlier); £3.20, children of five years but under sixteen, £1.60, pensioners £1. The AQUARIUM is open (free) from 10 a.m., the CHILDREN'S ZOO (also free) from 10.30. — WHEELCHAIRS (£1 all day; £5 deposit) and CHILDREN'S PUSHCHAIRS (50p; 30p deposit) are available. Dogs and other pets are not allowed in the gardens.

FEEDING TIMES: *Gorillas* (2, on plan), 4.30 in summer, 2.15 in winter (when possible); *Reptiles* (11), 2.30 (Fridays only); *Polar Bears* (12), 3, on most days; *Pelicans* (below 12), 2.45; *Sea-Lions* (15), 12 and 3.30 in summer, 2.30 in winter (not on Fridays); *Penguins* (20), 2.30; *Birds of Prey* (29), 3.15; *Elephant Bath Time* (17), daily at about 3.45 in summer, when warm enough. — ANIMAL RIDES near the Broad Walk (3) and in the Children's Zoo (21), every afternoon in summer (weather permitting).

RESTAURANTS: REGENT RESTAURANT (36), with waitress service, and REGENT CAFETERIA (below the Regent Restaurant), both licensed, lunches and teas; PAVILION BAR (35), light refreshments; MAPPIN CAFÉ (13) and GARDEN CAFÉ (32), these two unlicensed, light refreshments; and numerous refreshment kiosks.

The ZOOLOGICAL GARDENS, now officially named the LONDON ZOO, but known to Londoners simply as 'the Zoo', occupy an area of about thirty-six acres at the north end of Regent's Park. They have two entrances: the Main Entrance in the Outer Circle (which has a large car park) and the South Entrance, near the south-east angle, in the Broad Walk. The gardens may be reached by motorists via the Outer Circle (compare Route 17). They are divided by the Outer Circle and the Regent's Canal into three unequal portions which communicate with each other by two tunnels under the drive and three bridges over the canal.

The Zoo contains the finest and most representative collection of animals in the world, with over 8,000 inhabitants. It has a magnificent aquarium, an excellent mammal house, notable reptile and insect houses, many fine aviaries, and adequate open space for the larger mammals. The Mappin Terraces comprise a hugh reinforced concrete amphitheatre in which bears and other animals can be seen largely without the impediment of iron bars. Other interesting sections of the Zoo (especially for children) are the houses for monkeys and giraffes, the ponds for sea-lions and penguins, the giant panda and bear enclosures, the elephant and rhinoceros pavilion, the Children's Zoo, and the new Lion Terraces completed in 1976.

The Zoological Society of London, the owner of the gardens, was founded in 1826 by Sir Stamford Raffles and Sir Humphry Davy. The collections, first opened in 1828, were augmented in 1831 by the animals previously in the Royal Menagerie at the Tower of London. Four giraffes were purchased in 1836 for £2,300, in 1835 the first chimpanzee seen in Britain arrived, and in 1850 the first hippopotamus was shown. Reptiles were first housed at the Zoo in 1849, and in 1853 the society built here the first aquarium in the world. The collections were further augmented in 1876, when the Prince of Wales (later Edward VII) presented the society with the animals acquired on his Indian tour. Uncommon animals raised in captivity in the Zoo include the takin, the first to reach Europe alive (1909), and the first giant panda (1938). A few of the original buildings (by Decimus Burton) still survive, but the Zoo has now been landscaped afresh and new buildings, to the designs of Sir Hugh Casson and others, have been erected during the last twenty-five years.

The Zoo is most adequately explored by following the numbers given on the plan, an undertaking, however, requiring at least two hours for even a cursory survey. Visitors with less time at their disposal are advised to concentrate on the sections mentioned above. Opposite the MAIN ENTRANCE (1, on plan) are the popular PAVILIONS FOR APES AND MONKEYS (2), containing gorillas, chimpanzees, orang-utans, gibbons, mandrills, and other monkeys. On the south begins the BROAD WALK (3), where visitors may ride on camels and in llama traps. It leads past the Zoo Shop (4) and the GIBBON ENCLOSURE (5), which has several examples of these acrobatic animals. From the interesting COCKATOO AVIARY (6), on the north, a return is made towards the entrance via the Clock Tower (7) and the EASTERN AVIARY (8), with curassows and guans. Facing this is an enclosure (9) built for the GIANT PANDAS, Ching-Ching and Chia-Chia, presented by the Chinese government in 1974 (Ching-Ching died in 1985). To the west of the entrance is the West Tunnel (leading to the northern parts of the gardens).

To the south-west of the main entrance is the AQUARIUM (10), perhaps the finest in the world, with fresh-water, marine, and tropical halls, containing some 3,000 fish and other amphibious creatures. Notable are the pike, perch, carp, etc. (in the freshwater hall), the sea-horses, turtles, dogfish, and dragon fish (in the sea-water hall), and the lungfish, angel fish, electric eels, and glass catfish (in the tropical hall). The AMPHIBIAN HALL, close by, contains horned and tree frogs, giant toads, etc., and giant salamanders, from China and Japan. The largest amphibians, these reach over 5 ft in length. To the east of the Aquarium is the REPTILE HOUSE (11), where the animals live in natural conditions. Here can be seen alligators and crocodiles, lizards (chameleons, geckos, iguanas, etc.), cobras and rattlesnakes, pythons, and boa constrictors. Above the Aquarium rise the MAPPIN TERRACES (12), built in 1913, the lowest devoted to hogs, pigs, and peccaries, and those above to bears, including the favourite polar bears. On the highest terraces are Barbary wild sheep, moufflon and

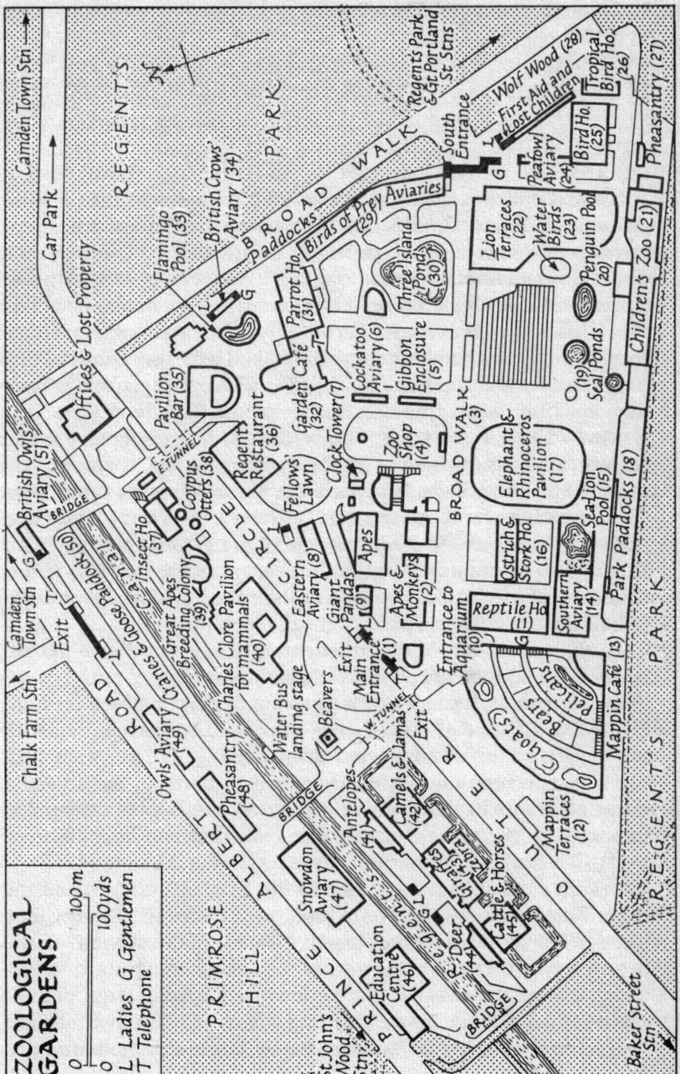
ZOOLOGICAL GARDENS
0 100m
0 100yds
L Ladies G Gentlemen
T Telephone
REGENT'S PARK
PRIMROSE HILL
BROAD WALK
PRINCE ALBERT ROAD
OUTER CIRCLE
Camden Town Stn
Car Park
Chalk Farm Stn
St John's Wood Stn
Baker Street Stn
Regents Park & Gt Portland St Stns
Offices & Lost Property
British Owls' Aviary (51)
Goose Paddock (50)
Cranes & Goose Paddock
Owls' Aviary (49)
Pheasantry (48)
Snowdon Aviary (47)
Education Centre (46)
Cattle & Horses (45)
Deer (44)
Giraffes (43)
Zebras
Camels & Llamas (42)
Antelopes (41)
Charles Clore Pavilion for mammals (40)
Great Apes Breeding Colony (39)
Coypus Otters (38)
Insect Ho (37)
Regent Restaurant (36)
Pavilion Bar (35)
British Crows' Aviary (34)
Flamingo Pool (33)
Garden Café (32)
Parrot Ho. (31)
Three Island Pond (30)
Birds of Prey Aviaries (29)
Paddocks
Wolf Wood (28)
Pheasantry (27)
Tropical Bird Ho. (26)
Bird Ho. (25)
Peafowl Aviary (24)
Water Birds (23)
Lion Terraces (22)
Children's Zoo (21)
Penguin Pool (20)
Seal Ponds (19)
Park Paddocks (18)
Elephant & Rhinoceros Pavilion (17)
Ostrich & Stork Ho (16)
Sea Lion Pool (15)
Southern Aviary (14)
Mappin Café (13)
Mappin Terraces (12)
Reptile Ho (11)
Entrance to Aquarium (10)
Giant Pandas (9)
Eastern Aviary (8)
Clock Tower (7)
Cockatoo Aviary (6)
Gibbon Enclosure (5)
Zoo Shop (4)
BROAD WALK (3)
Apes & Monkeys (2)
Main Entrance (1)
Apes
Fellows' Lawn
Beavers
Water Bus landing stage
Bears
Goats
Pelicans
First Aid and Lost Children
South Entrance
E. TUNNEL
W. TUNNEL
BRIDGE
Exit
Canal

other mountain sheep, and wild goats. Near the foot is a pelican pool and the Mappin Café (13).

Beyond the Reptile House is the SOUTHERN AVIARY (14), with various sea-birds, etc., and farther on is the SEA-LION POOL (15), best visited at feeding-time. To the left is the STORK AND OSTRICH HOUSE (16), and beyond this is the fine ELEPHANT AND RHINOCEROS PAVILION (17; designed by Sir Hugh Casson), with several African and Indian elephants. To the south are an enclosure for Wild Dogs and the PARK PADDOCKS (18), where kangaroos, wallabies, ponies, etc., are kept in the open air, and farther on are the SEAL PONDS (19) and the PENGUIN POOL (20; designed by Lubetkin and Tecton, 1934), always a centre of attraction. To the south-east of this is the CHILDREN'S ZOO and Farm (21), where young visitors have the opportunity of handling tame animals. Here also are the Pony Stables and a Nocturnal Hall with 'reversed' lighting, so that bush babies and other night creatures may be seen during the day.

The new LION TERRACES (22), east of the Penguin Pool, contain spacious paddocks for lions, tigers, leopards, jaguars, cheetahs, and lynxes. To the west of the terraces is a new aviary for WATER BIRDS (23). To the east is the PEAFOWL AVIARY (24), with many fine specimens, and in the south-east angle of the gardens are the BIRD HOUSE (25), containing hornbills, toucans, talking mynahs, ibises, and birds of paradise, the TROPICAL BIRD HOUSE (26), remarkable for its humming-birds, which fly about visitors' heads, and a PHEASANTRY (27). To the north-east of these is the WOLF WOOD (28), where a pack of wolves lives in a natural setting.

Near the SOUTH ENTRANCE is a post for first-aid and lost children. Beyond the entrance are the BIRDS OF PREY AVIARIES (29), with many eagles, vultures and hawks, facing the THREE ISLAND POND (30), which has various waterfowl. Farther north is the PARROT HOUSE (31), with its fine array of cockatoos, macaws, and longtailed parakeets. To the left is the Garden Café (32) and beyond are a FLAMINGO POOL (33) and the BRITISH CROWS AVIARY (34).

The East Tunnel, starting between the Pavilion Bar (35) and the Regent Restaurant and Cafeteria (36), leads under the Outer Circle to the section bounded by the Regent's Canal. In this section, on the left, are the fine INSECT HOUSE (37), which should not be overlooked; ponds for OTTERS (38), and for Coypus, large aquatic rodents; and a GREAT APES breeding colony (39; also by Lubetkin and Tecton, 1932). Next to this is the large and well-arranged

CHARLES CLORE PAVILION (40) for mammals (1967), with a great variety of interesting species (mongooses, porcupines, marmots, lemurs, squirrel monkeys, wallabies, etc.). A specially designed section, with 'reversed lighting', enables nocturnal animals, such as bats, badgers, bush babies, and flying squirrels, to become active during the day.

On the right, beyond the Pavilion, is the approach to the water-bus landing stage. Farther on is a new enclosure for BEAVERS, near the entrance to the West Tunnel (which has notable copies of the Lascaux and Altamira cave paintings). On the right is a new bridge over the canal, and farther on again are houses for ANTELOPES (41); CAMELS (42) and Llamas; GIRAFFES, the tallest living mammals, and ZEBRA (43); DEER (44); and HORSES and CATTLE (45). Deer and antelopes may also be seen on the slopes above the canal.

Another bridge over the Regent's Canal beyond these houses gives access to the northern section of the gardens. Here is the EDUCATION CENTRE (46), opened in 1976. Over 60,000 schoolchildren visit the Zoo every year for lecture tours. On the North Bank also is the SNOWDON AVIARY, (47), a 'walk-through' aviary designed by Lord Snowdon and built in 1963, with many African and Indian birds. Beyond the new bridge are another PHEASANTRY (48), the OWLS' AVIARY (49), and the CRANES AND GOOSE PADDOCK (50), facing an exit into Prince Albert Road. Farther on is an aviary for BRITISH OWLS (51). From this a third bridge across the canal returns to the middle section of the gardens opposite the East Tunnel.

SUBURBAN LONDON

The following section on Suburban London, including such pleasant regions as Chiswick, Hampstead, Highgate, Greenwich, and Dulwich, all with their points of interest, is arranged in districts, starting on the west from the Thames at Fulham, then working round north, east, and south to reach the river again at Putney. The relative positions of the various districts are shown on the road map on pages 40–41, and they are connected with Central London and with each other by numerous and frequent train and bus services.

Fulham

STATIONS: PUTNEY BRIDGE and FULHAM BROADWAY, on the District line.

FULHAM, approached from Chelsea (Route 8) by King's Road (Plan VI, F2, 3) and from South Kensington (Route 11) by Fulham Road (VI, F1, 2), stands on the north bank of the Thames, opposite Putney, and was once famous for its market gardens. In NEW KING'S ROAD is the site of the pottery established in 1671 by John Dwight, the maker of Fulham stoneware. A 19th-century bottle-kiln was brought to light in 1975. New King's Road ends at the junction of FULHAM HIGH STREET and Putney Bridge Approach. To the left, beyond Putney Bridge station, Ranelagh Gardens leads to the fashionable HURLINGHAM CLUB (founded in 1869), in a house of about 1760 (best seen from the river). Part of the grounds was converted in 1954 into a public park, with an athletics stadium.

Near the north end of PUTNEY BRIDGE (built in 1886 by Sir Joseph Bazalgette and widened in 1933) is ALL SAINTS' CHURCH, the parish church of Fulham, rebuilt in 1881 by Sir Arthur Blomfield, but retaining a 15th-century tower. It contains a 16th-century Flemish brass, a Gothic font of 1622, and many 17th-century monuments. In Fulham Palace Road, which leads north from Fulham High Street to Hammersmith Broadway (see below), is the approach to FULHAM PALACE, until 1973 the residence of the bishops of London, who owned the manor of Fulham from about 691 until 1868. The most interesting part is the courtyard on the west, built by Bishop FitzJames in the early 16th century; the rest of the buildings belong to the 18th and 19th centuries. The site of the moat is now a public garden, and between the palace grounds and the river is the BISHOP'S PARK, with a terrace that is a vantage point for watching the start of the Oxford and Cambridge Boat-Race.

Hammersmith and Chiswick

STATIONS: HAMMERSMITH, on the District, Metropolitan, and Piccadilly lines; RAVENSCOURT PARK (closed on Sundays), STAMFORD BROOK, and TURNHAM GREEN, on the District line.

HAMMERSMITH is reached from Kensington and the West End by way of Kensington High Street (Route 11; Plan VI, B 1) and its extension, HAMMERSMITH ROAD, which passes (on the left) the site of ST PAUL'S SCHOOL, a public school founded in 1509 by Dean Colet and moved here from St Paul's Churchyard in 1884, but moved again in 1968 to Barnes (see below). Field-Marshal Lord Montgomery's headquarters were established at the school during the planning of the invasion of Normandy in 1944. In Brook Green, on the right, is ST PAUL'S GIRLS' SCHOOL (590 pupils), founded in 1904, where Gustav Holst was director of music from 1905 until his death in 1934.

Hammersmith Road ends at HAMMERSMITH BROADWAY, a busy centre of traffic where several other roads converge. On the north of King Street, which goes on towards Chiswick (see below), is the LYRIC THEATRE, first opened in 1888 and rebuilt in 1978. ST PAUL'S CHURCH, a large but uninteresting structure of 1882, a little south of the Broadway, contains a fine late-17th-century pulpit and a monument of about 1665 with a bronze bust of Charles I, probably by Le Sueur. In Fulham Palace Road, which runs south-east beyond the Hammersmith Flyover, is the large CHARING CROSS HOSPITAL, established in 1818 (compare Route 21), but rebuilt here to the designs of Ralph Tubbs. The first part, with a sixteen-storey central towerblock, was opened in 1973; a second building, completed in 1976, contains the medical school, likewise founded in 1818 and combined in 1984 with the Westminster Hospital Medical School.

Hammersmith Bridge Road, running south-west from the Broadway, passes under the HAMMERSMITH FLYOVER, completed in 1961 as part of the Great West Road out of London. HAMMERSMITH BRIDGE is a characteristically Victorian suspension bridge of 1887, by Bazalgette, crossing the Thames to Barnes. To the east of the bridge are the RIVERSIDE STUDIOS, opened in 1978, with a theatre and an art gallery.

LOWER MALL, skirting the river west of the bridge, retains several picturesque houses of the 18th century, while farther west is UPPER MALL, with further picturesque old houses, including the charming SUSSEX HOUSE, of about 1726, and the DOVE INN, where James Thomson is said to have written part of *The Seasons*. KELMSCOTT HOUSE, built about 1780 (but much altered since), was from 1878 until his death in 1896 the home of William Morris, who founded his tapestry works and printing press here. In the garden, the first electric telegraph was constructed, in 1816, by Sir Francis Ronalds. A riverside path goes on to Hammersmith Terrace (see below).

On the left of King Street, west of the Broadway, is the HAMMERSMITH TOWN HALL, built in 1939 to the designs of Berry Webber. To the right, farther on, is RAVENSCOURT PARK, on the west side of which is the ROYAL MASONIC HOSPITAL, built in 1931–58 by Sir John Burnet, Tait & Partners. To the left of King

Street is ST PETER'S SQUARE, part of an interesting layout of 1825–30, closed on the south-east by ST PETER'S CHURCH, by Edward Lapidge (1829). On the other side of the Great West Road is HAMMERSMITH TERRACE (about 1750), where Sir Emery Walker (d. 1933), the typographer and friend of William Morris, lived for thirty years at No. 7. The road westward from here enters CHISWICK, a favourite place of residence in the 17th and 18th centuries, and now included in the Greater London Borough of Hounslow.

CHISWICK MALL is a delightful riverside street lined with many houses of the 18th century. WALPOLE HOUSE (about 1700), where the Duchess of Cleveland, mistress of Charles II, lived, is one of the claimants to be the original of Miss Pinkerton's school for young ladies in Thackeray's *Vanity Fair*. At the west end of the Mall is ST NICHOLAS'S CHURCH, rebuilt in 1884 by J. L. Pearson, except for the 15th-century tower. In the churchyard to the south is the tomb of William Hogarth (d. 1764), and J. McN. Whistler (d. 1903) is buried in the new graveyard to the west. CHURCH STREET, which has some interesting houses, leads to a busy roundabout on the Great West Road. To the left of this is the tiny CHISWICK SQUARE, of about 1680, opening to BOSTON HOUSE (1740), and on the left of the Great West Road, to the north-west, is the late-17th-century HOGARTH'S HOUSE (adm., p. 32), the summer home of the painter from 1749 until his death, now containing a collection of engravings of his paintings.

From the roundabout, Great Chertsey Road leads south-west to the gate of CHISWICK HOUSE (adm., p. 31), a delightful villa designed by Richard Boyle, Third Earl of Burlington, under the inspiration of Palladio's Villa Capra near Vicenza, and built in 1725–9. The decoration of the rooms was carried out by William Kent, the earl's protégé, who also laid out the gardens, now enclosed in a public park. In the house died the statesmen C. J. Fox (1806) and George Canning (1827).

King Street is extended by Chiswick High Road, north of the Great West Road, to Turnham Green Terrace (on the right). This ends at Turnham Green station, to the north of which is BEDFORD PARK, the earliest planned garden suburb in England, laid out from 1875 on by Edward Godwin, with houses by R. Norman Shaw, who also designed St Michael's Church and the Tabard Inn (about 1880).

Notting Hill and Shepherd's Bush

STATIONS: NOTTING HALL GATE, on the Central, Circle, and District lines; HOLLAND PARK, on the Central line; and SHEPHERD'S BUSH, on the Central and Metropolitan lines.

NOTTING HILL GATE (beyond I, F1) is a busy traffic centre from which Bayswater Road leads east to Marble Arch (see Route 12), Kensington Church Street south to Kensington High Street (Route 11), and Holland Park Avenue (see below) west to Shepherd's Bush. The CORONET CINEMA, on the south, was built in 1898 in an Edwardian Renaissance style by W. G. R. Sprague as the Coronet Theatre, and Ellen Terry, Sarah Bernhardt, Mrs Patrick Campbell, and Sybil Thorndike all played here. Pembridge Road leads north past Kensington Park Road to the long PORTOBELLO ROAD, famous for its street market in antiques (held on Saturdays).

KENSINGTON PARK ROAD forms the east boundary of the LADBROKE ESTATE, an early-Victorian planned suburb laid out from about 1850 on by Thomas Allom, with large Italianate houses and great expanses of trees. On the left of the road is KENSINGTON TEMPLE, built in 1848 by John Tarring as a Congregational chapel. The school of 1851 behind was converted in 1927 into the MERCURY THEATRE for the Ballet Rambert, founded in 1926 by Marie Rambert (d. 1982). The road passes the large LADBROKE SQUARE, with its attractive gardens, and the end of KENSINGTON PARK GARDENS, in which Sir William Crookes, the scientist, lived from 1880 until his death in 1919 at No. 7. This road, which (like other streets and crescents of the estate) has unusual communal gardens at the back, crosses the wide LADBROKE GROVE, the north-south axis of the estate. Its symmetrical unity is broken by HILLCREST (Nos. 51–7), a well-planned block of flats of about 1933 by Maxwell Fry. LANSDOWNE WALK, farther south, crosses Lansdowne Road, in which LANSDOWNE HOUSE, near the south end, is an unusual block of studio-apartments of about 1860 by William Flockhart. Charles Ricketts was among the artists who lived here. Lansdowne Walk goes on to CLARENDON ROAD (the west boundary of the estate), which runs south to Holland Park Avenue near Holland Park station.

HOLLAND PARK AVENUE, prolonging Notting Hill Gate to the west, passes (on the left) CAMPDEN HILL SQUARE, a layout of 1826, where John McDouall Stuart, the first explorer to cross Australia, died in 1866 at No. 9. AUBREY WALK, farther south, has a variety of interesting houses, some of which were originally coach houses for Campden Hill Square. Beyond Holland Park station, the main road passes NORLAND SQUARE, which with the streets to the north and ROYAL CRESCENT, farther on, forms a classical layout of 1837–46 by Robert Cantwell.

Holland Park Avenue passes the beginning of the WEST CROSS ROUTE, a branch of the M41, and ends at SHEPHERD'S BUSH, a large triangular green from which Shepherd's Bush Road runs south to Hammersmith Broadway. In WOOD LANE, which leads north from the green, is the vast TELEVISION CENTRE of the B.B.C., opened in 1960, to the designs of Graham Dawbarn. In Du Cane Road, on the left beyond Westway, is the HAMMERSMITH HOSPITAL, incorporating the

ROYAL POSTGRADUATE MEDICAL SCHOOL of London University (founded in 1934), new buildings for which, by Lyons, Israel, and Ellis, were opened in 1962. Farther on is WORMWOOD SCRUBS, a large open space best known for the neighbouring prison (1874), the largest in Britain, but the scene also of many early attempts at flying (from 1910 onwards) by Claude Grahame-White and other pioneers.

Paddington and Maida Vale

STATIONS: PADDINGTON (Plan I, D2) and EDGWARE ROAD (I, C3), both on the Bakerloo, Circle, District, and Metropolitan lines; WARWICK AVENUE (I, C2) and MAIDA VALE, on the Bakerloo line. — CRUISES on the Regent's Canal, see p. 56.

PADDINGTON is bounded on the east by Edgware Road and on the south by Bayswater Road. From this, Lancaster Terrace (see Route 12) leads north to ST JAMES'S CHURCH, the parish church of Paddington (I, E2, 3), rebuilt in a spacious Gothic style in 1883 by G. E. Street, who retained the tower of 1843. The fine west window, by Goddard and Gibbs (1952), is a war memorial depicting persons connected with Paddington. The church faces the junction of WESTBOURNE TERRACE (named after the stream which formerly flowed hence to Hyde Park) and SUSSEX GARDENS, wide boulevards (by S. P. Cockerell and George Gutch, 1828–35) that are interesting as examples of Regency town planning. Sussex Gardens extends north-east to EDGWARE ROAD (II, E2–I, B3), a long straight thoroughfare following the course of the Roman Watling Street, which ran to Verulamium, near St Albans.

Westbourne Terrace, which runs north-west from Paddington church, is crossed by Craven Road. This is extended north-east by PRAED STREET, passing the south side of PADDINGTON STATION (I, D2, 3), the principal terminus of the Western Region, mostly designed by Isambard Kingdom Brunel and first opened in 1838, but reconstructed in 1850–54. The Great Western Royal Hotel, masking the south front, was built by Philip Hardwick in 1852. Praed Street goes on to ST MARY'S HOSPITAL, founded in 1851, in the laboratories of which Sir Alexander Fleming discovered penicillin in 1928. The noted Medical School was established in 1854, rebuilt in 1933, and extended in 1969 to house the Wellcome Laboratories of experimental pathology. In the hospital were born Prince William (1982) and Prince Henry (1984), sons of the Prince and Princess of Wales.

Eastbourne Terrace, on the west of Paddington Station, leads to Bishop's Bridge Road, which runs east across the Paddington Basin of the Grand Union Canal (see below) to reach the long, winding HARROW ROAD (I, C1–3) beneath a raised motorway (WESTWAY; 1970), part of a new route into Central London. Farther east is PADDINGTON GREEN, the old village centre (much altered), with a statue of Mrs Sarah Siddons (d. 1831), the actress, who was buried in the churchyard to the north-west, now a playing field. The first regular omnibus service in London, started in 1829 by George Shillibeer, operated from Paddington Green to the Bank. The adjacent ST MARY'S CHURCH (I, C3), built in 1791 by John Plaw on the plan of a Greek cross, replaces that in which the painter Hogarth was married secretly in 1729.

Westward from Paddington Green, Harrow Road leads to Warwick Avenue, which goes on northward past WARWICK GARDENS, a green retreat laid out in 1954 overlooking 'LITTLE VENICE', a secluded basin of the Grand Union Canal, popular with pleasure craft and the starting point of the Regent's Canal (see Route 17). A long mural (1965) in WARWICK CRESCENT, on the south, commemorates Robert Browning (d. 1889), who lived near by (house demolished). In CLIFTON GARDENS, to the right from Warwick Avenue station (I, B, C2), Sir Ambrose Fleming (d. 1945), the pioneer of electrical technology, lived at No. 9. WARRINGTON CRESCENT, to the north, is part of an attractive layout of about 1880.

In MAIDA AVENUE, which skirts a pleasant reach of the Regent's Canal east of Little Venice, is a CATHOLIC APOSTOLIC CHURCH in an early Gothic style, by J. L. Pearson (1894). The road ends at the junction of Edgware Road and MAIDA VALE, a broad thoroughfare deriving its name from the Battle of Maida (in Calabria), in which Sir John Stuart defeated the French in 1806. It still retains some of its mid-19th-century villas, but is now mainly lined by palatial blocks of flats in a variety of styles. St John's Wood Road, on the right, ascends past Lord's Cricket Ground (Route 17). HAMILTON TERRACE, leading north from this road, is a wide, tree-lined boulevard laid out in 1830. In Kilburn Park Road, on the left near the north end of Maida Vale, is the lofty and spacious ST AUGUSTINE'S CHURCH, a vaulted Gothic building, one of the finest designs of J. L. Pearson (1880). In the transepts are paintings by Marco Palmezzano, Filippino Lippi, and Crivelli, given by Lord Northcliffe, the newspaper owner. William Friese-Greene (d. 1921), the pioneer of cinematography, lived at No. 136 in Maida Vale, near the beginning of Kilburn High Road, and W. P. Frith (d. 1909), the artist, lived at No. 114 in CLIFTON HILL, to the east.

Hampstead

STATIONS: CHALK FARM, BELSIZE PARK, and HAMPSTEAD, on the Northern line; HAMPSTEAD HEATH, on the North London line (London Midland Region); SWISS COTTAGE, on the Jubilee line; and FINCHLEY ROAD, on the Jubilee and Metropolitan lines.

HAMPSTEAD, one of the most favoured residential suburbs of London, is famous for its beautiful heath and its wealth of literary and artistic associations. The newer part spreads over the south and west slopes of a considerable hill, the top of which is crowned by the delightful old village with its tortuous streets and attractive houses. This is approached from St John's Wood (Plan II, A1) by way of Wellington Road and Finchley Road to Swiss Cottage (see below), and from Camden Town (beyond I, A3) by Chalk Farm Road (compare Route 17), near the farther end of which is the ROUND HOUSE, a former railway-engine shed (1847) converted in 1967 into an arts centre, but closed at present.

From Chalk Farm to the Whitestone Pond. From Chalk Farm station, the broad

HAVERSTOCK HILL ascends past Belsize Park station. In HOWITT ROAD, almost opposite, Ramsay MacDonald lived in 1916–25 at No. 9. Haverstock Hill, passing the former HAMPSTEAD TOWN HALL (1877), is continued by Rosslyn Hill. On the right is the imposing ST STEPHEN'S CHURCH of about 1869, by S. S. Teulon, for which an alternative use is being sought in 1985. In Pond Street, beyond, is the ROYAL FREE HOSPITAL, founded in 1828 and moved from Gray's Inn Road to new buildings from 1970 onward. An adjoining building of 1983 houses the Medical School, founded in 1874 and moved from Hunter Street, near Brunswick Square.

DOWNSHIRE HILL, on the right of Rosslyn Hill, with some good early-19th-century houses, goes down to ST JOHN'S CHURCH, a pleasant Regency building by William Woods (1823). The church stands at the corner of KEATS GROVE (formerly John Street), with further early-19th-century houses, including the charming KEATS HOUSE (adm., p. 32), built in 1815 and known as Wentworth Place when John Keats lived there, from December 1818 to September 1820, his most creative period. The poet and his friend, Charles Armitage Brown, occupied the east half of the house, and the Brawne family the other half. The rooms in these, and the Chester Room, built on the east in 1838, contain interesting relics of Keats, his betrothed Fanny Brawne, and his friends, books owned and annotated by the poet, and letters written by him and his acquaintances. In the garden in front is the mulberry tree under which the *Ode to a Nightingale* is often conjectured (incorrectly) to have been written. A library of books relating to Keats and his contemporaries has been arranged in converted rooms on the first floor of the house, which was otherwise restored to its former state, as far as possible, in 1975.

Keats Grove ends at SOUTH END ROAD, which leads south past Hampstead Heath station. In PARLIAMENT HILL, a street starting to the north of the station, 'George Orwell' (Eric Blair) lived in 1935 at No. 77. South End Road is extended in the other direction by EAST HEATH ROAD, skirting the lower part of the heath (see below). Sir Arthur Bliss, the composer, lived in 1929–39 at No. 1, and John Middleton Murry (d. 1957) and his wife, Katherine Mansfield (d. 1923), the writers, lived at No. 17. Paths on the right lead via the HAMPSTEAD PONDS, the source of the Fleet River, to PARLIAMENT HILL (319 ft), the southern extremity of the heath, affording a wide view over north London. Farther east are the HIGHGATE PONDS, extending up towards the grounds of Kenwood.

WELL WALK, running left from East Heath Road farther up,

passes the site of the wells that in the 18th century made Hampstead a fashionable spa. John Constable, the landscape painter, lived at No. 40 (then No. 5) from 1826 until the year of his death, while Keats lodged after June 1817 at a house whose site adjoins the WELLS TAVERN, of about 1849. In New End Square, on the right, is BURGH HOUSE (adm., p. 31), built about 1702, altered in the mid 19th century, and restored in 1977. It contains the Hampstead Museum of local history, arranges concerts, lectures, and art exhibitions, and is used also for community activities. FLASK WALK bears right from the end of Well Walk to gain (50 yds below the underground station) the HIGH STREET, the extension of Rosslyn Hill, retaining some of its original 18th-century houses (mostly disguised by modern shop fronts).

From the entrance to HAMPSTEAD STATION (1907), the deepest in London (192 ft), HEATH STREET, with many picturesque old houses, winds steeply up to the top of Hampstead Heath (see below). HAMPSTEAD SQUARE, on the right (with 18th-century houses), gives access to CHRIST CHURCH (1852), whose prominent spire is a landmark from many parts of London. Sir Flinders Petrie (d. 1942), the Egyptologist, lived at No. 5 in CANNON PLACE, to the north, and Sir Gerald du Maurier (d. 1934), the actor-manager, lived from 1916 at No. 14. SQUIRE'S MOUNT, between this road and East Heath Road, is a group of late-18th-century buildings (N.T.; no adm.).

In the other direction, Heath Street is prolonged by FITZJOHN'S AVENUE towards Swiss Cottage. On the right before the junction of these streets opens CHURCH ROW, the finest street in Hampstead, with delectable terraces of 18th-century dwellings. At the end is ST JOHN'S CHURCH, the parish church of Hampstead, rebuilt in 1745–7 by John Sanderson, with a western extension of 1844, converted into a chancel in 1878. Other 19th-century work includes the ornate decoration of the Renaissance-style ceiling (by Alfred Bell; 1855) and the altarpiece by Sir Thomas Jackson (1878). In the north aisle is a bust of John Keats, sculptured by Anne Whitney of Boston and given in 1894 by American admirers of the poet. John Constable (d. 1837), who painted many of his landscapes in and around Hampstead, is buried in the south-east corner of the churchyard, the fine 18th-century wrought-iron gates of which were brought from the demolished seat of the Duke of Chandos at Canons, near Edgware. In the newer cemetery north of the road are the graves of George du Maurier (d. 1896), the author; Sir Herbert Beerbohm Tree (d. 1917), the actor-manager (both at the south end); and Sir Walter Besant (d. 1901), the historian of London (near the west side).

HOLLY WALK, ascending west of the cemetery, passes ST MARY'S CHURCH, built for French Catholic refugees in 1816. ABERNETHY HOUSE (about 1819), in which R. L. Stevenson and his future biographer, Sir Sidney Colvin, lodged in 1874, stands at the corner of Mount Vernon, which leads to HOLLY HILL, the northward extension of High Street from the underground station. On the left are the large MEDICAL COUNCIL RESEARCH LABORATORIES, built in 1880 as a hospital, and on the right, at the beginning of HOLLY BUSH HILL, is the picturesque house (restored in 1957) built in 1797 by George Romney, the painter, but occupied only until the following year, when he returned to Kendal, in Westmorland, broken in health. From here HAMPSTEAD GROVE goes on north to Hampstead Heath, passing FENTON HOUSE (N.T.; adm., p. 32), a delightful mansion of about 1693 with an attractive walled garden and beautiful furniture, porcelain, and early keyboard instruments, including a harpsichord of 1612 played on by Handel (lent by the Queen Mother). NEW GROVE HOUSE, farther on, was occupied in 1874–95 by George du Maurier. ADMIRAL'S HOUSE (about 1700), in Admiral's Walk, to the left, was the home in 1856–64 of Sir George Gilbert Scott, the architect, and John Galsworthy, the novelist, lived at the early-18th-century GROVE LODGE, adjoining, from 1918 until his death in 1933. In LOWER TERRACE, ascending from the west end of Admiral's Walk to the Whitestone Pond (see below), No. 2, one of a pair of charming houses, was the first home in Hampstead of Constable (1821).

From Swiss Cottage to the Whitestone Pond. In Avenue Road, south of Swiss Cottage station, is the SWISS COTTAGE CENTRE, the only part completed of a civic centre for Hampstead, designed by Sir Basil Spence, Bonnington, and Collins. Opened in 1964, it includes the HAMPSTEAD THEATRE, a library, and a swimming pool. In Eton Avenue, east of the station, is the CENTRAL SCHOOL OF SPEECH AND DRAMA, incorporating the Embassy Theatre. FITZJOHN'S AVENUE, leaving Finchley Road on the right north of the station, ascends to the older part of Hampstead (see above). In MARESFIELD GARDENS, parallel on the west, Sigmund Freud, the pioneer psychoanalyst, lived for twelve months until his death in 1939 at No. 20, and Herbert Henry Asquith, the statesman, lived in 1887–92 at No. 27. Sidney and Beatrice Webb, the sociologists, lived at No. 10 in NETHERHALL GARDENS, farther west.

FINCHLEY ROAD, traversing the west side of the hill on which Hampstead stands, connects Swiss Cottage and Golders Green stations. It passes (at No. 527) NEW COLLEGE, formed in 1924 by the union of two colleges founded in 1673 and

1803, and now training candidates for the ministry (mainly Nonconformist). Benjamin Britten, the composer, lived in the late 1930s at No. 559 in Finchley Road, opposite the college. In Kidderpore Avenue, to the north, is WESTFIELD COLLEGE, founded for women in 1882 and now a school of London University, with a faculty of arts (men were admitted in 1963).

ARKWRIGHT ROAD, on the right, north of Finchley Road station, passes the CAMDEN ARTS CENTRE (adm., p. 31), where exhibitions are held frequently, and crosses FROGNAL, a long winding road ascending past UNIVERSITY COLLEGE SCHOOL, a public day school (520 boys), founded in 1830 and moved here from University College, Gower Street, in 1907. Famous pupils include Lord Leighton, Joseph Chamberlain, Viscount Morley, William de Morgan, and the Marquess of Reading. No. 97 in Frognal was the home of Kathleen Ferrier (d. 1953), the singer; No. 99 (now a convent) was the war-time home of General de Gaulle; and No. 103 (Upper Frognal Lodge), was the last home in London of Ramsay MacDonald (d. 1937). Sir Walter Besant died in 1901 at Frognal End, in FROGNAL GARDENS, to the right.

Frognal emerges at the upper end of Holy Hill (see above), which is extended by Branch Hill to the secluded WEST HEATH, overlooked by several 18th-century houses and by JUDGES' WALK, a fine avenue of trees leading towards the Whitestone Pond.

From the Whitestone Pond to Kenwood. At the north end of Heath Street is the WHITESTONE POND, commanding a varied and charming view said to extend into ten counties. The flagstaff just beyond marks the highest point (440 ft) of HAMPSTEAD HEATH, the finest 'lung' in the neighbourhood of London, a rugged sandy heathland (790 acres) spreading over the hills and valleys of a verdant range. Acquired by the L.C.C. between 1871 and 1927, it is still maintained largely in its natural state, partly grown with gorse and with a rich variety of trees. It is especially popular with Londoners on summer Bank Holidays, when a fair takes place near the Vale of Health. To the north of the flagstaff is JACK STRAW'S CASTLE, an old inn well known to Dickens and Thackeray, and commemorated by Washington Irving in *Tales of a Traveller*. Badly damaged by bombing, it was rebuilt in its former (18th-century) style in 1963.

Beyond the inn the road divides, the right branch (Spaniards Road) leading towards Highgate. It runs along a ridge above the VALE OF HEALTH, where Leigh Hunt took a cottage (probably Vale Lodge) after his release from prison and was visited by Keats, Shelley, Coleridge, and Lamb. In others of the houses here lived Rabindranath Tagore, the Indian poet (in 1912), D. H. Lawrence (in 1915), and the social historians, J. L. and Barbara Hammond (in 1906–13). The SPANIARDS INN, farther on in Spaniards Road, is a picturesque early-18th-century tavern, partly weather-boarded. Here the Gordon Rioters were overtaken while on their way to attack Lord Mansfield's house (1780). Outside is a restored 18th-century toll-house.

On the right, beyond the inn, is the entrance to KENWOOD HOUSE (adm., p. 33), a delightful mansion rebuilt in 1767–9 by Robert Adam for the first Earl of Mansfield, the famous Lord Chief Justice of George III. The wings on the north were added in 1793–6 by George Saunders, who also built the low service wing on the east, with the brewhouse, laundry, and coach house (now a tea-room). Kenwood House was bequeathed to the nation by the first Earl of Iveagh (d. 1927), together with his magnificent collection of paintings, which include many fine British portraits of the 18th and early 19th centuries by Gainsborough, Reynolds, Romney, Raeburn, and Lawrence, and other notable pictures by Claude de Jongh (Old London Bridge, 1639), Van Dyck, Frans Hals, Rembrandt, Jan Vermeer, Pater, Boucher, Guardi, John Crome, and Turner. The portico is characteristic of Adam's work; the finest of the rooms is the Library (sometimes called the Adam Room) in the east wing, with delicate plasterwork by Joseph Rose and ceiling paintings by Zucchi. Facing the beautiful rose-garden, to the west, is Dr Johnson's summer-house (originally at Streatham), moved here and restored in 1967. The lovely wooded grounds of Kenwood, laid out by Lord Mansfield and now the most beautiful part of Hampstead Heath, contain some splendid beeches and other fine trees.

North End Way descends from Jack Straw's Castle towards Golders Green, passing the OLD BULL AND BUSH INN, made famous by a music-hall song, and MANOR HOUSE HOSPITAL. Opposite this is IVY HOUSE, once the home of Anna Pavlova (d. 1931), the ballerina, and now part of the Middlesex Polytechnic. Also on the left is an entrance to GOLDERS HILL, the north-west extension of Hampstead Heath, a park with a secluded walled garden and deer enclosures. North End Road goes on to ST ALBAN'S CHURCH, built in 1932 by Sir Giles G. Scott, in GOLDERS GREEN, which has a station on the Northern Line, while a bus (No. 210) runs back across the Heath to Highgate.

HAMPSTEAD WAY, starting north of the Bull and Bush, passes WYLDES, a charming weather-boarded house (once a farmhouse), where William Blake, John Constable, John Linnell, Samuel Palmer, Charles Dickens, and Bernard Shaw all lived or stayed at various times. Hampstead Way goes on to HAMPSTEAD GARDEN SUBURB, a successful adventure in town planning, started in 1906 under the inspiration of Dame Henrietta Barnett and laid out by Sir Raymond Unwin, Berry Parker, and others. In the Central Square are ST JUDE'S CHURCH, the Free Church, and the Institute, all by Sir Edwin Lutyens (1908–11).

Highgate

STATIONS: ARCHWAY and HIGHGATE, on the Northern line.

HIGHGATE, another favoured suburb on the north side of London, stands mostly on the top of the twin hill to Hampstead, and like its neighbour it preserves many attractive old houses. From Hampstead the best approach is by Hampstead Lane, passing Kenwood (see above), and from Central London it is most conveniently reached via the Archway underground station and Highgate Hill. ARCHWAY ROAD, which runs northward from the station, was constructed in 1813 to avoid the precipitous slope of Highgate Hill. The lofty viaduct higher up was built over the road in 1897 in place of the former 'Highgate Archway'.

HIGHGATE HILL, ascending from Archway station, is the continuation of Holloway Road (compare below). On the left, in about 250 yds, is the WHITTINGTON STONE, set here in 1821 on the site of that on which Dick Whittington is supposed to have sat when he heard Bow Bells chiming 'Turn again, Whittington, thrice Mayor of London' (the cat was added in 1964). Farther up is ST JOSEPH'S RETREAT, the chief house in England of the Passionist Fathers, with a Romanesque chapel of 1888 dominated by its dome. Close by is an entrance to Waterlow Park (see below) and higher up (just inside the park) is LAUDERDALE HOUSE, built in the early 17th century, altered in the 18th century and restored after being gutted by fire in 1963. After 1660 it was owned by the notorious minister of Charles II, the Duke of Lauderdale, who is said to have lent it to Nell Gwyn. The house stands on a terrace enclosed by an attractive garden. Nearly opposite is CROMWELL HOUSE, which has no associations with Oliver Cromwell, but was built in 1638 and has an elaborate oak staircase. This is the finest of the old houses in Highgate Hill and its extension, HIGH STREET, though many notable 18th-century houses have survived. Above the junction of these streets is another entrance to WATERLOW PARK, a beautiful retreat with several small lakes on the secluded slopes of the hill.

Near the south-west gate in SWAIN'S LANE are the entrances to the two parts of HIGHGATE CEMETERY (open occasionally), where many famous people are buried, including Michael Faraday, Sir Rowland Hill, George Eliot, D. G. Rossetti, Herbert Spencer, and John Galsworthy. The grave of Karl Marx (d. 1883 at Hampstead), in the newer part to the east, is marked by a colossal head sculptured by Laurence Bradshaw (1956). Swain's Lane descends southward to Highgate Road, the continuation of Highgate West Hill (see below). In LISSENDEN GARDENS, farther south, are Parliament Hill Mansions, where Sir John Betjeman (1906–84), the Poet Laureate, was born at No. 52.

On the left of High Street, beyond Waterlow Park, is SOUTH GROVE, which leads past POND SQUARE (with further old houses) to the upper part of Highgate West Hill. On the left are the OLD HALL, built in 1691 (it is believed on the site of Arundel House, where Francis Bacon died in 1626), and ST MICHAEL'S CHURCH, built by Lewis Vulliamy in 1832, with a spire that is a well-known landmark. The east window contains glowing stained glass by Evie Hone (1955). The remains of Samuel Taylor Coleridge, poet and critic, were moved here from the crypt of Highgate School in 1961. THE GROVE, which runs north from the church approach, is the most delightful street in Highgate, preserving many charming houses of the late 17th and early 18th centuries. In one of these (No. 3) Coleridge lived from 1823 until his death in 1834.

The Grove ends at HAMPSTEAD LANE, which leads west to Kenwood (see above) and east to the upper end of High Street at the OLD GATE HOUSE TAVERN, named from a former toll-house. Facing this is HIGHGATE SCHOOL (620 boys), a public school founded in 1565 by Sir Roger Cholmeley, Lord Chief Justice, but rebuilt in 1866 and added to subsequently. In NORTH ROAD, which starts beside the school, A. E. Housman wrote *A Shropshire Lad* (1896) at No. 17, one of a row of Georgian houses. Farther north, on the same side, are the distinctive HIGHPOINT FLATS, designed by Lubetkin and Tecton in 1935–8 and called by Le Corbusier a 'vertical garden city'.

North Road, which retains other 18th-century houses, is prolonged by North Hill down to the outer end of Archway Road, while Southwood Lane, running parallel on the east at first, descends to Highgate station near HIGHGATE WOOD, owned by the Corporation of London.

Islington and Highbury

STATIONS: ANGEL (Plan IV, A3), on the Northern line; ESSEX ROAD, on the Eastern Region; HIGHBURY & ISLINGTON, on the Victoria line and the Eastern Region; CANONBURY (closed on Sundays) and HIGHBURY & ISLINGTON, on the North London line (L.M.R.).

ISLINGTON HIGH STREET, running north from the Angel (Route 31), is prolonged by Upper Street past an approach to the ROYAL AGRICULTURAL HALL, opened in 1862 (for the Smithfield Show) and to be restored as a Business Design Centre. The interior, 384 ft long, has an iron-framed roof with a span of 150 ft. Farther on is ISLINGTON GREEN, at the corner of which is a statue of Sir Hugh Myddelton (d. 1631), who brought the New River to London in 1613. On the right, noted for its antique shops and market, is the picturesque CAMDEN PASSAGE, where Alexander Cruden, the Biblical scholar, died in 1770. Essex Road (see below) bears right from the green, but Upper Street goes on past ST MARY'S CHURCH, the parish church of Islington, built in 1754 and destroyed by bombing in 1940, except for its baroque steeple. Handsomely rebuilt in 1956 by Lord Mottistone and Paul Paget, it is embellished with fine woodwork and a large reredos with eight painted panels by Brian Thomas. CROSS STREET, on the right farther north, with some houses of about 1780, passes Dagmar Passage, the approach to the LITTLE ANGEL THEATRE, the only permanent puppet theatre in London. In Almeida Street, on the left opposite Cross Street, is the small ALMEIDA THEATRE, built in 1837 (by Roumieu and Gough) as the Literary Institute.

Barnsbury Street, farther on, runs north of MILNER SQUARE, an unusual layout of 1841–3 by the same architects. To the west, beyond Liverpool Road, is the estate of BARNSBURY, laid out from 1820 on by Thomas Cubitt, the developer of Belgravia. Good terraces survive in RICHMOND AVENUE (south of Barnsbury Street) and in BARNSBURY SQUARE (to the north) and THORNHILL SQUARE (about 1850; to the west). In OFFORD ROAD, farther north, leading to Caledonian Road, No. 99 was the London home of Benjamin Britten in 1965–70.

Canonbury Lane, on the right beyond ISLINGTON TOWN HALL (1925), leads to CANONBURY SQUARE, a characteristic layout of about 1800. Samuel Phelps (d. 1878), the actor-manager, lived at No. 8. To the north-east, in CANONBURY PLACE (built by John Dawes in 1780), is CANONBURY TOWER (adm., p. 31), consisting chiefly of a tall brick tower with a gabled wing on the west and a lower brick wing on the east. The chief survival of a country residence of the priors of St Bartholomew's, it was mostly rebuilt about 1595 by Sir John Spencer, Lord Mayor of London. In 1616–25 it was leased by Francis Bacon, and in 1763–4 Oliver Goldsmith lodged here. Two rooms in the west wing retain their rich Elizabethan oak panelling, and a gabled 16th–17th-century range survives (though much altered) east of the courtyard. The tower, together with a modern hall in the courtyard, is now the home of the Tavistock Repertory Company. ALWYNE VILLAS, with Alwyne Place and Road, to the south, and the crescents of CANONBURY PARK, to the east, comprise an interesting layout of 1835–45, mostly of semi-detached villas.

COMPTON TERRACE, running north from Canonbury Lane, is a late-Georgian terrace of 1806, interrupted by the UNION CHAPEL of 1888. Upper Street ends at Highbury & Islington station, from which Highbury Place continues northward, skirted by the pleasant park of HIGHBURY FIELDS. This is faced on the north-west by HIGHBURY TERRACE, a notable Georgian survival of 1789. Farther on in HIGHBURY PARK, which has villas of about 1830, is the chief office (at No. 85) of the NATIONAL CHILDREN'S HOME, founded in 1869 and now caring for 7,000 handicapped children. To the east of Highbury Grove, which extends Highbury Park southward, is ABERDEEN PARK, an estate combining Victorian villas with new terraces by Darborne and Darke (1982), and to the south-east is HIGHBURY NEW PARK, with large villas of about 1850.

Holloway Road runs north-west from Highbury & Islington station through an uninteresting district to Highgate (see above), passing the POLYTECHNIC OF

NORTH LONDON, founded in 1892 and now 'recognized' by London University. ST GEORGE'S CHURCH (1868) in Tufnell Park Road, on the left farther on, was converted in 1970–75 into an Elizabethan-type theatre. In HORNSEY ROAD, which runs parallel to Holloway Road on the north-west, is the MICHAEL SOBELL SPORTS CENTRE (1973) with the largest indoor sports hall in Britain, 240 ft long.

Stoke Newington

STATIONS: ESSEX ROAD, on the Eastern Region, DALSTON JUNCTION (E.R. and L.M.R.), and STOKE NEWINGTON (E.R.); and thence by bus.

STOKE NEWINGTON, one of the smallest of the former London boroughs, is approached from Islington Green by the long ESSEX ROAD, which passes (on the right) HALLIFORD STREET, where Benjamin Britten lived at No. 8 in 1970–76 and was visited by Shostakovich. Essex Road is extended by the winding Newington Green Road to NEWINGTON GREEN. Hence the long ALBION ROAD, retaining some villas and terraces of 1830, runs north to the old village centre. Here is the OLD PARISH CHURCH of St Mary, rebuilt in 1563 and one of the few examples of an Elizabethan church, remarkable for its unusual brick south arcade. The north aisle, added in 1829 by Barry and destroyed in 1940, was restored in 1953 by C. M. Oldrid Scott, who also carried out other repairs. In the chancel is the tomb of John Dudley (d. 1580) and his wife Elizabeth, whose second husband was Thomas Sutton, the founder of Charterhouse. The spacious NEW PARISH CHURCH, on the south side of the road, was built in 1858 in a florid Early Decorated style by Sir G. G. Scott, and supports a prominent spire 245 ft high, added in 1890 by J. Oldrid Scott. Restored in 1957 after war damage, the church has stained-glass windows of the Life of Christ by Francis Skeat. CLISSOLD PARK, close by, containing a villa of about 1830, is skirted on the west by Green Lanes, which leads south to Newington Green and north past the NEW RIVER RESERVOIRS, with a curious castellated pumping station of 1856. The road goes on to FINSBURY PARK, one of London's oldest municipal parks (bought about 1850), just within the outer London borough of Haringey.

Church Street runs east from the Town Hall to the north end of STOKE NEWINGTON HIGH STREET, which follows the straight course of the Roman Ermine Street and preserves a fine group of Queen Anne houses at Nos. 187–91. It is extended south by Stoke Newington Road towards Kingsland Road (see Route 32).

Bethnal Green and Hackney

STATIONS: BETHNAL GREEN, on the Central line; HACKNEY DOWNS, on the Eastern Region.

BETHNAL GREEN, a populous district long engaged in silk-weaving but now occupied to a large extent in the furniture and leather trades, is reached from

Shoreditch High Street (Route 32) by the drab Bethnal Green Road. In St Matthew's Row, on the right, is ST MATTHEW'S CHURCH, built in 1743–6 by George Dance the Elder, remodelled in 1861, gutted by bombing in 1940, and restored in 1961. Facing the east end of Bethnal Green Road is ST JOHN'S CHURCH, an original design by Sir John Soane (1828), but altered internally after a fire in 1870. To the north, entered from Cambridge Heath Road, is the MUSEUM OF CHILDHOOD (adm., p. 33), a branch of the Victoria and Albert Museum, opened in 1872 as the Bethnal Green Museum, in a building designed by Henry Scott and J. W. Wild for the South Kensington Museum, and given its new title in 1974. It houses a fine collection of toys, dolls and doll's houses, children's costumes, books and games, as well as costumes and Spitalfields silks. Old Ford Road, starting north of the museum, leads in half a mile to VICTORIA PARK, the largest open space in east London, laid out in 1845, with a boating lake, a swimming pool, and (on the north-east side) a pair of alcoves from old London Bridge. Israel Zangwill (d. 1926), the writer and philanthropist, lived at No. 288 Old Ford Road, facing the park.

Cambridge Heath Road is extended northward by Mare Street, the chief street of HACKNEY, a once-squalid district where many blocks of flats have now sprung up. On the east of the street is ST JOHN'S CHURCH, the large parish church, built in 1797 on the plan of a Greek cross by James Spiller and handsomely restored in 1958 after a fire. It has 16th–17th-century monuments from the previous church, good 18th-century woodwork, and an unusual steeple added on the north in 1813. In the south-west corner of the churchyard rises the solitary tower, built in 1519, of the demolished old church. SUTTON PLACE, with a terrace of the early 19th century, leads east from the churchyard to Homerton High Street, in which Nos. 2–4 are SUTTON HOUSE (N.T.; no adm. at present), a Tudor manor house of the early 16th century that later became the home of Thomas Sutton, the founder of Charterhouse (Route 29). Though much restored, it contains good 16th-century panelling and stone fireplaces. In the north-east of the borough lie HACKNEY MARSHES, a large recreation ground bounded by the river Lea.

Whitechapel and Bow

STATIONS: ALDGATE (Plan V, E3), on the Circle and Metropolitan lines; ALDGATE EAST (V, E3), WHITECHAPEL, STEPNEY GREEN, MILE END, BOW ROAD, and BROMLEY-BY-BOW, all on the District and Metropolitan lines (Mile End is also on the Central line).

WHITECHAPEL is a district once largely inhabited by Jewish traders and craftsmen whose forerunners began to settle in this neighbourhood after the Russian persecution of 1881. Whitechapel High Street (Route 33) is prolonged by the broad WHITECHAPEL ROAD, the main thoroughfare, passing the WHITECHAPEL BELL FOUNDRY of Messrs Mears and Stainbank, founded in 1570. In Fieldgate Street, on the right, is the large EAST LONDON MOSQUE (1985), designed by John Gill Associated. On the left of the main road is BOOTH HOUSE, a Salvation Army hostel for homeless men (by H. and M. Lidbetter, 1967), and on the right is THE LONDON

HOSPITAL, the largest general hospital in the country, founded in 1740 but rebuilt here after 1748 and enlarged at various times. The Medical College, attached to London University, was founded in 1775. Charles Bradlaugh (d. 1891), the advocate of free thought, lived at No. 29 in TURNER STREET, west of the hospital, and J. R. Green, the historian, lived in 1866–9 at ST PHILIP'S VICARAGE, to the south. In Brady Street, on the left of the main road beyond Whitechapel station, is a disused JEWS' CEMETERY (entrance at No. 37) containing the tomb of Nathan Meyer Rothschild (d. 1836), the English representative of the famous family of financiers.

From Cambridge Heath Road, which runs north to Bethnal Green (see above), Whitechapel Road is extended by the wide tree-lined boulevard of MILE END ROAD, so called because it began one mile from the old City wall at Aldgate. On the left at the outset is a bronze bust of William Booth (d. 1912), who began the work of the Salvation Army in the neighbourhood in 1865. Just beyond are the TRINITY ALMSHOUSES, established in 1695 for twenty-eight 'decay'd masters and commanders of ships or ye widows of such'. The attractive rows of dwellings, extended in the 19th century and badly damaged by bombing, were taken over by the L.C.C., who restored them in 1958–60. The chapel, on the north, is now a welfare centre for handicapped people. Farther on is STEPNEY GREEN, which leads south-east to St Dunstan's Church (see below). ROLAND HOUSE (No. 29) was purchased in 1914 for the Scout Association as a centre for scouting in the East End.

Mile End Road goes on past the former SPANISH AND PORTUGUESE JEWS' HOSPITAL, established in 1665, rebuilt in 1913, and now an old people's home. Behind is a small Jewish Cemetery (disused) opened in 1656, the first to be acquired by the Jews after their resettlement in England. Farther on is QUEEN MARY COLLEGE, since 1907 a branch of London University, but founded in 1887 and formerly called the East London College. The central buildings, of this period, were until 1953 the People's Palace, a cultural and recreational centre for east London suggested by the 'Palace of Delights' in Sir Walter Besant's novel *All Sorts and Conditions of Men.* A large extension to the west (1936) is decorated with reliefs by Eric Gill. The college has faculties of arts, laws, science, engineering, and economics.

Mile End Road, with early-19th-century terraces, crosses the Regent's Canal. In Burdett Road, on the right, is ST PAUL'S, BOW COMMON, by Robert Maguire and Keith Murray (1960), one of the most successful churches in the modern idiom. The main road continues to BOW, so called from an arched ('bow') bridge built over the river Lea in the 12th century, and famous for its porcelain in the 18th century. In Priscilla Road, on the right, are the DRAPERS' ALMSHOUSES, built in 1706 and restored in 1982. In Bow Road are the former POPLAR TOWN HALL, by E. C. Culpin (1937), with a civic theatre, and the long parish church of ST MARY STRATFORD BOW, on an island in the busy traffic. Rebuilt in the late 15th century, it has excessively narrow aisles, a good contemporary font, and a fine embossed ceiling in the chancel. The upper part of the tower, recast in 1829, has been reconstructed again after war damage. A new flyover crosses the Lea to Stratford, now part of the borough of Newham.

Stepney and Poplar (London Docklands)

STATIONS: TOWER HILL (Plan V, F3), on the Circle and District lines; SHADWELL (closed on Sundays) and WAPPING, on the Metropolitan line (New Cross branch); STEPNEY (EAST), on the Eastern Region line from Fenchurch Street.

STEPNEY, once notorious as a congested and poverty-stricken borough, includes the greater part of the 'East End' of London, with a population formerly largely employed in the neighbouring docks or other seafaring activities. Streets upon streets were completely devastated during the Second World War, and the slums have now been almost wholly replaced by large and airier blocks of flats designed by the L.C.C. and the G.L.C. The whole of the dockland region is being replanned under an adventurous new scheme (see p. 320).

EAST SMITHFIELD, starting from the north end of Tower Bridge Approach (Route 34), is extended by THE HIGHWAY (previously Ratcliff Highway), a long street which formerly had an infamous reputation for its drinking dens for seamen, but now the northern boundary of the Docklands redevelopment. On the north rises ST GEORGE-IN-THE-EAST, one of the most imposing churches of Nicholas Hawksmoor (1715–23), gutted in 1941 and rebuilt within the surviving shell by Arthur Bailey (1964). Wapping Lane, on the right just beyond the church, leads past the site of LONDON DOCKS (1805; now filled in) to the eastward end of WAPPING HIGH STREET, running parallel to the Thames and still partly encompassed by huge warehouses. An alley beside the TOWN OF RAMSGATE, an inn over quarter of a mile west, admits to the Wapping Old Stairs made famous in a ballad. The notorious Judge Jeffreys was arrested near here in 1688, disguised as a sailor. The High Street is continued downstream by WAPPING WALL, passing a picturesque old inn, the PROSPECT OF WHITBY, where Turner and Whistler painted. Glamis Road returns to The Highway, crossing the exit from SHADWELL BASIN, a survival of the dock system.

The Highway goes on past the church of ST PAUL'S, SHADWELL, rebuilt in 1820 by John Walters, and the KING EDWARD MEMORIAL PARK, overlooking the river, with a memorial slab (1922) to Willoughby, Frobisher, and other intrepid navigators who set sail in the 16th century from Ratcliff. In Butcher Row, which crosses the entrance to Rotherhithe Tunnel (see below) farther on to the left, are the buildings of the ROYAL FOUNDATION OF ST KATHARINE (adm., p. 35), dating from 1950–52. A cloister containing monuments from the foundation's previous church adjoining Regent's Park (compare p. 199) leads to the simple chapel, which has finely carved 14th-century stalls, with interesting misericords, and a Jacobean pulpit. The 18th-century Master's House was previously the rectory of the demolished St James's church. The foundation runs a Retreat and Conference Centre, and interests itself in social welfare work in the neighbourhood.

Butcher Row ends on the north at Cable Street, which leads to the right to COMMERCIAL ROAD (Route 33), the main thoroughfare of Stepney. Belgrave Street, starting a little to the west, runs north to ST DUNSTAN'S CHURCH, the interesting parish church of Stepney and the only medieval church in East London (apart from Bow), standing in a leafy churchyard once surrounded by a huge bombed area. Baptisms which take place at sea are frequently recorded in the registers. Believed to have been founded in the 10th century, perhaps by St Dunstan himself, the church is mainly of the 15th century. Notable in the chancel are the carved 13th-century sedilia and the canopied tomb of Sir Henry Colet (d. 1510), whose son, John Colet, afterwards dean of St Paul's, was vicar here in 1485–1505. Below the east window, which contains striking glass by Hugh Easton showing Stepney after the 'blitz', is set a remarkable late-Saxon stone rood-panel of the Crucifixion. In the south aisle can be seen the medieval rood-stairs and a curious stone brought from Carthage in 1663.

Commercial Road runs westward past ALBERT GARDENS, a square laid out about 1810 and restored in the late 1970s. In the other direction, it continues past Stepney (East) station and LIMEHOUSE BASIN (formerly the Regent's Canal Dock; 1820), at the Dockland end of the Grand Union Canal. In Branch Road, between these, begins the approach to ROTHERHITHE TUNNEL, built in 1904–8 below the river to Rotherhithe. Close by in Commercial Road is the brick DANISH SEAMEN'S CHURCH, designed by Holger Jensen (1959) and containing wooden figures of St Peter and St Paul by C. G. Cibber, the Danish sculptor (1696). Farther east is the memorial hostel (1924) of the BRITISH SAILORS' SOCIETY, incorporated in 1818, and beyond this the LIMEHOUSE TOWN HALL (1879) now contains the NATIONAL MUSEUM OF LABOUR HISTORY (adm., p. 33), opened in d in 1975 and illustrating the history of the working-class movement from the reformers of the 18th and 19th centuries to the post-War Labour governments. ST ANNE'S, LIMEHOUSE, to the east, is a characteristic church by Hawksmoor (1714–30), dominated by its steeple.

From the end of Commercial Road, WEST INDIA DOCK ROAD bears to the right through Limehouse, a district which once had an unsavoury reputation. The narrow side streets, however, lost their character after the bombing and have mostly been swept away. On the left is Pennyfields, formerly the centre of the Chinese quarter, and on the right the RAILWAY TAVERN, better known as 'Charley Brown's', with an assembly of old curios. The road ends at the entrance to the WEST INDIA DOCKS, laid out by Ralph Walker and William Jessop in 1802–6 on a broad peninsula known as the ISLE OF DOGS, part of which, around the docks (closed in 1980), was declared an Enterprise Zone in 1982. The Isle is connected with Mile End station on the underground by a new bus service, the Docklands Clipper.

To the right of the dock entrance is the DOCKMASTER'S HOUSE (1807), originally an excise office, but now the Business Research and Information Centre of the London Docklands Development Corporation. Behind this is the SALVATION ARMY BUILDING, opened as a mission for Scandinavian seamen in 1902. Market Road runs east from the dock entrance to BILLINGSGATE MARKET, the principal fish market for London, moved in 1982 from Lower Thames Street (see Route 27) to a building of 1915 (formerly a warehouse) redesigned and extended by Newman, Levinson & Partners, with a cold store which has a capacity of about 1,160 tons. A bell is tolled at 5.30 each weekday morning to signal the start of trading.

To the left of Marsh Wall, the road which passes the west end of the three docks, is the LEDGER BUILDING (by George Gwilt, 1803), now the head-office of the Development Corporation. Beyond this are two warehouses, by George Gwilt and John Rennie, completed for the opening of the Import Dock in 1902 and to be converted into a museum. On the right of the road are the restored CANNON WORKSHOPS, built in 1825 as barracks by Sir John Rennie. Beyond the SOUTH DOCK, laid out by William Jessop (1805), but several times extended, Millharbour turns right and Tiller Road right again to reach West Ferry Road, which crosses the entrance to MILLWALL DOCKS (designed by John Fowler), added to the system in 1868. Farther on to the right is BURRELL'S WHARF, where the first large iron ships in Britain were built in the early 19th century by William Fairbairn. The *Great Eastern*, designed by I. K. Brunel, was constructed here in 1853–8 by John Scott Russell. Some of the original buildings survive.

At the south end of the Isle of Dogs are the ISLAND GARDENS, commanding a splendid view of Greenwich, with which the Isle is linked by a foot tunnel of 1902. East Ferry Road, running to the east of the Millwall Docks, passes the LONDON DOCKLANDS ARENA, a large shed which is to be converted (by 1986) to provide facilities for sports, exhibitions, and conferences. Beyond is the FOSTER OLSEN BUILDING, designed by Norman Foster and the first in Britain to employ heat and light reflecting mirror glass (1970). Prestons Road goes on via the BLUE BRIDGE, a draw-bridge of 1969 crossing the entrance to the South Dock, and the GUN INN, with a view of the Blackwall Reach of the Thames. The road, skirting POPLAR DOCK, built in 1830 but since enlarged, comes out near the east end of Poplar High Street.

The line of Commercial Road is extended by EAST INDIA DOCK ROAD through the southern part of POPLAR, which shared the marine interests of Stepney and also suffered disastrously during the war. On the north of the road is the district of LANSBURY, named in honour of the Labour leader George Lansbury (1859–1940), and the first part to be completed of a vast housing scheme planned by the L.C.C. over an area laid waste by bombing. It includes a modern market place, the Trinity Congregational Church, in a contemporary style by C. C. Handisyde and D. R. Stark (1951), and a large Roman Catholic Church by A. Gilbert Scott (1955), to an unusual design, with a massive brick tower raised over a central space. Farther east is ALL SAINTS CHURCH, the parish church of Poplar, built in 1823 by Charles Hollis, with an impressive Ionic portico and a successful steeple in the manner of Wren; the spacious and handsome interior has an unusual baldacchino over the altar. Near the gate of EAST INDIA DOCK, opened in 1802 (and closed in 1967), is the northern approach to BLACKWALL TUNNEL (1897), which passes beneath the Thames towards Greenwich (a duplicate tunnel was completed, downstream, in 1967). Near the river entrance to the dock, but within the boundaries of the Brunswick Wharf power station (visitors usually admitted) is the VIRGINIA SETTLERS' MEMORIAL, recast in 1970, commemorating the 105 adventurers who sailed in 1606 from Blackwall to found the first permanent British colony, at Jamestown, Virginia.

Bermondsey and Walworth

STATIONS: TOWER HILL (Plan V, F3), on the Circle and District lines; LONDON BRIDGE (IX, E2) and ELEPHANT & CASTLE (IX, D3), on the Northern line (Bank section) and the Southern Region (Elephant & Castle is also the terminus of the Bakerloo line). — RIVER LAUNCHES from Westminster to Tower Pier, see p. 56.

BERMONDSEY, now part of the borough of Southwark, borders the south bank of the river Thames (see Route 34) and is traversed by TOWER BRIDGE ROAD (IX, E, F3). The road crosses Tooley Street, which leads west towards London Bridge station and east towards Rotherhithe (see below). Tower Bridge Road goes on to ST MARY MAGDALEN, the parish church of Bermondsey, founded in 1290, rebuilt in 1679 and much restored in 1883. It has good 17th–18th-century woodwork (organ case, galleries, pulpit, and reredos) and preserves a carved 12th-century capital from Bermondsey Abbey, a flourishing house of Cluniac monks established on this site in 1082. Catherine of Valois, the widow of Henry V, died in the abbey in 1437 and Elizabeth Woodville, widow of Edward IV, in 1492. Just to the south is BERMONDSEY SQUARE, where a celebrated 'rag fair' (transferred from the Caledonian Market, Islington) takes place every Friday (from 7 a.m.).

Tower Bridge Road continues to the junction of Great Dover Street with the OLD KENT ROAD, long known as the resort of costermongers. The New Kent Road goes on from the junction to the ELEPHANT AND CASTLE (IX, D3), the meeting place of six busy streets, named from a tavern mentioned at least as early as the 16th century, and now rebuilt as part of a new plan (1960–65), centred round a broad carriageway linking two roundabouts. On the east of Newington Causeway, which runs north-east to the Borough High Street (see Route 35), is the huge ALEXANDER FLEMING HOUSE (by Ernö Goldfinger, 1963), the headquarters of the DEPARTMENT OF HEALTH and Social Security, established in 1968 by the merging of two ministries. Farther on (at No. 101) are the offices of the BRITISH TECHNOLOGY GROUP, formed in 1981 by combining the National Enterprise Board and the National Research Development Corporation. On the south of St George's Road, which leads north-west to Lambeth Road, is the LONDON COLLEGE OF PRINTING, built in 1964 and extended in 1969–73. On the east of the carriageway is an impressive SHOPPING CENTRE (1965), and facing this is the METROPOLITAN TABERNACLE, built in 1861 for Charles Haddon Spurgeon (d. 1892), the Baptist preacher, and largely rebuilt after a fire in 1898. Completely gutted by bombing, it was rebuilt again in 1959 behind its original classical façade.

Newington Butts, going on south-west from the southern roundabout, is extended by Kennington Park Road to Kennington. WALWORTH ROAD turns south-east from the roundabout, passing the former SOUTHWARK TOWN HALL (1866). The adjoining Central Library houses the CUMING MUSEUM (adm., p. 32), restored in 1959 after war damage and devoted largely to the history of Southwark, but containing also relics of Michael Faraday, the pioneer of electro-magnetism, who was born in 1791 in Newington Butts. Nos. 144–52, a late-18th-century terrace on the other side of Walworth Road, are now the headquarters of the LABOUR PARTY, founded in 1900. The ROBERT BROWNING SETTLEMENT, at No. 3 in Browning Street, on the left farther on, houses a collection of memorials of the poet (shown to visitors on application). Yet farther on, in Liverpool Grove, is ST PETER'S CHURCH, the parish church of Walworth, built in 1825 by Sir John Soane and restored in 1953 after war damage. Walworth Road goes on south towards Camberwell Green. Albany Road, on the left, skirts BURGESS PARK, newly created on a derelict site by the G.L.C.

Rotherhithe and Deptford

STATIONS: ROTHERHITHE, SURREY DOCKS, NEW CROSS, and NEW CROSS GATE, on the Metropolitan line from Whitechapel; DEPTFORD, on the Southern Region.

ROTHERHITHE and its neighbour Deptford stand on the south bank of the Thames, opposite Stepney and Poplar, and were once largely inhabited by dock-workers and others with seagoing connections. From Tower Bridge Road (see above), TOOLEY STREET runs east past the head of ST SAVIOUR'S DOCK, an inlet of the Thames. Mill Street, on the left beyond this, leads to BERMONDSEY WALL WEST, which, with the streets to the east, once wound through a forest of warehouses. Many of these are now derelict and others have been demolished, and the whole area downstream to the former Surrey Docks is included in the London Docklands Development scheme (see Route 34).

Tooley Street is continued by JAMAICA ROAD past West Lane, which leads to Bermondsey Wall East, with the picturesque (and now solitary) 18th-century ANGEL INN, facing the river. Jamaica Road is extended in turn by Brunel Road to Rotherhithe station. St Marychurch Street, on the left before this, leads to ST MARY'S CHURCH, the pleasant parish church of Rotherhithe, built in 1714–47 and containing good 18th-century woodwork. To the south is the 18th-century charity school, and empty warehouses of the early 19th century, in the neighbourhood, were converted in 1976 for the use of artists and craftsmen. ROTHERHITHE STREET, following the river eastward from the church, makes a half circle enclosing the site of the SURREY COMMERCIAL DOCKS, first opened in 1807 and once the centre of the timber trade, but closed in 1970 and now largely filled in. The chief survival is the GREENLAND DOCK, near the south end, reconstructed in 1894–1904 by Sir John Wolfe Barry and now used for water sports.

Lower Road, passing the southern entrance to ROTHERHITHE TUNNEL, runs south-east from the east end of Jamaica Road, passing the miscalled SOUTHWARK PARK. It is extended by Evelyn Street to DEPTFORD (pronounced 'Det-ford'), long famous for its naval dockyard, founded by Henry VII in 1485 and closed in 1869. The Emperor Peter the Great worked as a shipwright here in 1698, and occupied the residence of John Evelyn, the diarist, at Sayes Court, the site of which is indicated by the small SAYES PARK, on the left. The PEPYS ESTATE (farther left), begun in 1962, covers the site of the ROYAL NAVAL VICTUALLING YARD opened in 1745 and closed in 1961. Some of the Yard's 18th-century buildings have survived, and the quayside walk commands a wide view across the river to the Isle of Dogs and downstream to Greenwich. The royal dockyard lay to the south-east.

To the north of Creek Road, beyond the end of Deptford High Street, is ST NICHOLAS'S CHURCH, rebuilt in 1697 (except for the late-14th-century tower), but gutted by bombing and restored in 1957. The 17th-century woodwork, including a carving by Grinling Gibbons, has been returned, and a tablet has been put up to Christopher Marlowe, who was slain in a brawl at Deptford in 1593 and is buried in the churchyard. To the east of High Street is ST PAUL'S CHURCH, by Thomas Archer (1712–30), with a fine semicircular portico supporting a noble steeple, huge Corinthian columns inside, and rich plaster ceilings. ALBURY STREET, to the north of the church, has some early-18th-century houses, partly restored, with fine doorcases. Creek Road goes on east across the Deptford Creek, the mouth of the Ravensbourne, to Greenwich.

Deptford High Street continues southward to NEW CROSS ROAD, which leads west past the north end of Lewisham Way and the former DEPTFORD TOWN HALL, by Lanchester, Stewart, and Rickards (1904). Near this end of Lewisham Way is GOLDSMITHS' COLLEGE, founded by the Goldsmiths' Company and presented to London University in 1904. It has faculties of arts, education, music, and science. The building (of 1843) formerly housed the Royal Naval College (founded in 1733), moved here from Portsmouth. New Cross Road goes on west and north-west to the OLD KENT ROAD. In Asylum Road, on the left, are CAROLINE GARDENS, formerly the Licensed Victuallers' Benevolent Institution, built by Henry Rose from 1827 on, with a classical chapel in the centre. On the left of Old Kent Road (at No. 682) is the LIVESEY MUSEUM (adm., p. 33), in a building of 1890, restored after war damage and opened in 1974. In addition to the permanent exhibits, of local interest, the museum arranges special exhibitions (each lasting about three months) and is, with the Cuming Museum (see above), an archaeological centre for Southwark and Lambeth.

QUEEN'S ROAD continues westward the direction of New Cross Road to Peckham High Street (p. 527). In St Mary's Road, on the left, is the PIONEER HEALTH CENTRE, built in 1935 by Sir Owen Williams as an early experiment in combining medicine with social needs (now called the South-East London Practitioner Centre).

Greenwich, Blackheath, and Lewisham

STATIONS: GREENWICH and MAZE HILL, LEWISHAM and BLACKHEATH, all on the Southern Region. — RIVER LAUNCHES from Westminster, Charing Cross and Tower Piers, see p. 56. — GREENWICH PARK is open always; Restaurant in the National Maritime Museum (open in summer during museum hours), cafeteria near the Old Royal Observatory.

GREENWICH (pronounced 'Gren-nij'), one of the pleasantest suburbs of London, lies on the south bank of the Thames, nearly five miles below London Bridge by water. It has long been famous for its park, its hospital, and its observatory: the hospital now houses the Royal Naval College and the observatory has been moved to Sussex, but Greenwich has a maritime museum which should not be missed by any lover of the sea.

Greenwich High Road, the approach from the direction of London (A206), passes the station and the former TOWN HALL, by E. C. Culpin (1939), with a soaring clock-tower, 165 ft high. At the end of the road is ST ALFEGE'S CHURCH (adm., p. 32), traditionally on the place where Alphege, or Aelfheah, archbishop of Canterbury, was martyred by the Danes in 1011. Henry VIII was baptized in the medieval building; the present church, designed in 1712 by Nicholas Hawskmoor and completed by John James, who also added the steeple (1730), was carefully restored in 1953, after severe war damage, by Sir Albert Richardson. The chiaroscuro decoration of the apse, by Thornhill (much damaged), has been repainted by Glyn Jones. In the church are the tomb of Thomas Tallis (d. 1585), the 'father of English church music', and a monument to General Wolfe (d. 1759), whose flag is also preserved.

Church Street runs north from St Alfege's to GREENWICH PIER, the terminal point of the river launches. Close by is the permanent berth of the CUTTY SARK (adm., p. 32), the last and most famous of the sailing clippers, launched at Dumbarton on the Clyde in 1869 and brought here in 1954, partly for use as an educational centre of the Mercantile Marine; after careful refitting, she was opened to visitors in 1957. Below decks is an interesting exhibition of old figureheads, prints and paintings, and maritime relics. Farther west is berthed the GIPSY MOTH IV (adm., p. 32), the yacht in which Sir Francis Chichester sailed single-handed round the world in 1966–7.

A pedestrian tunnel near the pier gives access under the river to the Isle of Dogs (p. 517) and a footwalk runs along the riverside north of the Royal Naval College to the TRAFALGAR TAVERN (1837; restored in 1965), at the north end of Park Row. Farther east is TRINITY HOSPITAL, almshouses of about 1613, much restored in 1812.

In King William Walk, which leads south from the pier to the National Maritime Museum, is the main entrance to the ROYAL NAVAL COLLEGE for the higher education of naval officers (adm., p. 34), moved from Lewisham (see below) in 1873 and occupying the noble group of buildings erected mainly from 1696 onward as GREENWICH HOSPITAL. This stands on the site of the royal palace of Placentia, begun in 1428 by Humphrey, Duke of Gloucester, and a favourite residence of the Tudor monarchs. Henry VIII and his daughters Mary I and Elizabeth I were all born here, and Edward VI died here in 1553. A new palace begun in 1664 for Charles II by John Webb was proceeded with after 1694 as a home for disabled seamen. Sir Christopher Wren, who took over the design in 1696, was joined in 1700 by Nicholas Hawksmoor. The buildings, consisting of four separate blocks, were opened in 1705 (though not completed until 1752), but the hospital was abandoned in 1869 in favour of pensions. In the south-west block is the PAINTED HALL, completed in 1703 by Wren and so called from the effective wall and ceiling paintings by Sir James Thornhill (1708–27). The artist has depicted himself in the painting of George I and his family on the end wall. The CHAPEL, in the south-east block, was designed by Wren, completed in 1752 by Ripley, and remodelled in 1789, after a fire, by James Stuart and William Newton; it was redecorated in 1955. The fine pulpit, lectern, and font were made of wood from the old dockyard at Deptford; the altarpiece consists of a huge painting, 25 ft high, of St Paul shaking off the Viper, by Benjamin West. The organ, built in 1789 by Samuel Green, is one of the finest in Britain. In the angle between King William Walk and Romney Road (south of the college) is the SEAMEN'S HOSPITAL, built in 1763, by 'Athenian' Stuart, as the Greenwich Hospital infirmary and altered in 1811 after a fire.

In Romney Road is one of the entrances to the NATIONAL MARITIME MUSEUM (adm., p. 33), a fascinating survey of naval history from Tudor times to the present day. There is another entrance on the east from Park Row, approached from Maze Hill station via Park Vista. In the centre of the buildings is the QUEEN'S HOUSE, designed by Inigo Jones, the first example in England of the Palladian style, begun in 1616 for Anne of Denmark, consort of James I, and completed in 1635 for Henrietta Maria, the queen of Charles I. It is connected by colonnades with wings on the east and west, added in 1805–16 (by D. A. Alexander) to accommodate the Royal Hospital School for the children of sailors and marines. The school moved to Suffolk in 1933 and the museum was opened here in 1937. The arrangement is mostly chronological, starting in the Queen's House with the Tudor and Stuart period, continuing in the West Wing with exhibits up to the close of the Napoleonic Wars, and finishing in the East Wing, which brings the history up to the Second World War, but some of the galleries are being rearranged in 1985. The galleries contain notable silver, porcelain, glass, ship models, and mementoes of famous seamen, but are chiefly remarkable for the magnificent collection of naval scenes and seascapes by the Van de Veldes, De Loutherbourg, Turner, and others, and the portraits by Kneller, Lely, Hogarth, Reynolds, Gainsborough, Romney, Copley, and many other famous artists.

The rooms in the West Wing hold a fine assembly of portraits and personal relics of Lord Nelson (including the uniform worn by him at the Battle of Trafalgar), and of Captain Cook and other seafarers. In the Neptune Hall, to the south, are the *Reliant*, a 90-ft paddle tug (1907), the *Donola*, a Thames pleasure launch of 1893, and other craft, and displays showing the development of the steamship, boat-building, sailmaking, etc. On the west the hall opens to the Barge House, containing the state barge of Mary II (1689), a barge built for Frederick, Prince of Wales (1732), and two 18th-century barges used by the Commissioners of the Navy. Gallery A, on the Lower Ground Floor, illustrates the history of wooden shipbuilding and Gallery B the archaeology of water transport, with displays showing the excavation of the Bronze Age boats at North Ferriby (Yorkshire), the oldest known boats in Europe; the Sutton Hoo ship (see p. 351); and the boat of the Viking period from Graveney (Kent). Galleries C–E are confined to yachting. A wing extending to the west contains the interesting Navigation Room, with nautical instruments, globes, charts, etc., among them four chronometers made in 1736–64 by John Harrison.

Above are a gallery for special exhibitions and the Picture Department, with the Print Study Room (open on Wednesdays and Thursdays by appointment), containing many thousands of prints, drawings, and photographs. The Caird Library and Reading Room are in the West Central Wing, the Lecture Theatre on the upper floor of the East Wing.

Behind the museum rises GREENWICH PARK, a royal park laid out for Charles II by Le Nôtre, the landscape-gardener of Louis XIV, and notable for its sweet chestnuts, oaks, and hawthorns. The hill in the centre commands a wonderful view over Greenwich to east London and the Docks, with Tower Bridge and St Paul's to the left. The statue here of General Wolfe, by Tait Mackenzie (1930), was given by the Canadian nation. Near by is the OLD ROYAL OBSERVATORY (adm., p. 34). The observatory was established in 1675, primarily for the assistance of navigation, but owing to the growing pollution of the atmosphere it was transferred in 1948–57 to Herstmonceux, in Sussex, and the buildings became an annexe of the National Maritime Museum. Outside the courtyard gate is a twenty-four-hour clock of 1851 showing Greenwich Mean Time, which remains British Standard Time. The zero meridian of longitude passes through the Meridian Building, on the south of the courtyard, and is marked in the cobbled yard. Flamsteed House, west of the courtyard, was built in 1675 by Wren for John Flamsteed (d. 1719), the first Astronomer Royal. It has 17th-century living rooms on the ground floor, with a fine octagon room over them containing displays on astronomy and navigation. The mast on the turret above carries a time-ball that falls every day at precisely 1 p.m. In Flamsteed's Observatory (rebuilt), to the south, are his quadrant and sextant. The Meridian Building, a new observatory built in 1749 and since enlarged, contains instruments used by Edmond Halley and other early Astronomers Royal. The Great Equatorial Building (1857), to the south-east, has a prominent dome housing a twenty-eight-inch telescope. Farther south, in a building of 1891–8, is the interesting CAIRD PLANETARIUM (adm., p. 34), the second in Britain, opened in 1965.

Near the west gate of the park is MACARTNEY HOUSE (1694), where General Wolfe lived from the age of eleven, and lower down, in CROOMS HILL, are several fine 17th–18th-century houses, including the Manor House of 1697, and the GREENWICH THEATRE, converted from an old music-hall (by Brian Meeking) in 1965–9, with an art gallery incorporated. In Chesterfield Walk, which runs south alongside the park, is the RANGER'S HOUSE (adm., p. 34), a handsome brick house built in 1688–94, enlarged in 1749 by the Earl of Chesterfield, and later occupied by Field-Marshal Viscount Wolseley. It contains the fine Suffolk Collection, mainly of Elizabethan and Stuart portraits. To the east of the park, in Maze Hill, is VANBRUGH CASTLE, built for himself in 1717–26 by Sir John Vanbrugh and now a school. WOODLANDS (adm., p. 36), in Mycenae Road, nearly half a mile farther east, was built in 1774 for John Julius Angerstein (whose collection formed the nucleus of the National Gallery) and is now a local history and arts centre.

To the south of the park stretches BLACKHEATH, an open breezy common, once the resort of highwaymen and the rallying-point of the Kentish rebels in 1381 (under Wat Tyler) and 1450 (under Jack Cade). The first golf club in the world was founded on the common in 1608 (but has been moved to Eltham). Sir James Clark Ross (d. 1862), the Polar explorer, lived at No. 2 in ELIOT PLACE, to the south-west of the common. MONTPELIER ROW, facing the south side, has houses of the late 18th and early 19th centuries. Farther south are Blackheath station and BLACKHEATH VILLAGE. In Independents Road, near by, are the headquarters, opened in 1980, of the CHURCH ARMY, the evangelical and social organization founded in 1882 by Wilson Carlile. Sir Arthur Eddington (d. 1944), the scientist, lived at No. 4 in

BENNETT PARK, east of the station, and Nathaniel Hawthorne, the American author, stayed in 1856 at No. 4 in POND ROAD, east of Montpelier Row. THE PARAGON, at the south-east angle of the common, designed by Michael Searles about 1790 and restored after war damage, is a noble crescent of seven villas connected by colonnades. In MORDEN ROAD, starting at the east end, Charles Gounod, the composer, stayed in 1870 at No. 15. Farther east is MORDEN COLLEGE, a home for City merchants founded in 1695 by Sir John Morden; the delightful building, confidently attributed to Wren, is well seen from the footpath passing north of the grounds.

Lewisham Hill descends from the south-west corner of Blackheath to LEWISHAM, a borough of little interest centred round the Ravensbourne River. In GRANVILLE PARK, a road on the left, Samuel Smiles (d. 1904), the author of *Self-Help*, lived at No. 11. From LEWISHAM HIGH STREET, farther south, Loampit Vale and Hill and Lewisham Way run north-west to New Cross (see p. 520). The long High Street goes on south to ST MARY'S CHURCH, rebuilt by John Gibson in 1774–7 (except for part of the 15th-century tower) and poorly restored by Sir Arthur Blomfield, who added the chancel (1881). The Vicarage, a fine house of 1692, is to the north, opposite the impressive LADYWELL BATHS (1965). Farther on, at Catford, is the TOWN HALL, rebuilt in 1932. At LEE, three-quarters of a mile east of the High Street, the public library occupies the graceful 18th-century Manor House.

Woolwich, Charlton, and Eltham

STATIONS: CHARLTON, WOOLWICH DOCKYARD, and WOOLWICH ARSENAL, on the North Kent line (S.R.) to Dartford; ELTHAM (WELL HALL), on an alternative line via Lewisham.

WOOLWICH (pronounced 'Wool-ij'), on the south side of the Thames some way below Greenwich, is a busy industrial and garrison town long famous for the largest and oldest military arsenal in Britain. BERESFORD SQUARE, the market centre of the town, lies between Woolwich Arsenal station and the main entrance (1829 and later) to the ROYAL ARSENAL, established in 1717 as the Brass Gun Foundry. Nearly 40,000 workers were employed here during the Second World War, but closure of the arsenal took place in 1963–7. Some of the original buildings survive, and part of the grounds, on the north-east, is being taken into THAMESMEAD, a mainly residential town planned in 1967 by the G.L.C. and eventually to have a population of over 40,000. Amenities include lakes for sailing, etc., 230 acres of open spaces, and a riverside walk; a yacht harbour is to be built.

Beresford Street, running north-west from Beresford Square, is extended by Woolwich High Street past the approach to the WOOLWICH FREE FERRY, opened in 1889; its picturesque paddle-steamers were replaced in 1963 by diesel-powered ferries, and a new terminal was completed in 1966. On the left beyond the approach is ST MARY MAGDALEN'S, the spacious parish church, built on a rise facing the river in 1727–39 and enlarged by a new chancel in 1894. Farther on, to the north of Church Street, is the site of the ROYAL DOCKYARD (closed in 1869), founded by Henry

VIII, where the *Great Harry* was launched in 1515 and from which Sir John Franklin set out on his ill-fated expedition to the Arctic in 1845.

Church Street is extended by WOOLWICH ROAD to Greenwich, passing Maryon-Wilson Park. Across the river to the north (and reached by Eastmoor Road) is the imposing THAMES FLOOD BARRIER, begun in 1974 to combat the possible flooding of riverside London during an exceptionally high tide, and completed in 1982. Designed by Rendel, Palmer, and Tritton, the barrier is about 610 yds wide, with four gaps of 200 ft each and two of 103 ft each, closed by huge steel gates 66 ft tall and each weighing 1,300 tons, which can be raised by hydraulic machinery contained in massive piers with unusual boat-shaped roofs. It is estimated that some 50,000 ships pass through in a year. A Visitors' Centre (adm., p. 35) on the south bank affords a good view of the barrier and has a display explaining its working.

Green's End, ascending south-west from Beresford Square and passing the end of Powis Street, the chief shopping street of Woolwich, is extended past the TOWN HALL (by A. B. Thomas, 1906; now the civic centre of Greenwich) by Wellington Street, in which is the THAMES POLYTECHNIC, founded in 1890 (as the Woolwich Polytechnic) and reformed in 1970. Wellington Street is extended by Artillery Place to Repository Road, on the west of which is THE ROTUNDA, a prominent tent-like building designed by Nash and erected in St James's Park for the visit of the allied sovereigns in 1814. Moved here in 1819, it now contains an interesting artillery museum (adm., p. 34). In Stadium Road, the continuation of Repository Road, is the QUEEN ELIZABETH MILITARY HOSPITAL, moved from Millbank to a new building by Powell and Moya (1972–5).

Artillery Place is extended westward by Hill Reach towards the older part of CHARLTON, likewise included in the borough of Greenwich. At the centre is ST LUKE'S CHURCH, a pleasing little brick building of about 1630 with a gabled porch, enlarged by a north aisle in 1693 and by a new chancel in 1840. A little to the south stands CHARLTON HOUSE (adm., p. 31), an excellent Jacobean mansion with a three-storeyed porch, built in 1607–12 for Sir Adam Newton, tutor to Henry, Prince of Wales, restored after bombing, and now a public library and community centre.

Woolwich New Road, starting south of Beresford Square, ascends near the huge ROYAL ARTILLERY BARRACKS, built in 1775–1802 facing the north side of Woolwich Common. The road skirting the east side of the common passes the former ROYAL MILITARY ACADEMY, familiarly known as 'The Shop', founded in 1741. The buildings, by James Wyatt (1808), have since been enlarged, but in 1946 the academy was merged with the Royal Military College at Sandhurst (Berkshire). Academy Road climbs up to SHOOTERS HILL, where it reaches the old Canterbury road, on the site of the Roman Watling Street. A divergence on the left to an open space east of the cross-roads opens up a view over the river and the East End of London. Before the road reaches the highest point of the hill (425 ft), a lane on the right leads to CASTLEWOOD, a fine public park with a tower (1784) commemorating the capture of Severndroog, on the Malabar Coast, by Sir William James in 1755.

Well Hall Road, prolonging Academy Road, descends from Shooters Hill to the dormitory town of ELTHAM (pronounced 'El-tam'). In a public park on the right, beyond the London–Rochester road (A2), is WELL HALL (adm., p. 35), the surviving wing of a house of 1568 or earlier showing good Tudor brickwork. Now called the 'Tudor Barn', it contains a restaurant and an art gallery for loan exhibitions. At the crossing of the HIGH STREET, which retains some old houses, is ST JOHN'S CHURCH, rebuilt in 1872 by Sir Arthur Blomfield. In the churchyard are buried Thomas Doggett (d. 1721), the actor, founder of Doggett's Coat and Badge, and Sir William James (d. 1783; see above). To the south, a road on the right leads to ELTHAM PALACE, a favourite residence of the English kings from Henry III to Henry VIII. Edward III received John II of France here in 1363, on his return to voluntary exile, and Henry IV was married here by proxy to Joan of Navarre (1402). The palace, approached by a bridge (probably of the 15th century) over the former moat, is now the headquarters of the Institute of Army Education. Much the most interesting part is the restored Banqueting Hall (adm., p. 32) built in 1479–82 for Edward IV, which has a splendid hammerbeam roof, with massive pendants, and good oriel windows. The adjoining house was mainly built after 1931 by Seely and Paget, though the outer walls are partly of the 14th century. The 15th–16th-century houses on the north of the bridge were formerly the 'Chancellor's Lodging'. To the south-east Court Road skirts the Royal Blackheath golf course (see above), the club house of which (out of sight from the road) is the former ELTHAM LODGE, a fine house of 1665 by Hugh May.

Camberwell and Herne Hill

STATIONS: ELEPHANT & CASTLE, on the Bakerloo and Northern lines and the Southern Region, and thence by bus; DENMARK HILL and HERNE HILL, on the Southern Region.

CAMBERWELL, a mainly residential district, is reached from the Elephant and Castle (p. 518) by Walworth Road and its long extension Camberwell Road, which leads to CAMBERWELL GREEN, an open space shaded by a variety of trees. Thence Church Street runs east past the end of CAMBERWELL GROVE, an avenue with well-preserved late-Georgian houses. Joseph Chamberlain, the statesman, was born in 1836 at No. 188. Farther east is the tall ST GILES'S CHURCH, rebuilt in the Early Decorated style by Sir George Gilbert Scott (1844), with 14th-century sedilia and piscina, and grisailles of 13th-century glass in the west window. Farther on, in Peckham Road, are the SOUTHWARK TOWN HALL (1934; formerly the Camberwell Town Hall) and the SOUTH LONDON ART GALLERY (1898), which arranges good loan exhibitions (adm., p. 35). Peckham Road is extended by Peckham High Street towards New Cross (p. 520).

DENMARK HILL ascends to the south from Camberwell Green, passing KING'S COLLEGE HOSPITAL, founded in 1839 and moved in 1913 to new buildings here, enlarged in 1965–8 by George, Trew, and Dunn. The Medical School, founded in 1831, was affiliated to London University in 1909. In Champion Park, the turning on the left beyond the railway, is the WILLIAM BOOTH MEMORIAL TRAINING COLLEGE of the Salvation Army, with statues of the founder and his wife (by G. E.

Wade) flanking the entrance to the large buildings, which were designed by Sir Giles G. Scott (1929). The main road continues past RUSKIN PARK (commemorating the residence in this locality from 1823 to 1871 of John Ruskin) and Red Post Hill (on the left), leading to North Dulwich station (see below), to reach HERNE HILL. To the east of the station here is ST PAUL'S CHURCH, mostly rebuilt in 1858 by G. E. Street and much praised by Ruskin, who is commemorated by a tablet (1900). To the south-west of the station is the pleasant BROCKWELL PARK, with the hall of 1813 (by D. R. Roper) and a secluded old-world garden.

Dulwich and Crystal Palace

STATIONS: NORTH DULWICH, WEST DULWICH, SYDENHAM HILL, and CRYSTAL PALACE, all on the Southern Region.

DULWICH (pronounced 'Dul-lij'), one of the quietest and most attractive suburbs of London, still retains to a large extent a rural atmosphere. This it owes in the first place to the benefactions of Edward Alleyn (1566–1626), the actor-manager and 'master of the royal beasts', who purchased the manor in 1605 and in 1619 founded the College of God's Gift, a trust which now maintains Dulwich College and several other schools, as well as the Dulwich College Picture Gallery.

The road leading south from North Dulwich station goes through DULWICH VILLAGE, which has many good Georgian houses. In the angle between Gallery Road (leading towards West Dulwich station) and College Road are the OLD COLLEGE BUILDINGS, the 17th-century home of Alleyn's college, much altered in the 19th century and now comprising almshouses (part of the original foundation) and the offices of the trust. The chapel (entered from the cloister), recast in 1823, contains the grave of Edward Alleyn and a fine marble font of 1729 designed by Gibbs.

In College Road is the entrance to the DULWICH COLLEGE GALLERY (adm., p. 32), the nucleus of which was a bequest of Edward Alleyn. This was greatly enhanced by paintings collected by Noël Desenfans, a French picture dealer, for King Stanislaus of Poland (who abdicated before he could receive them) and bequeathed in 1807 to his friend Sir Peter Francis Bourgeois, the painter, who in 1811 left them to the college. The gallery, the first public art gallery opened in London (1814), was designed by Sir John Soane and has been well restored after its damage by bombing. The splendid collection is especially notable for its Dutch paintings (Rembrandt, Gerard Dou, J. van Ruisdael, Aelbert Cuyp, Hobbema, etc.) and its portraits by 17th–18th-century British artists (Lely, Kneller, Hogarth, Richard Wilson, Allan Ramsay, Gainsborough – especially of members of the Linley family – Reynolds, Romney, Hoppner, and Lawrence). The Italian School is represented by Raphael (two small panel paintings), Veronese, Domenichino, Guido Reni, Guercino, Carlo Dolci, Canaletto, and G. D. Tiepolo; the Flemish School by Rubens (including several fine sketches), Van Dyck, and the two Teniers; the Spanish School by Murillo (especially the lovely Madonna with the Rosary); and the French School by Poussin (several characteristic works), Charles Le Brun, Watteau, and Lancret.

Opposite the old college is an entrance to DULWICH PARK, best seen when its azaleas are in flower. Lordship Lane, east of the park, ascends towards FOREST HILL. In London Road here is the HORNIMAN MUSEUM (adm., p. 32), in a highly original building by C. Harrison Townsend (1897–1902), worth a visit also for its ethnographical collections and its musical instruments, and possessing a fine library.

College Road goes on south from the gallery past DULWICH COLLEGE, a public school (1,350 boys) administered by the Alleyn Trust. The Italianate brick buildings, by the younger Charles Barry (1866–70), have been several times extended. Famous 'Old Alleynians' include Sir Ernest Shackleton, the Polar explorer, one of whose rescue boats is preserved in the grounds. The road ascends through the only surviving toll-gate in London to UPPER NORWOOD. An elevated plateau here is the site of the CRYSTAL PALACE, an immense structure of glass and iron, designed by Sir Joseph Paxton for the Great Exhibition of 1851, but transferred from Hyde Park and redesigned by Paxton in 1854. In 1936 it was completely destroyed by fire, except for the two tall towers at each end, and these were pulled down in 1940. The soaring television transmitting mast, 708 ft high, was erected by the B.B.C. in 1958. Part of the grounds has been converted into a public park, with a children's zoo, a boating-lake, modern sculptures, and curious 'prehistoric' animals in bronze, the only relic of the 1851 exhibition. The NATIONAL SPORTS CENTRE here, built to the designs of Sir Hubert Bennett and opened in 1964, has facilities for athletics, a championship swimming pool, and an artificial ski slope. Sir Ernest Shackleton (d. 1922) lived at No. 12 in WESTWOOD HILL, north of Crystal Palace Park.

Kennington, Brixton, and Streatham

STATIONS: KENNINGTON and OVAL, on the Northern line; BRIXTON, the southern terminus of the Victoria line; STREATHAM HILL and STREATHAM, on the Southern Region.

KENNINGTON, a mainly residential area and its southern neighbour Brixton, with its greater emphasis on recreational facilities, form part of the extensive borough of Lambeth. Newington Butts, running south-west from the Elephant and Castle, is prolonged by KENNINGTON PARK ROAD, which has good Georgian terraces on both sides. The road, skirting KENNINGTON PARK, laid out in 1854, ends at the junction (on the right) of Harleyford Street. This leads to THE OVAL, the ground of the Surrey Cricket Club, formed in 1844. The gates are a memorial to Sir Jack Hobbs (d. 1963), the batsman.

In the angle between Camberwell New Road (south of Kennington Park) and Clapham Road is St Mark's Church, by D. R. Roper (1822). The interior, gutted by bombs in 1940, was restored in 1949–60. Field-Marshal Viscount Montgomery (d. 1976) was born in 1887 in the vicarage (since rebuilt) near the Oval. Camberwell New Road runs south-east to Camberwell Green. Foxley Road, on the right, where David Cox (d. 1859), the artist, lived at No. 34, leads to Vassall Road, with the church of St John the Divine, a notable building by G. E. Street (1874), with a spire added by his son, A. E. Street (1889). The interior, decorated by G. F. Bodley (1892), but gutted by bombing, was restored in 1958 by H. S. Goodhart-Rendel.

In Brixton Road, which starts to the east of St Mark's, Nos. 1–3 house the London Taxi Museum (adm., p. 33), containing a representative collection of London taxicabs from 1907 onward. The road passes Christ Church, an unusual Byzantine-style structure by Beresford Pite (1902). In Hackford Road, to the west, Vincent Van Gogh lived in 1873–4 at No. 87 as an art dealer. The main road goes on past Stockwell Park Road, where Lilian Baylis, the manager of the 'Old Vic' and Sadler's Wells Theatres, died in 1937 at No. 27, to the effective Lambeth Town Hall (by Septimus Warwick, 1908). The classical St Matthew's Church, a little to the south, built by Charles F. Porden in 1822, with its steeple at the east end, was converted in 1976 into a community centre. From here the long Brixton Hill ascends to the east of Blenheim Gardens, which has a restored windmill of 1816 (adm., p. 31) containing machinery from a mill in Lincolnshire. Farther on is Streatham (pronounced 'Stret-am'), a residential district mainly remarkable for its numerous huge blocks of flats. Like Balham, Tooting, Putney, and Roehampton, it is now included in the large borough of Wandsworth.

To the left, near the beginning of Streatham Hill, is the Italianate brick Christ Church, by J. W. Wild (1842), 'perhaps the most original of Victorian churches', with a campanile, good mosaics in the apse, and stained glass by Walter Crane (1891). Pullmann Court, beyond, is a successful layout of luxury flats by Frederick Gibberd (1935). In Streatham High Road, some way farther down, is St Leonard's Church, the parish church, rebuilt in 1831, altered at various times in the 19th century, and well restored after being gutted by fire in 1975. A new window by John Hayward illustrates the history of Streatham. The epitaph to Henry Thrale (d. 1781) is by Dr Johnson, who was a frequent visitor at Streatham Park, the home of the Thrales, which stood near the south side of Tooting Bec Common, half a mile west of the church.

Clapham and Wandsworth

Stations: Clapham Common, on the Northern line; Clapham, Clapham Junction, and Wandsworth Town, on the Southern Region.

Clapham, chiefly a residential district, is now part of the large borough of

Lambeth. It is reached from Kennington (see above) by CLAPHAM ROAD. On the right opens ALBERT SQUARE, with rather grand houses of 1847. Clapham Road is joined at Stockwell by South Lambeth Road from Vauxhall (Route 35) and extended by Clapham High Street. The street of Clapham Park, on the left, leads towards ST JAMES'S CHURCH, an interesting design by N. F. Cachemaille Day (1958).

Clapham High Street ends at the triangular CLAPHAM COMMON, on which the Greater London Horse Show is held. In the north-east angle is HOLY TRINITY CHURCH, built in 1776 by Kenton Couse, with a chancel added in 1903. A tablet on the south wall, outside, commemorates the 'Clapham Sect', an Anglican group that gathered in the houses round the common in the late 18th and early 19th centuries. In NORTH SIDE, Sir Charles Barry, the architect, died in 1860 at No. 29, a Georgian house on the site of that where Samuel Pepys died in 1703. Zachary Macaulay (d. 1838), the philanthropist, and his son, Thomas Babington (later Lord) Macaulay, lived at No. 5 in THE PAVEMENT, east of the church. OLD TOWN, with a row of three charming Queen Anne houses (Nos. 39–43), the continuation northward, leads towards ST PAUL'S CHURCH, built in 1815 on the site of a 12th-century structure. The chancel and transepts were added in 1879 in a Romanesque style by Blomfield; the north transept contains finely sculptured figures from the monument to Sir Richard Atkins (d. 1689) and his family.

The church stands above the long uninteresting Wandsworth Road, which is extended west by Lavender Hill, passing the CHURCH OF THE ASCENSION, a notable design by James Brooks, begun in 1876 but not completed until 1898. Farther on is the former BATTERSEA TOWN HALL (by E. W. Mountford, 1893), now containing the Battersea Arts Centre, where temporary exhibitions and other events are held. Lavender Hill ends at the cross-roads east of CLAPHAM JUNCTION, claimed to be the busiest station in the world, with more than 2,500 trains passing every working day.

Falcon Road leads north from the cross-roads to the High Street of Battersea (see below), while St John's Hill goes on west towards WANDSWORTH, mainly an industrial district, reached also from Clapham Common North Side by Battersea Rise, which passes to the north of SHELGATE ROAD, where Edward Thomas (d. 1917), the poet and essayist, lived at No. 61, and of the elongated WANDSWORTH COMMON. Its westward extension is crossed by TRINITY ROAD, where Thomas Hardy lived in 1878–81. Trinity Road goes on at length to cross ROUTH ROAD, in which No. 3 was the home of David Lloyd George (d. 1945).

St John's Hill is continued by East Hill. At the junction with North Side, in a Victorian mansion, are the headquarters of the NATIONAL BOOK LEAGUE, founded in 1925. ST ANNE'S CHURCH, to the south of East Hill, is a classical building by Sir Robert Smirke (1824), with a 'pepper-box' tower. East Hill is extended by WANDSWORTH HIGH STREET which crosses the river Wandle and is extended in turn by WEST HILL, ascending to Putney Heath (see below) and passing MAYFIELD SCHOOL (by Powell and Moya, 1955), an outstanding example of modern functional school architecture. Putney Bridge Road, running north-west from High Street, skirts WANDSWORTH PARK, which faces across the Thames to the Hurlingham grounds, in Fulham.

Battersea

STATIONS: BATTERSEA PARK and QUEENSTOWN ROAD, BATTERSEA (these two for Battersea Park), and CLAPHAM JUNCTION, all on the Southern Region.

BATTERSEA, on the south bank of the Thames opposite Chelsea, is mainly concerned with industry, but retains some semblance of an old quarter round the church and the former village square. Queenstown Road, running south from Chelsea Bridge (Route 8), skirts the east side of the attractive BATTERSEA PARK, which stretches along the river to Albert Bridge and contains a fine boating-lake, a sub-tropical garden, a small zoo, and sculptures by Henry Moore and others. It was laid out in 1858 on the site of Battersea Fields, where the Duke of Wellington fought a duel with the Earl of Winchilsea in 1829. A Japanese Peace Pagoda, 110 ft high, was built in the park, overlooking the river, in 1985. In the north-east part of the park, facing the river, are the FESTIVAL GARDENS, designed by John Piper and Osbert Lancaster and opened in 1951 as part of the Festival of Britain. Its attractions included an ornamental lake and a concert pavilion. Noël Coward, actor and playwright, lived in 1908–13 at No. 70 in PRINCE OF WALES MANSIONS, south-east of the park. Queenstown Road crosses BATTERSEA PARK ROAD, which leads east towards New Covent Garden (Route 35), passing (at No. 4) the BATTERSEA DOGS' HOME (established in 1860), the main collecting centre for lost and unwanted dogs in London.

Albert Bridge Road (compare Route 8) skirts the west side of Battersea Park. From Battersea Bridge Road, parallel to the west, Church Road leads west to ST MARY'S CHURCH, the parish church of Battersea (first mentioned in 1086), overlooking an industrialized reach of the river. Rebuilt in 1776 by Joseph Dixon, it retains from the previous church some 17th-century stained glass and several monuments, among them that of Henry St John, Viscount Bolingbroke (d. 1751), and his wife, with medallion portraits by Roubiliac. William Blake, the poet-visionary, was married here in 1782 to the 'heaven-provided' Catherine Boucher.

The RAVEN INN, facing the old village square at the south end of Church Road, dates partly from the 17th century. Hence VICARAGE CRESCENT bears right past two fine 18th-century houses, in the second of which (the Vicarage) lived Edward A. Wilson (d. 1912), the Antarctic explorer. No. 48, a warehouse remodelled in 1974, is now the ROYAL ACADEMY OF DANCING, and beyond is OLD BATTERSEA HOUSE, built in 1699. From the end of Church Road, the narrow High Street goes on towards Clapham Junction (see above), and York Road (extending Battersea Park Road across the High Street) runs south-west towards Wandsworth.

Putney and Roehampton

STATIONS: PUTNEY BRIDGE (in Fulham) and EAST PUTNEY, on the District line; PUTNEY, on the Southern Region.

PUTNEY, on the south bank of the Thames, opposite Fulham, is a well-known resort of rowing clubs, whose boat-houses stretch along the river bank, and has been the starting-point since 1845 of the Oxford and Cambridge Boat-Race to Mortlake. Near the end of PUTNEY BRIDGE (see p. 489) is ST MARY'S CHURCH, rebuilt in 1837, except for the 15th-century tower, gutted by fire in 1973, and finely restored in 1982. The early-16th-century fan-vaulted chapel was built for Nicholas West (d. 1533), bishop of Ely, who was born at Putney in 1461. The church was the scene in 1647 of the Putney Debates, under the chairmanship of Oliver Cromwell, which helped to shape the future of parliamentary democracy. Lower Richmond Road runs west from the bridge to PUTNEY LOWER COMMON, on the south-east side of which is ALL SAINTS' CHURCH, built in 1874 by G. E. Street and with many windows (the earliest of 1877) by William Morris and Burne-Jones.

PUTNEY HIGH STREET ascends from the bridge to Putney station and is continued from there by PUTNEY HILL. A. C. Swinburne, the poet, died in 1909 at The Pines (No. 11), where he had lived for thirty years with Theodore Watts-Dunton. Putney Hill leads to PUTNEY HEATH, once notorious as the resort of highwaymen and duellists, across which Portsmouth Road and Kingston Road (the extension of West Hill; see above) run towards ROEHAMPTON.

Roehampton Lane, on the west side of the heath, leads north past the ALTON EAST ESTATE, where eleven-storey blocks of flats (among the first tall flats in outer London) were built for the L.C.C. in 1952–5. On the right of Roehampton Lane is HOLY TRINITY CHURCH, by G. H. Fellowes Prynne (1898), with a spire over 200 ft high. Some old houses survive in ROEHAMPTON VILLAGE, close by. To the left farther on (and reached from Holybourne Avenue, opposite Roehampton High Street) is MANRESA HOUSE, a villa in the Palladian style designed by Sir William Chambers for Lord Bessborough (1760) and now incorporated in a teachers' training college. Gerard Manley Hopkins (d. 1889), the poet, lived and studied here when it was a Jesuit college. Behind is the less successful ALTON WEST ESTATE, built by the L.C.C. in 1954–66, skirting Richmond Park. MOUNT CLARE, to the north-west, was built in 1773 by Sir Robert Taylor and is now part of the training college.

Roehampton Lane goes on past DOWNSHIRE HOUSE, built before 1775, much altered since, and now likewise part of the college. On the right is QUEEN MARY'S HOSPITAL, founded for mutilated ex-soldiers, incorporating Roehampton House, built by Thomas Archer in 1712 and enlarged by Lutyens in 1913. GROVE HOUSE, reached from Clarence Lane, opposite, a building of 1777 by James Wyatt, is now the Froebel Institute. Roehampton Lane goes on past the ROEHAMPTON CLUB, a fashionable sports club (founded in 1901) with a golf course, to Upper Richmond Road and Barnes Common.

GREATER LONDON

In 1965 the boundaries of London were greatly extended and thirty-two boroughs (not counting the City of London) were created to make up the administrative unit of GREATER LONDON. The following are the new London Boroughs (those indicated * are Inner London Boroughs), with their estimated populations (1985), the addresses of the chief municipal offices, and the names of the former boroughs, urban districts, etc., now within their boundaries.

BARKING (population 151,200; Civic Centre, Dagenham, Essex): consisting of part of Barking (see Newham) and part of Dagenham (see Redbridge).

BARNET (pop. 296,500; Town Hall, The Burroughs, Hendon, London NW4): Barnet, East Barnet, Finchley, Friern Barnet, and Hendon.

BEXLEY (pop. 217,900; Civic Offices, Bexleyheath, Kent): Bexley, Crayford, Erith and part of Chislehurst and Sidcup (see Bromley).

BRENT (pop. 254,000; Town Hall, Forty Lane, Wembley, Middlesex): Wembley and Willesden.

BROMLEY (pop. 299,500; Town Hall, Bromley, Kent): Beckenham, Bromley, Orpington, Penge, and part of Chislehurst and Sidcup (compare Bexley).

CAMDEN* (pop. 172,000; Town Hall, Euston Road, NW1): Hampstead, Holborn, and St Pancras.

CROYDON (pop. 318,700; Town Hall, Taberner House, Park Lane, Croydon, Surrey): Croydon, and Coulsdon and Purley.

EALING (pop. 282,000; Town Hall, Ealing, W5): Acton, Ealing, and Southall.

ENFIELD (pop. 257,200; Civic Centre, Silver Street, Enfield, Middlesex): Edmonton, Enfield, and Southgate.

GREENWICH* (pop. 209,800; Town Hall, Wellington Street, Woolwich, SE18): Greenwich and that part of Woolwich south of the Thames (see Newham).

HACKNEY* (pop. 183,300; Town Hall, Mare Street, Hackney, E8): Hackney, Shoreditch, and Stoke Newington.

HAMMERSMITH AND FULHAM* (pop. 148,400; Town Hall, King Street, Hammersmith, W6): Fulham and Hammersmith.

HARINGEY (pop. 204,600; Civic Centre, High Road, Wood Green, N22): Hornsey, Tottenham, and Wood Green.

HARROW (pop. 198,800; Civic Centre, Station Road, Harrow, Middlesex): Harrow only.

HAVERING (pop. 241,200; Town Hall, Main Road, Romford, Essex): Hornchurch and Romford.

HILLINGDON (pop. 229,200; Civic Centre, Uxbridge, Middlesex): Hayes and Harlington, Ruislip-Northwood, Uxbridge, and Yiewsley and West Drayton.

HOUNSLOW (pop. 200,900; Civic Offices, Lampton Road, Hounslow, Middlesex): Brentford and Chiswick, Feltham, and Heston and Isleworth.

ISLINGTON* (pop. 162,900; Town Hall, Upper Street, Islington, N1): Finsbury and Islington.

KENSINGTON AND CHELSEA* (pop. 136,800; Town Hall, Hornton Street, Kensington, W8): a royal borough combining Chelsea and Kensington.

KINGSTON UPON THAMES (pop. 133,700; Guildhall, Kingston upon Thames, Surrey): a royal borough comprising Kingston, Malden and Coombe, and Surbiton.

LAMBETH* (pop. 246,800; Town Hall, Brixton Hill, Brixton, SW2): Lambeth and part of Wandsworth.

LEWISHAM* (pop. 233,600; Town Hall, Rushey Green, Catford, SE6): Deptford and Lewisham.

MERTON (pop. 167,900; Town Hall, Broadway, Wimbledon, SW19): Merton and Morden, Mitcham, and Wimbledon.

NEWHAM (pop. 212,300; Town Hall, East Ham, E6): East Ham, West Ham, part of Barking, and that part of Woolwich north of the Thames (compare Greenwich).

REDBRIDGE (pop. 227,000; Town Hall, High Road, Ilford, Essex): Ilford, Wanstead and Woodbridge, and parts of Chigwell and Dagenham (compare Barking). The northern part of Chigwell remains in Essex.

RICHMOND UPON THAMES (pop. 161,600; Municipal Offices, Twickenham, Middlesex): Barnes, Richmond, and Twickenham.

SOUTHWARK* (pop. 215,400; Town Hall, Peckham Road, SE5): Bermondsey, Camberwell, and Southwark.

SUTTON (pop. 170,100; Civic Offices, St Nicholas Way, Sutton, Surrey): Beddington and Wallington, Carshalton, and Sutton and Cheam.

TOWER HAMLETS* (pop. 144,500; Town Hall, Patriot Square, Cambridge Heath Road, E2): Bethnal Green, Poplar, and Stepney.

WALTHAM FOREST (pop. 214,500; Town Hall, Walthamstow, E17): Chingford, Leyton, and Walthamstow.

WANDSWORTH* (pop. 258,500; Town Hall, Wandsworth, SW18): Battersea and part of Wandsworth (compare Lambeth).

WESTMINSTER* (pop. 163,800; City Hall, Victoria Street, SW1): Paddington, St Marylebone, and the City of Westminster.

Places outside the London postal area retain in their addresses the names of the counties in which they were previously situated.

PLACES OF INTEREST in Outer London (apart from those now described in Suburban London) include Boston Manor, Syon House (with the National Gardening Centre), Osterley Park, and Heathrow Airport (all in the borough of *Hounslow*); Gunnersbury Park and Pitshanger Manor (*Ealing*); Wembley Stadium (*Brent*); Harrow-on-the-Hill with its famous school (*Harrow*); the Royal Air Force

Museum, Battle of Britain Museum, and Church Farm House Museum at Hendon (*Barnet*); Finsbury Park, the park of Alexandra Palace, and Bruce Castle Museum at Tottenham (*Haringey*); Forty Hall (*Enfield*); Walthamstow Museum and the William Morris Gallery, Walthamstow (*Waltham Forest*); Epping Forest, with the Queen Elizabeth Hunting Lodge (partly in *Waltham Forest*); Passmore Edwards Museum at Stratford (*Newham*); Eastbury Manor and Valence House Museum (*Barking*); Hall Place, Danson Park, and Lesnes Abbey (*Bexley*); Chislehurst Caves (*Bromley*); the Old Palace, etc. (*Croydon*); Wimbledon Common and the Lawn Tennis Club Museum (*Merton*); the royal borough of *Kingston upon Thames*; and Richmond with its charming houses and fine park, Ham Common and House, the Royal Botanical Gardens at Kew, Twickenham (Marble Hill House, Orleans House, etc.), Bushy Park, and Hampton Court Palace (all in the borough of *Richmond upon Thames*).

Among the many places of interest farther afield, yet within convenient reach of London, the following are especially worthy of mention: Windsor Castle, Eton and its college, the Chiltern Hills, St Albans Cathedral and Verulamium, Hatfield House, Waltham Abbey and the Lee Valley, Rochester and its cathedral, Knole, Chartwell, and the Greensand Hills, Down House and the North Downs, Epsom Downs with its racecourse, and Guildford and its cathedral.

DEFINITIONS OF ARCHITECTURAL TERMS

AISLE: wing or lateral division of a church, separated from the nave, chancel, or transept by a row of columns

ALTARPIECE: structure of wood or stone above an altar, usually carved and/or painted

AMBULATORY: aisle or corridor, especially one enclosing an apse

APSE: semicircular or polygonal end of a chancel or chapel

ARCADE: range of arches supported on piers or columns

AUMBRY: recess or cupboard for sacred vessels used during Mass or Communion

BALDACCHINO: canopy over an altar, generally supported on pillars

BALUSTER: small shaft or column of varying diameter, often ornamented. *Balustrade:* series of balusters supporting a coping or rail

BAPTISTERY: part of the church (containing the font) where baptism is administered

BARBICAN: outer fortification, resembling a gatehouse, defending the entrance to a castle or town

BAROQUE: style of architecture introduced from the Continent in the 17th century and characterized by a heavy extravagance in its ornamentation

BARREL VAULT: *see* Vault

BASILICA: rectangular building with colonnades on either side and a projecting apse

BASTION: projecting work in the line or at the angle of a fortification

BAYS: internal compartments of a building divided from each other only by piers or buttresses at the side

BOSS: projection, usually ornamented, covering the intersection of the ribs of a vault

BUTTRESS: structure of masonry or brickwork built against a wall to strengthen it. *Flying buttress:* one in the shape of part of an arch

CANOPY: ornamental projection above a recess, altar, etc.

CAPITAL: head of a pier or column (*see also* Orders)

CHANCEL: eastern part of a church, formerly divided from the nave or crossing by a screen

CHANCEL ARCH: enclosing arch at the west end of a chancel

CHANTRY: endowment for a priest to say Mass daily for a deceased person. *Chantry chapel:* one used for this purpose

CHAPEL: place of worship inside or attached to a church, with an altar

CHAPTER HOUSE: meeting place for the officiating clergy of a cathedral or of the members of a religious order

CHARNEL HOUSE: building or chamber attached to or under a church for the reception of the bones of the dead

CHOIR: part of the church where the service is sung

CLASSICAL: in the style of the ancient Greeks and Romans (*see also* Orders)

CLERESTORY: upper part of the nave, chancel, or transept of a church, pierced with windows

CLOISTER: series of covered passages, usually along the sides of a quadrangle, in a monastic or collegiate building

COFFER: sunk rectangular or polygonal panel, usually in a ceiling

COLLEGE: body of persons organized under one roof and devoted to common pursuits. *Collegiate:* containing a college or having one attached to it

COLONNADE: range of columns, spaced at regular intervals

COMPOSITE: *see* Orders

CORBEL: bracket or projection from a wall, usually of stone, to support a roof vault or other weight

CORINTHIAN: *see* Orders

CORNICE: moulded horizontal projection at the top of a wall or other part of a building

COVING: concave undersurface (like a large moulding) to a cornice, at the edge of a roof or ceiling, or under a rood-beam (hence also *coved*)

CROCKET: carved foliated ornament on a canopy, pinnacle, etc.

CROSSING: space at the intersection of the nave, transepts, and chancel

CRYPT: underground room, especially one below the east end of a church

DECORATED: the style of the middle period of English Gothic architecture, approximately 1280–1380 (*see* also Geometrical)

DEMI-FIGURE: the sculptured representation of the upper half only of a figure

DETACHED SHAFT: *see* Shaft

DORIC: *see* Orders

EARLY ENGLISH: the style of the earliest period of English Gothic architecture, approximately 1190–1280

EASTER SEPULCHRE: recess in a chancel or chapel to contain an effigy of Christ for Easter celebrations

FAN VAULT: *see* Vault

FERETORY: shrine or reliquary borne in a procession, or the place in a church where a shrine was kept

FINIAL: ornamented top of a pinnacle, canopy, roof, etc.

FLYING BUTTRESS: *see* Buttress

FOLIATED: carved or adorned with leaf shapes

FONT: vessel to contain water for baptism

FRESCO: wall painting done on the plaster while it is still wet

GEOMETRICAL: the style of the earlier part of the Decorated period, so called from the window tracery, which was almost wholly in the form of circles or parts of circles

GOTHIC: the style of architecture which followed the Romanesque and was characterized by the pointed arch. It is divided into Early English, Decorated, and Perpendicular

GRISAILLE: painting or staining in grey monochrome to simulate shapes or ornament in relief

GROINED: *see* Vault

HAMMERBEAM: beam projecting at right angles from the top of a wall to support the roof members

IONIC: *see* Orders

KEEP: the main tower or stronghold of a medieval castle

LANCET WINDOW: narrow window with a pointed arch

LECTERN: reading-desk from which parts of the service are said

LIERNE VAULT: *see* Vault

LINENFOLD: stylized representation of

linen in vertical folds, adopted as a pattern of decoration on panelling in the Tudor period

MISERICORD: bracketed projection on the underside of a hinged stall seat, which, when turned up, afforded support to a person standing

MOULDING: shaped edge of an arch, etc., with continuous grooves and projections, frequently ornamented with a regular pattern

NARTHEX: enclosed vestibule or porch at the west end of a church

NAVE: the main body of the church, separated by pillars from the aisles

NORMAN: *see* Romanesque

ORATORY: small private chapel in a house or castle

ORDERS: system of parts and ornamentation distinguishing the styles of classical architecture, the Doric, Tuscan, Ionic, Corinthian, and Composite

ORIEL WINDOW: bay window projecting usually from an upper storey

PEDIMENT: triangular or segmental gable surmounting a portico, door, or window in classical buildings

PERPENDICULAR: the style of the last period of English Gothic architecture, approximately 1380–1540

PIER: solid pillar supporting an arch. *Clustered pier:* one made up of columns, or shafts, generally banded together

PILASTER: rectangular column built against a wall, forming a kind of flat buttress

PISCINA: stone basin, usually set in the wall of a chancel or chapel, to contain water for purifying the vessels used in Mass or Communion (plural, *Piscinae*)

PORTCULLIS: gate made to slide in vertical grooves and close the entrance to a castle or ward

PORTICO: porch whose roof is supported by columns

POSTERN: small gateway at the back of a castle, forming a private entrance

PREDELLA: platform or horizontal panel (or series of panels) below an altar on which persons or scenes subsidiary to those on the altarpiece are represented

QUADRIPARTITE: divided regularly into four parts (as in the vaulting of a roof bay)

RAMPART: embankment or wall of earth or stone surrounding a fortified place

RELIQUARY: casket or other repository for sacred relics

RENAISSANCE: the style of architecture inspired by the classical revival in the 14th–16th centuries in Italy

REREDOS: altarpiece

RETRO-CHOIR: part of a cathedral or large church behind the high altar

REVESTRY: vestry

ROCOCO: style of architecture that followed the Baroque but was characterized by a lighter extravagance in its ornamentation

ROMANESQUE: the style of architecture characterized by the round arch. It was current in England in the 11th–12th centuries, and is divided into Saxon and Norman. *See also* Transitional Norman

ROOD: crucifix, usually placed above the entrance to the chancel in a medieval church. *Rood-beam:* beam supporting the rood. *Rood-loft:* gallery over the rood-screen. *Rood-screen:* screen across the west end of the chancel, under the rood-beam. *Rood-stairs:* stairs giving access to the rood-loft

SACRISTY: room in a church for keeping vestments, books, and sacred vessels

SANCTUARY: inner part of a chancel, where the altar is placed

SAXON: *see* Romanesque

SEDILIA (singular, *Sedile*): seats (usually three, of stone) for the officiating clergy, built on or into the chancel wall of the church

SHAFT: column supporting a capital, often grouped together to form a pier or arranged singly for decorative effect. *Detached shaft:* one (possibly of a group) standing free of the main pier, etc.

SHRINE: chest or casket to contain sacred relics, or a tomb or sepulchre in which relics are deposited

SPANDREL: flat surface between the shoulder of an arch and the moulding, etc., enclosing it, or between the shoulders of adjacent arches

STALL: seat made of wood or stone and enclosed at the back and sides, usually one of a row for the choir and officiating clergy

TESSELLATED: made up of small coloured cubes of stone

TRACERY: ornamental ribwork, especially in a window (*see also* Geometrical)

TRANSEPT: transverse part of a cruciform church

TRANSITIONAL NORMAN: style of the transitional period between the Romanesque and the Gothic, characterized by the change from the round to the pointed arch, which took place about 1150–90

TRIFORIUM: gallery or arcade in the wall above the arcade of the nave, chancel, or transepts, and below the clerestory

TRIPTYCH: altarpiece consisting of a central carved or painted panel, with folding doors on either side, the insides of which are also carved or painted. Similarly, *Polyptych*, with more than one central panel

TUSCAN: *see* Orders

TYMPANUM: space between the lintel of a doorway and the arch above it

UNDERCROFT: vaulted space below a large room or building, especially a church or chapel

VAULT: arched roof of stone or brick. *Barrel vault:* semicircular vault without ribs. *Fan vault:* vault whose ribs all spring from one point and spread out like a fan. *Groined vault:* roof having edges (groins) formed by the intersection of two or more vaults. *Lierne vault:* one having crossribs ('liernes') connecting the main ribs at or near the centres of their spans

WARD: open space or court of a fortified castle

INDEX

NAMES beginning with Academy, College, Institute, Ministry, National, Royal, Society, and School will, as a general rule, be found under their specific heads: for instance, Institute of Actuaries, under Actuaries, Institute of; Royal Aeronautical Society, under Aeronautical Society, Royal. With a few exceptions, only architects of before 1900 have been included in the Index. Abbreviations: Abp = Archbishop, Bp = Bishop.

I. PADDINGTON, BAYSWATER, AND HYDE PARK

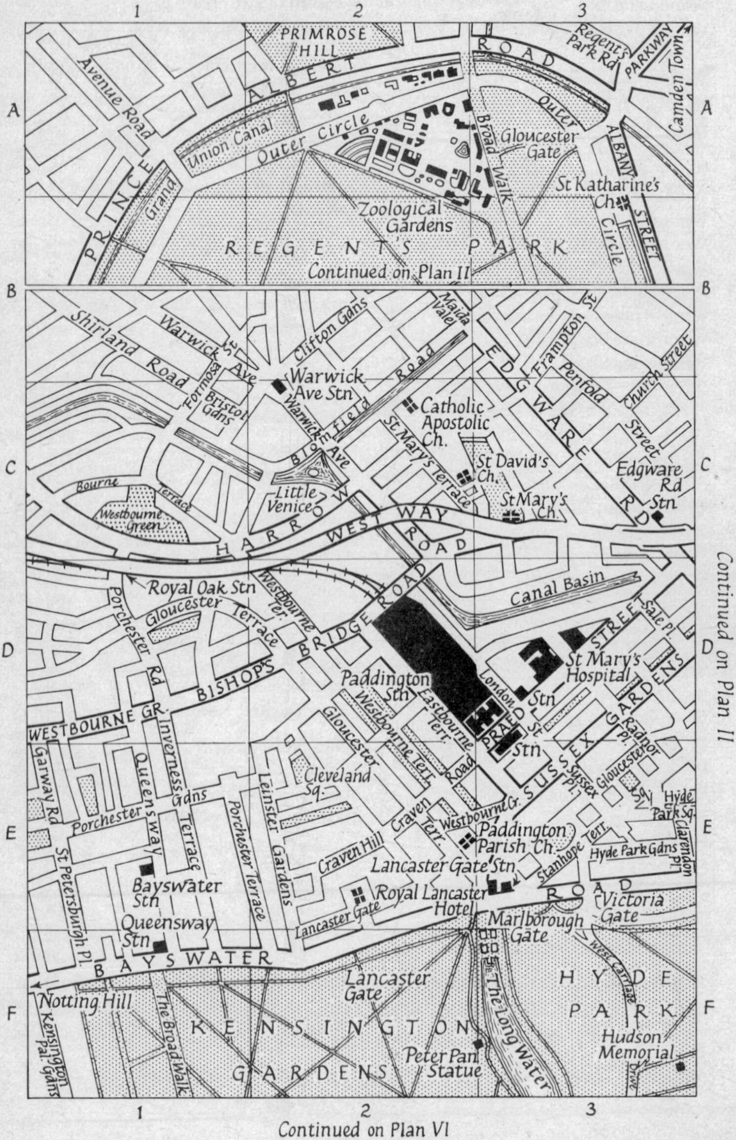

Continued on Plan VI

II. REGENT'S PARK, MARYLEBONE, AND MAYFAIR

Continued at top of Plan 1

Continued on Plan I

Continued on Plan III

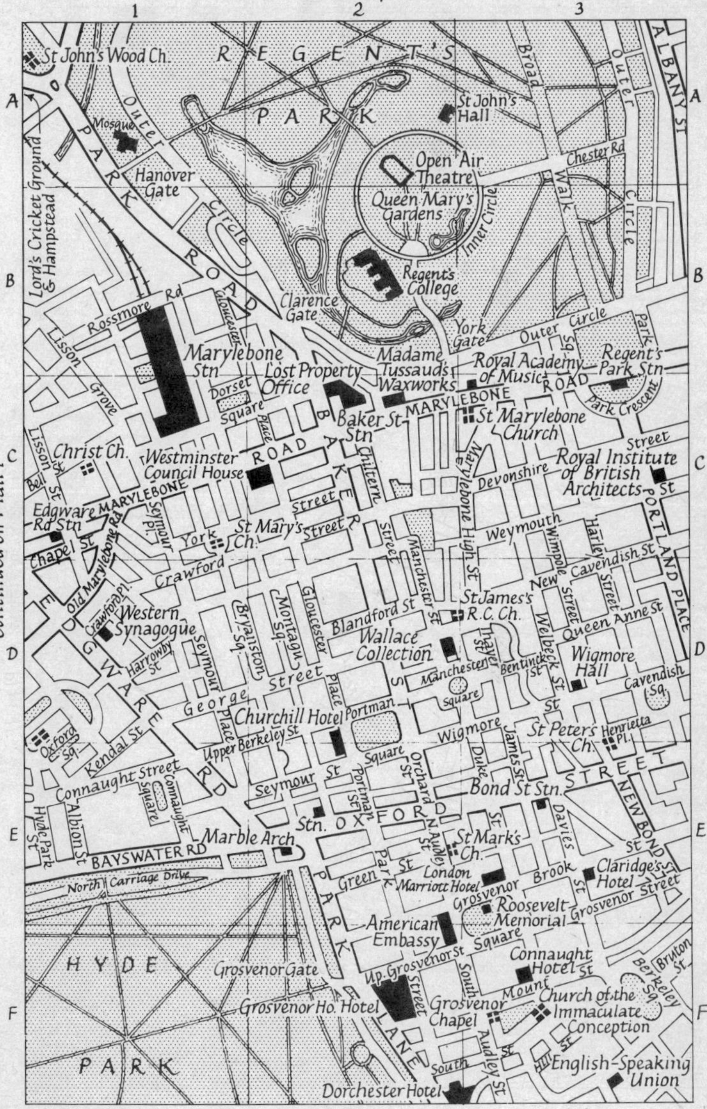

Continued on Plan VII

III. BLOOMSBURY, SOHO, AND CHARING CROSS

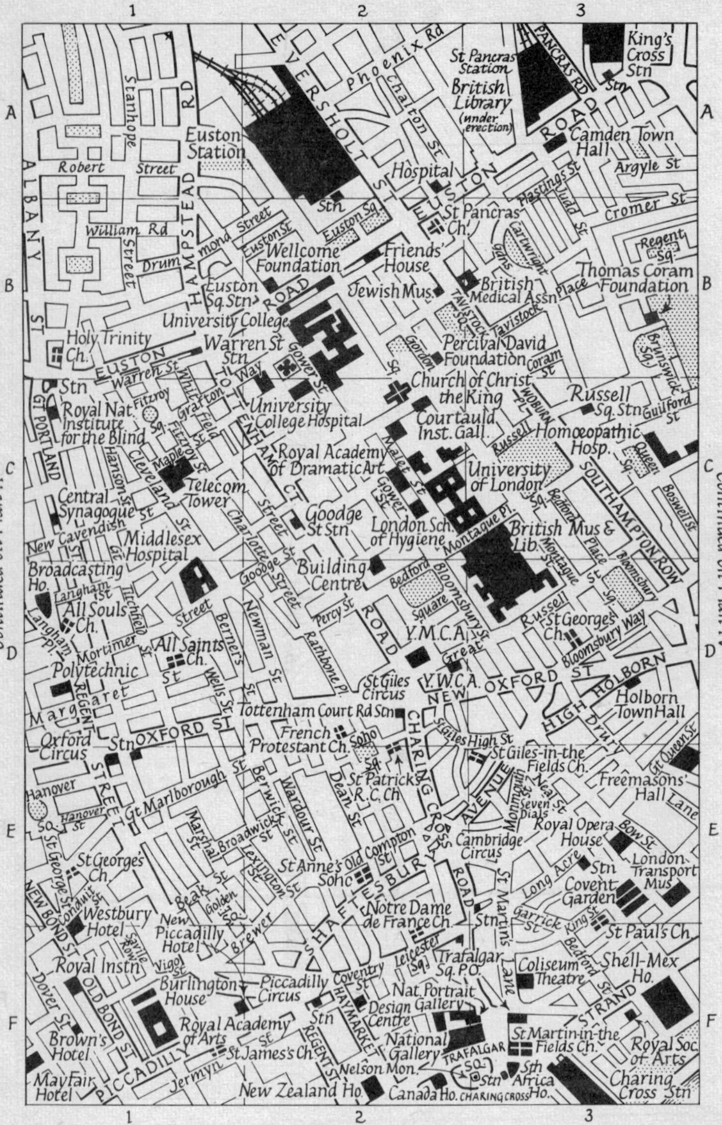

Continued on Plan II

Continued on Plan IV

Continued on Plan VIII

IV. FINSBURY, HOLBORN, AND THE STRAND

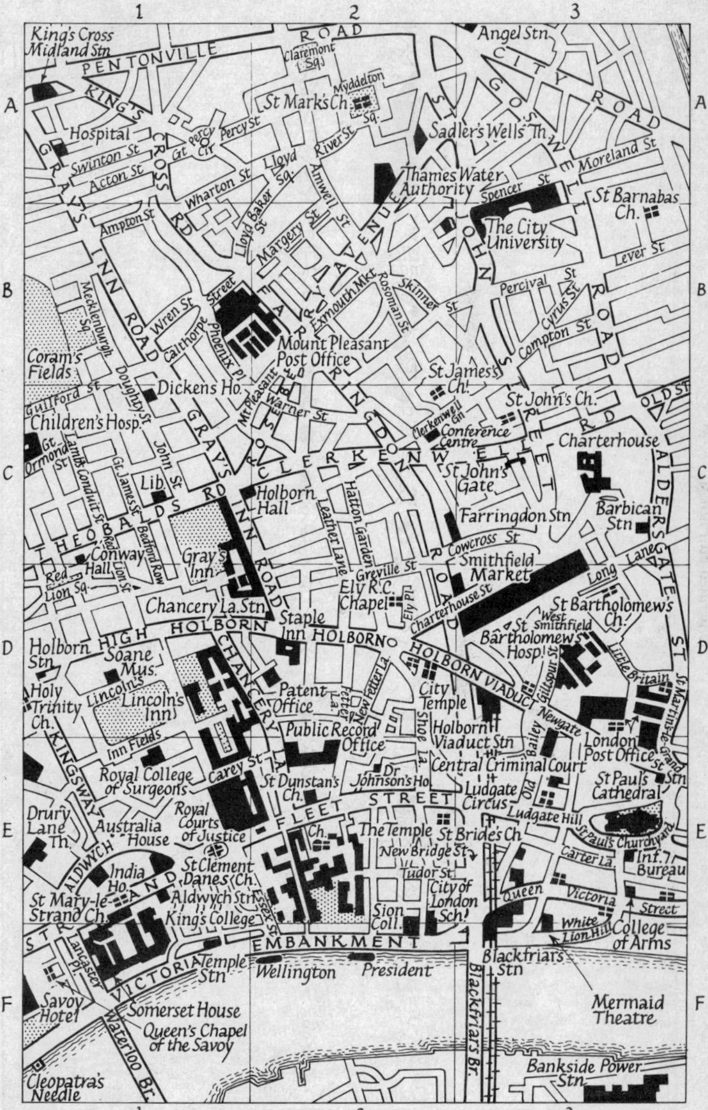

Continued on Plan III

Continued on Plan V

Continued on Plan IX

V. SHOREDITCH AND THE CITY

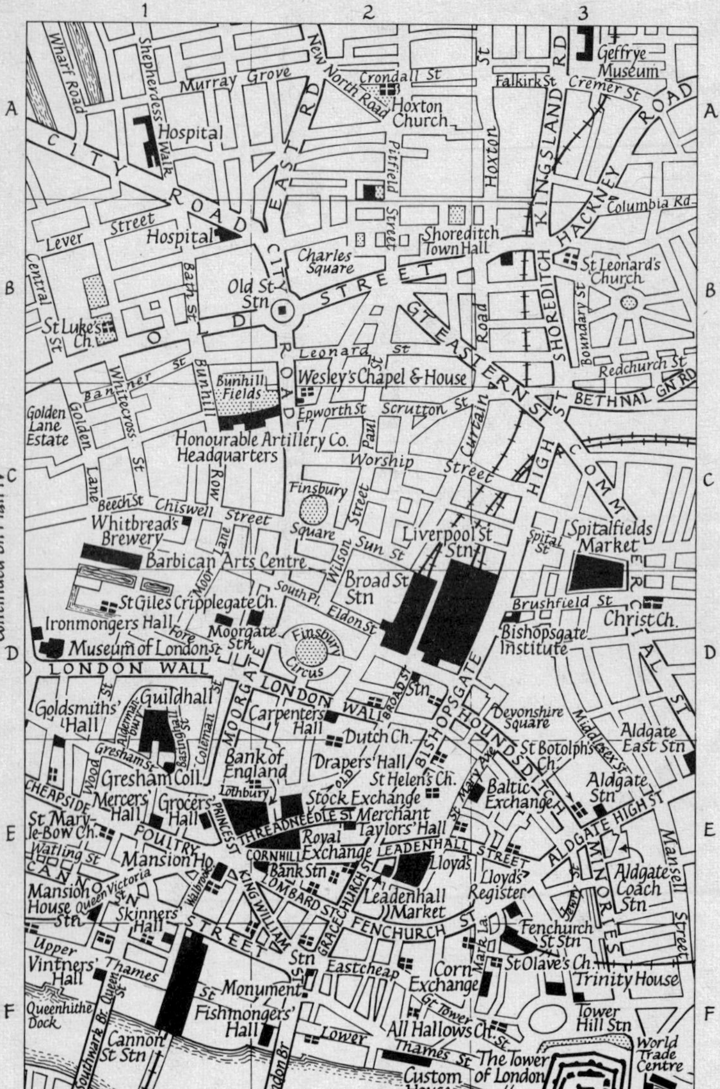

Continued on Plan IV

Continued on Plan IX

VI. KENSINGTON, BROMPTON, AND CHELSEA

Continued on Plan I

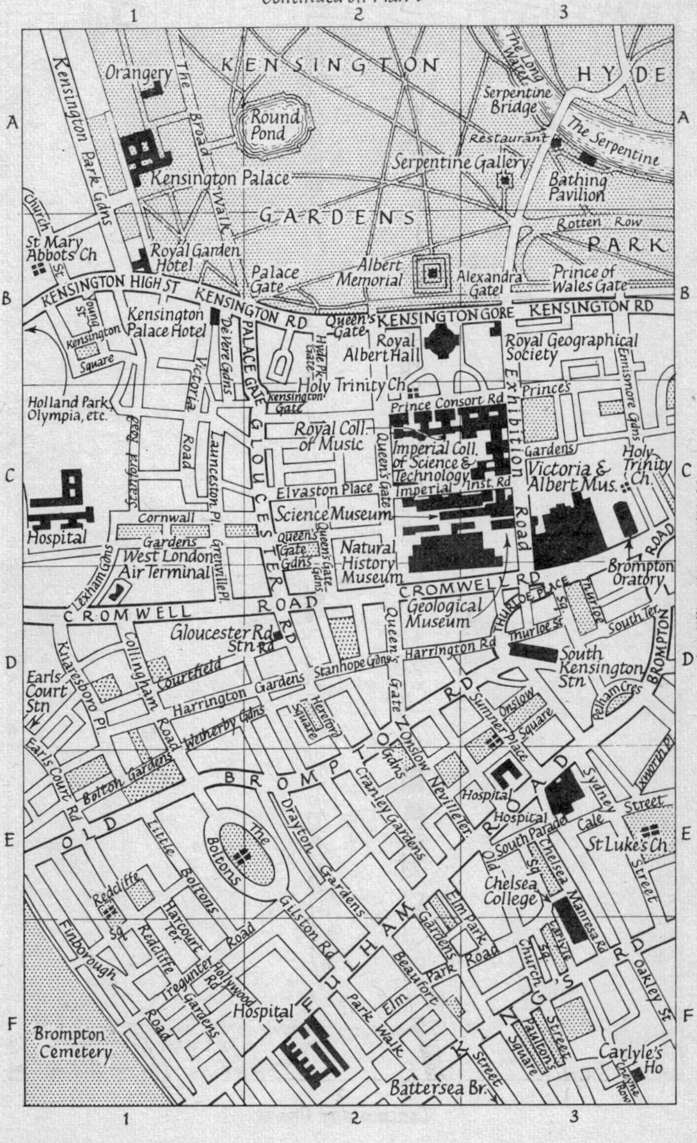

Continued on Plan VII

VII. HYDE PARK, BELGRAVIA, AND CHELSEA

Continued on Plan II

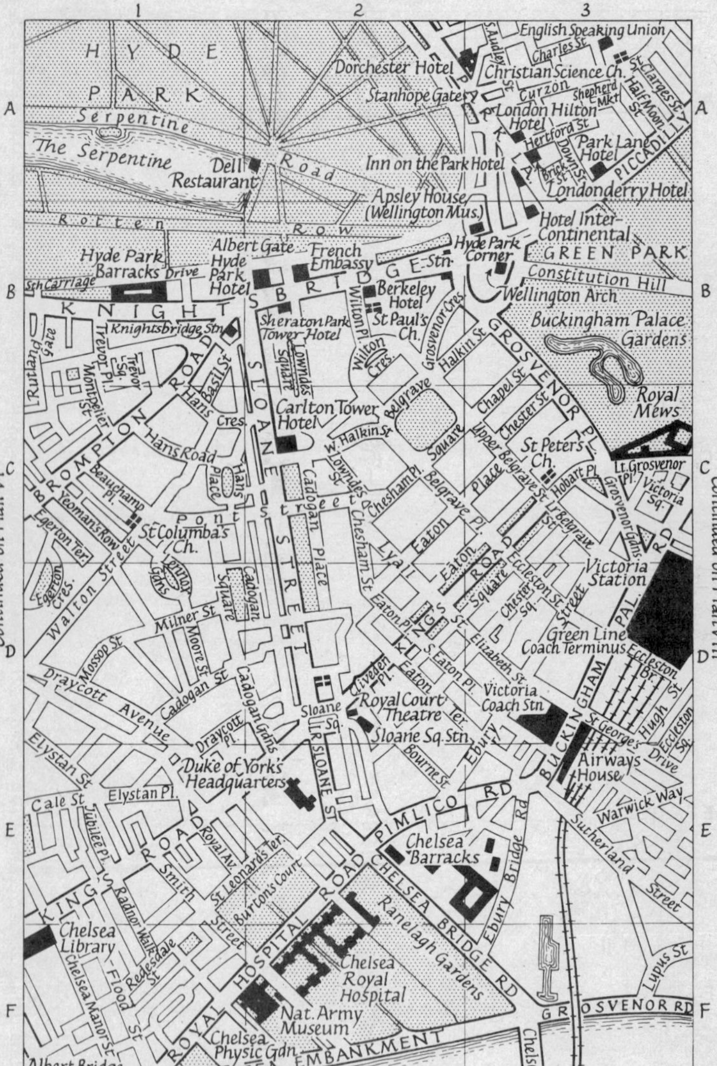

Continued on Plan VI

Continued on Plan VIII

VIII. ST JAMES'S, WESTMINSTER, AND PIMLICO

Continued on Plan III

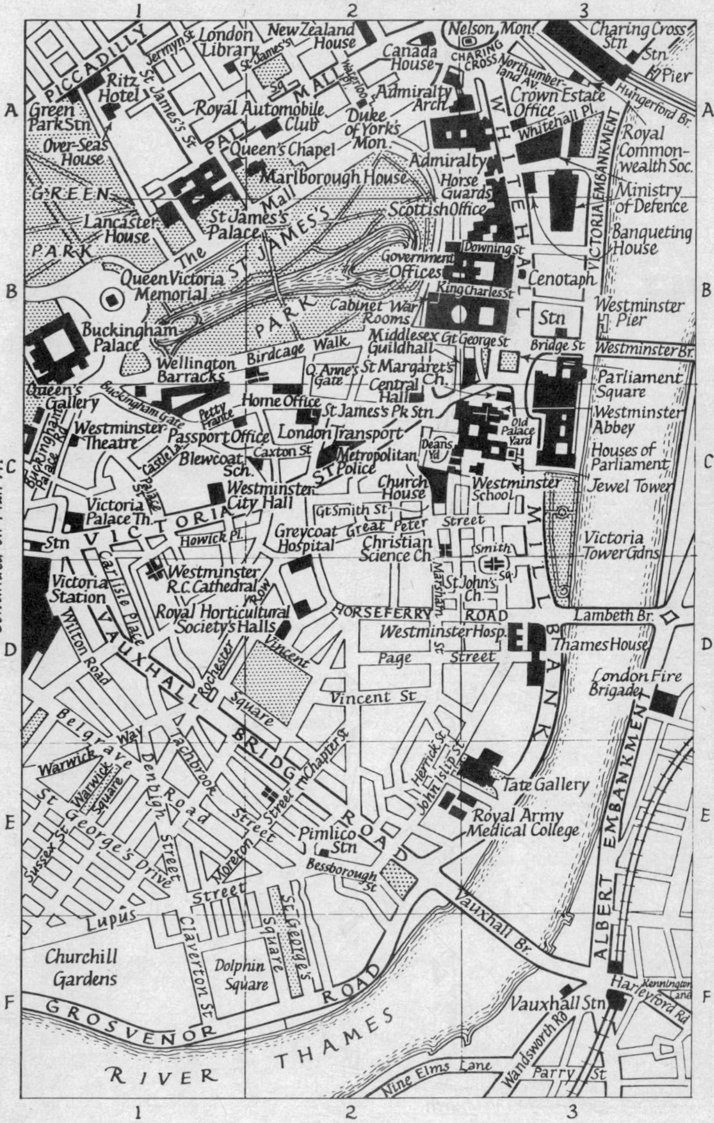

Continued on Plan VII

Continued on Plan IX

IX. LAMBETH, SOUTHWARK, AND BERMONDSEY

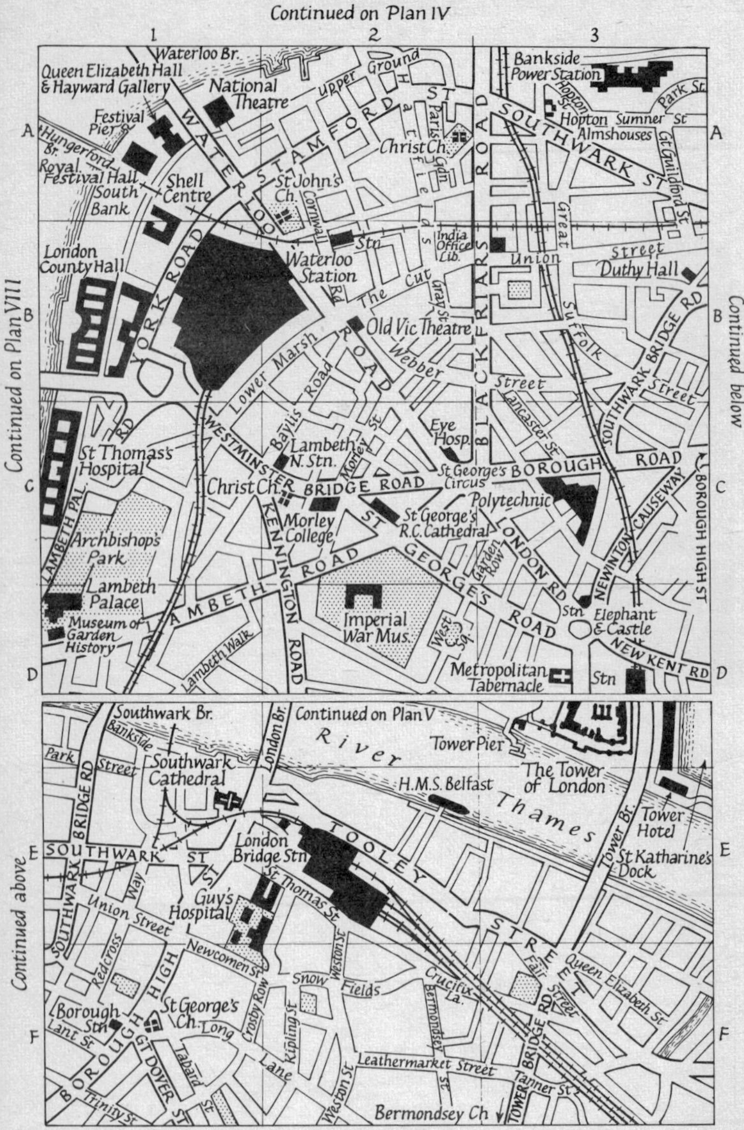